Praise for Kay Showker's
CARIBBEAN PORTS OF CALL

"Written by travel expert Kay Showker, is a first-of-its-kind guide that shows anyone how to plan a carefree vacation at sea and make the most of the limited time in each port of call."

—*Modern Bride*

"Add to cruise clients' enjoyment by tipping them off to fun things to do while ashore."

—*Travel Life*

"A handy reference and sale tool for agents and perfect as a bon voyage gift for clients. . . . The format is easy to follow and includes real 'insider' information."

—*Cruise Views*

"There are shelffuls of guidebooks on the Caribbean, and there are books that deal with cruising in general (and with ships in particular), but there has been no comprehensive work that effectively combines the two. Kay Shower's admirably fills that void."

—*Oceans*

"Very, very comprehensive, a complete and invaluable book."

—Joel Rapp, WABC Radio, New York

"What if you're doing the islands by cruise ship? Check out *Caribbean Ports of Call* to get an inside line not only on the cruise 'personalities' and itineraries, but also where to go, what to do, and what to skip when the ship pulls into shore."

—*Self* magazine

"Her book will become a standard in its field that fills a need people have referred to but not one has taken the time to prepare. For both the first-time cruiser as well as the aficionado, this book is perfect. It is absolutely indispensable to any person taking a cruise and can lend a totally added dimension to the cruise experience."

—Arthur Frommer, "Arthur Frommer's Almanac of Travel"
The Travel Channel

"Has much to offer both the most experienced old salt and the first-time passenger. . . . pulls together various aspects of Caribbean cruising that often are covered in separate books. . . . The bulk of the book more than lives up to it's title."

—*The Washington Times*

HELP US KEEP THIS GUIDE UP TO DATE

Every effort has been made by the author and editors to make this guide as accurate and useful as possible. However, many things can change after a guide is published—establishments close, phone numbers change, hiking trails are rerouted, facilities come under new management, etc.

We would love to hear from you concerning your experiences with this guide and how you feel it could be made better and be kept up to date. While we may not be able to respond to all comments and suggestions, we'll take them to heart, and we'll also make certain to share them with the author. Please send your comments and suggestions to the following address:

The Globe Pequot Press
Reader Response/Editorial Department
P.O. Box 833
Old Saybrook, CT 06475

Or you may e-mail us at:

editorial@globe-pequot.com

Thanks for your input, and happy travels!

CARIBBEAN PORTS OF CALL SERIES

CARIBBEAN PORTS OF CALL:
EASTERN AND SOUTHERN REGIONS

FROM PUERTO RICO TO ARUBA INCLUDING THE PANAMA CANAL

SECOND EDITION

KAY SHOWKER

A VOYAGER BOOK

The Globe Pequot Press

OLD SAYBROOK, CONNECTICUT

Every effort has been made to ensure the accuracy of the information in this book. But please bear in mind that prices (and exchange rates), schedules, etc., change constantly. Readers should always check with a cruise line regarding its ships and itineraries before making final plans.

Cover Photo courtesy Fraink/Waterhouse/H. Armstrong Roberts
Cover design by Schwartzman Design
Text design by MaryAnn Dubé

Library of Congress Cataloging-in-Publication Data:

Showker, Kay.
    Caribbean ports of call : eastern and southern regions : from Puerto Rico to Aruba, including the Panama Canal / Kay Showker. — 2nd ed.
        p. cm. – (Caribbean Ports of Call series)
    "A Voyager book"
    Includes index.
    ISBN 1-56440-981-3
        1. Antilles, Lesser — Guidebooks.   2. Caribbean Area — Guidebooks.   3. Cruise ships — Antilles, Lesser — Guidebooks.   4. Cruise ships — Caribbean Area — Guidebooks.   5. Ocean Travel — Guidebooks.
    I. Title
F2001.S56   1997
917.2904'52—dc21

97-22104
CIP

Manufactured in the United States of America
Second Edition/First Printing

*In memory of Audrey Palmer Hawks, a credit to
her homeland of Grenada and a beloved friend
who radiated the warmth and charm of the
Caribbean and the strength of its women.*

Contents

List of Maps

Eastern and Southern Caribbean Islands

Anguilla
Antigua/Barbuda
Aruba
Barbados
Bonaire
British Virgin Islands
Curaçao
Dominica
Grenada/Carriacou
Guadeloupe/Iles des Saintes (Les Saintes)
Martinique
Montserrat

Puerto Rico
Saba
St. Barts
St. Eustatius
St. Kitts/Nevis
St. Lucia
St. Maarten/St. Martin
St. Vincent and the Grenadines
  (Bequia, Mustique, Mayreau, Palm,
  Union/Tobago Cays)
Trinidad and Tobago
United States Virgin Island

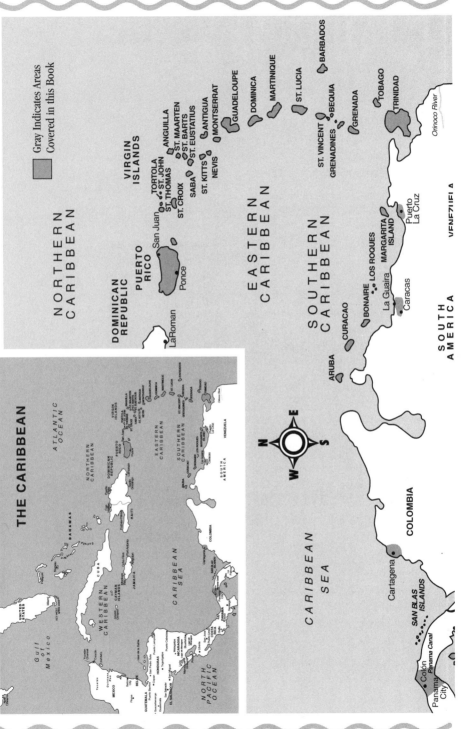

Eastern and Southern Ports of Call

INCLUDING THE PANAMA CANAL

Anegada, British Virgin Islands
Basse-terre, Guadeloupe, French West Indies
Basseterre, St. Kitts
Bequia, St. Vincent and the Grenadines
Bridgetown, Barbados
Cartagena, Colombia
Castries, St. Lucia
Charlestown, Nevis
Charlotte Amalie, St. Thomas, U.S. Virgin Islands
Christiansted, St. Croix, U.S. Virgin Islands
Codrington, Barbuda
Cruz Bay, St. John, U.S. Virgin Islands
English Harbour, Antigua
Falmouth, Antigua
Fort Bay, Saba
Fort-de-France, Martinique
Frederiksted, St. Croix, U.S. Virgin Islands
Gustavia, St. Barthélemy (St. Barts), French West Indies
Hillsborough, Carriacou
Iles des Saintes, Guadeloupe, French West Indies
Jost Van Dyke, British Virgin Islands
Kingstown, St. Vincent
Kralendijk, Bonaire
La Guaira (Caracas), Venezuela
Los Roques, Venezuela
Marie Galante, French West Indies
Marigot, St. Martin, French West Indies

Margarita Island Porlamar, Venezuela
Mayreau, St. Vincent and the Grenadines
Mustique, St. Vincent and the Grenadines
Norman Island, British Virgin Islands
Oranjestad, Aruba
Oranjestad, St. Eustatius
Panama Canal, Panama
Palm Island, St. Vincent and the Grenadines
Philipsburg, Saint Maarten
Pigeon Point/Rodney Bay, St. Lucia
Pigeon Point, Tobago
Plymouth, Montserrat
Pointe Bout, Martinique
Pointe-a-Pitre, Guadeloupe, French West Indies
Ponce, Puerto Rico
Port of Spain, Trinidad
Portsmouth/Prince Rupert Bay, Dominica
Puerta La Cruz, Venezuela
Road Town, Anguilla
Road Town, Tortola, British Virgin Islands
Roseau, Dominica
San Juan, Puerto Rico
Scarsborough, Tobago
Soufriere, St. Lucia
St. George's, Grenada
St. John's, Antigua
Virgin Gorda, British Virgin Islands
Willemstad, Curaçao

PART I

ISLANDS OF NEW DISCOVERY

ISLANDS OF NEW DISCOVERY

The popularity of cruising continues to boom, with almost five million people taking cruises annually and more than 50 percent of them cruising in the Caribbean. Proximity, prices, superb weather, and variety—of cultures, activity, scenery, sports, and attractions—all have made the Caribbean by cruise ship a particularly popular vacation choice.

To meet the ever-growing demand and to broaden the appeal of Caribbean cruising, the 1990s has seen a dramatic shift of cruise ships from their home base in Florida to San Juan and other ports in the Eastern Caribbean. An even larger number of ships introduced cruises to the Eastern Caribbean for the first time. Yet anyone who looked for information on this area of the Caribbean found little has been available. This book is designed to fill that important need.

Caribbean Ports of Call: Eastern and Southern Regions is a companion volume to *Caribbean Ports of Call: Northern and Northeastern Regions* and the *Caribbean Ports of Call: Western Region.* Like them it differs from other books on cruising or on the Caribbean in a significant way: It is written specifically for cruise passengers. It contains information to help you plan and organize your time and set your priorities so that you can use your visit to the best advantage. It is also intended to be taken along as a guide to the port.

The books are in three volumes for practical reasons. In addition to making each book portable, the ports were divided to reflect the patterns of Caribbean cruises.

Caribbean Ports of Call: Northern and Northeastern Regions covers the islands of the Northern and Northeastern Caribbean plus The Bahamas. It includes the ports of call on the itineraries of the majority of cruises lasting from two to seven days, which depart year-round from Florida to The Bahamas and the Caribbean.

Caribbean Ports of Call: Western Region covers the ports on the itineraries that depart regularly from Florida to the Bahamas and Western Caribbean for two to seven days; those that sail from other ports, such as New Orleans and Houston, for the Western Caribbean; and longer voyages that either include Central American ports or sail to the Western Caribbean enroute to the Panama Canal.

This volume, *Caribbean Ports of Call: Eastern and Southern Regions,* includes the islands of the Eastern and Southern Caribbean plus the northern coast of South America and the Panama Canal. It describes the ports in the Eastern Caribbean visited by ships departing from San Juan and elsewhere in the region; longer cruises departing from Florida and other U.S. ports; and cruises that include ports in the Southern Caribbean and Panama Canal.

HOW TO USE THIS GUIDE

Part I is an introduction to the Caribbean and particularly to the Eastern and Southern Caribbean, with an overview of their attractions and contrasts with the northern and western regions. It is also a guide for selecting and buying your cruise, with information on ways to save money on your cabin, no matter which ship you select, and it provides tips to help you get ready for your trip.

Part II is a guide to the cruise lines that sail in the Eastern and Southern Caribbean. It is designed to help you find the line and ship most likely to match your tastes and pocketbook. A chart at the end of the book capsulizes the ships and their ports, listing cruise ships/lines with their various ports of call and the price range of their cruises. This information is intended for general planning only.

Parts III through VI cover the ports of call in the Eastern and Southern Caribbean and the Panama Canal. For easy reference an alphabetical list of the ports follows the Contents. Every effort has been made to be consistent in the presentation of information for each port of call; but some slight variations are inevitable because of the differences in the islands.

All major port chapters open with At a Glance, a generic list of attractions with one star ★ to five ★★★★★ stars. The stars are not used in the sense of a restaurant critique; they are intended as an objective guide to what the island has to offer, that is, which of its attractions are comparatively the best. The purpose is to give an instant picture of the port to help you judge how best to use your time.

Major port chapters include an introduction to the country with a general map, Fast Facts, and Budget Planning. Brief descriptions of popular tours, or shore excursions, as cruise lines call them, are provided for those who like to tour with a group.

The Port Profile has information on embarkation, port location and facilities, and local transportation. The Author's Favorite Attractions are then listed; these can be used as a guide to tailor your own priority list. Sections on the capital city or main, historic, and other attractions are followed by those on shopping, sports, dining, entertainment, cultural events, holidays, and festivals.

For those who want to be on their own, each chapter has a walking tour with map, where appropriate, and descriptions of island attractions to see when you rent a car or hire a taxi.

Prices are not uniform in the Caribbean; they tend to be highest in the most popular places. You might sometimes have the feeling that there's a "soak the tourist" attitude, but try to remember that a place like St. Maarten, which has no industry and only minimal agriculture, must import almost all of its food and other supplies. Since the islands cater mainly to Americans, costs are high because American tastes often cost a great deal to satisfy.

MAPPING THE CARIBBEAN

The Caribbean roughly has the shape of a rectangle. The sides of the rectangle—north, east, south, and west—represent four regions that are quite different from one another, each with its particular qualities and special appeal.

The northern leg—Cuba, Jamaica, Haiti, Dominican Republic, and Puerto Rico—is known as the Greater Antilles. These are the largest, most developed islands, with the largest populations and closest to the United States, with direct air service (except for Cuba). Historically they have had the closest ties with the United States and from a visitor's standpoint, cater mainly to American tourists. Indeed, for most Americans, they *are* the Caribbean.

But far more numerous and more "Caribbean" in the tropical sense are the islands of the "other" Caribbean—the string of tiny jewels that starts east of Puerto Rico and arch south to South America. They are the islands of new discovery.

Sometimes called the Bali Hai of the Western Hemisphere, the islands of the Eastern Caribbean are serene, seductive hideaways with grand landscapes of savage beauty. Most are intensely green and very mountainous, often rising almost directly from turquoise seas to jagged, cloud-covered peaks.

Known in history as the Lesser Antilles, they fall into two groups: the Leewards on the north (comprised of U.S. and British Virgin Islands that bridge the northern and eastern Caribbean, Anguilla, St. Maarten/St. Martin, St. Barts, Saba, St. Eustatius, St. Kitts/Nevis, Antigua/Barbuda, Montserrat, and Guadeloupe); and the Windwards on the south (Dominica, Martinique, St. Lucia, St. Vincent and the Grenadines, and Grenada). Barbados, technically neither a Leeward nor a Windward island, is 100 miles to the east of St. Vincent. The islands on the south side of the Caribbean rectangle—Trinidad and Tobago, Aruba, Curaçao, and Bonaire—form what is known as the Southern Caribbean and are described more fully on page 5.

WHAT'S IN A NAME?

After battling with the French and Dutch for two hundred years in the 17th and 18th centuries, the British gained control over most of the Antilles in the late 18th century and divided them into two administrative groups, calling them by the nautical terms—the Leeward Islands and the Windward Islands. Following World War II, when some of the former British colonies obtained a measure of independence, they formed a loose alliance, called the Eastern Caribbean Associated States, with a common currency and protection in trade agreements under the British Commonwealth of which they are members.

Lesser Antilles and "Leewards and Windwards" are terms still used by mapmakers, but "Eastern Caribbean" has gradually replaced the nautical and colonial administrative terms as the popular name to define the small islands of the east, to differentiate them from the big islands of the north. Along with the former British colonies, the Eastern Caribbean now also includes the Dutch West Indies, the French West Indies, and the U.S. territories.

Until recently the islands of the Eastern Caribbean were visited only by yachts and small cruise ships and an occasional large ship en route to the Panama Canal or South America, but in the past decade, there have been significant changes for two reasons. First, since 1987, the number of cruise ships sailing to the Caribbean has almost doubled. As the competition for Caribbean cruises departing from Florida has intensified with the arrival of new ships, more ships and larger ships, cruise lines have felt the pressure to find new destinations.

Most lines have moved some of their fleet to San Juan, from which they sail through the Eastern Caribbean on a wide variety of itineraries. The development of San Juan as the major air hub of the Caribbean has also been an important consideration in its selection as an alternative home port. During the winter season, there are now as many ships based in San Juan as there are in either Miami or Fort Lauderdale. St. Thomas, St. Maarten, Martinique, and Barbados are being used as home ports, as well.

Meanwhile most islands of the Eastern Caribbean have improved and expanded their port facilities, roads, and transportation as well as shopping, sports, and other tourist facilities, specifically to attract more and larger ships. Small islands that were minor players in the past have developed into major ports.

PLANNING YOUR TIME

All cruise lines would like you to believe that their ships are the main reason to take a cruise, but they are the first to admit that most passengers select a cruise for its destinations. In the Eastern Caribbean the destinations are as different as the U.S. or British Virgin Islands, the French West Indies, and the Netherlands Antilles. Some, like Grenada and St. Lucia, are mountainous and lush with tropical greenery; others, like Aruba, are flat and dry, resembling the American southwest. Like Barbados and St. Croix some are steeped in history; others, like Bequia and Carriacou, are the hideaways time has left behind.

Together the ports on an Eastern Caribbean cruise provide a kaleidoscope of the region's history and cultures, scenery and sights, language and music. It is a window onto the islands with an ever-changing panorama. The Eastern Caribbean offers every warm-weather sport, along with magnificent weather in which to enjoy them, and a year-round calendar of feasts, festivals, and special events.

A cruise is the best and sometimes the only way to visit several Eastern Caribbean islands in one vacation—that's one of cruising's main attractions. But if you don't plan, you might come back thinking the islands are all alike. Each island has its own special features, personality, and appeal. This book explains their differences and will enable you to plan your activity in each port in order to have an interesting cruise full of variety.

Since cruise passengers are a diverse group with changing interests, this book is intended to address a variety of needs. Some readers may want to pursue sports, others may be more interested in history, art, and culture. Others may want to stroll around and shop. Any of these activities are available in Eastern Caribbean ports, but you will need to decide which activity you prefer to do at a particular destination. You also need to decide if you want to take an organized tour or see the sights on your own. Some Eastern Caribbean ports lend themselves to organized touring; others are best seen by walking or touring on your own.

San Juan, Barbados, and some Caribbean ports are both a home base and a port of call for cruise ships. Passengers arrive by plane to board their ships and often come early or plan to stay a few days after their cruises, when time is less of a constraint. They might want to plan both organized tours and independent travel.

To ensure that this book has the broadest possible application and can be used by many different kinds of cruise passengers, a great deal of specific information is provided on sports, sightseeing, shopping, culture, and how to see the port of call whether you take a tour or travel on your own. In any case the primary objective has been to help you organize and maximize your time in port to ensure that you get the most out of your visit.

THE CARIBBEAN
WITH A DIFFERENCE

Often called the Undiscovered Caribbean, most of the Eastern Caribbean are idyllic hideaways, still natural and unspoiled. It is of course difficult to generalize, since the islands are at various stages of development and sophistication, but with a few exceptions the Eastern Caribbean islands are less developed and hence less commercial than those of the Northern Caribbean.

For the most part these off-the-beaten-track destinations are little known to most Americans. They have retained a more local ambience, not one geared to American tourists. Their economies, generally, are based on agriculture. The people live closer to the land and are more self-reliant. There is a warm, easy natural quality about them.

The islands also differ from those of the north in origin, size, and history—elements that give them their character and ambience. Most islands are mountainous and volcanic in origin; some

still have smoking craters and other evidence of continuing volcanic activity. St. Lucia even boasts a "drive-in volcano." From their jagged, smoldering peaks, often shrouded in mist and white clouds brought by the trade winds, the terrain falls through exotic rain forests and lush green valleys crisscrossed by cascading rivers to coastlines scalloped with pearly beaches fringed by coral reefs floating in turquoise seas. On approach from a cruise ship, the panorama is breathtaking and fits the popular image of the tropics.

The island chain acts as a barrier between the Atlantic and Caribbean. On the east, or windward side, the rolling Atlantic Ocean pounds against rocky shores often covered with wind-sheared vegetation. On the west, or leeward side, the crystal waters of the calm Caribbean lap gently at the white—or black—sand beaches of reef-trimmed coves. These protected leeward waters have long been among the world's most popular yachting waters. Indeed, although the Eastern Caribbean is newly discovered for many cruise ships, it has been the favorite of yachtsmen for decades.

Most of the islands are less than 20 or 30 miles in length; yet often they have scenery so grand, it belies their small size. Sharp contrasts make up one of their most outstanding attractions. Martinique, for example, in a distance of only 50 miles drops from an active volcano at almost 5,000 feet and razorback peaks thick with rain forests to flowing meadows and pastureland—complete with grazing cows—to bone dry desert. On its east coast, white-capped Atlantic waves crash against weather-beaten shores. On the western Caribbean side, quiet, dreamy beaches hide in little coves—and all within a day's drive.

Sprinkled throughout this volcanic region are low-lying islands and coral atolls rung by pristine white sand beaches and coral reefs. These are often the popular destinations of day-sailing trips from the main ports of call.

The islands of the Eastern Caribbean are close together, like stepping stones. Cruise ships sailing on these routes are seldom out of sight of land and sometimes visit two islands in one day. These itineraries, unfortunately make for a hurried trip in a part of the world where the tranquil, relaxing pace is one of the most delightful attractions.

Added to the visual diversity of the land and the coral gardens of the sea, the Eastern Caribbean is a cultural kaleidoscope. It changes from the Spanish heritage in San Juan—from which most of the ships depart—to the Danish legacy in the U.S. Virgin Islands, to the Dutch in the Dutch Windwards, the French in the French West Indies, and the British in a dozen or so stops from Anguilla to Barbados. Throughout the region monuments, old forts, plantation homes, sugar mills, churches, and synagogues—often beautifully restored and used as art galleries, boutiques, restaurants, and museums—reflect that region's rich cultural heritage.

Out of this melting pot, the islands of the Eastern Caribbean have evolved a culture of their own—more creole or West Indian than the islands of the north—which is reflected in their festivals, dances, music, and cuisine. The islands have a year-round calendar of events that showcases the Eastern Caribbean's cultural diversity. Carnival, held at various times of the year in different islands, is a wonderful opportunity to see the region's creative talents at their best.

THE SOUTHERN CARIBBEAN

The southernmost islands—Trinidad and Tobago, Aruba and the Netherlands Antilles islands of Curaçao and Bonaire—are on the south side of the Caribbean rectangle and lie along the north coast of South America. Sometimes called the Deep Caribbean, they form separate units and are quite different in appearance, culture, and history from the islands of the Eastern Caribbean. The contrasts offered by these islands are delightful.

Due to their location they are normally ports of call on itineraries of longer than one week from Florida and San Juan and on cruises en route to South America or the Panama Canal.

They, too, are coming into their own now as ports of call on itineraries starting from Barbados or Curaçao. Also, some ships based in Jamaica, and others that visit it from Florida ports, drop south to Aruba or Curaçao. Adventure and nature-type cruises frequently combine the islands of the Deep Caribbean with journeys up the Orinoco or Amazon rivers.

THE SPICE OF LIFE

Each island is different, and discovering their differences is part of the fun and fascination of a Caribbean cruise. You can maximize the enjoyment of your cruise by taking advantage of the unique or unusual features of each port of call rather than repeating the same activity in each port. Planning activities that take in the cultural as well as the scenic variety the ports offer. Enjoy a sport or learn a new one in at least one port, and select an activity in each port that you cannot do elsewhere.

In other words, if you were to spend all your time on a walking tour in Old San Juan, you might want to have a gourmet lunch in Guadeloupe, take a snorkeling or diving lesson in St. Maarten, and go hiking in a rain forest in St. Lucia. If you plan to shop for perfume and other French products in Martinique, you should plan another activity as well, because most people finish their shopping in an hour or two and then don't know what to do with themselves.

FACTS TO REMEMBER

CLIMATE: While the sun keeps the islands warm, the trade winds that blow from the northeast and east throughout the year keep the temperatures comfortable and consistent, averaging about seventy-eight to eighty-two degrees year-round. The difference between summer and winter temperatures seldom varies more than five to ten degrees. December through March are normally the driest, coolest months, when temperatures on some islands might drop to sixty-five degrees on mountain peaks. July, August, and September are the hottest, wettest months, when temperatures reach eighty-six to ninety degrees and the humidity can be 100 percent. Fortunately, during this period, frequent tropical showers quickly cool the air.

The lay of the land has a direct impact on weather on every island. Some islands such as Antigua, Barbados, and St. Barts, which do not have the high mountains and thick foliage characteristic of most Eastern Caribbean islands, tend to be dry with low rainfall averaging only 46 inches annually. And even on the islands with high mountains, such as St. Kitts, the climate can vary from 148 inches of annual rain on forested mountain peaks to less than 40 inches per year in dry lowlands.

Trinidad and Tobago, Aruba, Bonaire, and Curaçao fall south of the Caribbean hurricane belt. Aruba, Bonaire, and Curaçao are similar in climate, which, typically, is much drier than in other parts of the Eastern Caribbean. On these islands where the terrain is low, the winds are strong and constant, reaching their greatest intensity in June and July.

 CLOTHING: Cotton and lightweight fabrics are recommended year-round. Informal, casual but conservative dress is appropriate throughout the islands. Bathing suits, tank tops, and revealing attire are not acceptable anywhere except on the beach. West Indians generally are conservative and are offended by tourists wearing such attire in public places. Some casinos require jackets.

In the French West Indies, on an island like St. Barts the dress code is informal, with slacks, shorts, or jeans by day and only a slightly more fashionable look at night. As in France topless is not only allowed, it's expected. Guadeloupe and St. Martin have topless and nudist beaches, but Martinique does not.

Remember that the sun is very strong. Wear a sun hat or visor for protection, and always use sunscreen lotion. For hiking at high altitudes, take a sweater and good hiking shoes.

 DEPARTURE TAX: All the islands covered in this book, with the exception of Puerto Rico, U.S. Virgin Islands, Guadeloupe, and Martinique, have departure taxes. Cruise passengers do not pay these taxes, unless they leave their ship during the cruise to return home by air. The amount is noted in Fast Facts for each island.

 ELECTRICITY: Aruba, St. Maarten, and U.S. Virgin Islands have 120 volts A.C., 60 cycles; Barbados, Bonaire, Curaçao, and Puerto Rico have 110-120 volts A.C., 50 cycles.

The French West Indies and all other islands (Anguilla, Antigua/Barbuda, British Virgin Islands, Dominica, Grenada, Montserrat, St. Kitts/Nevis, St. Lucia, St. Vincent, Trinidad and Tobago) have 220 volts A.C., 60 or 50 cycles. Appliances made in the United States need transformers or models with converters built into them. Hotels on most islands, however, have 110 volts A.C., 60 cycles or both currents. If in doubt inquire at the hotel front desk.

 ENTRY FORMALITIES: U.S. and Canadian citizens do not need visas, but if you leave your ship you will need proof of citizenship with photo (passport, birth certificate, naturalization papers). Most islands also require visitors to have a valid onward or return ticket.

In the French West Indies (Guadeloupe, Martinique, St. Barts, St. Martin), if proof of citizenship is a document other than a passport (such as a notarized birth certificate), it must have a raised seal and photo identification.

PORT SECURITY: No special identity or security measures are required on any island covered in this book. Passengers are allowed to come and go from their ships freely; every cruise ship has its own system for identifying its passengers. Large ships usually issue identity cards like a credit card, while small ship may simply use cabin keys or tabs.

TIME: All the islands covered here fall into the Atlantic Standard Time Zone, which is one hour ahead of Eastern Standard Time. When Daylight Savings Time is in effect in the United States, only a few of the islands change their time. In those months Atlanta Standard Time is the same as Eastern Daylight Time.

VACCINATION REQUIREMENTS: There are no innoculation requirements for U.S. and Canadian citizens to visit any island in the Caribbean.

SELECTING A CRUISE

TIPS AND ADVICE

With so many cruises going to so many different places, selecting one can be difficult. My suggestion is to start your planning at a travel agency. About 95 percent of all cruises are purchased through travel agents. It will not cost more than buying a cruise directly from a cruise line, and it will save you time.

USING A TRAVEL AGENT

A good travel agency stocks the brochures of the leading cruise lines; these show prices and details on the ship's itineraries and facilities. An experienced agent will help you understand the language of a cruise brochure, read a deck plan, and make reservations. The knowledgeable agent can help you make comparisons and guide you in the selection of a ship and an itinerary to match your interests. Your agent can book your dining room table and handle a particular request such as for an anniversary party or a special diet. Agents also know about packages and discounts that can help you save money.

In recent years, with the boom in cruising, there has been a rapid growth in travel agencies that sell only cruises. Such specialized agencies are more likely than general agencies, which sell all the products of travel, to have staffs with firsthand knowledge of many ships and should be able to give you a profile of the ship, its crew, and its personality. If not, you should go to another agency.

THE BUILT-IN VALUE OF A CRUISE VACATION

Of all the attractions of cruising, none is more important than value. For one price you get transportation, accommodations, meals, entertainment, use of all facilities, and a host of recreational activity. The only items not included are tips, drinks, personal services such as hairdressers, port tax, and shore excursions. There are no hidden costs.

Dollar for dollar, it's hard to beat a cruise for value. To make an accurate assessment of how the cost of a cruise compares with other types of holidays, be sure to compare similar elements. A holiday at sea should be compared with a holiday at a luxury resort, because the quality of service, food, and entertainment on most cruises is available only at posh resorts.

The average brochure price of a one-week Caribbean cruise is about $200 to $250 per day including airfare and all the ingredients previously described, but with current discounts and advance purchase plans these prices can be cut in half. Shorter three- and four-day Bahamas cruises range from $130 to $150 per day and there are plenty of low promotion fares available for them, too. No luxury resorts give you transportation to and from the resort, a hotel room, four full meals plus two or three snacks each day, nightly entertainment plus a myriad of activity—all for the one price of $150 to $250. Deluxe resorts can't match such an offering even in their off-seasons.

Stretching Your Budget

Air/sea packages provide cruise passengers further measurable savings in airfare. Because cruise lines transport so many passengers to and from their departure cities on a regular basis, they can buy air transportation in volume at low group rates and offer it as "free air." Since, more often than not, the air travel is on regularly scheduled flights, cruise passengers have the utmost flexibility in making their travel plans. The packages also provide savings on baggage handling, two-way transfers from the airport to the ship, and other features.

Air/sea combinations are available in two forms: an all-in-one package combining a cruise and air transportation in one price; or a second type in which the cruise is priced separately and an air supplement is added on to the cruise price, or a credit for air transportation from one's hometown to the ship's nearest departure port is offered. The amount of the supplement or credit varies from one cruise line to another. But, usually, the supplement is slightly more the farther away from the departure port you live. Still, the total cost is far less to you than if the cruise and air transportation were purchased separately. The details are spelled out in the cruise line's brochure. Ask your travel agent to explain how the package works as it can be confusing.

Is Free Air Free?

If you are skeptical—you don't get something for nothing—every cruise company publishes pamphlets that show the rates for every cabin on its ships, regardless of how passengers elect to get to the ship. If the cruise offers "free" air transportation and quotes one price for the package without a breakdown for each component, you can still know the value by reading the section intended for those prospective passengers who live in or near the departure port of the ship.

Although air/sea packages save you money, it goes without saying that some definitely represent larger savings than others, depending on the cruise line, the cruise, and the time of year. Every line's policy is different and policies vary not only from line to line, but even from cruise to cruise on any specific ship. The introduction of new cruise lines and the addition of new cruise ships, particularly in the Caribbean, have created a buyer's market with real bargains. It pays to shop around.

SELECTING A SHIP

The ship and the cruise line's reputation are other considerations in making your selection. Not only do ships differ; so do their passengers. You are more likely to enjoy a cruise with people who are seeking a similar type of holiday and with whom you share a community of interests and activities. A good travel agent who specializes in selling cruises is aware of the differences and should be able to steer you to a ship that's right for you. But before you visit an agent or begin to cull the colorful and enticing brochures, here are some tips on the items affecting cost that can help you in making a selection.

SELECTING A CABIN

The largest single item in the cost of a cruise is the cabin, also known as a stateroom. The cost of a cabin varies greatly and is determined by its size and location. Generally, the cabins on the top deck are the largest and most expensive; the

prices drop and the cabins narrow on each deck down from the top. (Elevators and stairs provide access between decks.) But the most expensive cabins are not necessarily the best. There are other factors to consider.

Almost all cruise ships cabins have private bathrooms, but the size and fittings vary and affect cost. For example, cabins with full bathtubs are more expensive than those with showers only. Greater standardization of cabins is a feature of most new cruise ships.

Outside cabins are more costly than inside ones. There is a common misconception that inside cabins are to be avoided. It dates back to the days before air-conditioning when an outside cabin above the water line was desirable because the porthole could be opened for ventilation. Today's ships are climate-controlled; an inside cabin is as comfortable as an outside one. What's more, on a Caribbean cruise particularly, you will spend very little time in your cabin; it is mainly a place to sleep and change clothes. An inside cabin often provides genuine savings and is definitely worth investigating for those on a limited budget.

For the most stable ride, the deck at water level or below has less roll (side to side motion) and the cabins in the center of the ship have the least pitch (back and forth motion). But these cabins also cost more than those in the front (fore) or the back (aft) of the ship. Fore (or the bow) has less motion and is therefore preferable to aft (or the stern) where sometimes there is vibration from the ship's engines.

A ship's deck plan shows the exact location of each cabin and is usually accompanied by diagrams of the fittings in the cruise line's brochures. It does not give the dimensions of the cabin, but one can have a reasonable estimate since beds are standard single size—about 3 x 6 feet. Some ships have double beds, but most have twin beds that can be converted to doubles on request.

A few ships have single cabins; otherwise, a passenger booking a cabin alone pays a rate that is one and a half times the price per person for two sharing a cabin. A few ships offer special single rates on certain cruises or reserve a few cabins for single occupancy at the same rate as the per person rate on a shared basis plus a small supplement. Your travel agent should be able to give you specific information about singles rates.

OTHER COST FACTORS

As might be expected, rates for the winter season in the Caribbean are higher than in the spring, summer, or fall. Cruises over Christmas, New Year's, and other major holidays are usually the year's most expensive, but often, real bargains are to be found on cruises immediately before or after a holiday season when demand drops and lines are eager to stimulate business.

The length of the cruise bears directly on its cost. Longer cruises provide more elegance and fancier dining and service. The cost also varies depending on the ship's itinerary. For example, it is more economical for a cruise line to operate a set schedule of the same ports throughout the year, such as the ships departing weekly from Florida to the Caribbean, than it is to change itineraries every few weeks.

Family Rates

If you are planning a family cruise, look for cruise lines that actively promote family travel and offer special rates for children or for third and fourth persons in a cabin. It means a bit of crowding but can yield big savings. Family rates vary from one cruise line to another. As a rule of thumb, children sharing a cabin with two paying adults get discounts of 50 percent or more of the minimum fare. Qualifying ages vary, too, with a child usually defined as 2 to 12, and sometimes up to 17 years. Some lines have teen fares, while at certain times of the year others have free or special rates for the third or fourth person sharing a cabin with two full-fare adults, regardless of age. Most lines permit infants under two years to travel free of charge.

CRUISE DISCOUNTS

In today's highly competitive market, discounts have become a way of life. Cruise lines use them to publicize a new ship or itinerary, to attract families, younger passengers, singles, and a diversity of people. Some low fares are available year-round but may be limited to a certain number of cabins on each sailing; others are seasonal or may apply to specific cruises.

You can take advantage of fare discounts in two ways. If you book early, you can usually benefit from early bird discounts, and of course, you can

be sure you have the cruise you want. On the other hand, if you are in a position to be flexible, you can wait to catch the last minute "fire sales." Cruise lines do not advertise the fact, but you can sometimes negotiate the lowest price on the day of sailing. To take advantage of this situation, you need to have maximum flexibility.

And remember, when you are buying a cruise, you will have already paid for *all* your accommodations, *all* meals (three meals a day is only the beginning; most ships have seven or more food services daily), *all* entertainment, and *all* recreational facilities aboard ship, and in most cases, round-trip airfare to the ship's departure port, baggage handling, and transfers. It is this all-inclusive aspect of a cruise that makes it a good value—a particularly significant advantage for families with children and those who need to know in advance the cost of a vacation.

SHORE EXCURSIONS

Sight-seeing tours, called shore excursions by the cruise lines, are available for an additional cost at every port of call in the Caribbean. A pamphlet on the shore excursions offered by the cruise line is usually included in the literature you receive prior to sailing. If not, ask for one.

A few lines encourage travel agents to sell their shore excursions in advance; most do not. Rather, you buy them on board ship from the purser, cruise director, or tour office. Most people seem to prefer buying them on board since, frequently, their interests and plans change once the cruise is underway.

A word of caution: When I began this series in 1987, I found that there was very little difference between the cruise ships' prices for tours and those of local tour companies, if you were staying in a hotel. However, in the last few years, the situation has changed so dramatically that I must alert readers to the change. In their need to keep their cruise prices down in the face of intense competition and rampant discounting, many cruise lines have come to regard shore excursions (as well as ancillary services such as shipboard shopping, bars, and spa facilities) as profit centers; some are selling their tours at exorbitant prices.

In a preliminary survey, I found prices jacked up 30 to 50 percent; some are even double the prices you would pay on shore. To help you in your selection and to gauge fair prices, each port of call in this book has descriptions of the main shore excursions offered by the majority of cruise lines, as well as some that you must arrange on your own. The approximate price of each excursion when you buy it directly from a tour company on shore is noted, where possible, along with the current price at which it is sold aboard ship. The prices were accurate at press time but, of course, they are not guaranteed.

Since tours vary from vendor to vendor and cruise ship to cruise ship, it is difficult to generalize. Therefore, when you check prices, it is important that you compare like items and, when necessary, factor in such additional costs as transportation from the pier to the vendor's office or starting point. The information and prices provided here are intended as guidelines. Even if they change, the increase is not likely to be more than a dollar or two. If you come across shore excursion prices that appear to be out of line in comparison with those found in this book, please write to me and enclose a copy of the tours with their descriptions and prices sold on your cruise.

PORT TALKS

All ships offer what is known as a port talk—a brief description of the country or island and port where the ship will dock as well as shopping tips. The quality of these talks varies enormously, not only with the cruise line but also with the ship, and can depend on such wide ranging considerations as the knowledge and skill of the cruise director to the policy of the cruise line as to the true purpose of the information.

You should be aware that most cruise lines in the Caribbean have turned these port talks into sales pitches for certain products and stores with which they have exclusive promotional agreements and in which the cruise lines take commissions or are paid directly by the stores. You will receive a map of the port with "recommended" shops. What that really means is that the shop has paid the cruise line for being promoted in port talks and advertising in the ship's magazine that

might appear in your cabin. Also, sometimes cruise directors receive commissions from local stores, even though they deny it. Hence, their vested interest could color their presentation and recommendations.

There are three ways to avoid being misled. If a cruise line, a cruise director, a guide, or anyone else recommends one store to the exclusion of all others, that should alert you to shop around before buying. The recommended store may actually be the best place to buy—but it may not. Second, if you are planning to make sizeable purchases of jewelry, cameras, or china, etc., check prices at home before you leave and bring a list of prices with you. Be sure, however, you are comparing like products. Finally, check the prices in shipboard shops, which are usually very competitive with those at ports of call.

Happily, because you have this book you do not need to rely on port talks for information, but if you do attend your ship's port talks and find that they have been more sales pitch than enlightenment, please write and tell me about your experience.

KNOW BEFORE YOU GO

LUGGAGE AND WARDROBE: There are no limits on the amount of luggage you can bring on board ship, but most staterooms do not have much closet and storage space. More importantly, since you are likely to be flying to your departure port you need to be guided by airline regulations regarding excess baggage. Life on a cruise, especially a Caribbean one, is casual. It is needless to be burdened with a lot of baggage; you will spend your days in sports clothes—slacks, shorts, T-shirts, bathing suits. Men usually are asked to wear a jacket at dinner.

The first and last nights of your cruise and the nights your ship is in port almost always call for casual dress. At least one night will be the captain's gala party where tuxedos for men and long dresses for women are requested but not mandatory. Another night might be a masquerade party; it's entirely up to you whether or not to participate.

A gentleman who does not have a tuxedo should bring a basic dark suit and white shirt. Add a selection of slacks and sport shirts, one or two sports jackets, and two pairs of bathing trunks. Women will find nylon and similar synthetics are good to use on a cruise because they are easy to handle, but these fabrics can be hot under the tropical sun. It largely depends on your tolerance for synthetic fabrics in hot weather. Personally, I find cottons and cotton blends to be the most comfortable. You will need two cocktail dresses for evening wear. A long dress for the captain's party is appropriate but not compulsory. Add a sweater or stole for cool evening breezes and the ship's air-conditioning in the dining room and lounges. Take cosmetics and sun lotion, but don't worry if you forget something. It will most likely be available in shipboard or portside shops.

You will need rubber-soled shoes for walking on deck and a comfortable pair of walking shoes for sight-seeing. Sunglasses and a hat or sun visor for protection against the strong Caribbean sun are essential. A tote bag comes in handy for carrying odds and ends; include several plastic bags for wet towels and bathing suits upon returning from a visit to a beach. You might also want to keep camera equipment in plastic bags as protection against the salt air and water and sand. And don't forget to pack whatever sporting equipment and clothes you will need. If you plan to snorkel, scuba, or play tennis, often you can save on rental fees by bringing your own gear.

DOCUMENTATION: Requirements for vaccinations, visas, and so on depend on the destinations of the ship and are detailed in the information you receive from the cruise lines. Among the Caribbean's many advantages is that normally no destination (except Cuba, which is not covered in this book) requires visas of U.S. and Canadian citizens arriving as cruise passengers.

MEAL TIMES: All but the most luxurious Caribbean cruise ships have two sittings for the main meals. Early sitting breakfast is from 7 to 8 A.M.; lunch is from 12 to 1 P.M.; and dinner is from 6:15 to 7:30 P.M. On the late sitting, breakfast is from 8 to 9 A.M.; lunch is from 1:30 to 2:30 P.M.; and dinner is from 8:15 to 9:30 P.M. If you are an early riser, you will probably be happy with the early sitting. If you are likely to close the disco every night, you might prefer the late one. Of course, you will not be confined to these meals as there are usually a buffet breakfast, lunch on deck, a midnight buffet, and afternoon tea.

REQUESTING A TABLE: Your travel agent can request your table in advance, if you want a table for two or for your family, as well as your preference for early or late seating. Some cruise lines will confirm your reservation in advance; others require you to sign up for your dining table with the maître d'hôtel soon after boarding your ship. In this day of computers, it's hard to understand why any cruise line would want to put a passenger through this unnecessary inconvenience, but some do.

ELECTRICAL APPLIANCES: Cabins on almost all new ships have outlets for electric razors and have hairdryers or are wired for them, but older ships are not. Instead, rooms with special outlets are provided. Few ships allow you to use electric irons in your cabin because of the potential fire hazard. Electric current is normally 115–120 volts—but not always—and plugs are the two-prong, American-type ones. Check with your cruise line for specific information.

LAUNDRY AND DRY CLEANING: All ships have either laundry service for your personal clothing (for which there is an extra charge) or coin-operated laundry rooms. Only a very few have dry cleaning facilities. In the Caribbean, this is not an important consideration since the clothes required are cotton or cotton blends and should be easy to wash.

HAIRDRESSING: Almost all Caribbean cruise ships have hairdressers for both men and women. Prices are comparable to those at deluxe resorts.

RELIGIOUS SERVICES: All ships hold interdenominational services; many also have a daily Catholic mass. Services will be conducted by the captain or a clergyman. At ports of call you will be welcome to attend local services.

MEDICAL NEEDS: All cruise ships are required by law to have at least one doctor, nurse, and infirmary or mini-hospital. Doctor visits and medicine are extra costs.

Seasickness: First-time cruise passengers probably worry more about becoming seasick than about any other aspect of cruising. Certainly they worry more than they should, particularly on a Caribbean cruise where the sea is calm almost year-round. Ships today have stabilizers, which steady them in all but the roughest seas. But if you are still worried, there are several types of nonprescription medicines such as Dramamine and Bonine that help to guard against motion sickness. Buy some to bring along—you may not need it but having it with you might be comforting. Also, the ship's doctor can provide you with Dramamine and other medication that will be immediately effective, should you need it.

Sea Bands are a fairly new product for seasickness prevention. They are a pair of elasticized wristbands, each with a small plastic disk that, based on the principle of acupuncture, applies pressure on the inside wrist. I use Sea Bands and have given them to friends to use and can attest to their effectiveness. They are particularly useful for people who have difficulty taking medication. Sea Bands are found in drug, toiletry, and health-care stores and can be ordered from Travel Accessories, P.O. Box 391162, Solon, Ohio 44139, 216–248–8432. They even make sequined covers in a dozen colors to wear over the bands for evening.

There are two important things to remember about seasickness: Don't dwell on your fear. Even the best sailors and frequent cruisers need a day to get their "sea legs." If you should happen to get a queasy feeling, take some medicine immediately. The worst mistake you can make is to play the hero, thinking it will go away. When you deal with the symptoms immediately, relief is fast, and you are seldom likely to be sick. If you wait, the queasy feeling will linger and you run a much greater risk of being sick.

Caution against the Caribbean Sun: You should be extra careful about the sun in the tropics. It is much stronger than the sun to which most people are accustomed. Do not stay in the direct sun for long stretches at a time, and use a sunscreen at all times. Nothing can spoil a vacation faster than a sunburn.

SHIPBOARD SHOPS: There's always a shop for essentials you might have forgotten or that can't wait until the next port of call. Many ships—particularly the new ones—have elaborate shops competitive with stores at ports of call. It's another reason to pack lightly, since you are almost sure to buy gifts and souvenirs during the cruise.

TIPPING: Tipping is a matter of a great deal of discussion but much less agreement. How much do you tip in a restaurant or a hotel? Normally, the tip should be about $3 per person per day for each of your cabin stewards and dining room waiters. On some ships, particularly those with Greek crews, the custom is to contribute to the ship's common kitty in the belief that those behind the scenes such as kitchen staffs should share in the bounty. On some ships, dining room staffs also pool their tips. Tipping guidelines are sometimes printed in literature your cruise line sends in advance, enabling you to factor the expense into your budget even before booking a cruise. The cruise director, as part of his advice-giving session at the end of the cruise, also explains the ship's policy and offers guidelines.

TELEPHONE CALLS—SHIP-TO-SHORE AND SHORE-TO-SHIP: Most new ships have telephones in cabins with international direct dialing capability and fax facilities in their offices. Be warned, however, the service is very expensive— about $15 per minute. If someone at home or in your office needs to reach you in an emergency, they can telephone your ship directly. Those calling from the continental United States would dial 011 plus 874 (the ocean area code for the Caribbean), followed by the seven-digit telephone number of your ship. Someone calling from Puerto Rico should dial 128 and ask for the long distance operator.

Instructions on making such calls, how to reach the ship, or who to notify in case of an emergency are usually included in the information sent to you by your cruise line along with your tickets and luggage tags. If not, your travel agent can obtain it. You should have this information before you leave home.

PART II

CARIBBEAN CRUISE LINES AND THEIR SHIPS

 A GUIDE

Every effort has been made to ensure the accuracy of the information on the cruise lines and their ships, their ports of call, and prices, but do keep in mind that cruise lines change their ships' itineraries often for a variety of reasons. Always check with the cruise line or with a travel agent before making plans. For specific information on the itineraries of ships cruising to the Eastern Caribbean, see charts at the end of this book.

AMERICAN CANADIAN CARIBBEAN LINE, 461 Water Street, Warren, RI 02885; 401-247-0955; 800-556-7450; fax 401-245-8303

Ships (Passengers): *Caribbean Prince* (83); *Grande-Carib* (100); *Mayan Prince* (90); *Niagara Prince* (84)
Departure ports: Various ports
Type of cruises: 12 days Panama Canal/San Blas; Central America; Virgin Islands; Trinidad/Orinoco/Tobago; and Aruba/Bonaire/Curaçao during Winter
Life-style tips: Family-style dining; mature and experienced passengers; light adventure; no frills. Emphasis is on natural attraction and local culture

If you are looking for tranquility, informality, and conversation with fellow passengers instead of floor shows and casinos, American Canadian Caribbean Line offers low-key cruises around the Bahamas archipelago, Belize, the southwestern Caribbean, and Central America during the winter and early spring.

In 1964, founder Luther Blount designed his first small ship for cruising Canada's inland waterways.

By 1988, the line had expanded to the extent that it could add Caribbean to its name. In the intervening years, ACCL remained faithful to the concept that small, intimate ships with limited planned entertainment can be successful. The ships' innovative bow ramps and shallow drafts give passengers direct access to beaches, coves, and places that are inaccessible to larger ships.

ACCL's ships are popular with mature, well-traveled passengers who like hearty American menus and the informal atmosphere of family-style dining. It is an atmosphere for instant friendships and complete relaxation. The line's large number of repeaters would seem to indicate that passengers agree with its concept and appreciate the "in-close" facility the ships bring to the cruise experience.

CARNIVAL CRUISE LINES, 3655 N.W. 87th Avenue, Miami, FL 33178–2428; 305–599–2600; 800–327–7373; fax 305–599–8630

Ships (Passengers): *Carnival Destiny* (2,642); *Celebration* (1,486); *Ecstasy* (2,040); *Elation* (2,040); *Fantasy* (2,044); *Fascination* (2,040); *Holiday* (1,452); *Imagination* (2,044); *Inspiration* (2,044); *Jubilee* (1,486); *Paradise* (2,040); *Sensation* (2,040); *Tropicale* (1,022)
Departure ports: Miami, San Juan
Type of cruises: 7 days to Eastern, Southern, Western, and Northern Caribbean, and the Panama Canal
Life-style tip: The "Fun Ships," youthful, casual, action-filled; high value for money

When Kathie Lee Gifford flashes her pretty smile across your television screen and says, "Carnival, the most popular cruise line in the world," that's not simply advertising hype. It's true—and the story of how it got to that position is the stuff of legends.

In 1972 Florida-based cruise executive Ted Arison and an innovative Boston-based travel agency bought the *Empress of Canada*, which they renamed the *Mardi Gras* to start a cruise line that would stand the stodgy old steamship business on its ear. But alas, the *Mardi Gras* ran aground on her maiden cruise. After staring at losses three years in a row, Arison took full ownership of the company, assuming its $5 million debt, buying its assets—i.e., the ship—for $1, and launched the "Fun Ships" concept that is Carnival's hallmark.

The idea was to get away from the class-conscious elitism that had long been associated with luxury liners and to fill the ship with so much action-packed fun that the ship itself would be the cruise experience. The line also aimed at lowering the average age of passengers by removing the formality associated with cruising and providing a wide selection of activity and entertainment to attract active young adults, young couples, honeymooners, and families with children at reasonable prices. In only a few months Carnival turned a profit and in the next two years added two more ships.

The line's next move was as surprising as it was bold. In 1978 when shipbuilding costs and fuel prices were skyrocketing—threatening the very future of vacations-at-sea, Carnival ordered a new ship, larger and more technologically advanced than any cruise ship in service. It changed the profile of ships and enhanced the "fun" aspects of cruises. But it was Carnival's next move that really set the trend of the eighties and beyond.

In 1982, less than ten years after its rocky start, Carnival ordered three "superliners," each carrying 1,800 passengers, with design and decor as far removed from the grand old luxury liner as could be imagined. Between 1985 and 1987, the three ships—*Holiday, Jubilee*, and *Celebration*—were put into service. The decor was so different, it was zany. The owners called it "a Disney World for adults." On the *Holiday*, the main promenade deck, called "Broadway," complete with boardwalk and a Times Square, runs double-width down only one side of the ship and is lined with bars, nightclubs, casinos, lounges, and disco with as much glitz and glitter as the neon on Broadway. At one end of the deck there's a marquee and an enormous theater spanning two decks where Broadway musical–style and Las Vegas cabaret–type shows are staged twice nightly.

In 1990, Carnival outdid itself with the *Fantasy*, the first of eight megaliners even more dazzling than the earlier superliners. A ship for the twenty-first century, the *Fantasy*, with its flashy decor and high-energy ambience, is something of a Las Vegas, Disneyland, and Starlight Express in one. The heart of the ship is an atrium, awash in lights, towering seven decks high. Here and in the entertainment areas, 15 miles of computerized lights are programmed to change color—constantly, but imperceptibly—from white and cool blue to hot red, altering the ambience with each change. The ships have full-fledged gyms and spas and so many entertainment and recreation outlets that you need more than one cruise to find them all. In December 1996 *Carnival Destiny*, the world's largest cruise ship, made her debut.

Now headed by Arison's son, Micky, Carnival is directed by a young, energetic, and aggressive team that seems determined to entice *everybody*—single, married, families, children, retirees, disabled (on the new ships), first-time cruisers, repeat cruisers, people from the north, south, east, and west, and from all walks of life—to take a cruise. To that end, the cruises are priced aggressively and offer early bird and special rates for third and fourth persons in the cabin.

Do all these ideas work? You bet they do! By 1998 Carnival will have 13 cruise ships in service, carrying almost two million passengers a year. That's up from 80,000 passengers in its first year. In 1987 Carnival Cruise Lines went public, and the following year it began *Carnival Air Lines;* and purchased the long-established Holland America Line, which in turn owned Windstar Cruises. Later it acquired partial ownership in the Seabourn Cruise Line, with ultra-luxurious ships. Although these lines operate under their own banners, the combination makes Carnival one of the world's largest cruise lines and gives it enormous marketing clout across the widest possible spectrum. Recently, Carnival acquired ownership in Airtour, a large European tour company, as an avenue for expanding in Europe. And in 1997, in a joint venture, Carnival and Airtour bought Costa Cruises, Europe's largest cruise line.

CELEBRITY CRUISES, 5201 Blue Lagoon Drive, Miami, FL 33126; 305–262–6677; fax 800–437–5111

Ships (Passengers): *Century* (1,750); *Galaxy* (1,750); *Horizon* (1,354); *Mercury* (1,750); *Zenith* (1,374)
Departure ports: Ft. Lauderdale, San Juan
Type of cruises: 7, 10, 11 nights to the Bahamas and Northern Caribbean; Eastern and Western Caribbean; Bermuda
Life-style tip: Modestly deluxe cruises at moderate prices

In 1989, when John Chandris, the nephew of the founder of Chandris Cruises, announced the creation of a new deluxe mid-priced cruise line, he said the goal was "to bring more luxurious cruises to experienced travelers but still at affordable prices." He was met with a great deal of skepticism; "deluxe" and "mid-priced" seemed a contradiction in terms. But three years later, he had made believers out of all his doubters.

Not only did Celebrity Cruises accomplish what it set out to do, it did it better than anyone imagined and in record-breaking time. A Celebrity cruise is not only deluxe; it offers the best value for the money of any cruise line in its price category.

Celebrity was a completely new product with a new generation of ships designed for the 1990s. It defined the ideal size of a cruise ship and the appropriate layout, cabins, decor, and ambience for its market and set new standards of service and cuisine in its price category.

Celebrity's ships are not as glitzy as some of the new megaliners but they are spacious and have a similar array of entertainment and recreation. The once-standard one-lounge-for-all has been replaced by small, separate lounges, each with its own decor, ambience, and entertainment, and a variety of bars to give passengers a range of options. They have stunning, stylish decor that has brought back some of the glamour of cruising in bygone days but with a fresh, contemporary look.

From its inception, Celebrity Cruises aimed at creating superior cuisine as one way to distinguish itself. To achieve their goal, they engaged as their food consultant Michel Roux, the award-winning master French chef who operates two Michelin three-star restaurants and five other restaurants in England, a catering service, and other food enterprises. He spent six months developing the menus for Celebrity Cruises and working with the ships' chandlers and chefs.

Roux accomplished miracles and set a new standard for other cruise lines. The food is sophisticated but unpretentious; quality is more important than quantity, although there's no lack of quantity either. Using the best-quality products, Roux keeps the menus seasonal to the extent possible, changing them every three months. To make sure the cuisine stays at his demanding level, he sails on each ship several times during the year.

Celebrity was launched in 1990 with the brand-new *Horizon* and the *Meridian* (which was sold in early 1997). The stylish, elegant *Horizon* is classic and very contemporary at the same time. It has mostly outside staterooms equipped with closed-circuit television that carries daily programs of events, first-run movies, and world news. The ship has a piano bar, a nightclub, a duplex show lounge with state-of-the-art sound and lighting systems, a disco, a casino, and an observation lounge. There are shops, a sports and fitness center, two swimming pools, and three Jacuzzis. The *Zenith*, which lives up to its name in every way, followed in 1992 and is almost identical to the *Horizon*.

Celebrity received awards for its ships and its cuisine from the first year of operation. Now, in the suites, butler service is available. As a send-off on the last day of the cruise, all passengers may enjoy a classic high tea with white-glove service and classical music.

Also, in 1992 Celebrity teamed up with Overseas Shipholding Group, one of the world's largest bulk-shipping companies, to form a joint cruise company and launch three new megaliners known as the Century series—designed, the cruise line believes, for the twenty-first century. Among the innovations, Sony Corporation is providing the most advanced technology in entertainment and interactive services yet seen on cruise ships. The first ship, *Century,* made her debut in December 1996, followed by the *Galaxy* in November 1996 and the *Mercury* in 1997.

In 1997 Royal Caribbean Cruise Line bought Celebrity Cruises and will operate it as a seperate brand.

CLIPPER CRUISE LINE, 7711 Bonhomme Avenue, St. Louis, MO 63105; 314–727–2929; 800–325–0010; fax 314–727–6576

Ships (Passengers): *Clipper Adventurer* (122); *Nantucket Clipper* (102); *Yorktown Clipper* (138)
Departure ports: St. Thomas, Grenada, Curaçao, Panama City
Type of cruises: 7 days to the Virgin Islands; 11 days to the Eastern and Southern Caribbean
Life-style tip: Small ships for nature-oriented travelers

Clipper Cruise Line is a special niche: nature-oriented cruises on comfortable small ships with pleasing interior decor, sailing to the little-known corners of the Caribbean and Central America in winter and other parts of North and South America during the other seasons. The ships' shallow drafts often enable them to sail into places where larger ships cannot go.

The ships carry Zodiacs that enable them to drop anchor frequently for passengers to enjoy a swim at secluded beaches, hike in a rain forest, or sail up a river to a remote village. Daily onboard seminars by a naturalist on the places to be visited are followed by discussions after the visit. The naturalist also acts as a guide for those who want to take nature walks, and bird-watch.

The crew is American, mostly fresh out of college, and unfailingly polite and friendly. The itinerary is leisurely and so is the activity. Scuba diving, windsurfing, golf, or tennis can also be arranged, depending on the itinerary. Absent, but not missed by its passengers, are the casinos, pools, staged entertainment, and organized diversions of large ships. Both the ship and passenger complement are small enough that you get to know everyone aboard in the course of a week.

Clipper's ships have outside staterooms—most with large windows. Some are entered from the outside (as on river steamboats) rather than interior corridors. Cabins and lounges are nicely decorated with quality furnishings. Passengers dine at one seating on good American cuisine prepared by a staff headed by a chef from the prestigious Culinary Institute of America.

Clipper Cruise Line passengers are not bargain hunters or those looking for last-minute specials. Rather, they are mature and well-traveled.

In 1997, Clipper was acquired by INTRAV, a St. Louis–based, NASDAQ-traded travel company, and added a third ship, *Clipper Adventurer,* which will begin sailing in 1998.

CLUB MEDITERRANEE, S.A., 40 West 57th Street, New York, N.Y. 10019; 212–977–2100; 1-800–CLUB–MED; fax 212–315–5392

Ships (Passengers): *Club Med I* (392); *Club Med II* (392);
Departure port: Martinique
Type of cruises: 7 days to Eastern and Southern Caribbean
Life-style tip: Casual and sports oriented

Club Med, a name synonomous with all-inclusive vacations and an easy life-style, took its popular formula to sea in 1990 with the introduction of the world's largest sailboat and geared it to upscale, sophisticated, and active vacationers. But theirs was no ordinary sailing ship.

Longer than two football fields, she is 610 feet long, and is rigged with five 164-foot masts. The $100-million ship was the last word in 21st century technology with seven computer-monitored sails. All 191 outside staterooms have a twin porthole and hand-rubbed mahogany cabinetwork. The spacious, 188 square-foot cabins are fitted with twin or king-sized beds. All cabins have private bath, closed circuit television, radio, safe, and minibar. A ship-to-shore phone is available in every cabin: It can also be used to order fresh towels and room service.

Guests are welcomed on the *Club Med I* with a fruit basket in their rooms. The ship has two restaurants: the Odyssey, located on the top deck, offers casual dining and has an outdoor veranda for breakfast and lucheon buffets; La Lousiane, on the deck directly below, is a more formal dining room with waiter service and a la carte menu. Complimentary wine and beer accompanies both luncheon and dinner and an extensive wine list is also available for an additional charge. Both restaurants have single unassigned seatings. Afternoon tea is served daily in the piano lounge with indoor and outdoor tables.

The ship has a fitness center with a panoramic view from the top deck, pine saunas and licensed massage therapists, tanning salon, two swimming pools, a discotheque, casino, twenty-four-hour room service and satellite telecommunications. Other facilities include a boutique, theater, hair salon, and observation deck. Passangers can take aerobics, stretch, and other fitness classes.

In the stern, the ship carries water-sports equipment and has a special sports platform that unfolds into the sea from which passangers can sail, windsurf, scuba dive, water-ski, and snorkel. There are qualified instructors to teach the fine points. Scuba diving excursions, however, are reserved for certified divers who have their C-card.

During the winter season, *Club Med I* is based in Martinique from where she sails on five alternating itineraries that visit almost all the islands of the Eastern and Southern Caribbean from the U.S. and British Virgin Islands on the north to Los Roques, off the coast of Venezuela, on the south. In April 1997, *Club Med I* was purchased by Windstar Cruises, whose owning company is Carnival Cruise Lines. The ship will leave the Club Med fleet in March 1998 at the end of her winter Caribbean season. She will be renamed, *Wind Surf,* and start her new life with Windstar Cruises in May 1998. Meanwhile, Windstar is negotiating for the purchase of *Club Med II,* which has a different group of owners and sails in the South Pacific.

COSTA CRUISE LINES, World Trade Center, 80 S.W. 8th Street, Miami, FL 33130-3097; 305–358–7325

Ships (Passengers): *CostaRomantica* (1300); *CostaVictoria* (1,950)
Departure ports: Miami, San Juan
Type of cruises: 7 days to Western, Northern, Eastern, and Southern Caribbean
Life-style tip: More European atmosphere and service than similar mass-market ships

"Cruising Italian Style" has long been Costa Cruise Lines' stock in trade, with a fun and friendly atmosphere created by its Italian staff and largely Italian crew. The emphasis is on good Italian food, which means pasta, pizza, and espresso (there are other kinds of cuisine, too); European-style service, par-

ticularly in the dining room; and, not to forget the Italians' ancestry, a toga party, which is usually a hilarious affair, one night of the cruise.

The Genoa-based company of the Costa family has been in the shipping business for more than 100 years and in the passenger business for more than 50 years. Costa began offering one-week Caribbean cruises from Miami in 1959; it was the first to offer an air/sea program, introduced in the late 1960s.

Costa launched the 1990s with one of the newest fleets in the Caribbean. Each ship introduced interesting new features in its design, combining classic qualities with modern features and boasting unusually large cabins for their price category. Among the ships' nicest features are canvas-covered outdoor cafes and pizzerias serving pizza throughout the day without additional charge.

Serena Cay (Catalina Island) is Costa's "private" island off the southeast coast of the Dominican Republic featured on Eastern Caribbean cruises. The island is near the sprawling resort of Casa de Campo, which has, among its many facilities, two of the best golf courses in the Caribbean, a tennis village, horseback riding, and polo.

Costa's ships have fitness centers and spas (most services are extra), along with a health and fitness program to suit individual needs. Costa's shore excursions, which tend to be expensive, stress outdoor activities.

In 1996, the line's largest ship, *CostaVictoria,* made her Caribbean debut in November, sailing weekly from Miami and alternating between the Western and Eastern Caribbean. In 1997, Costa was bought jointly by Carnival Cruise Line and Airtour, one of Europe's largest tour companies.

CRYSTAL CRUISES, 2121 Avenue of the Stars, Suite 200, Los Angeles, CA 90067; 310–785–9300, 800–446–6645; fax 310–785–3891

Ships (Passengers): *Crystal Harmony* (960); *Crystal Symphony* (960)
Departure ports: Worldwide
Type of cruises: 10- to 17-day transcanal
Life-style tips: Ultra luxury for sophisticated travelers

The launching of Crystal Cruises in 1989 was one of the most anticipated in the cruising world.

The new cruise line had begun spreading the word two years before its first ship had seen the water, and its owners spared no expense to ensure that the sleek *Crystal Harmony* would live up to its advance billing. Its goal was to create luxury cruises that would return elegance and personalized service to cruising and be designed for an upscale mass market at deluxe prices. The *Crystal Harmony* exceded expectations. Indeed, it has been so well received by passengers and by its competition that it has become the ship by which others in its class—or trying to be in its class—are measured. But for my money, the Crystal sisters are in a class all their own.

Crystal Symphony is essentially a copy of the *Crystal Harmony,* with some refinements and new features; for example, there will be no inside staterooms. The ships are magnificent, with exquisite attention to detail. The food is excellent and the service superb, with the staff at every level smiling and gracious and always willing to go the extra mile.

Built in Japan by Mitsubishi Heavy Industries, these are spacious ships for experienced travelers with sophisticated life-styles. The luxury is evident from the moment you step on either ship. The atrium lobby, the ship's focus, is accented with greenery and hand-cut glass sculptures. The piano bar features—what else?—a crystal piano.

Staterooms have sitting areas, minibars, spacious closets, and such amenities as hairdryers, plush robes, VCRs, and 24-hour hookup with CNN and ESPN; more than half have verandas. The ships' penthouses have Jacuzzis and butler service. Facilities include spa and fitness centers and full promenade decks for jogging. The indoor/outdoor swimming pools have swim-up bars and lap pools with adjacent whirlpools. The casinos are the first "Caesars Palace at Sea."

The ships' most innovative feature is the choice of two dinner restaurants—Japanese or Asian and Italian—at no extra cost. These restaurants are in addition to standard meal service in the main dining room and 24-hour room service.

In 1996, Crystal Cruises introduced low single supplement rates, ranging from only 10–15 percent more than the per-person, double-occupancy rate for a cabin in Category A through E, which includes deluxe cabins with verandas.

CUNARD, 555 Fifth Avenue, New York, NY 10017; 212–880–7500; 800–221–4770 (outside New York)

Ships (Passengers): *Sea Goddess I* (116); *Sea Goddess II* (116); *Queen Elizabeth 2* (1,810); *Royal Viking Sun* (740); *Vistafjord* (736)
Departure ports: Ft. Lauderdale, San Juan, St. Thomas, and Barbados
Type of cruises: 7 to 16 days for ships in Caribbean and transcanal on seasonal schedules
Life-style tip: Deluxe with a British touch, catering to affluent travelers

Cruise lines spend billions annually on promotion, but according to some tests, the only ship that the man-on-the-street can recall by name, unaided, is the *QE2.* That's perhaps not surprising when one considers that she is heir to a family of transatlantic liners reaching back over a century and a half and the only ship still on regular transatlantic service, from April to December.

The *Queens* have set the standard of elegance at sea in times of peace and served their country with distinction in times of war. Today, the *Queen,* which recently had a multi-million dollar makeover, sets the tone for Cunard. To many, she is the ultimate cruise experience. The *QE2* is a city-at-sea, dwarfing most other ships. She is proud, elegant, formal, and as British as—well, yes—the queen. The *QE2* isn't seen often in the Caribbean as her winters are taken mostly with an annual cruise around the world.

The other ships are important to the Cunard mix. The spacious and graceful *Vistafjord,* which has long epitomized luxury cruising, maintains the ambience of traditional cruising. Her Caribbean schedule is seasonal. The top-rated *Royal Viking Sun,* which Cunard bought in 1994, cruises the world, as do the ultra-deluxe *Sea Goddess* twins, built expressly to offer the most exclusive, elegant cruises in the world.

Their cabins, decor, itineraries, and cuisine were all planned to meet the expectations of a select group of very affluent people, offering highly personalized service and an unregimented ambience. The dining room has open seating and there is full meal service in staterooms around the clock. The ships have a stern platform that can be lowered to the level of the sea, enabling passengers to snorkel, swim, and enjoy other water sports from the boat. One of the twins sails on one-week itineraries of the Eastern Caribbean and longer transcanal ones.

Even though Cunard is one of the oldest lines afloat, it has been very much an innovator, responding to today's changing life-styles with gusto and recognizing the impact of the electronic revolution on people's lives—including their holidays. The *QE2* was the first ship to have a full-fledged spa at sea, a computer learning center, and satellite-delivered world news.

DOLPHIN CRUISE LINE,
901 South America Way, Miami, FL
33132; 305–358–2111; 800–222–1003
Ships (Passengers): *IslandBreeze* (1,146); *OceanBreeze* (772); *SeaBreeze* (840)
Departure ports: Miami, Montego Bay, Santo Domingo
Type of cruises: 7-day cruise to Eastern and Western Caribbean, Panama, Costa Rica
Life-style tip: Friendly, comfortable for all ages, and economical

Dolphin Cruise Line made major changes in 1995, selling the *Dolphin IV,* dropping Aruba as a home port for the *OceanBreeze,* and acquiring Carnival Cruises' *Festivale,* which it renamed *IslandBreeze.*

In early 1997 Dolphin was acquired by Cruise Holdings, Inc., a private investment company that operates several other cruise lines. (It also acquired majority interest in Seawind Cruise Line at the same time.) In late 1997 the lines *IslandBreeze* will introduce innovative, alternating Eastern and Western Caribbean cruises that depart Santo Domingo on Sundays.

During the winter season, *IslandBreeze* sails weekly from Montego Bay to Panama with a partial transit of the canal; during summer she sails from New York. The *SeaBreeze* continues on cruises that alternate weekly between the Western and Eastern Caribbean. The cruises can be combined into a two-week cruise at a special price.

When Dolphin Cruise Line started out in 1984, it had a hard time going up against the giants of Bahamas cruises, but affordable one-week packages, combining a three- or four-day cruise with

visits to Disney World/EPCOT or Miami helped it succeed. Early bird discounts and special low rates for children and third and fourth persons in a cabin also helped.

Dolphin cruises are family-oriented. The *SeaBreeze* has 32 cabins with adjoining doors, especially for families; the *OceanBreeze* has cabins with Pullman beds and a children's playroom. The ships have youth counselors on board seasonally to plan and supervise children's activities.

For active adults the ships have diving and snorkeling programs, as well as golf and tennis with instruction on board and play in port. Dolphin's sister line is Majesty Cruise Line, which caters to a more upscale traveler than Dolphin.

HOLLAND AMERICA LINE,
300 Elliott Avenue West, Seattle,
WA 98119;
206–281–3535; 800–426–0327
Ships (Passengers): *Maasdam* (1,266); *Nieuw Amsterdam* (1,214); *Noordam* (1,214); *Rotterdam VI*(1,075); *Ryndam* (1,266); *Statendam* (1,266); *Veendam* (1,266); *Westerdam* (1,476)
Departure ports: Ft. Lauderdale, Tampa, New York, New Orleans
Type of cruises: 7 days to Western and Eastern Caribbean; 10 days to Southern Caribbean, and 10 to 23 days to Panama Canal
Life-style tip: Classic but contemporary

Begun in 1873 as a transatlantic shipping company between Rotterdam and the Americas, Holland America Line stems from one of the oldest steamship companies in the world. Through the years and two wars her ships became an important part of maritime history, particularly significant as the westward passage of immigrants to America. The line also owns Westours, the Seattle-based tour company that pioneered tours and cruises to Alaska five decades ago; and it acquired the unusual Windstar Cruises in 1988. The following year the entire group was purchased by Carnival Cruise Lines, but all operate as separate entities.

Holland America now has one of the newest fleets in cruising, having added four magnificent, brand-new ships in three years: *Statendam, Maasdam, Ryndam,* and *Veendam.* They combine the Old World with the New in decor and ambience and boast million-dollar art and antique collections reflecting Holland's association with trade and exploration in the Americas and the Orient. Their Dutch officers and Indonesian and Filipino crews are another reminder of Holland's historical ties to Asia.

The ships have the space and elegance for the long cruises of two weeks or more for which they were designed. They feature a three-level atrium lobby with a large fountain, an elegant two-level dining room, small lounges and bars, disco, casino, a large state-of-the-art spa, a sliding-glass dome for the swimming pool, spacious cabins, and premium amenities. All suites and 120 deluxe cabins have private verandas, whirlpool baths, minibars, and VCRs. There are bathtubs in all outside cabins (485 cabins out of 633 total—an unusually high percentage).

The *Westerdam,* bought from Home Lines in 1988, was given a $60 million stretch job to increase her capacity. She combines the style and refinement of great ocean liners with state-of-the art facilities and fits well into Holland America's fleet.

The *Nieuw Amsterdam* and *Noordam* are reflective of today's cruise ships, although they were thought revolutionary when they were inaugurated in the early 1980s. Each ship has a square stern that increased its open deck space by 20 percent over traditional design, providing additional room for recreational and entertainment facilities. There are two outdoor heated swimming pools, fully equipped gym and spa, sauna, massage, and whirlpool. Stateroom doors are opened with a coded card rather than a key; movies, nightclub entertainment, and other events can be viewed on television in the cabins. Many of these features, dazzling when they were introduced, have become standard on new ships.

Holland America's *Rotterdam,* launched in 1959, will be replaced in 1997 by the *Rotterdam VI.* It has the feel of a grand transatlantic liner with rich interiors, cozy bars, and big public rooms. When the ship is not on a long cruise in distant parts of the world, she sails from Ft. Lauderdale to the Caribbean.

Life aboard the ships of Holland America proceeds at a leisurely pace. Traditionally the line has attracted mature, experienced travelers and families. During the winter, all the fleet sails on Caribbean and Panama Canal cruises, some departing from Tampa, a port Holland America helped to develop for cruise ships, and New Orleans to the Western Caribbean and the Panama Canal; others leave from Ft. Lauderdale.

NORWEGIAN CRUISE LINE,
95 Merrick Way, Coral Gables, FL 33134;
305–447–9660; 800–327–7030

Ships (Passengers): *Norwegian Dream* (1,754); *Leeward* (950); *Norway* (2,022); *Norwegian Crown* (1,000); *Norwegian Dynasty* (800); *Norwegian Majesty* (1,056); *Norwegian Sea* (1,540); *Norwegian Star* (1,198); *Norwegian Wind* (1,754)

Departure ports: Miami, Ft. Lauderdale, New York, San Juan, Los Angeles, Houston

Type of cruises: 3, 4, and 7 days to the Bahamas; Northern, Eastern, and Western Caribbean; Bermuda; Mexican Riviera

Life-style tip: Mainstream of modern cruising

Norwegian Cruise Line was started in 1966 by Knut Kloster, whose family has been in the steamship business in Scandinavia since 1906. Kloster is credited with launching modern cruising when he introduced the *Sunward* on year-round three- and four-day cruises from Miami to the Bahamas, thus creating the first mass-market packaging of cruises.

By 1971, Kloster had added three new ships and pioneered weekly cruises to Jamaica and other Caribbean destinations. He introduced a day-at-the-beach feature in the Caymans and bought a Bahamian island to add a day-on-a-private-island to the line's Bahamas cruises. The idea has since been adopted by most cruise lines sailing the Bahamas and Caribbean.

Yet, in its history loaded with "firsts," nothing caused as much excitement as the entry of the *Norway* in 1980. After buying her as the *France* for $18 million, NCL spent $100 million to transform her from the great ocean liner she had been to the trendsetting Caribbean cruise ship she became.

With space for 2,000 passengers, the *Norway* was the largest passenger ship afloat. Her size enabled NCL to create a completely new environment on board with restaurants, bars, and lounges of great diversity, shopping malls with "sidewalk" cafes, full Broadway shows and Las Vegas revues in its enormous theatre, full casino, and sports and entertainment facilities that can keep an active passenger in motion almost around the clock. Such innovations are now standard on all large ships.

The *Norway* was readied for the 1990s in a two-stage $65 million renovation that added a 4,000-square-foot health and fitness center, a jogging track, luxury staterooms, and two glass-enclosed decks. But the most spectacular addition was the Roman spa, covering 6,000 square feet and equipped with eight massage rooms, four herbal-therapy baths—cruising's first—and a gym. Spa services are not included in the cruise price; packages are available. Additional renovations in 1996 restored some of her original art deco features.

NCL added a fleet of new ships, beginning in 1988 with the debut of the *Seaward,* recently renamed *Norwegian Sea,* taking the line in a new direction. Each ship carries 1,200 to 1,400 passengers, going against the trend of larger ships but giving the line flexibility. These mid-range ships are aimed at upscale passengers who want the facilities of a superliner but prefer the more intimate feeling of smaller ships. Among their innovations, *Norwegian Dream* and her sister ship, *Norwegian Wind,* have four small dining rooms instead of the traditional one or two large ones. The concept gets away from the mega–dining room, and their mul-titiered design enables passengers to enjoy extensive views through panoramic windows. One of the sun decks is also tiered, getting away from the long lineup of deck chairs.

The *Norwegian Dream* was the first ship to have a sports bar and grill with multiple television screens featuring live broadcasts of ESPN and the NBA and NFL, which are now standard for all the fleet. Standard cabins have a separate sitting area; 75 percent are outside facing. In 1995 the line added the *Leeward;* it, too, has many of the NCL standard features.

NCL, which blankets the Caribbean, is known for its entertainment—some of the best in the business, ranging from comedy clubs and cabaret stars to Broadway shows. Although it did not orig-inate water sports programs for passengers, the line has developed them further than most, offer-ing instruction while the ships are at sea and in-water experience at ports of call. Year-round the ships have sports and fitness programs and theme cruises for golf, tennis, baseball, running, and others. NCL also has an extensive youth and children's program. In 1997 NCL expanded to South America and Europe and moved the *Norwegian Star* to her new base in Houston.

In 1984, Kloster Cruise Ltd., NCL's parent company, bought the prestigious Royal Viking Line, and in 1990, it acquired Royal Cruise Line. The moves turned out to be bad ones, saddling the company with mountains of debt and forcing it to sell RVL in 1994 and to close RCL in 1996. RCL's popular *Royal Odyssey* joined the NCL fleet as the *Norwegian Crown;* along with the *Royal Odyssey,* now the *Norwegian Star* whose capacity was increased by adding third and fourth berths to two hundred cabins. Then in a surprising move in early 1997, NCL acquired Majesty Cruise Lines, adding her two ships, *Crown Majesty* (renamed *Norweigian Dynasty*), and *Royal Majesty* (renamed *Norwegian Majesty*). Early in 1998, *Norwegian Dream* and *Norwegian Wind* will be "stretched" by adding 130-feet mid-sections to each.

PRINCESS CRUISES,
10100 Santa Monica Boulevard,
Los Angeles, CA 90067;
310–553–1770; 800–LOVE–BOAT

Ships (Passengers): *Crown Princess* (1,590); *Dawn Princess* (1,950); *Grand Princess* (2.600); *Island Princess* (640); *Pacific Princess* (640); *Regal Princess* (1,590); *Royal Princess* (1,200); *Sea Princess* (1,950); *Sky Princess* (1,200); *Sun Princess* (1,950)
Departure ports: Ft. Lauderdale, San Juan, Acapulco, Los Angeles
Type of cruises: 7 to 10 days, combining Western, Eastern, Southern Caribbean, and Panama Canal
Life-style tip: Casually stylish and modestly affluent

Princess Cruises, a West Coast pioneer begun in 1965, is credited with helping to create the relaxed and casual atmosphere that typifies life on board today's cruises. For one thing, one of its ships, the *Pacific Princess,* is the ship used in the popular television series *The Love Boat*. It's impossible to calculate, but that show probably did more to popularize modern cruising than all other cruise publicity combined. It was certainly a factor in dispelling cruising's elitist image and enabling people who might have never considered a cruise holiday to identify with it.

In 1988, Princess acquired the Los Angeles-based Sitmar Cruises, another innovative and well-established pioneer of West Coast cruising, creating one of the world's largest cruise companies and more than doubling Princess's capacity in one stroke.

The pride of the Princess fleet—its flagship, and one of the most stylish, elegant ships of the 1980s—is the *Royal Princess*, which was christened by the Princess of Wales. When she made her debut in 1983, the ship set new standards in passenger comfort with all outside cabins and refrigerators, televisions, and bathrooms fitted with tub as well as shower in every cabin category. The decor throughout is warm, inviting, and comfortable, and always with a touch of class. All suites, deluxe cabins, and some of those in lesser categories have private outside balconies—a first for cruising.

After a debut in Europe, the *Crown Princess* was officially christened by actress Sophia Loren in New York in 1990 during Princess Cruises' twenty-fifth anniversary. Very different in profile from other ships, the *Crown Princess* was designed by Renzo Piano, the architect of the Pompidou Center in Paris. Her sleek lines were inspired by the shape of a dolphin. The top of the head holds "The Dome," the forward observation and entertainment area, and the casino. The spacious ship has large cabins and a high percentage of them have verandas. Its twin, *Regal Princess*, was launched in 1991. The *Island Princess* and *Pacific Princess* are identical twins, more casual than their sisters.

Princess's latest venture—*Sun Princess*, dubbed a "Super Love Boat"—is the line's largest vessel. Designed by Njal Eide, the architect of the elegant *Royal Princess*, the ship is the most beautiful large ship afloat with exquisite interiors of the finest Italian workmanship. It introduced many new features, including two atrium lobbies and two main show lounges, a true theater-at-sea, and a restaurant offering 24-hour dining. About 70 percent of the outside cabins have verandas. *Sun's* identical twin, *Dawn Princess*, debuted in May 1997 and sails on Eastern and Southern cruises from San Juan in winter.

In recent years, Princess has had one of the strongest presences in the Caribbean in the winter season. The line has a private beach, Princess Cays (on south Eleuthera in the Bahamas), where the ships call. Newly expanded and upgraded, the facility has just about every water sport a passenger could want; nature trails with guided walks; games; kiosks for local crafts; and a large dining pavilion where passengers are served lunch.

Princess caters to a modestly affluent clientele from 35 years of age plus, with a median age of 50 to 55. It is very aggressive with promotional fares and seasonal savings.

Princess's British sister, P&O Lines, is seen in the Caribbean during winter as their ships make their annual round-the-world voyages. Catering mostly to an established British clientele, they are gaining American fans as they become better known, especially for their new ship *Oriana*, and for the *Adriana*, formerly Princess's *Star Princess*.

RADISSON SEVEN SEAS CRUISES, 600 Corporate Drive, No. 410, Ft. Lauderdale, FL 33334; 305–776–6123; 800–477–7500; 800–333–3333; fax 305–772–3763

Ships (Passengers): *Bremen* (164); *Paul Gauguin* (320); *Hanseatic* (188); *Radisson Diamond* (354); *Song of Flower* (180)
Departure ports: San Juan and worldwide ports seasonally
Type of Cruises: 3 to 14 days; transcanal, Eastern Caribbean, Europe, Asia
Life-style tip: Luxury for affluent travelers

"Futuristic" and "revolutionary" were some of the words used to describe the semi-submersible *Radisson Diamond*, one of the decade's most innovative ships, when it made its debut in 1992. Well, it is certainly novel. Viewed from the front, it looks more like a UFO than a cruise ship.

Measuring 420 feet in length and 103 in width and sitting high in the water, the SSC *Radisson Diamond* is the largest twin-hull cruise ship ever constructed; it marked the first time the design technology called SWATH (small waterplace area twin hull) was applied to a luxury ship of this nature. The design is intended to provide greater stability than that of a single-hull ship of similar size. Speedboats and water-skiers have been known to race through the space between the hulls, under the underbelly.

Diamond Cruises, a joint venture of Finnish, Japanese, and U.S. interests, formed a partnership with Radisson Hotels International to market the ship. In 1995, Radisson Diamond joined with Seven Sea Cruises to form a new company, Radisson Seven Seas.

The focus of the *Diamond* is a five-story atrium with glass-enclosed elevators and a grand staircase. The cabins, most with private balconies, are large, luxurious, and very comfortable. They are fitted with minibars, televisions, VCRs, and full baths with tubs. Perhaps because of its spaciousness and design, the ship has more the look and feel of a hotel than of a ship.

The dining room and its cuisine are, without doubt, the ship's most outstanding features. The dining room, one of the prettiest at sea, is decorated in exquisite silks and other fine fabrics in soft blues, beige, gray, and gold draped from the floor-to-ceiling windows and covering the handsome dining chairs. The room functions like a restaurant, with passengers dining at their convenience. And they dine leisurely on cuisine that is truly gourmet and some of the finest at sea. Table service is rendered by female rather than male waiters—an unusual case for cruise ships. The waitresses are exceedingly pleasant and efficient. The bar has women attendants as well. The ship has a no-tipping policy.

On the top deck the Grill, with a more informal atmosphere, offers breakfast and in the evening becomes an Italian specialty restaurant with superb cuisine. It's probably the ship's most popular feature.

The *Diamond* has a spa and fitness center with a gym, saunas, and a jogging track; and at the stern there is a hydraulically operated floating marina with equipment for water sports. The ship has good facilities for meetings at sea, with three boardrooms, a large meeting room that can be subdivided into six small rooms, and business-related services such as in-house publishing and teleconference facilities, fax machines, a broadcast center, and secretarial services.

Sailing from its Caribbean home port of San Juan in the winter, the *Diamond* has a series of imaginative itineraries of 3 to 14 days, including Panama Canal itineraries. The deluxe *Song of Flower* cruises in Europe and Asia; *Hanseatic*, a deluxe adventure ship, sails on unusual, ever-changing itineraries from pole to pole; *Bremen*, a deluxe exploration ship sails on various itineraries from Europe to Antarctica; and *Paul Gauguin* cruises in French Polynesia.

ROYAL CARIBBEAN INTERNATIONAL, 1050 Caribbean Way, Miami, FL 33132; 305-539-6573; 800-327-6700

Ships (Passengers): *Enchantment of the Seas* (1,950); *Grandeur of the Seas* (1,950); *Legend of the Seas* (1,808); *Majesty of the Seas* (2,354); *Monarch of the Seas* (2,354); *Nordic Empress* (1,606); *Rhapsody of the Seas* (2,000); *Song of America* (1,414); *Sovereign of the Seas* (2,276); *Splendor of the Seas* (1,800); *Sun Viking* (714); *Viking Serenade* (1,514); *Vision of the Seas* (1,800)
Departure ports: Miami, San Juan, New York
Type of cruises: 3 to 10 days to the Bahamas and Western, Eastern, and Southern Caribbean
Life-style tip: Active, wholesome ambience

Royal Caribbean Cruise Line, launched in the early 1970s, was the first line to build a fleet of ships designed specially for year-round Caribbean cruising. The ships were established as top-of-the-line so quickly that within five years RCCL needed more capacity and did so by "stretching" two of the vessels. They were literally cut in half and prefabricated mid-sections were inserted. Although the method had been used on cargo and other vessels, RCCL's work was the first for cruise ships.

For the 1980s it added superliners with unique design features, and in 1988 it got a headstart on the 1990s with the *Sovereign of the Seas,* the first of the new generation of megaliners and the largest cruise ship afloat at the time. Few ships in history have received so much attention.

The *Sovereign,* RCCL's flagship, is three football fields in length but, miraculously, she does not seem gigantic to passengers on board because of her superb design. A dramatic midship atrium spanning five decks and featuring glass-walled elevators was a "first" for cruise ships and was quickly copied in most new ships. The atrium functions similarly to the lobby of a hotel and provides a friendly focal point for the ship. The atrium also separates the forward section of the ship, which contains all of the cabins, from the aft, where all public rooms, dining, entertainment, sports, and recreation facilities reside—a revolutionary design borrowed from *Song of America*. The arrangement has a double advantage: quieter sleeping areas and shorter walking distances from one location to another in the public area.

It would be impossible for even the most active passenger to participate in all the daily activities offered on the *Sovereign*. Fitness folks have a third-mile outside deck encircling the vessel and one of the best-equipped health clubs at sea, complete with ballet bars, sophisticated computerized exercise equipment, and a high-energy staff to put them through their paces. The sports deck has twin pools and a basketball court.

For those with something less strenuous in mind, there are small, sophisticated lounges for drinks, dancing, and cabaret entertainment. Enrichment programs run the gamut from napkin folding to wine tasting. The library resembles a sedate English club, with its wood paneling and leather chairs. Two feature films run daily in twin cinemas; the shopping boulevard has a sidewalk cafe; the show lounge, a multitiered theater with unobstructed views, runs two different Las Vegas-style revues and variety shows.

Somewhere there's music to suit every mood, from big band, steel band, Latin, country, rock, or strolling violins to classical concerts. The Schooner is a lively piano bar; Music Man has entertainers from blues to country; and the disco projects holograms on the mirrored walls and music videos around the dance floor. Casino Royale offers blackjack, 216 slot machines, and American roulette. The chic Champagne Bar is a quiet corner where 50 people clink flutes and scoop caviar.

Sovereign's twins, *Monarch of the Seas* and *Majesty of the Seas*, arrived in 1991 and 1992,

with only a few changes, such as family suites for up to six people. When RCCL merged with Admiral Cruises in 1988, it acquired *Viking Serenade*, which it rebuilt, and for the first time, RCCL entered the short cruise market which had been Admiral's strength.

Designed as they are for Caribbean cruising, the ships have acres of open sun decks and large pools. The line offers low-fat, low-calorie fare and has a ShipShape program on all ships in the fleet. It is often combined with sports in port. Golf Ahoy! enables passengers to play golf at courses throughout the Caribbean. RCCL is the official cruise line of the Professional Golfer's Association of America.

All the ships have bright, cheerful Scandinavian decor, enhanced by Scandinavian art. The themes used throughout the fleet relate to hit musicals and operas. The officers are Norwegian, and the hotel and entertainment staff are a mini–United Nations. The cabins are compact—in fact, they are small, but given RCCL's success, it would seem not to matter; they are also functional and spotless. A top-deck lounge cantilevered from the funnel provides fabulous views from 12 stories above the sea. These lounges are RCCL's signature.

RCCL blankets the Caribbean year-round. It has cruises year-round on the West Coast and Mexico, and in Alaska and Europe in the summer. In 1995, the line added Asia. CocoCay, a small island in the Bahamas inherited from Admiral Cruises, is used for the ships' day at the beach. Labadee, RCCL's private resort on the north coast of Haiti, was created in 1987 and is very popular.

RCCL's enormous success results from its smooth and consistent operation, often winning "Ship(s) of the Year" and "Cruise Line of the Year" awards. Founded in 1969 as a partnership of three prominent Norwegian shipping companies, RCCL went public in April 1993. Not content to rest on its laurels, however, RCCL is adding a new group of 1,800 to 2,000 passenger ships.

The first ship, *Legend of the Seas*, built in France at the same shipyard that constructed RCCL's three megaliners, was launched in 1995, introducing the first miniature golf course at sea and a spectacular "solarium"—an indoor/outdoor swimming, sunning, and fitness facility. Its sister ships, *Splendor* and *Grandeur*, arrived in 1996, *Rhapsody* and *Enchantment* arrived in 1997, and others are slated for 1998.

RCCL caters to a moderately upscale market and enjoys a high repeat business. The atmosphere is friendly and casual, and the activities are so varied that there is something for everyone at almost every hour of the day. All RCCL ships have programs for children and teenagers, because the line believes that a happy kid on a cruise now will still be a customer in 2020.

With the arrival of the new ships, RCCL is making significant and innovative changes: *Nordic Empress* moves to San Juan for the winter, sailing on 3/4-night cruises to St. Thomas, St. Maarten, and St. Croix—a first. *Sovereign* sails on Bahamas cruises from Miami, the largest cruise ship to sail the route.

In 1997, RCCL bought Celebrity Cruises and plans to operate it as a seperate brand.

ROYAL OLYMPIC LINE,
1 Rockefeller Plaza, Suite 315,
New York, NY 10020;
212–397–6400; 800–872–6400

Ships (Passengers): *Stella Solaris* (620); *Odysseus* (400)
Departure ports: Ft. Lauderdale, Miami, Galveston, and Manaus, Brazil
Type of cruises: 10 to 14 days, Western, Eastern, and Southern Caribbean combined with South America and the Amazon or Panama Canal during winter
Life-style tip: Low-key deluxe cruises for an upscale market to off-the-beaten-track destinations

In August 1995, Sun Line merged with Piraeus-based Epirotiki Cruise Line to form a new company, Royal Olympic Cruises. The new line operates a fleet of ten cruise ships under two brands distinguished by the colors of the Greek flag: the "blue" ships of Sun Line are more traditional and upscale and include the *Stella Solaris, Stella Oceanis,* and Epirotiki's *Odysseus.* Three "white" ships of Epirotiki, the *Triton, Orpheus,* and *Olympic,* offer more casual cruises. The four other ships, are managed by Royal Olympic,

primarily on charter. At the present time, only the *Stella Solaris,* which recently has been completely renovated, sails in the Caribbean; other members of the fleet cruise mainly in South America in winter or the Greek Isles and Eastern Mediterranean year-round.

Sun Line Cruises has been a pioneer and innovator of Caribbean cruises, being the first to combine the small islands of the Eastern Caribbean with a cruise up the Orinoco River in Venezuela; to extend an Eastern Caribbean cruise to the Amazon River; and to combine the Amazon and Panama Canal in one cruise. While it was not the first cruise line to go to Rio for Carnival, it was one of the few to combine the annual event with the Eastern Caribbean.

One of Sun Line's most popular cruises is timed for the spring equinox at Chichén Itzá in the Yucatán. Frequently, as in the case of the Yucatán and Amazon voyages, Sun Line engages experts to lecture on the cruise's destinations.

Sun Line was started in the mid-1950s by a well-respected Greek family whose patriarch, the late Ch. A. Keusseoglou, had already made his mark as head of Home Lines. At Sun Line, Keusseoglou introduced some of the first ships designed specifically for cruising that eliminated class distinction on board and provided large, sunny public rooms and outdoor areas for relaxation and deck sports.

And while many cruise lines are adding bigger and bigger ships, Sun Line's ships remain small and intimate. The size of the staff in relation to the number of passengers is high. The ships and their staffs are Greek. Many of the personnel have had 20 years of uninterrupted service with Sun Line.

Sun Line specializes in long cruises, but most itineraries can be taken in one week segments. The combination of unusual itineraries, private club-like atmosphere, and members-of-the-family crew gives the ships special appeal to sophisticated and experienced travelers. Sun Line's passengers in the Caribbean winter season are affluent and tend to be age 45 and older. Often 50 percent are repeaters, an unusually strong testimonial for the line. Sun Line offers spa cuisine on its menus, and for its high percentage of single women passengers, it has a host program.

**SEABOURN CRUISE LINE,
55 Francisco Street, San Francisco, CA
94133; 415–391–7444; 800–929–9595;
800–527–0999 (Canada)**

Ships (Passengers): *Seabourn Legend* (214);
Seabourn Pride (214); *Seabourn Spirit* (214)
Departure ports: Ft. Lauderdale, Barbados,
Aruba, San Juan, Antigua
Type of cruises: 5 to 14 days in Eastern and
Southern Caribbean and Panama Canal in win-
ter; worldwide schedules year-round
Life-style tip: The ultimate luxury cruise

When Seabourn was formed in 1987, it set out
to create the world's most deluxe cruises on the
most elegant, luxurious ships afloat. To guide its
debut it engaged Warren Titus, whose stewardship
of Royal Viking Lines helped to set top-quality
standards for the entire cruise industry. Despite
very high per diem rates, Seabourn quickly won
enough fans to add a second ship. In 1996, following Royal Cruise Line's demise, Seabourn
acquired the former *Queen Odyssey,* which it
rechristened the *Seabourn Legend* in July 1996
in New York.

The ships and cruises were designed with a certain type of person in mind—one who normally
stays in the best rooms at a luxury hotel and
books a deluxe suite on a luxury liner. The staterooms are luxuriously appointed in soft, warm
colors and have television with CNN, VCRs, pre-
stocked bars, refrigerators, walk-in closets, and
large marble bathrooms with tub and shower.
Each has a roomy sitting area beside a large picture window with electrically manipulated shades
and outside cleaning mechanisms.

Passengers dine on gourmet cuisine served on
Royal Doulton china and have open seating. They
may also dine from the restaurant menu in their
suites, and there is a 24-hour room service menu
with a wide selection and a choice wine list.

Seabourn's ships have sleek profiles that resemble the most modern of yachts. A water sports
platform at the stern has a "cage" that can be lowered into the water for passengers to swim in the
open sea without fear. The ships carry windsurfers, snorkeling and dive equipment, and two
high-speed boats. The ships' itineraries take them
to all parts of the world, but at least one spends

some of the winter in the Caribbean. On selected
cruises Seabourn offers a low singles fare of 110
to 125 percent, rather than the standard 150 percent, and offers substantial discounts to
repeaters, including free cruises after 140 days of
sailing with Seabourn.

Seabourn is a privately held company; 75 percent is owned by its founder, Atle Brynestad, a
Norwegian industrialist, and 25 percent is owned
by Carnival Cruise Lines.

**SEAWIND CRUISE LINE,
Bay Point Office Tower, 4770 Biscayne
Boulevard, No. 700, Miami FL 33137;
305–573–3222; 800–258–8006;
fax 305–576–1060**

Ship (Passengers): *Seawind Crown* (624)
Departure port: Aruba
Type of cruises: 7 days for Southern Caribbean
Life-style tip: Mainstream cruising at
moderate prices

Launched in 1992, the Seawind was the first
cruise line to use Aruba as its home port from
which to provide weekly sails to the uncrowded
ports of the Southern Caribbean, a refreshing
alternative to the more traveled Caribbean routes.
The cruises are designed for passengers who prefer to travel at an unhurried pace. They have been
called a second-timer's cruise because of the
nature of the ship and its itineraries.

Seawind Cruise Lines was originally owned by
First Ocean Steamship Company, a complex
partnership between Nordisk, a large Swedish
travel comglomerate, and Waybell, a firm owned
by George Potamianos, whose family owns the
Epirotiki Line. Together the two own Panama-
based Trans World Cruises, which in turn owned
the Seawind Crown. In early 1997, Cruise
Holdings, a private investment group that had
been an investor in *Seawind,* obtained majority
control of the cruise line at the same time it
acquired Dolphin Cruise Line. The *Seawind
Crown* (the former *Vasco de Gama*) is a spacious ship, combining old-world elegance with
contemporary features such as refrigerators,
televisions, and hairdryers in every cabin. It was
given a $40 million overhaul in 1988, and in
1994 more cabins were added. The attractive
decor is mellowed by the fine wood paneling

and trim found on older ships. The ship has shops, a casino, and a variety of of small lounges.

The ship sails on 7-day itineraries from Aruba, departing on Sundays to Curaçao, Caracas, Barbados, and St. Lucia, making full-day stops at each port. Both cruises have 2 full days at sea. The two itineraries can be combined into a 14-day cruise with substantial discounts on the second week. The line also offers a "SEA-Aruba Cruise Resort Vacation" package for a pre- or post-cruise stay in Aruba.

SILVERSEA CRUISES, 110 East Broward Boulevard, Ft. Lauderdale, FL 33301; 800–321–0165
Ships (Passengers): *Silver Cloud* (306); *Silver Wind* (306)
Departure ports: Nassau, Ft. Lauderdale, Barbados
Type of cruises: Caribbean, seasonally
Life-style tip: Ultra-luxurious surroundings in a relaxing, friendly—not stuffy—atmosphere

Silversea Cruises was launched in late 1994 with the luxurious all-suite *Silver Cloud* designed by Oslo-based Petter Yran and Bjorn Storbraaten, the architects of the *Sea Goddess* and *Seabourn* ships. Her twin, *Silver Wind*, made her debut the following year.

The Silversea ships mirror Seabourn's in many ways but carry 306 passengers (100 more than Seabourn's), and 107 of the Silversea's 155 suites have verandas (Seabourn's suites do not).

Silversea's large suites, averaging 300 square feet, have a spacious sitting area, walk-in closet, fully stocked bar, hairdryer, TV with VCR, direct-dial telephone, and marble-floored bathroom with tub. Passengers are welcomed to their staterooms with fresh flowers, a bottle of champagne, a basket of fruit replenished daily, personalized stationery, and plush terry robes for use during their cruise.

There is open seating in the dining room and 24-hour room service. The ship has a tiered show lounge spanning two decks, with a nightclub at the upper level, plus a casino, a spa, and a library.

The ships sail in Asia, Africa, and Europe most of the year, but at least one is in the Caribbean for transcanal, Central, and South American itineraries in winter. The co-owners of the line are passenger and shipping veterans Francesco Lefebvre of Rome and the Vlasov Group of Monaco, who were once partners in Sitmar Cruises. Silversea sails under the Italian flag with Italian officers and a European staff.

STAR CLIPPER, INC., 2833 Bird Avenue, Miami, Florida 33133–4504; 800–442–0551; fax 305–442–1611
Ships (Passengers): *Star Clipper* (180); *Star Flyer* (180)
Departure ports: Antigua, St. Maarten
Type of cruises: 7 and 14 days on alternating itineraries in the Eastern Caribbean
Life-style tip: For active travelers looking for the romance of sailing to out-of-the-way places

Star Clipper is the brainchild of Swedish shipping entrepreneur, Mikael Krafft, whose passions for sailing and building yachts and his love of the Clipper Ship (which he says is one of America's greatest inventions) led him to create a cruise line with Clipper ships. Launched in 1991 the cruises are priced to fit between the budget-conscious niche of Windjammer Barefoot Cruises and the pricey voyages of Windstar Cruises and other lines with yachtlike ships.

Star Clipper is truly distinctive. Its newly built tall-ships—each accommodating 180 passengers in 90 staterooms—are direct descendants of the fast, sleek clipper ships that ruled the seas during the mid 1800s. Built in Belgium the vessels are 357 feet long with four masts and square-rigged sails on the forward mast—a Barguentine configuration—with a total of 17 sails (36,000 square feet of sail area). They are manned not computerized and capable of attaining speeds of 19.4 knots. At 208 feet tall they are among the tallest of the Tall Ships.

Today's clippers retain the romance of sailing under canvas coupled with the excitement of participating in the sailing of an authentic square rigger. They are further enhanced by the out-of-the-way Caribbean destinations that the cruises visit. Passengers quickly get to know the youthful crew who double in their duties as deck hands, sports instructors, and in other capacities.

Responding to a changing preference among some vacationers for a deemphasis on ostentatious food and the crowds of big ships, the cruises focus on an active, casual, and even educational, experience, so it's more like being on a private yacht. The food is good but not gourmet. Dress is very casual with shorts and deck shoes the uniform of the day, and only slightly less casual in the evening. Fellow passangers will be kindred souls—you hope—and 50 percent or more might be Europeans, depending on the time of the year. The cruises are also a great environment for families with children ages 7 to 17.

All cabins are carpeted, air-conditioned, and have private bathrooms with showers. Most cabins are outside facing and fitted with twin beds that can be converted to a bed slightly larger than the standard queen size. Eight inside cabins are furnished with upper and lower beds and eight cabins can accommodate three passengers. The top staterooms on the main deck have marble bathrooms with bathtubs and hairdryers. Cabins are equipped with multi-channel radio and video players. Video tapes are available from the ships library. There is storage for luggage, golf clubs, scuba gear, and other such items.

Facilities include a small piano bar, located midship on the main deck. It has brass-framed panoramic windows, carved paneling, and cushioned banquettes. The unusual lighting comes from the skylight overhead, it's actually the transparent bottom of the sun deck pool, one of the ship's two small pools. The piano bar is on the landing of a double staircase leading into the Clipper Dining Room on the deck below. All passangers dine at one seating, although when the ship is full the room can be very crowded. In addition to regular meal service, the dining room converts into a meeting room with screen projectors and video monitors.

Adjoining the aft end of the Piano Bar is the Tropical Bar, protected from the elements by a broad canvas awning, under which is found the bar, a dance floor, and the stage where the Captain holds his daily talks, and where much of the entertainment takes place during the cruise. Breakfast and lunch buffets are occasionally served here too. Also on the main deck is a library that resembles an English club with large brass-framed windows, carved paneling, and a marble fireplace. It doubles as a reception desk and is used for small meetings.

The *Star Flyer* is based in Antigua in winter, sailing on alternating 7-day cruises in the Eastern Caribbean. An unduplicated 14-day itinerary is possible with back-to-back cruises. The *Star Clipper* spends the winter in Southeast Asia and summer in the Mediterranean. The clippers can anchor in bays that large cruise ships cannot reach. Launches take passengers to isolated beaches, scuba and snorkeling spots, or to enjoy other water sports. Snorkeling gear, water skis, sailboards, and volleyballs are carried on board.

TALL SHIP ADVENTURES, INC.,
1010 South Joliet Street, Suite 200,
Aurora, CO 80012;
800–662–0090; fax 303–755–9007

Ship (Passengers): *Sir Francis Drake* (36)
Departure port: Tortola
Type of cruises: 3, 4, or 7 days of Virgin Islands
Life-style tips: Sailing under canvas in comfort

Begun in 1988 this cruise line offers short cruises on a classic, three-masted tall ship with comfortable accommodations for 36 passengers. The cruises, evoking the romance of the sea of bygone days, depart twice weekly year-round from Tortola on 3- and 4-day cruises of the British Virgin Islands and can be combined into a week's cruise. The ship's ports of call depend on the winds and weather but most are the hideaways where large ships cannot go.

The 162-foot-long ship is completely air-conditioned and has a wood-paneled lounge with bar, stereo, video, and television. In the evening the salon is transformed into a lovely dining room. Snacks are also served on the topside open deck. The cabins are air-conditioned and have twin or double beds and upper bunks and private toilet with shower.

The ship carries Sunfish sailboats, windsurfing and snorkeling equipment, and a power boat and diving equipment for use by certified divers.

WINDJAMMER BAREFOOT CRUISES,
Box 120, Miami Beach, FL 33119-0120;
305–672–6453; 800–327–2601

Ships (Passengers): *Amazing Grace* (96); supply ship); *Fantome* (126); *Flying Cloud* (76); *Mandalay* (72); *Polynesia* (126); *Yankee Clipper* (66)

Departure ports: Cozumel for Western Caribbean; various ports for Eastern Caribbean

Type of cruises: 6 days for Western Caribbean; 6 and 13 days for various Bahamas and Caribbean itineraries

Life-style tip: Barefoot adventure for sailors from 7 to 70 with good sea legs and happy spirits

Windjammer Barefoot Cruises, which celebrated its fiftieth anniversary in 1992, boasts the largest fleet of tall ships in the world. The history of each ship is part of the lore and pleasure of the cruise. The *Mandalay*, the queen of the fleet, was once the luxury yacht of financier E. F. Hutton and an oceanographic research vessel of Columbia University. The *Fantome*, extensively renovated in 1992, was originally built for the Duke of Westminster and was later owned by the Guinness family of brewery fame. They sold it to Onassis to be given to Princess Grace and the Prince of Monaco as a wedding present. But, as the story goes, Onassis was not invited to the wedding, so the present was never delivered.

Most cabins on all ships are fitted with bunk beds. They are cozy, not luxurious, and have private bath facilities and steward service. The food is good, not gourmet. The atmosphere is casual—shorts and beachwear on a full-time basis—and congenial. Most of your time will be spent enjoying the sun, swimming, snorkeling, steel band music, barbecues, and picnics on the beach.

The ships have super itineraries, including sailing from Grenada through the Grenadines, a route that is often called by yachtsmen the most beautiful sailing waters in the world. Other members of the fleet visit off-the-beaten-path destinations such as Saba and St. Eustatius, in the Eastern and Southern Caribbean. Most are 6 days long; some have different southbound and northbound legs that can be combined into a two-week cruise.

Windjammer offers several all-singles cruises as well as fitness cruises for high-energy folks during the year. The cruises appeal most to people with a sense of adventure who want something completely different from their routine structured lives in a relaxed and friendly atmosphere. Fellow passengers (who return about 40 percent of the time) come from all walks of life and many countries, although most are Americans. The company does not take children under 7 years of age.

It's not for everyone, but then, Windjammer doesn't try to be. If there's a Captain Mitty in you, though, then here's your chance to stand watch at the wheel or climb the masts, and to have the kind of tropical holiday of which dreams and travel posters are made.

**WINDSTAR CRUISES,
300 Elliot Avenue West,
Seattle, Washington 98119;
206–281–3535; 800–967–8103**

Ships (Passengers): *Wind Star* (148), *Wind Song* (148), *Wind Spirit* (148); *Wind Surf* (312)

Departure ports: Antigua, Barbados, Puerto Caldera

Type of cruises: 7 days to the Eastern and Southern Caribbean; Costa Rica, and Panama Canal

Life-style tip: Combination of sailing yacht and deluxe cruise ship, for active people

Imagine a deck one-and-one-half-times the length of a football field and half its width. Now, look up to the sky and imagine four masts in a row, each as high as a 20-story building and each with two enormous triangular sails. If you can picture these dimensions, you will have a mental image of the Windcruiser, which is the newest, most revolutionary vessel since the introduction of the steamship in the last century. The six great sails are manned by computers instead of deck hands. The computer is designed to monitor the direction and velocity of the wind to keep the ship from heeling no more than 6 degrees. The sails can be furled in less than two minutes.

The windcruiser marries the romance and tradition of sailing with the comfort and amenities of a Cruise Ship. The ship has 75 identical, outside 182-square-foot staterooms (so they are comparable in size to those on regular cruise ships). The well-designed cabins make optimum use of space, and are fitted with twin- or queen-size beds, mini-bar, color television, VCR, satelite phone communications, and individual safes.

Cabins, gym, and sauna are on the bottom two of four passenger decks. The third deck has a main lounge and dining salon; both are handsome rooms that have the ambience of a private yacht. The dining room, which has open seating, serves gourmet sophisticated cuisine. The ship has a tiny casino, boutique, and beauty salon. The top deck has a swimming pool, bar, and veranda lounge used for lunch during the day and a disco at night. Through the overhead skylight of the lounge, passengers can have a dramatic view of the majestic sails overhead.

The *Wind Star* has a crew of 81; the officer staff is Norwegian and dining staff are Italian, French, and other nationalities. Cabins are attended by stewardesses. The ship can cruise at a maximum speed of 12 knots. Electrical power and backup propulsion are provided on the 440-foot vessel by three diesel-electric engines.

The vessel has a shallow 13.5-foot draft that enables her to stop at less-visited ports and secluded beaches and coves. She is fitted with a water sports platform that gives passengers direct access to the sea. Sailboats and windsurfing boards are carried on board, as are Zodiaks (inflatable boats) to take passengers snorkeling, scuba diving, waterskiing, and fishing. The gear for these activities is available for use without additional charge. Any passanger lucky enough to hook a fish can have it cooked to order by the ship's chefs.

Cruises are planned to be partly cruise, partly yacht charter, and partly Club Med-type vacation. They are geared to working professionals who can afford to take a cruise and like the luxury of a cruise ship or resort, but who want a more active and unusual vacation than that associated with traditional cruises; thus they attract experienced cruise passengers and boat owners as well as people who may have shunned cruise ships in the past.

The *Wind Star* departs from Antigua and cruises the Caribbean from October or November to April (she sails in the Mediterranean in summer); *Wind Spirit* departs from St. Thomas and Barbados from mid-fall through winter, (she spends the summer in Alaska); and *Wind Song* recently moved to the Western Caribbean from Singapore where she will sail on a new Costa Rica itinerary.

Windstar Cruises was acquired by Holland America Line in 1987, and the following year both companies were purchased by Carnival Cruise Lines. Windstar, however, continues to operate as a separate entity with its own special type of cruises.

In April 1997, Windstar Cruises bought *Club Med I*, one of two identical ships in the Club Med fleet that are large versions of Windstar's ships, and at press time was negotiating for the second ship, *Club Med II*. After some remodeling, *Club Med I* to be renamed *Wind Surf*, will enter service for Windstar Cruises in May 1998 in the Mediterrean for the summer and will return to the Caribbean for the winter season beginning in November 1998.

PART III

GATEWAYS TO POINTS EAST AND SOUTH

Three of the islands covered in this section—Puerto Rico, St. Thomas, and St. Maarten—are bases, or home ports, from which many ships depart en route to destinations in the Eastern and Southern Caribbean. These, together with their neighboring islands—St. John, St. Croix, the British Virgin Islands, Saba, St. Eustatius, and Anguilla— form a bridge between the Northern and Eastern Caribbean. We have, therefore, grouped them as the Gateways to Points East and South.

Puerto Rico

SAN JUAN • PONCE

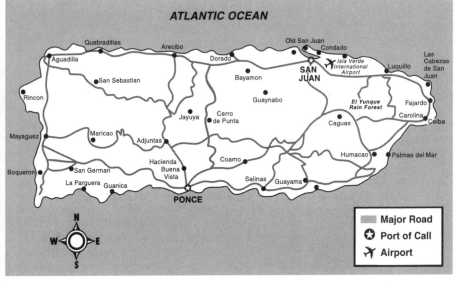

ATLANTIC OCEAN

	Legend
▬	Major Road
✪	Port of Call
✈	Airport

AT A GLANCE

Antiquities	★★★★★
Architecture	★★★★★
Art and Artists	★★★★
Beaches	★★
Colonial Buildings	★★★★★
Crafts	★★★★
Cuisine	★★★
Cultural	★★★★★
Dining/Restaurants	★★★★
Entertainment	★★★★★
Forts	★★★★★
History	★★★★
Monuments	★★★★★
Museums	★★★★
Nightlife	★★★★★
Scenery	★★★★
Shopping	★★★
Sight-seeing	★★★
Sports	★★★★★
Transportation	★★★★

CHAPTER CONTENTS

THE COMPLETE ISLAND

Cruise passengers sailing into San Juan Bay have a breathtaking view of Puerto Rico. From afar the green peaks of the thickly wooded Cordillera Central, rising to 4,398 feet, are outlined against the blue Caribbean sky. By the sea, palms etch miles of white-sand beaches. As the ship approaches the harbor, it passes the colossal fortress of El Morro to dock in Old San Juan, the oldest city now under the American flag. Beyond the ramparts of the fortress, the skyline of new San Juan is juxtaposed against the Old World grace of the colonial city.

Puerto Rico, the easternmost island of the Greater Antilles, is the only commonwealth among the states and possessions of the United States. Although it has been under the American flag since 1898, it was under Spanish rule for almost four centuries. From the intermingling of the two cultures comes modern Puerto Rico. It offers visitors the best of both worlds—the familiarity of home in a setting that is distinctly foreign. And it offers a great deal more.

Rectangular in shape, Puerto Rico is only 110 miles long and 35 miles wide, yet it has the range of scenery and geographic features of a country fifty times its size. From the quiet, palm-fringed beaches on the east, the land rises to two rugged mountain ranges that fall off in an ocean of rolling surf on the west. The mountainous spine, which peaks toward the center at more than 4,390 feet, separates the north coast on the Atlantic Ocean from the south coast facing the Caribbean Sea. The slopes are thick with rain forests; the foothills are covered with breadfruit, mango, and coffee trees, and rolling hills planted with sugar and pineapple.

The island has desert, salt flats, mangroves, and three phosphorescent bays that glow in the night. On the west end is the Maricao State Forest, one of the island's ten forest reserves; near the east end is the 28,000-acre Caribbean National Forest, known locally as El Yunque, the only tropical rain forest in the U.S. Forest Service system.

Puerto Rico has long been a popular port of call. Among the many reasons for its popularity is the variety of activity and attractions it offers.

Sports enthusiasts can enjoy Puerto Rico's miles of beaches for swimming, windsurfing and sailing, and even surfing. Anglers can try to beat one of the three dozen sportfishing world records previously set in Puerto Rican waters. Golfers have fourteen courses to test; tennis buffs can choose from one hundred courts in and near San Juan. A dozen or more places around Puerto Rico and its offshore islands are suitable for snorkelers and divers. There are caves to explore, hiking in the rain forest, and horseback riding and racing. Puerto Rico even has its own special breed of horses, Paso Fino.

In a country whose culture spans more than five hundred years, attractions for history buffs are abundant. Shoppers can be diverted at street markets and boutiques in the Old City, arcades in hotels, or the Texas-size shopping centers of the suburbs. But what will interest them most are the crafts made in Puerto Rico.

Entertainment and nightlife offer so much variety, you could stay in Puerto Rico a month, try a different restaurant and nightclub every night, and still have plenty left for your next visit. There are discos, cabarets, casinos, and the Puerto Rican specialty—lobby bars with salsa and other Latin beats, where you can catch the beat in the afternoon and dance the night away.

The variety of arts and cultural attractions is equally impressive. No week goes by without art exhibits in galleries and museums. The performing arts calendar is filled year-round with concerts, opera, ballet, and theater and highlighted by the annual Casals Festival in June.

For those planning a stay before or after their cruise, Puerto Rico offers a large variety of hotels in San Juan and around the island to suit any lifestyle or pocketbook. Remember, too, that it's part of the United States, so you can use your U.S. dollars, credit cards, and driver's license.

FAST FACTS

POPULATION: 3.6 million

SIZE: 3,421 sq. miles

MAIN CITIES: San Juan, Ponce, Mayaguez, Caguas, Arecibo

GOVERNMENT: Following the Spanish-American War, Puerto Rico was formally turned over to the United States in 1898. Puerto Ricans were made U.S. citizens and given the right to vote in local elections in 1917 and made a commonwealth in 1952. It is represented in the U.S. Congress by a resident commissioner with a voice but no vote, except in the committees on which he may serve.

CURRENCY: U.S. dollar

CUSTOMS REGULATIONS: Cruise passengers who disembark in San Juan to return to the United States by plane after visiting other islands and countries must go through U.S. customs here.

DEPARTURE TAX: None

LANGUAGE: Spanish. English widely spoken.

POSTAL SERVICE: Same as U.S. mainland

PUBLIC HOLIDAYS: January 1, New Year's Day; January 6, Three Kings Day; January 11, Patriot de Hostos; February, Presidents' Birthday; March 23, Emancipation Day; Good Friday; April 16, Patriot de Diego Day; May, Memorial Day; July 4, U.S. Independence Day; July 17, Munoz Rivera Day; July 25, Constitution Day; July 27, Barbosa Day; September 1, Labor Day; October 14, Columbus Day; November 11, Veteran's Day; November 19, Discovery of Puerto Rico (by Columbus); November, Thanksgiving; December 25, Christmas.

TELEPHONE AREA CODE: 787

AIRLINES: *From the United States mainland:* American, Continental, Delta, Northwest, Pan Am Carnival, Tower, TWA, United, and US Airways. *Regional:* American Eagle, LIAT.

INFORMATION:

In the United States,
Puerto Rico Tourism Company:
New York: 575 Fifth Avenue, 23rd Floor, New York, NY 10017; (800) 223–6530; fax: (212) 818–1868.
Los Angeles: 3575 W. Cahuenga Boulevard, No. 560, Los Angeles, CA 90068; (213) 874–5991; fax: (213) 874–7257.
Miami: Peninsula Bldg., 901 Ponce de Leon Boulevard, No. 604, Coral Gables, FL 33134; (305) 445–9112; fax: (305) 445–9450.

In Canada: 2 Bloor Street West, No. 700, Toronto, Ont. M4W 3R1;
(416) 368–2680; fax: (416) 358–5350.

In San Juan: La Casita, Puerto Rico Tourism Information Center, Comercio Street, Old San Juan; 722–1709; fax: 722–5208.
Hours: Tuesday to Saturday 9:00 A.M. to noon and 1:00 to 5:00 P.M. *Que Pasa* is the free quarterly official tourist guide.

BUDGET PLANNING

Costs in Puerto Rico are similar to ·those on the mainland. In San Juan they are comparable to those in a large metropolitan area, such as New York or Chicago; and those in the Puerto Rico countryside, to small-town America. The best way to save money is to walk, which is delightful in Old San Juan, and to use public transportation, which is inexpensive and plentiful. All but the most deluxe restaurants, are reasonably priced. Outside of San Juan they are cheap by any standard.

PORT PROFILE: SAN JUAN

LOCATION/EMBARKATION: One of the biggest attractions of San Juan for cruise passengers is the location of the port. Quite literally you step off your ship into the oldest, most interesting part of town. All ships pull in dockside unless there is an unusually large number in port. The piers are within walking distance of the city's main sight-seeing, shopping, dining, and transportation to other parts of the city. In recent years the port and its surrounding area have been extensively renovated and beautified.

The ride from the airport to the pier takes 25 to 40 minutes, depending on traffic. A taxi costs about $16. If you are arriving as part of an air/sea package, your cruise line arranges the transfer. Tourist Police (wearing white hats) are available to help visitors.

LOCAL TRANSPORTATION: Fleets of taxis are on hand to meet all ships. Taxis operate on meters and are comparable in price to those in stateside cities. You can hire them by the hour or half day, but settle the price in advance. A taxi dispatcher is available at the port to help passengers.

City buses to Condado and all parts of San Juan leave frequently from the bus station near Pier Three. A list of bus routes can be found in *Que Pasa*. Free motorized trolleys, sponsored by Goya and the Old San Juan Merchants Association, operate on two routes: from in front of the bus depot to Plaza de Armas via San Francisco and Fortaleza streets; and to Calle del Cristo and Fortaleza via Boulevard del Valle and Calle Norzagaray.

ROADS AND RENTALS: Puerto Rico has an excellent network of roads. You can drive around the entire island on a road that skirts the coast, drive through its mountainous center on the Panoramic Highway—one of the Caribbean's most scenic routes; and detour to rural mountain-town or seaside fishing villages along the way.

All major U.S. rental firms are represented in San Juan, but none has offices at the port. The nearest offices are in Condado, 10 minutes from the port. There are also many local companies with lower rates. A list appears in *Que Pasa*.

FERRY SERVICE: Ferries leave frequently from San Juan pier to Cataño across the harbor. Cost is 50 cents. On Sundays sight-seeing ferries operate cruises around the harbor.

DOMESTIC AND REGIONAL AIR SERVICE: American Airlines/American Eagle (721–1747), flies to Mayaguez and throughout the Eastern Caribbean. Flamenco (724–7110) flies to Puerto Rico's satellite island of Culebra, and Vieques Air Link (722–3736) serves Vieques. Air service to Ponce is very limited.

EMERGENCY NUMBERS: Medical service: 754–3535; Ambulance: 343–2550

Police: 343–2020; Tourist Zone Police, 24 hours, emergencies, 722–0738; Alcoholics anonymous: 723–4187

AUTHOR'S FAVORITE ATTRACTIONS

OLD SAN JUAN

SAN JUAN NIGHTLIFE

GOLF AT HYATT DORADO BEACH
    OR DEEP-SEA FISHING

HIKING IN EL YUNQUE

SHORE EXCURSIONS

The first tour listed is available on almost all cruise ships, but the others might not be or may vary in length and price. All sites are described elsewhere in the chapter.

City Tour—Old and New San Juan: 2–2.5 hours, $19. San Juan is a large, sprawling metropolis; a brief tour can be a useful introduction on a first visit.

El Yunque Rain Forest and Luquillo Beach, 4 hours, $25. A drive in El Yunque is combined with a stop at palm-fringed Luquillo Beach, the most popular *balneario,* or public beach.

San Juan Nightlife Tour: 3 hours, $35–$40. Sample San Juan nightlife at a cabaret with a Las Vegas–type show, casino, and drink, try "Ole Latino," a musical revue featuring Latin America dances, at the Condado Convention Center.

SAN JUAN ON YOUR OWN

San Juan, the air and cruise hub of the Caribbean, with a population exceeding one million, has the bustle of a large American city, the grace of its Spanish heritage, and the beat of the Caribbean. It also has a wonderful variety of big-city activity and attractions, yet it is only a stone's throw from quiet fishing villages and quaint mountain hamlets.

Beautifully restored Old San Juan is a living city bursting with activity from morning to night and ideal for walking. (For more than 350 years it was a walled and fortified city.) Then, beginning in this century with growth and expansion to new areas along Condado and Isla Verde beaches, the old part of San Juan became seedy. It might easily have been lost to the bulldozers, had it not been for some farsighted Puerto Ricans who banded together to save it, by first getting it made a protected historic zone in 1949. In 1955 the Society for the Development and Conservation of San Juan got a ten-year tax exemption for those restoring Spanish colonial buildings, and the Institute of Puerto Rican Culture designed a twenty-year plan to guide the preservation effort.

The renovations sparked a renaissance that has recaptured the town's old charm and ambience. Along streets paved with the blue cobblestones and in lovely old Spanish houses with flower-filled balconies and colonnaded courtyards, you can browse in shops, museums, and art galleries, enjoy lunch or refreshments at restaurants and cafes, and visit some of the oldest monuments in the Western Hemisphere.

AN OLD SAN JUAN WALKABOUT

Old San Juan was laid out in typical Spanish colonial fashion as a grid and built on a hill, which slopes from El Morro and San Cristobal fortresses on the north to the port on the south. With the exception of the perimeter roads that follow the contour of the old city walls, streets run north-south and east-west, making it easy to find one's way. If you prefer to have a guide contact *Colonial Adventure* (201 Recinto Sur Street, Old San Juan; 729–0114), which conducts 2- to 3-hour-long walking tours for $20.

From your ship the 25-minute walk west-north-west along the Old City walls to El Morro is a lovely introduction to Old San Juan and the way visitors in olden times had to approach it. If you want to conserve time and energy, take a taxi to El Morro ($6) and start your walking tour from there. Upon leaving the piers (**1**) turn left (west) to Plaza de Hostos, passing *La Casita* (**2**), where the Puerto Rico Tourist Office is located. On Saturdays and Sundays, 3:00 to 5:00 P.M., Festival La Casita, combining street theater with an arts fair, takes place here.

THE ARSENAL (3) South of Calle La Princesa is the 18th-century building known as the Arsenal, which houses the *Museum of Puerto Rican Culture,* with changing art exhibits. Here in 1898 the last Spanish general, Ricardo Ortego, turned over Puerto Rico to the United States. Hours: Wednesday to Sunday 9:00 A.M.–noon and 1:00–4:30 P.M.

LA PRINCESA (4) At the west end of Calle La Princesa is a former jail, built in 1837. It was restored to house the offices of the Puerto Rico Tourism Company. The beautiful building is also used as a gallery for contemporary Puerto Rican art. Calle La Princesa rounds the corner along the massive *City Walls,* which rise to 70 feet above the sea and once completely surrounded the city.

GATE OF SAN JUAN (5*) Walking north along the walls, you come to the small park and the Gate of San Juan, one of the four original gates to the city, built in 1639. On the south is La Fortaleza

(16), the residence of the governor of Puerto Rico for almost five hundred years. Originally it was the fort where the early Spaniards stored their gold and silver.

LA ROGATIVA (6*) After you pass through the Gate of San Juan, turn left to Plaza de La Rogativa.

The spectacular sculpture of La Rogativa is one of the most forceful, inspired works in iron ever conceived. It was done by Lindsay Daen to mark the city's 450th anniversary in 1971. La Rogativa, meaning The Procession, commemorates the saving of San Juan in 1797, after the British had laid

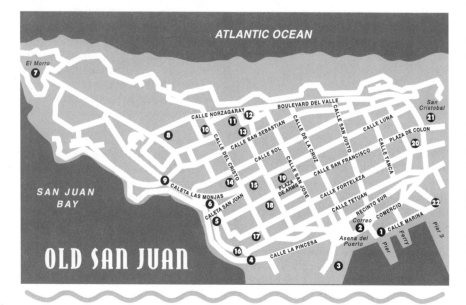

MAP LEGEND FOR WALKING TOUR OF OLD SAN JUAN

1. San Juan Pier and Plazoleta del Puerto
2. La Casita
3. Museum of Puerto Rican Culture (The Arsenal)
4. La Princesa Jail and City Walls
5. Gate of San Juan
6. Plaza de La Rogativa
7. El Morro Fortress
8. Ballaja Barracks (Museum of the Americas) and Casa Beneficencia
9. Casa Blanca
10. Plaza of Five Centuries
11. Church of San Jose and Dominican Convent
12. San Juan Museum of Art and History
13. San Jose Plaza and Casals Museum
14. Hotel El Convento
15. San Juan Cathedral
16. La Fortaleza
17. Pigeon Park and Christ Chapel; La Casa del Libro and National Center for Popular Arts
18. Department of State and Provincial Deputation Building
19. City Hall
20. Plaza Colon, Tapia Theatre, and Old Casino of Puerto Rico
21. Fort San Cristobal
22. To Municipal Bus Station

siege to it from the sea. As the saga goes, after two weeks city leaders thought their defeat was imminent and asked the bishop to lead a night vigil in honor of St. Catherine, the governor's patron saint. Marchers bearing torches started from San Juan Cathedral at the top of the hill above La Rogativa, proceeded through the streets, and returned to the church for Mass. The British commander, seeing the torchlights and hearing the ringing of church bells, thought reinforcements had arrived by land from the east. Rather than face an uncertain battle, he hoisted anchor and quietly slipped away under the cover of night. The next morning the townspeople found their prayers had been answered.

A path north of La Rogativa leads directly to El Morro.

EL MORRO (7*) A magnificent fortress begun in 1539, El Morro was part of the Spanish defense system that stretched from Puerto Rico on the Atlantic to the coast of South America. It was built to protect the ships carrying gold and silver from Mexico and South America to Spain.

El Morro is built on a promontory, or *morro,* in the shape of a head of a longhorn steer. The fortress was built with such strength that it withstood all attempts to take it from the sea for more than 350 years. During the Spanish-American War, the U.S. Navy bombarded El Morro; after the war, when the Spaniards left Puerto Rico, the U.S. Army occupied the site for several years.

El Morro was a living citadel, with seven levels of tunnels, storage rooms, barracks, artillery emplacements, plus kitchens, a chapel, and foundry. Be sure to go up to the level of the lighthouse for splendid views. The fort has been beautifully restored and is maintained by the U.S. National Park Service; it is listed on the National Register of Historic Sites. El Morro and its companion fort, San Cristobal; San Juan Gate and the City Walls; and La Fortaleza have been designated by UNESCO as landmarks on the World Heritage List. Orientation is available in English and Spanish; there is a museum and bookshop. Hours: daily, 8:00 A.M.–6:00 P.M.

BALLAJA BARRACKS AND CASA DE BENEFI-CENCIA (8) As the centerpiece of San Juan's Quincentennial effort, the Ballaja district was transformed by the $60 million restoration of the buildings and grounds that once comprised Fort Brooke (decommissioned in 1967). The district covers the 5 blocks from the Dominican Convent and Church of San José on the east to Casa Blanca, the ancestral home of the Ponce de Leon family, on the west. Now part of the San Juan National Historic Site, Ballaja contains some of Old San Juan's largest, historically significant buildings.

Most of the buildings date from the 19th century, but Ballaja was the name of the barrio or district as early as the 18th century. In 1857 after the construction of the Ballaja Military Barracks (El Cuartel de Ballaja) as the headquarters of the Spanish Army, the barrio became more integrated with its contingent areas, and the Dominican Convent (1523), Conception Hospital (1774), and other nearby buildings were taken over by the military. After the Spanish-American War, the U.S. Army occupied the buildings and added three small structures. All were turned over to the Commonwealth in 1976.

The Barracks, the largest, most imposing of the buildings, is used by the University of Puerto Rico and houses the *Museum of the Americas,* created by Ricardo Alegria, the founding director of the Institute of Puerto Rican Culture. Facing the Barracks, another huge building, dating from 1861, *Casa de Beneficencia,* is the new home of the Institute of Puerto Rican Culture. The facades of the two buildings define a triangle that has a small plaza and park. Here, the street leads directly to El Morro, which is in full view.

CASA BLANCA (9*) The first structure, a modest wooden house, was built in 1521, but after it was partially destroyed by fire, Ponce de Leon's son-in-law built a stone-and-masonry structure, which also served as a fort against Indian attacks. In 1540 when La Fortaleza was completed, Casa Blanca became the Ponce de Leon family home and so remained until 1779, when it was sold to the Spanish government as a residence for the army engineer corps. After the Spanish-American War, Casa Blanca was occupied by the U.S. military until 1967. The following year the house was declared a National Historic Monument and is used for exhibits.

PLAZA OF FIVE CENTURIES (10*) The historic and symbolic centerpiece of the Ballaja restorations is the *Plaza of Five Centuries,* a three-tiered urban park with trees and fountains, highlighted by a monumental commemorative sculpture. Beneath the plaza is an underground parking lot for 500 cars.

CHURCH OF SAN JOSÉ AND DOMINICAN CONVENT (11*) The east side of the plaza is bordered by the Church of San José and the Dominican Convent. The church is the second oldest Roman Catholic church in the Americas and one of the purest examples of Gothic architecture in the world. Built in the early 16th century as a chapel of the Dominican monastery on land donated by Ponce de Leon's family, it was used as a family church until the last century. Ponce de Leon was buried here after his remains were brought from Cuba in 1559; his body was moved to San Juan Cathedral in 1908. The Church of San José has undergone lengthy renovation to strip away centuries of coatings on the walls and reveal the beautiful apricot stone and magnificent cross vaulting of the ceiling. Hours: Monday to Saturday 8:30 A.M.–4:00 P.M.; Sunday Mass at noon.

Next to the Church of San José is the convent, which dates from 1523. It was one of the first buildings to be constructed after Ponce de Leon moved from Caparra, the site of his original settlement, to establish San Juan. The convent was converted into a barracks for the Spanish army and later became the U.S. Antilles Command headquarters.

SAN JUAN MUSEUM OF ART AND HISTORY (12) Next to the convent, but facing Calle Norzagaray, is a large structure originally built in 1855 as a marketplace. Restored in 1979, it is used as a cultural center for exhibitions of Puerto Rican art and cultural events, staged in its large courtyard. Hours: weekdays 8:00 A.M.–noon and 1:00–4:00 P.M. Audiovisual shows on the history of San Juan are presented at 11:00 A.M. and 1:15 P.M.

SAN JOSÉ PLAZA AND CASALS MUSEUM (13*) On the south side of the church is San José Plaza, with a statue of Ponce de Leon. Made in 1882, the statue is said to have been cast from the melted-down cannons used by the British during their attack on San Juan in 1797. On the east side of the plaza, a townhouse holds the Casals Museum, devoted to the great Spanish cellist who made his home in Puerto Rico for more than twenty years. Pablo Casals spearheaded the founding of the performing arts festival that bears his name. The island's leading cultural event, the festival is held annually in June. (Hours: Tuesday to Saturday 9:30 A.M.–5:30 P.M.; Sunday 1:00– 5:00 P.M.). The plaza, Calle San Sebastian, and adjacent streets are the setting for the *Festival of San Sebastian,* an annual art and music show in late January. Walk west on Calle San Sebastian to a set of stone steps, *Calle del Hospital,* leading to Calle Sol and a second set of stairs, *Stairway of the Nuns,* leading directly to Hotel El Convento.

HOTEL EL CONVENTO (14*) Built in 1646 as a convent for the Carmelite nuns, it was first made into a deluxe hotel in the 1970s, but altered several times in the 1980s. Now after extensive renovation, the hotel has reopened under new ownership. The first two levels have boutiques; the second and third to fifth floors house the new deluxe hotel. The lovely colonial architecture was retained and furnishings throughout are antiques or authentic reproductions from the 17th and 18th centuries. The project was directed by Jorge Rosello, the architectural genius behind El San Juan and El Conquistador hotels.

SAN JUAN CATHEDRAL (15) Facing El Convento on Calle del Cristo, San Juan Cathedral enjoys a commanding position at the top of the hill leading up from San Juan Gate. It was from here that the procession commemorated by La Rogativa set out in 1797 and miraculously saved the city. The present 19th-century structure stands on the site of the first chapel built soon after the city was founded. Ponce de Leon's tomb is on the north wall.

LA FORTALEZA (16*) Continuing south on Calle del Cristo, you'll pass some of the best shops and art galleries in the city; turn west on Calle Fortaleza. La Fortaleza, the official residence of the governor of Puerto Rico, is said to be the oldest executive mansion in continuous use in the Western Hemisphere. Hours: Monday to Friday 9:00 A.M.–4:00 P.M. Tours in English through the ceremonial rooms and the lovely grounds are available every hour. Tours to the second floor are available in English only at 10:00 and 10:50 A.M. Visitors must be properly dressed (721–7000).

PIGEON PARK (17) From Fortaleza, return to Calle del Cristo, and turn right at the corner onto the pretty little street with outdoor cafes leading to Pigeon Park (Las Palomas), where you can get a great view of San Juan harbor and spot your ship at the pier. *Christ Chapel,* with a silver altar, is said to have been placed here after a horseman, racing down the hill from El Morro, missed the turn in the road and was thrown over the wall to the sea below to seemingly certain death. But, miraculously, he did not die, according to the legend. On the east side of the street, adjoining 18th-century buildings house *La Casa del Libro,* a rare book museum, and next door, the *National Center for Popular Arts,* which sells the island's traditional crafts.

STATE DEPARTMENT (18*) At Calle San José, turn left (north) for a stop at the Department of State, whose interior courtyard is one of the loveliest examples of colonial architecture in San Juan. Note especially the staircase on the right of the entrance. Across the street is the *Provincial Deputation Building,* so called because it served for eleven days as the headquarters of Puerto Rico's first representative body, formed in 1897 when Puerto Rico gained autonomy from Spain.

CITY HALL (19) Across Plaza de Armas is City Hall, dating from 1602 and the site of many important events in Puerto Rico's history, including the abolition of slavery in 1873.

Here on the square, you can pick up the trolley to return to the port or walk east two blocks to Calle Tanca, which leads south directly to the pier where you started. One block farther east on Fortaleza is Plaza Colon.

PLAZA COLON (20) Dominated by the statue of Christopher Columbus (whose Spanish name is Colon) placed here in 1893 to mark the 400th anniversary of Columbus's discovery of Puerto Rico. On its south side is the *Tapia Theatre,* built early in the last century. It has been renovated many times, but claims to be the oldest theater in continuous use in the Western

Hemisphere. The theater has a year-round schedule of concerts and drama. Check *Que Pasa* or call 722–0407.

On the east side of the plaza is the *Old Casino of Puerto Rico,* built in 1915 to be the most elegant social hall in the Americas. Because of the war, however, the building never realized its potential and came to be used for many purposes, deteriorating all the while. It was renovated in 1985; its magnificent drawing rooms restored to their former elegance. Renamed the Manuel Pavia Fernandez Government Reception Center, it is used mainly by the Puerto Rico State Department for special occasions and receptions. Hours: weekdays 8:00 A.M.–4:00 P.M.

FORT SAN CRISTOBAL (21) Northeast of Plaza Colon is the entrance to Fort San Cristobal, part of the defense structure begun in 1633. The impressive fortress is larger than El Morro, with several levels of ramparts, moats, tunnels, and storerooms, and is considered a masterpiece of strategic military design. It, too, is maintained by the U.S. National Park Service. Hours: daily 8:00 A.M.–6:00 P.M. Orientation is available in English and Spanish.

 **SHOPPING**

Old San Juan with its pretty boutiques and specialty shops is the best area of the city for shopping. The Condado hotel area also has a large selection of stores, and you'll find Texas-style shopping centers, such as Plaza Las Americas in Hato Rey. Most open Monday to Saturday from 9:30 or 10:00 A.M. to 5:30 or 6:00 P.M.

Because cruise passengers frequently visit duty-free ports, such as the U.S. Virgin Islands, they are often understandably confused about Puerto Rico's status. Puerto Rico is NOT a duty-free port. Imported goods such as gold jewelry and Scottish cashmeres have the same duties levied on them here as in New York or Miami. Advertisements for "duty-free" merchandise mean only that you will not have to pay additional customs duties upon your return home, and, of course, you save state and local taxes. The best buys are for art, crafts, clothing, and rum made in Puerto Rico. And for those last minute needs, there's a Walgreen's (Plaza des Armes) a short walk from the port.

ART AND ARTISTS: On a walk in Old San Juan, you will see art galleries where you can discover many fine Puerto Rican and other artists living and working here. *Galeria M. Rivera* (107 Calle del Cristo) belongs to native son and former New Yorker Manuel Rivera. He makes small replicas of Old San Juan houses with the colors and architectural details of the originals you see in the Old City. They make charming souvenirs of your San Juan visit. Costs are $30–$50.

Galeria Palomas (207 Calle del Cristo) is a serious gallery with a collection of established as well as aspiring artists. *Galerias Botello* (208 Calle Cristo) belonged to Angel Botello, one of Puerto Rico's best-known artists with a very distinctive style. The gallery is now owned by Botello's son.

Galeria San Juan (204 Boulevard del Valle; 722–1808). Set in three restored 17th-century buildings, the gallery is the home and studio of American-born artist Jan D'Esopo, known for her Old San Juan street scenes. Hours: Tuesday to Saturday 10:00 A.M.–5:00 P.M.

The Butterfly People (152 Calle Fortaleza) is a second-floor art gallery with a pretty restaurant, where all art works on display have butterflies in their design. *Fenn Studio/Gallery* (58 Calle San José) is the studio-gallery of artist Patricia Fenn, who paints local scenes.

BOOKSTORES: The Bookstore (Calle San José) has the best selection of books on Puerto Rico in English.

CIGARS: Cigar stores, as well as cigar bars, have proliferated. Near Pier 3, opposite the new *Wyndham San Juan Hotel* is *Cigarros Antillas,* where you can watch a Dominican craftsman roll tobacco into shape and purchase the product. One cigar costs $2.50; box of twenty-five cigars, $55.

CLOTHING: A Ralph Lauren outlet is at the corner of Calle del Cristo and San Francisco. *London Fog Factory Outlet* (156 Calle del Cristo) has the best bargains of all. Snow and rainwear imperfects (but almost impossible to spot the imperfections) are up to 50 percent off

retail prices. *Big Planet* (205 Cristo St.; 725–1204) carries good quality sports wear.

T-shirt shops are everywhere. The most attractive have designs adapted from Taino Indian petroglyphs. Hand-painted T-shirt dresses and bathing coverups are also popular.

Not to be overlooked are Puerto Rican designers. *Nono Maldonado,* a former fashion editor of *Esquire,* who has boutiques on Ashford Avenue in Condado and at the El San Juan Hotel. *Lisa Cappelli* (206 Calle O'Donnell; Old San Juan; 722–5784) is a young designer who creates fun, fresh, funky outfits that are sold at several shops around town.

CRAFTS: An Artisan's Market is held on Saturdays from noon to 5:00 P.M. at the San Juan Convention Center. The carving of *santos*—small wooden figures representing a saint or depicting a religious scene—is considered Puerto Rico's most distinctive craft. The *santeros'* style and techniques have been passed from father to son for generations.

Musical instruments and masks are two of the oldest crafts. The *cuatro* is a five-double-string guitar inherited from the Spaniards; the guiro, or gourd, comes from a tradition that goes back to the Taino Indians. Mask making is found mainly in Loiza, a town east of San Juan that has maintained its African heritage. Papier-mâché masks, a Spanish tradition, are used in Carnival, particularly in Ponce. Hammocks are another skill taught to the early Spaniards by the Taino Indians. *Mundillo,* handmade bobbin lace, came with the Spaniards and Portuguese.

Aguadilla en San Juan (352 Calle San Francisco) and *Puerto Rican Art & Crafts* (204 Calle Fortaleza) specialize in Puerto Rican crafts. Calle Fortaleza has a tiny lane known simply as *La Calle,* a variety of attractive shops selling jewelry, leather handbags and belts, and other accessories, masks, and crafts.

JEWELRY: Calle Fortaleza has so many jewelry stores, especially for gold, you might think they were giving it away! (A check of stateside prices will convince you they are not.) Some cruise directors and guides direct passengers to certain stores, where they have something to gain. The practice is no different here than in other places around the world, so a good dose of skepticism on your part is healthy. If you plan to buy expensive jewelry, become familiar with prices at home, and do not buy in San Juan or any other Caribbean port without looking around and comparing prices. *Boveda* (209 Cristo) has unusual, one-of-a-kind mod jewelry, accessories, and women's clothing.

LEATHER: Several shops in Old San Juan import leather goods from Spain and South America. Prices are often much less than those in the United States. The best buys are in the small shops of *La Calle*, a-cul-de-sac near Calle del Christo and Fortaleza. *Coach* (158 Calle Cristo; 722–6830) has fine leather goods. Most cost about 20 percent less than mainland ones, but some go up to 40 percent.

DINING AND RESTAURANTS

Puerto Rico has a cuisine of its own, which you can enjoy at pretty restaurants set in townhouses of Old San Juan. Some dishes you might find on menus are black-bean soup; *asopao,* a spicy chicken stew; *pionono,* ripe plantain stuffed with ground beef; *mechada,* stuffed eye of round beef; *pernil,* roast pork; *arroz con gandules,* rice with pigeon peas; and *tostones,* fried plantain.

Entries range from moderate (under $10), to moderately expensive ($10 to $25), to expensive (more than $25).

OLD SAN JUAN

Amadeus (106 Calle San Sebastian; 722–8635) was one of the first to offer nouvelle Puerto Rican cuisine, sophisticated creations based on local products. Moderately expensive.

Cafe Berlin (407 San Francisco/Plaza Colon; 722–5205), a pastry shop and sidewalk cafe with light fare and vegetarian specialties. Great people-watching spot. Moderate.

Il Perugino (105 Cristo; 722–5481) has wide selection of veal dishes and fresh fish. Moderately expensive.

La Mallorquina (207 Calle San Justo; 722–3261), in operation since 1850, claims to be the oldest restaurant in Puerto Rico. Its menu has the most typical Puerto Rican dishes, along with Spanish and Cuban ones. Moderate.

Los Bigotes del Abuela (163 Calle San José, second floor), a delightful art deco cafe with a small veranda, is perfect for a snack or light meal of Puerto Rican and other cuisine during your walking or shopping tour. Another is *El Patio de Sam* (102 Calle San Sebastian). Inexpensive.

The Parrot Club (363 Calle Fortaleza; 725–7370) serves spicy Caribbean cuisine. Moderate.

CONDADO—ISLA VERDE

Aquarella (El San Juan Hotel; 791–1000), the new venture of Doug Rodriguez of New York's *Patria,* has ultra-modern decor—the right setting for the chef's unorthodox creations that emphasize seafood and South American dishes with Pacific Rim touches. Very expensive.

Augusto's Cuisine (Excelsior Hotel, Miramar; 725–7700) is headed by the former executive chef of the Caribe Hilton, August Schreiner, who creates his own European-inspired specialties. Expensive.

Chayote (603 Avenida Miramar, Olimpio Court Hotel; 722–9385) features fresh local fruits, vegetables, and fish. Expensive.

Cobia (Condado Plaza Hotel; 721–1000). Seafood lovers—do yourselves a favor and try this brand-new San Juan addition. Select from a great variety of fish and have it prepared to order—baked, fried, broiled, blackened, grilled, steamed, or as you like. Expensive.

Compostela (Avenue Condado 106, Santurce; 724–6088) is often named by San Juan's movers and shakers as the best in the city for classic Spanish cuisine with impeccable service by tuxedoed waiters.

Pikayo (1 Joffre Street, Condado; 724–4160) is located in the Tanama Princess Hotel. This new restaurant with stark contemporary decor ranks as the best among the fans who appreciate Chef Wilo Benet's innovative cuisine that fuses French and Californian with Caribbean creole.

Ramiro's (1106 Magdalena; 721–9049), set in a house across from the Condado Plaza Hotel, features *la nueva cocina criolla* along with Spanish cuisine. Expensive.

SPORTS

Puerto Rico has some of the best sports facilities in the Caribbean, near enough to the pier for cruise passengers to use them with ease. You should contact the hotel or sports operator in advance to make arrangements, particularly during the peak season. And don't overlook spectator sports, especially baseball. In the winter season, from October through February, all eight of the local professional teams have major league players in their lineups. Check newspapers or the Professional Baseball League of Puerto Rico (Box 1852, Hato Rey, San Juan 00919; 765–6285).

Horse races are held on Wednesday, Friday, Sunday, and holidays at *El Commandante* (724–6060). Buses leave from Plaza Colon, timed for the starting race, and return according to the racing schedule. Horse shows are often held when a village celebrates a saint's day or festival. The local breed, Paso Fino, is a small, spirited horse noted for its gait; shows are held year-round; check *Que Pasa.*

BEACHES/SWIMMING: All beaches are public, including hotel beaches. Those operated by the government or municipality have *balneario* facilities (lockers, showers, and parking) at nominal fees. Hotels on or near Condado Beach are the closest to the port; Caribe Hilton and Condado Plaza are the most popular. Isla Verde Beach, where The Sands and El San Juan Hotel are located, is 1 mile from the airport.

DEEP-SEA FISHING: San Juan is one of the world's favorite sportfishing spots. Half- or full-day and split-boat charters with crew and equipment are available; expect to pay about $300 and up for a half day and $600 and up for a full day for up to six people. Contact *Benitez Fishing Charters* (Club Nautico San Juan, Miramar; 723–2292).

GOLF: The quartet of Robert Trent Jones championship courses at *Hyatt Regency Cerromar Beach* (796–1010) and *Hyatt Dorado Beach* (796–1600) are not only among the best in the Caribbean, but in the world. Located at Dorado 15 miles west of San Juan, these courses are famous for their layouts and natural settings. Reserve in advance.

Westin Riomar (887–3964), a resort east of San Juan (a 40-minute drive from the port), has two 18-hole courses: one designed by George Fazio; and a new one by Greg Norman, his first in the Caribbean. Both are dotted with lakes, and have El Yunque as a backdrop and a palm-fringed beach in the foreground.

HIKING: The best trails are in the rain forest of the Caribbean National Forest of El Yunque and range from an easy 15-minute walk to arduous 8-hour treks. Information and maps are available from *El Portal,* the visitors and interpretive center which opened in 1996. Hours: daily, 9:00 A.M. to 5:00 P.M. Admission: $3 adults; $1.50 senior and children under 12. For Hiking Information, call Caribbean National Forest, (888–1810). See El Yunque section for more information.

HORSEBACK RIDING: East of San Juan near Luquillo Beach, *Hacienda Carabali* (889–5820) offers group riding along the coast and foothills of El Yunque. Reservations are required. The Caribe Hilton sells a riding excursion for the hacienda.

KAYAKING: Kayaks are available at the *Condado Plaza Hotel* water sports center where they can be rented by the hour.

SCUBA AND SNORKELING: Puerto Rico's best snorkeling and diving are found on the east coast around the coral-fringed islands facing Fajardo. Boats operated by water-sports centers at San Juan resort hotels depart daily for these locations. Equipment is available for rent for certified divers, and the centers offer diving courses. Several catamarans offer full-day picnic sails with snorkeling to Icacos for $60 per person. Check *Que Pasa. Caribe Aquatic Adventures,* Caribe Hilton; (729–2929 ext. 240) is one of the oldest dive operations on the island and a member of the Puerto Rico Water Sport Federation. It has daily dive trips and arranges kayaking, sailing, and windsurfing. The newest location, dubbed the Puerto Rican Wall and as exciting for divers as the Cayman Wall, is off the south coast at La Parguera.

TENNIS: Courts and full-time pros are available at more than a dozen San Juan hotels. Nearest the port is *Caribe Hilton*, with six night-light courts. *El San Juan Hotel* (Isla Verde) has three courts, while nearby, the new *Ritz-Carlton* (scheduled to open in early 1998) has two night-lit courts. *San Juan Central Park* (Cerra Street; 722–1646) has seventeen public courts with night lighting. Hours: open daily.

ENTERTAINMENT CULTURAL EVENTS

San Juan has a full calendar of seasonal concerts by the Puerto Rico Symphony Orchestra, San Juan Opera Company, several ballet and theater groups, Broadway productions, and performances by visiting artists. Most are given at the *Fine Arts Center* (El Centro de Bellas Artes), also known as the Performing Arts Center, a multiauditorium complex and one of the best-equipped facilities in the Caribbean. Another venue is the *Tapia Theatre*, in Old San Juan.

The year's biggest cultural event is the *Casals Festival of the Performing Arts* in June, but there are many arts and music festivals throughout the year. *Que Pasa* lists all major cultural and sporting events.

Three nights weekly the *LeLoLai Festival* highlights Puerto Rico's folklore with song, dance, and crafts. Each show has a different theme to reflect Puerto Rico's long and rich culture and blends the island's Spanish, African, and Taino Indian heritages. The festival, staged at participating hotels, is sponsored by the Puerto Rico Tourism Company and is usually available to cruise passengers as part of a shore excursion. For information and tickets: Convention Center, Ashford Avenue, Condado. Hours: Weekdays 9:00 A.M. to 5:00 P.M.

You also have a choice of small bars with Spanish guitars or jazz, in the Old City; or nightclubs, discos, cabarets, and casinos, in Condado or Isla Verde. Some of the liveliest action is at

lobby bars that have combos playing salsa and other Latin and disco beats, and there's even a *Hard Rock Cafe.*

In Old San Juan small-scale and low key *La Bistrot de San Juan* (152 Calle Cruz) is the place to hear jazz. Other jazz spots are *Café Matisse* (Condado; 723–7910) and *Vivas* (Condado Beach Hotel; 721–6090) where the jazz has a Latin flavor.

The Caribe Hilton's *Caribe Supper Club* has big-name entertainers, and *Juliana's* is the leading disco in the city. El San Juan Hotel's nightclub offers a headliner monthly, and The Sands' "Legends" is a popular long run show. "Ole Latino" is a Latin American musical revue at the Condado Convention Center (722–8433). Both are often stops on San Juan-by-night cruise ships shore excursions.

CASINOS: All of San Juan's casinos are in hotels, and some, like the Condado Plaza and El San Juan, are practically in the lobby. These two are also the most popular.

SAN JUAN'S ENVIRONS AND EAST

CATANO AND PALO SECO Across the bay from San Juan in Catano is the home of the *Bacardi Rum Distillery*, the largest single producer of rum in the world. Bacardi guides drive you around the distillery's manicured grounds and modern plant on a free 45-minute tour. There is a museum and gift shop. About a mile from the distillery is the fishing village of Palo Seco, noted for its waterfront seafood restaurants.

The ferry for Catano departs every half-hour from 6:15 A.M. to 10:00 P.M. from a small dock situated between Pier One and Pier Two. The ride takes about 20 minutes. On the opposite side of the bay, you can get a *publicos* (shared minibus) to the Bacardi Rum Distillery.

BOTANIC GARDENS: In the San Juan suburb of Rio Piedras, about a 30-minute drive from the port, are the Agricultural Experiment Station

Botanical Gardens, which is part of the University of Puerto Rico, and the Institute of Tropical Forestry, which is part of the U.S. Forest Service. Spanning both sides of a stream and a series of ponds, the gardens cover an area of 270 acres, 45 of which are developed in a park setting, providing a delightful introduction to the enormous variety of plants, flowers, and trees of Puerto Rico and the Caribbean. At Casa Rosada (766–0740), the headquarters, an orientation and a leaflet guide in Spanish are available.

EL YUNQUE: In the Luquillo Mountains, about 30 minutes east of San Juan, is the Caribbean National Forest, more commonly known as El Yunque—the only tropical rain forest in the U.S. Forest Service system. Long a research center on tropical flora and fauna, El Yunque has 240 species of trees, more than 200 types of fern, and 60 species of birds. One of its most important projects has been the effort to save the Puerto Rican parrot, decimated from an estimated million birds at the time of Columbus to only twenty-two in 1975. Now the bird's numbers are slowly being rebuilt.

You can drive through El Yunque on a tarmac road (No. 191) that goes into the heart of the rain forest, passing waterfalls, lookouts, and picnic areas. At the turnoff from Route 3, the main highway, you'll find the office of the Caribbean National Forest and *El Portal,* the new visitors' and interpretive center, open daily. Maps—essential for hiking—and an orientation are available.

La Mina/Big Tree Trail, a paved path leading to La Mina Falls, takes about an hour, round-trip. It runs along the Mina River and passes through a forest of stately tabonuco trees, one of the four types of forest found in the reserve.

LAS CABEZAS DE SAN JUAN In the northeastern corner of the island, about a 30-minute drive from El Yunque, is *Las Cabezas de San Juan Nature Reserve,* a 316-acre peninsula of forest land, mangroves, lagoons, beaches, cliffs, cays, and coral reefs, marked by a 19th-century lighthouse, *El Faro,* which serves as the visitors' center. Opened in 1991 by the Conservation Trust of Puerto Rico, there are nature exhibits in the lighthouse and walkways through the mangroves for self-guided tours. Guided tours are available. A spectacular view from the lighthouse extends 40 miles east to the Virgin Islands and west over El Yunque and the Caribbean.

FAJARDO South of the reserve on the coast is Fajardo, home to Puerto Rico's largest marina and an occasional port for small cruise ships. Nearby is *El Conquistador Hotel,* a large elaborate resort with a championship golf course and excellent tennis and water-sports facilities.

WEST OF SAN JUAN

RIO CAMUY CAVE PARK Of the 220 caves that have been documented, the Camuy Caves are the largest with a surface area of 268 acres. Seven miles of passageways have been explored, including chambers as high as a twenty-five-story building. The Camuy River, the third-largest underground river in the world, passes through the complex system.

At the visitor's center a film provides an orientation. At the cave entrance visitors accompanied by bilingual guides board a tram for the tour. The tram winds through a ravine with rain forest vegetation to the first of sixteen chambers, where passengers begin a 45-minute walk. The room is illuminated by natural light that penetrates the entrance. It leads to another huge chamber, tall enough to hold a 17-foot-high stalagmite. The trail winds along a path from which the Camuy River, 150 feet below, comes into view. The park (898–3100) is open Wednesday to Sunday. From Old San Juan it is a 1.5-hour drive west via Arecibo and inland on Route 129.

THE PANORAMIC ROUTE Crossing the center of Puerto Rico is a spine of tall green mountains, Cordillera Central, with peaks that are often concealed by clouds. The Panoramic Route, a 165-mile road made up of 40 different routes, winds through the mountains, from Yabucoa on the southeast to Mayaguez on the west coast, providing spectacular panoramas through forests and rural landscapes—light-years away from the bustle and glitter of San Juan. The route divides into three sections, each requiring a day to cover with stops along the way. There are trails, picnic areas, a spring-fed swimming hole, and man-made lakes—reservoirs created in the 1930s to harness the island's water resources.

PONCE

Puerto Rico's second-largest city, Ponce was founded in 1692 by a great-grandson of Ponce de Leon, for whom it was named. The site is thought to be an ancient one, since a huge Indian burial ground lies a short distance north of town.

Ponce is a treasure house of architecture, with streets of colonial houses with balconies and wrought-iron railings reminiscent of Savannah and New Orleans. Other houses are turn-of-the-century Victorian gems, with gingerbread trim reminiscent of Key West; still others built in the 1930s and 1940s are straight off the drawing boards of art deco architects. Its National Historic Zone, an area of 66 blocks in the town center, was renovated for Ponce's 300th Anniversary in 1992.

On the main square, the Old Firehouse, built in 1883 as an exhibition booth for an agricultural fair, is painted bright red and black, Ponce's colors. It's all the more startling, standing as it does next to the classic Cathedral of Our Lady of Guadalupe, which dates from 1670. The firehouse has a collection of memorabilia pertaining to the history of the building.

Ponce is especially proud of its Fine Arts Museum, housed in a building designed by Edward Durell Stone. The collection, one of the largest in the Caribbean, has more than one thousand paintings and four hundred sculptures representing all periods of Western art from ancient to contemporary. Hours: weekdays 10:00 A.M.–noon and 1:00–4:00 P.M. The Visitor's Information Center (Cristina and Mayor streets) is directly across from La Perla Theatre, where plays, concerts, and other events are held throughout the year.

INDIAN CEREMONIAL PARK One of the oldest, most important burial grounds ever discovered in the Caribbean is the Tibes Indian Ceremonial Park, 2 miles north of town. Here seven ceremonial plazas belonging to the Igneri culture, dating from A.D. 600 to 1000, were found. The Indo Museum has displays pertaining to the Taino Indians and other pre-Columbian cultures. A film on the first Puerto Ricans is shown every 45 minutes as an orientation to the site. Guides are available.

HACIENDA BUENA VISTA In the foothills of the Cordillera Central north of Ponce, is an old estate that was once one of the largest working plantations in Puerto Rico, growing coffee and other cash crops. Now a property of the Puerto Rico Conservation Trust, it has been extensively renovated as an interpretive center and museum. A footpath through the pretty woods leads to waterfalls along an aqueduct that once carried water to a huge waterwheel supplying the estate with its power. Multilingual guides and descriptive brochures for a self-guide tour are available.

The Virgin Islands

U.S. VIRGIN ISLANDS

CHARLOTTE AMALIE, ST. THOMAS; CRUZ BAY, ST. JOHN; FREDERIKSTED, ST. CROIX; CHRISTIANSTED, ST. CROIX

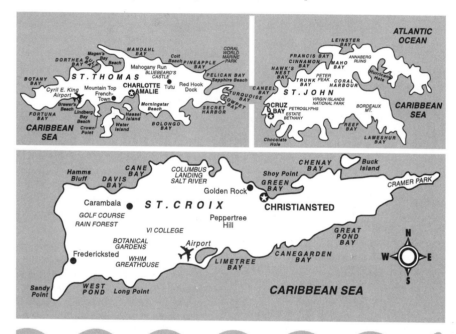

AT A GLANCE

Antiquities	★	Forts	★★★★
Architecture	★	History	★★★★
Art and Artists	★★	Monuments	★
Beaches	★★★★★	Museums	★★
Colonial Buildings	★★★★	Nightlife	★
Crafts	★	Scenery	★★★★★
Cuisine	★★	Shopping/Duty-free	★★★★
Culture	★	Sight-seeing	★★★
Dining/Restaurants	★★★	Sports	★★★★★
Entertainment	★★	Transportation	★★★★

BRITISH VIRGIN ISLANDS
TORTOLA, NORMAN ISLAND, JOST VAN DYKE, VIRGIN GORDA, ANEGADA

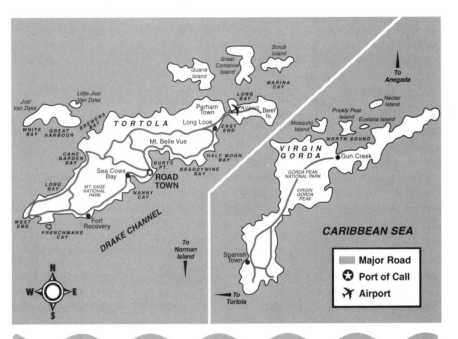

CHAPTER CONTENTS

U.S. VIRGIN ISLANDS

THE AMERICAN PARADISE

Their license plates say "American Paradise." They are our corner of the Caribbean, and, topside or beneath the sea, you will not find a more beautiful place under the American flag. Every turn in the road reveals spectacular scenes of white beaches washed by gentle turquoise water, backed by forest-green hills, and colored by a rainbow of flowers with such marvelous names as Catch-and-Keep and Jump-Up-and-Kiss-Me. Easy breezes carrying the light scent of jasmine cool the air.

The Virgin Islands are divided between the United States and Britain into two groups of about fifty islands and cays each. They are situated in the northeastern Caribbean adjacent to the Anegada Passage, a strategic gateway between the Atlantic Ocean and the Caribbean Sea, 40 miles east of Puerto Rico, where the Lesser Antilles begin.

The U.S. Virgin Islands constitute a "territory" rather than a state. Only three islands are inhabited: St. Croix, the largest, lies entirely in the Caribbean and is the easternmost point of the United States; St. Thomas, the most populated and developed, is 35 miles north of St. Croix, between the Caribbean and the Atlantic Ocean; and neighboring St. John, the smallest, is 3.5 miles east of St. Thomas. The islands are so close together that they can be visited in a day yet no three in the Caribbean are more different from one another than our American trio.

Columbus first sighted the Virgin Islands on his second voyage in 1493. He arrived at an island native Carib Indians called Ayay and named it Santa Cruz, or Holy Cross (we call the island by its French name, St. Croix). There Columbus sailed into the Salt River estuary on the island's north coast to replenish his ships' supply of fresh water. (Hence, St. Croix's claim: that it is the first land now under the American flag to have been visited by the great explorer.)

But the fierce Caribs did not welcome Columbus as the peaceful Arawaks had done elsewhere. Columbus made a hasty withdrawal and continued north through the archipelago. The admiral, like all those who have followed him, was dazzled by the islands' exquisite beauty. Seeing so many clustered together, he named the group after the ancient legend of St. Ursula and the eleven thousand virgins.

Columbus claimed the islands for Spain, but the Spaniards paid little attention to them for a century or more. Sir Francis Drake, the dashing corsair of English history, was among those who sailed the Virgins' waters—long enough to form the basis of England's claim to them. The islands' jagged coastlines, good harbors, and proximity to major shipping lanes made them natural havens for pirates and privateers. By 1625 the English and Dutch had recognized the islands' strategic location and began colonizing St. Croix.

The Danes took possession of St. Thomas in 1672, adding St. John in 1717 and St. Croix in 1733. Two decades later Denmark declared the islands a crown colony and subsequently made St. Thomas a free port that flourished as the center of contraband for the entire Caribbean, while St. Croix and St. John became rich with sugar plantations.

In 1917 the United States, concerned about protecting the Panama Canal, bought the Virgin Islands for $25 million—or about $300 an acre—a high price at the time. Island residents were made U.S. citizens in 1927; the present structure of territorial government was established by the U.S. Congress in 1954. In December 1996 the U.S. Department of the Interior transferred ownership of 50 acres of Water Island, a former World War II military installation, to the Virgin Islands government. Located a quarter mile off St. Thomas' Charlotte Amalie Harbor, the island's remaining 440 acres will be transferred as agreements with homeowners are finalized.

Although the islands are American—with fast-food shops and supermarkets, direct dial and cable television—they have retained enough of their past to give visitors a sense of being in a foreign yet familiar place.

FAST FACTS

POPULATION: St. Croix, 60,000; St. John, 3,000; St. Thomas, 50,000.

SIZE: St. Croix, 27 miles long, 85 sq. miles; St. John, 9 miles long, 21 sq. miles; St. Thomas, 13 miles long, 34 sq. miles.

MAIN TOWNS: Christiansted and Frederiksted, St. Croix; Cruz Bay, St. John; Charlotte Amalie, St. Thomas.

GOVERNMENT: Executive power is vested in the governor, who appoints the heads of his twelve departments. Residents were granted the right to vote for their governor in 1970. The legislature, which has convened since 1852, is a single body of fifteen senators from the three islands, elected for two-year terms. Residents vote in local elections and, since 1972, have sent a representative to Congress. They pay federal income tax, but cannot vote in national elections, and their congressman does not vote on the floor of the House of Representatives.

CURRENCY: U.S. dollar.

CUSTOMS REGULATIONS: Cruise passengers who disembark in the U.S. Virgin Islands and plan to return to the mainland by plane pass through customs here. The U.S. Virgin Islands have a special status, enabling U.S. residents to bring back up to $1,200 worth of goods—twice that of other islands in the Caribbean—free of customs tax. Persons over twenty-one years old are allowed five fifths of liquor, plus a sixth one of a Virgin Islands spirit (such as Cruzan Rum) and five cartons of cigarettes or 100 cigars. You can also mail home gifts (other than perfume, liquor, or tobacco), each valued up to $100.

**DEPARTURE TAX:** None

LANGUAGE: English. But don't be surprised if you have trouble understanding some Virgin Islanders. The local dialect is an English-Creole, which has had a profound influence on their speech. If you have trouble with the dialect, ask the person to speak slowly—and you should do the same.

PUBLIC HOLIDAYS: January 1, New Year's Day; January 6, Three Kings Day; third Monday in January, Martin Luther King's Birthday; February 18, Presidents' Day; Easter Thursday, Good Friday, Easter Sunday and Monday; March 31, Transfer Day (from Denmark to United States); May 27, Memorial Day; June 16, Organic Act Day (granting Virgin Island self-government in 1945); July 3, Emancipation; July 4, Independence; July 22, Hurricane Supplication; September 2, Labor Day; October 14, Columbus Day; October 21, Hurricane Thanksgiving; November 1, Liberty Day; November 11, Veteran's Day; Thanksgiving Day; December 25, 26, Christmas. Banks and stores are closed on the major holidays; stores remain open on local ones.

TELEPHONE AREA CODE: 809.

AIRLINES:

From the United States: American, Delta, U.S. Airways.

Intraregional: Air St. Thomas, American Eagle, LIAT, Seabourne Seaplane, Winair.

**INFORMATION:**

In the United States: U.S. Virgin Islands Tourist Information: 1–800–372–USVI

Chicago: 500 North Michigan Avenue, No. 2030, Chicago, IL 60611; (312) 670–8784; fax: (312) 670–8788.

Los Angeles: 3460 Wilshire Boulevard, Los Angeles, CA 90010; (213) 739–0138; fax: (213) 739–2005.

Miami: 2655 LeJeune Road, No. 907, Coral Gables, FL 33134; (305) 442–7200; fax: (305) 445–9044.

New York: 1270 Avenue of the Americas, New York, NY 10020; (212) 332–2222; fax: (212) 332–2223.

Washington: 444 N. Capital Street, No. 298 Washington, D.C. 20001; (202) 624–3590; fax: (202) 624–3594.

In Canada:
245 Britannia Road East, Missassauga, Toronto, Ont. L4Z 2Y7 Canada; (416) 233–1414; fax: (416) 233–9367.

In St. Croix:
P.O. Box 4538, Christiansted, USVI 00822; 773–0495.

In St. John:
P.O. Box 200, Cruz Bay, USVI 00830; 776–6450.

In St. Thomas:
P.O. Box 6400, Charlotte Amalie, USVI 00804; 774–8784; fax: 774–4390.

BUDGET PLANNING

Prices for sports and tours in St. Thomas and St. John generally are typical for the Caribbean; St. Croix is slightly lower. The largest expenses for visitors are taxi fares and fancy restaurants. On the other hand there is an ample selection of moderately priced, attractive restaurants serving local dishes; public transportation is plentiful and inexpensive; and beaches are free or have minimal charges.

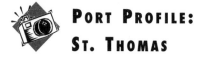

PORT PROFILE: ST. THOMAS

St. Thomas is the ideal cruise port. The green mountainous island rises dramatically from the deep turquoise sea to peaks of 1,550 feet that frame an irregular coastline of fingers and coves, idyllic bays, and white-sand beaches. Steeped in history, St. Thomas is as up-to-date as Fifth Avenue; it is small enough to see in a day, yet it has the diversity and facilities to offer cruise passengers a wide choice, with every kind of warm-weather sport a visitor could want. There are inviting restaurants—some in historic settings, others

with lovely views—and enough colonial buildings, old homes, forts, and monuments for history buffs easily to fill their day.

LOCATION/EMBARKATION: Set on a deep horseshoe bay Charlotte Amalie (pronounced Ah-*mahl*-ya) is the busiest cruise port in the Caribbean—a role it played for two hundred years during the colonial era as a major trading port on the sea lanes between the Old and New worlds.

The heart of town—both historic and commercial—hugs the shore and climbs the mountainsides overlooking the port. The harbor has three docks; the size of your ship usually dictates which one is used. On the east, about 1.5 miles from downtown, is the West Indian Company Dock, where the majority of ships arrive. Six cruise ships can berth here at one time.

Small ships (under two hundred passengers) often sail directly to the waterfront in town a few steps from the Virgin Islands Tourist Bureau (Territorial Building, Veterans Drive; 774–8784). On the west side is Crown Bay Dock, about 1.5 miles from town. Since more cruise ships call at St. Thomas than at any other port in the Caribbean, it is not surprising to find the port crowded. The system operates more or less on a first-come, first-served basis; the number of ships in port will determine whether your ship draws dockside or tenders.

At the West Indian Company Dock, there are telephones for local and long distance calls, a mobile U.S. Post Office, and a new tourist information center where you can get maps and information, and a large shopping complex, Havensight Mall, where many of the Main Street stores have branches. Crown Bay Dock's facilities are much more limited.

LOCAL TRANSPORTATION: The transportation system at the ports is well organized and convenient. You will find taxis, minibuses, and open jitneys for twenty passengers lined up by the dozens for transportation from the port to Emancipation Square in downtown Charlotte Amalie. Cost is $2.50 per passenger one-way. The square is located at the head of Main Street, the central shopping street. It is also the ideal place from which to start a walking tour. To return to your ship, jitneys and taxis leave frequently from the square to the docks; you can almost always share a taxi with other returning passengers. Be sure to give yourself ample time to return to your ship, particularly around the noon hour and from 4:00 to 6:00 P.M., when local traffic is extremely heavy and moves at a snail's pace. It can take 45 minutes to drive the 1.5 miles between town and the West Indian Company Dock.

Taxi rates, set by the government, are based on destination rather than mileage, a copy of the rates should be available from the driver. Rates for most locations beyond town are $6 to $11 one-way. Coki Beach is $7.50 for one person and $5 per person for two or more. Taxis are available for island tours. Drivers, who act as guides, are usually informed on the basics, but some are definitely better than others—be prepared to take potluck. Cost is $30 for two persons for a 2-hour tour, $12 for each additional passenger.

BUSES: Regular bus service connects Charlotte Amalie with Red Hook, at the eastern end of the island, where ferries leave for St. John and Bordeaux at the west end. Buses run about hourly, with the last returning to town about 10:00 P.M.; cost is $1. The open-sided "safari" buses, or jitneys, from Market Square to Red Hook leave hourly on the quarter hour until 5:15 P.M.; the last returns from Red Hook to town at about 9:00 P.M. A one-way fare is $2.

ROADS AND RENTALS: Roads on St. Thomas are generally well marked with route signs, but pay close attention because the roads are very winding and frequently branch onto small roads. In addition, driving is on the LEFT side of the road, and it is very easy to get distracted by the views.

Route 38 traverses the island east-west from Charlotte Amalie to the eastern end, forking northeast to Coki Point, and southeast to Red Hook. Route 40, known as Skyline Drive, runs parallel along the north side of the mountains, affording magnificent views, and leads to Mountain Top, the highest accessible point on St. Thomas.

You need a valid U.S. driver's license to rent a car here. Expect to pay about $45 to $65 per day for a compact with unlimited mileage from an international chain and about $40 from independent dealers. Jeep rentals cost about $65, but unless you have had experience with driving on

the left and on mountain roads, you may be wiser to rent a car. Some car-rental companies have agreements with local merchants offering discounts on rentals and/or merchandise. Some also have free pickup and delivery service at the port, but during the winter season, when demand is greatest, availability of cars is uneven and pickup service unreliable.

A list of rental firms is available in *St. Thomas This Week*, a free booklet widely distributed in tourist offices and elsewhere. Among them are *ABC Auto & Jeep* (776–1222; 800–524–2080); *Budget* (778–4663); *Caribbean AMC Jeep* (776–7811; 800–524–2031); *Discount* (776–4858).

FERRY SERVICE: Ferries between downtown and Frenchman's Reef Hotel leave every half hour 9:00 A.M. to 4:00 P.M., daily except Sunday; and from the downtown waterfront, 8:30 A.M. to 4:30 P.M. Cost is $4. St. John is connected by hourly service from Red Hook from 6:30 A.M. to 7:30 P.M.; the trip takes 20 minutes. Another ferry, less frequent but more convenient for cruise passengers, leaves from the downtown waterfront several times daily, beginning at 9:00 A.M. *Katron Hydrofoil* has daily service between St. Thomas and St. Croix: 7:15 A.M. and 3:15 P.M. from St. Thomas; 9:15 A.M. and 5:00 P.M. from St. Croix. The trip takes 1 hour 15 minutes. Cost is $37 one way; $70 round trip; seniors fares are $33 and $63.

Ferries to Tortola, B.V.I.—*Smith's Ferry* (775–7292) and *Native Son* (774–8685)— leave from Charlotte Amalie frequently and take 45 minutes; some continue to Virgin Gorda. You need a passport or proof of citizenship. Schedules are printed in *St. Thomas This Week*.

INTERISLAND AIR: *Seaplane Service* (777–4491) flies between St. Thomas and St. Croix almost hourly during the day. LIAT flies on regular schedules from St. Thomas to Tortola and Virgin Gorda. American Eagle connects St. Thomas and St. Croix with Puerto Rico. Air Anguilla and Winair connect Anguilla, St. Maarten, and neighbor islands to St. Thomas.

EMERGENCY NUMBERS:
Medical: St. Thomas Hospital, 776–8311;
Ambulance, Fire, Police: Dial 911;
Recompression Chamber: 776–2686;
Alcoholics Anonymous: 776–5283

AUTHOR'S FAVORITE ATTRACTIONS

CHARLOTTE AMALIE WALKABOUT

DAY SAIL WITH SWIMMING AND SNORKELING

EXCURSION TO ST. JOHN AND VIRGIN ISLANDS NATIONAL PARK

DEEP-SEA FISHING

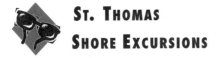

ST. THOMAS SHORE EXCURSIONS

What to do in St. Thomas largely depends on your personal interest—the choices are plentiful. Be sure to plan some activity: Despite all you have heard about the wonderful shopping here, most people complete their shopping in under two hours and then are disappointed if they have not planned something else, too. Shore excursions most frequently offered by cruise ships follow; prices may vary by cruise line. All sites are described elsewhere in the chapter.

St. Thomas Island Tour: 2.5 hours, $20–$26. Drive to Bluebeard's Castle for the view; Mafolie Hill and Drake's Seat for scenic panorama of Magens Bay and British Virgin Islands; and return to town. Same drive available by taxis for $30 for two.

St. John Safari: 4.5 hours, $30–$50. Recommended for those who have visited St. Thomas before or who prefer outdoor activity to shopping. The excursion goes by ferry to Cruz Bay, tours St. John, and visits Trunk Bay for a swim and snorkel. Bring a towel and plastic bag for swimsuits.

Underwater Life: 3 hours, snorkelers, $36; introductory dive lesson, $60. Some cruise ships send snorkelers and divers in separate groups; others combine them depending on the number of people and their proficiency. They are accompanied by an instructor. Children under eighteen usually have to be accompanied by an adult.

Sailing: 3.5 hours, $40–$50; full day $55–$75. Your yacht (with crew) sails to nearby uninhabited islands to anchor while you swim and snorkel. It has an open bar, and light snacks are served.

ST. THOMAS ON YOUR OWN

The historic district of Charlotte Amalie is listed in the National Register of Historic Places. Most restorations were done by private owners who gave the old structures new life as stores, business and government offices, hotels, restaurants, and residences—uses not far removed from their original purposes. A walk through these streets is a chance to learn something about the island's history and shop in lanes made charming by the past.

A CHARLOTTE AMALIE WALKABOUT

Historic Charlotte Amalie is a grid of three blocks deep from the waterfront on the south to the hillsides on the north, intersected by long east-west streets extending from old Hospital Gade on the east to just below General Gade on the west. A walk takes two to three hours, depending on your pace. Taxis from the cruise ports discharge passengers at or near Emancipation Garden at the head of Main Street.

EMANCIPATION GARDEN (1) A small park that was originally the town square was named to commemorate the abolition of slavery on July 3, 1848. It has a bandstand and an open-air market where T-shirts and souvenirs are sold. There is a bust of the Danish king Christian IX and a small replica of the Philadelphia Liberty Bell. At the southwest corner is the Tourist Hospitality Lounge operated by Project St. Thomas, a citizens' group. The lounge has rest rooms, telephones, and information on St. Thomas.

GRAND HOTEL (2) The building on the north side of the park, built in 1839 as the Commercial

Hotel, was the town's leading accommodation for more than a century. Originally the Greek Revival structure occupied an entire block overlooking the square. It is now a commercial building with shops and a new interior courtyard with a sushi bar and an outdoor cafe.

FORT CHRISTIAN AND MUSEUM (3) East of the park, Fort Christian is the oldest building in the Virgin Islands and a National Historic Landmark. The red-brick fortress, built between 1666 and 1680, was named for Denmark's King Christian V and was the center of the community for three centuries, housing the colony's first governors and later serving as a church, garrison, surgeons' quarters, shipwatch, prison, police station, and local courthouse. It now houses a small museum, and a gift and bookshop. Hours: weekdays 8:30 A.M. to 4:30 P.M.

LEGISLATIVE BUILDING (4) The lime-green Italian Renaissance structure on the waterfront is the home of the Virgin Islands Legislature. Here in 1917 the Danish flag was lowered for the last time, transferring ownership to the United States. Built in 1874 as barracks for the Danish police, it served as a U.S. Marine Corps barracks from 1917 to 1930 and as a public school until 1957. Open weekdays.

FREDERICK LUTHERAN CHURCH (5) Built in 1820 to replace an earlier one destroyed by fire, it is the oldest church on the island. The church was originally established in 1666, the year Erik Nielson Smith took formal possession of St. Thomas in the name of the Danish West India Company. The charter that the royal government granted to the company stockholders included a provision for the Lutheran church, the state church of Denmark. When St. Thomas became a Crown colony in 1754, the church quickly expanded its role, increasing the number of schools it operated and adding a hospital.

The *Parsonage* (23 Kongen's Gade) behind the church, is more than 250 years old and is one of the oldest structures in continuous use on the island. The original walls, partially exposed in several rooms, consist of bricks and stones brought from Denmark as ballast for sailing ships and exchanged for cargoes of sugar, cotton, and rum.

MORAVIAN MEMORIAL CHURCH (6) Farther east on Norre Gade is another 19th-century church. The two-story structure is built of local volcanic rock called blue-bitch stone and beveled sandstone cornerstones. Atop the hip roof is a bell tower with a delicate wooden cupola dating from 1882. Inside, the church has balconies supported by columns on three sides.

GOVERNMENT HOUSE (7) Built from 1865 to 1867 for the Danish Colonial Council, Government House is the official residence and office of the governor of the U.S. Virgin Islands. The first two floors are open to the public and have paintings and objets d'art relating to the islands' history and works by the French Impressionist Camille Pissarro, who was born in St. Thomas in 1830. Hours: weekdays 8:00 A.M.–noon and 1:00–5:00 P.M. Closed holidays.

A short detour east of Government House is the *Seven Arches Museum* (774–9295), a private residence open to the public as a lived-in museum. It is a modest example of Danish West Indian architecture; some rooms are furnished with antiques. A thick vine growing on the wall of the garden is full of iguanas. Hours: daily except Sunday and Monday, 10:00 A.M.–3:00 P.M.

THE 99 STEPS (8) The steep hills made it difficult to build roads; instead, access between the higher and lower parts of town was gained by a series of stone stairs. Two of the best preserved ones, built by the Danes in the mid-18th century, are west of Government House—one immediately west of the mansion and a second, known as the 99 Steps, a short walk beyond.

FORT SKYTSBORG (9) Both passageways lead to Fort Skytsborg, a five-story conical watchtower known as Blackbeard's Tower, built by the Danes in 1678. Legend has it that the infamous pirate used the tower to scout his prey and hide his treasures. The view from here is reward enough for climbing the 99 Steps.

HOTEL 1829 (10) At the foot of the 99 Steps on Kongen's Gade is Hotel 1829, formerly known as Lavalette House after its builder, a French sea captain. The initial "L" of the original owner can still be seen in the wrought-iron grillwork at the entrance. The two-story stucco townhouse, begun in 1819, was designed by an Italian architect in a Spanish style. It has had extensive restoration down to the two-hundred-year-old Moroccan tiles in the main dining room. The bar is in the original Danish kitchen, and there is a pleasant courtyard. Continue to Garden Street, and turn west onto Crystal Gade.

ST. THOMAS DUTCH REFORM CHURCH (11)

The Greek Revival building, constructed in 1846, has such classical features that it looks more like a temple than a church. Its two-story facade is surmounted by a large triangular pediment supported by four Doric columns. Its doors are framed by columns with classical cornices and moldings.

SYNAGOGUE HILL (12)

Farther along, Beracha Veshalom Vegemilith Hasidim Synagogue, built in 1833 on the site of two earlier structures, is one of the oldest synagogues in North America. (As early as 1684 Gabriel Milan, a member of a prominent European Jewish family, was appointed governor by the Danish Crown.) The Synagogue marked its 200th anniversary in 1996.

The synagogue is a freestanding, one-story structure of cut stone and brick. A wrought-iron fence encloses a small patio. Marble steps lead to its unusual entrance: the front doorway, a high pointed arch, which is covered by a porch supported by four columns from which plaster has been removed to expose its red-brick composition. Similar columns are repeated at the entrance and matching bricks frame the arched windows on either side.

Inside, the exposed walls are composed of native stone with a mortar made of sand and molasses. Mahogany pews face the center of the sanctuary; the *m'chitzot* that once separated the men and women can be seen behind the fourth row. The furniture and many of the fixtures and ornaments date from 1833. On the east wall the Holy Ark contains scrolls of the Torah, three of which are more than two hundred years old; one set of *rimonim* (handles of the scrolls) were saved from a fire in 1831; and the old mahogany doors have ivory insets. Above the Ark are the blue-and-gilded Tablets of the Decalogue; the lamp of eternal light hanging in front can be raised and lowered with a counterweight. Overhead in the center of the dome is a Magen David encircled with designs; from it hangs an eighteen-armed candle chandelier with Baccarat crystal hurricane shades.

There are four corner columns with Doric capitals, said to represent the four mothers of Israel: Sarah, Rebecca, Rachel, and Leah. Several interpretations are given for the sand floors, but according to the synagogue's historian, Isidor Paiewonsky, they are meant as reminders of the time when the Jews of Spain were forced to pray in unfinished basements. Hours: weekdays 9:30 A.M.–4:30 P.M.

The *Weibel Museum* (next to the synagogue; 774–4312) covers the three-hundred-year-old

MAP LEGEND FOR WALKING TOUR OF CHARLOTTE AMALIE

1. Emancipation Garden
2. Grand (Commercial) Hotel
3. Fort Christian
4. Legislative Building
5. Frederick Lutheran Church
6. Moravian Memorial Church
7. Government House
8. The 99 Steps
9. Fort Skytsborg or Blackbeard's Tower
10. Hotel 1829 (formerly Lavalette House)

11. St. Thomas Dutch Reform Church
12. Synagogue Hill
13. Market Square
14. Enid M. Baa Public Library
15. Pissarro Birthplace
16. Riise Alley
17. Post Office
18. Virgin Islands Tourist Information Office
19. Frenchtown
20. Bluebeard's Castle Hotel

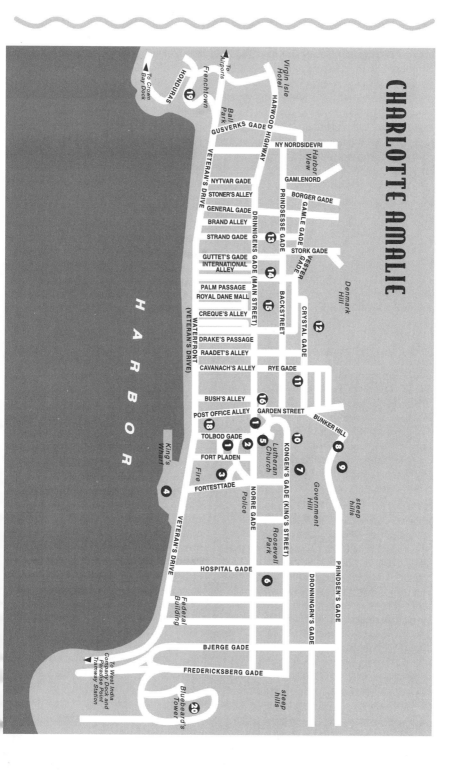

CHARLOTTE AMALIE

HARBOR

Virgin Isle Hotel

To Airports

To Frenchtown

To Crown Bay Dock

HONDURAS

Ball Park

GUSVERKS GADE

HARWOOD HIGHWAY

NY NORDSIDEVRI

Harbor View

GAMLENORD

VETERAN'S DRIVE

NYTVAR GADE

STONER'S ALLEY

GENERAL GADE

BRAND ALLEY

STRAND GADE

GUTTET'S GADE

INTERNATIONAL ALLEY

PALM PASSAGE

ROYAL DANE MALL

CREQUE'S ALLEY

DRAKE'S PASSAGE

RAADET'S ALLEY

CAVANACH'S ALLEY

BUSH'S ALLEY

POST OFFICE ALLEY

WATERFRONT (VETERAN'S DRIVE)

PRINDSESSE GADE

BORGER GADE

GAMLE GADE

STORK GADE

VESTER GADE

BACKSTREET

DRINNIGENS GADE (MAIN STREET)

CRYSTAL GADE

Denmark Hill

RYE GADE

GARDEN STREET

BUNKER HILL

TOLBOD GADE

FORT PLADEN

FORTESTTADE

King's Wharf

Fire

Lutheran Church

KONGEN'S GADE (KING'S STREET)

Police

NORRE GADE

Roosevelt Park

Government Hill

steep hills

PRINDSEN'S GADE

HOSPITAL GADE

Federal Building

DRONNINGRN'S GADE

BJERGE GADE

FREDERICKSBERG GADE

steep hills

Bluebbeard's Tower

To West India Company Dock and Paradise Point Tramway Station history of the Jews of St. Thomas. Hours: weekdays 10:00 A.M.–4:00 P.M.; weekends, 12:30–4:00 P.M.

MARKET SQUARE (13) Continuing west on Backstreet, Market Square is the site of the notorious slave market, one of the biggest in the West Indies. Today it is covered by an iron market shed built earlier in this century and used as the town's open-air fruit-and-vegetable market. Saturday is market day. One block west on Main Street is the Cathedral of St. Peter and St. Paul, built in 1844.

PUBLIC LIBRARY (14) East of Market Square on Main Street is the Enid M. Baa Public Library, built around 1800 as the Lange residence. The library is named for one of the island's first female university graduates, who served as librarian for many years and was instrumental in creating the von Scholten Memorial Collection with books, prints, and documents on the Virgin Islands and the West Indies.

PISSARRO'S BIRTHPLACE (15) No. 14 Dronningens Gade (Main Street) is the birthplace of Camille Pissarro (1830–1903), a Sephardic Jew who lived here until he went to Paris to study at the age of twelve. Pissarro lived in Paris most of his life, but he is known to have returned to St. Thomas at least once.

On both sides of Main Street, small lanes have been made into palm-shaded shopping plazas where shops are housed in 18th-century buildings that were houses of the old port; some are recent structures made to look old.

RIISE ALLEY (16) One of the first old structures to be renovated, helping to spark the renaissance of the historic district, was *A. H. Riise Store and Alley,* belonging to the Paiewonsky family whose patriarch is the island's leading historian and historian of the synagogue. In olden days each warehouse had its own lift to haul cargo from the ships at the waterfront and load it onto a flatbed car that ran on rails through the alleyway to Main Street. The sample here is the only one remaining. At the end of Riise Alley, the 18th-century building housing Gucci was the *Danish Harbor Office.*

At the end of Main Street by the Emancipation Garden is the *post office* (17), with murals by illustrator Stephen Dohanos. They were painted in the 1940s as a WPA project, before he gained his reputation as an illustrator for the *Saturday*

Evening Post. Next to the post office, the Continental Building is the old Danish Customs House. Next door is the Territorial Building, housing the *Tourist Information Office* (18).

FRENCHTOWN (19) At the west end of town is the old fishing village of Frenchtown, settled by French immigrants fleeing the Swedish invasion of St. Barts in the late 18th century. Some of their descendants continue to speak a Norman dialect. While many of the old structures have given way to new houses and buildings, Frenchtown has retained a community feeling, and fishermen can often be seen bringing in their catches to sell on the dock. This small area has a concentration of restaurants popular with islanders and a pretty village church, the Church of St. Anne. Frenchtown is known as Cha Cha Town for the pointed straw hat called *cha cha,* woven by the town's women.

PARADISE POINT TRAMWAY: Directly behind the West Indian Dock is the station (774–9809), where a cable car whisks passengers up a steep mountainside in four minutes to Paradise Point, the summit. There are spectacular views of Charlotte Amalie and St. Thomas. Cost is $10 round trip. The restaurant/bar at the peak is a popular spot for cocktails at sunset. Paradise Point can also be reached by road from the harbor.

DRIVING TOUR OF ST. THOMAS

Remember: KEEP TO THE LEFT. East of Charlotte Amalie the waterfront boulevard, called Veterans Drive (Route 30), forks and leads up to *Bluebeard's Castle Hotel* (20), high on a hill from which you can enjoy a spectacular view of Charlotte Amalie and spot your ship at the West Indian Company dock directly below. The hotel is set in gardens of tropical plants, and its 17th-century Danish watchtower for which it is named is the honeymoon suite. Look closely among the hibiscus and you might see an iguana, a reptile that looks like a miniature dinosaur. Unlike other Caribbean islands, where the iguana is elusive and endangered, it is something of a pet on St. Thomas and will often remain still for a photograph.

From Bluebeard's Routes 35/40 lead to *Drake's Seat*, a small lookout named for the British sea captain Sir Francis Drake, who is said to have used this vantage point to watch for the Spanish treasure galleons on which he preyed. You may not see any treasure ships, but you will be richly rewarded with a magnificent view of Magens Bay and neighboring islands; off to the east is Drake's Passage, a sea channel first explored by Drake in 1580. On Route 40, the *Estate St. Peter Greathouse and Botanical Garden* (St. Peter Mountain Road; 774–4999 or 690–4499) was once part of an 18th century plantation. It is now a 12-acre landscaped spread 1,000 feet above Magens Bay Beach. The estate's modern West Indian-style house is furnished with works by fifty local artists. Self-guided nature trails are also offered. Hours: daily 9:00 A.M.–5:00 P.M.; $8 adults and $4 children.

Crown Mountain Road (Route 33 west) circles Crown Mountain at 1,550 feet, the highest peak. Solberg Hill Road (Route 40 south) returns to Charlotte Amalie, providing extensive views of the town, harbor, and Hassel Island in the foreground and Water Island beyond.

West of Charlotte Amalie, Veterans Drive passes Frenchtown and the airport, continuing to the *University of the Virgin Islands* situated on 175 acres.

Shopping

Main Street and side lanes such as newly renovated Palm Passage have pretty stores and smart boutiques housed in renovated old warehouses from its heyday as a trading post. You will find top-brand watches, jewelry, cameras, electronic equipment, china and crystal, designer clothes and accessories, perfumes, and other gift items— all at prices ranging from 15 percent and more off those on the mainland. Store are open Monday through Saturday, 9:00 A.M. to 5:00 P.M. Some stores in Havensight Mall remain open until 6:00 P.M. Stores close on Sunday unless a cruise ship is in port, when some may open for half a day.

Duty-free shopping: The matter of "duty-free" needs some explanation. All stores in the U.S.

Virgin Islands are duty-free. Even so, the goods they sell are not entirely without import taxes. Local merchants pay taxes on the merchandise they import, but the levies are lower in the U.S. Virgin Islands than on the mainland.

A word of caution: Merchandise in St. Thomas is not always the bargain that is claimed. The proliferation of discount houses in the United States, particularly for cameras and electronic equipment, has cut into the traditional savings on duty-free merchandise. The only way to know a real bargain is to come prepared with prices from home and to do some comparative shopping before you buy. Cigarettes and liquor have the lowest prices and represent the greatest savings.

ART AND ARTISTS: *A. H. Riise Gifts and Art Gallery* (Main Street; 800–524–2037) has a collection of local as well as Haitian artists. In late March, August, and November, *Tillett's Gardens* (Route 38, Tutu; 775–1929), where some artists and jewelry designers work and sell their products year-round, holds an arts fair, *Arts Alive,* with more than fifty local artists and artisans. The colorful Mocko Jumbies, clowns, acrobats, and folkloric dancers are part of the entertainment. Admission is free.

BOOKS: *Dockside Bookshop* (Havensight Mall) and *Island Books* (Grand Hotel) have the largest selection of books and carry stateside newspapers—costing $2 or more.

CAMERAS/ELECTRONICS: All leading makes are available, but bring stateside prices for comparison. The largest selections are at *Boolchand's* (31 Main Street and Havensight Mall). Prices are comparable to those of discount houses in New York.

CHINA/CRYSTAL: *Little Switzerland* (Main Street) carries a wide selection of English china, French crystal, and similar high-quality goods. You can get a catalog by calling (800) 524–2010. *A. H. Riise Gifts* (Main Street) is something of a department store with a collection of boutiques for gifts, jewelry, perfume, china, silver, and crystal, as well as liquor.

CLOTHING: You can find boutiques with designer fashions in the narrow passageways between Main Street and the waterfront. *Fendi, DKNY,* and *Polo Ralph Lauren* (Palm Passage) have their own stores. *Nicole Miller* (Main Street) is a new addition, as is *Bisou-Bisou* (Palm Passage) which has young trendy fashions. *Local Color* (Hibiscus Alley) has handpainted T-shirts, dresses, and sportswear. Look for the label, *Sloop Jones,* which is based at Hansen Bay, St. John.

CRAFTS: Don't overlook locally made products, especially for gifts and souvenirs. You do not have to count these products in your $1,200 customs allowance. Products you will find include straw hats, mats and baskets; candles with scents of local herbs and spices; candies and preserved fruits and spices; pottery and ceramics; folkloric dolls; macramé and scrimshaw; and perfume and suntan lotions made from native flowers and herbs.

Down Island Traders (on the waterfront) sells preserves, herbs, and spices as well as imported teas and coffees. *Sheltered Workshop* (Municipal Hospital Complex), which is part of the island's vocational rehabilitation program, stocks hand-made dolls and other island crafts. *Caribbean Safari* (35 Back Street) has a selection of straw crafts from all over the Caribbean. *Cowboys and Indians* (Grand Hotel Court) specializes in Native American art.

JEWELRY: Stores such as *Cardow, Cartier,* and *H. Stern* (all on Main Street) have international reputations; *A. H. Riise Gifts* has a large jewelry department and is the exclusive Mikimoto dealer. *Blue Carib Gems* (Bakery Square Mall) has jewelry designed by Alan O'Hara, who uses gemstones and coral found in the Caribbean. Many smaller jewelry stores on Main Street and adjacent malls sell gold jewelry. Look around before you buy.

LEATHER/LUGGAGE: Royal Dane Mall has several shops with high-quality Italian and Spanish handbags. *Cosmopolitan* (Drake's Passage) carries Bally shoes for men and women and Bruno Magli for men. *The Leather Shop* (Main Street and Havensight Mall) is the dealer for Fendi. *Gucci* and *Louis Vuitton* have their own stores; *Coach* (Hibiscus Alley) recently joined them.

LINENS: Table linens are among the best bargains here. Most come from India and China. *Linen House* and *Mr. Tablecloth* (Palm Passage) have large collections, and you might also check out some of the general stores on Main Street.

LIQUOR: Prices are very competitive, but *Al Cohen's* near the port claims to have the best prices in St. Thomas. Check *St. Thomas This Week* or *Best Buys in St. Thomas,* free pamphlets distributed for tourists. The centerfold or back page has a list of current liquor prices.

PERFUMES: *Tropicana Shop* (Main Street) has nothing but perfume. *West Indies Bay Company* (Estates Thomas, previously at Havensight Mall) makes St. Johns Bay Rum for men, J'Ouvert for women, and other fragrances packaged in bottles with handwoven palm fronds in a traditional design used by Caribbean fishermen for their fish pots. The company offers factory tours.

DINING AND NIGHTLIFE

The Virgin Islands did not gain their reputation as Paradise in the kitchen. It's not that innkeepers and restaurateurs don't try. They try very hard, perhaps too hard, to create gourmet havens. But for a myriad of reasons (Herman Wouk's hilarious *Don't Stop the Carnival* was written from his trials and tribulations in trying to operate a hotel in St. Thomas), they are unable to maintain a consistently high level. Aspiring places can quickly become pretentious disappointments at very high prices instead.

With this caveat, the selection here is based less on the great gourmet experience you are unlikely to have than on the aesthetic one you are sure to experience, either thanks to a view, a historic setting, or both. Some of the best establishments are open for dinner only. Expensive means more than $30 per person. If wine is added, the bill can quickly climb to $50 per person and more. Most are open daily, but check locally.

WITH A VIEW OR HISTORIC SETTING

Hervé Restaurant and Wine Bar (Government Hill; 777–9703) is St. Thomas' hottest new restaurant and is set in a newly renovated 18th century building with a panoramic view of Charlotte Amalie. *Hervé* is Herve Paul Chassin, a St. Thomas restaurateur for 25 years. You lunch and dine in an informal ambience on contemporary American and classic French selections, all touched by a bit of Caribbean. The bar serves wines by the glass. Closed Sunday. Expensive.

Hotel 1829 (Government Hill; 774–1829) is a historic landmark with a long-established reputation for its classic international selections in a pretty setting. Very expensive.

Old Stone Farmhouse (Mahogany Run; 775–1377). St. Thomas habitués will welcome the recent return of this former island favorite. In its rustic yet elegant setting, you can select from an eclectic array of French, Asian, and Caribbean dishes as well as steak and seafood dishes. Expensive.

Light and Local

Beni Iguana (Grand Hotel Court; 777–8740) is a sushi bar in an old Danish courtyard with umbrella tables. There are cooked dishes and daily specials, as well. The bar serves domestic and Japanese beer and sake. Live classical and jazz guitar on Friday evenings. Closed Sunday. Moderate.

Craig and Sally's (Frenchtown; 777–9949) is a family-run restaurant/bar with owners Craig at the door and Sally in the kitchen. The bar, open daily 11:30 A.M. to 1:00 A.M. except Monday, serves wine by the glass. The restaurant offers an eclectic menu that's changed daily. Closed Saturday and Sunday lunch. Moderate.

Cuzzin's (7 Backstreet; 777–4711) is a lively restaurant-bar in the heart of Charlotte Amalie featuring West Indian dishes, sandwiches, and pasta. Moderate.

Gladys' Cafe (Royal Dane Mall; 774–6604) is a charming cafe in town that serves lunch plus dinner on Friday with jazz, 6:00 to 9:00 P.M. Lunch offers fresh fish, hamburgers, salads, and local specials. Gladys' own hot sauce, attractively packaged for gifts, is on sale for $6 a bottle. Moderate.

Paddy O'Furniture's Irish Brew Pub (East End; 779–1760), USVI's first "Irish brew pub" makes four different beers. Moderate. *Pitbull Irish Stout,* the most popular brew, combines four malts. The waterfront restaurant serves lunch and dinner and has take-out service. Closed Sunday.

Zorba (2B Commandant Gade, Government Hill; 776–0444). Rustic outdoor patio gives this unpretentious restaurant a flavor of Greece as much as does its good food. Inexpensive.

Evening Entertainment

Nightlife is small-scale—steel bands, combos, discos—and mostly revolves around hotels and restaurants.

A terrace at *Paradise Point* and *Room with a View* (Bluebeard's Castle; 774–1600) provide a good perch for cocktails at sunset; and offer a fabulous view of Charlotte Amalie. On different nights of the week, you will find entertainment at various hotels. Check local newspaper and tourist publications such as *St. Thomas This Week* for what's happening.

 Sports

St. Thomas boasts good facilities for almost every warm-weather sport—fishing, golf, tennis, parasailing, waterskiing, windsurfing—and those for sailing and diving are outstanding.

BEACHES AND SWIMMING: The coves and bays that sheltered pirates in the old days are among St. Thomas's biggest attractions for tourists today. The most celebrated—and the most crowded—beach is at Magens Bay on the north side of the island. Beaches closest to Charlotte Amalie are Morningstar, Limetree, and Bolongo on the south/southeast. Tranquil Honeymoon Beach on Water Island, which is earmarked to get a $3.3 million facelift, is open for visitors and can be reached by a short ferry ride from town. You'll find a list of beaches and facilities in *St. Thomas This Week.*

BIKING: *Island Bike Adventures* (phone/fax: 776–1727) offers an island tour in an open-air safari van enroute to your biking adventure. At the start you receive a 21-speed mountain bike, helmet, and water bottle plus an orientation to the bike and route. The guided tour, followed by a support vehicle, travels on secluded roads and trails and ends at Magens Bay beach for a swim. You can return to your ship or stay at the beach. You should be in good health, 13 years or older. Wear tennis shoes and light clothing. Currently the tour is sold only through cruise lines and costs about $50–$60 per person.

BOATING: Calm seas and year-round balmy weather have made the Virgin Islands a boating mecca. Every type of craft is available for chartered, bare boat, or crewed, and with all provisions. Many charter operators have stateside offices and toll-free numbers for information and reservations. *Yacht Haven Marina* is the homeport for the V.I. Charter Yacht League (774–3944) and the venue for the league's annual boat show in mid-November. On the east end at Red Hook are *American Yacht Harbor* (775–6454) and *Charter Boat Center* (Piccola Marina; 800–866–5714; 775–7990), among others.

Several dozen boats operate day sails that take passengers to pretty beaches for swimming and snorkeling. Some boats hold only six people, while party boats can take several dozen.

DEEP-SEA FISHING: Experts say the Virgin Islands are among the best places in the world for blue marlin, and the records set here support the claim. Other fish—maho, kingfish, sailfish, wahoo, tuna, and skipjack—are plentiful, too. *American Yacht Harbor, St. Thomas Sports Fishing Center* (775–7990), and a dozen or more boat operators offer half- and full-day trips; they provide bait, tackle, ice, and beer. *Boobie Hatch* (Red Hook; 775–6683) runs half-day trips for $325 to $375; full-day, $550 to $750 for up to six people. The time of year makes a difference in the prices; the marlin season is mainly July and August.

GOLF: *Mahogany Run Golf Course* (777–6006 for tee-off times) is St. Thomas' only 18-hole course. The championship layout is one of the Caribbean's most challenging. It was completely renovated in 1996 and a new watering system was installed to ensure optimum conditions year-round. Located about 20 minutes from Charlotte Amalie, the spectacular course (6,100 yards, par 70) by George and Tom Fazio extends over verdant hills and rocky cliffs overlooking the north

coast. It has a pro shop, driving range, and practice green. Greens fee: $75 plus $15 for cart, which is required. After 2:00 P.M. cost is $60. Ship golf package may cost $130, but will include transportation from the port.

KAYAKING: *Virgin Island Ecotours* (Nadir, Route 32; 779–2155; fax: 809–774–4601) offers 2.5-hour guided kayak tours of the Virgin Islands Marine Sanctuary Mangrove Lagoon, led by marine biologists and naturalists from the University of the Virgin Islands. It uses single or two-person ocean kayaks that are easy to paddle. No motorized vessels are allowed in the lagoon, so kayakers can enjoy quiet waters. Tours start from the Holmberg Marina and cost $50, with a 15-minute orientation and slide show to introduce kayakers to local flora and fauna. Kayaks may also be rented for individual exploration.

SNORKELING AND SCUBA DIVING: The Virgin Islands are rated by dive experts among the best in the world for both novice and experienced divers. Visibility ranges up to 150 feet, water temperatures average 82 degrees F in summer and 78 degrees F in winter, and there's great variety plus excellent facilities. Three dozen of the Virgin Islands' one hundred dive sites lie within a 20-minute boat ride of St. Thomas. Most dive operators have their own tanks and boats and offer packages ranging from half-day to week-long certification. A list of operators is available from the V.I. Tourist offices. Many cruise ships offer a half-day course as an introduction to scuba diving.

If you don't swim you might opt for the *Atlantis II*, a recreational submarine that departs from its station next to West Indian Company Dock for Buck Island (not to be confused with Buck Island off St. Croix), a 20-minute boat ride away. The 50-foot-long, air-conditioned ship with all systems duplicated to ensure safety, dives up to 150 feet. The dive lasts about an hour and costs $72 for adults, $36 ages 13–18, and $27 ages 4–12.

Coral World, an underwater observatory and park at Coki Point and once St. Thomas' most popular attraction, was badly damaged in the 1995 hurricane. In spring 1997, it was purchased by a group of local investors with the aim of renovating the facility and reopening it for the 1998 season. Check locally.

TENNIS: About three dozen hotels here have tennis courts. Those closest to the West Indian Company Dock and open to nonguests are at Marriott's *Frenchman's Reef Hotel* (774–1600), two courts, $10 per hour. Courts nearest to Crown Bay Dock are two public ones, lighted until 10:00 P.M.

WINDSURFING: *Morningstar Beach* is nearest the West India Company Dock, but the eastern end of the island has the best windsurfing. *Sapphire Beach* (775–6100) offers instruction on a simulator and instruction in the water. *West Indies Windsurfing* (775–6530), on the beach in Red Hook, has the best rentals.

On the southside of Red Hook, Vessup, known locally as *Bluebeard's Beach,* is a popular venue for windsurfing contests.

CULTURAL EVENTS AND FESTIVALS

The Virgin Islands observe all the U.S. national holidays, plus a few of their own. Leading the list is *Carnival,* which, on St. Thomas, is held during the last two weeks of April. It begins officially with a week-long calypso competition for the coveted title of the Calypso King; followed by a week of festivities with the crowning of a Carnival queen, and an elaborate all-day parade featuring the Mocko Jumbi Dancers.

From October through May, the *Reichhold Center for the Performing Arts* (693–1559) features concerts, opera, ballet, Broadway musicals, jazz, gospel, and plays at its wonderful outdoor theater.

ST. JOHN A GIFT OF NATURE

Serene St. John, the least developed of the U.S. Virgin Islands, is truly America the Beautiful. Almost one-half of the heavily forested, mountainous island—9,485 acres—is covered by national

park on land donated in 1956 by Laurance Rockefeller. The island is edged by lovely coves with pristine, white-sand beaches and some of the most spectacular aquamarine waters in the Caribbean. Beneath these waters is a tropical wonderland, also protected by the park.

Development is restricted; it has occurred mainly in the area of the lilliputian port of Cruz Bay and in the southwest corner. On the north coast is the super deluxe Caneel Bay, set on an old sugar plantation in the magnificent gardens fronting seven—yes, seven—of the prettiest beaches in the Caribbean. The tennis facilities are great, too.

Several cruise ships call at St. John, but the majority of its visitors come on day trips from St. Thomas; it is one of the most delightful excursions available for cruise passengers, whether as an organized tour, a day sail, or on your own. The day's target for most visitors is a circle route along North Shore Road (Route 20) and Centerline Road (Route 10), the two main roads, with stops for a swim, picnic, and short hikes.

FERRY SERVICE: Ferries depart Red Hook hourly from 6:30 A.M. to midnight for Cruz Bay and return from 6:00 A.M. to 11 P.M. Others depart from the Charlotte Amalie waterfront at two-hour intervals from 7:15 A.M. to 3:45 P.M. There is also ferry service from St. John to Jost Van Dyke and Tortola, B.V.I.

TRANSPORTATION: Taxis with driver/guides can be hired in Cruz Bay at the pier, or you can rent a car or jeep for about $45 per day. A two-hour island tour costs $30 for one or two persons; $12 per person for three or more. Several St. Thomas tour companies provide service in St. John and combine the two islands into one package. Drivers take and return you to the ferry docks on both islands. After a tour of St. John, your driver leaves you at a beach to fetch you later.

 ## CRUZ BAY

Tiny, yacht-filled Cruz Bay hugs a narrow strip of land between the harbor and the mountains. Most of the buildings and houses are West

Indian–style in architecture and painted a medley of pastel colors. Until recently the structures were small and blended into the landscape as naturally as the bougainvillea. Regretfully, new construction is drastically altering the character of the town by crowding the space around the harbor and turning the once-natural setting into a tacky, T-shirt and fast-food mall. Nonetheless, the town—three streets wide and four streets deep—is worth exploring and easy to do on foot. Facing the pier is a park, and on its north are the Taxi Association and Tourist Information Center.

PARK SERVICE VISITOR CENTER: Northwest of the harbor is the Virgin Islands National Park Service Visitor Center, open from 8:00 A.M. to 4:00 P.M. The center is well organized and offers a variety of activities including ranger-led tours, hikes, snorkeling trips, cultural and wildlife lectures, and film presentations. A schedule is available in advance from the park service (776–6201). Reservations during the winter season are strongly recommended. Write Virgin Islands National Park, Box 806, St. Thomas 00801 (775–6238).

HIKES AND TOURS: *Trail Guide for Safe Hiking* is a park brochure outlining twenty-one trails with a map and tips on preparations. Most trails are designed in clusters of two or three contiguous paths to be taken in segments as short as 10 minutes, or, when strung together, as long as 2 to 4 hours. The most popular is Reef Bay, a 2.5-mile trail that takes about two hours to cover in a downhill direction.

Among the historic programs is the Annaberg Cultural Demonstrations (3 hours), which visits the partially restored ruins of the Annaberg Plantation, where you can learn about tropical food, plants, weaving, baking, charcoal making, and other skills islanders once needed to subsist.

Cruise-ship excursions usually stop at Trunk Bay, a lovely beach on the north shore, about 20 minutes from town and the site of an underwater trail laid out for snorkelers by the park service. Unfortunately, the reef is now badly deteriorated from overuse. Snorkelers and divers on their own have many other reefs around St. John to explore. At Honeymoon Beach, one of the palm-studded coves of Caneel Bay, snorkelers can swim with spotted eagle ray.

SHOPPING AND DINING IN ST. JOHN

St. John's beauty and tranquility have made it something of an artists' community. Several artists have stores in town sandwiched between the T-shirt and junky-merchandise shops.

The Pink Papaya (Lemon Tree Mall; 776–7266) is the gallery and gift shop of Virgin Islands artist Lisa Etre, whose distinctive style reflects her West Indian environment in a sophisticated way. In addition to original paintings and prints, elements from her drawings are used in designs on tableware, greeting cards, and lovely gifts.

Mongoose Junction, a 10-minute walk north of the pier, is a shopping plaza designed as an artist's enclave with rustic wooden buildings incorporating the trees in a natural setting. You will probably want to browse, as each shop is different. Among the boutique/studios of local artists and transplanted mainlanders, *Donald Schnell Studio* (800–253–7107) features ceramics of natural materials—coral sand, woods—by an American artist who comes originally from Michigan. *The Clothing Studio* has hand-painted tropical wear from $6 T-shirts to $150 dresses. *Fabric Mill,* belonging to interior designer Trisha Maize, carries unusual fabrics and accessories. *Batik Kitab* features St. John artist, Juliana Aradi, who works on silk, cotton, and linen.

South of the pier *Wharfside Village* is a multi-level mall of West Indian–style structures awash in cool pastels, with more than forty shops and restaurants. *Rusty Nail Originals* (693–7740) is one of the newest shops, and has gifts, books, handcrafted jewelry, and island clothing. *Pusser's Landing,* an English bar/restaurant, anchors the group. *Coral Bay Folk Art Gallery* sells work by local and Caribbean artists and is the only place that sells native St. John whisk baskets.

Asolare (Cruz Bay; 779–4747) reopened after extensive renovation and is an island favorite for Pacific Rim cuisine, which can be enjoyed along with spectacular views.

SPORTS IN ST. JOHN

St. John Water Sports (Box 70, Cruz Bay, St. John 00830; 776–6256) offers reef and wreck dives departing daily at 9:00 A.M. and 2:00 P.M. Cost is $45 for a one-tank dive or $65 for a two-tank dive. Resort course is $55. *Cruz Bay Watersports* (Box 252, St. John 00830; 776–6234) has similar programs as well as day sails with snorkeling, drinks, and lunch for $60. For a new experience, try SNUBA. It's something like scuba without the serious gear. *Snuba of St. John* (Trunk Bay; 693–8063) has daily guided tours, starting at 9:30 A.M., for $45.

KAYAKING: In recent years kayaking has become very popular and is available in St. John from *Big Planet Sea Kayaking Center* (Mongoose Junction II; 776–6638), which offers a four-hour guided tour of the beautiful coastal waters with time for swimming, snorkeling, and exploring isolated beaches accessible only by boat, for $45. Another is *Low Key Watersports* (800–835–7718; 693–8999), which will tailor the trip to your interest.

ST. CROIX THE SLEEPING VIRGIN

St. Croix, 40 miles south of St. Thomas, is the largest of the U.S. Virgin Islands and served as the capital for more than two hundred years, but today it is less developed and generally less known to tourists than St. Thomas.

St. Croix has much to offer: scenery, sight-seeing, sports, shopping, historic towns, pretty beaches, good restaurants, and some attractions that not even St. Thomas or St. John can boast. It has two 18-hole golf courses, a "rain forest," botanic gardens, wildlife refuges for birds and leatherback turtles, and three parks, including the only underwater park in the U.S. National Park Service.

A low-lying island of gentle landscape and rolling hills, St. Croix is vastly different from its mountainous sisters. From the time Columbus sighted the island in 1493 to the United States' purchase in 1917, it saw seven flags fly over the land. Whereas St. Thomas prospered on trade, St. Croix became a rich sugar producer and developed a plantation society that prevailed long after the abolition of slavery. Today many of the sugar mills and plantation homes have been restored as hotels and restaurants; and the colonial hearts of Christiansted, the main town, and Frederiksted, the old capital, are on the National Historic Registry.

Frederiksted, on the west coast, has a deep-water harbor used by most cruise lines and is convenient to popular attractions included on most shore excursions. Christiansted, 17 miles east of Frederiksted on the north shore, has a pretty yacht-filled harbor trimmed by a colorful, historic waterfront anchored by a grand fort—all beautifully restored. Although Christiansted is more developed than Frederiksted for shopping, restaurants, and water sports, unless the harbor is dredged, it is limited to receiving small, shallow draft ships—a situation many local people prefer.

St. Croix has good roads and transportation, and travel is easy regardless of which port is used. Your ship's port of call can, however, influence your selection of activities by its proximity and convenience to certain attractions. A more serious limitation is the length of time your ship is in port. Often ships calling at Frederiksted arrive about 7:00 or 8:00 A.M. and depart by 1:00 or 2:00 P.M. Such brief stopovers restrict tours to 3 or 3.5 hours and limit the range of possibilities.

Most ships offer only one excursion: *St. Croix Island Tour* (3.5 hours, $20; or by taxi, $60). If a second shore excursion is available, it would most likely be a Buck Island Tour. For those on a first visit, we recommend an island tour, preferably by taxi with a driver/guide. A 2-hour-long tour costs $30; a 3-hour tour costs $40. It is not worthwhile renting a car unless your ship remains in port for a full day.

Taxi and tour prices are posted at the Visitor's Bureau office by the pier. The St. Croix Combined Taxi and Tour Association (Box 2439, Frederiksted, USVI 00841; 809–772–2828, fax: 772–3718) has more than 75 members, who must take tourism/guide refresher courses every six months. Maurice Hamilton (772–1180) drives a minivan and makes a particularly pleasant and knowledgeable guide.

St. Croix Bike and Tours (Pier 69, Frederiksted; 772–2545) offers guided mountain-bike excursions. *Crusian Helicopters* (690–4356) can take you flight-seeing.

FREDERIKSTED

A WILLIAMSBURG IN THE MAKING

Frederiksted was an almost deserted town in the 1970s, but federal legislation granting tax benefits to historic preservation galvanized community action and many old buildings were renovated. Despite the setback due to Hurricane Hugo in 1989, city fathers dream of someday making Frederiksted a Williamsburg of the Caribbean. Cruise passengers have a choice of staying close to town to enjoy the beach and stroll through its historic center; taking an island tour; or enjoying a specific sport—diving, horseback riding, golf, or hiking.

The old district of Frederiksted, directly in front of the pier, is laid out in a grid running seven blocks from Fort Frederik and the Customs House on the north, to the Library and Queen Cross Street on the south, and five blocks deep from the waterfront (Strand Street) east to Prince Street. *Fort Frederik,* which dates from 1752, was the site of the emancipation of the slaves in 1848. Other important buildings include *Government House,* built in 1747; *St. Paul's Anglican Church,* 1817; and *St. Patrick's Roman Catholic Church,* 1848. Many historic homes and commercial buildings line the old streets.

SANDY POINT NATIONAL WILDLIFE REFUGE Just 3 miles south of Frederiksted is a protected area that is one of only two nesting grounds for the leatherback turtle in the United States. From March through June the enormous turtles—up to 6 feet in length and 1,000 pounds in weight—come ashore to dig holes where each lays as many as eighty eggs. Afterward they cover the eggs with sand for protection and lumber back to the

sea, returning to repeat the ritual as many as six times during nesting season. After about two months the hatchlings emerge from the sand pits and dash to the sea under the cover of night. Earthwatch, a United States–based, nonprofit research organization and the St. Croix Environmental Association, maintains a turtle watch in which visitors can participate from April through June and in August. Reservations must be made in advance. Inquiries should be made to the association (773–1989). The group also conducts guided environmental tours.

CHRISTIANSTED

THE PICTURE-PERFECT PORT

Christiansted is one of the Caribbean's prettiest little towns. In an area of about five square blocks, you will find some of the best-preserved and most interesting landmarks in the Virgin Islands. Alongside them are shops, making it easy to combine a walking tour with a shopping excursion.

SCALEHOUSE: The Visitor's Bureau is located at the foot of King Street in Scalehouse, once part of the Customs House where goods were weighed for tax purposes. It is thought to date from 1855. In 1989 the winds and sea surge of Hurricane Hugo were so powerful they lifted the base of the heavy huge scales out of the ground. Hours: weekdays 8:00 A.M. to 5:00 P.M.

FORT CHRISTIAN: Overlooking the harbor is the best preserved of the five Danish forts in the West Indies. Built in 1749, Fort Christian is now under the supervision of the U.S. National Park Service. You can get a brochure for a self-guided tour, and park rangers who know their history well are on hand to answer questions and provide fascinating tidbits not available in brochures. For one thing, they'll show you the cell where Alexander Hamilton's mother was jailed for her "improprieties." Tut tut! New interpretative exhibits have been installed in some of the rooms to demonstrate life in the fort in the mid-18th century. Hours: weekdays 8:00 A.M.–5:00 P.M.; weekends and holidays 9:00 A.M.–5:00 P.M.

Between the fort and Scalehouse is the old

Customs House and Post Office, built in 1751. It is used now as a library.

GOVERNMENT HOUSE: One block west on King Street, an imposing 18th-century townhouse that was built as a private home was later used as the residence and offices of the Danish governor. A handsome outside staircase leads to a beautiful ballroom on the first floor.

STEEPLE BUILDING: The first church the Danes built after acquiring St. Croix in 1733 stands at the corner of Church and Company streets. Completed in 1750, it was a Lutheran church until 1831, and afterward served as a school, hospital, and storehouse. It now has a small museum with Amerindian and other types of artifacts.

BUCK ISLAND: The Buck Island Reef National Monument, 3.5 miles northeast of St. Croix, is a volcanic rock of about 300 acres surrounded by 550 acres of underwater coral gardens of unusual beauty and scientific interest. The reef around Buck Island makes up the only underwater park in the U.S. National Park Service. A park-service pamphlet explains the reef and pictures some of the fish that swimmers are likely to see; it is usually distributed to participants of snorkeling excursions.

Glass-bottom boats, catamarans, and motorboats with snorkeling equipment operate daily from King's Wharf in Christiansted to Buck Island. (See snorkeling in the sports section.) The ride to Buck Island takes about 30 minutes. The time spent at the reef is usually an hour, but it can be longer, depending on your interest.

A Drive around St. Croix

A driving tour by bus or car is usually made in a circular fashion from Frederiksted to Christiansted via Mahogany Road (Route 76), a scenic east-west road through the Rain Forest, a stretch of lush tropical vegetation very different from the rest of the island. The return uses Centerline Road, the island's main east-west highway, convenient for stops at three of St. Croix's main attractions.

ST. GEORGE VILLAGE BOTANICAL GARDEN On the north side of Centerline Road, about 5 miles east of Frederiksted, are 16 acres of tropical gardens, landscaped around the ruins of a Danish sugar-plantation workers' village dating from the 18th and 19th centuries. The garden began in 1972 as a cleanup project of the local garden club, but when the debris was cleared away, the members recognized the site as one of historic significance. Archaeologists excavated the area and found beneath the colonial ruins an Arawak settlement dating from A.D. 100 to 900. It is believed to have been the largest of the ninety-six Indian villages that existed on St. Croix at the time of Columbus.

Designed to incorporate the colonial ruins, the garden combines natural growth, landscaped plantings, and open land. The standout is the cactus garden.

Among the restored ruins you will see the bake oven, which is operating again, and the blacksmith's shop, where volunteer smiths using original tools produce items sold in the gift shop. An excellent map is available and walkways are signposted for self-guided tours. The garden is open daily. There is a $5 admission charge. The garden (Box 338, Frederiksted, 00840; 772–3874) is privately supported and volunteer managed.

CRUZAN RUM DISTILLERY At the pavilion of the Virgin Islands' leading rum maker, visitors are offered a free tour, rum cocktails, and recipe booklets. Hours: Tours weekdays from 9:00 to 11:30 A.M. and 1:00 to 4:00 P.M.

WHIM GREATHOUSE St. Croix's pride is Whim Greathouse, a restoration project of the St. Croix Landmarks Society. The beautifully restored plantation house, built in 1803, is furnished with lovely antiques; and the old kitchens, mill, and other buildings give visitors a good picture of life on a sugar plantation in the 18th and 19th centuries. You will also see the cook house, bathhouse, apothecary, 1856 steam engines, animal mill, windmill, boiling shed, rum still, and sugar factory. It has a museum, gift shop, and furniture showroom. Hours: daily 10:00 A.M. to 5:00 P.M. For information call 772–0598. Admission: $5 for adults; $1 children. The society offers tours of historic homes annually in February and March. In March it stages an annual antiques auction.

COLUMBUS LANDING SITE AND THE SALT

RIVER BAY NATIONAL PARK: On the north shore at the mouth of the Salt River, Salt River Bay is an estuary, an important Arawak Indian site, a major dive location, and the site of Columbus's landing. The site was designated a national park in 1992 to commemorate the Columbus Quincentennial. Southeast of the estuary at Triton Bay, the Nature Conservancy has a twelve-acre preserve.

ST. CROIX AQUARIUM (Caravelle Arcade, Christiansted; 773–8895) is both a visitor attraction and marine education center, and offers guided tours by a marine biologist.

SHOPPING IN
ST. CROIX

St. Croix's best shopping is in Christiansted, where 18- and 19th-century warehouses have been made into attractive, palm-shaded shopping plazas. The streets paralleling King Street—Company Street on the east, Strand Street on the west—also have attractive shops. The historic buildings around Market Square, between Company and Queen streets, have recently been renovated and house many new, smart shops. Shopping in Frederiksted is limited, but a few Christiansted stores have branches there. Cruzans, as the people of St. Croix are called, maintain their prices are better than those in St. Thomas because they do not have to pay St. Thomas's high rents nor the high commission demanded by some cruise directors.

ART AND ARTISTS: St. Croix has an active art community of local artists and mainlanders who live there part of the year. *Gilliam-King Gallery* features local artists, Trudi Gilliam who specializes in metal sculpture with a distinctive style, influenced by the sea and local environment; and Judith King, who can be seen here at work. Open Tuesday to Friday.

BOOKS/MAPS: *Jeltbrups Book Store* (30 King Street) and *The Bookie* (3 Strand Street) sell books and periodicals.

CHINA/CRYSTAL: *Little Switzerland* is known throughout the Caribbean for its stock of high-quality English china, French crystal, Swiss watches, Hummel figurines, and other gift items.

You can request a catalog in advance by calling (800) 524–2010.

CLOTHING/SPORTSWEAR: *1870 Town Shoppes* (52 King Street), set in a historic townhouse built in 1870, has fashionable sportswear at moderate prices. *Java Wraps* (Pan Am Pavilion), a long established Caribbean chain, sells resortwear; its sister store on Company Street stocks antique furniture and household items.

CRAFTS: *Many Hands* (Pan Am Pavilion) displays handcrafts by three hundred artisans living in the Virgin Islands. The products range from jewelry and ceramics to sculpture, and paintings. *St. Croix Leap* (Mahogany Road, Route 76; 772–0421) is a great place to stop if you are touring the eastern end of the island. You can watch craftsmen make bowls, vases, and other practical home products from native woods. The items can be purchased. Crafts and original art are duty-free upon your return through U.S. Customs.

JEWELRY: *Colombian Emeralds* (43 Queen Cross Street), as the name implies, specializes in emeralds from Colombia, which produces about 90 percent of the world's supply. Unmounted emeralds can be brought into the United States duty-free. *Sonya Ltd.* (Company and Church streets; 772–0421) specializes in handwrought gold and silver jewelry.

PERFUME: *St. Croix Perfume Center* (Kings Alley) has as complete a selection as any store in town—and at competitive prices.

The newest shopping plaza, King's Alley Walk (Christiansted) has a variety of stores, including *The White House*, which specializes in women's clothing in shades of white, off-white, ivory, and beige; the *Caribbean Bracelet Co.*, where you can buy bracelets made in the Dominican Republic; *Patrick's Watches* for repair or purchase; *Cruzan Cellars*, which stocks duty-free Caribbean rum; and a variety of other clothing and gift outlets. When you need a break, *Sippers Ice Cream* has ice cream and desserts; *St. Croix Chop House & Brew Pub* offers steaks, chops, and fish; and *A Taste of Asia* features Thai-Caribbean cuisine.

In the shopping plazas and at the King Christian Hotel facing the waterfront, there are car-rental firms and water-sports operators who make excursions to Buck Island and offer diving and other sports.

SPORTS IN ST. CROIX

BEACH/BOATING: Frederiksted has a pretty public beach only a few minutes' walk from the pier and, south of town at Sandy Point, one of the most beautiful stretches of sand in the Caribbean.

GOLF AND TENNIS: Equidistant between Frederiksted and Christiansted, on the north side of the island, is *Carambola Beach Resort and Golf Club* (6,856 yards, par 72), a lovely, eighteen-hole layout designed by Robert Trent Jones. It has a clubhouse and pro shop. Call in advance for tee-off times (809–778–3800).

A mile east of Christiansted, *Buccaneer Beach Hotel* (773–2100) sprawls over 240 landscaped acres with great views, beaches, spa, and water-sports facilities. It has an 18-hole golf course, and its eight Laykold courts are the largest complex on the island.

HIKING AND BIKING: In the northwest corner of St. Croix, an area known as the *Rain Forest* has winding roads with light traffic and paths in the woods that lead to seasonal streams and waterfalls. The most scenic route, Western Scenic Road, begins (or ends) at Hams Bay on the northwest coast. The coastal road (Route 63) north passes Butler Bay, where a nature preserve of the St. Croix Landmarks Society is popular for bird-watching. Caledonia Valley, on the south side of the ridge, has the island's only year-round stream and is popular for bird-watching. *Take-a-Hike* (778–6997) offers guided walking tours; advance arrangements are necessary. *St. Croix Bike and Tours* (772–2545) has guided mountain-bike excursions.

HORSEBACK RIDING: *Paul and Jill's Equestrian Stable* (772–2880), next to Sprat Hall Estate 2 miles north of Frederiksted, is operated by a member of the family that has owned Sprat Hall, one of the island's most historic inns, for more than two hundred years. The stable offers 2-hour scenic trail rides for about $50.

Buccaneer Hotel (near Christiansted) has riding over trails on its property. Both facilities require advance reservations.

SNORKELING AND SCUBA DIVING: St. Croix is almost completely surrounded by coral reefs. In addition to Buck Island, there are forty-seven dive sites near St. Croix. The greatest variety of coral and fish is found along 6 miles of the north shore where the reef is only 500 yards from the coast in water about 35 feet deep. It is most accessible from Christiansted, which is also the location of *Mile-Mark Watersports* (800–524–2012), *Dive St. Croix* (773–3434), and other dive operators.

Miles-Mark Watersports (800–524–2012), has several daily excursions to Buck Island: A power-boat leaves at 9:30 A.M. and returns at 1:00 P.M.; cost is $35 per person; catamaran or trimaran for 20 passengers runs from 10:00 A.M. to 4:00 P.M. and includes a beach barbecue, $60 per person; and on a smaller scale, a day sail for up to six people costs $55 per person.

On the south of St. Croix, *Anchor Dive Center,* in the Salt River National Park, has daily dives to what it calls the "seven wonders of St. Croix."

The Salt River Dropoff at the mouth of the river is a prime diving location made up of two sites: the east and west walls of a submerged canyon, which shelve and plunge more than 1,000 feet. The walls are encrusted with corals, sponges, and forests of black coral and attract large schools of fish. Frederiksted is not without interest, particularly for shipwrecks and the abundance of tiny seahorses around the harbor.

THE BRITISH VIRGIN ISLANDS

YACHTMAN'S HAVEN

The British Virgin Islands, an archipelago of about fifty green, mountainous islands, cays, and rocks are spread over 59 square miles of sapphire waters along the Anegada Passage between the Caribbean Sea and the Atlantic. Mostly volcanic in origin and uninhabited, they have scalloped coastlines and idyllic little coves with white-sand beaches. In olden days their strategic location made them a favorite hiding place of pirates who plundered ships carrying treasures and cargo between the Old and New worlds. Today the islands of this British Crown Colony are favorite hideaways for yachtsmen drawn by the good anchorage; vacationers drawn by the beaches; and for a growing number of cruise ships determined to get away from the crowd.

The largest and most populated islands are Tortola, the capital; Virgin Gorda; and Anegada. Others such as Peter Island or Guana Island have become popular after being developed as private resorts, but for the most part the British Virgin Islands are almost as virgin as the day Christopher Columbus discovered them.

The B.V.I., as the aficionados call them, say frankly that they do not appeal to everyone. They have no golf courses or casinos, and what little nighttime activity exists is very low-key. But what these islands lack in flashy entertainment is more than made up for in facilities for boating, scuba diving, deep-sea fishing, and windsurfing.

The British Virgin Islands are next-door neighbors of the U.S. group, and without a map it's hard to tell the difference. On the other hand, when you ask someone from the B.V.I. if there is a difference between their islands and ours, they will delight in answering, "Yes, the British Virgins are still virgin."

ARRIVING IN THE BRITISH VIRGIN ISLANDS

Most visitors arrive in the B.V.I. by water on a cruise ship, ferry boat, or a private yacht—their own or one they have chartered. Frequent ferry service connects Tortola with St. Thomas and St. John in about 1 to 1.5 hours. Round-trip fare is $32. Less frequent service is available between either St. Thomas or Tortola and Virgin Gorda.

Tortola is the home of the largest yacht charter fleet in the Caribbean, where boats with or without crew can be chartered for a day or a year. Lying in close proximity astride Drake's Passage, the islands create a sheltered waterway that is one of the world's prime sailing locations. From their base in Tortola, boats crisscross the passage to visit Peter and Norman islands directly across from Road Town; Virgin Gorda to the east/northeast; and Jost Van Dyke on the northwest. These are also the stops made most often by cruise ships.

LOCAL TRANSPORTATION: Tortola's three entry points—Road Town, the main town on the south coast; the Soper Hole West End ferry landing; and the airport on Beef Island at the east end—are linked by paved roads. Beef Island is connected to Tortola by a bridge. Paved roads wind over the mountains to Brewers Bay, Cane Garden Bay, and other resort areas on the northwest coast. More remote areas are accessible by dirt roads, some requiring four-wheel drive. Taxis are plentiful in Tortola; they used fixed rates, based on distance.

SIGHT-SEEING: Taxis and travel agencies offer half-day tours by minivan. Major car-rental firms, as well as independent ones, have offices in Tortola; two companies rent cars on Virgin Gorda; no service is available on the other islands. Remember: In this British colony driving is on the LEFT.

Virgin Gorda has an open-air jitney bus that shuttles between Spanish Town, the Baths, and some resort areas. With it you can see most of the island on your own in less than 3 hours.

INFORMATION: *In the United States:* British Virgin Islands Tourist Board, 370 Lexington Avenue, New York, NY 10017; (212) 696–0400; (800) 835–8530; fax: (212) 949–8254.

In Tortola: BVI Tourist Board, Box 134, Road Town, Tortola; (809) 494–3134; fax: (809) 494–3860. National Parks Trust, Fishlock Road, Road Town, Tortola; (809) 494–3904.

TORTOLA AND ITS NEIGHBORS

Tortola is a sleepy little place with not a great deal of activity, but that's as it should be. Road Town is the only sizable residential center. It has shops, hotels, restaurants, and bars with local bands. Most are located along the south shore road and on Main Street, a picturesque street of small, pastel-painted shops.

If you want to know more about the B.V.I., visit the Virgin Islands Folk Museum, operated by the Virgin Islands Historical Society.

BOTANIC GARDENS One of Road Town's most prized attractions is the tropical Botanic Garden, created on a neglected site formerly occupied by the B.V.I. Agricultural Station. The 3-acre spread, opened in 1987, is the work of the B.V.I. National Trust and volunteers from the Botanic Society and Garden Club. The garden is divided into about twenty collections of rare and indigenous tropical plants.

SAGE MOUNTAIN NATIONAL PARK In the 1960s Sage Mountain, on Tortola, and Virgin Gorda's Spring Bay and Devil's Bay were donated to the B.V.I. government by Laurance Rockefeller. The gift led to the creation of the B.V.I. National Parks Trust and the start of a land- and sea-conservation program with eleven of twenty-three proposed areas under management.

The 92-acre Sage Mountain National Park is located on the peaks of the tall volcanic mountains that cross the center of Tortola, reaching 1,780 feet, the highest elevation in either the U.S. or British Virgin Islands. Its vegetation, characteristic of a rain forest, is thought to be similar to that of the island's original growth. A road leads to the park entrance, where you will find panoramic views. Two graveled, signposted trails, each about an hour's hike, wind through the forest past huge elephant ears, hanging vines, lacey ferns, and a variety of trees common to the Caribbean, such as kapok, mahogany, and white cedar.

NORMAN ISLAND Across Drake's Passage from Tortola is uninhabited Norman Island, said to be the "Treasure Island" of Robert Louis Stevenson's novel. The island has old ruins, a salt pond with abundant bird life, and footpaths. One path is a thirty-minute hike up Spy Glass Hill, from which you can get a fabulous 360-degree view. In olden days pirates used this vantage point to watch for Spanish treasure ships, hence its name. The island is apparently still a convenient base for illegal activity; B.V.I. authorities have seized boats smuggling drugs here. At Treasure Point partly submerged caves can be enjoyed by snorkelers as well as divers.

RHONE NATIONAL MARINE PARK Southeast of Tortola at Salt Island lies the Wreck of the Rhone, the most famous—and popular—shipwreck dive in the Virgin Islands, if not the entire Caribbean. The movie *The Deep* was filmed here. The wreck, lying at 20- to 80-foot depths west of Salt Island, has been made into a marine park covering 800 acres. Along with nearby reefs and caves, the park includes Dead Chest Island on the west, where seabirds nest on the tall cliffs.

The 310-foot Royal Mail Steamer *Rhone* sank in 1867 during a terrible hurricane. Anchored in calm seas off Peter Island, the ship was loading passengers and stores for its return trip to England when a storm blew in suddenly. The ship lost its anchor when its cable broke, and, no longer safe at anchor, with her rigging torn by the winds, she steamed at top speed for open water to ride out the storm. But the hurricane struck again from another direction, forcing the *Rhone* onto the rocks at Salt Island. She split apart and sank. Parts of the ship can be seen by snorkelers.

Salt Island has a few residents who still tend the salt ponds, trails that lead up a hill to a wonderful view, and a good beach.

JOST VAN DYKE Off the northwest coast of Tortola and directly north of St. John, Jost Van Dyke's good anchorage and beautiful beaches make it a popular stop for yachts and small cruise ships that sail regularly through the Virgin Islands. Most anchor at yacht-filled Great Harbor, the main settlement surrounded by green hills. Two of the best-known beach bars in these parts are *The Soggy Dollar* at the Sand Castle Hotel; and *Foxy's Tamarind Bay*. They are favorites of the yachting crowd, where a beach party with calypso music is the order of the day—any day.

 # VIRGIN GORDA

Virgin Gorda is known for *The Baths,* an extraordinary grotto created by toppled gigantic rocks that have puzzled geologists for years. They are completely different from any other rock formation of the area. Worn smooth by wind and water over the millennia, the enormous rocks have fallen in such a way as to create labyrinths and caves that are fun to explore, although they are not real caves, of course. Where the sea rushes in and out, the formations near the shore catch the water, creating pools of crystal-clear water shimmering from the sunlight that filters between the rocks. They are delightful for a refreshing splash—hence their name. The area can be reached by land or sea, and the reefs fronting the Baths are popular for snorkeling.

Virgin Gorda rises from its boulder-strewn coast and sandy beaches on the south in a northerly direction to 1,370-foot Gorda Peak near the island's center. The top of the mountain is protected by the Virgin Gorda Peak Park, which covers 265 acres of forests. The park has a self-guided hiking trail leading to an observation point; it is actually the end of a paved road leading to Little Dix Bay—one of the Caribbean's famous resorts and the sister resort to Caneel Bay on St. John. Equally as expensive, exclusive, and low-keyed, the resorts were begun by Laurance Rockefeller as Rockresorts and were among the Caribbean's first ecologically designed hotels, encompassing the natural environment in which they are set and harmonizing their architecture with it.

On the south end of the island is the Devil's Bay National Park, a secluded coral sand beach, which can be reached by a scenic trail in a 15-minute walk from the area of the Baths.

Virgin Gorda's other famous spots are *Bitter End,* a hotel/restaurant/bar that is probably the most popular watering hole in the Caribbean for the yachting crowd; and Necker Island, across the bay from Bitter End that belongs to English rock recording czar Richard Branson, who built his sumptuous nest on its summit. This ten-bedroom perch is available for rent at a mere $9,900 per day!

ANEGADA

Unlike the other B.V.I., which are green and mountainous, Anegada is a flat, dry coral atoll fringed by miles of sandy beaches and horseshoe-shaped reefs. The most northerly of the B.V.I., it was once a pirates' lair, where the low-lying reefs caught pursuers unaware. An estimated three hundred ships are thought to have gone down here. Today those wrecks and the reefs attract divers, and the fish attracted to the reefs make the island's waters a prime fishing location.

In addition to sailing, the B.V.I.'s healthy and abundant reefs are popular for snorkeling and scuba diving. The B.V.I. waters are also popular for live-aboard dive boats, which carry passengers in cruise ship–style comfort. Some are based in Tortola year-round, while others visit from time to time. Dive operators, based in Tortola, offer a full range of excursions. Glass-bottom boat tours are available, too.

The B.V.I. waters teem with fish, and the islands are adjacent to the 50-mile Puerto Rican Trench. But surprisingly, deep-sea fishing has only recently been developed here. Sport-fishing boats are available for charter in Tortola and Virgin Gorda, which are both a 45-minute boat ride from the trench.

You can get windsurfing equipment at most resorts. Experienced surfers say the northwest coast of Tortola, where the swells roll in from the Atlantic and break against the north end of Cane Garden Bay, is the Virgin Islands' best surfing location.

St. Maarten/St. Martin

AND NEIGHBORS

PHILIPSBURG, ST. MAARTEN; MARIGOT, ST. MARTIN; FORT BAY, SABA; ORANJESTAD, ST. EUSTATIUS; SANDY GROUND, ANGUILLA

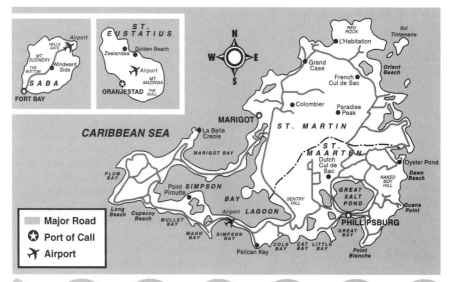

AT A GLANCE

Antiquities	★
Architecture	★
Art and Artists	★★
Beaches	★★★★★
Colonial Buildings	★
Crafts	★
Cuisine	★★★
Culture	★
Dining/Restaurants	★★★★★
Entertainment	★★★
Forts	★
History	★
Monuments	★
Museums	★★
Nightlife	★★★
Scenery	★★★
Shopping	★★★
Sight-seeing	★★★
Sports	★★★★★
Transportation	★★

CHAPTER CONTENTS

THE DUTCH WINDWARD ISLANDS

AND THEIR NEIGHBORS

Centered at a cluster of lovely hideaways in the northeastern Caribbean are three of the most distinctive islands in the entire region. They share their seas with a neighbor that recently became the most talked-about gem in the ocean.

Sint Maarten (commonly written as St. Maarten), the capital of the Dutch Windward Islands and the major cruise-ship port of the group, is an island of green mountain peaks that swoop down to scalloped bays and stretches of powdery white-sand beaches and the shimmering, turquoise sea. Situated on an island of only 37 square miles, Sint Maarten shares more than half of the land with French St. Martin. Their split personality—Dutch on one side, French on the other—enables visitors to dine, tour, sail, and play tennis in two languages, under two flags, without ever leaving the island.

Saba, pronounced *Say*ba, another member of the Dutch group, is unique. The five-square-mile volcanic peak, 28 miles southwest of St. Maarten, rises straight up from the sea. Its history reads like a fairy tale.

St. Eustatius, known as Statia, is the third of the Dutch Windwards and is 10 minutes by plane south of Saba. This island of 8 square miles was once the richest free port in the Americas, though today it takes some imagination to picture it.

Anguilla, a British colony 5 miles north of St. Martin, was the best-kept secret in the Caribbean until the addition of some highly publicized super-deluxe resorts brought trendsetters flocking to this spot of tranquility. You can easily discover Anguilla for yourself on a day trip from St. Maarten.

BEFORE CONCORDIA

Before Columbus got to St. Maarten in 1493 and claimed it for Spain, the island was inhabited by the Carib Indians. More than a century later—after the island had bounced among the Dutch, French, and Spanish—a young Dutchman of later New York fame, Peter Stuyvesant, tried to wrestle it from Spain. He lost a limb instead—only to see the Spaniards abandon their claim to the island to the Dutch just four years later, in 1648.

When the Dutch sent their commander from St. Eustatius to take possession, they found the French waiting to do battle. But the Dutch and French soon agreed to stop fighting over the island and split the spoils instead. Legend says the accord has lasted more than three centuries; in fact, the island changed hands another sixteen times. The place where the agreement was reached is known as Mt. Concordia, nonetheless, and the old accord is celebrated as an annual holiday. More important: The two sides have no real border between them. The only way you know you are crossing from one country to the other is by a welcome sign on the side of the road.

Yet the two sides of this island are noticeably different, beginning with the spelling of the names: Sint Maarten and Saint Martin. Signs are in Dutch and French (also in English), and the people speak Dutch or French (also English). Two currencies—guilders and francs—circulate, but everyone takes dollars (even vending machines on the Dutch side take U.S. coins). There are two governments, two flags, and two sets of stamps—which your philatelic friends will love. Most important, each side has a distinctive, unmistakable ambience.

Small as it is St. Maarten has as many diversions as places ten times its size. The beaches are gorgeous, the water spectacular, and the sports facilities excellent. There's golf, scuba, tennis, windsurfing, fishing, riding, sailing, snorkeling, and biking. St. Maarten has bouncing showplaces and quiet corners, fancy restaurants, discos, and eight casinos.

Located in the heart of the Caribbean between the Virgin Islands and the French West Indies, St. Maarten is an air- and sea-transportation hub for the northeastern Caribbean. Its central location enables cruise passengers to explore the neighboring islands—Anguilla, Saba, and Statia—by air or boat in a day.

Note to Readers: This chapter is oriented to St. Maarten for practical reasons. An estimated 80 percent of all cruise ships arrive in Philipsburg; hence most passengers are likely to want information on the facilities and services convenient to it. Separate entries for French St. Martin have been made when it seemed pertinent and clearer to do so.

ST. MAARTEN FAST FACTS

POPULATION: St. Maarten: 32,000; Saba: 1,090; St. Eustatius: 2,089.

SIZE: 16 sq. miles

MAIN TOWN: Philipsburg

GOVERNMENT: The three Dutch Windward Islands, together with Bonaire and Curaçao in the South Caribbean, make up the Netherlands Antilles. The government is a parliamentary democracy, headed by a governor who is appointed by and represents the queen of the Netherlands. The central government is in Curaçao; each island has its own representative body called the Island Council.

CURRENCY: Netherlands Antilles guilder, written NAf. US $1 equals NAf 1.80.

DEPARTURE TAX: US $12 airport and $6 port departure tax on boat trips to neighboring islands; $2 to Anguilla.

ELECTRICITY: St. Maarten and St. Martin have separate systems: the Dutch side uses 110–120 volts A.C., 60 cycles.

LANGUAGE: Dutch is the official language, but Papiamento is the local language. English is a common second language.

PUBLIC HOLIDAYS: January 1, New Year's Day; Good Friday; Easter Monday; April 30, Coronation Day (Dutch); May 1, Labor Day; Whit Monday; Ascension Thursday; November 11, St. Maarten's Day; December 25 and 26, Christmas.

TELEPHONE AREA CODE: St. Maarten and St. Martin have separate telephone systems, and that's where the island's two-country quaintness can lose some of its charm. A call between the two is an international phone call; sometimes it's easier to call New York from Philipsburg than to call Marigot, less than 8 miles away. So much for Concordia! To call St. Maarten from the United States, dial 011–599–5 plus five-digit local number. To call from the Dutch to the French side, dial 06 plus local number.

AIRLINES:

From the United States: ALM, American, BWIA, Continental; and American/American Eagle from San Juan to St. Maarten.

Interisland, from Princess Juliana International Airport in St. Maarten, Winair (Windward Islands Airways) has daily service to Saba, St. Eustatius, Anguilla, St. Barts, St. Kitts, and St. Thomas; Air Guadeloupe flies daily to Guadeloupe. Air Guadeloupe and LIAT also have service to neighboring islands.

INFORMATION:

In the United States:
St. Maarten Tourist Office, 675 Third Avenue, No. 1806, New York, NY 10017; (212) 953–2084; 1–800–STMAARTEN; fax: (212) 953–2145.

In Canada:
St. Maarten Tourist Board, 243 Ellerslie Avenue, Willowdale, Toronto, Ontario M2N 1Y5; (416) 223–3501; fax: (416) 223–6887.

In Port:
St. Maarten Tourist Bureau, Walter Nisbeth Road, No. 23, Philipsburg; 22337; fax: 22734.

St. Martin
Fast Facts

POPULATION: 25,000

SIZE: 21 sq. miles

MAIN TOWNS: Marigot and Grand Case

GOVERNMENT: St. Martin is a subprefecture of Guadeloupe. Along with Guadeloupe, Martinique, and St. Barts, it is part of the French West Indies, whose nationals are French citizens with the same rights and privileges as their countrymen in metropolitan France. St. Martin has a town council elected by the people and headed by a mayor; the subprefect is appointed by the French government.

CURRENCY: French franc. US $1 fluctuates around 5 Ff.

ELECTRICITY: St. Martin's electricity system is separate from the Dutch side and is 220 volts A.C., 50 cycles.

LANGUAGE: French is the official language; English, although widely used, is not spoken by the local French people with the same fluency as those with a Dutch language background.

PUBLIC HOLIDAYS: January 1, New Year's Day; Good Friday; Easter Monday; May 1, Labor Day; Whit Monday; July 14, Bastille Day; Ascension Thursday; November 11, St. Martin's Day; December 25 and 26, Christmas.

TELEPHONE AREA CODE: St. Martin and St. Maarten have separate telephone systems. To call St. Martin from the United States, dial 011–590 plus the six-digit local number. To call from the French to the Dutch side, dial 3 plus local number.

AIRLINES:

From the United States and intraisland: See St. Maarten Fast Facts.

From Esperance Airport, a small domestic airport in St. Martin, Air St. Barts flies daily to St. Barts. American Eagle has service from San Juan to St. Martin.

INFORMATION:

In the United States: French West Indies Tourist Board, 610 Fifth Avenue, New York, NY 10020; (212) 757–1125.

In Canada: French Government Tourist Board, 1981 Avenue McGill College, No. 490, Montreal, P.Q. H34 2W9; (514) 288–4264; fax (514) 844–8901 and 30 St. Patrick Street, Suite 700, Toronto, Ont., M5T 3A3, Toronto, Ont. M5G 169; (416) 593–6427; fax (416) 979–7587.

In Port: St. Martin Tourist Office, Sur le Port, Marigot (87–27–21; fax: 87–56–43).

Budget
Planning

If you choose the beachcomber's St. Maarten, costs are reasonable. You can take advantage of the beaches near the pier, snack at one of the modest places in town, and do your shopping on Frontstreet, you will find where bargains galore. If you choose the elegant side, however, for haute cuisine and shops with designer clothes, you will find St. Maarten/St. Martin to be expensive. Top French restaurants cost $200 or more for dinner for two persons; chic shops with fashions by Armani, Valentino, and other top designers may be 20 percent lower than U.S. prices, but they are still expensive. It pays to look around, and do not be shy about asking the price. It will not endear you to the French to know some restaurants have two sets of prices—one for their local clientele and one for tourists.

Taxis, unless you share with others, are expensive. If you plan to tour on your own, a car rental is the best deal.

AUTHOR'S FAVORITE ATTRACTIONS

SELF-DRIVE EXCURSION AROUND ST. MAARTEN/ST. MARTIN
DAY-SAIL PICNIC TO NEARBY ISLAND
AMERICA'S CUP REGATTA

SHORE EXCURSIONS

Cruise lines usually offer several excursions but St. Maarten is easy to see and enjoy on your own.

Island Tour, 3 hours, $19 by bus (or by taxi, 2 hours, $40 for two people; each additional person is $10). For first-time visitors reluctant to drive, a bus tour is a quick look at the island.

America's Cup Regatta, 3 hours, $55 to $70 per person, depending on the cruise line. Experience the fun and thrill of racing an authentic America's Cup yacht in an actual race. It's the most popular excursion in St. Maarten. You don't need experience, but you do need to be in good physical condition.

Diving or Snorkeling Package, 3 hours, single tank, $56; snorkeling, $28–$49 per hour. Most cruise ships offer a variety of snorkeling and dive packages; some include an island tour, while others include sailing around the island to the uninhabited islets off the northeast coast.

PHILIPSBURG

As your ship approaches St. Maarten, the tall green mountains make the island seem much larger than it is; and when you walk down the streets of Philipsburg, its capital, the crowds make it seem larger than it is, too.

Philipsburg, situated on a crest of land facing Great Bay, was founded in 1733 as a free port and named for John Philips, who served as the commander from 1735 to 1746. It is still a free port.

Frontstreet and the lanes leading to Backstreet are lined with trendy boutiques and air-conditioned malls selling duty-free goods from around the world. The Dutch side, which saw its first hotel open in 1947, developed sooner than its French counterpart. In addition to the international airport and cruise-ship port, the Dutch side has the majority of hotels, banks, and stores.

PORT PROFILE

LOCATION/EMBARKATION: Philipsburg's little harbor on Great Bay seems like a doll's town. Most ships anchor at sea and tender passengers to Little Pier, officially named Captain Hodge Wharf, located directly in front of Wathey Square, the town center. Construction of a new $1.7-million pier in Philipsburg, has extended the Hodge Wharf and has added a tourist information office, telephone booths, restrooms, shopping kiosks, and taxi stand. The wharf will accommodate up to seven tenders at one time. St. Maarten has also announced plans to build a new $30-million port.

Some ships use Bobby's Marina, slightly east of town; and others pull dockside at A. C. Wathey Pier (not to be confused with Wathey Square) at Point Blanche, the easternmost tip of Great Bay, about a mile from Frontstreet. Taxis and buses await cruise ships, but from Bobby's Marina, it's only a short walk to Frontstreet. At Great Bay Marina and Bobby's Marina, you can sign up for diving or a picnic sail to a secluded beach or a day sail to a neighboring island. Most boats leave about 9:00 or 9:30 A.M.

LOCAL TRANSPORTATION: Taxis do not have meters; rates, which must have government approval, are based on destination for two passengers per trip. A charge of $2 is added for each additional person. There is a 25 percent surcharge after 10:00 P.M. and 50 percent between midnight and 6:00 A.M. Always ask for the fare in advance. Cab drivers usually quote prices in U.S. dollars, but to avoid misunderstandings be sure to ask which currency is quoted. Your driver will expect a 10 to 15 percent tip.

Approximate fares in U.S. dollars from

Philipsburg: west to Little Bay, $4; airport/Pelican Resort, $8; Maho/Mullet Bay, $10; La Samanna, $16; east to Oyster Pond and Dawn Beach, $16; north to Marigot, $10; Grande Case or Orient Beach, $20.

For budget-minded travelers, public buses run between Philipsburg and Marigot throughout the day. The fare is $1.50. Other buses run hourly between Mullet Bay, Simpson Bay, Cole Bay, and Grand Case. Bus stops on the Dutch side are marked "Bushalte"; on the French side, "Arret"; or you can usually stop an approaching bus by waving to it.

ROADS AND RENTALS: St. Maarten's narrow, winding roads are barely adequate for the traffic around town and the airport. Driving is on the right. Most companies have pickup and delivery service and offer unlimited mileage. You should book in advance, particularly in high season, and don't be surprised if your confirmed reservation is not fulfilled. As we have noted many times in this book, while intentions are good, execution often falls short of them. Expect to pay about $40 for a standard shift and $50 for automatic with air-conditioning.

Among the rental companies are *Budget* (54274; fax: 54308); *Cannegie* (52 Frontstreet; 22397) has cars and jeeps; Avis, Hertz, and National are also represented.

MOTORBIKES: *Super Honda Bikes* (25712) and *Carter's Joy Rides* (44251) charge $35 per day for 150/cc bike and $50 per day for 250/cc bike with helmet. *Rent-A-Scoot* (87–20–59), on the French side, has scooters from $19, motorbikes from $32, and Harley's from $100. We do not recommend bikes even for experienced, careful drivers, however, because St. Maarten's roads are narrow, hilly, and replete with potholes and blind curves. You are likely to have to stop dead for a cow or goat that has strayed onto the road, particularly in the rural northeast side—and animals have the right of way.

FERRY SERVICE: To St. Barts, *White Octopus* and other catamarans depart from Bobby's Marina at 9:00 A.M. and return at 5:00 P.M. daily except Sunday. The trip is sold as a round-trip excursion and takes 1.5 hours. Reservations: 23170. The *Voyager* (24096; 87–10–68), a high speed ferry, departs from Marigot for St. Barts daily, except Thursday and Sunday, at 5:30 P.M. Cost is $56; on Thursday it departs for Saba at 8:30 A.M. and returns at 5:30 P.M. Cost is $63. Ferries have a start-and-stop history here. Always check in advance before making plans.

INTERISLAND AIR SERVICE: See St. Maarten Fast Facts.

EMERGENCY NUMBERS:
Medical: Philipsburg Hospital, 22300;
Ambulance: 22111;
Police: St. Maarten, 22222

MARIGOT A
FRENCH DELIGHT

Marigot is less than a 20-minute drive from Philipsburg, but the differences make it light-years away. Marigot is so unmistakably Gallic you don't need the language, the signs, the food, the wine, or the khaki-clad gendarme to tell you so. The ambience is St. Tropez in the tropics—complete with sidewalk cafes, fishing boats, and a topless beach or two. You will find boutiques with French perfumes and fashionable sportswear, and gourmet shops and grocery stores where you can stock up on French products.

The little French capital is definitely worth a stroll. Despite modern incursions from new hotels, stores, and a marina with a large shopping and restaurant complex, the town retains its old character thanks to many West Indian–style houses, colonial buildings, and the main streets beautified with flowers.

At the tiny harbor filled with fish and ferry boats, there is an outdoor market for fruit and vegetables, and souvenirs. The waterfront has recently been expanded by landfill, adding a larger market area and parking space. Outdoor cafes offer delicious croissants and *pains au chocolat* to be enjoyed with espresso or cappuccino.

In Marigot a taxi service is located at the port near the St. Martin Tourist Information Bureau. Sample fares from Marigot: to Grand Case Beach Club, $10; to Philipsburg $10. A 25 percent surcharge is added after 9:00 P.M. and 50 percent after midnight.

FERRIES: From Marigot harbor, service to Anguilla leaves approximately every half hour, takes 15 minutes, and costs $10 one-way plus $2 departure tax. You can buy tickets at a kiosk by the dock. The ferry dock in Anguilla is on the south side of the island. Don't forget to bring your passport or travel identification documents. The *Voyager* has frequent departures from Philipsburg for St. Barts. (See St. Maarten section.)

INTERISLAND AIR SERVICE; See St. Martin Fast Facts.

EMERGENCY NUMBERS:
  Medical: Marigot Hospital, 87–50–07;
  Ambulance: 87–86–25;
  Police: St. Martin, 87–50–04

INFORMATION: St. Martin Tourist Information Bureau on the waterfront in Marigot.

ST. MAARTEN ON YOUR OWN

Philipsburg sits on a thin crest of land hemmed in by two bodies of water: Great Bay on the south and Great Salt Pond on the north, and anchored by high hills at both ends of the crest. As a result the downtown is only two blocks deep with two main streets: Frontstreet (Vorstraat, in Dutch) with traffic one-way east; Backstreet (Achterstraat), one-way west. The pond once provided the island with its major source of income: salt, once an important commodity in world trade.

With growth, two new roads—Cannegieter Street and Walter Nisbet Road (better known as Pondfill Road and Ring Road)—were added through landfill of Great Salt Pond in order to relieve the downtown traffic congestion. They have barely kept up with the pace.

A stroll around town takes less than an hour unless you get sidetracked with shopping. Frontstreet and the little lanes, or *steegjes,* that connect it to Backstreet have boutiques, restaurants, air-conditioned shopping malls, and small hotels.

COURTHOUSE On the north side of Wathey Square, a white clapboard building with green trim is the old Courthouse, built in 1793 and rebuilt in 1825. Originally the house of the colony's commander, in subsequent years it was used as the council chambers, courts, fire hall, and jail. Today the upper floor is still used by the courts, and the building serves as the town hall.

GUAVABERRY TASTING SHOP St. Maarten liquor made from rum and a local fruit, guavaberry, can be purchased from a shop at the east end of Frontstreet housed in a historic building dating from the late 18th century. Once the home of a St. Maarten governor, it is said to occupy the former site of a synagogue. The shop sells many flavors, any of which you can sample before you buy.

ROYAL GUEST HOUSE Across the street is the *Pasanggrahan Hotel,* once the Royal Guest House, which hosted Queen Wilhelmina of the Netherlands when she was en route to exile in Canada after the Nazi invasion of her country. The modest inn, hidden behind its tropical gardens, was the favorite of those who discovered St. Maarten before the boom. The front porch and restaurant are directly on Great Bay Beach.

MUSEUM OF ST. MAARTEN At the east end of Frontstreet is the Museum of St. Maarten, created in 1989 by the St. Maarten Historic Foundation. Located on the second floor of a small shopping complex, the modest museum has displays from excavations on the island and artifacts donated by residents. Next door is the gallery-museum of Mosera, one of St. Maarten's leading artists. Hours: Monday to Saturday from 10:00 A.M. to 4:00 P.M. Admission is $1.

FORT AMSTERDAM Philipsburg does not have any "must see" historic sites, but a pavement at the foot of Frontstreet goes over the hill to Little Bay to the ruins of Fort Amsterdam, on the finger of land separating Great Bay and Little Bay. The fort dates from the 17th century.

A DRIVE AROUND THE ISLAND

The best way to see and enjoy St. Maarten is to rent a car and drive around the island on your own, and when you find a pretty beach or a scenic view, stop for a swim, a photo, or a picnic. One road circles the island, and secondary ones go inland or to secluded beaches. You can leave Philipsburg by the Ring Road, which runs west along Great Salt Pond and over Cole Bay Hill.

COLE BAY HILL CEMETERY The Scottish adventurer John Philips is buried on the hill overlooking the town he founded. The hill separates Philipsburg from the west end of the island where its best-known resorts are located. From an observation platform at the summit you can see neighboring Saba, St. Eustatius, St. Kitts, and Nevis. The valley below overlooking Cay Bay was where Peter Stuyvesant unsuccessfully battled the Spaniards in 1644.

SIMPSON BAY LAGOON After several winding miles the road intersects with Welfare Road, where you can turn north to Marigot or continue west along Simpson Bay Lagoon, the island's main setting for water sports. The road parallels the airport on the south; at the end of the runway is Maho Bay, the smart "suburb" of St. Maarten with attractive shops, good restaurants and entertainment.

The main road west continues to Cupecoy and the French side, where secondary roads lead to La Samanna, a very expensive luxury resort on Long Beach, one of the island's most magnificent stretches of sand. The western end is hilly and provides good views of the island and coastline. West of Cupecoy is the dividing line between the two parts of the island.

ST. MARTIN MUSEUM At Sandy Ground on the south side of Marigot is the new *St. Martin Museum,* also called "On the trail of the Arawaks." Three permanent exhibits are on view. The first displays artifacts from the archaeological excavations in St. Martin over the past decade, some dating back to 1800 B.C.; a second display covers early explorers and colonization; and the third presents the island from 1900 to the 1960s. The exhibits are labeled in French and English. There are also changing exhibits of works by local artists. Hours: 9:00 A.M.–1:00 P.M.; 3:00–7:00 P.M. Historic tours of St. Martin can be reserved through the museum: Tel./fax: 29–22–84; they depart at 9:00 A.M. and return at 11:00 A.M. Cost is US $30.

PARADISE PEAK After Marigot en route to Grand Case, country roads on the east lead to the village of Colombier and Paradise Peak, the island's highest mountaintop. There is a short trail at the top, from which there are panoramic views.

Five miles north of Marigot is Grand Case, a small town with an international reputation as a gourmet haven. The road through town passes at least a dozen restaurants that could command your attention. At the north end of town a dirt road west leads to Grand Case Beach Club, an American-operated beachfront hotel.

FRENCH CUL DE SAC From Grand Case the road cuts east across the north tip of the island, the most mountainous part, to French Cul-de-Sac and the eastern side of the island fronting the Atlantic Ocean. A very hilly road continues north to Le Mendian Habitation, on one of St. Martin's prettiest beaches.

ORIENT BEACH From the main east-coast route, secondary roads lead to Orient Beach, (a nudist beach at its eastern end).

Continuing south, you will pass through the most rural part of the island. A side road takes you into the interior to Orleans, the village of the island's best-known native artist, Roland Richardson.

THE BUTTERFLY FARM On the Galion Beach Road on Paradise Peak's eastern flank (about a 30-minute drive from Philipsburg) is the island's newest attraction, *La Ferme des Papillons* (87–31–21). In 1,000 square meters of tropical gardens fenced with wire mesh like an aviary, you can see hundreds of rare exotic butterflies flitting about freely. The gardens have a montage of blossoms to provide nectar for the butterflies and special plants to feed the caterpillars.

A guide leads visitors through the exhibit area, identifying species, pointing out courtship and mating displays, and relating interesting facts and stories about these beautiful creatures. Visitors also see the stages of the butterflies' life cycle, from laying their eggs to caterpillars hatching, growing, and forming their chrysalis. Visitors may wander through the gardens to take photos and video film or sit in the shaded areas to absorb the tranquil atmosphere, watch the butterflies, and listen to the soothing pan music heard quietly in the background. Guests are warmly welcomed by the English owners William and Karin Slayter, general manager John Coward, and a staff that is always on hand to answer questions. They also can provide information on butterfly gardening, the unique farming techniques used at the Butterfly Farm, and tips for photographers. Hours: 9:00 A.M.–5:00 P.M. Admission US $9.95 adults; US $4.50 children. A shop sells unusual butterfly gifts.

OYSTER POND/DAWN BEACH Immediately after crossing the Dutch/French border, the road takes a sharp turn to the east, and after another mile it forks east to Dawn Beach and Oyster Pond resort areas. (The return to Philipsburg can be made via Naked Boy Hill Road, a winding road south along Great Salt Pond.)

This drive can easily be taken in the reverse direction. If it is an afternoon drive, time your return to the western side for late afternoon to watch a St. Martin sunset. Don't miss it!

SHOPPING

On this half-Dutch, half-French island with its duty-free goods and smart boutiques, shopping is as much an attraction as are its restaurants and sports. You can buy delftware and Gouda cheese as easily as Limoges and Brie, not to mention Japanese cameras, Italian leather, Chinese linens, Colombian emeralds, and a host of other quality products from around the world. Savings range from 20 to 40 percent off U.S. prices, but, as we always emphasize, the best way to know if you are getting a good buy is to come with prices from home. St. Maarten shopkeepers are very competitive; it pays to shop around. Yet even the most ardent shoppers will probably find they can check out the best in either Philipsburg or Marigot in an hour or two.

Attractive shopping complexes with quality stores are also in the resort areas west of Philipsburg. The Maho Bay shops are centered around Maho Beach Hotel and the attractive Cinnamon Grove Plaza is designed around an outdoor courtyard with boutiques in low-rise buildings of colorful West Indian–style architecture. The shopping arcade at Simpson Bay Yacht Club has such attractive stores as *Antilles Batik,* which sells the well-known line Java Wraps; the *Dutch Delft Shop,* which carries the full line of delftware; *Island Time,* featuring Calvin Klein fashions for men and women; and stores for leather goods and home decorating. There is also an outdoor deli/cafe and yogurt-and-ice cream shop.

Stores named below are on Philipsburg's Frontstreet unless otherwise indicated. Some close for lunch from 12:00 to 2:00 P.M. When cruise ships are in port on Sundays and holidays, some shops—not the best—open briefly.

ART AND ARTISTS: *Art Gallery Maboo* (36 Cinnamon Grove) features a wide selection of artists living in the Caribbean. *Greenwith Galleries* (23842) specializes in fine art of the Caribbean and represents thirty-six artists living in St. Maarten and nearby islands. *Simpson Bay Art Gallery* (Airport Road; 43464), situated in a lovely stone and wood "dollhouse," features the fanciful and sometimes whimsical works of Mounette Radot, a French artist who has lived on St. Maarten for many years. She also shows the work of local artists. Open daily, including Sunday. *Mosera Fine Arts Gallery* (Speetjens Arcade; phone/fax: 20702) is the gallery of Mosera Henry, one of St. Maarten's most talented artists, who is originally from St. Lucia. In addition to his works, exhibits of other artists are shown and poetry readings and plays are held from time to time. Hours: weekdays 10:00 A.M. to 2:00 P.M.; 3:00 to 5:00 P.M.

Among other St. Maarten artists are Ria Zonneveld, who creates unusual clay busts with a touch of whimsy; Ruby Bute, Cyrnic Griffith, one of the best-known painters of local scenes; Harriet Sharkey; and Roland Richardson, who has a home studio in Orleans (87–32–24). The French side is particularly active with more than a dozen galleries. Most are located in Marigot or Grand Case; many show French or other Europeans and Americans living in St. Martin for part or all of the year.

In Grand Case, members of an artist family from New York have a gallery in their home (phone 87–77–24). They include Gloria Lynn, a painter of local scenes; husband Martin Lynn, a sculptor; and son, Robert, also a painter.

On the main road at Orient is *The Potters* where you can watch master potters and their apprentices at work and buy their products.

BOOKS/MAPS: In addition to crafts, *Shipwreck Shop* carries books, magazines, maps, postcards reproduced from paintings and prints by island artists, and stamps.

CAMERAS/ELECTRONICS: *Boolchand's* has three downtown stores where you will find the leading names in Japanese cameras and electronic equipment. Bring prices from home for comparison. The shops also carry linens, jewelry, and Bally and Adidas shoes.

CHINA/CRYSTAL: *Little Switzerland,* a familiar name throughout the Caribbean, carries only the highest-quality English china, French crystal, Swiss watches, Hummel figurines, and other gift items. You can request a catalog in advance by calling (800) 524–2010.

CLOTHING: *Liz Claiborne, Ralph Lauren,* and *Tommy Hilfiger* are the most familiar name-labels with their own stores here. *Bye-Bye* has sportswear; *Beach Stuff* carries bathing suits and resortwear. *Dalila* and *Batik Caribe* (Promenade Arcade) have fabrics as well as beachwear of hand-dyed batiks on 100 percent cotton. *Lil' Shoppe* (Little Pier) features swimwear by Gottex.

La Romana is the top fashion store for Fendi, Armani, and the other priests of Italian high fashion. But make no mistake, these are designer clothes at designer prices, and the unfriendly sales staff will do little to make you want to part with your money.

CRAFTS: *Impressions* (Promenade Arcade) specializes in authentic native arts and crafts from the Caribbean, folklore, occult artifacts, and herbs and spices. One of the shop's best artists is Moro from Haiti, who makes carved and painted wood pieces that are very original and distinctive. Another unusual craft, bread and fruit baskets made from fired coconut shells, comes from Nevis. *Seabreeze* (Promenade Arcade) carries hand-painted T-shirts by Ruby Bute as well as her postcards. *The Shipwreck Shop* stocks Caribbean crafts.

FOOD SPECIALTIES: Dutch cheese and chocolates, as well as liquor, liqueurs, and wines are available at *Emile's Place* (Wathey Square).

JEWELRY: *H. Stern* is known from New York to Rio for fine jewelry of original design. Its merchandise comes with an international one-year exchange guarantee. If emeralds are your passion, *Colombia Emeralds* has the largest collection, and the staff is quick to remind you that unmounted emeralds can be brought into the United States free of customs duty. The merchandise also carries a guarantee honored by the company's Miami office. *Oro de Sol* carries Bulgari, Piaget, and other top-name watches. *Artistic* sells Mikimoto pearls. For more modest shopping, *Treasure Cove,* in a restored West Indian house, has gold jewelry and semiprecious stones.

LEATHER/LUGGAGE: Gucci is the most familiar name, but there are several other stores, such as *Maximo Florence,* that carry high-quality Italian-leather handbags and accessories.

LINENS: *New Amsterdam* (you'll recognize it by the brightly painted tulips on the facade) specializes in hand-embroidered linens, quality gifts, and jewelry. The second floor features large selections of men's and women's sportswear, bathing suits, and shoes.

LIQUOR: *Caribbean Liquors and Tobacco* (side street at the east end of Frontstreet) has a full line of liquors and wine.

PERFUMES: *The Yellow House* (west of post office), *Lipstick,* and *Penha* have the large stocks of cosmetics and French perfumes. The latter store also carries sportswear and fashion jewelry.

Marigot

Shops along rue de la République, Liberté, and the Port La Royale Plaza at the marina have goods as familiar as Dior and Cacharel, Chanel, and Yves St.-Laurent. In recent years shopping in Marigot has become as good as that in Philipsburg with many of the high-quality Philipsburg stores branching to the French side. Store hours are Monday to Saturday from 9:00 A.M. to 1:00 P.M. and 3:00 to 7:00 P.M. Some stores open when ships are in port on Sundays and holidays.

Dining and Restaurants

The number and variety of good restaurants on this small island are astonishing. The best gourmet selections, which have won the island international recognition, are on the French side, particularly in the tiny village of Grand Case. But be prepared for the bill. Many are as expensive as top French restaurants in New York. The restaurants listed below in Philipsburg are located on Frontstreet unless otherwise indicated. Moderate means under $20 per person, expensive means $35 or more; and very expensive means $50 or more per person. Expensive gourmet restaurants close one day during the week, usually Sunday or Monday, but it is best to check in advance, as opening hours and days vary.

St. Maarten

Antoine's (at the water's edge; 22964) is a seaside terrace popular for a classic French menu. Expensive.

Cheri's Cafe (Maho Shopping Center; 53361), lively open-air cafe and bar, the current "in" spot, with music and dancing every evening. Food is served from 11:00 A.M. to midnight; the varied menu has salads, fresh fish, steaks, and hamburgers. Moderate.

Saratoga (Simpson Bay; 42421) created by two Culinary Institute of America graduates who trained under Alice Waters, the famous California chef. It specializes in New American cuisine with California and Southwest influences and has a delightful terrace setting overlooking the bay. Expensive.

Turtle Pier Bar (Simpson Bay Lagoon; 52230), in a delightful setting on the lagoon, has its own boat dock and sun deck where you can enjoy light fare or nightly entertainment. Moderate.

Saint Martin

Marigot and Environs

Bar de la Mer (on the waterfront), a casual, friendly, cafe and bar serving salads, pizzas, and steak, is a great people-watching and rendezvous place. They lend backgammon sets, too! Moderate.

Le Poisson d'Or (87–50–33), with only fifteen tables in a beautiful setting of an old stone warehouse, serves haute cuisine. Very expensive.

Mini Club (87–50–69) is an old-time rustic favorite, especially on Wednesday and Saturday

evenings for the large buffet ($35). Moderate.

La Rhumerie (Colombier; 87–56–98), situated in a private house in a small village between Marigot and Grand Case, is tops for creole cuisine. Expensive.

Grand Case and Environs

Alabama (87–81–66) is a local favorite for French cuisine. (This is despite its unlikely name.; one owner, Karin, is from Austria and the other, Pascal, is from France.) Fish and steak dishes with wonderful sauces and great desserts are served for very reasonable prices. Closed Mondays.

Auberge Gourmande (Grand Case; 87–73–37) offers the best value of the town's leading dozen restaurants. Moderately expensive. The owner's other restaurant, *Le Tastevin* (across the street; 87–55–45) has a contemporary French menu. Expensive.

Captain Oliver's Restaurant & Marina (Oyster Pond; 87–30–00) has a delightful waterfront setting where you—and its loyal local patrons—can enjoy French and continental cuisine. Moderate.

Cha Cha Cha (87–72–32) is in a beautiful building that once housed the *gendarmerie*. You may dine inside selecting from a varied menu with moderate prices, or in the garden, where tapas are served. Each of the delicious dozen or so tapas costs $2.75. There's also an outdoor bar where a Spanish combo is often featured. Moderately expensive.

Chez Martine (Grand Case; 87–51–59), elegant yet cozy French restaurant with exquisite cuisine. Expensive.

Sports in Philipsburg and Environs

In most cases you should contact the hotel or sports operator in advance to make arrangements, particularly during the peak season when demand is likely to be high.

BEACHES/SWIMMING: St. Maarten is famous for its beaches—more than three dozen lovely white-sand stretches and coves where you might easily spend the day. Some are busy with people, facilities, and concessioners; others are quiet and secluded. Some of the beaches on French St. Martin are nude or topless, but none are on St. Maarten. If you take a taxi to one of the more secluded beaches, arrange with the taxi driver a specific time to return, and agree in advance on the price of the round-trip fare.

The beaches are listed here by their proximity to Philipsburg. A taxi to west-side beaches costs about $10; those to the east side about $15; and north to Orient Bay, $20.

Great Bay, a mile-long strand directly in town on Great Bay, has calm and generally clean water, but with heavy port and town activity, it is no longer as attractive as it once was. *Little Bay,* west of town within walking distance from the pier, is a smaller beach with lovely water; there are several hotels on the beach with water sports. *Simpson Bay* and *Maho Bay,* by the airport, have hotels with concessioners handling water-sports activities. Farther west, *Cupecoy Beach*—with sandstone cliffs as a backdrop—is quiet, less accessible. There are no facilities other than a beach bar on the cliffs where you can rent snorkel gear. The far end of the beach is used for bathing in the buff.

Long Beach, at the far western end of the south shore is one of the Caribbean's most beautiful beaches, and rounding the point are *Plum Bay* and *Rouge Beach,* two secluded beaches more easily reached by boat. No facilities. Both are topless beaches.

On the east side of St. Maarten, *Oyster Pond* and *Dawn Beach* constitute a long, wide stretch along Guana Bay where the Atlantic washes the shore. The south end is popular for surfing. *Orient Bay,* on the northeast, is a nudist beach.

BOATING: St. Maarten offers excursions on two types of boats: large catamarans, holding up to twenty-five or more passengers, which go to St. Barts for the day, allowing passengers 2 to 3 hours for sight-seeing, lunch, or the beach; and small sailboats for six to ten passengers, which sail to a secluded beach for a swim, snorkel , and picnic. Boats leave from *Bobby's Marina* (22366) about 9:00 or 9:30 A.M. and return about

5:00 or 5:30 P.M. Prices are $60 to $70 per person plus $5 departure tax.

DEEP-SEA FISHING: Charters with tackle, bait, sandwiches, and drinks cost approximately $375–$450 for half day; $700–$900 for full day and are available from *Bobby's Marina.* The season for dolphin, (mahi mahi) kingfish is December to April; tuna, year-round.

GOLF: *Mullet Bay Resort* (Box 309; 52801; 800–468–5538) has the island's only golf course. Some cruise ships have special arrangements with the resort, and sell golf packages.

HORSEBACK RIDING: *Bayside Riding Club* (Orient; 87–80–93) takes small groups with a guide on rides. Reservations must be made in advance. At the north end in French St. Martin, *Caid and Isa* (Anse Marcel; 87–45–70) offers similar excursions.

SNORKELING/SCUBA: St. Maarten is a good place to learn to snorkel, because there are reefs near shore in shallow water so clear that visibility to 150 feet is normal. It is also a good place to try your first scuba dive. A one-day resort course is available from *Ocean Explorers Dive Center* (Simpson Bay; 45252), $50. *Tradewinds* (Great Bay Marina; 75176) is an operator near the port.

Experienced divers will enjoy St. Maarten's wrecks, as well as a variety of reefs characterized by a descending series of gentle hills and valleys and a rich display of colorful fish. Near the entrance to Great Bay harbor lies the British man-of-war *HMS Prostellyte,* sunk in 1801. The hull is gone, but divers can see coral-encrusted anchors, cannons, and other of the ship's fittings.

Off the northeast coast, *Ilet Pinel* offers shallow diving; *Green Key* is a barrier reef rich in sea life; *Flat Island,* also known as Tintamarre, has sheltered coves and a sunken tugboat. The area comprising Flat Island, Ilet Pinel, Green Key, and *Petite Clef* is protected in the Underwater Nature Reserve. The water-sports operator at Orient Beach has snorkeling trips to Green Key island, 2 hours, for $30.

WINDSURFING: The best windsurfing is at *Orient Bay,* where the water-sports operator rents boards for $20 per hour and has a lesson package, too. Windsurfing boards are also available at most beachside resorts.

ENTERTAINMENT IN PHILIPSBURG AND ENVIRONS

St. Maarten's small-scale nightlife offers music varying from piano bars to discos and calypso bands at large resorts and restaurants specializing in Caribbean cuisine. On the Dutch side the Maho area is the center of the action; on the French side Port Royal Marina draws the crowd.

Small as it is, the Dutch side has ten casinos! Most are in or connected with a hotel and open at 1:00 P.M. Those closest to the Philipsburg pier are on Frontstreet: *Rouge et Noir* at Seaview Hotel and the *Coliseum Casino,* with a gallery of slot machines and a shopping arcade. The decor, complete with Venus and Cupid statues, is so outrageous it's camp.

FESTIVALS: The year's major festival is *Carnival,* beginning mid-April and ending with *Coronation Day,* April 30, a public holiday.

SABA THE STORYBOOK ISLE

Saba, pronounced *Say*-ba, located 28 miles southwest of St. Maarten, is the most curious island in the Caribbean. It is a cone-shaped volcanic peak rising straight up from the sea to 3,000 feet. It has no flat land and no beaches.

When Dutch engineers surveyed the island's steep mountainous terrain in the 1930s, they concluded that construction of a road would be impossible. Undeterred, a local resident, Lambertus Hassell, decided to prove them wrong even though he had no technical training. He sent away for and studied an engineering correspondence course, organized the island's citizens, and in 1943 completed the first ¾-mile of road up the mountain face to the capital, The Bottom.

Twenty years later, in 1963, the last stretch was finished. The road drops 1,312 feet in twenty hairpin turns ending at the island's airport, which was cut out of the mountainside, too. It looks something like the deck of an aircraft carrier at sea. Landing here in one of Winair's STOL aircraft is an experience you will never forget.

But then, everything about Saba is unusual and unforgettable. The population of about 1,200 is made up mostly of the descendants of Scottish, Irish, and Dutch settlers. And what a hardy bunch they must have been! Before the airport and road were built, people and goods were hoisted up the side of rock cliffs. The alternative was to climb the steep mountain paths to reach the island's several villages.

HELL'S GATE AND WINDWARDSIDE Today the hand-laid road that zigzags up the mountain from the airport leads first to Hell's Gate and continues to Windwardside, a lilliputian village of gingerbread houses with white picket fences. Were it not for the tropical gardens surrounding them, you could imagine yourself on the set of *Hansel and Gretel* rather than on a Caribbean island. One of the homes, a sea captain's house built in the mid-19th century, is *The Saba Museum,* furnished with antiques and has a display of pre-Columbian artifacts found on Saba. It is open Monday to Friday from 10:00 A.M. to noon and 1:00 to 3:30 P.M. There is $1 donation for admission.

MOUNT SCENERY From Windwardside a series of 1,064 steps rise through the misty rain forest rich in flora and fauna to the summit of 2,855-foot Mount Scenery—well named for the magnificent panoramas of the Caribbean and neighboring islands that are there to reward hikers. Most trekkers take a picnic lunch and make a day of the climb to enjoy the views and lush vegetation along the way. If you have less time and energy, you can hike to one of several other locations on trails that have been developed recently by the new Saba Conservation Foundation (Box 18, Fort Bay, Saba, N.A.; 4–63295).

The town's ten-room *Captain's Quarters* is the oldest of the island's tiny inns and guesthouses and has a lovely hillside setting with a swimming pool and open-air bar/restaurant. Neighboring *Juliana's* and *Scout's Place* also have pools and open-air restaurants. But the most popular stop for lunch or dinner is *Brigadoon Restaurant* (4–62380), the excellent terrace restaurant of former New Yorker Penny Johnson and her Saban husband, Gregory, in Windwardside. The menu has selections of seafood and creole specialties that have been given a sophisticated touch and are served with fruits, vegetables, and herbs from the owners' farm.

THE BOTTOM From Windwardside the road descends to The Bottom, another doll-like village of white clapboard houses with red gabled roofs and neat little gardens. The former *Government Guesthouse,* one of the town's most historic buildings, is Cranston's Antique Inn.

SABA ARTISANS' FOUNDATION At the Saba Artisans' Foundation you can find needlework, silk-screened fabrics, beachwear, and other island specialties.

SABA MARINE PARK Saba's steep volcanic cliffs drop beneath the sea as vertical walls encrusted with a fantastic variety of reefs and other marine life. To protect this treasure the Saba Marine Park was developed with the help of the Netherlands Antilles National Park Foundation, the World Wildlife Fund of the Netherlands, and others. The park is comprised of the entire shoreline and seabed from the high-water mark to a depth of 200 feet and two offshore seamounts. It has twenty-six self-guided underwater trails and areas designated for recreation. The park was developed under the guidance of Tom van't Hof, who also directed the marine parks in Bonaire and Curaçao and has written a guidebook to the park. The main dive areas are on the west coast. *Ladder Bay* to *Torrens Point* is an all-purpose recreational zone and includes Saba's only "beach," a stretch of pebble shore with shallow water. The most frequented sites are at Tent Bay to the southwest, where the wall drops to 80 feet and is covered with colorful tube sponges and black coral. The reef is a long, shallow ledge at 50 feet with overhangs where snorkelers and divers can see huge barrel sponges, barracudas, French angelfish, and more.

Saba Deep (63347; fax: 63397) and *Sea Saba* (62246), and *Wilson's Dive Shop* (800–328–2288; 62541) are the island's three fully equipped dive operators with their own dive boats. Each offers several dive trips daily and arranges fishing excursions. The Saba Bank, 3 miles southwest of Saba, is a 32-mile region of shallow water where fishing is terrific.

SIGHT-SEEING Taxis with driver/guides are available at the airport for tours of the island, or, for those who arrive by boat, at Fort Bay, the port on the southwest corner of the island. Guided nature tours of Mt. Scenery and other locations can be arranged through the Saba Tourist Office in Windwardside.

 AIR AND FERRY SERVICE: From St. Maarten, morning and afternoon flights on Winair are available daily, making it possible to visit Saba on a day trip ($50 round-trip). *The Edge,* a high-speed ferry, offers excursions to Saba from St. Maarten. Inquire at Pelican Marina in St. Maarten (Simpson Bay; 42640).

 TELEPHONE AREA CODE: To phone Saba from the United States, dial 011–599–4 plus the local number.

 **INFORMATION:**

In the United States:
Saba Tourist Information Office, c/o Classic Communications International, 10242 Northwest 47th Street, No. 31, Ft. Lauderdale, FL 33351; (954) 741–2681; (800) 722–2394; fax: (954) 741–1243.

In Saba:
Saba Tourist Office, Windwardside, Saba, N.A.; 4–62231.

 **ST. EUSTATIUS**

A CRUEL TWIST OF FATE

Statia, as St. Eustatius is known, is 10 minutes by plane south of Saba. You may need all the imagination you can summon to believe it today, but this island of only 8 square miles was once the richest free port in the Americas, with a population of 8,000 (it has 1,700 today), where everything from cotton to contraband from around the world was traded. In the first two hundred years after Columbus discovered it, the island changed hands twenty-two times!

FORT ORANJE During the American Revolution the neutral position of Holland, which had claimed the island in 1640, was suspect to the British because St. Eustatius was used as a transit point for arms and goods destined for the rebels. On November 16, 1776, after the island's garrison at Fort Oranje saluted the *Andrew Doria* flying the American flag—the first foreign port to do so after the United States declared its independence—the gesture so enraged the British that they sacked the town and destroyed the harbor. (The late Barbara Tuchman's book *The First Salute,* published in 1988, is based on this incident.)

In one of history's saddest cases of overkill, the British navy left the Dutch flag up long enough to lure 150 merchant ships into the harbor, then confiscated their cargo, burnt the town to the ground, and, as the coup de grâce, destroyed the harbor's breakwater. The grand houses and warehouses tumbled into the sea. The island never recovered.

(More recent research debunks this version of the events, which has become the embellished truth of local lore.)

Under President Franklin D. Roosevelt, the United States expressed its belated thanks, and the fort and other buildings dating from the 18th century were restored with U.S. help. Although we can wonder why, Statia-America Day, celebrated on November 16, is one of the island's main events.

ORANJESTAD The little town of Oranjestad is divided into two parts. Upper Town, a pretty little community of palm-shaded, cobblestone streets lined with West Indian gingerbread-trimmed houses and flowering gardens, grew up around the old fort atop a 150-foot cliff overlooking the sea. Lower Town, the site of the famous old harbor, is the docking area today, and to the north is the island's main beach. Only a few feet beneath the sea rests centuries-old debris that has led researchers to call Statia "an archaeologist's nightmare and a scuba diver's dream." The two

parts of town are connected by the cobblestone pedestrian walk and a paved road.

ST. EUSTATIUS HISTORICAL FOUNDATION MUSEUM A colonial house near the fort contains the town's museum, which displays artifacts from Indian settlements dating from A.D. 300, as well as 17th- and 18th-century artifacts found in the underwater ruins of warehouses, wharfs, and shipwrecks. You can get a brochure with a map for a self-guided tour of the fort and surrounding historic buildings. These include the old Government House, a Dutch Reform church, a synagogue that was probably the second or third created in the Western Hemisphere, and other ruins from the 18th century.

THE QUILL The crater of an extinct volcano that dominates the south end of the island, the Quill can be seen distinctively in the island's silhouette. A series of eight signposted trails has been developed, enabling you to hike up to and around the crater's rim, down into the cone, and around the outside of the cone at about midgirth. The hikes were designed as a series of contingent trails that can take from 1 hour up to a full day.

The most popular trail leads from town up the western slope of the crater to the rim in about an hour. It meets another trail, which is a steep path down to the floor of the crater, passing through steamy thick foliage where trees, protected from winds and hurricanes, grow tall. Their trunks and branches are entwined with enormous elephant ears, other vines, and sometimes tiny orchids. The crater's interior is planted with bananas, but over the years it has been cultivated with coffee, cacao, and cinnamon trees, which now grow wild.

DIVING HAVEN Scuba divers have a heyday exploring the ruins of the houses and warehouses in the old harbor that have lain undisturbed for two hundred years. Farther out the sea bottom is littered with hundreds of shipwrecks, some dating back three hundred years. Atop this jumble corals grow, attracting a great variety of fish and marine life. That combination of coral reefs, marine life, and historic shipwrecks, all untouched by commercial development, is what makes Statia extraordinary and so exciting to divers. Most diving is in 20 to 80 feet of crystal-clear water, which makes it accessible to snorkelers, too.

Sixteen sites have been charted to date. The most popular, dubbed the Supermarket, is located about a half-mile off the coast from Lower Town at a 60-foot depth. It has two shipwrecks less than 50 yards apart, with patches of beautiful coral and colorful sponges growing over them. There are also rare fish here; the flying gurnards are the most intriguing. About 12 inches long, these fish are black with white spots and iridescent blue pectoral wings, and they move through the water like hovering birds.

Dive Statia, the island's water-sports operator, has its own boats making two or three dives daily.

 INTERISLAND AIR SERVICE: St. Eustatius is a 10-minute flight south of Saba or 17 minutes from St. Maarten. Winair has five flights daily; round-trip airfare is $50. The airport is located midisland, about 1.5 miles from town. There you can arrange a tour by taxi or rent a car. Donkeys can be hired for climbing up to the crater.

 TELEPHONE AREA CODE: To phone St. Eustatius from the United States, dial 011–599–3 plus the local number.

 **INFORMATION:**

In St. Eustatius:
St. Eustatius Tourist Bureau, Fort Oranjestraat 3, Oranjestad, St. Eustatius, N.A.; phone 3–2209 or 2213.

ANGUILLA

TRANQUILLITY WRAPPED IN BLUE

Anguilla is a British colony that has the distinction of rebelling to *remain* a colony. Until its super-deluxe resorts were spread across the pages of slick travel and fashion magazines, Anguilla was the best-kept secret in the Caribbean. The small coral island 5 miles north of

St. Martin is especially noted for its three dozen gleaming white-sand beaches—which you can have practically to yourself—and the clear, blue-green waters surrounding it.

Known to its original Arawak Indian inhabitants as *Malliouhana,* the island takes its name from the French word for eel, *anguille,* or the Spanish, *anguilla*—they were both here—because of its shape. In the past when it had only a few tiny hotels and guesthouses, the tranquil island appealed to true beachcombers who cared little for social conveniences. Yachtsmen, too, have long been attracted to the spectacular waters around Anguilla, as have snorkelers and scuba divers from neighboring islands. Two large reefs with huge coral formations growing to the surface of the sea lie off the island's shores.

Even with all the attention, the island's unspoiled quality remains. But then, the Anguillans are as unspoiled and appealing as their island. Until the tourism boom began, most were fishermen supplying the restaurants in St. Martin. The 16-mile-long island has no golf courses or casinos, and there still are as many goats and sheep as people.

Two of the super-deluxe hotels have attracted much of the attention. *Cap Juluca,* a sybaritic fantasy in Moorish design, graces one of the most magnificent powdery white-sand beaches in the Caribbean. Its terrace restaurant, *Eclipse,* overlooking the sea with St. Martin in the distance, has an imaginative selection of light cuisine with a French flair, designed for warm Caribbean days.

The other posh resort, *Malliouhana,* on the island's northwest coast overlooking two spectacular beaches, is Mediterranean in design with graceful interiors by Larry Peabody, known for his stylish decor in other Caribbean resorts. The resort has three terraced swimming pools, three tennis courts, and a full range of water sports. If you want to do any more than look—perhaps have a meal—you will need to make arrangements in advance and be prepared to spend US $100 for lunch.

For such a small island, Anguilla has an extraordinary number of good restaurants; there were fifty at last count.

Hibernia (Island Harbour; 497–4290) is not only the best restaurant in Anguilla, but easily one of the best in the Caribbean. The French owner is a serious chef who smokes his own fish and knows how to combine creole flavors with fine French cuisine—all to be enjoyed on a terrace overlooking the Caribbean. Entrees range from US $20. *Koal Keel* (497–2930), in one of the oldest houses on the island, should also be at the top of your list. The ancient cistern is now a wine and brandy cellar where tastings are held. Other parts of the house have a rum and cigar shop and a bakery.

The Dive Shop, a PADI training facility, is located on the beach at Sandy Ground (497–2020). It is open daily and offers a full range of water-sports equipment, as well as a regularly scheduled picnic excursion by sail or motorboat several days a week. Similar trips can be arranged on request. A second operator, *Anguillan Divers Ltd.,* is at Island Harbour on the east end of the island.

Concerned about the phenomenal growth in the 1980s, Anguilla created a National Trust with a permanent staff to oversee the preservation of the island's cultural and national heritage and direct already-active volunteer organizations. These include the Archaeological and Historical Society, which organized in 1979 the first scientific survey of the island, which unearthed thirty-three sites of antiquity; the Horticultural Society, which organizes periodic cleanup and beautification drives; the Marine Heritage Society, the driving force behind the creation of marine parks; and various cultural groups working to preserve Anguilla's folklore, music, and other traditions.

In 1990 the Anguillan government took its first major step at marine-resource management. Six wrecks resting by Anguilla's shores were towed to sea and sunk to create artificial reefs that have become nurseries for fish and new sites for divers. Their removal also eliminated a potential boating and marine hazard in Road Bay, the island's main harbor.

TRANSPORTATION: American Airlines/American Eagle has daily service from San Juan to Anguilla, and Winair has several flights daily making the 5-minute trip from St. Maarten to Anguilla for a round-trip fare of US $50. Air Anguilla (776–5789) and Tyden Air (497–2719) provide service to neighboring islands.

Ferries from St. Martin take 15 minutes and cost US $10 one way plus US $2 port tax. They leave almost every 30 minutes during the day from Marigot harbor. The ferry dock in Anguilla is located on the south side of the island where you can hire a taxi or rent a car, essential for touring the island because there is no regular bus service.

Connors Car Rental (497–2433) has reasonable rates. A local driver's license, arranged by the rental agency, costs US $6. Driving is on the *left.*

 TELEPHONE AREA CODE: 809; 264 (effective date not yet announced)

 **INFORMATION:**

In the United States:
Anguilla Tourist Information Office, Medhurst & Associates, 1208 Washington Drive, Centerport, NY 11721; (516) 425–0900; fax: 425–0903.

In Anguilla:
Anguilla Tourist Board, P.O. Box 1388 The Valley, Anguilla, B.W.I.; (264) 497–2759; fax: (264) 497–2710; (800) 553–4939.

Anguilla Life, a quarterly published by veteran Caribbean writer Claire Devener, is a valuable source of information. Contact East Caribbean Publishing Co., Box 109, Anguilla, B.W.I.; 497–3080.

PART IV

THE EASTERN CARIBBEAN

Antigua

St. John's, Antigua;
Falmouth, Antigua;
English Harbour, Antigua;
Codrington, Barbuda

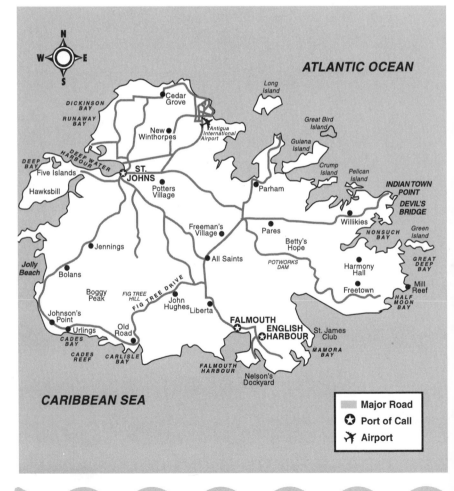

ATLANTIC OCEAN

Long Island

DICKINSON BAY

RUNAWAY BAY

Cedar Grove

Great Bird Island

New Winthorpes

Antigua International Airport

Guiana Island

DEEP WATER HARBOUR

DEEP BAY

Five Islands

Crump Island

Pelican Island

INDIAN TOWN POINT

Hawksbill

ST. JOHNS

Potters Village

Parham

DEVIL'S BRIDGE

Willikies

Green Island

NONSUCH BAY

Freeman's Village

Pares

Betty's Hope

Jennings

GREAT DEEP BAY

Jolly Beach

Bolans

All Saints

POTWORKS DAM

Harmony Hall

Mill Reef

Boggy Peak

FIG TREE HILL

FIG TREE DRIVE

John Hughes

Liberta

Freetown

HALF MOON BAY

Johnson's Point

Urlings

Old Road

CADES BAY

FALMOUTH

ENGLISH HARBOUR

St. James Club

MAMORA BAY

CADES REEF

CARLISLE BAY

FALMOUTH HARBOUR

Nelson's Dockyard

CARIBBEAN SEA

Major Road
Port of Call
Airport

AT A GLANCE

CHAPTER CONTENTS

A BEACH FOR EVERY DAY OF THE YEAR

Relaxed and quietly sophisticated, Antigua is a mecca for those who love the sea. Shaped roughly like a maple leaf, the protruding fingers provide Antigua's coastline with sheltered bays, natural harbors, and extra miles of beautiful beaches—one for every day of the year, the Antiguans say. The coral reefs that fringe the island are a magnet for snorkelers and scuba divers. Together these assets have made Antigua one of the most popular beach and water-sports centers in the Caribbean. As a bonus, low humidity coupled with year-round trade winds create a wonderful climate for tennis, golf, horseback riding, and a variety of other sports—and, of course for sight-seeing.

Antigua, pronounced An-*tee*-ga, is the largest of the Leeward Islands. Barbuda, her sister island 32 miles to the north, is largely undeveloped; the third member, Redonda, 36 miles to the southwest, is uninhabited. Located at the heart of the Caribbean, east of Puerto Rico and the Virgin Islands between the French and Dutch West Indies, Antigua is a transportation hub of the region.

Settled by the British in 1632, Antigua was Britain's most strategic Caribbean colony for two centuries due to her protected harbors and position on the trade routes, with the winds blowing almost year-round from the east. The island's historic character is most evident at English Harbour where the buildings of the old wharf, known as Nelson's Dockyard, have been restored. The British legacy is also seen in the island's passion for cricket, afternoon tea, and driving on the left side of the road.

Of the eighty or more archaeological sites found here, the oldest dates back more than four-thousand years to the Ciboney, a Stone-age people about whom little is known. The most extensive excavations have been those of the Arawak Indians who arrived in Yarumaqui, as they called

Antigua, about A.D. 500. They remained about five centuries and moved north, probably to flee pursuing Carib Indians, a warlike people after whom the Caribbean is named.

Wadadli, the Carib name for the island, was sighted by Columbus in 1493. He did not come ashore, but he did name the island, Santa Maria de la Antigua, after the virgin saint of the Cathedral of Seville in Spain. Attempts by the Spaniards, and later the French, to settle the island were unsuccessful. Then in 1632 English settlers from St. Kitts led by Edward Warner, the son of Thomas Warner, who founded the first settlement on St. Kitts, came ashore near Old Town on the south coast where they established a colony. Except for a brief French occupation in 1666, Antigua remained British for the next three hundred years.

The first settlers cleared the land and planted tobacco, a crop they learned from the Arawaks. But in time tobacco was replaced by sugar, and slaves were imported from Africa to work the cane fields. The island was divided into estates, and a plantation society developed that lasted well into the twentieth century. Much of this history is reflected today in village, family, and location names.

In 1784 Horatio Nelson, who later became one of Britain's most celebrated admirals, took command of the Leeward Islands Squadron in which the future king, William IV, served as captain of HMS *Pegasus*. Antigua became the New World headquarters for the Royal Navy, and English Harbour, as it is known today, was strongly fortified.

After the abolition of slavery in 1834, the sugar-based economies of the Caribbean declined, while the introduction of the steamship changed the course of trade between the Old and New Worlds. For the next century Antigua, like so much of the Caribbean, was largely ignored by her colonial masters. During World War II, the island became a U.S. military base, and the impact was immediate. It brought jobs, new roads, piers, an airport, and technicians who helped to train Antiguans in skills that served the local population well after the war.

In 1958 Britain granted Antigua and her other colonies semiautonomous status in the West

Indies Federation. In 1967 Antigua, with Barbuda and Redonda, became an Associated State within the Commonwealth, governing her own internal affairs. Finally in 1981 full independence was achieved. In less than a decade on her own, Antigua has been transformed from an agricultural economy to a service one with tourism the major source of jobs and revenue.

FAST FACTS

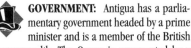

POPULATION: 66,000

 SIZE: Antigua, 108 sq. miles; Barbuda, 62 sq. miles.

 MAIN TOWN: St. John's

GOVERNMENT: Antigua has a parliamentary government headed by a prime minister and is a member of the British Commonwealth. The Queen is represented by a governor general.

CURRENCY: Eastern Caribbean dollar. US $1 equals EC $2.60. Major credit cards and U.S. dollars are widely accepted. Since both currencies are rendered in "dollars," be sure to determine which currency is being discussed whenever you negotiate the price of a service or commodity.

 DEPARTURE TAX: EC $30 (US $12).

LANGUAGE: English has been the language of Antigua for three centuries and adds to the ease of getting around.

PUBLIC HOLIDAYS: January 1, New Year's Day; Good Friday and Easter Monday; Labor Day, first Monday in May; Whit Monday; Queen's Official Birthday, second Saturday in June; Carnival, first Monday and Tuesday in August; November 1, Independence Day; December 25, Christmas; December 26, Boxing Day. Although not a public holiday, Sailing Week in late April is one of the biggest events of the year and commands the attention of most people.

TELEPHONE AREA CODE: 268

AIRLINES: *From the United States,* American, Air Jamaica, and BWIA, fly directly. Antigua's airport, which is headquarters for LIAT (Leeward Islands Air Transport, the regional carrier owned by eleven Eastern Caribbean island-states), offers frequent service to the neighboring islands of the Eastern Caribbean and daily to Barbuda, a flight of 10 minutes.

 INFORMATION:

In the United States:
Antigua and Barbuda Department of Tourism, 610 Fifth Avenue, Suite 311, New York, NY 10020, (212) 541–4117; fax (212) 757–1607; 2252 2nd Avenue, No. 300; Miami, FL 33131, (305) 381–6762; fax (305) 381–7908.

In Canada:
Antigua and Barbuda Department of Tourism, 60 St. Clair Avenue E., Toronto, Ont. M4T 1N5, (416) 961–3085; fax (416) 961–7218.

In Antigua:
Antigua Tourist Board, Thames Street, Box 363, St. Johns, Antigua, W.I.; 462–0480. Antigua Historical and Archaeological Society, Museum of Antigua and Barbuda, P.O. Box 103, Market Street, St. John's; 463–1060. National Parks Authority, Box 1283, St. John's, Antigua; 463–1053.

BUDGET PLANNING

Taxi fares are high, and unless one has others with whom to share them, sight-seeing by taxi is expensive. Car rental is more reasonable and recommended. Aside from taxis, prices in Antigua are moderate and restaurants serving local or West Indian cuisine are inexpensive.

PORT PROFILE: ST. JOHN'S

LOCATION/EMBARKATION: St. John's, the capital, is located on the island's northwest Caribbean coast at the head of a deep-water harbor. A pier at the foot of town enables passengers to walk off their ships directly into Heritage Quay, a shopping, food, and entertainment complex. Antigua Deepwater Harbour, another pier on the north side of the harbor about a mile from town, is still used for large ships and when there are more ships than the town pier can accommodate. Yachts and some small cruise ships often arrive at English Harbour, one of the prettiest yacht basins in the Caribbean, or at neighboring Falmouth Harbor, both on the southeastern coast.

LOCAL TRANSPORTATION: The distance from the pier at Deepwater Harbor to St. John's is short enough to walk, but most visitors prefer to take a taxi because the only place to walk is in the road. Taxis are plentiful and cost US $6; they can be shared by up to three people for the ride into town. A taxi with the driver acting as guide can be hired for touring. Rates are set by the government and tend to be expensive, costing $16 per hour (about US $60) and up for an island tour. Be sure to set the price in advance and to confirm whether the price quoted is in U.S. or E.C. dollars. Local buses are not useful for cruise passengers.

ROADS AND RENTALS: If you have an adventurous spirit, the ideal way to tour the island is by self-drive car. Antigua has an extensive network of roads, but driving can be a bit difficult due to narrow, winding roads that are not well marked or in the best condition. Also, traffic in this former British colony moves on the LEFT. A good map is essential, but even with it, roads can be confusing: Expect to get lost several times. Happily, the Antiguans are friendly and helpful, although not very precise in giving directions; you might need to ask for directions several times. Basically, the road system fans out from St. John's on major arteries that loop around each area of the island—north, southeast, south-west—making it easy to leave from the capital by one route and return by another.

Rental cars and jeeps are reasonably priced, costing from about US $50 per day for a small car with unlimited mileage. During the winter season demand is often greater than supply, and cars can be difficult to obtain; reservations are recommended. Avis, Budget, and other international companies are represented. You'll need a local driver's license, but the car-rental agency will obtain it for you upon presentation of a valid U.S. or Canadian one; the fee is US $20. Before starting out be sure to have a full tank of gasoline; there are very few gas stations outside of St. John's.

INTERISLAND AIR SERVICE: See Fast Facts.

EMERGENCY NUMBERS:
Medical: Holberton Hospital,
Hospital Road, St. John's;
24-hour service, 462–0251;
Ambulance, 462–0251
Police: 462–0125

AUTHOR'S FAVORITE ATTRACTIONS

DRIVE TO ENGLISH HARBOUR VIA FIG
TREE DRIVE
VIEW FROM SHIRLEY HEIGHTS
DAY SAIL TO BIRD ISLAND

SHORE EXCURSIONS

With advance arrangements local travel companies can tailor a tour to your specifications by using a private car with a driver/guide. But whether on an organized tour in a minibus or by car, local guides are not well trained and cannot be depended upon for much commentary. The shore excursions most often available on cruise ships follow; prices are per person and may vary from ship to ship. Details on the sites are described later in this chapter.

Historic Antigua, 3 hours, $30 ($70 for up to 4 persons by car with drive/guide). Drive across the heart of the island to English Harbour, Clarence House, and Shirley Heights.

Scenic and Historic Antigua, 4 hours; $40 ($90 for up to 4 persons by car). The above tour with the addition of a drive along the southwest coast and through Fig Tree Road.

Picnic Party Cruise, 3 hours, $35. A day sail to an uninhabited island for a picnic, swimming, and snorkeling available on small yachts for six or ten people and on large boats such as the *Jolly Roger,* a replica of a pirate ship.

ANTIGUA ON YOUR OWN

Antigua's capital was a sleepy West Indian town that was transformed into a new town by the tourist boom over the past decade.

A ST. JOHN'S WALKABOUT

One of the island's oldest ports, settled in the early 17th century, St. John's was once a scruffy town of hard-drinking sailors and traders and an unsavory reputation to match. It was laid out formally in 1702 and given city status in 1842. Through the centuries the town suffered destruction by fires, hurricanes, and earthquakes, yet enough of its historic buildings and West Indian architecture remain to give it character. The most historic and interesting area is a grid of six blocks in the heart of town, best seen on foot in an easy hour's walk.

REDCLIFFE QUAY (1) On the waterfront on the west side of town is a group of former warehouses and other buildings that have been restored and made into attractive boutiques, restaurants, and offices. To the west is pretty *Heritage Quay* (**2**), a shopping, food and entertainment center of two stories built around an open-air plaza. Although modern in design, its architecture incorporates colonial and West Indian elements that blend into the old town. The *Tourist Information Office*

and the *post office* (**3**) (Thames Street) are a block to the north.

MUSEUM OF ANTIGUA AND BARBUDA (4) The oldest structure in use in St. John's now houses the Museum of Antigua and Barbuda (Market and Long streets). An 18th-century court house built from white stone quarried from an island off the northeast coast, the building has been repaired and rebuilt many times over the centuries. It housed the island's parliament until 1974 when the building was damaged by an earthquake. The latest renovations, completed in 1988, were undertaken by the Antigua Historical and Archaeological Society with the aid of Canada, UNESCO, and private donors, to create the museum.

The collection includes Arawak and pre-Columbian artifacts found in Antigua; other displays interpret Antigua's history from the colonial period to independence. The museum's main purpose is to educate the island's children about their history, but it is very much worth a visit for others, too. Hours: Monday to Thursday, 8:00 A.M.–4:00 P.M., Fridays to 3:00 P.M.; Saturday 10:00 A.M.–1:00 P.M.; 462–3946. The Historical and Archaeological Society, which operates the museum, sponsors cultural and natural history tours and invites membership.

ST. JOHN'S CATHEDRAL (5) On the highest rise of town stands the Cathedral of St. John the Divine (Newgate Street and Church Lane), dating from 1847. It is on the site of an earlier church, built in 1745 and destroyed by an earthquake in 1843. The first church, dedicated in 1683, was a wooden structure built by the island's largest plantation owner, Sir Christopher Codrington. The iron railings at the entrance date from 1789. The figures of John the Baptist and John the Evangelist at the south gate, originally destined for Dominica, were the spoils of war for an English man-of-war, taken from a French ship in the early 19th century. The church has two towers, topped with silver cupolas; the interior is faced with pitch pine, a type of pine that yields pitch and is intended to strength the structure to withstand hurricanes and earthquakes.

Behind the church is *Government House* (**6**), dating from the 17th century. Originally two houses, one of which was the residence of the minister for the parish of St. John's, it was bought as a residence by Lord Lavington of Carlisle Estate in 1801. Today it is the official residence of the governor general of Antigua and generally is not open to the public.

PUBLIC MARKET (7) By the waterfront on the south end of Market Street is the Public Market, a particularly lively, colorful scene on Fridays and Saturday mornings and a good place for an

introduction to Antigua's local produce and some of the exotic fruits and vegetables of the Caribbean. Next door is the Industrial School for the Blind, where a limited selection of handcrafts are on sale.

St. John's Point, the tip of a 2-mile scenic headland on the north side of the harbor, has the remains of *Fort James,* built in the early 18th century, with ten of its original thirty-six cannons.

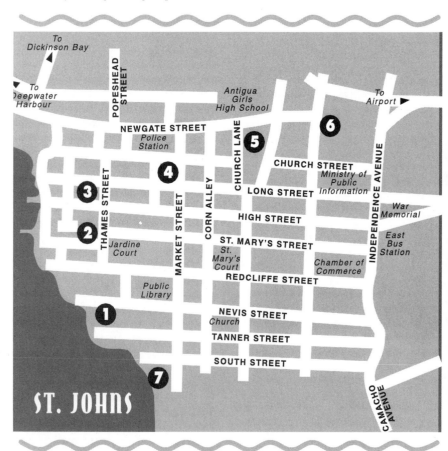

MAP LEGEND FOR WALKING TOUR OF ST. JOHNS

1. **Redcliffe Quay**
2. **Heritage Quay and town pier**
3. **Tourist Information Office and Post Office**
4. **Museum of Antigua and Barbuda**
5. **St. John's Cathedral**
6. **Government House**
7. **Public Market**

Its counterpart, *Fort Barrington,* crowns a promontory known as Goat Hill, on the south side of the harbor. The forts were part of the extensive British military installations to protect the main harbors and attest to the island's strategic importance in colonial times.

A DRIVE
AROUND ANTIGUA

SOUTH TO FALMOUTH AND ENGLISH HARBOUR

Southwest of St. John's along the Caribbean coast are some of Antigua's prettiest beaches. The most immediate road west from St. John's leads to the Royal Antiguan, the island's largest hotel. Secondary roads take you to the Five Islands area, a part of the island with beautiful beaches and reefs and offshore islets popular for boating and water sports.

The main road from St. John's to the southwest coast runs inland through Jennings, the turnoff to 595-foot. *Green Castle Hill,* the remnant of a volcano with rock formations whose origin is unknown. A trail climbs to the top, from which there is a grandstand view over the south end of the island. Immediately before Johnson's Point on the southwest tip are Jolly Beach, a large resort, and *Dark Wood Beach,* an exquisite stretch of white sand on the quiet Caribbean, popular with cruise ships for their crews on R&R.

BOGGY PEAK The small village of Urlings sits on the southern flank of Boggy Peak, the highest point on the island (marked by a communications tower), and overlooks Cades Bay. A road inland leads to the top of the hill. The area is famous for the Antigua black pineapple, an unusually sweet, delicious variety cultivated here. Offshore is the 2.5-mile-long Cades Reef, part of which is a marine park.

OLD ROAD The hamlet of Old Road, at Carlisle Bay, marks the site of the first English settlement in 1632. Curtain Bluff Hotel, perched on a small bluff overlooking two lovely beaches, is one of Antigua's most attractive resorts, embraced in magnificent flowering gardens.

FIG TREE DRIVE At Old Road the main route turns inland onto Fig Tree Drive (*fig* is the Antiguan name for the banana plant) and winds through the hills between Old Road and the village of *John Hughes.* The 3-mile, sometimes bumpy stretch, overhung with tropical vegetation, is called "The Rain Forest" locally, because the area is more lush than the dry landscape typical of most of Antigua.

Antigua's hilly south coast between Old Road and Falmouth is popular for hiking on footpaths leading to hilltops and cliffsides for panoramic views and to beautiful, secluded beaches, otherwise accessible only by boat.

LIBERTA AND MONK'S HILL At the tiny village of Sweet's en route to Falmouth, the main road bends southeast to Liberta, one of the first settlements founded by freed slaves after the emancipation in 1834. The church of *St. Barnabas,* the parish church, dates from the 19th century. East of Liberta a road leads to Monk's Hill and *Fort George,* built by the British in the 17th century primarily as a place of refuge for women and children in times of attack. The road—used for walking or driving—is marked with a sign to the village of *Table Hill Gordon* a steep hike of about an hour to Monk's Hill.

FALMOUTH The port of Falmouth, set on a pretty bay, was once Antigua's capital. It is surrounded by former sugar plantations whose old mills dot the landscape here as they do throughout Antigua. The restored *St. George's Church,* dating from the 17th century, is one of the island's oldest churches. The *Antigua Yacht Club* is located here, too.

ENGLISH HARBOUR A small inlet on the southeast coast barely visible from the sea is one of the best natural harbors in the Caribbean, deep enough for oceangoing ships. Thanks to its deep water, hidden opening, and protective hills sheltering it from hurricanes and providing strategic positions for defense, the harbor became the main base of the British Admiralty in the West Indies. Throughout the 18th and 19th centuries, it was used as a base of operations by such famous British admirals as Nelson and Rodney and played a major role in helping to establish British naval superiority over the French.

The naval base, constructed between 1725 and 1746, occupied a narrow promontory that juts into the bay and separates English Harbour from Falmouth Harbour. A series of fortifications were added at the harbor and on the ridge surrounding it. The hills on the east are known as *Shirley Heights,* named for the governor of the Leewards who built the hilltop installations. After the Battle of Waterloo and peace in 1815, English Harbour's strategic importance began to decline. It was formally closed as a royal dockyard in 1889 and fell into decay until 1931 when an effort was launched to preserve the site.

NELSON'S DOCKYARD English Harbour, today one of the busiest yacht basins in the region, is obviously still appreciated by sailors. Serious reconstruction of the old dockyard, now called Nelson's Dockyard after the British admiral, began in 1951. The first phase took a decade, and the harbor was officially reopened in 1961, but another decade was needed to complete the task. The beautifully restored historic buildings house charming shops, museums, inns, restaurants, and a marina. *The Admiral's House,* Nelson's former residence, contains a museum of colonial history. Admiral's Inn is a hotel with a terrace restaurant overlooking the harbor. The old Copper and Lumber Store is also a hotel furnished in colonial style. An entrance fee which includes a guided tour of the Dockyard, which is now part of the national park.

CLARENCE HOUSE The 18th century residence of Prince William Henry, Duke of Clarence and later King William IV, who was based here as commander of the HMS *Pegasus* in 1787, stands on a hill overlooking English Harbour. The Georgian manor, furnished with antiques loaned by the British National Trust, is now the country house of the governor of Antigua and can be visited. A guide is on duty.

DOW'S HILL INTERPRETATION CENTRE Operated by the national park, the center is a must stop for those interested in the island's history, culture, and natural attractions. "Reflections in the Sun," a multimedia presentation traces the history of Antigua and Barbuda from prehistoric times to the present. The center is on a hilltop above Nelson's Dockyard en route to Shirley Heights.

SHIRLEY HEIGHTS The military installations on the hillside east of the harbor also have been restored and contain a small museum and a restaurant. The main attraction, though, is the magnificent view overlooking English and Falmouth harbors, the hills, and south coast of Antigua. On a clear day you can see as far away as Redonda and Montserrat, 32 miles to the southwest. The heights are a popular place to watch a fabulous Antiguan sunset. Jammin' at the heights has become a Sunday tradition when half the island is on hand to dance, hang out, and watch the sunset.

The *Lookout Trail,* a nature walk created by the National Parks Authority, leaves from Galleon Beach Hotel on the east side of English Harbour. A descriptive pamphlet for a self-guided hike, available from the Parks Authority, explains the traditional uses of the trees and plants you'll see along the way. The hike is not difficult and takes about 40 minutes to go up and 15 minutes to descend. Wear sneakers or similar shoes.

A secondary road winds over the heights to *Dow's Hill,* a site used by NASA for a tracking station during the Apollo program. The former NASA building now houses the *Antigua University of Health and Sciences.* Here a footpath leads to Bat's Cave, a small cavern with hundreds of bats.

The fastest return to St. John's from English Harbour is across the center of the island via All Saints, a pretty little village where pottery making is a traditional craft.

NORTH OF ST. JOHN'S

Antigua's main resort center is north of the capital, along the Caribbean coast. The stretch of sand closest to St. John's, known as Runaway Beach, is often used by cruise ships for their "day-at-the-beach" excursions. Dickinson Bay and Hodges Bay, farther north, have the largest concentration of hotels. Water sports are available from vendors at resorts along the beach. You'll find good snorkeling here and in the pristine waters of the uninhabited islets offshore.

PARHAM Directly east of St. John's on the northeast coast, the little settlement of Parham was the first capital of Antigua. *St. Peter's Church,* built in

1840 to replace an earlier church destroyed by fire, was designed by Thomas Weekes, a famous architect of the time, who was brought from Britain for the purpose. About a mile northeast of Parham is Crabbs Slipway and Marina, a boating center and a port of entry for yachts. The area is popular for biking tours.

GREAT BIRD ISLAND NATIONAL PARK An uninhabited islet offshore, with a pretty little beach, is popular for day-sailing excursions. The limestone cliffs of Great Bird Island are home to the red-billed tropic bird that can be seen gliding on the wind currents blowing in from the Atlantic. Bird Island and nearby cays have good snorkeling.

EAST TO THE ATLANTIC COAST

From St. John's two roads lead east to the Atlantic coast. The more northerly one passes through the villages of Pares and Willikies to Indian Town Creek, a national park on the northeast corner of Antigua. En route feeder roads and tracks extend to the north coast, an area sheltered by cays and reefs that provide calm waters for sailing, snorkeling, and fishing.

BETTY'S HOPE Near Pares a signposted road turns inland to the ruins of the first large sugar plantation in Antigua, Betty's Hope, founded in the 1650s and granted to Sir Christopher Codrington, a prosperous planter from Barbados, in 1668. Codrington is credited with introducing large-scale sugar cultivation and innovative processing methods in Antigua. The success of Betty's Hope, named for Sir Christopher's daughter, is said to have led other planters to turn from tobacco and indigo to sugar cane as their main crop. Codrington and his son served as governor general of the Leeward Islands, developing the plantation as the seat of government. The estate remained in the Codrington family until 1944. The ruins include two windmill towers and arches of the boiling house, among other structures.

In 1990 a $10-million restoration project was launched to restore Betty's Hope for use as a cultural center and historic attraction. The fund-raising activities are spearheaded jointly by the government, business and civic leaders, Partners of the Americas (Rochester, New York, Antigua's sister city), and Antigua Historical Society. There is an interpretive center in the old stables. Hours: 10:00 A.M. to 4:00 P.M., Monday to Saturday. Admission: US $2.

INDIAN TOWN NATIONAL PARK The main road beyond Willikies ends at Pineapple Beach, an all-inclusive resort on Long Bay. Tracks branch out across the northeastern peninsula to pretty coves. In deep cove known as Indian Town Point is Devil's Bridge, a natural bridge that has been carved out of the rocks by the relentless waves of the Atlantic. Alongside it "blowing holes" send jets of water high into the air. The south side of the peninsula overlooks Nonsuch Bay, one of the prettiest bays on the Atlantic coast, protected by coral reefs. Offshore Green Island is a nature preserve. The reef between Green Island and tiny, uninhabited York Island is a popular area for day-trippers.

The southerly of the two roads from St. John to the east coast skirts Potworks Reservoir for almost 2 miles. The largest of Antigua's numerous man-made catchments and one of the largest bodies of freshwater in the Eastern Caribbean, it has a pretty wooded setting, popular for bird-watching.

SHOPPING

The best shopping is found in the heart of St. John's along St. Mary's, High, Redcliffe, and Market streets, the oldest thoroughfares, where many shops are housed in colorful historic buildings of West Indian architecture. Here you will find a variety of locally made clothing, straw products, pottery, paintings, batiks, and jewelry with local semiprecious stones. Locally made rum and liquor prices are some of the lowest in the Caribbean. The downtown area is relatively small, and shops are within easy walking distance of one another. Stores are open daily (except Sunday), 9:00 A.M. to 5:00 P.M. Many take an hour's noontime lunch break.

Heritage Quay, a shopping and entertainment complex, was built with cruise-ship passengers in mind. The center has more than forty stores with high quality merchandise such as English bone china, French crystal and perfumes, Italian leather, and Swiss watches at duty-free prices.

ART AND ARTISTS: *Harmony Hall* (Brown's Bay Mill, Nonsuch Bay; 463–2057) is a branch of the well-known art gallery in Jamaica. It stocks quality Jamaican, Antiguan, and other Caribbean artists and holds exhibitions year-round, seeking out the best local artists and artisans. The gallery has a delightful setting on an old sugar plantation. It's almost an hour's drive from St. John's, but worth a stop, if you plan to spend a day rambling about the island.

Island Arts (Heritage Quay; 462–2787) is the gallery of artist and filmmaker Nick Maley and specializes in Caribbean art and handcrafts. Has original oils and prints by Katie Shears, who specializes in wildlife, and other local artists. Signed limited editions, pretty silk-screened gifts, and hand-painted T-shirts are other specialties.

BOOKS/MAPS: *The Map Shop* (St. Mary's Street) stocks maps of Antigua and the Caribbean and reproductions of antique maps, as well as postcards and stationery. It also sells British Admiralty charts.

CHINA AND CRYSTAL: *Little Switzerland* (Heritage Quay) is a branch of one of the best-known chains in the Caribbean for fine china and crystal, jewelry, and perfumes. *The Lady Hamilton* (Church Street) specializes in English crystal and ceramics, antique maps, souvenirs, collector's stamps, and swimwear.

CLOTHING: *Base* (Redcliffe Quay) is the boutique of American Bruce Cannella and Englishman Stephen Giles. They design trendy, sexy, slightly funky, but easy to wear, body-hugging or loose-fitting separates and dresses, mostly in a cotton/lycra knit, for their boutique here and in South Beach, Miami. All the clothes are made in Antigua and are moderately priced. *Benetton* (Heritage Quay), the well-known Italian clothing and accessories chain, has sportswear in bright coordinated colors. *Sunseekers* (Heritage Quay) stocks a large selection of swimwear.

Island Woman Boutique (Redcliffe Quay) carries locally designed leisure wear for men and women, jazzy swimwear from Jamaica and Brazil, fun design T-shirts, and stuffed batik animals for children. *Noreen Philips* (Long Street, next to the Lemon Tree) designs sophisticated evening wear,

which the shop claims can be made in 2 hours. *The Gallery Boutique* (English Harbour and St. James's Club Village), the shop of designer Janie Easton, stocks casual and sportswear by the owner and others. Particularly attractive are the fashions by John Warden, a designer from St. Kitts.

CRAFTS AND SOUVENIRS: You can watch Antiguan pottery being made at *Seaview Pottery* and *Cockleshell Pottery,* both near St. John's. *Jacaranda* (Upper Redcliffe Quay) stocks island spices, herbs, teas, and cosmetics, along with prints by Bajan artist Jill Walker. *Shipwreck Shop,* (St. Mary's Street and Jardine Court) specializes in gifts indigenous to Antigua and the Caribbean, local art, books, and magazines.

Sugar Mill Boutique (St. Mary's Street) specializes in silk-screened originals with designs of flowers, fish, and shells of the Caribbean by Antiguan artists. It also carries swimwear.

JEWELRY: *The Goldsmitty* (Redcliffe Quay) makes fine, handcrafted gold jewelry of original design, often using local stones. *Colombian Emeralds* (Heritage Quay), a major gem dealer, has stores throughout the Caribbean.

LEATHER AND LUGGAGE: At Heritage Quay, *Gucci* has one of its most attractive Caribbean stores ; *Land, The Leather Collection* is a quality-leather store for handbags and luggage.

LINENS: *The Linen Shop* (Heritage Quay) specializes in imported hand-embroidered tablecloths, table mats, sheets, towels, and bedspreads at low prices.

PERFUMES: *La Perfumerie* (Heritage Quay) offers an excellent selection of French perfumes. *Scent Shop* (High Street) has perfumes along with Cartier watches, jewelry, pens, and leather goods; Baccarat, Waterford, and other crystal.

DINING AND RESTAURANTS

Antigua is an island of many different life-styles, reflected in its variety of restaurants—from rustic taverns by the beach, English pubs, and unpretentious establishments for West Indian food to elegant dining rooms where jacket and tie are required. Seafood is a specialty with fresh local lobster and conch at the top of the list. Exotic Caribbean vegetables include christophene (a type of squash), dasheen (a leafy plant similar to spinach), plantains, and breadfruit. The Antigua black pineapple is one of the sweetest, best-tasting kinds anywhere; mangoes, papaya, and coconuts are abundant. Rum turns up in many recipes and drinks. Normally restaurants open daily for lunch and dinner, unless noted otherwise. This being the laid-back Caribbean, however, it is always wise to check in advance.

St. John's and Environs

Coconut Grove (Siboney Hotel Dickinson Bay, 462–1538). Pretty, romantic beachfront setting, specializing in seafood. Live music during the winter season. Reservations advised. Moderate.

Hemingways (St. Mary's Street). Second-floor bar and restaurant is situated in one of the oldest houses of West Indian gingerbread, with an attractive veranda overlooking the town center. Great variety of tropical drinks are featured along with salads, seafood, and sandwiches. Moderate.

Home (Gambles Terrace, Luther George Place; 461–7651), made famous by CNN, which featured owner/chef Carl Thomas for his seafood and local dishes.

The Lemon Tree (Long and Church streets; 461–2507). One of the town's most stylish restaurants with an eclectic menu of snacks and light fare. It walked away with five gold and three silver medals in the 1989 Antiguan Culinary Exposition. Piano bar and occasional live entertainment. Closed Sundays. Moderate.

Munchies Cafe (Old Parham Road; 462–2186). A popular snack shop for beef and chicken rôti, fish and chips, hamburgers, beer, stout, and a choice of seventeen flavors of ice cream. Inexpensive.

English Harbour

Admiral's Inn (Nelson's Dockyard; 463–1027). Built in 1788 as offices for the naval engineers, the inn's tree-shaded dining terrace overlooking the harbor provides one of Antigua's most pleas-

ant settings for seafood and light lunches. The soups are especially good. Moderate.

Alberto's (Willoughby Bay; 460–3007). The favorite of Antigua's foreign residents was a hit from opening day for its cuisine and delightful ambience in a terrace setting open to the breezes. Seafood is the specialty. Expensive. Closed Monday.

NIGHTLIFE

Nightlife revolves around hotels, small bars, and discos. Almost any evening there will be a barbecue, with steel band music, at one of the hotels.

The casinos are: *King's Casino* (Heritage Quay); *Royal Antiguan* south of St. John's on Deep Bay; *Halcyon Cove Beach and Casino* on Dickinson's Beach; and the *St. James's Club* on the southeast coast at Mamora Bay. Ribbit—The Club, the leading disco, south of town is open Thursday to Sunday from 10:30 P.M. until the wee hours.

SPORTS

Antigua has some of the best sports facilities in the Caribbean for swimming, sailing, and tennis. In most cases you should contact the sports operator or hotel in advance to make arrangements, particularly during the peak season, when demand is likely to be high.

BEACHES/SWIMMING: Many people would say the best reason to visit Antigua is its beaches—frequently ranked by Caribbean aficionados as the best in the region—and there are plenty of them. Antigua's maple leaf shape gives it extra miles of shore, with beaches in little coves hidden between rocky fingers and long, powdery white sands that often stretch for a mile. Some beaches can be reached only by hiking or from a boat; others have bars, restaurants, music, and facilities for water sports.

The beaches closest to the port are at *Runaway* and *Dickinson bays* on the north, *Deep Bay* and *Hawksbill* on the south (where one of Hawksbill's four beaches is clothing optional). All are on the

Caribbean, or leeward, side where the sea is calm and gentle. The beaches on the Atlantic, or windward coast, often have wave action and surf, but many coves are protected by reefs and have calm water.

BIKING: *Sun Cycles* (461–0324) rents 18-speed bikes for $18 per day. Free delivery and pick up are available in the St. John's area.

BOATING: Tradewinds blowing 90 percent of the year from the east, the spectacular water surrounding the island, the variety of anchorages and sheltered coves with pretty beaches and reefs, plus splendid facilities all have made Antigua one of the major boating centers of the Caribbean. You can choose from among day trips to offshore islands or longer charters. There are daily cruises around Antigua and picnic sails to nearby islands. The large boats have steel-band music and make quite a party of it.

English Harbour is the main marina and headquarters for *Nicholson's Yacht Charters,* one of the Caribbean's oldest, most respected operations, with an international reputation. Its founders spearheaded the renovation of Nelson's Dockyard. The Yacht Club is on the southeast corner of Falmouth Harbour.

Regattas are held year-round, but for true salts Antigua is the place to be in late April or early May when the island hosts *Sailing Week,* the Caribbean's most prestigious annual-yachting event attracting sailing greats and would-be greats from around the world. Since its inception in the 1960s, Sailing Week has become to sailing what Wimbeldon is to tennis.

GOLF: The *Cedar Valley Golf Club* (462–0161), located 3 miles from St. Johns, has the island's only 18-hole course (6,077 yards, par 70). Green fees are U.S. $20 for 18 holes; golf cart, $25; rental clubs, $13. There is a pro shop and snack bar. *Jolly Harbour* (462–6166) has a brand new 18-hole course.

HIKING: The *Historical and Archaeological Society* organizes monthly hikes. Inquire at the Antiquities Museum in St. John's. Antigua has a web of dirt roads and tracks that wander from main roads to beaches where you can swim or into woodlands and along ponds for bird-watching. The only marked trails on the island are those leading to

the heights above English Harbour. Short hikes in the hills of the south coast between Old Road and Falmouth take 30 minutes or an hour to reach lovely beaches accessible only by hiking or by boat. If you bring a picnic lunch, you can make a day of it with time for swimming and snorkeling. Rendezvous Bay, one of the island's most spectacular beaches, can be reached from Falmouth by four-wheel-drive vehicles or a hike of about 45 minutes.

HORSEBACK RIDING: Beach and trail rides are available from *St. James's Club* (460–5000), where riders trek through the southeast countryside. You need to reserve 24 hours in advance. *Spring Hill Riding Club* (Falmouth; 460–2700) is another.

SNORKELING/SCUBA DIVING: Antigua is surrounded by coral reefs in crystal clear, shallow water, ideal for snorkelers. Almost all beaches and offshore islands have reefs within swimming distance or a short boat ride from shore. With a few exceptions diving is in shallow water at sites of less than a 60-foot depth, where colorful reef fish are abundant. North of St. John's above Dickinson Bay is *Paradise Reef,* a popular area for snorkeling. Fronting the palm-fringed beaches on the east coast are miles of reefs that break Atlantic waves and provide calm waters for snorkelers.

South of the capital along the west coast at *Hawksbill Rock,* there is a cave in 15 feet of water. *Sunken Rock,* which drops to a depth of 122 feet, is a deep dive for experienced divers. Along the drop off divers see sting rays, barracuda, and occasional dolphin.

Cades Reef, a 2.5-mile-long reef about a mile off Cades Bay on the south coast, is typical of the reefs around Antigua. It is dominated by staghorn and elkhorn coral in the shallow areas and rich with colorful reef fish, such as parrotfish and blue tang. Visibility ranges from 80 to 150 feet. The reef is one of Antigua's main dive sites; part of it has been designated a marine park. Antigua and Barbuda are only now becoming known for wreck diving. The most popular of the six wrecks close to Antigua is the *Andes,* a three-masted, fully rigged merchant vessel that sank in 1905. It is located south of St. John's harbor by Deep Bay in only 20 feet of water.

Among the half dozen dive shops, the most convenient to the port is *Big John's Dive Antigua* (Rex Halcyon Cove Hotel; 462–3483).

TENNIS AND SQUASH: Antigua's low humidity makes it very suitable for tennis, a sport very popular here. More than a dozen hotels have courts. *Curtain Bluff* often hosts Tennis Week in January, when tournaments feature top seeded players. *Temo Sports* (Falmouth Bay; 460–1781) is a tennis and squash complex. It has locker rooms and showers, snack bar, and pro shop. Courts must be reserved.

WINDSURFING: The same tradewinds that made Antigua a haven for ships of yesteryear and attract yachts today have made her a windsurfing mecca, too. Most beachside hotels have boards for rent. The quiet seas and gentle breezes along the Caribbean shores are ideal for beginners. Strong winds varying from 12 to 25 knots and seas with 2- to 3-foot chops on the Atlantic side attract experienced enthusiasts. Antigua has several internationally known windsurfing schools. *Windsurfing Antigua Week,* the annual international competition, is usually held in January. The *Lord Nelson Hotel* on the northeast coast is the favorite center for experienced windsurfers.

FESTIVALS AND CELEBRATIONS

Antigua *Sailing Week* in late April or early May is the most important annual yachting event in the Caribbean and attracts sailors from around the world. More than one-hundred top-class racing yachts take part, and, for a week or so, English Harbour is crammed with boats and people who come to be part of the activities. Along with racing the week is full of frolic and festivities and topped off with a fancy-dress ball at Admiral's Inn—the social event of the season.

Carnival in Antigua began two decades ago as festivities to celebrate the visit of Queen Elizabeth II. The Antiguans had so much fun doing it, they repeated the celebration the following year, and the next, until it grew into an annual event. Since independence in 1981, Carnival has become an

11-day arts festival highlighting the island's culture and heritage with parades and other competitions. It is held in late July and early August prior to *Emancipation Week,* which begins the first Monday in August.

BARBUDA

B arbuda, Antigua's sister island, is a nature lover's paradise. Scalloped with miles of pink sand beaches and fringed by reefs, the coral island is a sparsely settled wilderness interspersed with lagoons, marshes, and mangroves, which are home to the largest frigate-bird sanctuary in the Eastern Caribbean. Located 26 miles north of Antigua, the largely undeveloped island is only 143 feet above sea level at its highest point. Codrington, where most of the island's 1,500 people live, is the only village.

CODRINGTON LAGOON A large estuary along the west coast is the mating ground for thousands of magnificent frigatebirds. During the mating season, from late August to December, the sight is fantastic. Every bush appears to have a dozen or more females on it, and a few feet overhead dozens of males with wing spans up to 8 feet glide through the air in display, ballooning their red throat pouches to get the attention of the flapping females.

Boats are available in Codrington for the short trip to the middle of the lagoon, where you can watch and photograph the birds within a few feet of the bushes. In addition to the frigatebird, Barbuda is said to have 170 bird species. Other wildlife includes white-tailed deer and boar.

South of Codrington in the area of Palmetto Point are the island's most beautiful pink-sand beaches. Offshore, Palaster Reef is a marine reserve established in 1972 to protect the reef, its pristine waters and historic shipwrecks. George Jeffries (Barbuda; 460–0143) takes up to three people on a four-hour tour, including the frigate bird sanctuary, for US $90 or US $25 per person for four or more.

St. Barthélemy (St. Barts)

GUSTAVIA

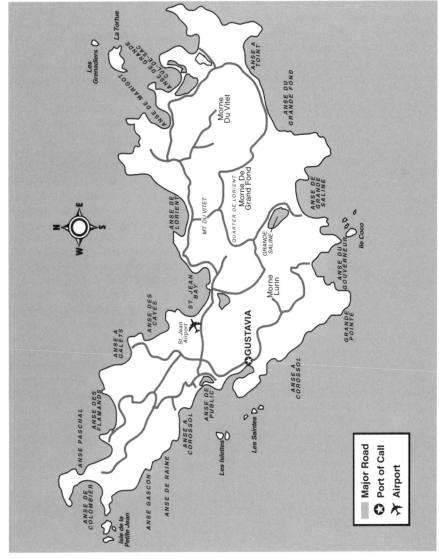

AT A GLANCE

CHAPTER CONTENTS

St. Barthélemy (St. Barts)

THE DARLING OF THE JETSET

A seductive paradise of scenic beauty at first sight, serendipitous upon acquaintance, St. Barthélemy—or St. Barts, as it is better known—is a stylish hideaway, 15 miles southeast of St. Maarten. The smallest of the French West Indies, St. Barts is a tiny Eden of green mountains and miniature valleys overlooking two dozen gorgeous white-sand beaches and turquoise water.

Discovered three decades ago by the Rockefellers and Rothschilds, it is something of a St. Tropez-in-the-Tropics attracting jet-setters and a host of show-biz celebrities and all those who follow in their wake. But the lot of them are mere Johnny-come-latelies. The island was probably inhabited first by the Arawaks. Christopher Columbus came upon the island in 1493 and named it for his brother's patron saint, Bartolomeo. The first French colonists arrived in 1648 from St. Kitts and were followed by the Knights of Malta. After raids by the fierce Carib Indians, the island was abandoned until 1673, when it was again settled by Frenchmen from Normandy and Brittany.

In 1784 the French sold St. Barts to Sweden in exchange for trading rights elsewhere. The Swedes renamed the harbor Gustavia in honor of their king, declared it a free port, and profited handsomely from the enterprise. France repurchased the island in 1878, retaining its free port status to this day.

In addition to being the only Caribbean island the Swedes ever possessed, St. Barts has other features that make it different. Too dry and rocky to be coveted for agriculture, the little island attracted only small farmers who had to scratch for a living. It was never converted to a sugar economy like that of most other Caribbean islands; slaves were never imported; and the plantation society typical of the colonial Caribbean never developed here.

Rather St. Barts is a minuscule remnant of ancient France, with neat little villages surrounded by meadows marked with centuries-old stone fences, and fair-skinned farmers and blue-eyed fishermen who speak a dialect of their 17th-century Norman ancestors that even Frenchmen cannot understand. Against this background of a conservative, closely knit society with Old World traditions, St. Barts has become a modern playground of worldly French sophistication for the rich and famous from both sides of the Atlantic.

FAST FACTS

 POPULATION: 5,043

SIZE: approximately 10 sq. miles

MAIN TOWN: Gustavia

GOVERNMENT: St. Barts and neighboring St. Martin make up a Sous-Préfecture of Guadeloupe, which in turn is an Overseas Department and Region of France whose people have full French citizenship like those on the mainland. St. Barts is administered by a *sous-préfect* who resides in St. Martin and has a representative on St. Barts.

CURRENCY: French franc. US $1 fluctuates at about 5 Ff. U.S. dollars are widely accepted, and prices are often quoted in dollars.

 DEPARTURE TAX: 10 Ff to the French side of St. Martin or Guadeloupe; 30 Ff to other destinations.

FIREARMS: Yachts are permitted to have firearms aboard, but they must be declared. Otherwise visitors are not allowed to bring them into St. Barts.

 LANGUAGE: French is the official language; the local dialect stems from old Norman speech and is hard to understand, even for Frenchmen.

PUBLIC HOLIDAYS: January 1, New Year's Day; May 1, Labor Day; May, Ascension Thursday; May, Pentecost Monday; July 14, Bastille Day; August 15, Assumption Day and St. Barts/Pitea Day, which commemorates the twinning in 1977 of St. Barts and Pitea, Sweden; November 1, All Saints Day; November 2, All Souls Day; November 11, Armistice Day; December 25, Christmas.

 TELEPHONE AREA CODE: 509. To call St. Barts from the United States station-to-station, dial 011–590 plus the St. Barts number; person-to-person, dial 01–590 plus the St. Barts number. To call St. Barts from other French West Indies islands, dial direct. To call Dutch St. Maarten from St. Barts, dial 3 plus the St. Maarten number. To call the United States from St. Barts, dial 19, wait for a second dial tone and dial 1 plus area code plus number.

 AIRLINES: From the United States to St. Barts, there are no direct flights. Travelers fly to St. Maarten, San Juan, and other gateways to connect with Winair (27–61–01), Air St. Barts (27–71–90), Air Guadeloupe (27–61–90), or Air St. Thomas (809–776–2722). The flight from St. Maarten takes 10 minutes. St. Barts's small airport and short landing strip can handle nothing larger than twenty-seat STOL aircraft. It is not equipped for night landing.

INFORMATION:

In the United States:
New York: French West Indies Tourist Board, 444 Madison Avenue, New York, NY 10022; (212) 757–1125. Tourists may also phone "France on Call," (900) 990–0040, for 95 cents per minute.
French Government Tourist Offices:
Chicago: 676 N. Michigan Avenue, IL 60611; (312) 751–7800.
Los Angeles: 9454 Wilshire Boulevard, Beverly Hills, CA 90212; (213) 272–2661.

In Canada; French Government Tourist Board:
Montreal: 1918 Ave. McGill College #490, Montreal, P.Q. H3A 2W9; (514) 288–4264;

fax: (514) 844–8901.
Toronto: 30 Patrick Street, No. 700, Toronto, Ont., M5T 3A3;
(416) 593–6427; fax: (416) 979–7587.

In Port:
Office du Tourisme, Quai General de Gaulle, Gustavia, 27–87–27; fax: 27–74–47.
Mailing: St. Barts Tourist Office, B.P. 113, Gustavia, 97098 Cedex, St. Barthelemy, F.W.I.
Hours: Weekdays 8:30 A.M. to 6:00 P.M., and until noon on Saturday.

BUDGET PLANNING

St. Barts offers the best that money can buy—and you will need plenty of it. It is one of the most expensive islands in the Caribbean, particularly so for its restaurants, which are comparable to top New York ones and often costing $100 and more per person for lunch or dinner. On the other hand, day-sailing excursions and car rentals are reasonable. French products are slightly less than in the United States but generally, more than on the neighboring St. Martin.

PORT PROFILE: GUSTAVIA

EMBARKATION/LOCATION: The pretty, yacht-filled harbor of Gustavia is located on the south side of the island. Small cruise ships usually steam directly into the harbor but do not dock; instead they tender passengers the short ride to the wharf. Larger ships remain outside the harbor and tender passengers to the dock. Bordering the harbor on three sides are fashionable boutiques and outdoor cafes with an unmistakable French ambience.

LOCAL TRANSPORTATION: There is no public bus system, but since the island is so small—only 25 miles of road—you can walk to many locations. There is a taxi station on rue de la République and another at the airport. You can also call for a taxi (27–66–31). Taxi fare for up to three persons per car from Gustavia to St. Jean

Beach is about 25 Ff for rides up to 5 minutes long and 20 Ff each additional 3 minutes. After 8:00 P.M. and on Sundays and holidays, fares have a 50 percent surcharge.

ROADS AND RENTALS: The best way to tour St. Barts is by car, which can be rented for about U.S. $60 per day in winter and U.S. $35 in the summer with unlimited mileage. Gas is extra and costs about $3.25 per gallon. Advance reservations are necessary, especially during the winter season, but be aware that some agencies require a 2- or 3-day minimum rental. The island has two gas stations; neither is open on Sunday. Not all car-rental companies take major credit cards. The most popular vehicles are open-sided Mini-Mokes, Gurgles, and Volkswagen Beetles—all well suited for the narrow, winding roads and hilly terrain— but drivers of these vehicles need to know how to operate a stick shift. Driving is on the right side of the road. The speed limit is 28 mph, which suits the roads and terrain—but not the French drivers from the mainland who race around St. Barts as if they were practicing for the Grand Prix.

Motorbikes, mopeds, scooters, and 18-speed mountain bikes are available from *Rent Some Fun* (27–70–59). You'll need to show a motorbike or driver's license, and French law requires drivers to wear helmets. Rentals cost about 140 Ff a day, plus a US $100 deposit.

Most car-rental firms are located at the airport. There are independent dealers and major names. *Avis/St. Barth Car,* (27–71–52); *Budget/Jean-Marc Greaux* (27–67–43); *Hertz/Henri's Car Rental* (27–71–14); *National/Europcar Caraibes* (phone 27–73–33).

FERRY SERVICES: *Gustavia Express* (tel. 27–77–24; fax 27–77–23) leaves Gustavia for Philipsburg on Monday, Wednesday, and Friday at 8:00 A.M. and returns at 5:00 P.M. The trip takes 1 hour. On Tuesday, Thursday, and Saturday it departs from Gustavia for Marigot at 7:15 A.M. and for Marigot, at 3:45 P.M., with returns at 9:00 A.M. and 5:30 P.M. These trips take 1.5 hours. On Sunday there is a 5:30 P.M. departure from Gustavia for Philipsburg and a 6:30 P.M. return trip. A one-way fare is US $36 from Philipsburg, US $40 from Marigot, plus US $6 port tax. Reservations: 27–77–24; fax: 27–77–23.

INTERISLAND AIR SERVICE: See Fast Facts

EMERGENCY NUMBERS:
> *Medical:* Gustavia hospital, 27–60–00 or 27–60–35
> *Police:* 27–66–66

AUTHOR'S FAVORITE ATTRACTIONS

A LEISURELY DRIVE AROUND THE ISLAND
SNORKELING AT ST. JEAN BAY
A DAY SAIL TO ILE FOURCHUE

SHORE EXCURSIONS

Cruise lines normally offer only two tours: an island tour of St. Barts and a day-sailing excursion. Island tours are operated by minibus or by taxi, with the driver acting as guide. Three tours of St. Barts depart by minibus from the pier in front of the tourist office. A 45-minute trip goes to Colombier, Flamands, Corossol, and Public, returning to Gustavia, with one stop; costs, 150 Ff for three persons, 200 Ff for more than three. A 1-hour excursion goes to St. Jean, Salines, Grand Fond, Cul de Sac, Marigot, and Lorient, with two stops; costs 200 Ff for up to three people, 250 Ff for more than three; and the third, 1.5-hour trip adds the villages of Colombier and Corossol, with three stops, and costs 250 Ff for three persons; 300 Ff for more than three. The Office du Tourisme can provide a list of independent driver/guides.

ST. BARTS ON YOUR OWN

The delightful little town of Gustavia with its Lilliputian port has a pretty setting: yachts bobbing in the harbor and red-roofed houses climbing the surrounding green hills. Only 3 blocks deep, the town has no must-see historic sites and can be explored easily on foot in an hour, stopping now and then to check out the boutiques and to enjoy refreshments at one of the sidewalk cafes that lend a French air to the setting. A few street signs in Swedish are reminders that the Swedes were here, too.

A GUSTAVIA WALKABOUT

Old fortifications are located on both sides of the harbor. On the south, a 5-minute walk passes Fort Karl en route to Petite Anse de Galet, also known as Shell Beach, where there is good shelling. On the north Fort Gustave offers a nice view of the harbor.

The *Town Hall (Mairie de St. Barth)* and some restaurants are housed in old buildings dating from the 18th century. *St. Barth Municipal Museum* (Musee Municipal de St. Barthélemy), on the south side of the harbor, depicts the island's history through photographs, documents, costumes, and antiques. It is open daily.

A steep road by the landmark clock tower on the east side leads over the hill where a rough road continues to Anse du Gouverneur, a cove with one of the island's most beautiful, secluded beaches bracketed by jagged cliffs. You can see Saba, St. Eustatius, and St. Kitts in the distance.

A DRIVE AROUND THE ISLAND

The quickest way to get into the St. Barts mode is to rent a Mini-Moke (a canopied jeep) and wander about following your whim. Stop at a beach for a swim or in a village to sip an aperitif, ramble down a country lane, or turn up a road to a hillside for a view. St. Barts can be easily toured by car in half a day. The narrow roads—yesterday's donkey tracks—twist and turn through tiny villages and along rocky shores to secluded, picture-book beaches.

WEST OF GUSTAVIA

On the north side of town, the road forks northeast to the airport and northwest to *Corossol,* the most traditional of the island's tiny fishing villages where the old Norman dialect can be heard. Some of Corrosol's elderly women still wear long blue-and-white-checkered dresses and the *caleche,* a stiff-brimmed bonnet derived from 17th-century Breton style. It is sometimes called *quichenotte,* meaning "kiss me not." The women are very shy and disappear at the first sign of strangers who might try to take their pictures. If you put away your camera and take a interest in the straw hats they want to sell you, you will find the reception quite different. The straw—the finest, most supple in the Caribbean—is handwoven from the fan-shaped fronds of latania palms. Also in Corossol is the *Inter Oceans Museum,* a private collection of shells, open daily 10:00 A.M. to 4:00 P.M. Admission: 20 Ff.

Farther along the road winds its way to Anse des Flamands on the north coast, where you will see another of the island's beautiful coves with a wide, half-mile stretch of white sand fringed by latania palms and framed by weather-worn rocks washed by intensely turquoise seas. It is home to several small resorts and one of the island's favorite celebrity-watching spots, *Taiwana,* a beach club and popular restaurant.

Anse de Colombier on the northwest end is a pretty cove accessible only by foot or boat. En route to Colombier, you pass the boutique and workshop of St. Barts's best-known fabric designer, Jean-Yves Froment, who specializes in beachwear and casual attire.

THE NORTH COAST AND EAST END

From Gustavia a hilly, twisting road heads northeast, passing the airport and skirting St. Jean Bay on its way to the eastern end. The bay, rimmed by white-sand beaches and bathed by calm, reef-protected turquoise waters, is divided about midpoint by a small promontory topped by tiny Eden Rock, the island's first hotel, which was recently renovated. From where you can enjoy fabulous views and absorb something of the St. Barts legend, in the place where it began. The bay is the hub of St. Barts's resort and water sports activity.

Lorient at the eastern end of St. Jean Bay is the site of the first French settlement in 1648. Its palm-fringed beach is used by local families, and its long rolling waves make it popular with surfers and windsurfers. Jutting out to sea between Lorient Bay and Marigot Bay on the east are the jagged cliffs of Milou and Mangin, where Atlantic waves crash against rock. Pointe Milou, almost barren a decade ago, is now a fashionable residential area of elegant homes and resorts.

Rising behind Lorient are the island's highest peaks: 898-foot Morne de Grand Fond on the west and 938-foot Morne du Vitet on the east. One road passes between the mountains to the south coast, another loops around Morne du Vitet via Grand Cul-de-Sac and the south coast, and a third winds up Morne du Vitet. They all pass centuries-old rural landscapes of farmhouses, grazing cattle, and patchwork fields outlined by stone fences.

Grand Cul-de-Sac, a large bay on the northeast, is another resort and water sports center, where shallow, reef-protected waters are ideal for novice windsurfers and snorkelers. Another road passes over the mountain to Anse de Toiny, with wild landscape that reminds people of the Normandy coast.

 **SHOPPING**

St. Barts is a duty-free port. Perfumes and famous brand crystal, silver, and china; jewelry; liquor, and tobacco are sold for about 20 percent less than U.S. prices. But as we have said earlier, St. Barts is not a place for bargains. As in most of France, stores close for lunch.

ART AND ARTISTS: *Le 'Ti Marche* in Gustavia is a little market devoted to the arts and artisans of the island. Set up in stalls on rue du Roi Oscar II near the City Hall, the market is open every morning except Sunday. Among the items available, *Belou's "P"* is a line of fragrant body oils, toilet waters, and rum punches, created and bottled by hand by Helene Muntal and Franck Garcia, a duo from Paris who now live on St. Barts.

Other products on sale include exquisite straw work, woven from lan-tana palm, by the older women in the fishing village of Corossol; lovely jewelry by Annelisa Gee, who also sells it at her boutique "Made in St. Barth," in St. Jean's; and paintings by artists living in St. Barts.

BOOKS AND MAPS: For books in French and English, try Librairie Charles Barnes (Rue Courbet, Gustavia).

CHINA/CRYSTAL: Several shops around the island carry French china, crystal, and silver; convenient to the port is *Carat* (Quai de la République), which has Baccarat, Lalique, Christofle, and other high-quality brands.

CLOTHING AND ACCESSORIES: Boutiques of Hermés, Gucci, Donna Karan, and other famous designers are found in Gustavia, St. Jean, and the *La Savane Commercial Center* opposite the airport. A canvas tote bag stamped "Loulou's Marine" is sold at the well-known nautical supply shop in Gustavia.

CRAFTS AND SOUVENIRS: The women of Corossol and Colombier are famous for their handwoven baskets, broad-brimmed hats for men and women, and handbags, made of delicate, supple straw with designs that resemble old lace. Other locally crafted products include sandals and shell jewelry.

LIQUEURS AND WINE: Fine French vintages stored in temperature-controlled rooms are found at *La Cave du Port Franc* (Gustavia). The store also sells contemporary paintings and antique objets d'art.

PERFUMES AND COSMETICS: The well-known French labels are available in boutiques, but more unusual are the locally made perfumes, lotions, and suntan oils of natural products. Beauty lotions and suntan oils made from island plants and other natural materials also make unusual gifts. One line, *La Ligne de St. Barth,* (27–82–63; fax: 27–70–93) is produced and sold by Brigit and Hervé Brin, whose ancestors settled on St. Barts hundreds of years ago. Their boutique and laboratory in Lorient are well worth a visit. Another line is *Belou's "P"* (Parfums et Punchs), created by Helene Muntal and Franck Garcia, in Anse des Cayes (27–85–45; fax 27–94–48). The couple who are also therapists, make beautifully bottled fragrant oils, each named for a different island beach. The products are sold at the *'Ti Marche* in Gustavia and *La Villa Creole* in St. Jean.

DINING AND RESTAURANTS

St. Barts is the gastronomic capital of the Caribbean, where dining is one of the main attractions. Renowned chefs from France frequently visit the island, and some teach classes here during the winter season. Young chefs trained in France's best restaurants come to work in St. Barts, bringing with them a high standard and creativity. By combining local ingredients, Gallic traditions, and modern trends, they have created a new French Caribbean cuisine.

Restaurants are small, and each has something special, either in food, setting, or atmosphere. About half of the sixty or so restaurants are open only for dinner or only during the winter season. Most close on Sunday. For three courses without wine, expect to pay about $25 per person for a modest meal, $40 per person for a moderate one, and $60 per person and up for an expensive one. Some restaurants do not accept credit cards; inquire in advance.

GUSTAVIA AND ENVIRONS

L'Escale (Quai de la Marine; 27–70–33). Survey the boat-filled harbor, and select from many types of pastas and pizza; or chicken, beef, and seafood grilled on a wood fire. Moderate.

La Marine (rue Jeanne d'Arc; 27–70–13). Picnic-style tables and benches on a waterside terrace. Seafood is a specialty. Moderate.

WEST OF GUSTAVIA

La Case de L'Isle (Hotel Isle de France; 27–61–81). The intimate beachside eatery, on Anse des Flamands, is the island's latest winner. Managed by American Evelyn Weber, the chef de cuisine is 28-year-old Jean-Claude Dufour from Bordeaux, who spent 10 years working for the Troisgros family in France. Moderate.

New Born (En route to the Manapany Hotel at Anse des Cayes; 27–67–07). Authentic Creole

dishes such as *accras* (codfish fritters), *boudin* (sausage), *blaff* (poached fish), and *calalou* are served a stone's throw from the beach in simple, pleasant surroundings. Moderate.

François Plantation (Colombier; 27–61–26). A hillside villa hotel houses one of St. Barts's brightest dining stars. A long arbor covered with blooming vines leads to a plant-filled bar and elegant, terraced dining room with a wine cellar that is partly under a decorative waterfall. The cuisine is French, classic, and haute, and the ambience sophisticated. Dinner only. Expensive.

ST. JEAN AND BEYOND

Club Lafayette (Grand Cul-de-Sac; 27–62–51). Fun fashion shows with clothes from the Club Lafayette boutique are part of the weekend entertainment. Closed May through November. For a table between 12:30 and 2:00 P.M., reservations are suggested. No credit cards. Very expensive.

Eden Rock (27–72–94). This completely renovated landmark—St. Barts' first hotel—is worth a visit for the beautiful view, to have a drink at the harbour bar, and to dine in the original bar perched over St. Jean Bay or in the new Yorkshire Bar at ground level. Lunch is moderately priced; dinner is expensive.

L'Indigo (Guanahani Hotel; 27–66–60). Since Guanahani's famous *Le Bartolomeo* serves only dinner, you might try *L'Indigo,* its poolside cafe. It's a good choice for casual daytime dining in an air of relaxed sophistication. Expensive

Hostellerie des Trois Forces (Vitet; 27–61–25) Grilled shrimp, lobster in basil sauce, fish with fennel, and other dishes are turned out from a wood-burning fireplace and served in the cozy atmosphere of a rustic country inn. The proprietor is an amateur astrologist and yoga practitioner; hotel rooms are named for the signs of the zodiac. Moderate to expensive.

Le Tamarin (Grande Saline; 27–72–12). An informal, very "in" dining place in a bucolic setting off the bumpy road to the Plage de Saline: Guests dine at tables on a porch or on the grass. It's always busy for lunch, but you can enjoy drinks under a centuries-old tamarin tree or try archery while you wait for a table. Moderate.

NIGHTLIFE

Leisurely dining is the main evening pastime. St. Barts has no movie houses or casinos. Young locals and visitors gather at such popular hangouts in Gustavia as *Bar de l'Oubli* (across from *Loulou's Marine*), where the open porch is a great people-watching spot reminiscent of Saint-Tropez. Its neighbor, *Le Select,* is a long-standing local hangout for snacks, drinks, and people watching. The garden restaurant, *Cheeseburger in Paradise,* is next door; it's named for Jimmy Buffet, an island habituee. There's a late night cabaret show at the popular *West Indies Cafe* (Sereno Beach Hotel; 27–64–80). *St. Barth Magazine,* a lively French/English publication, is the best source of information on current nighttime attractions.

SPORTS

St. Barts has good facilities for water sports. You should always contact the hotel or sports operator in advance to make arrangements, particularly during the peak season. There are about a dozen tennis courts, but no golf course.

BEACHES/SWIMMING: St. Barts is scalloped with more than two dozen pearly beaches bathed by calm turquoise waters—and few are ever crowded, even in peak season. Signs prohibiting nudism are all around the island, but the teensiest monokini is the fashion. All beaches are public and free.

Anse du Gouverneur, near the port, and *Anse de Grande Saline,* also on the south coast, are the most secluded beaches; *St. Jean* on the north coast and *Grand Cul-de-Sac* on the northeast are the most developed ones, with hotels, restaurants, and water sports.

BOATING: St. Barts's popularity for yachting is due in part to its location midway between Antigua and Virgin Gorda, two major sailing centers. Gustavia's harbor, which runs 13 to 16 feet in depth, has mooring and docking facilities.

Loulou's Marine (Gustavia; 27–62–74) is known throughout Caribbean yachting circles as one of the best-stocked marine supply stores in the Leeward Islands. The staff speaks English, and its bulletin board is something of a message center.

Annually St. Barts hosts the colorful *Route du Rose,* a regatta of tall ships that leaves St. Tropez in early November and arrives in Gustavia in early December. It is accompanied by a *Salon du Rose,* a week of festivities sponsored by the producers of Provence rosé wine, ending with a regatta around the island.

Sunfish sailing is especially pleasant in St. Barts, because most of the bays have gentle waters. Boats can be rented at St. Jean, Grand Cul-de-Sac, Public, and Colombier beaches.

Yacht Charter Agency (27–62–38) and *La Marine Service* (27–70–34) have half-day sails and other excursions to nearby beaches and islets. Bare-boat rentals, with gas and ice, cost about 1,300 Ff per day at Marine Service. Full-day sailing excursions to Ile Fourchue, a desolate island of wild moonscape terrain off the northwest coast, depart Gustavia at about 9:00 A.M. and return about 4:00 or 5:00 P.M. The cost is about US $96 per person (minimum of four) and includes swimming, snorkeling, cocktails, and picnic lunch with wine. The island is interesting to explore but hot; bring a generous supply of water, sun protection, and sturdy shoes for hiking. A half-day cruise with swimming, snorkeling, and open bar costs US $52.

DEEP-SEA FISHING: Fishing charters can be arranged through *Yacht Charter Agency* (27–62–38) and *La Marine Service* (27–70–34). The latter charges 2,000 Ff for a half-day, including fishing gear for four persons. Popular catches are tuna, bonito, dorado, marlin, and barracuda. Check with local fishermen before eating your catch; not all fish in these waters are edible.

HIKING: St. Barts's pretty landscapes and country roads with light traffic make walking and hiking popular pastimes. Almost any location is within easy reach, although the hilly terrain and hot sun make distances deceiving.

HORSEBACK RIDING: *Ranch des Flamands* at Anse des Flamands. Contact Laure Nicolas

(27–80–72). A 2-hour-long excursion departs at 9:00 A.M. and costs US $35.

SNORKELING/SCUBA DIVING: St. Barts is almost completely surrounded by shallow water reefs, better suited for snorkeling than diving, and often within swimming distance of shore. St. Jean Bay has the most accessible reefs. Equipment can be purchased at *Loulou's Marine* (27–62–74) or rented from *La Marine Service* (27–70–34) for about 60 Ff per day.

The best dive locations are on the west coast at about 50- to 60-foot depths within easy reach of Gustavia. Immediately outside the harbor is Gros Ilet, a rock poking about 75 feet above the sea, where you can see grouper, snapper, moray eel, lobster, and large schools of reef fish.

Dive operators run boat trips daily. *La Marine Service* (27–70–34) offers PADI and French certification. Dive trips cost about 250 Ff per person, gear included. *Dive with Dan* (Emeraude Plage Hotel, St. Jean; 27–74– 68) also offers PADI certification. The staffs, certified as instructors by their French federation, are familiar with American methods and standards, and the shops maintain American as well as French tanks and regulators.

SURFING: Lorient, east of St. Jean Bay, is the most popular surfing area. You can rent boards at water-sports centers and get advice about water conditions at the same time.

WINDSURFING: Shallow waters and gentle winds make conditions at St. Jean and Grand Cul-de-Sac ideal for learning to windsurf. Rentals are available at beachside watersports centers. *St. Barth Wind School* (Tom Beach Hotel; 27–71–22) and *Wind Wave Power* (St. Barth's Beach Hotel; 27–62–73) offer rentals and lessons. Rentals average about US $15 to $18 an hour. Lorient is the most popular site for the experienced sportsmen.

FESTIVALS AND CELEBRATIONS

St. Barts celebrates *Mardi Gras* in the French tradition and has some festivals and events special to the island.

The *St. Barts Music Festival,* under the direction of Frances DeBroff, president of the Pittsburgh Symphony Association, is an annual affair in late January/early February featuring chamber music, dance, and other arts. Artists from the United States and Europe perform in the church of Lorient and at the wharf in Gustavia.

The *Festival of St. Barthélemy,* August 24, is the colorful feast day of the island's patron saint. Similarly the *Feast of St. Louis,* August 25, is celebrated in the village of Corossol.

St. Kitts and Nevis

BASSETERRE, ST. KITTS;
CHARLESTOWN, NEVIS

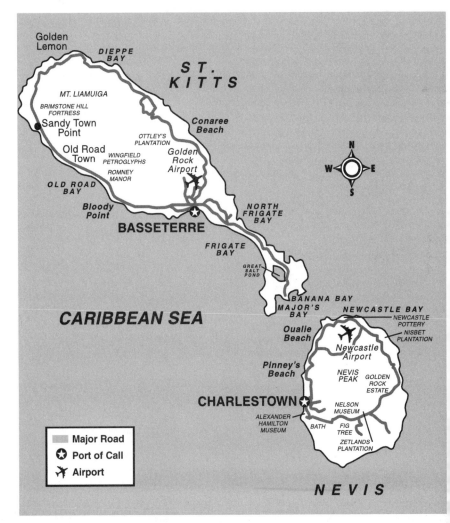

Golden Lemon

DIEPPE BAY

ST. KITTS

MT. LIAMUIGA

BRIMSTONE HILL FORTRESS

Sandy Town Point

Conaree Beach

OTTLEY'S PLANTATION

Old Road Town

WINGFIELD PETROGLYPHS

Golden Rock Airport

ROMNEY MANOR

OLD ROAD BAY

Bloody Point

NORTH FRIGATE BAY

BASSETERRE

FRIGATE BAY

GREAT SALT POND

BANANA BAY

MAJOR'S BAY

NEWCASTLE BAY

CARIBBEAN SEA

NEWCASTLE POTTERY

NISBET PLANTATION

Oualie Beach

Newcastle Airport

Pinney's Beach

NEVIS PEAK

GOLDEN ROCK ESTATE

CHARLESTOWN

NELSON MUSEUM

ALEXANDER HAMILTON MUSEUM

BATH

FIG TREE

ZETLANDS PLANTATION

Major Road
Port of Call
Airport

NEVIS

AT A GLANCE

CHAPTER CONTENTS

St. Kitts and Nevis

THE SECRET CARIBBEAN

Graceful islands of gentle beauty, St. Kitts and Nevis enchant visitors with their lovely landscapes and unspoiled qualities. Christopher Columbus, who came upon the islands in 1493, selected St. Kitts from all his discoveries to name for his patron saint, St. Christopher. Located in the Leeward Islands west of Antigua, St. Kitts and Nevis call themselves "The Secret Caribbean," being discovered only now by tourists and cruise ships. The irony is that these islands were the first the English settled, and St. Kitts—as St. Christopher came to be known—had the title of the "mother colony" throughout its colonial history.

Here the British gained great wealth from the land that produced the highest-yielding sugar crop in the world. Little wonder that the native Carib Indians called the island Liamuiga (Lee-a-*MOO*-ee-ga), meaning "fertile land." To protect their valuable possession, the British built their most massive fortress in the Eastern Caribbean. From their base in St. Kitts, the British settled Nevis, Antigua, and Montserrat.

Shaped like a paddle, St. Kitts rises from a grassy coastal skirt through intensively cultivated green hills to a central spine of mountains covered with rain forests. Mount Liamuiga, a dormant volcano whose peak, at almost 4,000 feet, is usually hidden under a cap of white clouds, dominates the north. Different in climate and terrain from the main body of St. Kitts, the Southeastern Peninsula, a hilly tongue of land forming the "handle of the paddle," is covered with dry woodlands and salt ponds and scalloped with the island's best beaches.

After a century as a Spanish possession, the first English settlers arrived in St. Kitts in 1623 to stake a claim for Britain. They established a colony near the place known today as Old Town. The following year the French arrived and claimed the northern and southern parts of the island. Like the British, they used it as a base for further colonization, laying claim to Guadeloupe, Martinique, St. Martin,

and St. Barts—the islands that make up the French West Indies today.

For more than a century Britain and France fought over St. Kitts for possession of this rich prize, but they first had to battle the Carib. It was not until 1783, under the Treaty of Versailles, that the British finally got St. Kitts and Nevis for themselves. The islands remained British colonies until 1983 when full independence was established.

FAST FACTS

POPULATION: St. Kitts, 36,578 Nevis, 9,423.

SIZE: St. Kitts, 65 sq. miles; Nevis, 36 sq. miles.

MAIN TOWNS: Basseterre, St. Kitts; Charlestown, Nevis.

GOVERNMENT: St. Kitts and Nevis, officially known as the Federation of St. Christopher and Nevis, belong to the British Commonwealth. They are governed by a parliamentary government headed by a prime minister. Each island has a legislature and assembly. The queen is represented by a governor-general.

CURRENCY: East Caribbean dollar EC $2.70 equals US $1. U.S. dollars are widely accepted.

DEPARTURE TAX: EC $27 (US $10)

LANGUAGE: English

PUBLIC HOLIDAYS: January 1, New Year's Day; Good Friday; Easter Monday; Labor Day, first Monday in May; Whit Monday; Queen's Birthday, second Saturday in June; August Monday, first Monday in August; September 19, Independence Day; December 25, Christmas; December 26, Boxing Day; late December, Carnival Day at the end of the two-week festivities that begin a week before Christmas.

TELEPHONE AREA CODE: 869. From the United States and Canada, dial 869–465 for St. Kitts and 869–469 for Nevis, followed by the four digit local number. International telex service is operated by Skantel; international collect calls can be made from their office in Basseterre.

AIRLINES:

From the United States and Canada: St. Kitts is served from New York and Miami and by American Airlines/American Eagle via San Juan.

Interisland: Other international carriers connect with regional ones via St. Maarten, and Antigua to St. Kitts. Nevis is served by Nevis Express (469–9755), LIAT, and Winair.

INFORMATION:

In the United States: St. Kitts and Nevis Tourist Board, 414 East 75th Street, New York, NY 10021; (212) 535–1234.

In Canada: St. Kitts and Nevis Tourism Office, 11 Yorkville Avenue, Suite 508, Toronto, Ont. M4W 1L3; (416) 921–7717.

In Port: St. Kitts: St. Kitts–Nevis Department of Tourism, Pelican Mall, P.O. Box 132, Basseterre, St. Kitts, W.I.; 465–2620/4040.

Nevis: St. Kitts–Nevis Tourist Office, Charlestown, Nevis, W.I.; 469–5521, ext. 2049/2037.

BUDGET PLANNING

St. Kitts and Nevis are among the least expensive islands in the Caribbean. If you can share the cost, a taxi is the best way to tour in the short time usually available to cruise passengers. Restaurants (with local cuisine) are moderately priced. As for shopping, the island compares favorably in price with St. Thomas for duty-free goods, but you are likely to find the locally made products of more interest.

PORT PROFILE

LOCATION/EMBARKATION: Cruise ships arrive in St. Kitts at Basseterre, the capital, on the southwest side of the island. Most ships are now using Port Zante, the new facility in town where land reclamation—the first phase of a $22 million port development project—has been completed, extending Basseterre's waterfront from the shore behind Pelican Mall about 800 feet into the bay. The 26 acres of new land has an arrival center and shopping mall, yacht club and marina, and other businesses are being added in a park setting. All the buildings must conform to the Victorian-colonial-style of Basseterre's historic town center, after which the port's architecture has been adopted. When the entire project is completed, cruise passengers should find the arrival in St. Kitts to be one of the most delightful in the Caribbean. Meanwhile, some ships may need to use the old port, Deep Water Harbour on the south end of a wide bay about a mile or so from the town center.

In Nevis cruise ships and ferries from St. Kitts arrive in Charlestown, the main town. Its waterfront is being renovated, too. The pier for cruise ships to dock or tender has been rehabilitated, and the historic Cotton Ginnery has been renovated to house small arts-and-crafts shops. A small museum and other facilities are planned, too. Land reclamation has provided parking areas and passenger gazebos in a parklike setting. The construction of a new cruise port, farther south on the coast, is scheduled to start next year.

LOCAL TRANSPORTATION: On St. Kitts private buses operate between villages, but generally, they are not used by cruise-ship passengers due to the short time their ships are in port. Taxis, operating on set rates, are available for touring on both islands. Drivers are a loquacious lot and likely to sprinkle their commentary with local lore. Sample rates: one-way from Basseterre to Frigate Bay, EC $25 (US $10); Deep Water Port, EC $22 (US $8); to Half Way Tree (near Brimstone Hill), EC $30 (US $11); to Dieppe Bay, EC $50 (US $19); to *Ottley's,* EC $23 (US $9). For a taxi from one point to another within Basseterre, EC $8 (US $3). Waiting time charged for every 15 minutes, EC $3 (US $1). Taxi rates are published in Tourism Department pamphlets.

ROADS AND RENTALS: A good road circumnavigates the main body of St. Kitts, hugging the coast all the way; and a wonderful, scenic road opened in 1989 crosses the Southeast Peninsula to the tip, a stretch of about 7 miles. The coastal road makes it easy to drive—or bike—around the island and provides access to the mountainous interior, where you'll find splendid hiking. There are no cross-island roads through the central mountains, but there are footpaths. Maps are available from the Tourism Department.

Nevis has about 20 miles of narrow, winding roads that encircle the island, but not always along the coast; some cut across the foothills of Mt. Nevis. The south side of the island is honeycombed with country lanes and footpaths, ideal for rambling. Local people use the roads for walking as much as for driving, since traffic is light.

To drive you must obtain a local driver's license by presenting your valid U.S. or Canadian license and paying a fee of EC $50 (US $20) at the Traffic Department (Central Police Station, Cayon Street, Basseterre, or the police station in Charlestown). Normally the transaction takes only a few minutes. Driving in this former British colony is on the LEFT.

Car-rental rates are comparable to U.S. ones. Some agencies require that drivers be at least 25 years of age. Most offer pickup and delivery service. Some agencies have Mini-Mokes or Jeeps, mopeds or motorbikes, as well as popular Japanese and European cars.

In St. Kitts: *Avis/Brown's* (465–3338); *Byrons* (465–2165); *Caines* (465–2366); *Economy* (465–2361); and *T.D.C.* (465–2511). The latter two as well as *Island Moped & Auto* (Sprott Street) have mopeds and bicycles.

In Nevis: *Avis* (469–5648); *Budget* (469–5390); *Multiline* (469–5389); *Skeete's* (469–5458); *T.D.C.* (Main Street; 469–5430).

FERRY SERVICE: The government operates a passenger ferry, *Caribe Queen*, between Basseterre and Charlestown. It takes 45 minutes. The service operates daily except Thursday and Sunday from 7:00 A.M. to 6:00 P.M. There is

usually one early morning and one midafternoon departure in each direction. Fare: EC $20 (US $8) round-trip. Schedules are available from the Tourist Office on both islands.

INTERISLAND AIR SERVICE: See Fast Facts.

EMERGENCY NUMBERS:

> *Medical:* Joseph N. France General Hospital, Basseterre; 465–2551;
> Alexandra Hospital, Nevis, dial operator.
> *Police:* Dial 99

AUTHOR'S FAVORITE ATTRACTIONS

BRIMSTONE HILL NATIONAL PARK
HIKING ON MT. LIAMUIGA
DRIVE AROUND ST. KITTS OR NEVIS

SHORE EXCURSIONS

Island/Brimstone Hill Tour, 2.5 hours, US $25. The most frequent shore excursion is an island tour that takes in the scenic west coast with a stop at Caribelle Batik and Brimstone Hill. You could take a similar route on your own, with a stop at *Rawlins Plantation Inn* on the north coast for lunch or a swim.

Mt. Liamuiga Rain Forest, 5–6 hours, US $30–$35. You can take a guided hike to the crater rim of Mt. Liamuiga through local companies; make arrangements in advance. Half-day rain-forest hikes can also be arranged here and in other areas of St. Kitts.

ST. KITTS ON YOUR OWN

The capital of St. Kitts is unmistakably British despite its French name. Hard by the sea along a wide bay, Basseterre, which means "lowland" in French, is considered one of the best remaining examples of a traditional West Indian town in the

Eastern Caribbean. Despite fires, hurricanes, and earthquakes, many examples of Georgian and Victorian architecture have survived and give the town its historic character.

A BASSETERRE WALKABOUT

The historic town center, laid out in a modified grid, is easy to cover on foot and to combine with a shopping tour.

THE CIRCUS (1) One block inland from the waterfront, the palm-shaded Circus is a small replica of Piccadilly Circus in London with a Georgian clock tower and a memorial to Thomas Berkely, a former president of the Leeward Islands Legislative Council. The round-about is in the heart of the business district at the intersection of Fort and Bank streets and Liverpool Row—all with shops, car rentals, tour companies, and restaurants.

INDEPENDENCE SQUARE (2) East of The Circus at the end of Bank Street is Independence Square, a public park with flowering gardens and a central fountain. The square was the site of the slave market in the 18th century and is surrounded by some of the town's best-preserved colonial buildings, many with balconies and gingerbread trim. Its side streets have shops, the island's best art gallery, and restaurants. On the east side stands the *Church of the Immaculate Conception.*

ST. GEORGE'S ANGLICAN CHURCH (3) Originally built as Notre Dame by the French in

MAP LEGEND FOR WALKING TOUR OF BASSETERRE

1. The Circus
2. Independence Square
3. St. George's Anglican Church
4. St. Kitts and Nevis Department of Tourism

5. Treasury Building and Post Office
6. Market
7. Fisherman's Wharf and Pelican Cove Marina
8. Port Zante

1670, the church was destroyed by fire in 1706 by the British, who rebuilt it four years later and renamed it for the patron saint of England. Over the next century it suffered from fires and natural disasters and was rebuilt several times (the last time was in 1869).

At the foot of The Circus on the waterfront is a landmark building known as the *Treasury* (**5**), dating from 1894; the post office is located here. The St. Kitts Philatelic Bureau is west of the Treasury on Bay Street. St. Kitts and Nevis each issues its own stamps, which make them prized by stamp collectors—and a nice source of revenue for the government. Next door the *Pelican Mall* is a small shopping center with quality shops. The St. Kitts and Nevis Tourist Office (**4**) is on the second floor.

Farther west along the bay, *the Market* (**6**), liveliest on market day (Saturday), is a good place to learn about local fruits and vegetables. At the west end of the bay, *Fisherman's Wharf* and *Pelican Cove Marina* (**7**) are the main dive and water sports centers. From the gardens of the Ocean Terrace Inn on the hillside above the wharf, you can have a splendid view of Basseterre and see your ship docked at the new *Port Zante* (**8**).

A DRIVE AROUND ST. KITTS

The road north from Basseterre along the leeward coast hugs the shoreline and borders the tracks of the sugar train fringing the sugar fields; Mt. Liamuiga towers in the background on the north. Most of the coast is rockbound except for an occasional small cove with a tiny beach or stretch of golden sand, particularly between Old Road Town and Half Way Tree.

BLOODY POINT Stonefort Ravine, north of Boyd's, was the scene of a terrible massacre in 1626. The British and French joined forces to wipe out almost an entire population of 2,000 Caribs, after receiving word of an attack planned by the Carib Indians against the new colonists who had settled farther up the coast. The site is known today as Bloody Point, because it is said that the ravine ran with blood for three days.

OLD ROAD TOWN On the shores of Old Road Bay in 1623, Sir Thomas Warner, his family, and fourteen followers landed to establish the first British settlement in the West Indies. It served as the capital of St. Kitts until 1727. The tomb of Warner, who died in 1648, lies in a churchyard nearby at Middle Island.

ROMNEY MANOR Inland from Old Road Town en route to Romney Manor and Wingfield Estate, former plantations in the foothills of the central mountains, there are small boulders with Carib petroglyphs. The land of Wingfield Estate once belonged to a Carib tribe whose chief, Tegreman, befriended Warner and permitted him to make a settlement on St. Kitts—much to the chief's later regret.

Romney Manor, a 17th-century plantation house partially rebuilt after a fire in 1996, is the home of *Caribelle Batik*, surrounded by lovely gardens and shaded by an enormous *saman*, or rain tree, as it is known locally, said to be more than 350 years old. At Caribelle Batik you can watch artisans—mostly girls from the surrounding villages—at work, recreating drawings taken from the Carib petroglyphs, scenes of Caribbean life, and West Indian motifs. Caribelle Batik uses the ancient Javanese method of making batik; its sole concession to the 20th century is the use of colorfast dyes rather than traditional vegetable dyes, which fade.

BRIMSTONE HILL NATIONAL PARK Begun in 1690 by the French, and completed by the British over a century, Brimstone Hill has been dubbed the Gibraltar of the West Indies. Perched on an 800-foot spur of Mt. Liamuiga overlooking the west coast, the fortress covers thirty-eight acres. It's one of the most massive fortifications built during the colonial era. Made into a park in 1965, the fort has been beautifully restored with British assistance; it has three redoubts, officer's quarters, hospital, ordnance stores, kitchen, and drainage system. A museum was added in 1982.

In addition to being beautiful, the view from the ramparts brings into focus St. Kitts's strategic location to the colonial powers. Beyond the green cultivated fields on the north lie the islands of Saba, St. Eustatius, and St. Barts. On the south, beyond the sugar cane fields that cover the hills forming the backbone of St. Kitts are the peaks of Nevis and Montserrat.

MT. LIAMUIGA The brooding volcano known in colonial times as Mt. Misery rises behind Brimstone's gray stone walls. From its rain-forested peaks, the mountain slopes down through a quilt of green cultivated hills to a sapphire sea. The rim of the crater, at 2,625 feet, is not the actual peak which is located east of the crater, but it is the area that can be climbed.

The trail is a gradual ascent along deep ravines under a dense canopy of trees more than 50 feet high and dangling with curtains of vines, ferns, and philodendron. There are magnificent views down the coast and across St. Kitts to the surrounding islands. At the rim you have the unusual opportunity to walk down (crawl is more accurate) into the crater of a dormant volcano, but it is an arduous trek requiring stamina and agility.

Hikers usually approach the volcano from the north, at Belmont Estates where a dirt road leads to the trailhead at about 1,500 feet elevation. The hike to the crater rim takes about 2.5 hours on the ascent and about 1.5 on the descent. There are no facilities whatever on the trail. If you want to go down into the crater, it is essential to have a local guide, because it is easy to become disoriented and lost.

BLACK ROCKS On the northern tip of St. Kitts at Dieppe Bay, the coast is fringed by coral stone and black-sand beaches. The *Golden Lemon,* owned by a former New York magazine editor/ decorator, has long been considered one of the prettiest inns in the Caribbean.

At Belle Vue, on the windward coast, huge boulders of molten lava from prehistoric volcanic eruptions rest at the edge of the sea, where the pounding surf has shaped and weathered them into spectacular, wild scenery. You can return to Basseterre along the east coast via Conaree and the international airport. At Ottley's, a plantation acquired in 1989 by an American family from New Jersey, was converted into a hotel using the greathouse, dating from 1832, as the centerpiece. *Ottley's Plantation Inn* (800–772–3039; fax (869) 465–4760).

FRIGATE BAY AND THE SOUTHEASTERN PENINSULA

On the south side of Basseterre, a narrow strip of land stretches southeasterly in a series of knolls, ponds, and coves with St. Kitts's prettiest white-sand beaches. In the late 1970s the first phase of a long-range resort development of the peninsula began with the first mile or so in an area known as Frigate Bay. The remaining 7-mile strip was accessible only on foot or by boat until the completion of the first road through the area in 1989. The road affords lovely views throughout the drive and ends at the peninsula's most beautiful beaches. Major's Bay, a horseshoe cove, has a half-mile crest of white sand, Banana Bay, and Turtle Beach, home of the *Turtle Beach Bar* (469–9086), a rustic seaside restaurant/bar with a full array of water sports facilities including diving, deep-sea fishing, and guided kayaking. These beaches front the island's best snorkeling reefs. Behind them are two saline lakes, Little Salt Pond and Great Salt Pond, separated by a sliver of land that is a popular area for bird-watchers.

SHOPPING IN ST. KITTS

The development of tourism and the island's growing economy is reflected in the increasing number of shops in Basseterre, particularly those offering island crafts and duty-free gifts. Generally, store hours are from 8:00 A.M. to noon and 1:00 to 4:00 P.M. daily except Sunday. Most shops of interest to visitors are found in a compact area, from the waterfront near the Nevis ferry pier to The Circus and Independence Square. Some stores are situated in renovated historic buildings, others in new shopping plazas like Palms Arcade at The Circus and the small, pretty TDC Mall on lower Fort Street, where shops and a restaurant are set around an open courtyard.

ART AND ANTIQUES: *Spencer-Cameron Art Gallery* (Independence Square). Located in a restored colonial building dating from the 1860s, the art gallery and workshop of artist Rosey Cameron-Smith has works by artists from St. Kitts/Nevis and around the Caribbean. Rosey arrived in St. Kitts in 1977, en route to South America to visit friends, and never left. Finding herself in demand as an artist, she created collections for several hotels and then went into business producing silk-screened fabrics with island-inspired designs.

BOOKS AND RECORDS: *Wall's Deluxe Record & Bookstore* (Fort Street, above The Circus) has local guidebooks, stationery and greeting cards, cookbooks, magazines, and Caribbean music. *The Wayfarer* (Central Street) stocks books, magazines, and newspapers.

CHINA/CRYSTAL: *Little Switzerland* (Pelican Mall) carries fine china, crystal, famous name watches, and jewelry.

CLOTHING AND ACCESSORIES: *Grendale Boutique* (Central Street), set in its own courtyard, offers island inspired clothing, jewelry, gifts, and local souvenirs. *Island to Island* is the label for clothing designed and produced in St. Kitts by John Warden whose signature is casual yet elegant fashions in linen, flax, or cotton. The outfits are sold at *Palm Craft* and other quality boutiques or by appointment (465–1713; fax: 465–7569).

CRAFTS: *Caribelle Batik* (Liverpool Row at The Circus) is the in-town outlet for the batik maker at Romney Manor. The shop features colorful, handmade and original wall hangings and fashionable sportswear, all on fine sea-island cotton. *The Crafthouse* (Shoreline Plaza, Bay Road) is a government-sponsored center for local craftspeople to work and improve their skills as well as to display their wares. In addition to crafts and souvenirs, they sell perfume, gold jewelry, and fashion accessories. *Palm Crafts* (Fort Street) features island crafts of shell, straw, and coconut as well as homemade jams and local spices and potpourri.

JEWELRY: *Linen and Gold* (Pelican Mall) offers handcrafted items in gold and other jewelry and accessories. *Objects of Art* (The Circus) is a store and factory where jewelry is created from local shells, corals, and volcanic rock.

PERFUMES: *A Slice of the Lemon* (Palms Arcade) sells perfumes as well as watches and jewelry, china, crystal, and leather goods at duty-free prices that claim to beat those in St. Maarten.

DINING IN ST. KITTS

St. Kitts has a delicious local cuisine that reflects the Caribbean melting pot as well as any place in the region. Carib, African, European, Asian, and Middle Eastern influences are reflected in the taste and variety of dishes, which use exotic vegetables such as breadfruit and christophene (a type of squash); eggplant and okra, herbs, and fresh seafood. Peter Mallalieu, a fifth-generation Kittitian and food specialist, says such dishes as *pepperpot*, a meat stew, was learned from the Caribs; *konki*, a cassava, yam, and coconut bread steamed in banana leaves, came with the African slaves; *paelau*, a rice-and-peas dish served for celebrations, mingles Spanish and East Indian traditions; and *kibbe* and *rolled grape leaves* arrived with the Lebanese traders at the turn of the last century.

Restaurants are open daily except Sunday, unless otherwise noted. Not all take credit cards; inquire in advance. For dinner, not including wine, inexpensive means under US $15 per person; moderate, US $15–25; expensive, over US $25. Lunch is generally US $5 less.

The Ballahoo Restaurant (The Circus; 465–4197.) A good place to relax after shopping, it is popular with locals and tourists for seafood and local fare and for its location, which offers seating on a second-floor balcony overlooking the town. Moderate.

The New Pizza Place (Central Street; 465–2546). In addition to pizza, you can get rôti, chicken, and fried conch to enjoy in its courtyard or to take out. Inexpensive.

Rawlins Plantation (465–6221). The dining room of this small plantation inn is famous for its luncheon buffets of West Indian cuisine by owner Claire Rawson, who is a Cordon Bleu chef. The inn is in a magnificent setting at the foot of Mt. Liamuiga. Moderately expensive.

Royal Palm (Ottley's Plantation Inn; 465–7234). Innovative cuisine by chef Pamela Yahn, who creates Caribbean-inspired dishes with Asian flavors, can be enjoyed in a spectacular *al fresco* setting. Expensive.

Victor's (9 Stanfort Street; 465–2518). This long-time favorite for West Indian cuisine is usually crowded at lunch. Reservations required for Sunday lunch. Inexpensive.

NIGHTLIFE

St. Kitts is very low-key. Nighttime entertainment takes the form of live dance music by a small combo on the patio of one of the main hotels, bars, or discos. There is a casino at *Jack Tar Village* at Frigate Bay.

SPORTS IN ST. KITTS

BEACHES/SWIMMING: Beaches are open to the public, but access may be private along some stretches. St. Kitts's best beaches are on the southeastern peninsula.

The northern Atlantic coast has stretches of black sand, which are more of a natural curiosity than good bathing beaches. On the east coast south of Black Rock, swimmers should be cautious, because there are strong currents and undertow. Conaree Beach, on the east coast, has surf.

BIKING: St. Kitts, with a good road on the lowland skirt of the mountains, reasonably light traffic, and friendly people, is well suited for biking. Inquire in advance through the Tourist Board about the availability of equipment.

BOATING: Several boats offer day trips, but boating as a sport is not well developed in St. Kitts. *OTI Pelican Watersports* (Fisherman's Wharf; 465–2754) offers a day excursion to secluded Friar's Bay for a swim, snorkeling, and fine view of Nevis. *Tropical Tours* (Cayon Street; 465–4039; fax: 465–6400) has a picnic party cruise on the *Celica III,* a large catamaran, with live calypso, swimming, and snorkeling. Both companies arrange deep sea fishing charters, too. Although the waters around St. Kitts are rich in fish, sports fishing is not developed. Local fishermen catch mackerel, barracuda, kingfish, snap-

per, grouper, and marlin among others.

GOLF: An 18-hole championship course is located at Frigate Bay adjacent to the Jack Tar Royal St. Kitts Hotel and Casino. Visitors may use the course upon payment of appropriate fees.

HIKING: The variety of hiking on St. Kitts ranges from easy rambling on country lanes to arduous trekking on volcanic peaks. With a map you can easily find your way in the lowlands and foothills. In the rain-forested mountains, however, you should have a local guide, as vegetation often obscures trails. Guided hikes are available from *Greg's Safaris* (465–4121) and *Kriss Tours* (465–4042).

HORSEBACK RIDING: Plantation roads through lush sugar and banana fields in the shadow of brooding volcanic peaks are ideal for horseback riding. *The Stable* (Trinity Inn, Conaree; 465–3226) offers half-day excursions on the windward coast and in the rain forest.

SNORKELING/SCUBA DIVING: Under the sea St. Kitts remains largely unexplored. It has extensive reefs and a diversity of sites offering walls, canyons, and caves and drift diving in some locations. But the biggest attraction is wrecks. Of 350 unexplored wrecks known to be in St. Kitts waters, only 12 have been identified. Historic records show that approximately one hundred ships were lost in Basseterre harbor in one hurricane alone.

The reef in front of Banana Bay is in about 15 feet of water and is one of the island's best snorkeling locations. It has star coral, elkhorn and brain corals, and a large variety of colorful reef fish.

A long barrier reef, known as the Grid Iron, stretches for more than 6 miles from Conaree on the east coast of St. Kitts to Newcastle Bay on Nevis at depths varying from 6 to 50 feet. It helps protect the Narrows, the shallow seabed connecting St. Kitts and Nevis. Here, a large circular reef spread over an area of about a half mile, ranges from 18 feet to 50 feet. On the south side of the reef, an area known as Monkey Shoals is thick with black coral at 35 feet. It also has a few nurse sharks, rays, and lobster.

Facilities for diving and other water sports can be found at Fisherman's Wharf. *Kenneth's Dive Centre* (Bay Road; 465–2670) is headed by

Kenneth Samuel, a PADI dive master, who offers basic instruction. *OTI Pelican Watersports* (465–2754) has a range of water sports, including diving and sport fishing.

TENNIS: Tennis courts are available at most resorts. Those closest to the port are *Ocean Terrace Inn;* arrangements to play must be made in advance. The largest complex in the Frigate Bay area is at *Jack Tar Village.*

WINDSURFING: The best locations on St. Kitts are Frigate Bay and Banana Beach Bay. Equipment is available from water-sports operators and beachfront hotels.

 **NEVIS**

S eparated from St. Kitts by a 2-mile channel and linked by ferry, Nevis appears to be a perfect, dark-green cone rising with graceful symmetry from the sea. Mount Nevis, more than 3,000 feet, is usually crowned with white clouds, as though the mountain were covered with snow. Apparently the illusion was enough to inspire Columbus to name it Las Nieves, after a range of snowcapped mountains in Spain.

After its discovery by Columbus in 1493, little happened to Nevis until 1627, when it was granted to the Earl of Carlisle. The following year Thomas Warner sent one hundred settlers from St. Kitts to establish a settlement at Jamestown. After it was destroyed by a tidal wave in 1680, the capital was moved 2 miles south to Charlestown, where it is today. Although the colony started with tobacco as its first export, by the 18th century sugar had became the main crop, bringing with it large plantations and great wealth.

The rich plantation society soon made Nevis the social hub of the Caribbean, with an international reputation as the "Queen of the Caribbees." The Bath House Hotel, built in 1778 immediately south of Charlestown amid elaborate gardens, was said to be the finest building in the Caribbean: It had a casino, where planters and traders won and lost fortunes and made big deals, and a tony brothel for the officers of visiting ships.

It became the most fashionable spa in the region, attracting English and other European aristocrats who came to its mineral springs to cure their rheumatism, gout, and similar ailments. But even before the Europeans, the Carib must have appreciated the waters, too, because their name for Nevis was Oualie (pronounced *wally*), meaning "land of beautiful water."

The springs still flow, and tourists still come to Nevis, but not for the old spa, a historic ruin that awaits renovation, but for the former plantation houses that are now some of the finest small resorts in the Caribbean. Nevis is ideal for travelers who like to wander about, curious to learn what lies down an unnamed lane or over the next hill, stopping to chat with folks they meet along the way. It's what the West Indians call "limin'," or doing nothing in particular. The best way to see the small island is on a stroll around Charlestown, where cruise ships and the ferry from St. Kitts arrive, followed by a drive around the island by taxi, or on a hiking excursion.

CHARLESTOWN Located on the west side of the island, Charlestown is a West Indian colonial village so perfectly caught in time it could be a movie set. Only 2 blocks deep and about 4 blocks long, its streets are lined with a medley of pretty old buildings, many with gingerbread trim, and only a few modern intrusions.

On the south side of the pier is the Market, best on Saturday morning, market day, when folks from all around the island come to town to buy and sell. A few steps away are the Tourist Board Office, which has maps and books on Nevis for sale, and *Nevis Philatelic Bureau,* one of the busiest places in town.

The street directly in front of the pier leads to Main Street: with the *Nevis Handicraft Cooperative* on the south, and the post office and landmark Treasury building, dating from the 18th century, on the north. A turn south on Main Street leads past the shops to the courthouse and public library, a handsome stone building dating from the late 19th century; the original 18th-century building was destroyed by fire in 1873. In front is a memorial to the fallen sons of Nevis in the First and Second world wars. Farther along, at the corner of Government Road, an old Jewish cemetery

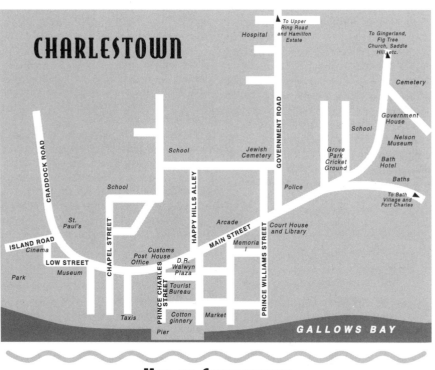

CHARLESTOWN

To Upper
Ring Road
and Hamilton
Estate

Hospital

To Gingerland,
Fig Tree
Church, Saddle
Hill, etc.

Cemetery

GOVERNMENT ROAD

Government
House

School

Nelson
Museum

School

Jewish
Cemetery

Grove
Park
Cricket
Ground

Bath
Hotel

Baths

School

Police

To Bath
Village and
Fort Charles

St.
Paul's

HAPPY HILLS ALLEY

Arcade

MAIN STREET

Court House
and Library

ISLAND ROAD

Cinema

CHAPEL STREET

Memoria
l

PRINCE WILLIAMS STREET

LOW STREET

Customs
Post House
Office

D.R.
Walwyn
Plaza

Park

Museum

PRINCE CHARLES STREET

Tourist
Bureau

Taxis

Cotton
ginnery

Market

Pier

GALLOWS BAY

MAP OF CHARLESTOWN

has tombstones dating from the 17th century, and the ruins of what may be the oldest synagogue in the Eastern Caribbean.

North on Main Street you pass some attractive shops, particularly *The Sandbox Tree* (Chapel Street) with art, antiques, beachwear, and island fashions, including made-to-order originals from silk-screen fabrics. *Knick Knacks Boutique* (469–5784), in an 18th century building on a lane off Main Street behind the Bank of Nevis, sells some of the most delightful, fun crafts by local artists to be found in the Caribbean. Best of all are cloth and carnival dolls by owner Jeannie Rigby. Also check out *Nevis Craft House,* with local crafts. On the west side of Main Street is the *Hamilton Museum,* the home of Alexander Hamilton, the first U.S. secretary of the treasury, who was born here in 1755.

Lord Nelson Museum (in a new location east of town) contains memorabilia of the famous admiral.

PINNEY'S BEACH North of Charlestown the road to Newcastle, where the airport is located, skirts the coast along 4-mile-long Pinney's Beach, an idyllic, palm fringed stretch of golden sand where the well-known Four Season Resort is located. At Cades Point a steep road leads to a hilltop high above Tamarind Bay, from which there are breathtaking views of St. Kitts and the Caribbean. It is the best place on the island to watch a spectacular Caribbean sunset. (Nevis habitués will know it as the site of the Cliffdwellers Resort, destroyed by Hurricane Hugo in 1989.)

Nevis's coast is sprinkled with springs and seasonal lagoons that fill after heavy rains, often catching fish when the waters spill over to the sea. At Nelson's Spring, a freshwater pond on the north end of Pinney's Beach, cattle egrets flock in the late afternoon to roost. This area had not been developed until 1991, when the *Four Seasons Resort* opened Nevis's first international deluxe resort. Located 3 miles north of Charlestown, it's most outstanding feature is its golf course. Another mile north is *Oualie Beach Resort,* which has one of the island's main dive and water-sports center.

NEWCASTLE On the north coast Nisbet Plantation, once the estate of Frances Nisbet, the wife of the famous British Admiral Lord Nelson, is now an antique-filled plantation inn, *Nisbet Beach Resort,* with a magnificent lawn that flows to the beach between double rows of stately palms and flowering gardens. With a little imagination you can easily envision the opulent life here in Nevis's heyday.

Nearby at Newcastle Pottery, you can watch pottery made from Nevis's rich red-clay soil being shaped and fired in traditional ways. The pottery is available for sale.

BATH STREAM On the south side of Charlestown are the ruins of the famous Bath spa and stream whose waters supply the spa. There is a small bathhouse still in use by local people. Plans to renovate and rebuild the spa have been discussed often, but languish for lack of funds.

FIG TREE VILLAGE The main road turns inland to Fig Tree Village and St. John's Church, where the book of records is open to the page that recorded the marriage of Lord Nelson and Frances Nisbet in 1787. Admiral Nelson, who was headquartered at the British naval base in Antigua, was first attracted to Nevis for its fresh water to supply his ships. Then he discovered Frances Nisbet, a widow of a wealthy plantation owner. The best man at their wedding—the Duke of Clarence—later became King William IV of England. The marriage took place at the Montpelier greathouse, which belonged to Frances Nisbet's uncle at the time. It is now restored as an inn, set in beautiful gardens. It can be reached on a side road south of Morning Star village, *Nelson Museum* contains memorabilia of the famous admiral; visitors are welcome.

GINGERLAND Beyond Morning Star, the area known locally as Gingerland has *Hermitage Plantation, Croney's Old Manor Estate,* and *Golden Rock Estate*—former plantations whose greathouses or sugar mills have been converted into inns. All are situated at about 1,000 feet elevation, on the southern slopes of Mount Nevis.

RAINFOREST TRAIL A trail through the rain forest on the side of Mount Nevis leaves from Stonyhill, above Golden Rock Estate, and winds north through groves of cacao, breadfruit, and nutmeg trees and overlooks the Atlantic coast. Vervet monkeys can be seen frequently on the walk. *Golden Rock Estate* has a map for a self-guided walk.

MOUNT NEVIS Dominating the landscape in every direction is cloud-covered Mt. Nevis. Dormant since its last eruption in 1692, it continues to emit hot sulphurous gases. The crater is a half-mile wide and almost 800 feet deep. A very difficult trail of about 2 miles leads to the crater rim—for experienced hikers only. New less strenuous trails are being developed, though, at a lower level on the mountainside. (See Hiking section.)

SPORTS

Four Seasons resort on Pinney's Beach has the best facilities, but they are expensive.

BEACHES/SWIMMING: All beaches are open to the public, and the 4-mile stretch of reef-protected *Pinney's Beach* is the standout. *Oualie Beach,* north of Pinney's Beach, is another fine, more-open strand of golden sand with surf and is popular for windsurfing.

DEEP-SEA FISHING: *Mt. Nevis Beach Club* (469–9395) and *Oualie Beach Club* (469–5329) arrange sports-fishing trips.

GOLF: The 18-hole championship layout by Robert Trent Jones is part of the *Four Seasons* resort. It overlooks Pinney's Beach and the Caribbean, with lofty Mt. Nevis as a backdrop.

HIKING: Nevis's web of country lanes and footpaths provides a delightful variety of hiking for ramblers. With a map it is easy to find your way. *Rainforest Trail* on the slopes of Mt. Nevis can be covered without a guide. The Nevis Historical and Conservation Society (469–5786), with help from the U.S. Peace Corps, has developed six easy to strenuous trails on Mount Nevis accessible from various locations and has a brochure describing them. *Eco-Tours Nevis* (469–2091) offers three walking tours on a regular schedule throughout the week. Cost US $10 to US $20 per person.

HORSEBACK RIDING: Nevis's lush countryside and hills are a wonderful setting for horseback riding. Inquire at the Nevis Equestrian Centre, (Cole Hill; 469–2638).

SNORKELING/SCUBA DIVING: Nevis's underwater world is even less explored than that of St. Kitts. The island is completely surrounded by reefs, some within swimming distance of shore. The best snorkeling locations are off *Pinney's Beach.* The *Grid Iron,* the barrier reef that stretches across the Narrows between Nevis and St. Kitts, starts at Newcastle Bay on the north coast of Nevis. *Scuba Safaris* (Oualie Beach; 469–9518) has PADI and NAUI instructors and offers diving trips for US $70. It also has glass-bottom boat cruises.

TENNIS: Four Seasons' tennis complex is one of the largest in the Eastern Caribbean.

WINDSURFING: The best location is the north-west coast from Cades Bay to Newcastle. Equipment can be rented from the *Oualie Beach Club.*

Montserrat

PLYMOUTH

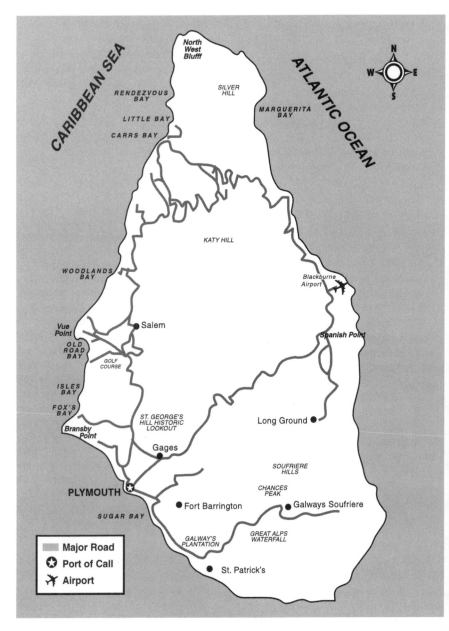

CARIBBEAN SEA

ATLANTIC OCEAN

North West Blufff

SILVER HILL

RENDEZVOUS BAY

MARGUERITA BAY

LITTLE BAY

CARRS BAY

KATY HILL

WOODLANDS BAY

Blackburne Airport

Vue Point

• Salem

OLD ROAD BAY

Spanish Point

GOLF COURSE

ISLES BAY

FOX'S BAY

ST. GEORGE'S HILL HISTORIC LOOKOUT

Long Ground •

Bransby Point

Gages

SOUFRIERE HILLS

PLYMOUTH

CHANCES PEAK

• Fort Barrington

• Galways Soufriere

SUGAR BAY

GALWAY'S PLANTATION

GREAT ALPS WATERFALL

• St. Patrick's

Major Road

Port of Call

Airport

AT A GLANCE

CHAPTER CONTENTS

A QUIET CORNER OF THE CARIBBEAN

NOTE TO READERS: *Since July 1995, volcanic eruptions in the southern half of the island have plagued Montserrat, and the area south of the Belham Valley has been declared off limits to both visitors and residents. The residents and businesses who were in this area, including those in the capital of Plymouth, have had to leave and move north. Most have resettled north of Plymouth in the area of Salem where life continues as normal as can be expected.*

It is hard to know at this writing when the situation will change because volcanoes are unpredictable. We have retained this chapter because some small cruise ships continue to call, and some tourists visit. Indeed for naturalists, environmentalists, and adventurous travelers, now is probably the most interesting time of all to visit Montserrat.

Known as the Emerald Isle of the West, Montserrat has the distinction of being the only place in the Caribbean settled by the Irish. The title also comes from the island's physical resemblance to Ireland, as velvet green as ever a place could be. The early settlers also left their mark in the names of people and places, evident throughout the island. And to honor them all, a shamrock is mounted on the governor's mansion, visitors' passports are stamped with a shamrock, and St. Patrick's Day is a public holiday.

This quiet corner of the Leeward Islands, 27 miles southwest of Antigua, promotes itself as "The Caribbean as it Used to Be," in praise of its uncommercialized ambience and natural environment. Mostly of volcanic origin, pear-shaped Montserrat rises quickly from a narrow belt of lowlands and foothills to mountains covered with tropical rain forests dominated by 3,002-foot Chance's Peak, the highest point.

Montserrat was sighted by Christopher Columbus in 1493, and, according to tradition, he gave the island its name because its serrated peaks reminded him of the mountain range surrounding Santa Marie de Monserrate, a monastery near Barcelona. The Spaniards apparently had no interest in the island, and the hills and forests were left to the Carib Indians until the middle of the 17th century, when the first European settlers arrived.

The Irish came to Montserrat in 1632, fleeing religious persecution on nearby St. Kitts. The French and British subsequently fought over the island until 1783, when Montserrat was ceded to Britain in the Treaty of Versailles. It remains a British crown colony.

Sugar and a plantation society based on the labor of African slaves dominated the island throughout the 18th century. Limes and, later, cotton were introduced after emancipation in the early 19th century. Today bananas are the main crop, with some production of limes and cotton.

FAST FACTS

POPULATION: 7,000

SIZE: 11 miles long and 7 miles wide; 39 sq. miles.

MAIN TOWNS: Plymouth; Salem

GOVERNMENT: Montserrat is a British crown colony, whose governor is appointed by the Queen.

CURRENCY: Eastern Caribbean dollar. US $1 equals EC $2.64. U.S. dollars are used widely, but credit cards are not.

DEPARTURE TAX: US $10

LANGUAGE: English

PUBLIC HOLIDAYS: January 1, New Year's Day; March 17, St. Patrick's Day; Good Friday; Labour Day; Whit

Monday; June 9, Queen's Birthday; August Monday (first Monday); December 25, Christmas Day; December 26, Boxing Day; December 31, Festival Day.

 TELEPHONE AREA CODE: 664. When calling from the United States, dial 491 plus the local four-digit number.

 AIRLINES: International carriers connect with LIAT flights in Antigua for the 15-minute flight to Montserrat. Blackburne Airport is on the east coast, 8 winding miles from Plymouth.

 **INFORMATION:**

In the United States:

Montserrat Tourist Board, c/o Caribbean Tourism Organization, 20 East 46th Street, New York, NY 10017; (212) 682–0435.
Caribbean Connection, P.O. Box 261, Trumbull, CT 06611;
(203) 261–8603; (800) 893–1100.

In Port:

Montserrat Tourist Board, P.O. Box 7, Plymouth, Montserrat; 491–2230.
Montserrat National Trust, Parliament Street, Plymouth, Montserrat; 491–7430.

 **Port Profile:**

LOCATION/EMBARKATION: The cruise ship port of entry is Plymouth, on the west coast but for now, cruise ships anchor offshore and tender passengers to Old Road Bay.

LOCAL TRANSPORTATION: Taxis and car rentals are available from the Vue Pointe Hotel, the major hotel and base of most tourist activity.

ROADS AND RENTALS: Montserrat has a network of paved roads that serve most parts of the island. The main road winds north around hillsides that skirt the island's main beaches. Blackburne Airport, on the rockbound east coast, is linked to the west coast by a magnificent road that was an engineering feat that took three years to complete. North from the airport, it zigs and

zags along the east coast with fabulous seascapes and views of Antigua in the distance. After about 5 miles the road turns west and winds through the hills of the north, joining the main north-south leeward road at Carrs Bay.

Given the difficult nature of the driving if you're unfamiliar with the narrow mountain roads and left-hand drive, you might prefer to hire a taxi. This way you are free to enjoy the beautiful scenery and listen to the driver, who is likely to be an animated storyteller as well as a guide. You can obtain information on their services by contacting Caribbean Connection, Box 261, Trumbull, CT 06611 (203) 261–8603; (800) 893–1100.

EMERGENCY NUMBERS:

Medical:
Hospital, 491–2552/3;
Dental surgeon, 491–5604;
Ambulance, 491–2253
Police: Dial 999

 **Shore Excursions**

Sightseeing excursions are available by taxi, for four persons, or by small minibuses for up to eight people, but most visitors might prefer to enjoy a sport—golf, diving, or hiking—because sights such as the *Great Alps Waterfalls, Galways Soufrière,* and *Galways Estate Ruins,* a landmark restoration project of a former sugar plantation, are off limits at present.

You might also visit some hideaways of the rich and famous, and lunch on local specialties at one of their favorite hangouts, *The Village Place,* a casual bar and restaurant in Salem.

 **MONTSERRAT ON YOUR OWN**

At press time Plymouth was off limits to visitors. Check locally to learn if the ban has been lifted.

The capital Plymouth is a small West Indian town of British colonial architecture interspersed with modern buildings. On the south side of town is the house of the governor, a Victorian mansion surrounded by pretty gardens. (The governor has taken up temporary residence in Olveston.)

North of town the last few hundred yards of Parliament Street become Church Road and end at the gate of *St. Anthony's Church*, the state church. Built originally in 1636, the church was ravaged by earthquakes, war, and hurricanes and rebuilt many times. The present building, constructed in part with stones from previous churches, dates from early in this century.

MONTSERRAT MUSEUM North of Plymouth is the Montserrat Museum. Housed in the mill of a former sugar plantation, it covers Montserrat's history from pre-Columbian times to the present. There are natural-history exhibits as well. The museum, operated by the Montserrat National Trust with a volunteer staff. (Temporarily closed.)

The trust is also responsible for the renovation of historic sites around the island; excavation of pre-Columbian sites; conservation programs that have established the Woodlands Beach Picnic Area and the Fox's Bay Bird Sanctuary; and flora and fauna research that brings scientists and other experts to the island. Under its guidance a national park system is being established with a grant from the World Wildlife Fund.

FOX'S BAY BIRD SANCTUARY On the coast 3 miles northwest of Plymouth is a fifteen-acre protected wildlife area established by the trust in 1979. The sanctuary is a mangrove and bog with a central pond that is the nesting area for coots, gallinules, and other waterfowl. There are several species of heron, of which the cattle egrets number more than one thousand. The sanctuary is encircled by a nature trail that ends at the beach where there are facilities for swimming and picnicking.

Montserrat has almost one hundred species of birds, some migratory. The endemic black-and-yellow Montserrat oriole, the national bird, dwells in mountainous areas. Among the island's thirty breeding species are three species of hummingbirds. (Check locally to learn if the area is off limits.)

CASTLE PEAK Up the hill from the Vue Pointe Hotel, which has a great view of the rumbling volcano, is the volcano's scientific observatory.

Travellers interested in volcanoes are welcome to visit and speak to the experts who man the center 24 hours a day.

Castle Peak is also the name of the island's newest volcano. It seems to be teasing the islanders with its capricious behavior of alternating between activity and quiet since July 1995. Indeed volcano watching has become a full time pastime for both visitors and residents. No other Caribbean island offers such an intimate and awesome look at Mother Nature as this. Some lava has flowed into the sea on the southeast coast. When the volcano is active, you may see the dome's red glow on a starlit night; when it's quiet, you may not even be aware of its occasional ash cloud that is normally swept south by the winds.

SOUTHERN MONTSERRAT

Due to volcanic activity, Montserrat's most popular attractions in the southern third of the island are considered unsafe and off limits to visitors and even to residents without special permission.

GALWAYS ESTATE: Three miles south of Plymouth are the ruins of a sugar plantation that was started in the mid-17th century and operated more than 250 years. In 1990 it was selected by the Smithsonian Institute as a preservation project for the Columbus Quincentennial; excavations have been underway for almost a decade, under the auspices of the Montserrat National Trust, aided by specialists from the University of Tennessee and Boston University, as well as Earthwatch and Partners for Liveable Places, among others.

Before excavation began in 1981, the foliage, allowed to run wild after the plantation was abandoned, had become so dense that structures could no longer be recognized. The ruins include a sugar mill and boiling house, windmill tower, cattle mill, greathouse, cisterns, and other structures, many of them built of beautifully cut stone.

GALWAYS SOUFRIÈRE The southern third of Montserrat is dominated by the Soufrière Hills, several of whose peaks are covered with rain forest. Galways Soufrière is an active boiling volcanic fissure at 1,700 feet. Known as the *Devil's Playground*, the barren landscape is a treacherous field of unstable rocks with a witch's brew of boiling mud, hissing steam, and the strong smell of sulphurous vapors.

GREAT ALPS WATERFALL Water from Galways Soufrière forms the White River, which begins with falls of 70 feet, Great Alps Falls, on the south side of the mountain. The cascade tumbles through lush vegetation into a shallow rock pool. Depending on the time of year and the rainfall, it can be a heavy rush of water or a gentle shower.

SHOPPING

Many of the stores, formerly in Plymouth, have moved to new locations, mainly in and around Salem, a hamlet north of Plymouth.

While most services of a centralized business community are available, finding a grocery store or bank is something of a treasure hunt, unless you ask a local resident who will happily help you with directions, give you a ready smile, and may even escort you.

One of the best known stores is *Arrows Man Shop,* which belongs to Montserrat's international calypsonian and soca star, The Mighty Arrow, whose real name is Alphonso Cassell. "Hot, Hot, Hot" is one of his best-known hits. His autographed recordings are also available, and he might even be there to autograph your copy.

DINING AND RESTAURANTS

Montserrat's native cuisine is West Indian with British and French influences. The most popular dish is mountain chicken, or frogs' legs, as we know them. Known locally by its creole name, *crapaud,* the large frog is hunted at night after rainy spells. Also hunted for its meat is the *agouti,* a rabbit-size, tailless rodent that was once abundant in the Lesser Antilles and is now extinct on most islands. Goat Water, another popular dish, is an adaptation of Irish stew substituting goat meat for beef and seasoned with rum and cloves.

Belham Valley Restaurant, on a hillside overlooking the golf course, is considered one of the best on island. It is open for lunch and dinner. *The Kitchen Table* (Salem) serves rôtis, patties similar to turnovers stuffed with meat or chicken and potato, flavored with curry; and local dishes, along with hamburgers. *Emerald Cafe* (Salem) specializes in fish and salads, and *Oasis Cafe* (Salem) has mountain chicken.

Other fun places to eat are *The Village Place* in Salem; and *The Gourmet Garden* in Olveston, next to *Duchers Studio,* which has nice gifts to take home. Ask a resident and you'll find *Alla* (known to one and all when she formerly was at *The Attic*) at lunch time selling her famous rôtis from a colorful roadside stand. Seek out, too, the new location for *Harbour Court Ice Cream,* which specializes in tropical flavors such as mango, coconut, and passionfruit.

SPORTS IN MONTSERRAT

BEACHES/SWIMMING: *Vue Pointe,* the main hotel and base of most tourist activity, has a freshwater pool, shuffleboard, and access to scuba diving and windsurfing. The island's best and most-accessible beaches stretch north along the Caribbean coast. Most are secluded strands of black or gray sand bracketed by rock cliffs with calm, clear water for swimming and snorkeling in shallow water. None has been developed commercially: They are *Isles Bay; Woodlands Beach,* where the National Trust has a picnic site; *Carrs Bay,* and *Little Bay,* where the sand is a butterscotch color.

The only white-sand stretch, *Rendezvous Beach,* is surrounded by steep cliffs and is usually reached by boat from Little Bay, directly to the south. Alternatively, you can hike on an inland path from Little Bay to Rendezvous in about 40 minutes, or make a steep 30-minute climb over the bluff separating the two bays. During the winter season, a boat departs from Vue Point Hotel (5711) to Isles Bay.

GOLF: The *Montserrat Golf Club* (also known as the Belham Valley Golf Club; 5220) is situated on two hundred acres in a beautiful tropical setting of the Belham Valley. The club is a favorite gathering place for residents and expatriates, open to visitors year-round. The 11-hole golf course is arranged to play as two 9-hole ones. Visitors green fees are US $30 per day.

HIKING AND BIKING: The Montserrat Government and the National Trust with aid from the World Wildlife Fund (U.K.), are developing a national park system with walking and hiking trails. Inquire at the Tourist Board in Salem. Visitors can make arrangements for a guide there, too. New trails are being developed on the north end of the island, particularly the path between *Little Bay* and *Rendezvous Bay,* and in the Centre Hills. Mountain bikes are popular on the island and can be rented at *Island Bikes.* Vue Pointe and other hotels have walking and hiking maps for jaunts on or near their properties.

TENNIS: Courts are available at *Vue Pointe Hotel.*

WATER SPORTS: Arrangements for deep-sea fishing, windsurfing, and boating can be made at Old Road Beach next to the Vue Pointe Hotel or next door at *Isles Bay.* Snorkeling or diving trips for experienced divers are available with Montserrat's only certified, licensed PADI instructor, *Wolf Dive Shop,* who rents filled tanks, belts, and other equipment for reasonable fees.

FESTIVALS AND CELEBRATIONS

The *Christmas Festival* is Montserrat's version of Carnival and begins officially on December 20. But actually it starts in November with preview activities when masqueraders begin rehearsing their quadrilles and polkas. There are calypso contests and performances by bands, groups, and schools. Once an adult art rooted in African folklore, masquerading is now done by children, who perform on holidays and for arriving cruise ships. Competitions, concerts, pageants, and parties keep revellers on the go during the festival until New Year's Day. The Queen's Parade, from Sturge Park, a five-acre green on the north side of town, to Marine Drive, is held on December 31.

Guadeloupe

POINTE-À-PITRE, GUADELOUPE; BASSE-TERRE, GUADELOUPE; ILES DES SAINTES, MARIE-GALENTE

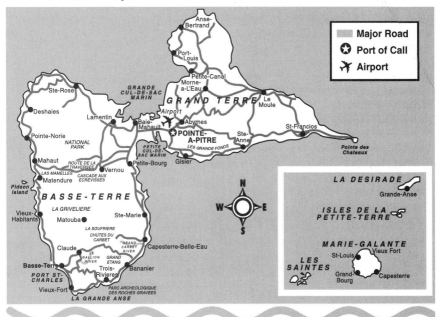

AT A GLANCE

Antiquities	★★
Architecture	★★
Art and Artists	★★
Beaches	★★
Colonial Buildings	★★
Crafts	★★
Cuisine	★★★
Culture	★★
Dining/Restaurants	★★★★
Entertainment	★★
Forts	★★★
History	★★
Monuments	★
Museums	★★★
Nightlife	★★
Scenery	★★★★★
Shopping	★★
Sight-seeing	★★★★
Sports	★★★★
Transportation	★★★

CHAPTER CONTENTS

THE CARIBBEAN IN MINIATURE

Guadeloupe is actually two islands shaped like butterfly wings. The two parts—Basse-Terre and Grande-Terre—are separated by a narrow channel and connected by a short bridge. No two islands in the Caribbean are more different.

Guadeloupe is also a small archipelago comprised of Marie-Galante, Les Saintes, and La Désirade. Together they make up a Caribbean-in-miniature with the full range of natural features and beauty for which the region is known, along with good facilities to enjoy them.

Grande-Terre, the eastern wing of Guadeloupe, is a flat, dry limestone island, densely populated and developed. It has Guadeloupe's largest town, Pointe-à-Pitre, the business and commercial capital and main cruise port. The south coast is the main resort area, with long strands of white-sand beaches along its quiet Caribbean shores where many cruise passengers often elect to spend their day.

In contrast Basse-Terre, the western wing, is a volcanic island dominated by a spine of steep, forest-green mountains climbing to 5,000 feet and mostly covered by the 74,100-acre Natural Park. From their lofty peaks, where up to 400 inches of rain fall annually, spectacular waterfalls rush over rocky cliffs, crash through canyons, and career through the mountains, forming the rivers and streams that irrigate an emerald skirt of sugarcane and banana fields along Basse-Terre's east coast. Basse-Terre is both the name of the island and of its main town, which is also the capital of Guadeloupe, on the southwest coast. Offshore are the Iles des Saintes, or Les Saintes, also of volcanic origin.

When Christopher Columbus came upon the islands in 1493, he sailed north from Dominica to the island he named Marie-Galante for his flagship, which had brought him there. He arrived in Guadeloupe at the place known today as Sainte-Marie de la Capesterre, on the east coast of Basse-Terre, claimed the island for Spain. Several attempts by the Spaniards to settle Guadeloupe were repulsed by the fierce Caribs, and a permanent European settlement was not established until after France took possession of the island in the early 17th century. Under the patronage of Cardinal Richelieu, French entrepreneurs formed "La Compagnie des Iles d'Amérique" to develop Guadeloupe. In 1635 it sent two noblemen, Charles Liénard de l'Olive and Jean Duplessis d'Ossonville, and a group from Normandy and Touraine to make a settlement.

For the next five years they fought the Caribs and drove them away to neighboring islands. The French cleared the land, introduced sugar and other crops, and imported slaves from Africa to work the land. In 1674 Guadeloupe was officially annexed by France, but for the next century it continued to be the scene of intense rivalry between France and Britain.

During the French Revolution Guadeloupe was occupied by Britain, but it was reconquered in 1794 by Victor Hugues, who abolished slavery. When Napoleon came to power, however, he reinstituted slavery. Through the efforts of Victor Schoelcher, a national hero today, slavery was abolished permanently in 1848. In the following years indentured workers from India were imported to work the cane fields.

In 1946 Guadeloupe was officially designated a French *département* with the same status as a *département* of metropolitan France, in the way that the Hawaiian Islands are a state of the United States. In 1974 Guadeloupe and her satellite islands, along with St. Barts and French St. Martin, were given the further status of *région*. Martinique is a separate *région*. Together they form the French West Indies, whose people are culturally French and citizens of France in all respects.

FAST FACTS

POPULATION: 408,000

SIZE: 583 sq. miles

MAIN TOWNS: Basse-Terre, Pointe-à-Pitre

GOVERNMENT: Guadeloupe is a *région* of France with a prefect appointed by the French Minister of the Interior. The prefect is assisted by two general secretaries and two sub-prefects, one for Pointe-à-Pitre and the other for St. Martin and St. Barthélemy, 125 miles to the north.

CURRENCY: French franc. US $1 fluctuates around 5 Ff. U.S. and Canadian currency are widely accepted. Banks are open Monday to Friday from 8:00 A.M.–noon and 2:00–4:00 P.M.

DEPARTURE TAX: None

FIREARMS: Yachts are permitted to have firearms on board, but they must be declared.

LANGUAGE: French and Creole. English is spoken in hotels by the manager and front-desk staff, but the personnel in stores, restaurants, and other tourist facilities are likely to speak French only. Non-French speakers should carry a French phrase book and a pocket dictionary when they strike out on their own.

PUBLIC HOLIDAYS: January 1, New Year's Day; Easter Monday; May 1, Labor Day; Ascension Thursday; Pentecost Monday; May 27, Slavery Abolition Day; July 14, Bastille Day; July 21, Schoelcher Day; August 15, Assumption Day; November 1, All Saints Day; November 11, Armistice Day; December 25, Christmas.

TELEPHONE: To phone station-to-station from the United States, dial 011–590 plus the local number; for person-to-person dial 01–590 plus local number. To phone from Guadeloupe, *Télécartes* (sold at post offices and outlets marked TÉLÉCARTE VENTE ICI are used in special booths marked *Télécom* throughout the island.

AIRLINES: American Airlines from U.S. cities via San Juan; Air France from Miami. Minerve Airlines flies directly from New York during the winter season. LIAT (82–12–26) provides scheduled service between Guadeloupe and major islands in the Eastern Caribbean. Air Guadeloupe (82–21–61) serves the French West Indies islands daily; Caraibes Air Tourisme flies to Les Saintes twice daily.

INFORMATION:

In the United States: (888) 4–GUADELOUPE
New York: French Government Tourist Board, 444 Madison Avenue, New York, NY 10022; (212) 838–7855; fax: (212) 838–7855.

Also French Government Tourist Offices:
Chicago: 676 N. Michigan Avenue, Chicago, IL 60611; (312) 751–7800
Los Angeles: 9454 Wilshire Boulevard No. 715, Beverly Hills, CA 90212; (213) 271–6665.

In Canada:
Montreal: 1981 Avenue McGill College, No. 490, Montreal, P.Q. H3A 2W9; (514) 288–4264; fax: (514) 844–8901.
Toronto: 30 Saint Patrick Street, No. 700, Toronto, Ont. MGT 3A3; (416) 593–6427; fax: (416) 979–7587.

In Port:
Guadeloupe Tourist Office (Office Départemental du Tourisme), 5 Square de la Banque, 97181 Cedex Pointe-à-Pitre, Guadeloupe, F.W.I.; 82–09–30; fax: 83–89–22.
Maps, magazines, and brochures are available.

BUDGET PLANNING

Guadeloupe is an expensive island, particularly for taxis and restaurants. An average meal for one person in an ordinary restaurant can cost $25, and in one of the better establishments, it will be

$40 and up. All service charges—taxes and tips—are included in the prices. You do not need to add more tip unless you want to. If you speak French and have the time to use local buses, you can travel economically. Otherwise you should plan to take one of the shore excursions offered by your cruise lines, or if you can share with others, hire a taxi or rent a car for touring.

PORT PROFILE:

LOCATION/EMBARKATION: Pointe-à-Pitre, Basse-Terre, and the offshore islands of Les Saintes are regular cruise ports; Marie-Galante is an occasional one. Pointe-à-Pitre has five berths and can accommodate the largest liners; Basse-Terre has one. Most cruise ships use Pointe-à-Pitre, where they dock directly in the heart of downtown only a block from the shopping district and the Tourist Office. The port complex, St. John Perse Center, opened in 1991 and has a hotel, restaurants, bars, several government ministries, and shops.

LOCAL TRANSPORTATION: Inexpensive easy-to-use public buses linking the main towns of Guadeloupe operate from 5:30 A.M. to 7:30 P.M. In Pointe-à-Pitre buses for Gosier and the south coast depart from Darse Station, near the dock and Tourist Office; those to the north and central regions depart from Mortenol Station. Buses connecting Grande-Terre with Basse-Terre leave from the Bergevin Station on the north side of town. Buses stop at signs marked *arret-bus*, or you can wave to the driver to stop. Few drivers—very few—speak English.

Due to their short time in port, cruise passengers usually prefer to use taxis, but they are expensive. They are plentiful at the port upon the arrival of cruise ships. Most drivers are looking for cruise passengers they can take on island tours, so expect a certain amount of hustling. (Do not count on them to speak English.)

The taxi stand closest to the port is Place de la Victoire near the Tourist Office. From Pointe-à-Pitre to the airport is about $20, and to Gosier hotels $20. A 40 percent surcharge is added from 9:00 P.M. to 7:00 A.M. and all day Sunday and holidays. For radio cabs call 82–15–09.

ROADS AND RENTALS: Guadeloupe has a network of excellent roads covering 1,225 miles. You can make a complete loop around either Basse-Terre or Grande-Terre and explore their interiors, except for certain parts of Basse-Terre. But due to the nature of the terrain, distances can be deceiving and often take double the amount of time you are likely to plan.

A self-drive car is the best way to tour the island; rates for car rentals are comparable to those in the United States and Europe. A valid driver's license is needed. Driving is on the right, and traffic regulations and road signs are like those in Europe. Drivers here tend to speed.

Car-rental companies in Pointe-à-Pitre open weekdays from 8:00 A.M. to noon and 2:30 to 5:00; Saturdays to noon or 1:00 P.M. Among the major car-rental companies are *Avis* (82–33–47); *Budget* (90–26–37); *Hertz* (91–00–63), and *Kemwel* (91–55–66; fax: 91–22–88). There are also independent companies; you can get a list from the Tourist Office.

Bicycles and motorbikes can be rented from *Dingo* (Place de la Victoire, two blocks from the port, 83–81–19). Vespas cost 100 Ff to 150 Ff per day with unlimited mileage.

FERRY SERVICES: From Pointe-à-Pitre to Les Saintes, *Express des Iles* (83–12–45) operates daily except Tuesday and Thursday; fare is about $32 round-trip. To Marie-Galante, ferries leave most days at 8:00 A.M. from Pointe-à-Pitre; fare is about $32 round-trip for the 2-hour crossing. (Both locations have daily air service from Pointe-à-Pitre.)

From Trois-Rivières on Basse-Terre (1.5 hour's drive from Pointe-à-Pitre), ferries leave twice daily at 8:00 A.M. and 4:00 P.M. for Les Saintes; the trip takes about 30 minutes. They also depart from the town of Basse-Terre to Les Saintes.

EMERGENCY NUMBERS:

Medical: Centre Hospitalier de Pointe-à-Pitre 82–98–80.

The Tourist Office can assist in locating English-speaking doctors.

Ambulance/SOS service: 24 hours a day, 82–89–33.

Police: Pointe-à-Pitre, 82–00–05; Basse-Terre 81–11–55.

AUTHOR'S FAVORITE ATTRACTIONS

HIKING IN THE NATURAL PARK
DAY TRIP TO LES SAINTES

SHORE EXCURSIONS

If you enjoy spectacular scenery, hiking in a rain forest, and picnicking in the woods, Basse-Terre will be your first choice. If beaching or biking are preferences, you will have the best of both in Grande-Terre. A Tourist Office booklet entitled "Guadeloupe Excursions" maps out six itineraries for self-drive tours. Similar tours can be made by taxi, and some are available as motorcoach tours. From my experience guides in Guadeloupe score the best in the Caribbean for knowledge about their island. Tours begin in Pointe-à-Pitre; prices and duration will vary, depending on the cruise line and tour company. Places mentioned here are described later in the chapter.

Basse-Terre to the Carbet Falls/Grand Etang, 4 hrs., 400 Ff. After skirting the east coast of Basse-Terre to St.-Sauveur, you turn inland to Carbet Falls. Longer versions include Grand Etang, an inland lake, or the town of Basse-Terre.

Basse-Terre to the Soufrière Volcano, 8 hours, 800 Ff. Same as above tour but instead of turning inland to Carbet Falls, it continues to Basse-Terre and winds up the mountains to La Soufrière Volcano.

Natural Park/Southern Basse-Terre, 8 hours, 800 Ff. The route crosses the Natural Park from east to west, where there are trails and picnic sites. On the west coast it turns south to Vieux Habitants, along the magnificent scenery of the Grande Rivière to La Grivelière, a coffee plantation. The return is via Basse-Terre, Archaeological Park, and east coast.

Grand Tour of Grande-Terre, 4–5 hours, 500 Ff. From the resort town of Gosier, the drive follows the south coast to Pointe-des-Châteaux; east coast to Le Moule; and around to the west coast at Petit-Canal and Morne-à-l'Eau.

GUADELOUPE ON YOUR OWN

Pointe-à-Pitre is the commercial center and main city of Guadeloupe. As early as the mid-18th century, its value as a well-protected, deep-water harbor was recognized by the English and the French, who took turns at building the city and fortifying the nearby hills. And it thrived despite fires, earthquakes, and hurricanes. Today the city has a slightly tatty look with an architectural diversity of wooden houses with wrought-iron balconies, in the small narrow streets of the old town juxtaposed against modern commercial and government buildings.

A POINTE-À-PITRE WALKABOUT

Pointe-à-Pitre can be explored easily on foot. *The St. John Perse Center* (1), a hotel and shopping complex at the port, was designed with cruise passengers in mind. The center is accessible to local citizens as well.

A short walk will put you in the heart of Pointe-à-Pitre at *Place de la Victoire* (2), a garden square shaded by royal palms and sandbox trees. They were planted in 1794 by Victor Hugues on the day after his victory against the British. The square is bordered by colonial-style houses that lend an Old World atmosphere to the town. Many have been renovated to house boutiques and sidewalk cafes.

The *Tourist Office* (3) is on the southwest corner of the square. One of the town's several markets, a lively vegetable-and-fish market, is on the south by the harborfront. Walking west along rue Peynier, you will cross the main shopping streets of rue Nozières, rue Frébault, and rue Schoelcher, where boutiques stock perfume, china, and other French goods. At the corner of Peynier and Frébault is the *Central Market* (4), a large town plaza where lady vendors sell tropical flowers, fruits and vegetables, spices, and crafts. West of the market, in a pink ornate colonial building on

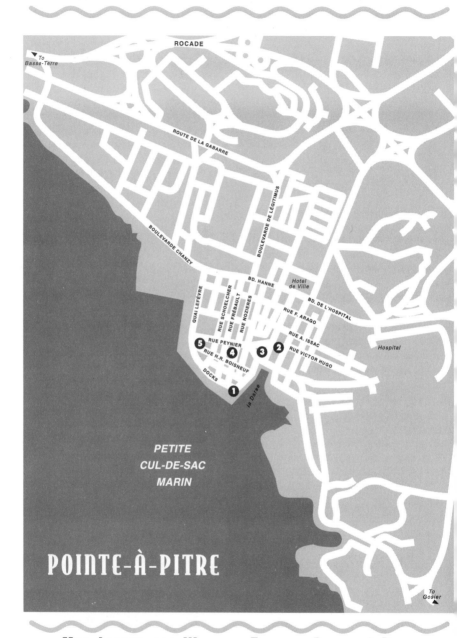

Map Legend for Walking Tour of Pointe-à-Pitre

1. St. John Perse Center
2. Place de la Victorie
3. Tourist Office
4. Central Market
5. Schoelcher

rue Peynier, is the *Schoelcher Museum* (5). It is dedicated to the leading French abolitionist of his time, who led the fight to end slavery in the French West Indies. Nearby on rue René-Boisneuf, a plaque at No. 54 marks the birthplace of Nobel Prize–winning poet St. John Perse and the *Saint-John Perse Museum,* which opened for his centennial in 1987.

A DRIVE AROUND THE ISLAND

To Basse-Terre: From Pointe-à-Pitre you cross Pont de la Gabare, the bridge over the Rivière Salée, the channel separating the two parts of Guadeloupe. After 2 miles you'll come to the Destrellan traffic circle, where you can turn south on highway N 1 to Basse-Terre town and the Soufrière Volcano; or turn north on N 2 to Le Lamentin, Ste.-Rose, and the beaches and fishing villages of northern Basse-Terre. A third option is to go to the N 1/D 23 intersection at Versailles and turn west on Route de la Traversée, the east-west highway that crosses the heart of the Natural Park.

SOUTHERN BASSE-TERRE

Basse-Terre's southeastern coast, from Petit-Bourg to Capesterre-Belle-Eau and Bananier, stretches in green fields of banana plantations from the sea, bordered by small villages and pretty beaches, to the brooding peaks of the Soufrière mountains. The coast south of Petit-Bourg is popular for swimming and scuba diving; offshore, tiny Ilet Fortune is a nudist beach. Farther along, Ste.-Marie has a monument commemorating Columbus' landing in 1493. At Changy a Hindu temple is one of several reminders of the multiracial makeup of the French West Indies.

Capesterre-Belle-Eau has a cassava-processing plant where you can watch cassava flour and bread being made. Cassava was a staple of the Amerindians, who taught early European explorers to use it and it continues to be a basic food of the West Indies. En route from Capesterre to St. Sauveur, the road passes through Allée Dumanoir, one of the most photographed settings of

Guadeloupe, where the route is lined with stately century-old royal palms.

CARBET FALLS (Chutes du Carbet) A detour inland at St. Sauveur takes you to the imposing Carbet Falls and the Grand Etang, a inland lake whose tranquil waters mirror the lush landscape surrounding it. From the eastern slopes of the Soufrière volcano, waters cascade more than 800 feet in three stages, forming the tallest falls in the Caribbean and creating the Grand Carbet River that empties into the sea at Capesterre-Belle-Eau.

GRAND ETANG (Grand Pond) Situated at 1,312 feet altitude, Grand Etang is the largest of several ponds in the area, covering fifty acres in a hot, humid atmosphere and creating a greenhouse that nurtures giant philodendron and ferns, orchids, anthurium, bromeliads, and other rain-forest vegetation not normally found at lower altitudes. The quiet pond—a striking contrast to tumbling Carbet Falls—was created when lava from a volcanic eruption blocked the St. Sauveur River.

ARCHAEOLOGICAL PARK (Parc Archéologique des Roches Gravées) Near Trois-Rivières on the road to the ferry for Les Saintes, there is an outdoor museum with petroglyphs of the Carib Indians, the pre-Columbian inhabitants of Guadeloupe. The drawings date from about A.D. 300 and depict animal and human figures. A footpath is bordered with cassava, cacao, calabash, pimiento, and other plants the Indians cultivated.

All along the drive of southern Basse-Terre, the dark green Soufrière mountains loom high on the western landscape. To go directly to the Soufrière volcano, turn north on D9 via Choisy, a hamlet surrounded by vast banana plantations, to St. Claude and La Savane à Mulets, a plateau and parking area where the hike to the volcano's summit begins.

BASSE-TERRE The capital of Guadeloupe, which sits at the foot of the Soufrière Mountains, is one of the best kept secrets in the Caribbean. A delightful town almost untouched by tourism, it was founded in the early 17th century and occupied several times by the British during the two centuries of rivalry between France and Britain over the Caribbean. To the south on a promontory was Fort St.-Charles; the Gallion River, which originates on the slopes of La Soufrière, runs under the fort's ramparts on its way to the sea. The fort was surrounded by the Carmel quarter, the traditional military and government section. Today it has the Palais d'Orléans with the Prefecture, the Palace of Justice, and the General Council building—all handsome examples of colonial architecture.

To the north was Saint-François parish, the commercial district with the streets laid out in a grid. It is still the commercial section, and behind the Town Hall on avenue Général de Gaulle are the main downtown streets. Rue du Docteur Cabre leads to the *Cathedral of Our Lady of Guadeloupe*, with a facade that's been classified as a historical monument.

SAINT CLAUDE The drive from Basse-Terre town to La Savane à Mulets, at 3,747 feet at the base of La Soufrière, takes 30 minutes and passes through the pretty hillside town of St.-Claude. A wealthy residential community, its West Indian houses are set in flowering gardens against rainforest greenery and cascading streams. A visitor's center, *La Maison du Volcan*, has displays relating to La Soufrière and the other volcanic regions of the Eastern Caribbean, as well as on volcanology throughout the world.

SOUFRIÈRE VOLCANO The forest green, deeply creviced mountains that dominate southern Basse-Terre are part of the National Park and take their name from the highest peak, La Soufrière, the brimstone-belching volcano at 4,813 feet. It is surrounded by other volcanic peaks more than 4,000 feet—all with waterfalls, hot springs, rain and cloud forests, and trails.

Although rumblings had been recorded since the 15th century, La Soufrière had been dormant for centuries when she began to erupt in 1975. Warnings had come as early as 1956, when tremors sent up rocks and ash and caused new fractures. La Soufrière continues to boil and bubble, but it is quiet enough to be climbed. A visit to the summit of an active volcano, the center of nature's most awesome force, is a rare and fascinating opportunity.

You can go by car as far as the base of the cone at La Savane à Mulets, from which four marked trails—Red, Yellow, Green, and Blue—lead to the summit. When combined the trails take 3.5 hours to cover. One trail (Red) leads from La Savane parking lot directly to the top in a series of switchbacks that gain 1,000 feet in 45 heart-pounding minutes. Composed of solidified lava, the crown has a deep split through the center, where continuing volcanic action can be seen. It is an eerie landscape of weird-shaped rocks, bubbling mud, and jagged fumaroles emitting hot gases and steam.

You should wear sturdy shoes and protection against the rain and wind, and be extremely cautious walking around fumaroles at the summit. Some parts of the trails are very difficult; mist and clouds often make it difficult to see your way. If you do not have the time or stamina to go to the summit, you can choose from several easy walks in the La Savane area.

MATOUBA Two miles northwest of St.-Claude, the town of Matouba, at 2,234 feet in altitude, was settled by the East Indians brought to the French West Indies as laborers in the mid-19th century after the abolition of slavery. The hot springs of Matouba are well known for their therapeutic properties.

VIEUX-FORT At the southern tip of Basse-Terre, where the Atlantic Ocean meets the Caribbean Sea, is an old town that takes its name from the fort that once guarded the strategic point. Today the town is known for a delicate embroidery art made by the women of the village. The volcanic Carib Mountains rise behind the town.

NATIONAL PARK OF GUADELOUPE (PARC NATIONAL DE GUADELOUPE) The spine of forested mountains that run almost the length of Basse-Terre constitute the 74,100-acre National Park. You'll find exhibits throughout on particular aspects—volcano, forest, coffee, sugarcane, archaeology, and wildlife—of the park, but explanations are in French only. The exhibits are intended as learning centers as well as outdoor museums. The centers are accessible on paved roads and are usually the starting point for one of the park's 200 miles of signposted trails.

ROUTE DE LA TRAVERSEE The highway through the center of the park starts from the banana and sugarcane fields on the east coast at Versailles and climbs to 600 feet at Vernou, a fashionable residential district of pretty villas with tropical gardens overlooking the serpentine Lézarde River Valley. After Vernou the highway winds through the park to a pass, *Col des Deux Mamelles,* where it crosses the ridge to the west coast. The scenic drive provides access to more than a half-dozen walks and hikes from a 10-minute stroll to a 10-mile trek.

ECREVISSES FALLS (THE FALLS OF THE CRAYFISH) About a mile from the park entrance on the south side of the Route de la Traversée, a path along the Corossol River leads in a 10-minute walk to the *Cascade aux Ecrevisses.* The pretty waterfall is the most accessible one in the park and is usually included on motorcoach tours of eastern Basse-Terre. It is also popular for swimming and picnicking. (Do not leave valuables unattended. Young boys, finding tourists easy prey here, sometimes sneak out from the woods to grab a handbag or camera and disappear into the foliage.)

THE FOREST HOUSE AND BRAS DAVID TROPICAL PARK About halfway on the Route de la Traversée is the Forest House (*La Maison de la Forêt*) in the Bras David Tropical Park, which takes its name from a nearby river. It has picnic grounds, trails, and a nature center with outdoor displays. Three short trails start south of the highway.

LES MAMELLES When the Route de la Traversée crosses over the main ridge, it passes several peaks where there are roads or footpaths for hiking. On the south are the Deux Mamelles: Petit-Bourg, 2,349 feet; and Pigeon, 2,526 feet. The latter has a path of 45 minutes with a lookout at 1,969 feet that takes in a grandstand view of the mountains and the coasts. From the pass of the Deux Mamelles, the Route de la Traversée winds down to the coast under a 2-mile umbrella of flamboyant trees that are magnificent when they are in bloom, from May to October.

At Mahaut on the west coast, you can turn north to Pointe-Noire and Deshaies or south on the scenic road known as the Golden Corniche, which winds along pretty little coves between cliffs and gorges to Basse-Terre town.

PIGEON ISLAND/COUSTEAU UNDERWATER NATURE PARK At Malendure Beach you can take a 5-minute boat ride to Pigeon Island or a glass-bottom boat excursion to the Underwater Park of Pigeon Island, also known as the Cousteau Underwater Reserve, Guadeloupe's main diving location.

MAISON DU CAFE Inland from Vieux-Habitants, a scenic drive winds along the Grand Rivière through the wooded mountains with magnificent views of the park, the Soufrière volcano, and the coast. It ends at the Maison du Cafè, one of the interpretive centers of the park, and La Grivelière, a small coffee plantation that has been in the same family for more than a century. A tour is available. Vieux-Habitants, one of the island's oldest villages, has the oldest parish church in Guadeloupe (1650), which was recently restored. South of the village and at Rocroy are two of the nicest beaches on this coast.

NORTHERN BASSE-TERRE

You can approach northern Basse-Terre from either the east or west coast. On the east coast the drive skirts miles of banana and sugar plantations and mangroves; on the west coast the wooded highlands of the park fall almost directly to the sea. The fishing villages of the north coast are popular for their creole and seafood restaurants. Domaine de Séverin in Ste.-Rose and Grosse-Montagne in Lamentin are long established rum makers where guided tours are offered.

From Mahaut at the western end of Route de la Traversée, the road north passes Pointe-Noire, a town known for its wood craftsmen. Here the House of Wood is a display center and forestry museum. Farther north, Deshaies has a marina, and nearby Grande-Anse, a long crescent of golden sand, has a campground. About a mile west is Plage de Cluny, a nudist beach.

AROUND GRANDE-TERRE

Grande-Terre, Guadeloupe's eastern wing, is flat in comparison to Basse-Terre and is as popular for biking as Basse-Terre is for hiking. From Pointe-à-Pitre the highway east passes Bas du Fort, with its large yacht-filled marina and the *Guadeloupe Aquarium* (Place Creole). Here you can see exhibits of Caribbean marine life and walk through the glass tunnel of a 21,000-gallon tank with sharks. Admission: 38 Ff adult; 20 Ff children. Hours: 9:00 A.M.–7:00 P.M. daily.

After passing the campus of the university, the road continues along the south coast to Guadeloupe's main resort centers—Gosier, Ste.-Anne, and St.-François—are set on attractive beaches or on hillsides overlooking the sea; they offer the full range of water sports. Petit-Havre, between Gosier and Ste.-Anne, and Raisins-Clairs Beach at St.-François are public beaches. St.-François, a fishing village, is known for its seafood restaurants.

POINTE DES CHATEAUX The easternmost point of Grande-Terre at Pointe des Châteaux, which is marked by a large white cross, has a dramatic setting with big Atlantic waves rolling in from the north and smashing against the cliffs of the rocky headlands. Immediately before the point a short track crosses to the north side to Tarare Beach, a nudist enclave. Offshore the uninhabited islets of Iles de la Petite-Terre are popular destinations for yachts. On La Désirade, inhabitants live a simple life as fishermen and boat builders.

LE MOULE Once the capital of Guadeloupe, Le Moule was the site of fierce fighting between the early French settlers and the Caribs. Today it is the main town on the Atlantic coast with a horseshoe beach and a picturesque church that is a historic monument. The neighboring village, La Rosette, has the *Edgar Clerc Archaeological Museum* (Musee D'Archéologie Precolombienne Edgar Clerc), where Amerindian artifacts gathered from the islands of the Eastern Caribbean are displayed. Hours: daily except Tuesday 10:30 A.M.–6:30 P.M.; 23–57–57. Admission is free.

The region around Le Moule is covered with cane fields and dotted with sugar mills, some with their original machinery, as well as the ruins of old plantation houses. There are several rum distilleries in the area. The contrast between the pastoral landscape of Grande-Terre and the brooding peaks of Basse-Terre is particularly noticeable here.

LES GRANDS FONDS Across central Grande-Terre, between Pointe-à-Pitre and Abymes on the west and Le Moule on the east, is the roller-coaster terrain of *mornes* and *fonds,* the hills and valleys that characterize this region, known locally as *montagnes russes.* Les Grands Fonds is inhabited by the descen-

dants of the Blancs Matignon, a small group of white settlers who retreated here after the abolition of slavery in 1848. They form a unique ethnic and social group, but today they are distinguishable from the rest of the population only by race.

MORNE-À-L'EAU South of Abymes in the town of Morne-à-l'Eau is one of the island's best-known landmarks, an amphitheater-shaped cemetery in checkerboard black and white. It is a place of pilgrimage on All Saints Day, November 1, when people from all over the island—as well as visitors—come to light candles for their deceased.

PETIT CANAL The *Monument to Liberty* in the small village of Petit-Canal is one of the most poignant sites in the Caribbean. It stands on a hillside at the head of fifty-three steps—one for each plantation that once flourished in Guadeloupe. During slavery plantation owners punished their rebellious slaves by putting them in barrels with spikes driven into the sides and rolling them down these steps.

North of the fishing villages of Port-Louis, the inviting beaches are all but deserted on weekdays. On the north side of Anse Bertrand, *Folie Plage* (22–11–17) is a well-known creole restaurant, particularly popular with local residents on Sunday outings.

EXPLORING THE OFFSHORE ISLANDS

ILES DES SAINTES (or Les Saintes) Off the south coast of Basse-Terre is an archipelago of eight tiny volcanic islands with quiet bays and rocky coves etched with white-sand beaches. These idyllic hideaways, where time seems to have stood still, have been discovered in recent years by day trippers from Guadeloupe and a few small cruise ships.

Only Terre-de-Bas and Terre-de-Haut, the largest of the group, are inhabited, and only the latter has tourist facilities. Most inhabitants are descended from the settlers from Brittany who were often the pioneers of the French West Indies. Many are fishermen who still wear the *salako,* a broad-brim, flat straw hat covered with white cloth, which they inherited from their seagoing ancestors.

Mountainous Terre-de-Haut, usually called Les Saintes, has one village, Bourg des Saintes, and one road, a flower-filled lane that runs from one end of the 3-mile-long island to the other. From the harbor situated on the north side of the island, the walk in either direction is delightful. On a hilltop overlooking the village is *Fort Napoleon,* built in the 17th century to defend Pointe-à-Pitre harbor. The fort has a botanic garden and, surprisingly, contains a museum of modern art. South of town, 1,020-foot Le Chameau is the island's highest hill, where a track zigzags up to an old watchtower and a panoramic view of Terre-de-Haut and her neighbors, Basse-Terre and La Soufrière.

West from the harbor the road leads up a hill along a tango of small, colorful houses with gingerbread trim and flowering gardens to delightful beaches with small hotels, good restaurants, and water-sports facilities. On the east end of the island, pretty St.-Pierre Bay has a white-sand beach; there is an entrance fee. On the south side of the island where the small airport is located, the beach is usually too windy and rough for swimming, but there is a path to a cliff with a beautiful view of the coast.

The island has taxis; daily ferry service from Trois-Rivières and Basse-Terre takes 30 minutes, from Pointe-à-Pitre about an hour. There is also air service from Pointe-à-Pitre.

MARIE-GALANTE Located 27 miles south of Grande-Terre, Marie-Galante is an occasional cruise port of call. Similar in appearance to Grande-Terre, the slightly pear-shaped island has green rolling hills and long, reef-protected white-sand beaches along the west and south coast. The east side is mostly rockbound. Historic Marie-Galante is called the island of a hundred windmills. Some of the old mills that dot the landscape still produce cotton and sugar, the island's mainstay. Château Murat, an old plantation manor house, is now a museum.

The three main towns—St. Louis on the west, Grand-Bourg on the southwest, and Capesterre on the southeast—are connected by good roads. Each town has narrow streets with tiny stores and pastel houses. The good roads, low terrain, and light traffic make biking a delightful mode of travel for the island.

One of the main roads crosses the southern third of the island from St. Louis and the beaches

of the west coast over rolling hills to the eastern part of the island. About midway the road branches to *Trou à Diable,* a grotto of stalactites. From St. Louis and Anse-Canot on the northwest coast, there are scenic routes along *La Grande Barre,* a high green ridge dividing the northern half of the island into two plateaus. Anse Canot and Vieux-Fort have beautiful beaches with reefs.

Marie-Galante is the most populous of the off-shore islands and has restaurants and small hotels. Daily flights from Pointe-à-Pitre take 15 minutes; ferries take 1.5 hours.

 # SHOPPING

Perfumes, china, crystal, leather goods, cosmetics, clothing and accessories, fine wines, and liqueurs are some of the French products famous labels that will attract your immediate attention, but don't overlook local products. You will find rum, coffee, spices, handcrafted pottery, straw, gold jewelry, madras dolls and shell figurines, and much more. French perfumes are about 20 percent lower in price here than in the United States. When you pay in U.S. travelers' checks, 20 percent is also sometimes deducted on certain luxury items in specialized shops.

The main downtown shopping streets run about 6 blocks deep from the port between rues Frébault, Nozières, and Schoelcher. All are picturesque with colorful old, balconied houses between the chic boutiques with fashions from Paris and the trendsetting Côte d'Azur. Don't expect much English to be spoken.

Shops in town are open on weekdays from 8:30 or 9:00 A.M. to 12:30 or 1:00 P.M. and from 2:30 or 3:00 to 5:30 or 6:00 P.M.; on Saturday to 1:00 P.M. Bas-du-Fort has two large commercial areas where stores remain open until 7:00 P.M. and on Saturday afternoons.

In addition to the chic boutiques, it's fun to visit the open-air markets. The main market is found at Place du Marché, north of rue Peynier. Here in the mélange of colors, sounds, and aroma, creole-speaking market women in madras dress sell exotic flowers and fruits, vegetables, and fresh spices, and they know how to drive a hard bargain.

ART AND ANTIQUES: *Tim Tim* (15, rue Henri IV), a small shop in a colonial mansion, has books, engravings, jewelry, and antique clothes and creole furniture, collected by the owners, novelist Andre Schwarz-Bart and his wife, Simone.

BOOKS AND MAPS *Librairie Antillaise* (41, rue Schoelcher and 29, rue Henri IV) and *Librairie Generale* (46, rue Schoelcher) are main outlets for books in French. For books on Guadeloupe and the French West Indies in English, try the gift shops in hotels.

CHINA AND CRYSTAL: *Rosébleu* (lower Frebault) and *A La Pensée* (lower Frebault) stock crystal, silver, porcelain, and other luxury gifts.

CHEESE AND GROCERIES: *Cora Shopping Center* on the east side of Pointe-à-Pitre is a large supermarket where you can find pâtés, cheese, canned delicacies, and kitchen gadgets, as well as inexpensive beachwear. *The Galfa Club* is a small branch of Paris's *Galeries Lafayette* department store.

CLOTHING AND SHOES: Designer labels and well-known brands are found at *Valerie* or *Lady's* (both on rue René-Boisneuf), *Citronnelle* (rue Jean-Jaures), and *Chloe* (rue Lamartine). *Falbala* (rue Schoelcher) is a tiny shop with lacy lingerie. Another fashionable boutique is *Paul et Virginie* (rue Schoelcher). Stylish sandals and inexpensive shoes are found at *Bata* and *100,000 Chaussures* (both rue Frébault). *L'Atelier de Melodie* (rue Frébault) has pretty hand-painted T-shirts and dresses.

CRAFTS AND SOUVENIRS: Handicrafts such as dolls dressed in madras, known as *doudou* dolls; madras table linens; aprons; cards with colorful collages; straw hats and bags; baskets of spices; shells; and wooden carvings can be found at *Au Caraibe* (4 rue Frébault) and *Macabou* (rue Nozières). Shop at *Hibiscus D'Or* (rue Schoelcher) for costume jewelry and unusual gifts.

MUSIC: Zouk is the French West Indies's answer to calypso or *soca*. Kassav is the best-known group of the zouk artists. Two locations of *Debs* (rue de Nozières and rue Frébault) sell their records. Although the selection of zouk recordings is greater here, the prices are higher than in New York.

LIQUOR AND WINE: *Antilles Delices* (45, rue René-Boisneuf) has old rums, tropical liqueurs, and gourmet gifts.

PERFUME: *Phoenicia* (rue Frébault and rue de Nozières) has a wide selection of perfumes and cosmetics, as well as ties, scarves, and small accessories. *L'Artisan Parfumeur* (rue Schoelcher) specializes in exotic fruit and flower-based scents. *Vendome* (rue Frébault) is the exclusive dealer for Orlane, Stendhal, and Germaine Monteil cosmetics and also has a small collection of imported fashions.

DINING AND RESTAURANTS

Although other French islands are becoming famous for their gourmet restaurants, Guadeloupe has traditionally been the culinary capital of the French West Indies—and it is the only island in the Caribbean with an annual feast honoring the patron saint of cooking. The island's distinctive creole cuisine reflects its multifaceted heritage: the French interest in careful preparation of fine cuisine, the ingredients inherited from the Arawaks, and the spices and traditions introduced by Africans, Indians, and Asians. Fresh seafood is an important element, as are conch and stuffed land crabs. To start your meal the traditional way, try a "ti-punch," a small but potent mixture of rum, lime juice, and sugarcane syrup that is meant to stimulate the appetite.

Cruise-ship passengers normally do not have the luxury of spending 2 or 3 hours over a meal as the French traditionally do, but if trying new and exotic cuisine is high on your list of priorities, you might want to spend part of your day enjoying a creole meal. It is easy to combine sight-seeing with lunch in an out-of-the-way place, since some of the best restaurants are rustic establishments on the south coast of Grande-Terre, the north coast of Basse-Terre, and in small villages along the way. Prices are on the high side. An inexpensive three-course meal for one person, without wine, costs less than $30, moderate, $30 to $45; and expensive ($45 and over). Inquire in advance about the use of credit cards, and serving hours.

Cote Jardin (7 La Marina; 90–91–28). This new restaurant quickly went to the head of the list of Guadeloupean's movers, shakers, and gourmets for its excellent cuisine and service in a lovely indoor garden setting. Expensive, but worth it for those who appreciate fine dining.

Issac Street (5 rue Alexandre Issac; 90–32–80). The restaurant specializes in Creole cuisine and has a tourist menu daily. Moderately expensive.

Le Barbaroc (Petit-Canal; 22–62–71). A rustic little restaurant in a village on the west coast of Grande-Terre offers old creole recipes that owner Félicité Doloir, named one of 1983's outstanding cooks of the world by H.J. Heinz and Company, has researched and recreated. With advance notice she takes guests on a countryside tour to show them native plants, herbs, and other local products and explain their use. She will offer you *moabie*, a nonalcoholic drink made from tree bark. Moderate.

Sucre Sale (Rue Assainessmont; 21–22–55). Creole cuisine is the specialty of this modest restaurant. Moderate.

La Rocher de Malendure (Bovillante, Basse-Terre; 98–70–84). Enjoy views of Pigeon Island and the sea from a rustic, terrace setting amid tropical gardens while you lunch on fresh seafood. This provides an ideal stop on a day tour of Basse-Terre. Moderately expensive.

NIGHTLIFE

In addition to hotel discos and nightclubs, there are nightspots for zouk, the pop music craze. Guadeloupe has two casinos: one in Gosier and the other in St.-François. The legal age is twenty-one, and proof of identity (passport or driver's license with photo) is required. Jacket and tie are not required, but dress is fashionable.

SPORTS

BEACHES/SWIMMING: Guadeloupe has a great variety of beaches, from long stretches of white sands and sheltered coves to black-sand beaches and surf-washed Atlantic shores. Public beaches are free, though some may charge for parking, but unlike hotel beaches they have no facilities. Generally, hotels welcome nonguests but charge for the use of facilities. There are several officially designated nudist beaches, the most popular being Pointe Tarare near Pointe des Châteaux. Topless is common at hotels, but less so on village beaches.

BOATING: Strong winds and currents make yachting a challenging sport in Guadeloupe. Boats of all sizes are available for charter by day, week, or month, with crew or bare boat. Safe anchorages and pretty beaches make Les Saintes and Marie-Galante popular destinations for day excursions. Full-day picnic sails are organized by local travel companies.

Guadeloupe has three good marinas: *Port de Plaisance Marina* (Bas-du-Fort; 82–54–85), the largest, is located 10 minutes from Pointe-à-Pitre and is considered in yachting circles to be one of the best in the Western Hemisphere for its facilities. *The Capitainerie* (harbormaster) is open weekdays 8:00 A.M.–1:00 P.M. and 3:00–5:00 P.M., and Saturday to 11:30 P.M. (82–54–85).

BIKING: Cycling is a national sport whose popularity gets an annual boost from the Tour de la Guadeloupe, a 10-day international race in August that is as hotly contested as the Tour de France on the mainland. For visitors, biking is best in Grande-Terre and Marie-Galante. *Cyclo-Tours* (84–11–34) and *Dingo* (83–81–19) in Pointe-à-Pitre have bikes for rent.

DEEP-SEA FISHING: Sports-fishing boats are based at *Port de Plaisance Marina* (Bas-du-Fort; 82–74–94); *Guadeloupe Chartaire* (Pointe-à-Pitre; 82–34–74), and the *Fishing Club Antilles* (Bouillante; 90–70–10).

GOLF: *Golf of St.-François* (88–41–87) on the southeastern end of Grande-Terre is within walking distance of the Hamak and Meridien hotels. The 18-hole course, designed by Robert Trent Jones, Sr., has a clubhouse with pro shop, lockers, and restaurant and an English-speaking pro.

HIKING: Basse-Terre's National Park, with its spectacular scenery and good trails, offers some of the best hiking in the Caribbean. The 200 miles of signposted trails range from easy walks through tropical rain forests to arduous treks through wild mountain terrain. Many short hikes lead to pretty picnic spots, waterfalls, and mountain pools. The Tourist Office in Pointe-à-Pitre has brochures on the park. Guided hikes can be arranged through the *Bureau des Guides de Moyenne Montague,* Maison Forestière, Matouba 97120; 81–24–83.

HORSEBACK RIDING: *Le Criolo* (St.-Felix; 84–38–90), a riding school with horses and ponies, offers tours and picnic excursions. *La Manade* (81–52–21; fax: 81–90–73), with a horseback-riding facility at Saint Claude on the northern flank of Soufrière Mountain, offers rides on trails in the tropical forest.

SNORKELING/SCUBA DIVING: The snorkeling locations nearest to the port in Pointe-à-Pitre are the reefs fronting Gosier and the offshore island, Ilet du Gosier. Equipment is available from watersports operators based at beachside hotels in Grande-Terre.

The most popular dive area is Pigeon Island off the west coast of Basse-Terre. It is actually two tiny volcanic islands with abundant marine life. Each dive location is different in character. The west side has a wall that begins at the surface, drops to 25 feet, slopes to 40 feet, and drops again. Here soft corals, large brain coral, seafans, and sponges and colorful fish are abundant, making it interesting for undersea photographers and popular with snorkelers.

The north side has a reef beginning in shallow water suitable for novice divers; it drops off to small canyons and walls, interesting for experienced divers. On the northeast side, a wall begins at the surface and drops to 40 feet. It is rich in sponges, pillar corals, and a great variety of fish. Ilet à Fajou, off the north coast of Basse-Terre, is another location visited on day trips from Grande-Terre.

Individual dives range from about 150 Ff to 320 Ff, depending on distance to dive sites. *Aqua-Fari* (Callinago; 84–26–26), and other dive operators in Grande-Terre, usually take groups to Pigeon Island. On Malendure Beach, facing Pigeon Island, there are three dive operators: *Les Heures Saines* (98–86–63), *Chez Guy et Christian*

(98–82–43), and the *Aux Aquanautes Antillais* (98–87–30). On Les Saintes, *Centre Nautique des Saintes* is located on Terre-de-Haut.

American visitors should be aware that the French, who pioneered the sport of diving, use a system for dive tables and apparatus that is different from the American one. As a safety matter, divers (including certified ones) are checked on the use of the equipment before they are permitted to don tanks. Courses for certification by CMAS (Confédération Mondiale des Activités Subaquatique), the French national scuba association, are rigorous.

TENNIS: Most hotels have courts. Those closest to Pointe-à-Pitre are *La Creole Beach* in Gosier; *Novotel Fleur d'Epée* and *Marissol* near Bas-du-Fort. Each has two courts.

WINDSURFING: Guadeloupe was a pioneer of windsurfing in the 1970s, and it is a frequent venue for international meets. Lessons and rental equipment are available from most beachfront hotels. *Loisirs Nautiques* (Callinago; 84–25–25) and *Nauticase* (Salako Hotel) rent boards for 60–70 Ff per hour. Beginner's lessons cost about 80 Ff.

FESTIVALS AND CELEBRATIONS

Fête des Cuisinières (Festival of the Women Cooks), one of the Caribbean's most colorful festivals, takes place on the second weekend in August. It is the feast day of St. Laurent, the patron saint of cooking. But this is no ordinary feast. For days the women cooks of the island prepare their specialties and make their costumes for a special parade. The celebration begins with a High Mass at the Cathedral in Pointe-à-Pitre to bless the food, which is placed at the altar. Afterward the women promenade through the streets in their creole finery, carrying their elaborately decorated plates of island specialties and gaily decorated baskets of fruits and vegetables trimmed with miniature kitchen utensils. The parade ends at a local school for a ceremony attended by the mayor and other dignitaries, followed by a feast and dancing. Visitors are invited to participate.

Other celebrations include *Carnival,* held in the traditional pre-Lenten period. For the last 5 days of Carnival, all business stops and by Shrove Tuesday, or Mardi Gras, festivities reach a frenzy with parades of floats, costumed red devils, and dancing in the streets of Pointe-à-Pitre. In the French West Indies Carnival continues through Ash Wednesday when participants dress in black and white, King Carnival is burned on a funeral pyre, and a night parade with torches is held to bury "Vaval."

Dominica

ROSEAU, PORTSMOUTH/PRINCE RUPERT BAY

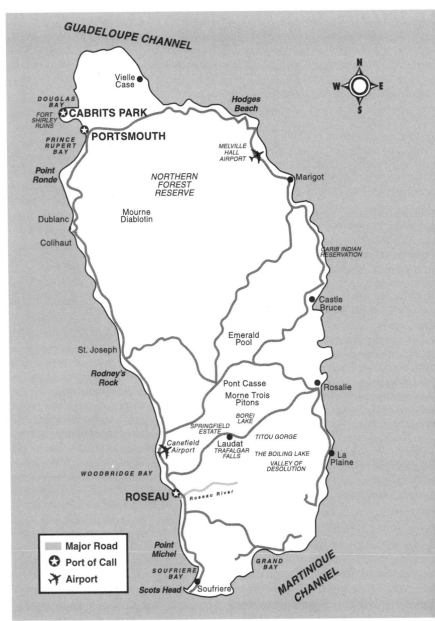

GUADELOUPE CHANNEL

Vielle Case

DOUGLAS BAY

Hodges Beach

FORT SHIRLEY RUINS

CABRITS PARK

PRINCE RUPERT BAY

PORTSMOUTH

MELVILLE HALL AIRPORT

Point Ronde

NORTHERN FOREST RESERVE

Marigot

Dublanc

Mourne Diablotin

Colihaut

CARIB INDIAN RESERVATION

Castle Bruce

Emerald Pool

St. Joseph

Rodney's Rock

Pont Casse

Morne Trois Pitons

Rosalie

BOREI LAKE

SPRINGFIELD ESTATE

TITOU GORGE

Canefield Airport

Laudat

TRAFALGAR FALLS

THE BOILING LAKE

La Plaine

VALLEY OF DESOLUTION

WOODBRIDGE BAY

ROSEAU

Roseau River

Point Michel

GRAND BAY

SOUFRIERE BAY

MARTINIQUE CHANNEL

Scots Head

Soufriere

▨ Major Road
✪ Port of Call
✈ Airport

AT A GLANCE

CHAPTER CONTENTS

Dominica

THE GIFT OF NATURE

Covered from end to end with towering volcanic mountains and spectacular tropical scenery, Dominica is the gift of nature. Mists rise from the green valleys and fall softly over the blue-green peaks densely carpeted with rain forests and exotic plants that host more than 135 species of birds. Natural wonders hide in the mountain vastness, and rivers and streams cascade over cliffs and rush down steep mountains.

Located in the heart of the Eastern Caribbean between Guadeloupe and Martinique, Dominica—not to be confused with the Dominican Republic—bridges the Leeward and the Windward islands. The most mountainous of the Lesser Antilles, the land rises steeply from the shore to peaks that reach almost 5,000 feet. The native Carib Indians called their island by the descriptive name of *Wai'tukubuli*, meaning "tall is her body." Moisture-laden trade winds from the east hang over the mountains, where they condense and release 250 inches of rain per year.

Dominica does not fit the usual image of a Caribbean island. Tourism's role is secondary in the economy. The island has no large resorts or shopping centers and does not want them. There are only a few beaches, and except for a stretch on the north coast, they consist mostly of black, volcanic sand—a matter of little importance, since the exquisite beauty of Dominica's interior more than compensates for the absence of beach-scalloped shores.

Columbus came upon Dominica on a Sunday in 1493 and named it for the day. The French and British fought over the island but in 1686 agreed in a treaty to recognize Dominica as a neutral territory to be left to the Caribs forever. But neither honored the agreement, and in practice Dominica became a sort of no-man's land of endless battles, with the French and British encroaching increasingly on Carib lands.

In 1805 Britain took possession of Dominica, and after almost two centuries of more turbulence, the island became independent in 1978. The French influence on the culture lingers to this day almost as much as that of the British. It is particularly apparent in the creole speech, the cuisine, and the names of people and places.

FAST FACTS

POPULATION: 75,000

SIZE: 29 miles long and 16 miles wide; 290.8 sq. miles

MAIN TOWNS: Roseau, Portsmouth

GOVERNMENT: Dominica is a democratic republic headed by a president. The constitution provides for seven ministers including a prime minister who is the leader of the party with a majority in the House of Assembly. The cabinet, comprising the prime minister, ministers of government, and attorney general, is the chief policy-making body.

CURRENCY: Eastern Caribbean dollar. US $1 equals EC $2.67. Credit cards are accepted at major hotels but are not widely used.

DEPARTURE TAX: EC $30 (US $11)

LANGUAGE: English is the official language, but creole, a French-based patois, is spoken widely.

PUBLIC HOLIDAYS: January 1, New Year's Day; Carnival, Shrove Monday and Tuesday; Good Friday; Easter Monday; May 1, Labor Day; May/June, Whit Monday; first Monday in August, August Monday; November 3–4, National Day Celebrations; December 25, Christmas; December 26, Boxing Day.

TELEPHONE AREA CODE: 767. Direct telephone and fax services to all parts of the world are operated by Cable and Wireless Ltd.

AIRLINES: There is no direct service from the U.S. mainland to Dominica. Rather, you must fly to San Juan, Antigua, or another of the Caribbean's main gateways, and transfer to American Eagle, Cardinal Airlines, LIAT, or other local airlines that fly to Dominica.

Dominica has two airports: Canefield, 3 miles north of Roseau, accommodates aircraft up to a 19-seater twin otter; and Melville Hall on the northeast coast, 29 miles from Roseau and 20 miles from Portsmouth, takes larger aircraft. LIAT operates daily flights to both airports.

INFORMATION:

In the United States: Dominica Tourist Office,
10 East 21st Street, No. 600,
New York, NY, 10010;
(212) 475–7542; fax: (212) 475–9728.

In Port: Dominica Tourist Board,
Cork Street; Box 293, Roseau, Dominica, W.I.;
448–2351; fax: 488–5840.
Forestry and National Parks, Botanic Gardens,
Roseau, Dominica, W.I.;
448–6008; fax: 448–0070.

BUDGET PLANNING

In some ways Dominica is one of the least expensive islands in the Eastern Caribbean but it is also one of the least developed for tourism. Restaurants serving locals are cheap; some catering to tourists are outrageously expensive. Outside of the capital and Portsmouth, tourist facilities are extremely limited or nonexistent. If the shore excursions offered by your cruise ship do not suit your interests, it is best to arrange a tour or hike with one of the local travel companies rather than go on your own.

PORT PROFILE:

LOCATION/EMBARKATION: Dominica has three ports. Roseau, the capital on the southwest coast, has a new passenger port in the heart of town. (The exit gate is directly in front of the museum.) A second, deep-water harbor and commercial port is at Woodbridge Bay, about one mile north of town and is sometimes used by cruise ships. The third port is Portsmouth, the second-largest town, and is located 25 miles north of Roseau on Prince Rupert Bay, a wide bay adjacent to the historic Cabrits Peninsula National Park. Dominica built the port in an effort to develop Portsmouth and the Cabrits as a tourist attraction. A $7-million dock and modern terminal, designed in West Indian architecture typical of the 18th century, was added. Here passengers disembark directly into the national park.

LOCAL TRANSPORTATION: Dominica's public transport is provided by private taxis and minivans in Roseau and between towns and villages.

ROADS AND RENTALS: Dominica has more than 300 miles of excellent roads that were built in the mid-1980s with the help of the United States. They connect Roseau with the main towns and villages of the country in a few hours' drive, making many of the island's most scenic parts—heretofore almost inaccessible—easy to reach. No highway completely encircles the island, but it is possible to loop around the northern end. Three highways connect Roseau on the west coast with the main east-coast villages of Rosalie, Castle Bruce, and Marigot.

And now for the bad news. The secondary roads and tracks feeding from the tarmac roads range from passable to terrible, and none are well marked. You must have a good map to find your way, but even detailed maps do not show all the important places. To see the most beautiful parts of Dominica, you need to leave your car and hike into the interior to the forests, lakes, waterfalls, and mountain heights.

Cars are available for rent; you need a visitor's driving permit, which can be obtained upon presentation of a valid driver's license to the Police

Traffic Department (High Street, Roseau) and payment of EC $30. Rental rates start at about US $40 per day; a deposit, payable by credit card, is sometimes required. Driving in this former British colony is on the LEFT. And, be aware, driving here is hazardous. Some car-rental firms in Roseau are *Avis Rent a Car* (448–2481; fax: 448–6881); *Budget* (449–2080; fax: 449–2694); *Norman Rentals* (448–5749; fax: 448–3962); and *Valley Rent-a-Car* (448–3233; fax: 448–6009).

EMERGENCY NUMBERS:
   Medical: Harlsbro Medical Centre,
      Hillsborough Street; contact through local
      operator or Dial 999
   Police: Dial 999

AUTHOR'S FAVORITE ATTRACTIONS

TRAFALGAR FALLS AND PAPILLOTE NATURE
   CENTER
INDIAN RIVER BOAT RIDE
HIKING IN THE RAIN FOREST

SHORE EXCURSIONS

Dominica has good, reasonably priced tour companies, and their tours are recommended for first-time visitors. You can waste a great deal of time trying to find your way in Dominica's mountainous terrain, where distances are very deceiving; routes often taking two or three times the normal amount of time to cover. Descriptions of sites mentioned here are provided elsewhere in the chapter. All rates are per person.

City/Trafalgar Waterfalls, 4 hours, US $25. Drive to Morne Bruce for a spectacular view of Roseau and harbor, visit the Botanic Gardens, and continue to Trafalgar Falls and a short walk in the rain forest.

Trafalgar/Emerald Falls/Carib Reserve, full day, US $40. The Trafalgar Falls, Emerald Falls Trail, and a drive on the scenic Imperial Road to the Carib Indian Reservation. Return via the Layou River Valley to Layou, a town on the Caribbean coast.

Trafalgar/Freshwater Lake/Emerald Falls, full day, US $40. The first tour described above combined with a hike to Freshwater Lake can be followed by a drive through the central mountains to Emerald Falls Trail and return via the Layou Valley.

Whalewatching (see Sports).

Hiking Safaris, 6 hours, US $50; US $200 for four people. To hike in the rain forest, you must have a guide. They can be obtained through the Dominica Tourist Office or from tour companies listed below. Most local companies specialize in safari-type excursions with nature guides who convey passengers in minivans or jeeps to points in the mountains from where hikes begin.

   In Roseau, *Dominica Tours* (Box 34, 448–2638; fax: 448–5680); *Ken's Hinterland Adventure Tours* (Box 447, Roseau; 448–4850; fax: 448–8486); *Nature Island Tours* (448–3397; fax: 448–4042); *Rainbow Rover Tours* (Box 3, Roseau; 448–8650; fax: 448–8650); *Wilderness Adventure Tours* (81 Bath Road; 448–2198; fax: 448–3600). Arrangements must be made in advance.

DOMINICA ON YOUR OWN

Dominica's capital is situated on a flat river delta at the mouth of the Roseau River on the site of a former Indian village. It takes its name from a wild reed, *roseau*, that once grew here in abundance. The French, the first Europeans to settle here, built a fort around which their colony developed. When the British took control of the island, they expanded the French fort and renamed it Fort Young, for the first British governor.

A ROSEAU WALKABOUT

A typical West Indian port, Roseau sprawls along the waterfront and climbs Morne Bruce and the other steep hills that frame it. The town has retained much of its old character, despite the

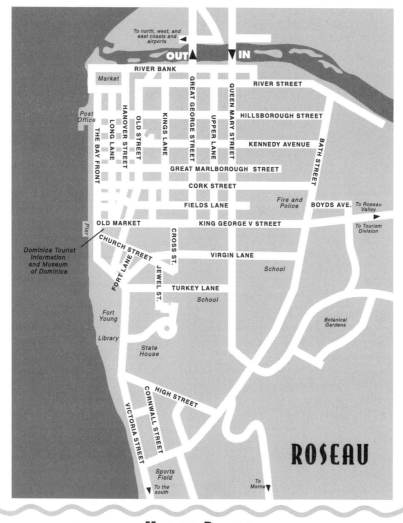

To north, west, and
east coasts and
airports

OUT   IN

RIVER BANK

Market

RIVER STREET

Post
Office

HILLSBOROUGH STREET

KENNEDY AVENUE

GREAT MARLBOROUGH STREET

CORK STREET

Fire and
Police

BOYDS AVE.   To Roseau
Valley

FIELDS LANE

To Tourism
Division

OLD MARKET

KING GEORGE V STREET

Dominica Tourist
Information
and Museum
of Dominica

VIRGIN LANE

School

TURKEY LANE

School

Fort
Young

Botanical
Gardens

Library

State
House

HIGH STREET

ROSEAU

Sports
Field
To the
south

To
Morne

RIVER BANK · GREAT GEORGE STREET · QUEEN MARY STREET · HANOVER STREET · OLD STREET · KINGS LANE · UPPER LANE · BATH STREET · LONG LANE · THE BAY FRONT · Pier · CHURCH STREET · FORT LANE · CROSS ST. · JEWEL ST. · CORNWALL STREET · VICTORIA STREET

MAP OF ROSEAU

devastation caused by Hurricane David in 1979. The oldest part is laid out in a modified grid of about 10 blocks and can be covered easily in an hour or so.

MUSEUM AND MARKET At the waterfront in front of the cruise dock is the *Museum of Dominica,* with a small beautifully displayed collection that traces the island's history from pre-Columbian times to the present. Next door is the tourist information office and directly behind it is

an outdoor market of Dominican crafts on the spot that was once the island's slave market.

The new fruit-and-vegetable market at the north end of Bay Street is a wonderful place to visit, particularly on Saturday mornings, when it is jammed with people from the countryside selling exotic fruits and flowers in a kaleidoscope of colors.

FORT YOUNG South of the museum on Victoria Street is Fort Young, constructed in 1770 to replace the original fort built by the French. It served as the main defense of the town and the harbor; some of its cannons can be seen at the entrance. In more recent times the building was used as the police headquarters and later was made into a hotel.

GOVERNMENT HOUSE Across from the Fort Young Hotel is Government House, built in the 1840s to replace an earlier building on the same site. It was altered and improved over the years as the official residence of the queen's representative. After independence it became the residence of the president of Dominica.

Also opposite the Fort Young Hotel is the 19th-century St. George's Anglican Church and the public library, one of several built in the Caribbean by the Andrew Carnegie Foundation in 1905.

THE CATHEDRAL East of Old Market Square on Virgin Lane, the Roman Catholic Cathedral of Our Lady of Fair Haven was built in 1854 to replace an earlier church and cemetery on the site. The side walls have old stained-glass windows, while behind the main altar are modern ones. One of the old windows in the west wall depicts Columbus's discovery of the New World.

The town center has a number of wooden houses with second-story balconies and gingerbread trim. One of the oldest was once the home of novelist Jean Rhys.

DOMINICA BOTANIC GARDENS Originally laid out in 1890 on 110 acres at the foot of the wooded cliffs of Morne Bruce, the Dominica Botanic Gardens have been reduced to forty acres. And despite urban growth, they are still the largest area of open space in town. Near the entrance to the gardens, which were devastated by Hurricane David in 1979, is a poignant reminder of David's visit: a yellow school bus crushed by a toppled African baobab tree. The wreck now supports new life; in 1985, after the tree had sprouted new branches, it began to flower again.

The gardens retain about 150 of the original 500 species of trees and shrubs; a replanting program has been in progress for many years. Among the significant trees is Carib Wood, whose red blossom is Dominica's national flower; it blooms from March to May. Others to note are the

pretty orchid trees near the entrance and two unusual bottle palms, whose name comes from the shape of the trunk, which is similar to the shape of the original Coca-Cola bottle. The gardens' most curious tree is the no-name tree, so called because specialists have not been able to identify it.

Spectacular views of Roseau and the coast can be seen from Morne Bruce, an elegant residential hillside above the Gardens and from Reigate Hall, a cliffside hotel farther up the mountain.

A DRIVE AROUND THE ISLAND

Roads east and north of Roseau lead to the edge of the national park, from which hiking trails ascend the mountains through rain forests to the lakes and waterfalls. Information on trail conditions and brochures prepared by the Park Service are available from the Dominican Tourist Board. Seven of the following nature sites are being developed with access roads, forest trails, interpretive centers, restroom facilities, picnic shelters, and ancillary services; they are due to be completed by fall 1998: Soufrière Sulphur Springs, east of Soufrière; Fresh Water Lake; Middleham Falls and nature trails; and Emerald Pool, all located within the Morne Trois Pitons National Park. Similar improvements are to be made at Trafalgar Falls and Morne Diablotin National Park. Another project will create a model Carib Indian Village in the Carib Indian Reservation area.

DOMINICA NATIONAL PARK Established in 1975 on sixteen thousand acres in the central and southern highlands, Dominica National Park has magnificent scenery and a great variety of plant and animal life. Known also as the *Morne Trois Pitons National Park* after the highest of four peaks in the park, it has hiking trails ranging from a comfortable 30-minute walk to the Emerald Pool to a tortuous 4-hour trek to the Boiling Lake. On the north side of Roseau, a road inland winds through the lush Roseau River Valley to the tiny village of Laudat on Mount Micotrin and the "gateway" to the main attractions in the park's central region.

TRAFALGAR FALLS One of the most beautiful, accessible sites in the park is also the one closest to Roseau. Spectacular Trafalgar Falls are actually three separate cascades, which tumble down the steep sides of Mount Micotrin into pools several hundred feet below. The falls are quite far apart. The trail is an easy, 15-minute walk and provides a good introduction to tropical rain forests.

At the base of the cliff and the entrance to the trail at a 1,000-foot elevation is the Papillote Inn, a wilderness retreat and nature sanctuary with a rainforest garden. Begun in 1969 by former New Yorker Anne G. J. Baptiste, the proprietor of the inn, the garden follows the natural contour of the mountainside, although some terraces were added. More than fifty species of nesting birds can be seen from the inn's terrace or nearby. The rustic inn organizes guided nature walks and trail hikes.

FRESHWATER AND BOERI LAKES Laudat is also the start of hikes to Freshwater Lake at 2,779 feet and Boeri Lake at 2,800 feet. The two bodies of water were once a single lake in the crater of an ancient volcano until Morne Micotrin, a young cone, formed in the crater and separated the water. Freshwater Lake, the largest of Dominica's five lakes and the source of its hydroelectric power, is surrounded by dense forests. Hummingbirds are seen often. The walk from the Laudat trailhead to Freshwater Lake takes about 40 minutes. The views across the park as you approach are wonderful.

North of Freshwater Lake, a steep, narrow trail of about 1 hour's hiking, winds up the mountain along the ridge separating the two lakes to Boeri Lake. It passes through different types of forests with giant tree ferns and many types of plants, and along small streams and hot and cold springs. Throughout the hike there are sweeping views across the island to the Atlantic coast. Boeri Lake has a magnificent setting between Morne Micotrin on the south and Morne Trois Pitons on the north, where it is difficult to believe you are in the Caribbean. The lake and its wooded surroundings look more like Vermont than the tropics.

TITOU GORGE—VALLEY OF DESOLATION—THE BOILING LAKE South of Laudat, the Titou Gorge, a narrow, deep defile, is the start of the trail to the Valley of Desolation and the Boiling Lake, the world's second-largest solfatara lake. The Boiling Lake is 6 miles east of Roseau as the crow flies, but to reach it on the ground takes 4 hours over a 6-mile rollercoaster trail. Some of the most difficult hiking in the Caribbean, this is an undertaking for experienced hikers and then only with a guide. As an alternative, you can go as far as Titou Gorge or go halfway on the trail to the edge of the Valley of Desolation, a hike of 3 hours round-trip.

First studied by British scientists in the 1870s, the Boiling Lake resembles a huge caldron of bubbling gray-khaki water smothered in mist. It is thought to be a flooded fumarole, or hole in a volcanic region, that releases hot gases and boiling vapors from the molten lava below.

SOUFRIÈRE On the south end of Dominica, 5 miles from Roseau, is the fishing village of Soufrière. It is situated on a wide scenic bay that ends at Scotts Head, a promontory that offers great views of the Martinique Channel where the Atlantic and Caribbean collide. Martinique is in view on the south. Scotts Head has some of the island's main dive sites. According to local legend, the cliffs above Soufrière Bay were used by Carib men to punish unfaithful wives—they threw them into the sea.

Along the small stretch of road from town to Scotts Head Village, you can see fishermen mending their nets and repairing their boats. On Friday nights the area is transformed into a street fair attracting Dominicans from the capital and all over the area coming for a raucous good time.

At Pointe Michel, a village between Roseau and Soufrière settled by survivors of the catastrophic 1902 eruption of Mt. Pélé in Martinique, farmers grow the grass used to make Dominica's distinctive rugs. The tough grass, *khuskhus*, is put on the road for cars to run over in order to make it more pliable to weave. In Jamaica the roots of this plant are used to make a perfume.

MIDDLEHAM TRAILS North of Roseau the road to Pont Casse, a junction in the center of the island, winds east along hairpin curves through the steep mountains. It passes Springfield Estate, an old plantation at 1,200 feet, and skirts the Middleham Estate on the northwest edge of the national park. Here a 950-acre tract was donated to the park in 1975 by John D. Archbold, the American owner of Springfield Plantations. It has some of Dominica's finest rain forests with trails.

EMERALD FALLS NATURE TRAIL At the north end of the national park near the Pont Casse junction, a sign on the road to Castle Bruce marks the turnoff for Emerald Falls Nature Trail, the national park's most accessible trail. An easy 30-minute walk on a good half-mile footpath, it passes through lush forest to a beautiful cascade that drops 20 feet into a grotto of black rock with emerald walls of ferns, orchids, and dense foliage. (The pool is large enough for a swim. Bring a towel; there are no facilities.)

The trail has lookouts over the magnificent Belle Fille Valley, an area of banana groves backed by jungle-thick mountains, and a stretch of the wild east coast at Castle Bruce. A short paved section of the trail is part of the old road—an ancient Indian trail—to Castle Bruce used by the Caribs before the main road was built in the 1960s.

THE IMPERIAL ROAD The 20-mile stretch known as the Imperial Road, between Pont Casse and Marigot on the northeast coast, crosses the heart of the Central Forest Reserve, one of two reserves in northern Dominica. The other, the enormous Northern Forest Reserve, is dominated by the island's highest peak, Morne Diablotin at 4,748 feet. The northern reserve is the last refuge of the rare Imperial parrot, known locally as the *sisserou,* and its smaller relative, the red-necked parrot, or *jacquot.*

The Central Forest Reserve protects a small gommier forest with gigantic trees up to 120 feet in height. The gommier is a beautiful hardwood used to make furniture, but for centuries it has been used by the Amerindians to make oceangoing canoes. The top branches of the gommier are the principal nesting places for Dominica's endangered parrots. Before strong conservation measures were put in place, commercial logging was destroying the forests at an alarming rate. The trend has been stopped but poaching of trees and birds does continue.

From the gommier forest the road drops into lime and banana plantations laced with ferns along the Pagua River. At Pagua Bay a wide crest of golden sand bracketed by rocky cliffs is washed by the crashing waves of the Atlantic, wind-sheared vegetation clings hard to the cliffs. The bay is the north boundary of the Carib Indian Reservation.

THE CARIB INDIAN RESERVATION Dominica is the only place in the Caribbean where the Carib, after whom the Caribbean is named, have survived. In 1903 approximately 3,750 acres, including eight hamlets in the northeastern part of Dominica from Castle Bruce to Pagua Bay, were set aside as a reserve for the Caribs. The land is held in common by the 3,202 descendants of the Caribs who inhabited the island at the time of Columbus. To be eligible claimants must have at least one parent of Carib origin and must reside in the reservation. About 10 percent of the descendants are considered predominantly of Carib stock but there are probably no pure-blooded Caribs today. Those who survived the wars or were not hunted down by the earlier settlers eventually intermingled with other people who came to the island. Today the Caribs you meet usually have rather distinct Asian features and straight black hair and bear some resemblance to the Amerindians of South America. Until recently some lived in traditional thatched huts, but those dwellings have been replaced by modern houses.

Visitors are often misled by descriptions in brochures and some guidebooks and go to the Carib reserve expecting to see a Stone Age people living as they did when Columbus arrived five hundred years ago. The Carib villages, as well as most of the people themselves, are indistinguishable from others on the island. A few Carib traditions that link them with their past have survived nevertheless. The Carib straw craft is instantly recognizable by its design and fabric and is different from any other straw woven in the Caribbean.

Another legacy—but one that is getting harder to find—is the oceangoing canoe that the Indians make from the trunk of the gommier tree. On the beach at Castle Bruce, you can sometimes see boatmen making dugout canoes in the same method used by the Indians since before Columbus. A modified version is still made and used as fishing boats in other Eastern Caribbean islands.

PORTSMOUTH The small, sleepy village of about 2,000 people overlooks Portsmouth Bay, known in history as Prince Rupert Bay. This wide natural harbor has a freshwater source, Indian River, on the south end. Behind the town rises Mount Diablotin, Dominica's highest peak. The natural harbor, a freshwater supply, and a defensive headland—the Cabrits Peninsula on the north side of the bay—were reasons enough for the area to be strategically important to the British and French and heavily fortified during their colonial wars. Indeed, one of the most decisive naval battles of the colonial wars was fought here in 1782. The British victory helped Britain establish its sea supremacy over the French and hence, the trade routes and wealth of the West Indies.

Portsmouth has a few modest beachfront hotels and a rustic restaurant on the beach. Windsurfing and snorkeling are the main watersports to enjoy here.

CABRITS HISTORICAL AND MARINE PARK The silhouette of the 260-acre Cabrits Peninsula can be recognized by its two steep hills, remnants of ancient volcanoes. The peninsula, a freshwater swamp that joins it to the mainland, and an 800-acre marine reserve in adjoining Douglas Bay make up the Cabrits Historical and Marine Park, which is part of the Dominica National Park. "Cabrit" is said to come from the word meaning goat in several European languages. Early exploration ships had the habit of leaving goats here to graze so that they would have fresh meat to eat on future visits.

From 1770 to 1815, on a promontory of the peninsula, the British built Fort Shirley, one of their most impressive military installations in the Caribbean. Since 1982 the extensive ruins have been under restoration following the original plans, which were found preserved in England. In addition to the battlements, there is a museum in the former powder magazines and trails—one leading to the ghostly remnants of the commander's house, now choked by enormous roots of ficus and sandbox trees.

When restoration began, the growth all but obscured the ruins. Prior to the area becoming a national park, the Forestry Division had planted trees on an experimental basis; even earlier, orchards of tropical fruit trees were cultivated here, so that now the park has an interesting variety of Caribbean flora. The adjoining swamp hosts a variety of plants and birds; and on the park's beaches, two species of sea turtles nest here from April to September. The marine park of Douglas Bay is a popular snorkeling area.

In the terminal reception hall, passengers are introduced to the attractions with audio-visual displays. (The Cabrit project was the 1990 winner of the Caribbean Heritage Award, a grant given by American Express to encourage historic preservation.)

THE INDIAN RIVER South of Portsmouth at the mouth of the Indian River a rowboat with a nature guide can be rented for a trip up river. The tranquil estuary is so thick with tropical vegetation, it forms a tunnel over the river so dense only slim rays of light filter through the foliage, dancing on the leaves and water, creating a hauntingly beautiful setting. About 30 minutes up the river, your boatman stops at a clearing where he leads his group on a hike, identifying the birds and flora along the way.

 # SHOPPING

Dominica is not a place for duty-free shopping for designer fashions and fancy electronics, but it is definitely worthwhile if you are interested in handcrafts. Dominica's crafts are not only good but distinctive, particularly the products of the Carib Indians and grass rugs. In recent years, crafts in Dominica have been flourishing with many shops specializing in art and crafts by local artists. *Discover Dominica,* a free tourist brochure sponsored by the government division of tourism, lists about a dozen local art and crafts shops with a brief description of their specialties: batiks, jewelry, tie-dye, pottery, and more.

The main handcraft centers in Roseau are: *Dominica Handcrafts* (Hanover Street); *Caribana Handcraft* (Cork Street) which specializes in products made by the Caribs; *Island Craft Co-Operative* (King George V Street); and *Tropicrafts Ltd.* (Queen Mary Street). The latter is the factory and shop for grass rugs made of *verti-vert*, as the khuskhus plant is known here. The craft was started in a Catholic convent by Belgian nuns who taught their students to make straw rugs using the designs they copied from traditional lace. Other good buys include soaps made locally from fresh coconut oil, leather crafts, cigars, and cassette recordings of traditional "jing-ping" folk music.

DINING AND RESTAURANTS

Dominica has a creole cuisine incorporating a great array of locally grown vegetables, fruits, and herbs that reflects its African and French heritage more than its British one. The most popular specialty is "mountain chicken," or frogs' legs, known locally by its creole name, *crapaud;* crayfish, or "river shrimp," and stuffed land crabs are others. Among the common vegetables are bananas, plantains, and dasheen, a root vegetable with green heart-shaped leaves, which can be seen growing throughout the country. The root is used like potatoes, and the young spinachlike leaves are used to make callaloo, a thick soup.

Evergreen Hotel Terrace Restaurant (Castle Comfort; 448–3288). In a delightful terrace setting overlooking the Caribbean, you can enjoy well-prepared local specialties at reasonable prices as well as a magnificent view.

La Robe Creole (3 Fort Street, Roseau; 448–2896). The Dominican cuisine turned out by Erica Burnett-Biscombe is reason enough to visit Roseau. Particularly outstanding is the callaloo and crab soup and the mountain chicken. Fish and meats are grilled over charcoal. Expensive.

The Orchard (King George V and Great George streets, Roseau; 448–3051). The menu has creole favorites like black pudding, rôti,

crabbacks, conch, and lobster. No credit cards. Moderate.

Reigate Hall Hotel (on a cliffside overlooking Roseau, about a winding mile or two from town; 448–4031) is known for its restaurant, which has a magnificent view and its specialties, mountain chicken and callaloo.

SPORTS

BEACHES/SWIMMING: Except for the golden strands of the northeast, most of Dominica's beaches are steel-gray volcanic sand. But the best swimming in Dominica is not always at seaside beaches. Lakes, rivers, and waterfalls of the interior provide some of the most pleasant spots. On the west coast at Layou, a 10-minute walk along the lush banks takes you to a spring-fed pool popular for swimming.

HIKING: The best and sometimes the only way to see Dominica's attractions is hiking. The easiest short walks are the Emerald Pool Nature Trail; Trafalgar Falls near Roseau; and Cabrits National Park. Longer, more strenuous hikes go to Freshwater Lake, Boeri Lake, and Middleham Falls. For hiking in the rain forest, you must have a guide; fast-growing vegetation often obscures trails, and it is easy to get disoriented and lost.

KAYAKING: Contact *Nature Island Tours* (448–3397; fax: 448–4042), which offers kayaking excursions.

SNORKELING/SCUBA DIVING: Dominica has only recently been discovered as a dive location. It has reefs on the north and west coasts. Hodges Beach, a white-sand beach on the northeast coast, faces three small offshore islands with banks of brain corals and an abundance of tropical fish. On the northwest shore the best snorkeling is found in Douglas Bay, where there is a large reef about 180 feet from shore in 20 to 50 feet of water.

On the south side of Roseau and about 300 feet north of the Anchorage Hotel, a reef approximately 180 feet from shore starts at about a 45-foot depth. Wall diving at Pointe Guignard, less than a mile north of Soufrière, holds the greatest interest for divers due to the variety of attractions: caves, lobsters, black and brown coral, sponges, and diverse marine life.

On the south end of the island, Scotts Head has a variety of diving locations from the Caribbean around to the Atlantic side of the promontory. These are mainly drop-offs and reef dives with characteristics similar to those of Pointe Guignard. The beach on the north side of Scotts Head is rocky, but it is popular for snorkeling, as the coral is within swimming distance. The area is small and features mostly finger corals, but it has a large variety of small, colorful reef fish.

Dive Dominica (448–2188) is a qualified dive operation offering a full range of services, including PADI instruction and a ten-passenger dive boat. Deep-sea fishing can also be arranged.

WHALEWATCHING: Seven species of whales and four dolphins species have been identified in waters off Dominica. Although whalewatching is available year-round, the best months are from October to April when sperm whales cavort only 3 to 8 miles offshore. Whalewatching excursions are well-organized and readily available from *Castle Comfort Diving Lodge/Dive Dominica* (P.O. Box 2253, Roseau; 448–2188; fax: 448–6088) and other local companies that offer daily tours. The cost is about US $40 per person.

WINDSURFING: The best areas for windsurfing are Hodges Beach on the north coast, Douglas Bay on the northwest, the west coast south of Roseau, and Soufrière Bay.

FESTIVALS AND CELEBRATIONS

Creole Day, which coincides with Dominica's Independence Day, is the year's main celebration. Schoolchildren, teachers, and other adults don the tradional, colorful madras costume for a day filled with parades, competitions, and other festive activities.

Martinique

FORT-DE-FRANCE

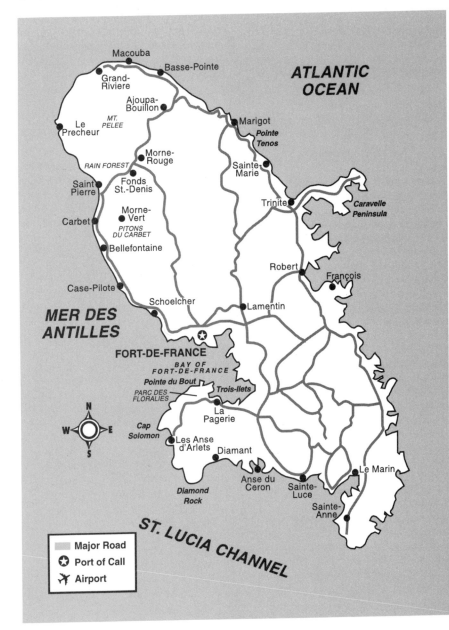

ATLANTIC OCEAN

Macouba
Basse-Pointe
Grand-Riviere
Ajoupa-Bouillon
Marigot
Pointe Tenos
Le Precheur
MT. PELEE
Morne-Rouge
Sainte-Marie
RAIN FOREST
Saint Pierre
Fonds St.-Denis
Trinite
Caravelle Peninsula
Carbet
Morne-Vert
PITONS DU CARBET
Bellefontaine
Robert
François
Case-Pilote
Schoelcher
Lamentin

MER DES ANTILLES

FORT-DE-FRANCE
BAY OF FORT-DE-FRANCE
Pointe du Bout
Trois-Ilets
PARC DES FLORALIES
La Pagerie

N
W   E
S

Cap Solomon
Les Anse d'Arlets
Diamant
Le Marin
Anse du Ceron
Sainte-Luce
Diamond Rock
Sainte-Anne

ST. LUCIA CHANNEL

Major Road
Port of Call
Airport

AT A GLANCE

CHAPTER CONTENTS

Martinique

THE ISLE OF FLOWERS

Beautiful and beguiling, Martinique is a paradox of razorback ridges and undulating meadows, steep peaks and soft hills, and possess the diversity of a continent rather than a small Caribbean island. Its three distinct regions of greatly varied terrain leave visitors with the impression that it is a much larger island.

Volcanic mountains, their peaks hiding under a hood of clouds, dominate the northern end of the island, where windswept cliffs hang high above the sea and the land climbs steeply along deeply creviced mountain slopes to the cone of Mt. Pelée, an active volcano more than 4,500 feet high. From these rain-forested slopes, the land drops to skirts of fertile green fields of banana and pineapple plantations. The central region rises in spiked peaks and ridges carved by rivers and streams that fall quickly to meadows with grazing cattle and sugarcane fields. Even greater in contrast is the dry, flat south end with parched lowland and saline flats bordered by white-sand beaches.

Some authorities say that when Columbus first sighted the island in 1493, he named it for a saint, as was his usual custom. Others claim that the name derives from a Carib word, *madinina*, meaning "isle of flowers"—a theory that's easy to believe, since masses of flowers color the landscape in every direction.

Columbus is believed to have come ashore at Carbet, on the Caribbean coast, on his fourth voyage, in 1502. The first settlers did not arrive until 1635, however, under Pierre Belain d'Esnambuc, a French nobleman from Dieppe. For the next quarter of a century, many other settlers arrived, and battles with the native Carib Indians were frequent. So, too, were skirmishes with the British and Dutch for control of the island. Then in 1763 Louis XV, in the Treaty of Paris, gave up Canada—which he reportedly called "a few snowy acres"—rather than his territory in the West Indies. The decision was later to be as pivotal for

the young United States as it was for France, which used Fort-de-France as a supply base to aid the Americans during the American Revolution.

By the early 19th century the voices of emancipation had grown strong. Through efforts led by Victor Schoelcher, an Alsacian deputy and one of the leading French abolitionists of the time, slavery in the French West Indies was abolished in 1848. Soon after, indentured workers from Asia were imported to work the sugar plantations. Some of this ethnic diversity—French, African, Asian—remains, but for the most part it has blended into an exotic combination creating Martinique's character today—which is as distinctive as her landscape.

FAST FACTS

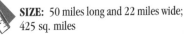

POPULATION: 359,572

SIZE: 50 miles long and 22 miles wide; 425 sq. miles

MAIN TOWN: Fort-de-France

GOVERNMENT: In 1946 Martinique was made a French *département* with representation in the French Parliament. More recently it was made a *région*. Martinique, along with Guadeloupe and her dependencies— St. Barts and St. Martin—make up the French West Indies. Its people are French citizens sharing the same culture and privileges as those in mainland France. The electorate sends four deputies and two senators to the French Parliament. It is governed by two elective bodies: the Conseil Général, with thirty-six representatives, and the Conseil Régional, with forty-one members.

 CURRENCY: French franc. US $1 fluctuates between 5 and 6 Ff. U.S. and Canadian travelers' checks and credit cards are readily accepted.

DEPARTURE TAX: None.

 LANGUAGE: French and creole. English is spoken in most tourist facilities, but a French phrase book and pocket dictionary are useful.

 PUBLIC HOLIDAYS: January 1, New Year's Day; Easter Monday; May 1, Labor Day; Ascension Thursday; Pentecost Monday; May 22, Slavery Abolition Day; July 14, Bastille Day; August 15, Assumption Day; November 1, All Saints Day; November 11, Armistice Day; December 25, Christmas Day.

 **TELEPHONE AREA CODE:** 596. To phone station-to-station from the United States, dial 011–596 plus the local number. In Martinique, "Télécartes," sold at post offices and outlets indicating "Télécartes en Vente Ici," are used in special booths marked "Télécom" and make local and international calling easier and less expensive.

 **AIRLINES:** American Airlines, American Eagle, and Air France via Miami or San Juan; Air Canada from Montreal and Toronto; LIAT from neighboring islands; and Air Martinique.

 **INFORMATION:**

In the United States: (800) 391–4909
   New York: Martinique Promotion Bureau, 444 Madison Avenue, New York, NY 10022; (212) 838–7800; fax: 838–7855.

Also, French Government Tourist Offices:
   Chicago: 676 N. Michigan Avenue, Suite 3360, Chicago, IL 60611; (312) 751–7800.
   Dallas: 2305 Cedar Spring Road, Suite 205, Dallas, TX 75201; (214) 720–4010.
   Los Angeles: 9454 Wilshire Boulevard, Suite 715, Beverly Hills, CA 90212; (301) 271–6665.

In Canada, French Government Tourist Board:
   Montreal: 1981 Avenue McGill College, Suite 480, Montreal, P.Q. H3A 2W9; (514) 844–8566; fax: (514) 844–8901.

Toronto: 1 Dundas Street W., Suite 2405, Toronto, Ont. M5G 1Z3; (416) 593–4717.

In Port:
Office Départemental du Tourisme (Martinique Tourist Office), Boulevard Alfassa, 97206 Fort-de-France, Martinique, F.W.I.; 63–79–60; fax: 73–66–93.
Hours: weekdays 7:30 A.M.–12:30 P.M.; and 2:30–5:30 P.M. (Friday to 5:00 P.M.); Saturday 8:00 A.M. to noon.
The office has maps, literature, and an English-speaking staff.

 # BUDGET PLANNING

Taxis and leading restaurants are expensive. Collective taxis and the ferry to Pointe du Bout are cheap. Sports facilities are comparable to prices in other popular Caribbean locations. The most economical way to tour the island is on an organized motorcoach tour or on your own, by rented car, if you can share the expense with others. Don't overlook the many walking excursions to be taken in Fort-de-France and the endless hiking opportunities around the island.

PORT PROFILE:

LOCATION/EMBARKATION: The main commercial harbor of Fort-de-France is located on the south side of the bay, a few minutes' drive from the city center. The newest passenger port, Pointe Simon, is on the north side within walking distance of town. Sometimes the largest ships anchor in the bay and tender passengers to the pier at the foot of town. Small ships sometimes dock at Pointe du Bout, the main resort area on the south side of the bay.

Two ships, regardless of the size, can pull dockside at Pointe Simon. The terminal building has an information desk to help arrange island tours; public phones that accept credit and phone cards; and restrooms.

A team of young English-speaking Martinic members of the new "Welcome Brigade,"

(Brigade d'Accueil) circulate in town to provide visitors with information and assistance. They are easily recognizable by their uniforms: white polo shirts, blue vests, and jeans, Bermuda shorts, or skirts. Members report regularly to fixed posts—near Pointe Simon dock, the old cruise ship terminal, and south edge of La Savane—and are on duty from 8:00 A.M. to noon (Tuesday 12:30 to 4:30 P.M.); schedules are also adjusted to coincide with cruise ship arrivals.

Other improvements include intensive English and tourism courses for taxi drivers; folklore presentations and local entertainment on board ships; and more information—maps, brochures, videos—about Martinique for distribution on board ship.

LOCAL TRANSPORTATION: Taxis are plentiful but tend to be expensive. There are taxi stands at the port, in town, and at major hotels. Sample fares from the port terminal: to Fort-de-France, about 63 Ff; to Pointe du Bout, 149 Ff. Between 8:00 P.M. and 6:00 A.M., there is a surcharge of 40 percent. Collective taxis, eight-seat limousines with the sign *TC,* are less costly and are used widely by tourists, particularly those who speak some French. The collectives depart frequently from the main terminal, on the waterfront at Pointe Simon, to outlying areas, discharging passengers en route. Public buses serve all parts of the island.

ROADS AND RENTALS: Martinique has some of the best roads in the Caribbean, although those over the mountainous interior are very winding. Essentially the network fans out from Fort-de-France and intersects with cross-island highways.

The Tourist Office has seven "Circuits Touristiques" for self-drive tours, which depart from Fort-de-France and vary in driving time from a half to a full day. They use one road on the outbound and a different one for the return, covering the north of the island in three circuits, the central in one, and the south in three. Each is named—North Caribbean, North Atlantic, and so on—with a color coded map to match the route's road signs.

With a valid driver's license you can rent a car for up to 20 days. There are many car-rental companies and most have French-made cars such as

Peugeot, Citroen, and Renault. Those in Fort-de-France are *Avis* (70–11–60); *Budget* (63–69–00); *Hertz* (60–64–64). They are open weekdays 8:00 A.M.–noon and 2:30–5:00 or 5:30 P.M.; Saturday to noon.

Bicycles and motorbikes can be rented from *Discount* (Pointe du Bout; 66–33–05); and *Funny* (Fort-de-France; 63–33–05). The Regional Natural Park of Martinique in cooperation with local bicycle organizations has designed off-the-beaten-track biking itineraries. For information call 73–19–30.

FERRY SERVICE: Fort-de-France is linked to Pointe du Bout, the main resort center, by frequent ferries that run daily from early morning until after midnight. One-way fare between Fort-de-France and Pointe du Bout is 11 Ff, round-trip, 24 Ff adults; 10 Ff children. In Fort-de-France all ferries (known locally as *vedettes*) depart the Quai d'Esnambuc, the pier at the foot of the town center.

INTERISLAND AIR SERVICE: See Fast Facts.

EMERGENCY NUMBERS:
Medical: La Meynard
(Quartier La Meynard; 55–20–00)
on the east side of Fort-de-France is one of the main hospitals. The Tourist Office can assist in locating English-speaking doctors.
Police: 63–00–00

AUTHOR'S FAVORITE ATTRACTIONS

A DRIVE ALONG ROUTE DE LA TRACE
TRACE DES JÉSUITES RAIN FOREST TRAIL
AJOUPA BOUILLON/BASSE-
POINTE/GRAND'RIVIÈRE DRIVE
FORT-DE-FRANCE WALKABOUT

SHORE EXCURSIONS

Any of the seven self-drive circuits designed by the Tourist Office could be made by taxi, and local tour companies offer some by motorcoach. The most popular are likely to be sold as shore excursions on your ship. Sites mentioned here are described later in the chapter.

To St. Pierre along the West Coast, 3.5 hours, 390 Ff. The classic island tour runs north 18 miles along the Caribbean coast through picturesque fishing villages to St. Pierre, known as the "Paris of the West Indies" until 1902—when Mt. Pelée erupted and turned it into the Pompeii of the New World. Return via the volcanic observatory to the Route de la Trace or *Leyritz Plantation, St. James Rum Distillery* and *Balata Gardens.* The tour is made in the reverse direction.

Route de la Trace to North Coast, 6 hours, 500 Ff with lunch. Depart on Route de la Trace for the north end of the island at Grand'Rivière via the pretty town of Ajoupa Bouillon and Basse-Pointe. Return via the Atlantic or Caribbean coast.

To Trois-Ilets and La Pagerie, 3 hours, 420 Ff. South of the capital, a westbound circuit follows the expressway on a wide swing around Fort-de-France Bay to Rivière-Salée, where a detour west leads to Trois-Ilets, Pointe du Bout, and the Caribbean coast beaches. Visit *Pagerie Museum* and a fish barbecue of *Les Salines* beach.

MARTINIQUE ON YOUR OWN

The pretty capital of Martinique stretches from the Bay of Fort-de-France to the foothills of the Pitons du Carbet, rising more than 3,500 feet in the background. A natural port and commercial center, Fort-de-France did not become the capital until 1902, after the old capital, St. Pierre, was buried under volcanic ash from Mt. Pelée.

A FORT-DE-FRANCE WALKABOUT

Fort-de-France is a delightful place to explore on foot. Its narrow streets, reminiscent of the French Quarter in New Orleans, are lined with pastel-colored houses and lacy wrought-iron balconies housing boutiques with fashions from Paris. The main business and shopping district is a 6-block area bounded by rue de la Liberté and rue de la République, from rue Victor Hugo to rue Perrinon—all to the west of La Savane.

LA SAVANE (1) A large public square by the bay is the heart of the city, with spacious lawns shaded by royal palms, flamboyant, and other flowering trees. The houses, hotels, and cafes around the square are in buildings dating from the 19th century that help give the city its colonial character. The square, a good people-watching spot, serves both as a playground and promenade often used for parades and other events on special occasions and public holidays.

One of the park's main attractions is a statue of Marie Josephe Rose Tascher de la Pagerie, better known in history as Napoleon's Josephine. The white Carrara-marble statue by Vital Dubray shows her in the flowing high-waisted dress of the First Empire and looking across the bay to Trois-Ilets, where she was born. A relief on the base depicts Josephine's coronation. At the southeast end of the park, the 17th-century Fort St. Louis, surrounded by water on three sides, commands the harbor. It is now open for visitors; admission is 25 Ff.

The southwest corner also has a lively open-air market where you can find madras-costumed dolls, ceramics, shell figures, and wicker and straw products, as well as inexpensive costume jewelry and Haitian paintings. *Centre des Metiers d'Art*, west of the park beyond the Tourist Office, also has a small selection of local crafts, particularly bright patchwork tapestries, a Martinique specialty.

SCHOELCHER LIBRARY (2) On the northwest corner of La Savane is the city's architectural showpiece, the Schoelcher Library (rue de la Liberté; 72–45–55). A Romanesque-Byzantine gem built for the Paris Exposition of 1889, it was dismantled and shipped piece by piece to Fort-de-France, where it was reconstructed on the site of the old Hotel du Petit Gouvernement, where the Empress Josephine once resided. Named for the French abolitionist Victor Schoelcher, who donated his library of nine thousand volumes to Martinique in 1883, the building has an elaborate fanciful facade. Hours: weekday 8:30 A.M.–noon and 2:30–6:00 P.M.; Saturday to noon.

MUSEE DEPARTEMENTAL DE LA MAR-TINIQUE (3) Situated in a beautifully restored colonial house on the west side of La Savane, the Archaeological Museum (9, rue de la Liberté; 71–57–05) has artifacts from pre-Columbian Amerindian cultures and representations of the island's everyday life and folklore in literature, art, music, clothing, and crafts. Hours: Weekdays 9:00 A.M.–1:00 P.M. and 2:00–5:00 P.M.; Saturday 9:00 A.M.–noon. Admission: 15 Ff adult; 5 Ff children.

Two companion galleries are the *Musee de l'Esclavage* (Route de Didier), on the history of slavery; and *Archival Services of Martinique* (Tartenson; rue St.-John Perse; 63–88–46) with a collection of maps and engravings from the 16th and 17th centuries.

CATHEDRALE ST.-LOUIS (4) Also west of La Savane, rue Blenac leads to the Cathédral St.-Louis, on the site of previous churches destroyed by war or natural catastrophes. The present church, built in 1978 following the design of the earlier 19th-century church, is earthquake-proof. Its fine stained-glass windows were restored.

Another block west at the rues Isambert and Blenac is the open-air vegetable market **(5)**, particularly lively on Saturday mornings. It is the best place to see the exotic vegetables and herbs that inspire island cooks to the taste treats of creole cuisine.

Sightseeing Aids: The cultural Admission Ticket (Tickets d'Acces Culturel), known as TAC, is a pass to most of Martinique's museums and cultural attractions. It can be purchased at island museums for 35 Ff and is valid for one year.

Walking Tours: *Azimut Tourisme Urbain* (74, Route de la Folie, 97200 Fort-de-France; 60–16–59; fax: 63–05–46) has four walking excursions of Fort-de-France accompanied by multilingual guides. (Azimut also has a kiosk in the craft market at La Savane.) *Traces* is a 2.5-hour historic/architectural tour; *Verso* reveals the unknown heart of the city; *Ship-Shop* is a shopping/sight-seeing excursion designed for cruise-ship passengers; and *Bet Afe* (creole words for "firefly") is Fort-de-France-by-night with dinner and entertainment.

A DRIVE AROUND MARTINIQUE

NORTH TO MT. PELÉE ALONG THE WEST COAST

The coastal road passes the large suburb of Schoelcher—once merely a small fishing village named for the French abolitionist—to Case-Pilote, one of the oldest settlements on the island, named after a Carib chief who befriended the French. Carbet, the probable site of Columbus's landing in 1502, has an 18th-century church and the *Amazona Zoological Gardens,* a private zoo with about seventy species of birds and animals endemic to the Amazon basin. Hours: Daily 9:00 A.M.–6:00 P.M.; admission 15 Ff.

Nearby at Anse Turin, a village where Paul Gauguin lived for four months in 1887, is the *Gauguin Art Center and Museum* (77–22–66), a small memorial to the noted French painter. The contemporary structure is in a rustic setting designed to encompass the natural surroundings that inspired Gauguin and contains reproductions of the dozen pictures he painted on the island, including *Two Women of Martinique* and *The Bay of St.-Pierre.* There are books about the painter, biographical information, and some of his letters. Hours: daily 10:00 A.M.–5:00 P.M. Admission: 10 Ff.

Valley of the Butterflies (78–19–19), at Carbet's Botanical Garden, is situated among the ruins of the earliest 17-century settlements of Martinique. Admission: 38 Ff adults; 28 Ff children.

Farther north at Fond Capot you can enjoy panoramic views of the Caribbean, Mt. Pelée, and the Pitons du Carbet. All along the serpentine coast, roads climb inland to pretty mountain villages and trails on the Pitons du Carbet. The landscape and cool climate has earned it the name of Little Switzerland.

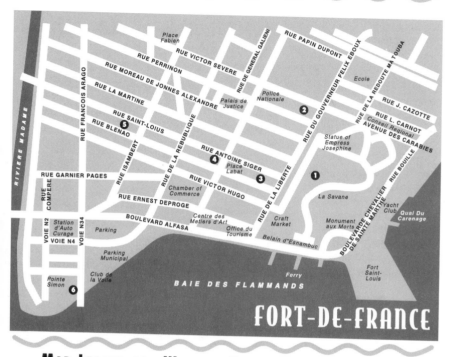

FORT-DE-FRANCE

MAP LEGEND FOR WALKING TOUR OF FORT-DE-FRANCE

1. La Savane
2. Schoelcher Library
3. Musée Départemental de la Martinique
4. Cathédral St.-Louis
5. Open-air vegetable market
6. Pointe Simon

ST. PIERRE The once-fashionable capital, St. Pierre was totally devastated by the eruption of Mt. Pelée on May 8, 1902, when a cloud of burning gas with temperatures over 3,600 degrees F, ash, and stones rained down it. In minutes the entire population of 30,000 perished, except for one survivor, a prisoner named Cyparis who was protected by the walls of his underground cell. The town never recovered. Today St. Pierre is only a village.

The eruption was not a total surprise. An increase in Mt. Pelée's volcanic activity had been observed for several years prior to the tragedy. In early April of 1902, tremors and steam were observed, and later in the month, ash fell over the mountain during five days of rumblings. In early May ash fell on the town itself for the first time. Nearby rivers and streams swelled, and birds fled.

Yet no one heeded the warnings, least of all the municipal authorities who were preparing for an election on May 8.

St. Pierre Museum (Musée Volcanologique 77–15–16), created by American volcanologist Franck A. Perret, is a poignant memorial to the fatal eruption. A number of clocks on display—all stopped at the same time—mark the historic moment. Photographs and documents of the old town and exhibits of molten glass and twisted metal reveal its ferocity. Among the bizarre relics are petrified spaghetti, teapots fused with lava, and twisted musical instruments, melted by the heat. Hours: daily 9:00 A.M.–noon and 3:00–5:00 P.M. Admission is 10 Ff.

The *Cyparis Express,* known as the Little Train of St. Pierre, offers tours of the historic town. On weekdays the tour lasts 1 hour; on weekends 30 minutes. Price is 40 Ff. Resting on the seafloor in St. Pierre Bay are twelve ships that were destroyed in the harbor at the time of Mt. Pelée's eruption. Because the bones of survivors were found, the site is a memorial grave kept intact. Jacques Cousteau headed the team that researched the site and made a film of it.

LE PRECHEUR North of St.-Pierre the coastal road skirts the spectacular scenery of Mt. Pelée's western flank. Le Prêcheur, one of the oldest villages on the island, is a base for climbing the mountain. Beyond Le Prêcheur a secondary road twists along the coast to Anse Céron, a beautiful beach with heavy surf and a tiny offshore island, La Perle, a dive site.

Inland, *Habitation Céron* (Anse Céron, Le Prêcheur; 52–94–53), the manor house of a 17th-century sugar plantation in a beautiful park setting by a stream, has impressive remains of its ancient mill. Surrounded by fields where coffee, cocoa, tapioca, and bananas once flourished, the principal crop today is avocados. Céron, historically, is connected to Françoise d' Aubigue, the celebrated Madame de Maintenon who secretly wed France's King Louis XIV. Individuals are welcome and day trips for small groups can be organized by bus or boat from Fort-de-France. The outing includes a Creole luncheon, a swim, and guided tour of the estate by the English-speaking owner, Madame Laurence des Grottes.

From St.-Pierre two routes cross the island. One passes the *Observatoire du Morne des Cadets,* the observatory that monitors Mt. Pelée's activity, and the village of Fonds St.-Denis, where the slopes on both sides of the road are covered with gardens. Fonds St.-Denis is a frequent winner of an annual, islandwide contest for the village with the most beautiful flowers. After Fonds St.-Denis, the cross-island highway joins the Route de la Trace.

NORTH OF FORT-DE-FRANCE OVER THE PITONS

Behind Fort-de-France are the Pitons du Carbet traversed by the most scenic route on the island, Route de la Trace, known simply as the Trace, a central highland road that winds through the rain forests of the Regional Natural Park of Martinique (PNRM) to the foot of Mt. Pelée. As the narrow road leaves Fort-de-France and snakes up the mountains, you can enjoy sweeping views of the city and the bay. In the distance on the north is *Sacre-Coeur de Balata,* a miniature of Montmartre in Paris set, incongruously, in the tropical landscape of the Pitons.

BALATA GARDENS On a hillside at 1,475 feet, overlooking the capital, is a private botanical park created by its owner, an artist and landscape designer. It is centered around a restored creole house furnished with antiques and has more than a thousand varieties of tropical plants. At the entrance are hedges of brilliant magenta bougainvillea, a flower that grows profusely in Martinique in many colors and named for Louis de Bougainville, who imported it from Brazil in 1768. Walkways through the gardens have lookouts that take advantage of the fabulous views of Fort-de-France and Cap Salomon; one path leads to a lily pond framed by a dramatic view of the Pitons. Along the way, look closely and you probably will see hummingbirds flitting about the hibiscus. Hours: daily 9:00 A.M.–6:00 P.M. Admission: 30 Ff; signs and literature are in French.

ABSALON MINERAL SPRINGS On the west side of the Trace, the Absalon Mineral Springs are the starting place of trails through the central mountains. In the immediate vicinity of the springs is a loop trail of about 3 hours' hiking.

A mile north of the springs, the Trace reaches its highest altitude at 2,133 feet. A tunnel on the north side of the Pitons, Deux Choux, marks a junction of the Trace with D 1, a major east-west artery. The road west runs through a deep gorge known as the Porte d'Enfer, or Gate of Hell, to Fonds St.-Denis and St.-Pierre, on the coast.

TRACE DES JESUITS East of the Trace and the cross-island highway is the Jesuits' Trail, one of the most popular rain-forest hikes in Martinique. The signposted trail, maintained by the Forestry and Park departments, starts less than a mile north of Deux Choux and passes through beautiful forest under a canopy of giant hardwoods, such as mahogany and gommier, typical of the Eastern Caribbean. The gommier, also known as white gum, has a tall, straight trunk whose sap the early

Jesuit missionaries used in making incense—hence the trail's name. The Amerindians used the trunks of the gommier for their dugout canoes. Today a boat called gommiers, or *gomye,* used by local fishermen, derives from the tradition.

It is about an hour's walk to the Lorrain River, which is a pleasant spot for a picnic. The complete hike takes about 3 hours and is ideal if you have limited time or want a relatively easy hike to see a tropical rain forest up close. Scheduled hikes led by park guides are available.

MT. PELÉE Towering over the northern part of Martinique from almost any location is cloud-capped Mt. Pelée, the island's highest peak, at 4,584 feet. The outward signs of volcanic activity have subsided, but the volcano is still boiling and belching. The hike to the summit takes a strenuous 5 hours round-trip.

At Le Morne-Rouge you can turn west to St.-Pierre and return to Fort-de-France via the Caribbean coast. Or turn east to continue to Grand'Rivière on the north coast.

AJOUPA BOUILLON The route east snakes through a beautiful part of the highlands under a canopy of tall tree ferns, bamboos, and palms to Ajoupa Bouillon. It is a delightful mountain hamlet, dating from the 17th century, where flowering hedges and colorful gardens border the highway. A narrow dirt road and trail marked GORGE DE LA FALAISE leads to a trail to a narrow river canyon with a beautiful waterfall. Admission: 35 Ff (US $7), adults; 15 Ff (US $3), children. Guide, 35 Ff.

LES OMBRAGES On the east side of Ajoupa Bouillon is one of the island's most beautiful attractions, Les Ombrages—tropical gardens and rain-forest trail in a magnificent natural setting. Heliconia and other colorful flowers natural to the rain forest have been added along a signposted footpath, which follows the natural contours of the land, winding beside a brook under a canopy of enormous trees and stands of bamboo that reach more than 60 feet in height. The privately maintained park provides a map for the 45-minute self-guided hike. There is an admission fee of 20 Ff for adults.

BASSE-POINTE From Ajoupa Bouillon the highway winds through green hillsides of banana, sugarcane, and pineapple plantations to Basse-Pointe, the main town on the northern Atlantic coast. Basse-Pointe (which means "low point") is situated at the base of windswept cliffs that plunge into the sea. They are covered with heavy foliage sheared by the *alizés,* or northeast winds, that blow off the Atlantic. Basse-Pointe has a high concentration of East Indians brought to Martinique to work the cane fields after slavery was abolished. There is a Hindu temple in the area.

Musée de Poupées Végétales (Plantation Leyritz, 75–53–92), created by resident artist Will Fenton, has a display of fifty or so elegantly dressed miniature dolls of celebrated women, such as Mme. de Pompadour and Josephine Baker. The dolls are made from six hundred different natural fibers and plants. Hours: Daily 8:00 A.M.–5:00 P.M. Fee: 15 Ff with visit to the Leyritz gardens and plantation house, which dates from the 18th century.

Farther north, Macouba has one of the oldest churches of the island, and from there the road weaves north through banana, coffee, and tobacco fields to Grand'Rivière, crossing some of the most spectacular scenery on the island. Big volcano rocks that have tumbled down the mountains from Mt. Pelée rest at the edge of black-sand beaches where huge white-capped waves crash against the vertical-sided cliffs carpeted with wind-sheared foliage.

GRAND'RIVIÈRE On the isolated north coast is an old fishing village where time has stood still. Grand'Rivière is set against the deep green, wind-sheared cliffs of Mt. Pelée under palms and giant breadfruit trees. Village fishermen returning with the day's catch must perform a feat of great skill by riding the swells and, with split-second timing, pulling their boat onto the beach to avoid being slammed against the rocks by the crashing waves. From Grand'Rivière a trail through the forests of Mt. Pelée's northern flank rounds the coast.

EAST OF FORT-DE-FRANCE TO THE ATLANTIC COAST

Fort-de-France is separated on the south and east by a wide savannah, grazed by cattle and oxen and edged by a landscape of tumbling hills. The region is watered by the Blanche River and other streams that flow from the Pitons into the Lézarde

River, Martinique's longest river, which empties into Fort-de-France Bay at Le Lamentin.

Le Robert, a fishing village on the Atlantic, is connected to Fort-de-France by an expressway. Le François is one of the prettiest spots on the east coast, with offshore islets and shallow, calm water; boat excursions are available. Two islets have plantation houses that have been converted into inns.

CARAVELLE PENINSULA AND NATURE RESERVE Jutting into the Atlantic directly east of Fort-de-France at La Trinité is Presqu'ile de la Caravelle, a peninsula with a nature reserve on the eastern half. A road of about 5 miles crosses the peninsula to the ruins of Château Dubuc, a 17th-century plantation house, where there are trails to the easternmost point of the peninsula, marked by a 19th-century lighthouse. The chateau museum is open weekdays 8:30 A.M.–12:30 P.M. and 2:30–5:30. Admission: 10 Ff adults; 5 Ff children.

La Trinité, once one of the island's most prosperous towns, sits in the elbow of the Caravelle peninsula on a sheltered bay with beaches for safe swimming, overlooking the rockbound north coast. Between Ste.-Marie and Marigot at Pointe Ténos, there is a wooded park with a picnic area and marked trails overlooking a beautiful bay with wild windswept scenery.

At Ste.-Marie, the *Rum Museum* at the Saint James Distillery (75–30–02) is set on a sugar plantation in an old creole plantation house. It has displays of engravings, artifacts, and machinery on the history of sugar and rum production from 1765 to the present; visitors can sample Saint James products. Hours: Weekdays 9:00 A.M.–5:30 P.M.; weekends 9:00 A.M.–1:00 P.M.

Nearby the *Banana Museum* is the first of its kind in the Caribbean. Located on Habitation Limbe, an authentic 17th-century banana plantation, the exhibits cover the history, cultivation, and medicinal properties of the banana and its importance to the island's economy. Banana beverages and pastries are available. Admission: 30 Ff (US $6). Hours: daily 9:00 A.M. to 5:00 P.M.

Farther north, *Fonds Saint-Jacques* is one of the best-preserved estates on Martinique. Built by Dominican Fathers in 1658, it was the home from 1693 to 1705 of Père Labat, the French Dominican priest who was an explorer, architect, engineer, historian—and even warrior against the British. The chapel, windmill, and workshops remain, and there is a museum, *Musée du Père Labat.* Hours: Daily 9:00 A.M.–noon. Admission is free; guided tours are available.

SOUTH OF FORT-DE-FRANCE ALONG THE CARIBBEAN

The Caribbean coast south of the capital bulges with a peninsula that stretches west to Cap Salomon and is scalloped by pretty coves and white-sand beaches. While there are good roads to the area, the quickest and most direct way to get there from Fort-de-France is the 20-minute ferry ride across the bay to Pointe du Bout, a small finger of land with luxury hotels and a marina. Small cruise ships dock here occasionally, and boats sail from here daily on excursions down the coast for swimming and snorkeling. Some of Martinique's main attractions are only a few miles from Pointe du Bout.

LES TROIS-ILETS On the bay, halfway between Pointe du Bout and Rivière-Salée, is the historic town of Les Trois-Ilets, one of the prettiest villages in Martinique. In its heyday the town prospered from the nine refineries that served the nearby sugar plantations. Much of that history has been preserved in nearby attractions.

MAISON DE LA CANNE (Pointe de la Vatable; 68–32–04). Opened in 1987, the House of Sugar is a modern museum in the ruins of an old distillery, with exceptionally good exhibits on sugar and rum in a park setting, labeled in French and English for a self-guided tour. Hours: Daily except Monday 9:00 A.M.–5:00 P.M. Admission: 15 Ff adults; 5 Ff children.

POTTERY CENTER (Centre Artisanal de la Poterie) East of Trois-Ilets a pottery-making center, established in the 18th century, was restored in 1987 to serve as an artisan's center. Using the rich terra cotta-colored clay of the area, potters make a mixture of three types of clay, which they fashion on hand-thrown wheels into objects such as carafes, bowls, ashtrays, and copies of pre-Columbian artifacts.

LA PAGERIE South of Trois-Ilets is La Pagerie, the former sugar plantation where Empress Josephine was born. The remaining stone structures of the estate house now contain the *Musée de La Pagerie* (68–34–55), set in landscaped gardens. The museum has a collection of furniture (including the bed that Josephine slept in until her departure for France at age sixteen), portraits of her and of Napoleon, invitations to great balls in Paris, medals, bills attesting to her extravagance as the empress, and letters—notably a passionate one from the lovelorn Napoleon. Hours: Daily except Monday from 9:00 A.M.–5:30 P.M. Admission: 20 Ff adults; 5 Ff children.

The Caribbean coast from Pointe du Bout south to Ste.-Anne has a series of pretty coves and beaches. Anse (or cove) Mitan is one of the island's main restaurant, bar, and water-sports centers.

The road winds south over hilly terrain to Les Anses d'Arlets, a large bay with mile-long palm-shaded white-sand beaches cupped by Cap Solomon, the westernmost point of Martinique's Caribbean coast. Popular weekend yacht havens today, these idyllic coves inspired Paul Gauguin, who lived here in 1887. Grande Anse, a fishing village, has colorful gommiers, fishing boats made in the traditional manner of the Amerindian dugouts.

DIAMOND ROCK Two miles off the south coast, at Diamond Bay, is a steep-sided volcanic rock jutting from the sea to 590 feet. The multisided rock has the shape of a cut gem, hence its name, Diamond Rock. It is the only known rock in history to be declared a warship. In the early 19th century, during the endless battles between Britain and France, the British landed two hundred sailors with cannons and arms on the rock, declaring it the *HMS Diamond Rock.* For eighteen months, they were able to hold the French at bay, bombarding any French vessel that came within range. When the French learned—through an "indiscretion"—that the British defenders had grown weary of their isolation, they devised an ingenious scheme to regain the rock. They loaded a boat with rum and caused it to run aground on the rock. As expected, the British garrison quickly consumed the rum, and the French took the rock without difficulty.

Two miles of tree-shaded beach stretch along the bay overlooking Diamond Rock, and at the eastern end is Le Diamant, one of the island's oldest villages. You can rent a boat to go to the rock, but the crossing is often rough. Diamond Bay is one of Martinique's main windsurfing locations. From Le Diamant you can return on the expressway to Fort-de-France, or continue south to Ste.-Luce, a fishing village and popular resort. The route south of Ste.-Luce to Ste.-Anne passes Le Marin, a picturesque old village with a large, yacht-filled marina.

SAINTE-ANNE An idyllic colonial village with a tree-shaded square anchored by an 18th-century stone church, the popular resort of Ste.-Anne has good seafood restaurants and water-sports facilities, as well as a pretty beach. At the south tip of the island, *Grande Anse des Salines* is a mile-long crescent of powdery white sand shaded by coconut palms that bow to the sea. The beach is trimmed with almond and white pear trees and huge sea grape with bent, knotted trunks. A similar tree, the manchineel, is marked with bands of red paint as a warning: Its small green apples are poisonous. Do not sit under the tree, particularly while it is raining, because the water washes sap from the leaves and bark that can cause a rash and severe blisters. The Caribs used its sap to coat their arrowheads.

SHOPPING

French perfume, crystal, jewelry, sandals, leather goods, designer scarves, and liqueurs, as well as locally made dolls, patchwork tapestries and other crafts, and rums are among the good buys. At the time of purchase, when you pay with traveler's checks or certain credit cards, shops selling duty-free items to tourists deduct the 20 percent tax on perfumes and other luxury items that local residents must pay. Downtown stores are open weekdays from 8:30 A.M. to 6:00 P.M.; Saturday to noon.

ART AND ARTISTS: *Galerie Artibijoux* (89, rue Victor Hugo) specializes in Haitian painting and some local artists. It stocks a few French and English art books and has a small costume-jewelry section. *The Gold Dolphin* (7, boulevard Chevalier, Ste.-Marthe) is a gallery with an exposition salon. Paintings by native-born Martiniquais and other artists who live on the island are shown year-round in some hotels.

Caribbean Art Center (boulevard Alfassas, next to the Tourist Office) has colorful patchwork tapestries that are considered original works of art; the best carry such artists' names as Réné Corail and Balisier. Prices range from $150 and up. *Boutique Tam Tam* (60, rue Victor Hugo) is a new shop with tasteful, inexpensive crafts from Haiti, South America, and Bali.

CHINA AND CRYSTAL: *Cadet Daniel* (72, rue Antoine Siger) stocks Christofle silver, Limoges china, and crystal from Baccarat, Lalique, and others. *Roger Albert* (rue Victor Hugo) is another long-established emporium for crystal.

CLOTHING: In fashion-conscious Martinique a new crop of boutiques blossoms each season. Here are a few that carry stylish pret-à-porter (ready-to-wear): *La Chamade* (38, rue Victor Hugo), *Georgia* (56, rue Victor Hugo), and *Ah! Nana*. For the hottest new look in sportswear from Paris and Côte d'Azur, try *Parenthése* (6, rue Schoelcher). *Samourai* (rue Antonie Siger) and *New Borsalino* (27, rue Blenac) are exclusive men's shops. The latter has handsome Italian-made, linen sports shirts in a variety of fashion colors for $75 to $100.

Mounia (rue Perrinon) carries top French designers including Claude Montana, Dorothée Bis, and Yves St. Laurent. Owned by Mounia, a beautiful Martiniquaise who was one of the top models for St. Laurent. Shows presenting collections by young Martinique designers are held in Fort-de-France hotels in spring and fall. Among the prominent names are Yves Gérard, Daniel Rodap and Gilbert Basson, whose ready-to-wear label is "Gigi," and *Paul-Herve Elizabeth*, who recently returned from Paris and has opened his elegant *Le Showroom* (rue Blenac).

The streets alongside the cathedral and open-air vegetable market are lined with shoe stores. Most carry reasonably priced shoes of mediocre quality for men and women, but a terrific buy are stylish, inexpensive summer sandals, averaging $15 to $25. Try *Sergio Valenti* (corner of rues Isambert and Blenac), and *Vankris* (46,

rue Lamartine).

JEWELRY *Gerbe d'Or* and *L'Or et L'Argent* sell pretty island-made 18-karat gold baubles, including the beaded *collier chou*, or "darling's necklace," the traditional ornament for the Creole costume. You can find great costume jewelry for low prices at *Cleopatre* (72, rue Victor Hugo) and in some of the stalls at the craft market (La Savane). *Cadet Daniel* carries the work of Emile Mothie, a top designer of both classic and modern Creole jewelry.

LEATHER AND LUGGAGE *Roger Albert* (rue Victor Hugo) has a leather goods department, but the best, most attractive selections can be found at *La Calèche* (41, rue Victor Hugo).

LIQUEUR AND WINE: Martinique rum is some of the Caribbean's best and least expensive—about $7 a fifth for light, $9 for dark; aged rums are higher. *La Case à Rhum* (rue de la Liberté) has a good selection. The dozen or so members of Le Comité de Défense du Rhum welcome visitors at their distilleries from January to July to see the processing and sample their products.

MUSIC: Records and tapes from folk music to zouk, the French West Indies answer to calypso, are found at *Georges Debs, Hit Parade,* and other downtown shops, but prices are often higher than at record/video shops in New York.

PERFUMES: Martinique boasts the lowest prices for French perfume in the Caribbean; but prices are now so standardized by French suppliers, I have found little difference. The best savings are to be found on quantities of an ounce or more. The exchange rate of the franc fluctuates, however, so check prices in advance at home to know how much of a bargain you can get. *Roger Albert* (rue Victor Hugo) has the largest selection but the least helpful staff.

SPICES AND GROCERIES: Gourmet chefs can have a field day here buying spices in the open-air markets and pâté or canned quail at local supermarkets. *Au Printemps* and *K-Dis,* two department stores, sell shredders, graters, and other culinary collectibles. French wines and champagnes are sold in grocery stores. One of the best products is fruit preserved in rum, attractively packaged in glass jars and sold at the St. James Distillery in Ste.-Marie.

In the village of Bezaudin, near Ste.-Marie, *Ella,* a "boutique gourmande" specializes in exotic homegrown spices, preserves, and syrups. Another homemade delicacy, *rillettes landaises au foie gras,* is prepared at Habitation Durocher, a duck farm near Lamentin. At Christmas its specialty is a *terrine de foie gras* made with Armagnac and packaged in attractive crockery made by Pottery Center of Trois-Ilets.

DINING AND RESTAURANTS

Martinique has excellent restaurants, most offering traditional French and creole cuisine. Fresh seafood is always on the menu, prepared in creole style or in a more sophisticated French manner. Classic French dishes are often served with exotic tropical fruits and vegetables, such as guava, soursop, cassava, christophene, and breadfruit. Specialties vary according to the morning's catch. Typical are *soudons* (small clams), *z'habitants* or *cribiches* (freshwater crayfish), *lambi* (conch), *oursin* (sea urchin), and *langouste* (clawless Caribbean lobster). Prices for a three-course meal for one person, without wine, can be inexpensive (under $30) to moderate ($30–$45) to expensive ($45 and up). Most restaurants include tax and service charges in the menu prices. Restaurants close one day each week, but there is no uniformity about it. Check in advance and also inquire about the use of credit cards.

FORT-DE-FRANCE

La Belle Epoque (2.5 km Route de Didier; 64–41–19). Nine tables on a spacious terrace of a pretty turn-of-the-century house is the setting to enjoy light, creative dishes by young Martinican chef Yves Coyac. Elegant and excellent. Open Tuesday to Saturday. Expensive.

Le Blenac (3 rue Blenac; 70–18–41). Situated just off La Savane, this tiny, tidy, and inexpensive restaurant is a good place to sample Creole staples. Daily specials for 45–50 Ff.

La Mouina (2.5 km Route de la Redoute; 79–34–57). French and refined creole dishes are served in the dining room and on the terrace of a lovely, colonial villa in a country setting overlooking an orchard and the town. Closed Saturday and Sunday. Expensive.

La Plantation (Lamentin, near the airport; 50–16–08). The dining room of the eight-unit Martinique Cottages is one of Martinique's best restaurants for its French and Creole specialties. Its country garden setting, so near to town, is delightful.

Le Planteur (1 rue de la Liberté; 63–17–45). On the second floor with views of La Savane and the boat-filled bay, the restaurant is the creation of Andre-Charles Donatien, a Martinican chef who learned cooking basics in his family's kitchen in Carbet and fine-tuned them in Burgundy. His recipes have earned him a Gault-Millau "Golden Key."

La Foulard (Schoelcher; 61–15–72). By the sea north of Fort-de-France, this is a long-established favorite for excellent seafood and French and Creole specialties. Expensive.

SOUTH OF FORT-DE-FRANCE

Aux Filets Bleus (Ste.-Anne; 76–73–42). Choose your lobster, pick a table, and go for a swim. Reservations are recommended. Closed Sunday and Monday evenings. No credit cards. Moderate.

NORTH OF FORT-DE-FRANCE

Le Colibri (Morne-des-Esses; 69–32–19). Clotilde Palladino's small home is the setting of a family restaurant. English is limited, but the creole food is so good and the atmosphere so pleasant you won't notice. Take one of the seven back terrace tables, relax, and enjoy the view and a 'ti punch while your meal is prepared to order. Phone ahead. Moderate.

La Factorerie (Quartier Fort, St.-Pierre; 78–12–53). Set in a hillside garden next to the ruins of the Eglise du Fort, the al fresco restaurant belongs to an agricultural training school that teaches students to serve, sow, and raise crops. Two daily three-course menus, plus a variety of à la carte selections are available. Closed Saturday and Sunday. No credit cards. Inexpensive.

Chez Mally (Route de la Côte Atlantique, Basse-Point; 75–51–18). An unpretentious little restaurant on the ground floor of Mally Edjam's home serves lunch only. You'll need a reservation and your dictionary. The menu of creole specialties is in English, but Mally speaks only French and creole. When arranged in advance Mally will prepare such wonderful creations as papaya soufflé, sea urchin, crayfish, soups, fresh vegetables, and more. No credit cards. Inexpensive.

NIGHTLIFE

Although popular as a base and departure port for chartered yachts, only one or two cruise ships use Martinique as a departure port. However, several ships arrive in the afternoon and remain for the evening, providing time for passengers to enjoy some early-evening nightlife. Fort-de-France has more than a half dozen little night spots with zouk or jazz, in addition to the nightclubs and discos in the larger hotels. There are also several piano bars.

Les Grands Ballets de la Martinique, the island's leading folkloric troupe, performs at different hotels each night and often comes on board cruise ships to perform. Under the direction of Jean-Pierre Bonjour, the group is one of the best in the Caribbean. Dancers in traditional costume perform a spirited mazurka brought to the islands from the ballrooms of Europe; the exotic beguine, born in the French West Indies; and an erotic "Calenda," danced to the beat of an African drum. Shows often end with the traditional song of farewell in the French West Indies, "Adieu Foulard, Adieu Madras," a bittersweet melody that tells of a creole girl's hopeless love for her French naval officer, who must sail away.

The new *Casino Bateliere Plaza* north of Fort-de-France near the Bateliere Hotel, is housed in a handsome building with a gaming room at one end and slot machines at the other. Hours: daily 9:00 P.M. to 3:00 A.M. Entrance for gaming room, 69 Ff. No fee for slots, which open at 11:00 A.M. The casino at the *Hotel Meridien Trois-Ilets* (Pointe du Bout) is open nightly from 9:00 P.M. to 3:00 A.M. Photo identification is required. Dress code is casual. The legal gambling age is 18.

SPORTS

BEACHES/SWIMMING: The beaches south of Fort-de-France are white sand, while those of the north are mostly gray and black sand. The best beaches are found on the south Caribbean coast with the mile-long crest at Grand Anse des Salines, the standout. Swimming on the Atlantic coast is generally not recommended except at coves protected by coral reef, such as Cap Ferré. Public beaches do not have changing cabins or showers, and hotels normally charge nonguests for use of facilities. You won't find any nudist beaches here, but large hotels generally permit topless bathing.

BIKING: *V T Tilt* (Anse Mitan, Trois-Ilets; 66–01–01) has a fleet of specialized bicycles, and a nine-seat vehicle that can accommodate nine bicycles. The company organizes trips that highlight Martinique's diverse landscape, explore places not visited by most tourists, and offer contact with the Martiniquais.

BOATING: Close to shore, Sunfish and Hobie Cats can be rented from hotel beach vendors. Yachts, bareboat or with crew, can be chartered for the day or week. Day-sailing excursions on large catamarans and schooners leave from Pointe du Bout and other marinas for St.-Pierre in the north and Diamond Rock in the south, stopping for snorkeling and picnic; cost is about $55.

Martinique's irregular coastline and many coves have long made it a favorite of yachtsmen. Fort-de-France Bay is a popular departure point for yacht charters sailing to the Grenadines. Yacht-club members (showing membership cards) may use the facilities of the *Yacht Club de la Martinique* (Ste.-Marthe; 63–26–76). *A Cruising Guide to Martinique* is a French/ English publication designed for experienced yachtsmen.

The Martinique Tourist Office can provide information on boat rental and charter companies in Fort-de-France, including trips on Martinique fishing yawls.

DEEP-SEA FISHING: Deep-sea fishing must be arranged a day or two in advance. The most popular catches in Martinique waters are tuna, bar racuda, dolphin, kingfish, and bonito. A full-day charter for up to six persons costs approximately 3,000 Ff (about $600).

GOLF: *Golf de l' Impératrice Josephine* (Trois-Ilets; 68–32–81), a 5-minute drive from the Pointe du Bout ferry, is an 18-hole course (par 71) designed by Robert Trent Jones, Sr. Set on 150 landscaped acres of the rolling terrain overlooking the sea, it has a clubhouse, pro shop, and restaurant. Greens fees are 270 Ff, cart 250 Ff, and club rents 100 Ff. It also has three tennis courts with night lights. Cruise ships often have golf packages for this course.

HIKING: Thirty-one marked trails, most designed as self-guided hikes, laid out by the Regional Natural Park (PNRM), National Forestry Office (ONF), and Le Club des Randonneurs (Hiking Club) are detailed (in French) in a guide, with maps, available from the Tourist Office. For information on trail conditions, call PNRM (73–19–30). Sunday hikes with PNRM guides are organized year-round on a published agenda. They are mainly intended to acquaint local people with the natural environment, but visitors are welcome (commentary is in French).

HORSEBACK RIDING: *Ranch de Galochat,* or *Ranch Jack* (near Anses d'Arlets; 68–63–97), and *La Cavale* (near Diamant; 76–22–94) offer riding excursions, along scenic beach routes and through tropical hillsides. A 1-hour ride costs about $16 per person; half-day ride with guide, about $50 per person.

KAYAKING: There are several locations but Belle Fontaine, about 10 miles north of Fort-de-France, is one of the best. Equipment is available there from *Basalt* (55–01–84).

SNORKELING/DIVING: Martinique is surrounded by reefs, but take the advice of local experts before snorkeling or diving on your own—many places have rough seas and tricky waters. There is a great variety of sea life, with walls, caves, and reefs with colorful sponges and corals.

In the south, Pointe du Bout, Anse Mitan, the small bays around Les Anses d'Arlets, and Ste.-Anne offer super snorkeling, most directly from the beach. Area hotels have glass-bottom boats and equipment for rent. Les Anses d'Arlets is for novice divers, Diamond Rock for advanced ones.

North of Fort-de-France, Cap Enragé Pointe, is popular for walls and caves where are large schools of soldierfish, trigger lobster. La Perle Island, north of Prêcheur for experienced divers, has moray eels, lo grouper, and other fish.

Dive operators are located in the main tour centers and serve the hotels of a particular area. The Pointe du Bout operators have American and French licensed instructors and provide instruction for beginners. A list of operators is available from the tourist office.

TENNIS: Hotels with tennis facilities nearest the port are the Bakoua and Meridien, each with two courts, on the south; and La Batelière with six courts, north of the capital.

WINDSURFING: Beachfront hotels have windsurfing equipment, and many offer lessons. Beginners start in the calm coves of the Caribbean southwest coast; advanced ones find Diamond Bay challenging. Boards rent for 60–100 Ff per hour; a half-hour private lesson costs 60–80 Ff. Martinique is a frequent venue for international windsurfing competition.

FESTIVALS AND CELEBRATIONS

Carnival is a five-day celebration, when all business comes to a halt, and the streets are filled with parades and revelers costumed as "red devils." Carnival continues to Ash Wednesday, when more devils, costumed in black and white, jam the streets for King Carnival's funeral procession and burial at La Savane.

In July the annual *Festival de Fort-de-France* is a month-long celebration of the arts that attracts major names in theater, art, music, and dance from the Caribbean and around the world. The festival is organized by SERMAC (Service Municipal d'Action Culturelle, Place José-Marti; 71–66–25).

In the first week in December of alternating years, the *International Jazz Festival* (odd years) and *International Guitar Festival* (even years) attract international artists. The festivals are sponsored by the Centre Martiniquais d'Animation Culturelle; 61–76–76).

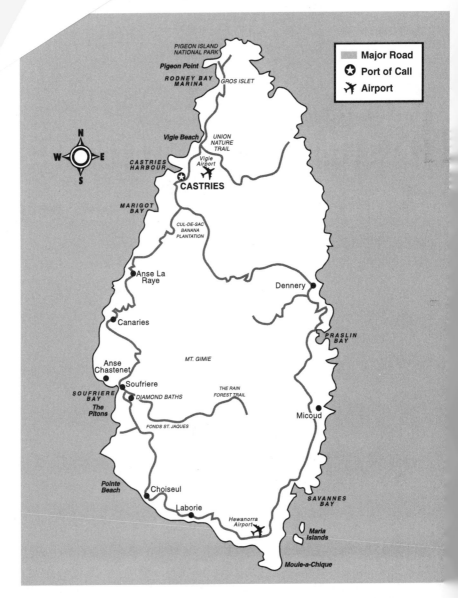

OWN 179

é, near Case
here there
sh, and
a site
ster,

Major Road
Port of Call
Airport

PIGEON ISLAND
NATIONAL PARK
Pigeon Point
RODNEY BAY
MARINA   GROS ISLET

N
W   E
S

Vigie Beach   UNION
NATURE
TRAIL

CASTRIES   Vigie
HARBOUR   Airport
CASTRIES

MARIGOT
BAY

CUL-DE-SAC
BANANA
PLANTATION

Anse La
Raye

Dennery

Canaries

PRASLIN
BAY

MT. GIMIE

Anse
Chastenet

Soufriere

SOUFRIERE   THE RAIN
BAY   FOREST TRAIL
The   DIAMOND BATHS
Pitons

Micoud

FONDS ST. JAQUES

Pointe
Beach   Choiseul

Laborie   SAVANNES
BAY

Hewanorra
Airport   Maria
Islands

Moule-a-Chique

AT A GLANCE

CHAPTER CONTENTS

THE BALI HAI OF THE CARIBBEAN

An island of surprises with scenic wonders on a grand scale, St. Lucia is a nature lover's dream, where every turn in the road—and there are many—reveals spectacular landscapes of lushly covered mountains and valleys colored with tropical fruits and flowers. Among its most celebrated natural attractions are a drive-in volcano and the ultimate postcard image of the tropics: the magnificent Pitons, sugarloaf twins that rise dramatically at the water's edge.

St. Lucia, mostly volcanic in origin, is the second largest of the Windward islands. From the north, where the hills are up to about 1,640 feet, the terrain rises to a central mountain range with peaks over 3,000 feet and quickly drops south to rolling hills and a coastal plain. In some places on the coast, cliffs rise almost directly from the sea, hiding tiny coves bathed by quiet Caribbean waters; in others rocky fingers bracket long stretches of white-sand beaches where Atlantic rollers wash the shores.

St. Lucia was inhabited by the Arawaks about A.D. 200 and the Caribs about A.D. 800. It has traditionally commemorated December 13, 1502, as the date of Columbus's discovery of the island on his fourth voyage. Some historians say Columbus was never there, however, and that it was Juan de la Cosa, Columbus's navigator, who actually made the discovery in 1499.

The first European colonists to arrive here were sixty-seven English settlers who were blown off course on their way to Guyana in 1605. They landed near Vieux Fort, on the south coast. Within a few weeks the Caribs had massacred most of them, but allowed the nineteen survivors to leave the island in a canoe. Thirty years later the English tried again but failed. Then in 1650 two Frenchmen purchased St. Lucia, along with Martinique and Grenada, for the grand sum of £1,660 from the French West India Company, which had come to possess them. The following year French settlers arrived, and for the next 150 years the English and French fought over St. Lucia. By 1815, when the British finally won, St. Lucia had changed hands fourteen times.

But their constant presence in St. Lucia gave birth to a fascinating blend of English and French traditions, which, in turn, were overlaid by the African ones that came with the slaves who were imported to work the sugar plantations. Today the language, feasts, festivals, and cuisine of this richly textured society reflect the curious cultural mix.

After slavery was abolished in 1838, sugar production declined. Britain reorganized her colonies of St. Lucia, Barbados, Grenada, St. Vincent, and Tobago into one administrative unit, called the Windward Islands Government. During World War II the United States established a military base on the island and built an airport at Vieux Fort, which is now the international jetport. St. Lucia got her independence in 1979. Although sugar has long since been replaced by bananas as the main crop, St. Lucia remains an agricultural country. Over the last decade tourism has gained steadily.

Fast Facts

POPULATION: 140,000

SIZE: 27 miles long, and 2 to 14 miles wide; 238 sq. miles

MAIN TOWNS: Castries, Vieux Fort

GOVERNMENT: St. Lucia, a member of the British Commonwealth, has a parliamentary government with two chambers: the seventeen-member House of Assembly, whose members are elected for a five-year term, and a Senate, whose members are nominated. The prime minister is the leader of the major political party in the Assembly. The head of state is the governor-general, appointed by the queen on the advice of the prime minister.

CURRENCY: Eastern Caribbean dollar. US $1 equals about EC $2.70. US and Canadian dollars, traveler's checks and most major credit cards are accepted by stores, restaurants, and hotels.

DEPARTURE TAX: EC $16 (US $6), if flying to another Caribbean island; EC $27 (US $11) if returning to a destination other than one in the Caribbean.

 LANGUAGE: English is the official language, but creole, a French-based patois, is the common language; many people also speak French.

 PUBLIC HOLIDAYS: January 1–2, New Year's holiday; February 22, Independence Day; Carnival; Good Friday; Easter Monday; May 1, Labour Day; late May/early June, Whit Monday; May 25, Corpus Christi; August 7, Emancipation Day; October 2, Thanksgiving; December 13, National Day; December 25, Christmas; December 26, Boxing Day.

 TELEPHONE AREA CODE: 758. From the United States, dial 758 plus 45, plus the five-digit local number. International direct-dial telephone, fax, and telex services are available at the cruise-ship terminal.

 **AIRLINES:** St. Lucia has two international airports: Vigie Airport at Castries served by American/American Eagle from San Juan; Air Martinique and LIAT; and Hewanorra International at Vieux Fort for wide-bodied aircraft and served with direct flights from the United States by Air Jamaica, American, and BWIA.

INFORMATION:

In the United States: St. Lucia Tourist Board, 820 Second Avenue, New York, NY 10017; (212) 867–2950; (800) 456–3984; fax: (212) 867–2795.

In Canada: St. Lucia Tourist Board, 4975 Dundas Street, No. 457, Elobicoke "D," Islington, Ont. M9A 4X4; phone/fax: (905) 273–3601.

In Port: St. Lucia Tourist Board, Pointe Séraphine, P.O. Box 221, Castries, St. Lucia, W.I.; 452–4094.
St. Lucia National Trust, P.O. Box 525, Castries, St. Lucia, W.I.; 452–5005.

 # BUDGET PLANNING

In recent years St. Lucia has become an expensive island for tourists. Taxi and tour prices, particularly, seem to be out of line when compared to other islands of the Eastern Caribbean. Shopping and restaurants (except those in deluxe hotels) are moderate. Restaurants may add a service charge or tax of about 10 percent to the bill.

 # PORT PROFILE:

LOCATION/EMBARKATION: The busy port of Castries, the capital, is located on the northwest coast overlooking a deep natural harbor with a narrow neck and sheltered by an amphitheater of green hills. In colonial days this anchorage was of immense strategic value. Today's cruise ships sail into the pretty harbor to an attractive new facility, Pointe Séraphine (22036). It has berths for two cruise ships and a jetty for tenders, a shopping plaza with duty-free shops, and an outdoor cafe. The Tourist Board's information desk (27577) can arrange sports activities. Numerous tour and car-rental agencies, as well as taxi and minibus operators, also have desks where passengers can make arrangements. There is shuttle-bus service to town. Pointe Séraphine is close to Vigie Airport.

Some of the largest ships dock on the south side of the harbor at the commercial port. While this location is not as attractive as Pointe Séraphine, it has the merit of being directly at the foot of town, within walking distance of shops and Derek Walcott Square.

Cruise ships also stop at Soufrière, a small picturesque port at the foot of the Pitons on the southwest coast and at Rodney Bay, so that passengers can visit Pigeon Island and the northern part of St. Lucia. Some small cruise ships stop in both ports.

LOCAL TRANSPORTATION: Public transportation is operated privately rather than by the government. A popular (though not comfortable) mode of travel are jitneys, wooden-seat buses that connect Castries with other towns and villages. They leave from the Castries Market on Jeremie Street in the town center.

Taxis are plentiful, but expensive. Rates are not fixed, but they are fairly standard. (Always agree on the fare with the driver before departure.) The one-way fare from Pointe Séraphine to Castries is EC $12; from Castries south to Caribelle Batik, EC $20; Hewanorra Airport, EC $110 (US $45); and north to Rodney Bay Marina, EC $30.

ROADS AND RENTALS: St. Lucia has some of the best and worst roads in the Caribbean. It is easy to tour St. Lucia by staying on the good roads, but to see some of the best scenery and to visit the rain forest, you will have to negotiate the bad ones, too. No roads encircle the island completely, but you can make a loop around the southern half, which has the main attractions. A new road that winds along the west coast from Castries to Soufrière offers some of the Caribbean's most spectacular scenery.

An alternative is a 45-minute motorboat trip, available daily from Castries to Soufrière, which provides wonderful views from the sea. South of Soufrière the west-coast road to Vieux Fort is good and takes about 45 minutes.

You might enjoy your sight-seeing more if you do not have to concentrate on those narrow, winding roads, particularly since driving in this former British colony is on the LEFT. Local travel companies offer well-organized tours, for small groups, to the main attractions. Or, if you have others with whom to share costs, you could hire a taxi to tour. Be sure to set duration, in addition to the price, in advance. The cost is about US $120 per day for up to four people, or $20 per hour for one to four persons.

If you prefer to do your own driving, you will need a temporary driver's license, which can be arranged by your rental company. The cost is EC $30 (US $12). Car-rental companies in Castries include *Avis* (452–2700; *Budget* (452–0233) has Suzukis for US $50 and Jeeps for US $70 per day; *Hertz* (452–0679); and *National* (450–8721). Rental cars cost US $55 and up per day; gasoline, US $2.50 per gallon. *Sycle World* (452–6055) rents motorbikes for US $37 and scooters for US $20 per day.

EMERGENCY NUMBERS:

Medical: Victoria Hospital in Castries has 24 hour emergency service. Dial the operator from any island location to be connected with the nearest medical facility or police.

Ambulance, dial 999

Police: Dial 999

Author's Favorite Attractions

VIEW OF THE PITONS FROM DASHEENE
SAILING INTO SOUFRIÈRE
HIKING ON THE RAINFOREST TRAIL

Shore Excursions

St. Lucia divides conveniently for touring into southern circuit and a west/north-coast tour. The following tours may be offered as shore excursions by your cruise ship, but their length and cost will vary, depending on the port—Castries, Soufrière, or Rodney Bay.—from which your tour commences.

Often Caribbean cruise ships northbound from the Panama Canal or Barbados, stop at Soufrière long enough to tender passengers to shore to pick up their tour and return overland. Meanwhile their ships sail on to Castries, where they dock and the passengers on tours rejoin their ship there. The reverse procedure may be followed on southbound cruises.

Soufrière and Drive-in Volcano, 3 hours, $50. From Castries the tour drops south along the west coast to Soufrière, with views of the Pitons, visit the drive-in volcano, Diamond Falls, and returns to Castries via the east coast.

Day-sail to Soufrière, full day, US $65. Sail down the west coast from Castries to Soufrière on a yacht or party boat, such as the *Unicorn,* miniature clipper ship with a stop for swimming and snorkeling.

North St. Lucia and Pigeon Island, half-day, $50. After a city tour with stops at Columbus Square, Bagshaw's Art Studio, and views from Morne ortune, the tour heads north to Pigeon Island ational Park. Some tours allow time for a swim.

pecial Excursions. Rain-forest hikes, a visit to a anana plantation, or an arts-and-cuisine tour are ome special ways to spend your day, provided you ake arrangements in advance, either with help om the Tourist Board or a local travel company.)uring the winter season the Forestry Department 450–2231) and local travel companies organize ikes on the Rainforest Trail.

St. Lucia Naturalist's Society (c/o St. Lucia ational Trust; 452–5005) conducts regular field rips. Some tour companies in Castries include: *Iinvielle & Chastanet* (452–2811); and *St. ucia Representative Services* (452–8232).

ST. LUCIA ON YOUR OWN

astries dates from the mid-18th century, but it is now a fairly new town, rebuilt in 1948 after fire destroyed many of its historic homes and hurches, including 80 percent of its old wooden ouses.

A CASTRIES WALKABOUT

EREK WALCOTT SQUARE The square in the enter of the city, formerly known as Columbus quare, was renamed in honor of St. Lucia's ative son Derek Walcott, who won the 1992 obel Prize for Literature. It is shaded by an enor- .ous saman, or rain tree, said to have been lanted by Governor Sir Dudley Hill in 1833. Some sources claim the tree is more than three undred years old.) The square, which was the ace d'Armes under the French, has a cenotaph, r monument, to the fallen of two world wars. On ovember 11, Remembrance Day, wreaths are id in an official ceremony.

On the east side is the *Cathedral of the mmaculate Conception,* one of the largest urches in the West Indies, built in 1897 and consecrated in 1931. It became a cathedral in 1957, when the Castries diocese was established. Facing the square on the south side, Brazil Street has several 19th-century buildings, the best known being a white-and-green Victorian building with gingerbread trim, which houses the restaurant *Rain.* It is one of the few colonial houses to have survived the 1948 fire. The building is said to have been a setting in Sinclair Lewis's *Arrowsmith,* which takes place on a fictitious Caribbean island, "St. Huberts," that was, in reality, St. Lucia. Farther east at Brazil and Chisel streets is the *Anglican Holy Trinity Church,* dating from the early 19th century. West of the square on Bourbon Street is the *Central Library,* built in 1925 by the Andrew Carnegie Foundation.

CASTRIES MARKET (2) One of the most interesting places in town is Castries Market (Jeremie Street) with a bright red facade and a clock over the entrance. Built in 1894 by engineers from Liverpool, the structure has had only minor repairs over the years and is virtually unchanged architecturally. Recently expanded the clean well organized market is a feast for the eyes as well as the table, with its colorfully dressed vendors selling an array of exotic fruits, vegetables, and spices. Saturday is market day, when farmers bring their produce to sell, crowding into the market and spilling over into adjoining streets. There are also vendors selling kitchen and other useful items, such as brooms made of palm fronds, clay pots, and straw craft, often made by the person selling them.

GOVERNMENT HOUSE On the south side of town is an ornate Victorian mansion perched on the side of Morne Fortune (which means "hill of good fortune" and is often referred to locally simply as The Morne). It is the official residence of the governor general. You will consider it *your* good fortune, too, if you are there to see a St. Lucia sunset.

FORT CHARLOTTE Due to its strategic importance, the hills surrounding Castries harbor were rung with batteries and forts built by the French and British. The best preserved is Fort Charlotte, which crowns the summit of Morne Fortune at 853 feet. Fort Charlotte was begun by the French in 1764 as part of a plan to build the "Citadelle du Morne Fortune," but was completed by the British in 1794. Many of the original fortifications are still in place. The view from Morne Fortune takes in Castries and stretches from Pigeon Island on the north to the Pitons on the south.

A Drive Around The Island

South to Soufrière

South of Morne Fortune the road winds around hairpin turns, up and over steep hills to the lower reaches of the beautiful Cul-de-Sac Valley, intensively green with vast banana plantations.

MARIGOT BAY At Marigot a corkscrew road drops down precipitously to Marigot Bay, a teardrop lagoon with one of the most beautiful settings in the Caribbean. At sunset the scene is exquisite. The bay, almost completely hidden by steep, heavily wooded hills, is a natural harbor that used to make a dandy hideout for pirate ships and warships in the olden days. Today it is a popular anchorage for yachts and serves as an Eastern

Caribbean base of The Moorings, one of the lea ing yachting companies in the Caribbean (home base is Clearwater, Florida). The Mooring resort, its pretty beach and water-sports faciliti all but hidden in the bay's tropical splendor, h frequently been used as a movie location.

After the Marigot turnoff, the main road cross the Roseau River Valley and passes the fishi villages of Anse la Raye and Canaries, skirti deserted beaches framed by high rocky clif some accessible only by boat. A small side ro leads to the old fishing village of Anse La Ray where you can tour *La Sikwi Sugar Museu* (452–6323), a cultural theater, a restored 4 foot water wheel, and botanical gardens advanced arrangements. There is a small adm sion fee. The serpentine route makes its w along the magnificently lush Duval Ravine a over the hills to the ridge overlooki Soufrière—one of the most fabulous views in t Caribbean. There, on the south side of Soufriè the majestic peaks of The Pitons jut out of the s

THE PITONS Petit Piton (2,438 feet), the nor ern peak, and Gros or Grand Piton (2,619 fee

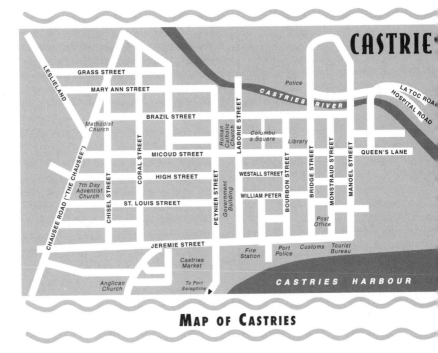

Map of Castries

on the south, are ancient volcanic spikes or extrusions. They rise from either side of a steep, wooded, hillside that shelters a deep bay.

The view of The Pitons is magnificent from several hilltops above Soufrière. One of the best, particularly for photographs, is at Dasheene, a hotel perched on a cliff south of Soufrière.

Of all the views, nothing beats the approach from the sea, an experience offered by several cruise ships and available on day-sails from Castries. To sail into Soufrière Bay, watching The Pitons grow in their dimensions as the ship nears, and to anchor directly in front of them where their peaks tower a half-mile overhead is to enjoy one of the most extraordinary experiences in the world of travel—on par with seeing the Pyramids of Egypt and the Taj Mahal. Here the sight is all the more fabulous because it is a natural phenomenon. If your arrival is timed for the late afternoon before sunset, the scene is more magical still as the peaks, bathed in the light of the setting sun, have an almost ethereal quality.

By the beach and on the hillsides between the Pitons is *Jalousie,* a resort that took its name from a former plantation on the site. Acquired by Hilton International in 1996, the hotel was controversial from the day it opened because the resort marred one of the Caribbean's most magnificent natural sites. Nor is the controversy helped by *Bang Between the Pitons,* a beach bar/restaurant whose owner, Colin Tenant, was the original developer of Mustique, as well as *Jalousie. Bang* is a collection of quaint gingerbread houses that serve as bar, boutique, and restaurant and offer local dishes.

SOUFRIÈRE The quaint little port of Soufrière has a spectacular setting at the foot of The Pitons with the mountains of the St. Lucia Rain Forest rising behind it. The town is the oldest settlement on St. Lucia and was an important center of trade and commerce under the French. At its prime in the late 18th century, there were as many as one hundred sugar and coffee plantations in the vicinity. During the French Revolution, which took as bloody a turn here as it did in France, members of the aristocracy were put to the guillotine erected in Soufrière's town square. Even after almost two centuries of British rule, the French legacy is still very apparent in the names of people and places,

their speech, and to some extent, the architecture of the old town.

Although a great deal of the town's historic houses have been lost to fires and hurricanes over the centuries, there are enough Victorian and French colonial buildings around the main square to give the town character. Restoration of the historic center has been under way since 1989 and will take many years to complete.

Soufrière and southern St. Lucia are known for their wood craftsmen. The furnishings of the Tourist Bureau's visitor's center at the pier were created entirely by local craftsmen using cedar, mahogany, teak, and other local woods. In addition to its fabulous setting, Soufrière is surrounded by scenic wonders and is the gateway to some of St. Lucia's most interesting natural attractions.

DRIVE-IN VOLCANO Southeast of Soufrière is the remnant of a volcanic crater, which St. Lucians have dubbed "the world's only drive-in volcano." Actually, a road does lead into an area of barren, grayish earth and gravel, with pools of boiling mud. At regular intervals clouds of steam, accompanied by hissing sounds, shoot 50 feet in the air, as sulphuric gases are released from the earth's inner core. Where water flows the rocks have been streaked with yellow, orange, green, purple, and brown, indicating the presence of sulphur, iron, copper, magnesium, and zinc washed from them by the water. A slight, but not offensive, sulphur odor can be detected. There is a small entrance fee and a park guide must accompany visitors.

The Eastern Caribbean is replete with the remnants of volcanic craters, solfatara, and sulphur springs, but few are as showy and easy to visit as this spot in St. Lucia, and none are more fascinating.

DIAMOND FALLS AND MINERAL BATHS After fresh rain water collects in the boiling crater, where it is saturated with minerals and heated to about 180 degrees F, it runs down the mountainside, dropping about 1,800 feet in six waterfalls. You can actually follow the course of the water on mountain trails, but an easier way to see at least one of the falls—lowest and prettiest of the six— is to visit the Diamond Falls and Mineral Baths, less than a mile east of Soufrière . From the entrance to the privately owned Diamond Waterfalls, a narrow bricked path bordered by hedges of tropical plants and shaded by stately palms and gigantic tree ferns leads to the bathhouse and the falls. The beautiful cascade roars out of dense tropical foliage down a mineral-streaked gorge into a stream that flows through the gardens to underground pipes and a series of pools, each a different temperature.

The Baths were built originally in 1784 for the soldiers of Louis XVI. The French governor of St. Lucia had had the water analyzed and found their curative properties to be similar to those of Aix-les-Bains in France. The Baths were almost totally destroyed during the French Revolution, and in 1836 the British governor tried to restore them, but without success. Only in recent times, after restoration by their present owner, have the baths functioned again; a part of the original 18th-century baths is still in use. The water reputedly has curative powers for arthritis and rheumatism, but even if you do not take the baths, you will find the peaceful gardens a cool, refreshing respite for sun-weary travelers. There are separate fees for the entrance and use of the baths.

ANSE CHASTANET On the north side of Soufrière is one of the most enchanting resorts in the Caribbean, with a setting so idyllic you will forgive, if not forget, the terrible road leading there. The road has the merit, however, of having a splendid view of Soufrière and The Pitons. Anse Chastanet is built along a precipitous hillside overlooking a lovely beach. Sunsets here must be seen to be believed. Some of the hotel's furnishings have been made by local wood craftsmen. Take particular notice of the columns of the dining terrace; they are made of local wood and beautifully carved with wildlife scenes by a local self-taught woodcarver, Lawrence Deligny. Anse Chastanet Beach fronts some of the best reefs in St. Lucia only 20 feet from shore. The hotel's dive facilities are open to nonguests for a fee.

ST. LUCIA RAIN FOREST The Central Forest Reserve, part of the 54,252 acres of forest and woodlands that cover St. Lucia, is a nature reserve of the central highlands, commonly called the St. Lucia Rain Forest. The Rainforest Walk, a 7-mile trail, crosses the island through the reserve, between the villages of Mahaut on the east and Fonds St. Jacques on the west. From the high ridge there are panoramic views of the central

mountains, The Pitons, and Mount Gimie, the highest peak on the island (3,117 feet). Don't be surprised to see farmers emerge from the valleys and mountainsides carrying sacks of produce. Even the high mountains of St. Lucia have been lumbered and cultivated since plantation days.

The forest, with up to 150 inches of rain per year, has a great variety of ferns, bromeliads, wild orchids, anthuriums, and other rain-forest vegetation. Overhead the canopy is often so dense that little sunlight gets through. On the approach to the trail, the air is perfumed by pretty white flowers called wild orchids that grow profusely by the roadside. Bird life is abundant and includes three species of hummingbirds and the highly endangered St. Lucia green parrot, the national bird. Since 1979 St. Lucia has had a tough conservation program to save the parrot, and bring it back from the edge of extinction.

The Rainforest Trail can be approached from either the east or west coasts, and many people hike straight from coast to coast. The hike is not difficult and takes 3.5 hours, but there are no facilities on or approaching the trail. Permission from the Forestry Department is needed. Forestry Department hikes with naturalists provide the most practical way to go.

Contact the Tourist Office in Soufrière or Anse Chastanet Hotel, which organizes hikes with one of the best naturalists in St. Lucia. The drive from Soufrière to Fonds St. Jacques takes about 30 minutes, but the road to the top of the ridge and the trailhead, once passable by car, is so rutted it must now be taken by jeep or on foot. The ridge road runs for about 2 miles to the signposted entrance of the reserve and the start of the trail. From here the hike west to the eastern exit takes about 3.5 hours. If your time is limited, an alternative would be to hike for only an hour or two and return to waiting transportation at the western entrance. Wear comfortable walking shoes; trails are often muddy, and showers are frequent.

TO THE SOUTH COAST

CHOISEUL The 45-minute drive to the southern end of the island passes through the fishing village of Choiseul, known as the arts and crafts center of St. Lucia, where many villagers work in their home as wood carvers, potters, and straw weavers. Their products can be purchased at the *Choiseul Arts and Craft Centre* (459–3226), a teaching center, and *Victoria Arts and Crafts,* a roadside stand.

On the north side of the town by the roadside, you will pass a rock with a clearly visible Amerindian petroglyph often pictured in St. Lucia brochures. After the fishing village of Laborie, the landscape is flat and dry—a complete contrast to most of the island.

MOULE-A-CHIQUE PENINSULA Vieux Fort is the main town of the south and the site of the Hewanorra International Airport. Hewanorra, meaning "land of the iguana," was the original Arawak name for St. Lucia. Regrettably, very few iguana remain. On the tip of the island, a narrow finger of land, Moule-à-Chique Peninsula, ends in an 800-foot-high promontory overlooking the sea, where the Atlantic Ocean and the Caribbean Sea collide. The view takes in the dramatic seascape with St. Vincent in the distance on the south and the Maria Islands on the east.

MARIA ISLANDS NATURE RESERVE At the end of the airport runway by Sables Bay is the Maria Islands Nature Centre and a half-mile offshore the two small islands of the Maria Islands Nature Reserve. Created in 1982 and operated by the National Trust, the reserve is home to a variety of wildlife including the Maria Islands Ground Lizard and the kouwes, a small harmless nocturnal snake said to be the rarest snake in the world. The Maria Islands are also a bird refuge, and the waters around the islands are rich in marine life. A visit to the islands must be arranged with the National Trust, but you do not need permission to snorkel, which is best on the southwest side of Maria Major, the largest of the two islands.

THE EAST COAST

Although there are no must-see attractions on the east coast, the scenery along the route is lovely. In some parts there are dramatic rock formations created by pounding Atlantic waves, and other parts have deep bays with quiet waters. Savannes Bay, immediately north of Vieux Fort, is a protected area, with the island's most extensive mangroves.

At quiet Praslin Bay you are likely to see men making dugout canoes from the gommier tree in the same manner used by the Arawak and Carib Indians five hundred years ago. Farther north en route to Dennery, the largest town on the east coast, the road passes through some of the island's most beautiful, lush scenery, with huge banana groves swooping down from rain-forested mountain peaks to the edge of the sea, where the Atlantic breaks against rocky fingers and barrier islets near the coast.

NORTH TO PIGEON ISLAND

St. Lucia's main resorts and some of its best beaches lie along a stretch of coast between Castries and Rodney Bay. Some of the hotels are all-inclusive resorts whose sports and other facilities are available only to their guests; others accommodate day visitors. Inquire at the Tourist Information Desk at Pointe Séraphine.

UNION NATURE TRAIL A few miles inland from Sandals Halcyon Beach Hotel on Choc Beach, a nature center at Union has a 45-minute trail for a self-guided walk; an herb garden featuring bush remedies used in St. Lucia, and a small zoo of local wildlife, developed in 1987 by the Forestry Department to acquaint children with their natural heritage and provide a convenient place to introduce these attractions to cruise passengers and other visitors. There is a small admission fee.

GROS ISLET Normally a quiet fishing village on the northwest coast, Gros Islet comes to life on Friday nights. A street fair and outdoor disco has become the island's biggest weekly event, with visitors joining residents in a "jump up," the street dancing of Carnival, which has come to mean a big party.

PIGEON ISLAND NATIONAL PARK Pigeon Island has a long and colorful history going back to the Arawaks. It was used as a hideaway by pirates who preyed on merchant ships in the 16th century and was a strategic British fort in the 18th century. It has been a quarantine station, whaling station, U.S. naval station, and even a hideaway of an English actress. As part of a resort development plan for northern St. Lucia, a causeway was built in 1971 to connect Pigeon Island with the mainland by closing the north end of Rodney Bay and creating a long sandy beach. After the causeway was constructed, the island was made into a park. It has trails leading to a promontory, now known as Pigeon Point, with the ruins of Fort Rodney and grandstand views of Rodney Bay and the north coast. The Pigeon Island Museum and Interpretive Centre is housed in the former British officer's mess, which was completely remodeled to the original 1808 plans. The history is brought to life in exhibits and an audio-visual re-enactment of Rodney's famous victory over the French. The park is open daily from 9:30 A.M. to 4:30 P.M. Admission: $2. The Rodney Bay Ferry offers a half-day excursion to Pigeon Island for EC $40 adults and EC $25 children under 12.

Ships that stop at Rodney Bay often arrange a barbecue on the beach with water sports, a visit of the park, or tours of the northern part of St. Lucia. At the south end of the bay is Rodney Bay Marina, a resort complex and yacht basin.

 **Shopping**

Pointe Séraphine has an attractive shopping complex set around a Spanish-style courtyard with two dozen shops selling duty-free goods. Selections are small, but prices are among the best in the Caribbean. You will find fine china, crystal, perfume, liquor, cigarettes, jewelry, leather goods, as well as locally made fashions and crafts.

Although Pointe Séraphine is primarily for cruise-ship passengers, it is open to other visitors and to St. Lucia residents. Cruise passengers must show their cabin key, landing card, or passport to claim duty-free privileges; island residents pay duty on their purchases. Liquor and cigarettes are delivered to the ship. Store hours are Monday to Friday from 9:00 A.M. to 4:00 P.M. and Saturday to 1:00 P.M., but the hours are usually extended when cruise ships are in port.

There are other shopping centers: Sunset Shopping Plaza and Rodney Bay Marina Shopping Complex. Beach and street vendors who are licensed by the government and permitted to operate in certain areas usually sell coral and freshwater pearl jewelry. They can sometimes be overzealous, but normally they are good natured and will move on after a smile and a "no, thank you." Artists, often Rastafarians, sell their woodcarvings

on the street or beach, too. And don't overlook the Castries Market—it's fun, even if you buy nothing.

ART AND ARTISTS: *Eudovic Art Studio* (Box 620, Goodlands, Castries; 452–2747). Joseph Eudovic is the dean of St. Lucia's wood sculptors and possibly the best of his style in the Caribbean. His works stand on an international level, with many being museum pieces. He carves from the trunks and limbs of local trees—gliricidia, red cedar, eucalyptus, and mahogany—allowing the natural wood to inspire the shape. Each piece is lyric with tension and energy that seem to be struggling to break out, but, at the same time, lines that flow with a calm and grace only a master craftsman can achieve. They evoke the movements of a ballet dancer, graceful and restrained but full of energy. Prices range from US $300 to $3,000.

Eudovic is also a teacher, and other artists and students work at his studio. Visitors are welcome to view works in progress. The small shop also has beautiful trays, masks, and other gifts made from local woods and coconut. Eudovic's wife makes madras-costumed dolls that are whisk brooms and brushes. The 15-minute drive south of Castries is well worthwhile for serious art lovers.

Another well known artist, Llewellyn Xavier, whose work is in the permanent collection of New York City's Museum of Modern Art, has his studio at Silver Point, Cap Estate (Gros Islet; phone/fax: 450–9155). Call for an appointment.

In Castries *Artsibit Gallery* (Brazil and Mongiraud streets; 27865) carries local and Caribbean art, as well as posters and prints. The St. Lucia's Artists Association, organized in 1987 to help local artists and create a permanent national collection, exhibits its members' work here.

BOOKS AND MAPS: *Sunshine Bookshop* (Brazil Street) has the largest stock in town. *Noah's Arkade* (Pointe Séraphine) and gift shops at hotels usually carry tourist books on St. Lucia.

CHINA AND CRYSTAL: *Little Switzerland* (Pointe Séraphine) has duty-free china and crystal.

CLOTHING AND ACCESSORIES: Several companies design and manufacture clothing in their factories in St. Lucia. Among them, *Islanders* makes men, women and children's mix-and-match outfits of cotton jersey, twill, and linen. *Base* (Rex St. Lucian Hotel), a branch of the

Antigua-based designer, specializes in body-hugging cotton knits with great style. *Benetton* (Pointe Séraphine), the ubiquitous Italian chain, is here as is *Pickwick & Co.*, which has the best of Britain in cashmere, china, and other goods.

CRAFTS AND SOUVENIRS: Batiks, hand-printed fabrics, and silk-screen designs are among the island's nicest products and are available as shirts, skirts, dresses, and a large variety of gifts. The oldest and most distinctive producer is *Bagshaws* (La Toc Road and Pointe Séraphine), which has been in business more than three decades and still uses the colorful designs created by the late founder. The enterprise is now operated by daughter-in-law Alice Bagshaw, a dynamic American who has lived on the island most of her adult life.

Bagshaws makes sportswear, leisure wear, and gift items with two dozen distinctive silk-screen designs on a variety of fabrics, including sea island cotton. The fabrics are designed, printed, and sold only in St Lucia. Prices are reasonable. The retail shop is next to the art studio, where you can watch artisans at work.

Caribelle Batik (Old Victoria Road) has its workshop in a century-old house on The Morne, where you can watch artists at work making batik using antique Asian hot-wax methods on cotton. Their batik wall hangings, *pareos* (beach wraps), shirts, skirts, sundresses, evening wear, and more are sold at *Sea Island Cotton* (Rodney Bay), and other quality shops.

The *Noah's Arkade* stores (Pointe Séraphine, Castries, and Rodney Bay) carry a large variety of crafts: wooden bowls, trays, and carvings; straw mats, baskets, and hats; ornamental shells and shell jewelry; and hammocks, as well as postcards and books on St. Lucia. *Handicraft St. Lucie* (Sunset Shopping Plaza) is an art gallery with souvenir items of red clay pottery, straw, and wood carvings.

HERBS AND SPICES: *Caribelle Batik* (Sunset Plaza) stocks Sunny Caribbee Herbs and Spices. *Erma of St. Lucia* (Rodney Bay Marina) has local products, perfumes and spices from Grenada, and unusual crafts that owner Erma Compton uncovers in her travels throughout the Caribbean and South America.

JEWELRY: *Colombian Emeralds* (Pointe Séraphine) with stores throughout the Caribbean,

has fully guaranteed sapphires, rubies, diamonds, and emeralds. *Y. de Lima* (William Peter Boulevard) is one of the top stores for fine jewelry, also selling cameras and film. *Touch of Class* (Pointe Séraphine) has jewelry and electronics.

LIQUOR AND WINES: Rums made in St. Lucia are *Denros Bounty, Admiral Rodney,* and *Five Blondes.* The latter is particularly popular with visitors as souvenirs for its label, which pictures . . . yes, five blondes. (Presumably the name originally referred to blond or light rum). Stores at Pointe Séraphine are well stocked and competitively priced; some are even lower than in St. Thomas.

PERFUMES AND COSMETICS: *Images* (Pointe Séraphine) has the best selection of perfume and cosmetics. Perfumes are made locally by *Caribbean Perfumes* (The Morne) and come in three floral scents.

DINING AND RESTAURANTS

Dining choices in St. Lucia range from elegant restaurants in the hills overlooking Castries to rustic seafood ones in villages by the sea. All have the personal stamp of their owners and reflect the island's diverse makeup. European and American fare is readily available, but it is the island's creole cuisine that deserves your attention. Be sure to sample such dishes as callaloo soup, stuffed breadfruit, banana bread, fried plantain, pumpkin soup, flying fish, and stuffed crab backs. Prices are not high, except in deluxe restaurants. Generally, lunch per person at an inexpensive restaurant will be under US $15; moderate, US $15 to $25; and expensive, over US $25. Most restaurants are open daily; some close on Sundays, others close on Mondays or Tuesdays. Check in advance.

CASTRIES AND ENVIRONS

Chez Paul and The Rain Bar (Derek Walcott Square; 451–3111). A few years ago Paul Simmons took over the landmark restaurant, *Rain,* then he changed the menu and prices but not the ambience and decor; Victorian with white-and-green gingerbread inspired by Somerset

Maugham's *Rain*. The menu features Pacific Rum and French cuisine with some local dishes. Moderate to expensive.

The Green Parrot (Morne Fortune; 452–3399). A local favorite with a grand view of Castries offers West Indian dishes, along with steaks, watched over by Chef Harry, a St. Lucian who trained at London's prestigious Claridges Hotel. There is also a pool and darts room with an English Pub atmosphere. Expensive (Harry has a beach bar/restaurant at Anse Jambette, a popular stop for day-sailing excursions south of Castries.)

Jimmie's (Vigie Cove; 452–5142). Open-air waterside dining on seafood and local specialties in a pleasant, casual setting. Moderately expensive.

The Lime (Rodney Bay; 452–0761). Popular at lunch for roti and light fare, it is a favorite for "limim" at Happy Hour and in the evening for the Rodney Bay crowd. Moderate.

Mortar and Pestle (Rodney Bay; 452–8756). A pavilion at the water's edge provides a rustic setting with walls and ceiling of pinewood and stone to enjoy Caribbean specialties. There is a dish from most every island. Expensive.

San Antoine (Morne Fortune; 452–4660). On a hillside in a restored colonial mansion set in pretty gardens overlooking Castries, this is St. Lucia's leading gourmet restaurant. Owners Nick and Pat Bowden have designed a sixty-page menu, complete with recipes of the restaurant's popular selections. Expensive.

Soufrière

Hummingbird (459–7232). Drinks and lunch with a view of The Pitons and a pool for a cool swim makes this an easy place to linger. The menu has seafood and creole specialties. Expensive.

Nightlife

St. Lucia is low-key, with nightlife revolving around hotels and a few restaurants with light entertainment. There are romantic cocktail and moonlight cruises and everyone on the island heads for Gros Islet on Friday night.

The newest addition to St. Lucia's nightlife is *The Derek Walcott Theatre* (at The Great House). It offers music, dance, and drama productions in a small, open-air theater located in the ruins of the old Cap Estate House. An annual performance by the Trinidad Theatre Workshop and Sunday brunch productions are among the theater's highlights.

Sports

BEACHES/SWIMMING: St. Lucia claims to have more than 120 beaches, many accessible only by boat. The beaches closest to Castries are north of the port and easy to reach by bus or taxi. The prettiest ones are in the secluded coves south of the capital, reached by motorboat in about 30 minutes.

BOATING: Sailing is one of St. Lucia's most popular sports, where yachtsmen can enjoy safe harbors on the island's deeply indented coastline. There are three boating centers. Marigot Bay is the base for *The Moorings St. Lucia* (451–4256), a major Caribbean boat charterer. It offers day-sailing in Marigot Bay. The resort has a dive shop and water-sports center. Rodney Bay Marina at Gros Islet has *Stevens Yachts* (452–8648), one of the oldest yachting specialists in the Eastern Caribbean; and *Trade Wind Yacht Charters* (452–8424)). Both offer day-sails and longer charters.

Castries is the base for large party boats that sail on picnic and snorkeling excursions, such as the *Unicorn* (452–6811), US $65; and *Surf Queen* (Vigie Marina; 452–8351) US $50. Both depart about 9:00 A.M. and return about 4:30 or 5:00 P.M. Soufrière is the most popular destination; Anse Jambette is also popular.

Aqua Action, usually held in late May or early June, is a week-long festival for water sports, with marathons and lots of parties thrown in. It is held at Rodney Bay under the aegis of the St. Lucia Yacht Club. The main event is the annual Southern Caribbean Match Racing Championship, held over three days on a course of 4 miles. The most hilarious event is a sort of soapbox-derby-of-the-sea, with participants making their own craft as cheaply as possible. Anything will do, as long as it has no engine and floats.

DEEP-SEA FISHING: Fully equipped sportfishing boats are available for half-day and full-day charters. Contact: *Michael Hackshaw* (Vigie Marina; 452–7044); or *Mako Water Sports* (Rodney Bay Marina; 452–0412). The main seasons are December to June for open-sea species, such as wahoo, sailfish, tuna, and kingfish; and July to December, when the catch is best closer to shore. Fishing is an old tradition and a way of life for many St. Lucians.

GOLF: The golf course at *Sandals La Toc* (452–3081), about 5 miles from the port, is reserved for its guests and available to others only by prior arrangement. A 9-hole course, *Cap Estate Golf Club* (450–8523) is about 1 mile from Rodney Bay. Greens fees are about US $30.

HIKING: The central mountains, particularly the short trail of the Barre de l'Isle, St. Lucia Rain Forest Trail, and Union Nature Trail, are the most popular for hiking. (See previous sections in this chapter for details.) These hikes do not require a great deal of experience or endurance. Wear comfortable shoes, and keep cameras in waterproof covers.

HORSEBACK RIDING: St. Lucia can be explored by horseback on trips organized by *Trim's Riding Stable* (452–8273) at Cap Estate. The stable offers picnic rides along the Atlantic coast and trail rides overlooking the Caribbean and horse-and-carriage tours of Pigeon Point.

SNORKELING/SCUBA DIVING: Although St. Lucia has lovely, unspoiled reefs with abundant fish along 24 miles of its Caribbean coast, it is a newcomer to diving: Many sites are yet to be explored. Some of its best reefs with spectacular coral and marine life are found at Anse Cochon and in the few miles between Anse Chastanet Beach and The Pitons. Here, many dive sites are found in calm and protected waters near the shore; some in only 20 feet of water are close enough to reach directly from the beach. Indeed, the proximity to shore of shallow-water reefs makes St. Lucia a good place to learn to snorkel and dive.

The Pitons drop as deep into the water as they rise above the ground, and their walls offer an exciting and unusual experience for divers, who see huge sponges, underwater caves, and a great variety of fish.

Scuba St. Lucia (Anse Chastanet; 459–7355) is the leading dive shop and offers beach and boat dives four times daily. It has resort courses for beginners, certification courses, night dives, underwater photography and others. Facilities include changing rooms, fresh-water showers, beach bar/restaurant, and boutiques. *The Moorings St. Lucia* (Marigot Bay) and *Windjammer Landing*, north of Castries, have dive operations as well.

TENNIS: The largest tennis complex is at *St. Lucia Raquet Club* (Club St. Lucia; 450–0551). Facilities include instruction, professional services, and nine flood-lit courts.

WINDSURFING: Sables Bay facing the Maria Islands is the most popular location for windsurfing, but the entire south coast, bordering both the Atlantic and the Caribbean, is ideal. Strong Atlantic winds and choppy waves are a challenge to experts, while the Caribbean's gentle breezes are suitable if you are learning or improving your skills. Most beachside hotels offer rental equipment and instruction.

FESTIVALS AND CELEBRATIONS

St. Lucia's festivities are a blend of its French, British, and African heritage—to the extent that it is hard to tell where one ends and another begins. Two festivals unique to the island are the *Feast of St. Rose de Lima*, August 30, and *Feast of St. Marguerite Mary Alocoque of France*, October 17. Both were founded by St. Lucian singing societies, La Rosa and La Marguerite, and are held on the feast days of the patron saints for which they are named.

Each festival is preceded by months of nightly singing practices called *séances*, which take place in festive settings. A king and queen, who serve as leaders for the events, are selected for each festival. Strict protocol is observed, with participants and visitors bowing to the chosen leaders upon entering the practice hall. A church service is followed by a costumed procession of members clad as kings and queens, princes and princesses, policemen and soldiers—singing and dancing in the streets. The parades are topped off with sumptuous banquets and dancing, with the king and queen leading the grand waltz at midnight.

St. Vincent and the Grenadines

KINGSTOWN, BEQUIA, MUSTIQUE, MAYREAU, TOBAG CAYS, PALM ISLAND, UNION ISLAND

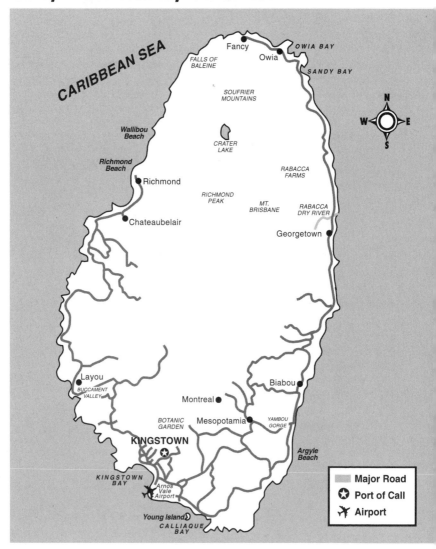

CARIBBEAN SEA

Fancy

Owia

OWIA BAY

FALLS OF BALEINE

SANDY BAY

SOUFRIER MOUNTAINS

Wallibou Beach

CRATER LAKE

Richmond Beach

RABACCA FARMS

Richmond

RICHMOND PEAK

MT. BRISBANE

RABACCA DRY RIVER

Chateaubelair

Georgetown

Layou

BUCCAMENT VALLEY

Biabou

Montreal

BOTANIC GARDEN

Mesopotamia

YAMBOU GORGE

KINGSTOWN

Argyle Beach

KINGSTOWN BAY

Arnos Vale Airport

Young Island

CALLIAQUE BAY

	Major Road
	Port of Call
	Airport

AT A GLANCE

CHAPTER CONTENTS

St. Vincent and the Grenadines

BREATHTAKING NATURE AND GENTLE BEAUTY

Majestic emerald mountains rising almost directly from a sapphire sea anchor a chain of three dozen exquisite gems that make up the country of St. Vincent and the Grenadines. Situated in the Windward Islands between St. Lucia and Grenada, they are the idyllic Caribbean hideaways for nature lovers, boating enthusiasts, and true beachcombers.

St. Vincent, the capital and largest of the group, is surprisingly different in composition and appearance from the Grenadines. It is covered almost end to end with intensely green, deeply creviced mountains that peak at 4,500 feet in an active volcano that displayed its awesome power as recently as 1979. Roads twist through the steep mountains, providing spectacular views of the interior, thick with tropical forests and cultivated with banana and arrowroot. On the Caribbean coast sheer cliffs drop to the sea, and white- or black-sand beaches hide in the crevices of an irregular coastline. On the windward side the Atlantic crashes against the rockbound shores.

The Grenadines, by contrast, are low-lying islets trimmed with palm-fringed, pristine beaches facing coral gardens. They stretch south from St. Vincent to Grenada over 65 miles of sparkling seas that yachtsmen often call the most beautiful sailing waters in the world. Now cruise ships are discovering them, too. Out of thirty-two islands and cays, eight are ports of call.

Discovered by Columbus on his third voyage in 1498, St. Vincent was probably inhabited first by the Ciboneys and later by the Arawak and Carib Indians. Pre-Columbian artifacts have been found throughout the islands, and Amerindian petroglyphs can be seen on rock faces in many places. The island was still occupied by Caribs in 1672 when it was claimed by Britain.

In 1675 a slave ship sank in the channel between St. Vincent and Bequia. Survivors reached both islands and, in time, were assimilated with the Carib. Their offspring came to be called the "Black Caribs," a name sometimes still used to refer to the villagers on St. Vincent's northeast coast where their descendants concentrated.

Britain and France fought over St. Vincent for a century, but the Caribs put up such fierce resistance that neither country was able to colonize it. In 1748 the European combatants declared St. Vincent a neutral island. Under the Treaty of Paris, however, St. Vincent was ceded to England in 1763 and, together with Grenada, the Grenadines, and Dominica, formed the Windward Islands Federation. The Grenadines were divided administratively, Grenada got Petit Martinique and Carriacou, at the south end of the chain, and St. Vincent was made responsible for all the islands north of Carriacou.

Except for a brief period of French occupation from 1779 to 1783, St. Vincent remained in British hands. With French support the Caribs made a final attempt in 1795 to regain their territory, but the rebellion was squashed. Hundreds of Caribs were shipped off to Balliceaux, an islet east of Bequia, and then deported to the island of Roatán, which was part of British Honduras at the time. St. Vincent and the Grenadines became independent in 1979.

FAST FACTS

POPULATION: 115,000

SIZE: St. Vincent, 18 miles long and 11 miles wide; 133 sq. miles; Bequia, 7 sq. miles; Mustique, 4 sq. miles.

MAIN TOWNS: Kingstown, St. Vincent; Port Elizabeth, Bequia; and Clifton, Union Island.

GOVERNMENT: St. Vincent and the Grenadines, a member of the British Commonwealth, has a parliamentary government headed by a prime minister. The parliament is made up of a House of Assembly, elected every five years. The governor-general is appointed by the queen on the advice of the prime minister.

CURRENCY: East Caribbean dollar. US $1 equals about EC $2.70.

DEPARTURE TAX: EC $20 (US $7.50)

LANGUAGE: English

PUBLIC HOLIDAYS: January 1, New Year's Day; January 22, St. Vincent and Grenadines Day; Good Friday; Easter Monday; May 1, Labor Day; May 22, Whit Monday; July 3, Caricom Day; first Tuesday in July, Carnival Tuesday; August Monday; October 27, Independence Day; December 25, Christmas Day; December 26, Boxing Day.

TELEPHONE AREA CODE: 809

AIRLINES: There are no direct flights from the United States to St. Vincent. American Airlines, BWIA, and Air Canada, connect in San Juan, Barbados, and Antigua with American Eagle, LIAT, and Mustique Airways. St. Vincent has an information desk in the arrivals hall at the airport in Barbados, open daily from 1:00 to 8:00 P.M. to assist passengers traveling to/from St. Vincent and the Grenadines.

INFORMATION:

In the United States, St. Vincent and the Grenadines Tourist Information Office, 801 Second Avenue, New York, NY 10017; (212) 687–4981 (800) 729–1726; fax: (212) 949–5946; 6506 Cove Creek Place, Dallas, TX 75240; (214) 239–6551; (800) 235–3029; fax: (214) 239–1002.

In Canada, St. Vincent and the Grenadines Tourist Information Office, 32 Park Road, Toronto, Ont. M4W 2N4; (416) 924–5796; fax: (416) 924–5844.

In Port:
Kingstown: St. Vincent and the Grenadines Department of Tourism, Egmont Street, P.O. Box 834, Kingstown; 457–1502; fax: 456–2610.
Hours: Weekdays 8:00 A.M.–noon and 1:00–4:15 P.M.;
Tourist Information Desk, E. T. Joshua Airport; 458–4685.

Bequia: Bequia Tourist Bureau, Port Elizabeth; 458–3286.
Hours: Sunday to Friday 9:00 A.M.–12:30 P.M. and 1:30 P.M.–4:00 P.M.; Saturday to 12:30 P.M.

Union Island: Union Island Tourist Bureau; 458–8350.
Hours: daily, including weekends, 8:00 A.M.–noon and 1:00–4:00 P.M.

BUDGET PLANNING

St. Vincent is one of the least expensive destinations in the Caribbean, but the limited tourist development limits your options as well. On the other hand, its unspoiled quality is part of the attraction. Plan to enjoy St. Vincent and the Grenadines for their unrivaled natural beauty, and leave your shopping for other ports. Some of the Grenadines—Bequia and Union—are also inexpensive, but those that have been developed as deluxe, private-island resorts, such as Petit St. Vincent and Young Island, are expensive. The islands frequented by cruise ships—Bequia, Mustique, Canouan, and Mayreau—are visited for their beaches and water sports; activities are generally prearranged by the cruise line.

PORT PROFILE:

LOCATION/EMBARKATION: The port is on the southeastern corner of St. Vincent at Kingstown Bay. It is a vital commercial artery for this predominantly agricultural country as well as being its cruise and ferry port. A new pier exclusively for cruise ships was part of a major reclamation project to improve the appearance, access, and facilities of the port area. A walkway from the pier leads directly into the city center, 2 blocks from the Department of Tourism and main shopping street.

LOCAL TRANSPORTATION: Minibuses to all parts of St. Vincent depart from Market Square, 1 block from the pier in Kingstown; or you can wave at a passing bus to stop for you. Sample fares from Kingstown to the main locations: Arnos Vale, EC $1; Mesopotamia, EC $2; Georgetown, EC $3. Cruise-ship passengers seldom use buses except for short distances near Kingstown.

Taxi rates are fixed by the government. The hourly rate is EC $30 (US $15). Taxis can be hired for sightseeing. Some examples of one-way fares from Kingstown to popular destinations: Airport, EC $20; Young Island dock, EC $20; Blue Lagoon, EC $30; Mesopotamia EC $35; Lists of bus and taxi fares are available from the Department of Tourism.

ROADS AND RENTALS: On St. Vincent the main road system is confined to the southern, most populated, third of the island between Kingstown and Layou on the west and Georgetown on the east. Most are narrow roads that wind through the mountains and along irregular coastlines. No road circumnavigates the island, and only roads on the south coast cross the island between the east and west coasts. There are very few roads in the central area, and almost none in the northern third. The east-coast road north of Georgetown is best covered by four-wheel drive.

Cars and jeeps are available for rent in Kingstown for US $45–$50 per day; gas, $2.50 per gallon, but you might enjoy your sight-seeing more if you do not have to negotiate the winding roads. Taxis can be hired by the hour or for the day; be sure to agree on the route and price in advance. Guides for hiking can be obtained through the Forestry Division or the Government Tourist Office. Local tour companies organize hikes to Soufrière; you should consult them about trail conditions.

Rental companies include: *Avis* (458–4613), *Star Garage/Hertz* (456–1743; fax: 456–2726); and some independent dealers. A local driving license is required and can be obtained for EC $40 (US $15) upon presentation of your U.S. or Canadian driver's license at the Licensing Authority, Halifax Street; or at the police station on Bay Street. Driving in this former British colony is on the LEFT.

Ports of call in the Grenadines have at least one road from the pier to the main community or resort, as well as tracks and footpaths. Bequia, Mustique, and Union have taxis.

FERRY SERVICE: Between Kingstown and Bequia ferries leave at 2- and 3-hour intervals from 6:00 A.M. to 7:00 P.M. Cost is EC $10 (US $4) one-way. Ferries to Canouan, Mayreau, and Union operate several days a week. You will find schedules in the Tourist Department's information booklet.

EMERGENCY NUMBERS:
   Medical: General Hospital, Kingstown; 456–1185
   Police and Coast Guard: Dial 999

Author's Favorite Attractions

Botanic Gardens
Buccament Nature Trail
Falls of Baleine

Shore Excursions

Due to the small number of cruise ships calling at Kingstown, shore excursions are generally limited to a 3-hour island tour with a visit to the Botanic Gardens and a drive to the Mesopotamia or Buccament valleys. For those who stay longer, consider a boat excursion to the Falls of Baleine—a magnificent waterfall accessible only by boat—passing spectacular scenery, with stops for swimming and snorkeling. The trip is offered as a day excursion by tour and water-sports companies in Kingstown. Another option is to hike to the summit of the Soufrière volcano. The excursion from Kingstown takes 6 hours.

For travelers arriving by yacht or coming to St. Vincent to begin a sailing excursion through the Grenadines, these tours can be arranged through your chartering company.

ST. VINCENT ON YOUR OWN

Kingstown is the only sizable town on St. Vincent. Founded in the early 18th century, the historic town stretches around Kingstown Bay and climbs the surrounding hills. It is laid out in a grid of 3 streets deep and about 10 blocks long. The historic sites, along with browsing in a few shops, can be covered on foot in an hour or so.

A KINGSTOWN WALKABOUT

From the pier you can walk directly up Egmont Street to the Government Tourist Office or east on Upper Bay Street, where former warehouses have been renovated to house shops and restaurants. The Cobblestone Inn is the most attractive structure, with a pretty interior courtyard containing with some of the town's best shops, as well as *Basil's Bar and Restaurant,* a popular place to take a respite from the hot St. Vincent sun.

One block west of the harbor at the corner of Long Lane Upper and Bedford streets is the market: a colorful, chaotic scene on market day, Saturday mornings. At the north end of the market, on Halifax Street, is the *Courthouse and Parliament* building, a large colonial structure and small square at the town's center.

West of the parliament Halifax Street becomes Grenville Street, which has two landmark churches. *St. George's Anglican Cathedral,* at the corner of North River Road, is the oldest church in St. Vincent (1820) and is noted for its stained-glass windows. But more curious is *St. Mary's Catholic Church*, an extraordinary mixture of Romanesque, Gothic, Renaissance, and baroque styles with pointed arches, round arches, turrets, square and wedding towers. It was created from pictures of famous European cathedrals by a bishop-architect in 1823,

enlarged in 1877 and 1891, and restored in the early 1940s. The interior is as ornate as the exterior. North of the church is *Victoria Park,* a parade ground.

BOTANIC GARDENS About a mile north of town are the oldest botanical gardens in the Western Hemisphere, established in 1765 on twenty hillside acres north of town. The gardens were begun mainly to grow herbs and spices, which in those days were the source of most drugs; the first curators were medical men as well as horticulturists.

After being allowed to deteriorate in the mid-19th century, the gardens were reactivated by 1890 as part of a larger agricultural and botanical scheme. Today they are beautifully maintained, though not well signposted, and have enormous variety; they rank among the most outstanding in the Caribbean. They have nine varieties of ixora, a flowering bush whose small clustered blossom is the national flower. Along with huge mahogany and teak, you might see African tulip, yellow *poui,* flamboyant, or others in bloom, depending on the month. In October, for example, the nutmeg are laden with fruit, and the cannonball tree, an ugly wiry tree, shows its magnificent, delicate coral blossom.

The gardens' prized species is a breadfruit tree planted in 1793 from the original plant brought to the Caribbean from Tahiti by Captain Bligh of *Mutiny on the Bounty* fame. When he arrived in Kingstown in 1793 on the HMS *Providence* on his second voyage, he off-loaded 530 breadfruit plants, of which 50 were planted in the gardens. The gardens' specimen is said to be a third-generation sucker of an original plant. As a clone of the original root, it can be referred to as an "original." The main entrance to the gardens is on the south, where an allamanda arch opens onto a manicured grass path bordered by hibiscus hedges and shaded by enormous Honduras mahogany. Guides are available. The famous breadfruit tree is near the north entrance.

On the west side of the garden is the *Archaeological Museum,* built in 1981 and once the home of the curator. It houses a small collection of pre-Columbian artifacts found in St. Vincent and the Grenadines. It is open on Wednesday mornings and Saturday afternoons.

On the east side of the gardens is an aviary for the St. Vincent parrot, the national bird and one of the most endangered parrot species. In this century alone the number decreased from thousands to an estimated five hundred birds today. Their habitat is being destroyed by clearing of the forest for agriculture, logging, hunting, and by the lucrative international pet market for exotic birds. The bird has magnificent coloring, with a distinctive white head and a brownish mauve body and green, deep lavender, and gold on the tail, neck, and wings.

A major effort to preserve the parrot is under way by the Forestry Division with the aid of Peace Corps volunteers, World Wildlife Fund, and RARE, the Philadelphia-based tropical-bird conservation group. A reserve has been established on about six hundred acres of rain forests in the Upper Buccament Valley. The program has involved the entire population—from schoolchildren, dressed as parrots, dancing to a calypso tune written especially for "Vincy," the parrot's nickname; to businessmen who use the parrot in their promotions.

FORT CHARLOTTE From its 650-foot-high perch about 2 miles west of town, Fort Charlotte commands a magnificent view across Kingstown Bay to some of the Grenadines. Built around 1791 during the reign of King George III and named for his queen, the fort was completed about 1812 and was occupied by British troops until 1873. The gun emplacements, which are intact, point inland. This and the moat location, between the promontory and the main island, indicates that the builders may have been more concerned about attacks from the land—from the Caribs or the French—than from the sea. Today an area of the fort is used as a women's prison.

FORT DUVERNETTE Built about 1800 to protect the entrance to Kingstown, the fort sits atop a volcanic spike, 195 feet above the sea. Fort Duvernette is next to Young Island at the entrance to Young Cut, a narrow channel on the south coast where water sports are centered. A

visit can be arranged through Young Island Resort.

A DRIVE AROUND THE ISLAND

THE SOUTH COAST TO THE MESOPOTAMIA VALLEY

From the capital Queen Elizabeth Drive, one of the main arteries, runs east over Sion and Dorsetshire Hills, providing fabulous views over Kingstown and Fort Charlotte. At Arnos Vale, by the airport, the road splits. One branch skirts the coast along Calliaqua Bay, where most of the hotels and popular beaches are located; and the other climbs the mountains. The east end of Calliaqua Bay, known as the Careenage or Blue Lagoon, is the center for sailing charters.

MESOPOTAMIA VALLEY The southern third of St. Vincent has two high mountain ridges bridged at two 3,000-foot peaks—Grand Bonhomme and Petit Bonhomme. They form the heads of two large, intensively cultivated valleys: the Mesopotamia Valley on the east and the Buccament Valley on the west. The high slopes of the Mesopotamia Valley are thick with tree ferns and bamboo and planted with nutmeg, cacao, and coconut. The panoramic views are spectacular. The lower reaches of the valley are the country's breadbasket, planted with West Indian staples that include breadfruit, banana, plantain, and root crops such as eddo and dasheen—all plants with huge leafs that enhance the valley's lush appearance. High on the windward slopes of Grand Bonhomme at Richland Park are the Montreal Gardens, a botanical garden and nursery.

YAMBOU GORGE You can return from the gardens via the Yambou Gorge, where the streams that drain through the Mesopotamia Valley tumble over volcanic rocks on their way to the sea. On the coast large Atlantic rollers break against the rocks and the black-sand beaches at Argyle. Views along the way across the ridges and through the valley to the sea are magnificent.

The West Coast to the Buccament Valley

West of Kingstown the Leeward Highway snakes along the west coast and after about 5 miles crosses the Buccament Valley. The former Pembroke Estate was once a prosperous one-thousand-acre sugar plantation whose aqueduct supplied water to power the mill. It is now part of the setting for the Aqueduct Golf Course; the hotel nearby has a casino and restaurant. A road inland along the Buccament River leads to the head of the valley and a rain forest trail on the slopes of Grand Bonhomme.

NATURE TRAIL A loop trail of 1.5 miles, developed by the Forestry Department with the aid of Peace Corps volunteers in 1988, rises from about 1,000 feet to almost 2,500 feet and passes under towering teak, mahogany, silk cotton, gommier, and other hardwoods that form a dense canopy overhead. The forest floor is carpeted with enormous ferns; tree trunks and their limbs are festooned with epiphytes (leafy air-plants) and entangled in a curtain of vines. The buttress roots of the oldest trees are among the largest seen in any Caribbean rain forest. The trail has lookouts for viewing parrots.

TABLE ROCK Less than a half mile before the signposted entrance to the Nature Trail, a short footpath east of the main road leads to Table Rock, where enormous lava rocks that tumbled down the mountainside rest in the river bed. The water has carved channels and basins where you can swim, except during the rainy season when the rushing water is too strong. The setting is delightful for a picnic, too.

Beyond Buccament the Leeward Highway snakes north along steep ridges that drop into the sea, passing fishing villages on the way to Chateaubelair, where the road ends. This region of jagged peaks, high bluffs, and deep ravines is the less-accessible part of the island.

FALLS OF BALEINE St. Vincent's prettiest waterfalls are almost at the edge of the sea on the northwest coast, about 7 miles north of Richmond Beach and 18 miles from Kingstown as the crow flies. At the head of a steep-sided gorge on the northern face of the Soufrière volcano, the falls cascade more than 70 feet in one stage through thick tropical foliage into a rockbound pool ideal for swimming.

Access to the falls from Kingstown is by boat. The 45-minute trip is as fascinating as the falls are enjoyable and provide a view of St. Vincent's spectacular scenery from the sea. The falls are located about 500 yards from a small pebble beach. The boat anchors about 10 to 20 yards from the beach, and you wade ashore or may have to swim from your boat, depending on the tide. Sneakers are advisable as the rocks and pebbles can be hard on bare feet. Water sports operators in Kingstown offer the excursion almost daily.

Exploring the East Coast

SOUFRIÈRE VOLCANO The northern third of St. Vincent is dominated by the Soufrière Mountains, which have one of the most active volcanoes in the Eastern Caribbean. Five eruptions between 1718 and 1979 are documented, but archaeological evidence indicates the volcano probably erupted as early as A.D. 160. During an 1812 eruption—one of the worst, killing two thousand people—ash fell as far away as Barbados, 90 miles to the east. In 1902, the same year as the devastating eruption of Mt. Pelée in Martinique, an eruption of Soufrière created the present width of the crater: 1 mile in diameter. In 1971 another eruption caused an island of lava to form in the center of the crater lake.

The most recent, in April of 1979, sent ash and stone thousands of feet into the air and rivers of molten lava down the mountainsides. More than twenty thousand people were evacuated, but, miraculously, no one was killed.

Once again the volcano is safe to climb and may be approached from either the eastern or western side on a trail running along the southern ridge of the crater. The eastern trail is used most frequently and can be followed by experienced hikers on their own. It starts 1 mile north of Georgetown at Rabacca where the peak first comes in view. A guide and jeep can be provided by a local safari outfitter.

From Kingstown to the start of the eastern trail is 26 miles and takes 1.5 to 2 hours to drive. It is followed by a 2.5-mile drive on a very rutted plantation road north of the Rabacca Dry River, passing through the extensive banana and coconut groves of Rabacca Farm—formerly the three thousand-acre Orange Hill Estate, once the largest coconut plantation in the Caribbean—to the base of the crater at about a 700-foot altitude. From there a 3-mile trail ascends gradually through a rain forest to the crater rim. Along the way are wonderful vistas, sometimes looking back to the coast. The hike to the rim takes about 3 hours.You should check with the Forestry or Tourism Offices about trail conditions. Bring water and a picnic lunch, and start early to avoid the heat of the sun (but temperatures at the summit are chilly). There are no facilities of any kind once you leave the coast.

RABACCA DRY RIVER A remarkable phenomenon of the St. Vincent volcanic eruptions are the "dry rivers": riverbeds that were filled and choked with scoriae, or lava cinder, and gravel after the eruptions of 1812 and 1902. Water flowing into the river seeps through the scoriae and disappears, becoming a subterranean river as it nears the coast. At the mouth of the river, the surface is bone dry.

The best examples of dry rivers are at Wallilabou, on the west coast, and on the east coast at the Rabacca Dry River, which enters the sea at Rabacca, north of Georgetown. Where the main highway crosses the riverbed, the dry river is more than a half-mile wide and covered with several feet of loose ash; no water is visible on the surface. But toward the mountain, where the terrain begins to rise, water can be seen. Depending on the time of the year, it might be a small stream or a raging torrent after a sudden downpour.

SANDY BAY AND FANCY On the north coast at the base of La Soufrière are the villages of Sandy Bay, Owia, and Fancy. Traditionally, Sandy Bay had the largest concentration of the descendants of the "Black Caribs," who came from the union of African slaves and indigenous Amerindians. After Sandy Bay the coastal road deteriorates and becomes a dirt track.

Shopping

The town center of Kingstown is small, and the shopping of interest to cruise passengers is mod-

est, involving only a few stores on Bay and Halifax streets. Stores are open weekdays from 8:00 A.M. to 4:00 P.M. and Saturday to noon. Most stores close for lunch between noon and 1:00 P.M.

The best selection of crafts, as well as books on St. Vincent, can be found at *Noah's Arkade* (Upper Bay Street). *Boutique Giggles* (Cobblestone Inn Arcade) carries accessories, locally crafted black coral and other jewelry, T-shirts, and Gotter swimsuits. *Artisans Local Art & Craft* (Bondie Building, Bay Street; 458–4436) specializes in local crafts.

The *St. Vincent Crafts Centre* on the east side of town is a marketing outlet and craft shop for locally made jewelry, dolls, baskets, and other crafts made from straw, clay, coconut, wood, and bamboo; quality is not consistent.

For china, crystal, perfume, and other duty-free gifts, *Stechers Jewelers* (Cobblestone Inn Arcade) has the best selection. *Y. De Lima* (Egmont and Bay streets) is a department store with jewelry and gifts.

Dining and Restaurants

Kingstown has only a few restaurants outside of hotels. Prices are moderate. Check locally about days and hours for serving lunch and dinner.

The French Restaurant (Villa; 458–4972). St. Vincent's best restaurant offers a selection of classic French dishes with an emphasis on seafood. There's a small, lively bar inside; dining is on a terrace by water overlooking Young Island. If you want West Indian cuisine, try *The Pepperpor* (457–4337), a new restaurant by the same owner.

Basil's Bar and Restaurant (*Cobblestone Inn* 457–2713). The famous watering hole on Mustique has a twin. Situated in a pretty, historic building within walking distance of the pier in Kingstown, the pub offers classic cuisine and seafood.

Camelot (Kingstown Park; 456–2100; fax 456–2233). Situated on a hillside in Kingstown's oldest guest house (which dates from 1765), the newly renovated old manor recently opened a the island's new hotel and promises to have the best dining room in town.

The Lagoon & Green Flash Bar (Blue Lagoon; 458–4308). In a romantic setting on a beautiful lagoon, the restaurant is part of the marina specializing in yacht charters. The menu features seafood.

Sports

BEACHES/SWIMMING: The white-sand beaches on the south and black-sand ones on the west are the safest for swimming. The windward, or east, coast is generally too rough and the shoreline too rocky for swimming. All beaches are public. On the south coast a 2-minute dock-to-dock boat ride across the cut takes you to Young Island, a private-island resort. Except for a few thatched-roof pavilions by the beach, most of the villas are hidden under curtains of tropical foliage. The resort does not provide changing facilities for day visitors, but you can swim at the beach and lunch in the restaurant.

BOATING: A sailing trip through beautiful waters of the Grenadines usually starts from St. Vincent. Yachts for up to eight people can be chartered, with or without crew, from *Lagoon Marina and Hotel* (Blue Lagoon; phone/fax 458–4308); and *Barefoot Yacht Charters* (Blue Lagoon; 456–9526; fax: 456–9238).

DEEP-SEA FISHING: Sportfishing is not a developed sport, although the seas around St. Vincent and the Grenadines have abundant fish. Watersports operators can arrange deep-sea fishing upon request, and in the Grenadines you can often go out to sea with a local fisherman.

HIKING AND BIKING: St. Vincent has some of the most spectacular scenery in the Caribbean, and it's best seen by hiking. There are easy trails in lush, mountainous settings and arduous ones over rugged terrain. For local people the lack of roads in many places makes walking and hiking a necessity. Guides for hiking are available through the Forestry Division and the Department of Tourism. Local travel companies organize hiking to Soufrière. *T's Tours* (Sharp

Street; 456–5837; fax: 809–456–5779). Owner Tessa Davy offers hiking trips and sightseeing tours. She does not take credit cards. *Sailor's Cycling Tours* (P.O. Box 684; 457–1712; fax: 809–456–2821) organizes bike tours to remote areas.

SNORKELING/SCUBA DIVING: The best snorkeling in St. Vincent is found along Young Island Cut and the west coast, but even better snorkeling is in the Grenadines, where shallow-water reefs surround almost every island, and huge schools of fish travel through the archipelago.

Diving in St. Vincent has only been explored in the past decade, and experts have been excited by what they have found. Reef life normally found at 80 feet in other locations grows here at depths of 25 feet, and there is an extraordinary amount and variety of tropical reef fish. *Dive St. Vincent* (457–4714; fax: 457–4948); and *St. Vincent Dive Experience* (456–9741) are located on St. Vincent's south coast; in Bequia, *Bequia Beach Club* (458–3248; fax: 458–3689) and *Dive Bequia* (458–3504). Generally, prices for dive excursions and use of equipment are lower than in other Caribbean locations.

TENNIS AND SQUASH: *Grand View Hotel* (458–4811; fax: 457–4174) on the south coast has a sports center with tennis and squash courts, gym, and an outside pool. Nonguests may use the facilities upon payment of a fee.

WINDSURFING: Equipment is available for rent from hotels on the south coast. In the Grenadines, all beachside resorts have windsurfing equipment.

Festivals and Celebrations

St. Vincent's Carnival, or *Vincy Mas*, as the Vincentians call it, is a ten-day festival held from the last Sunday in June to the first Tuesday in July. It is one of the biggest celebrations in the Eastern Caribbean, and people from neighboring islands participate.

The last two weeks in December have Christmas celebrations. Starting on the sixteenth people parade and dance through Kingstown every day (except Sundays) for the following nine mornings.

THE GRENADINES

The three dozen enchanted islands and cays that make up the Grenadines are like stepping-stones across the 65 miles between St. Vincent and Grenada. These idyllic islands-in-the-sun, where the news comes with the mail boat, are about as far off the beaten track as one can get in the Caribbean.

Scalloped with porcelain-white beaches protected by coral reefs, the Grenadines float on a deep turquoise sea. Long admired by yachtsmen, in recent years they have drawn the attention of cruise ships. Eight islands have settlements; the others are sanctuaries for birds and hideaways for those who love the sea.

BEQUIA

Lying 9 miles south of St. Vincent across the Bequia Channel, Bequia (pronounced beck-wee) is the largest of the Grenadines and a cruise-ship port of call. An island of rolling green hills, Bequia has only a few roads, but walking on unpaved roads and footpaths is easy. The island has many pretty beaches with reefs that are often within swimming distance from shore.

Bequia is known throughout the Eastern Caribbean for its skilled seamen, boat builders, and fishermen—descendants of New England whalers, European traders, pirates, and ship-wrecked slaves. A haven for yachtsmen from around the world for its excellent anchorage at Admiralty Bay, Bequia has become a mecca for artists, writers, and assorted city dwellers who have opted for the laid-back island life. Unlike some of the Grenadines, Bequia has not been developed for tourists. Most hotels and guest-houses—some in former plantation houses with flowering gardens—are small and unpretentious.

Port Elizabeth, the main town and port where ships dock, can easily be covered on foot. The tourist information office at the pier has free maps and literature. A short walk north of the harbor takes you to the workshops of the island's

best carvers of model boats, a craft for which Bequia is famous.

If you walk south from the pier along the main street, you will find a bookshop, *Noah's Ark,* and other small stores. By the bay, *Friendship Bay Hotel* belongs to the present prime minister of St. Vincent and the Grenadines, who hails from Bequia. The hotel is one of the oldest on the island, and its bar is something of an institution for residents and visiting salts. Next door *The Gingerbread* is a tiny hotel with a delightful restaurant open to the breezes, an ice-cream parlor, and *Dive Bequia,* one of the two local dive shops.

Some of Bequia's best snorkeling is found at Friendship Bay on the south coast where a half-mile beach is protected by reef; Spring Bay on the east coast is another. Windsurfing is available from *Paradise Windsurfing* (Friendship Bay; 809–458–3222), which offers five different locations. The breakers at Hope Bay are popular for bodysurfing. Sportfishing is not organized, but local fishermen hook tuna, marlin, wahoo, king-fish, or other big fish with ease.

Every spring the *Bequia Easter Regatta* attracts sailors and spectators from distant lands who join local fishing boats in four days of competition and celebration. Bequia's fishing vessels are wooden craft still made by hand. There are also competitions for model "gum boats" made by young Bequia craftsmen and gaily rigged miniatures made from coconut husks by children. The festival includes sports competitions, music, food and exhibition of island products.

Twice-daily ferry service connects Port Elizabeth and Kingstown in about 1 hour. Bequia has an airstrip; Mustique Airways flies daily from Barbados.

MUSTIQUE

Developed in the early 1970s by British and international investors, Mustique was put on the map by the British royal family, Mick Jagger, Raquel Welch, and a host of international celebrities who vacation here. Princess Margaret's home, a six-acre perch overlooking Galizeau Bay on the south coast, is available for rent. *Basil's Bar and Restaurant,* the parent of the Basil restaurant in

t. Vincent, is the best celebrity-watching spot on he island. It also has water-sports equipment for ent. Cruise ships anchor at Grand Bay (which the oyals renamed Britannia Bay). During the winter eason they are likely to line up with sleek yachts hat match the posh homes of the celebrity residents.

Mustique has a more manicured appearance han her sister islands and is one of the few Grenadines with paved roads. From the north end overed with gentle hills, the land rises to a steep ange in the center and south. Sandy Bay on the orth coast has a mile-long crest of white sand vith spectacular water whose colors run the full pectrum of blue and green. Off the western point f the bay lies the wreck of the *Antilles.* Other ood beaches are found at Pastor Bay on the east nd Landing Cove on the west. There is good snor-

keling, particularly at Britannia and Lagoon bays.

In colonial times the island had seven sugar plantations, one of whose estate houses is now the *Cotton House,* the only deluxe hotel in Mustique. There are frequent flights from St. Vincent, which take 10 minutes, and direct service from Barbados.

CANOUAN

Located between Mustique and Union, the island is a popular stop for yachts, with a marina for one hundred boats. *Canouan Beach Hotel* is the largest hotel in St. Vincent and the Grenadines, and *Tamarind Beach Hotel* (458–8044; fax: 458–8851) is the newest. Both have facilities for water sports. There is one main road and a tiny airport.

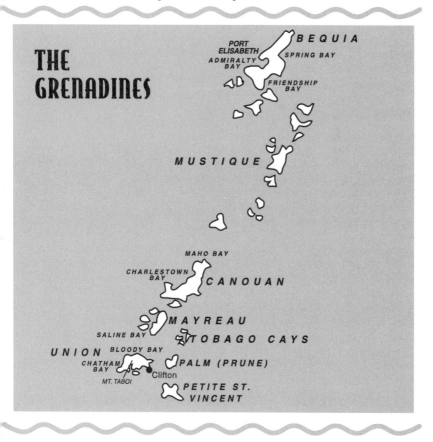

THE GRENADINES

BEQUIA
PORT ELISABETH
ADMIRALTY BAY
SPRING BAY
FRIENDSHIP BAY

MUSTIQUE

MAHO BAY
CHARLESTOWN BAY
CANOUAN

MAYREAU
SALINE BAY
TOBAGO CAYS
UNION
BLOODY BAY
CHATHAM BAY
MT. TABOI
Clifton
PALM (PRUNE)
PETITE ST. VINCENT

One of the driest islands of the group, Canouan is encircled by beautiful beaches. Charleston Bay on the west is the main port. The mushroom-shaped harbor has a mile-long beach. From the bay a half-mile-long footpath over the hill leads to more beautiful beaches and to some of the best snorkeling in an area called The Pool, where the colors of the water are fabulous.

MAYREAU

Until Salt Whistle Bay resort opened in 1987, Mayreau had no facilities. The resort is situated on a palm-fringed crescent of beach; at the north end, a short trail crosses over to the east side and a long stretch of beach. The island's tiny village is on a hill from which there is a lovely view over Tobago Cays and Horseshore Reef, an area with extraordinary multihued aquamarine waters for which the Grenadines are famous. Mayreau is popular as a cruise-ship stop for its beautiful beaches and reefs. The wreck of a British gun-boat, about 300 yards off Grand Col Point on the west coast, is a favorite of divers.

TOBAGO CAYS

East of Mayreau about halfway between Canouan and Union is one of the most beautiful spots in the Caribbean and a highlight of cruising the Grenadines. Tobago Cays are four uninhabited palm-fringed islets etched by pristine white-sand beaches and incredibly clear aquamarine waters. The setting is so serene it seems unreal. From a beach on any islet, you can walk or swim to clusters of reef to view the spectacular marine life. The water flowing between the islands has strong currents, which bring huge schools of fish. On the east the cays are encircled by Horseshoe Reef, the northern half of which has spectacular reefs; parts are shallow enough to wade.

In 1989 at the tenth anniversary of its independence, St. Vincent and the Grenadines's prime minister declared the 1990s as the Decade of the Environment, placing conservation at the top of his priority list. One of its first projects is the Tobago Cays National Park—and not a minute too soon. The islets were declared a marine

reserve a decade ago, but lack of attention and careless use by fishermen and boaters, coupled with the lack of strong government regulation, put tremendous stress on the coral gardens. Upgrading them to a national park provides the mechanism for the government to acquire the territory and manage it.

PALM ISLAND

A private resort on a 110-acre island, Palm Island was known as Prune Island until Texan John Caldwell came along. Known as the Johnny Appleseed of the Caribbean, Caldwell obtained a ninety-nine-year lease (for which he pays US $1 per year) from the St. Vincent government and built a fabulous resort, where he replaced the scrub and swamp—not to mention mosquitoes—with two thousand palm trees and hundreds of other flowering trees and plants. He also planted another three thousand palm trees on neighboring islands.

Palm is popular with yachtsmen and is an occasional stop for small cruise ships. It is surrounded by pretty beaches protected by reefs that are only a wade or a short swim away. The resort has complete water-sports facilities available to day visitors for a fee. To arrange for diving contact the resort in advance: (809) 458–4804. The resort has a yacht for six available for day charter or for a week's cruise.

PETIT ST. VINCENT

Another deluxe, private-island resort, Petit St. Vincent often appears on the Caribbean's "ten best" list. Half of the 113-acre property was left in a natural state, and the other half was turned into a manicured park setting. The island is scalloped with pretty spectacular beaches, and on its north side are two sandbars with gorgeous white sand—Punaise and Mopion—floating in fantastically beautiful water and reefs. In fact, the islands are the western extreme of a 3-mile reef that runs along the north and east sides of Petit St. Vincent to Petit Martinique, one of Grenada's Grenadines. The shallow water offers some of the best snorkeling in the area. Petit St. Vincent welcomes visiting yachts but not cruise ships.

UNION ISLAND

Located about halfway between St. Vincent and Grenada, Union Island is 1.5 miles from Palm Island and 4 miles from Tobago Cays. The second-most populated of the Grenadines, Union's 2,500 inhabitants live mostly in Clifton, which is the government and commercial center as well as port. It has a bank, police station, doctor and clinic, and several buildings dating from the early 1800s. A footpath leads to Fort Hills, where there is a gun emplacement with old cannons and a panoramic view.

The T-shaped island has a spine of jagged, slab-faced mountains running north-south along the T-bar with Mt. Tabor, at 999 feet, the highest peak in the Grenadines. A road connects Clifton, on the east coast, and Ashton, a fishing village on the south coast. Bloody Bay on the northwest coast and Chatham Bay on the west coast are popular anchorages.

Union has small hotels and an air strip served by scheduled flights from St. Vincent, Grenada, St. Lucia, and Martinique. Union celebrates Easter with boat races, calypso competitions, and cultural shows. In May the Big Drum Festival is a cultural event to mark the end of the dry season and culminates with the Big Drum Dance, a celebration also seen on Carriacou.

Grenada

St. George's, Grenada;
Hillsborough, Carriacou

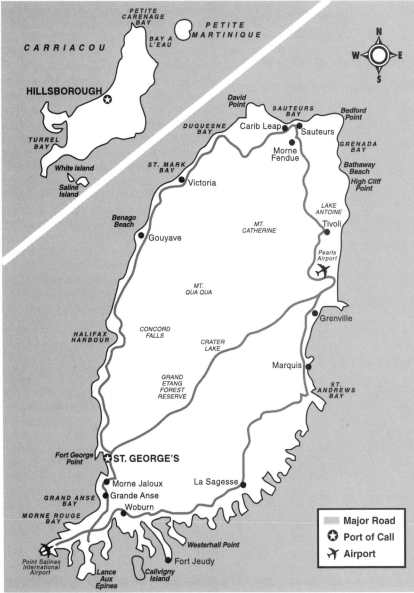

CARRIACOU

PETITE CARENAGE BAY

BAY A L'EAU

PETITE MARTINIQUE

HILLSBOROUGH

TURREL BAY

White Island

Saline Island

David Point

SAUTEURS BAY

Bedford Point

DUQUESNE BAY

Carib Leap

Sauteurs

Morne Fendue

GRENADA BAY

ST. MARK BAY

Victoria

Bathaway Beach

High Cliff Point

Benago Beach

MT. CATHERINE

LAKE ANTOINE

Tivoli

Gouyave

Pearls Airport

MT. QUA QUA

Grenville

HALIFAX HARBOUR

CONCORD FALLS

CRATER LAKE

Marquis

GRAND ETANG FOREST RESERVE

ST. ANDREWS BAY

Fort George Point

ST. GEORGE'S

La Sagesse

Morne Jaloux

Grand Anse

GRAND ANSE BAY

Woburn

MORNE ROUGE BAY

Westerhall Point

Point Salines International Airport

Lance Aux Epines

Calivigny Island

Fort Jeudy

▒	Major Road
✪	Port of Call
✈	Airport

N W E S

AT A GLANCE

CHAPTER CONTENTS

THE SPICE ISLAND

Mountainous and lush, Grenada is a tapestry of tropical splendor that leaves you breathless with its beauty. Here, where the air is filled with the scent of cinnamon and nutmeg, thick vines climb the telephone poles and trail along overhead wires; the banana trees by the side of the road grow as tall as the palm trees that shade the beaches. Waterfalls cascade through the forested mountains decorated with 450 species of flowering plants and 150 species of birds. Nutmeg, ginger, vanilla, and almost every herb and fruit of the tropics fill the landscape.

The Spice Island, as Grenada is known, is the southernmost island of the Windwards, located 100 miles north of Venezuela. Off her north coast are her dependencies of Carriacou and Petit Martinique—two islands of the Grenadines chain that stretches north to St. Vincent. The trade winds that cool the island—only 12 degrees north of the equator—bring more than 160 inches of rain annually to the interior, creating lush forests and rivers that rush down the mountains to the sea.

From its forested, volcanic peaks, Grenada drops to a varied coastline of steep cliffs with hidden coves of black sand, wide bays with long stretches of white sand, deep harbors sheltering sailing craft, and lagoons and estuaries that host wildlife. Beneath the sea volcanic action continues nearby. Kick 'em Jenny, a volcano, lies submerged only 500 feet under the water off Grenada's north coast.

Sighted by Columbus on his third voyage in 1498, Grenada was probably occupied first by the Ciboneys and later the Arawaks, who were driven north by the fierce Carib Indians around A.D. 1000. English traders attempted to establish a colony on Grenada's west coast in 1609, but they failed due to Carib resistance. In 1650 the French had better luck and established a settlement on the southeast coast at the present site of La Sagesse, which paved the way for it to become a French possession two decades later.

Because of her strategic location, Grenada was coveted by the British, too. Consequently, the island changed hands several times between the French and the British until 1783, when it was ceded to Britain under the Treaty of Versailles. The British expanded sugar production, stepped up the importation of slaves, and established a plantation system. In 1795 Julien Fedon, a mulatto planter of French origin inspired by the ideas of the French Revolution, led a bloody but unsuccessful rebellion against the British. After slavery was abolished in 1834, attempts to continue sugar cultivation by importing indentured laborers from Asia failed. In 1877 Grenada became a British crown colony, and in 1974 it gained full independence.

A few years later in 1979, a bloodless coup led by Maurice Bishop and six of his followers known as the New Jewel Movement, threw out the government of Sir Eric Gairy, a controversial character with a secret police known as the "Mongoose Gang." Bishop and his group might have been a welcome relief had they not changed the island's name to the People's Revolutionary Government of Grenada and begun waltzing with Cuba. The Cubans wasted no time in sending experts to train Grenada's security forces and help with her most pressing need: the construction of a new airport. The airport became a bone of contention for the United States, which saw Cuba's involvement as a camouflage to turn Grenada into a military base, enabling Cuba to control the two ends of the Caribbean.

Thus in 1983, when an internal struggle for power resulted in the assassination of Bishop and an attempt by a pro-Cuban faction to seize power, the United States saw an opportunity, and, with the endorsement of the Eastern Caribbean states, intervened militarily to stop the coup and restore order. The following year a parliamentary government was returned to power. The irony is that the United States completed the construction of the airport, which it had claimed Grenada did not need, and President Reagan landed there sixteen months after its opening, pointing with pride to its completion.

Despite its turbulent history, Grenada is an easy living sort of place, with hotels set in flowering gardens alongside beautiful beaches, old fishing villages, and gentle folk whose diverse heritage matches the colorful tapestry of their tropical landscape. British traditions run as deep as

African and Asian ones, but the French legacy, too, has endured: in the names of the people and places, the patois that is more French than English, and the cuisine, which is some of the best in the Caribbean.

 ## FAST FACTS

 POPULATION: 110,000

 SIZE: Grenada, including Carriacou and Petit Martinique, covers 133 sq. miles. Grenada itself is 12 miles wide and 21 miles long.

MAIN TOWNS: St. George's and Grenville, Grenada; Hillsborough, Carriacou.

GOVERNMENT: Grenada has a parliamentary form of government and is a member of the British Commonwealth. Parliament consists of two chambers: a Senate of seven appointed members and a House of Representatives of fifteen elected members. The cabinet, headed by the prime minister, is responsible to parliament. The queen is represented by a governor-general.

 CURRENCY: Eastern Caribbean dollar (EC). One US $1 equals EC $2.64. U.S. dollars and traveler's checks are widely accepted.

 DEPARTURE TAX: EC $35 (US $13 adults); US $2.50 ($6.50 ages 6 to 11)

 LANGUAGE: English

 PUBLIC HOLIDAYS: January 1, New Year's Day; February 7, Independence Day; Good Friday; Easter Monday; May 1, Labor Day; May, Whit Monday; June, Corpus Christi; First Monday and Tuesday in August, Emancipation Holidays; October 25, Thanksgiving Day; December 25, Christmas Day; December 26, Boxing Day.

TELEPHONE AREA CODE: 809 or 473

 AIRLINES: American Airlines via San Juan; BWIA from New York, Miami, and various Caribbean islands. LIAT from Barbados and Trinidad. Airlines of Carriacou and Region Air serve Carriacou from Grenada.

 ## INFORMATION:

In the United States:
New York: Grenada Tourist Office, 820 Second Avenue, Suite 900D, New York, NY 10017; (212) 687–9554 or (800) 927–9554 for travel information.

In Canada:
Grenada National Tourist Office, 439 University Avenue, Suite 820, Toronto, Ont. M5G 1Y8; (416) 595–1339.

In Port:
Grenada Tourism Department, The Carenage, St. George's, Grenada, W.I.; 440–2001/2279; fax: 440–6637.

 ## BUDGET PLANNING

Grenada is not an expensive island, with the notable exception of taxis, but since many cruise ships do not stay a full day in port, a taxi with the driver/guide might be your best way to tour—particularly if you have others with whom to share the cost. If you plan to do nothing more than go to the beach, public buses run frequently from town to Grand Anse Beach.

PORT PROFILE:

LOCATION/EMBARKATION: St. George's, the capital and port, has one of the most picturesque settings in the Caribbean. The harbor has two sections: one is the docking area for large cruise ships; the other is a well-sheltered inner harbor used as a yacht basin. Currently, there are berths for two large cruise ships; approval has been given for a major port expansion. There is a Welcome Center at the pier, where you can get information and make phone calls using a major credit card. Simply dial 111 from pay phones.

LOCAL TRANSPORTATION: Grenada does not have a fully developed public transportation system. Instead private minibuses provide in-town and intra-island services at low rates. They leave frequently from Market Square and Esplanade in St. George's.

Taxis are available at the port and in town, but they tend to be expensive unless you can share the cost with others. Rates are set by the government in cooperation with the taxi union. Sample taxi fares from the pier: to town center, US $3; Grand Anse/Morne Rouge, US $7; Golf Course, US $6; Point Salines Airport, US $12. It costs $15 per hour to hire a taxi.

ROADS AND RENTALS: One road circumnavigates the island, and another crosses it from coast to coast over the central highlands. By combining the routes it is easy to make a loop around the northern or southern half of the island. The time most cruise ships remain in port is usually insufficient, however, to cover both circuits in one day. The best roads are those between St. George's and the south coast, and the cross-island highway. Major arteries deteriorate farther north along both the west and east coasts. Secondary roads and dirt tracks reach most villages throughout the island. If you have a good map (on sale at the Grenada National Museum), you can rent a car, but if you are not accustomed to left side of the road driving, you are probably better advised to hire a taxi, with the driver acting as guide. Often roads are narrow, winding, and in poor condition and Grenadians drive fast, making for a daunting experience.

Cars and open-sided mini-Mokes cost about US $40 to US $60 per day to rent. In winter you should reserve in advance. You need a valid driver's license to obtain a local permit from the traffic department for US $11. Driving in this former British colony is on the LEFT. Rental agencies in St. George's include: *Avis/Spice Island Rentals* (440–3936); *Juliana Aird & Co.* (440–2504); and *McIntyre Bros* (440–2044).

FERRY SERVICE: The new *Osprey Express,* high-speed hovercraft, takes passengers daily from St. George's to Hillsborough, Carriacou, and to Petit Martinique in about 1.5 hours.

EMERGENCY NUMBERS:
   Medical: General Hospital,
      St. George's; 440–2051;
   Ambulance, St. George's area; Dial 434
   Police: Dial 911

AUTHOR'S FAVORITE ATTRACTIONS

CONCORD FALLS
GRAND ETANG TRAILS
WEST COAST DRIVE

SHORE EXCURSIONS

The island can be toured in a loop around its northern or southern half—it is not advisable to try to cover both in one day. The following tours are typical of the those offered by cruise ships or local tour companies. The places mentioned are described later in this chapter:

Grand Etang and the Central Highlands, 2–3 hours, US $20–$25 for four persons or more. After climbing the lush hillsides with grand views of the harbor, the route crosses the central spine of mountains with the Grand Etang National Park. From the visitor's center there are self-guided signposted trails in the rain forest.

The West Coast, 3 hours, US $25. A drive along the west coast reveals some of the island's most fabulous scenery. Stops are usually made at Dougladston Estate, a nutmeg plantation, and at the processing plant in Gouyave. You can return via the scenic Belvidere Road and the Grand Etang; or turn inland to the Concord Valley, and hike the 45-minute trail to the Concord Falls.

West Coast and North Coast Loop, 6 hours, US $32. The West Coast tour continues to Sauteurs and historic Caribs Leap, stopping for lunch at Morne Fendue, and returning to Grenville via the east coast and the cross-island highway. Some cruise ships charge US $65 per person when passengers travel by car.

City Tour and Bay Gardens, 3.5 hours, US $18. Tour St. George's, Richmond Hill, and Bay Gardens for a walk through the botanical gardens, and visit The Tower, a private estate house.

The Southern Route, 4–5 hours, US $35. The above tour continues to Westerhall Point, a deluxe residential area with a dramatic seascape, and to Grand Anse Beach. Alternatively, you could continue southeast to La Sagesse, a nature reserve and estuary, for a swim or a walk in the woods.

Tours are available from *Carin Travel Service* (444–4363), *Arnold's Tours* (444–0531), and *Spice Land Tours* (800–222–0133; 440–5127). In addition to tours, *New Trend Tours* (440–1236) can also arrange a "People-to-People" volunteer. The volunteer, who shares your interests or profession, can spend a few hours or the day with you. *Henry Safari Tours* (445–5313) and *Telfor Bedeau* (440–8163) specialize in hiking and nature tours.

Published prices for a taxi with a driver/guide for up to four persons: *Annandale Falls*, 1 hour, US $25; *Morne Jaloux/ Woburn/Grand Anse Beach*, 1.5 hours, US $30; *Bay Gardens*, 1 hour with tour, US $16; *Grand Etang*, 2 hours, US $30; *Grand Etang/Grenville*, 2.5 hours, US $50; *Dougladston/Gouyave/Spice Factory*, 2.5 hours including tours, US $40.

GRENADA ON YOUR OWN

The capital of Grenada is set on a deep bay with a tango of yellow, blue, and pink houses topped with red-tile roofs, clinging to the slopes of the green hills that frame the harbor. One of the Caribbean's most beautiful natural harbors and an important trading center since its founding by the French in the early 18th century, St. George's is a popular port of call for cruise ships and yachts sailing the Grenadines.

A ST. GEORGE'S WALKABOUT

Like its history, St. George's character is part French and part English, yet distinctively West Indian. It is divided into two parts separated by a promontory crowned by Fort George. The lower town hugs the inner harbor, known as the Carenage, and the new town is "over the hill" along the seaside Esplanade. The two are connected by a tunnel under the hill, used by motor vehicles, and by a road and narrow sidewalk over the hill, used by cars and pedestrians. Both parts are best seen on foot, which takes about 2 hours, but it could take longer if you stop frequently to admire the views or browse in shops and historic sites along the way.

THE CARENAGE (1) A perfect horseshoe in shape, the Carenage is one of the best anchorages in the West Indies and always busy with boats of all sizes and description. It is also the center of life for the town, where schooners load with Grenada's bountiful harvest of fruits and vegetables for markets in Barbados and Trinidad. Most of the schooners are made in the neighboring Grenadines by local shipwrights.

On the south side of the Carenage, a second harbor known as the *Lagoon* (2) is the yacht basin, marina, and commercial port. The Lagoon is actually the submerged crater of an ancient volcano. On its east are the *Botanical Gardens,* begun in 1887; buildings on the grounds house government offices.

North of the *pier* (3), Lagoon Road/Wharf Road skirts the Carenage past the post office, the *Department of Tourism Bureau* (4), the public library, and small shops on the waterfront. Near the Department of Tourism, overlooking the water, is a shaded pedestrian plaza with seats and pretty flowers around a statue, "Christ of the Deeps." It was given to Grenada by Costa Cruise Line in appreciation of the island's help to the passengers and crew of the *Bianca C,* which caught fire in the harbor in 1961. For a different view of St. George's, "water taxis" cross the harbor from the pier to the north side of the Carenage for about US $ .50 a ride.

Climbing the hill above the Carenage are old churches that combine West Indian and European architectural elements and government buildings dating from the early 1800s. *York House* holds the supreme court; the neighboring *Registry Building* was built about 1780; and *Government House*, remodeled in 1802, is a fine example of early Georgian architecture. *St. George's Anglican Church* (**5**), rebuilt in this century, has wall plaques from the 18th and 19th centuries; *St. Andrew's Presbyterian* dates from 1830; and *St. George's Methodist Church* from 1820.

GRENADA NATIONAL MUSEUM (**6**) On the hill up from the Carenage in an 18th-century building that was once part of a French army barracks and prison is the National Museum. Here artifacts from archaeological excavation around the island and exhibits trace Grenada's history from the Ciboneys to colonial times. The museum sells books, pamphlets, and maps of Grenada. Hours: weekdays 9:00 A.M. to 4:30 P.M., Saturdays 10:00 A.M. to 1:00 P.M., closed Sundays. Admission: US $2.

MARKET SQUARE (**7**) A walk from the Carenage up Young Street over the hill or a drive through Sendall Tunnel (**8**) takes you to the other side of St. George's, with Market Square at the center of town. The market is one of the liveliest, most colorful in the Caribbean, particularly on Saturday morning. Vendors, each with their tiny plot and brightly colored umbrella, sell brooms, baskets, and an array of exotic tropical fruits, vegetables, and spices. West of the square the *Esplanade* (**9**), a strip of coastal road along the outer harbor, has fish and meat markets.

At strategic hilltops around the harbor, the French and the British built a series of fortifications in the 18th century to defend the island. Today they stand as testimony to the rivalry that raged between the two powers throughout most of Grenada's colonial history, as well as offering grandstand views.

FORT GEORGE (**10**) The harbor entrance is guarded by an imposing fort built in 1706 by the French as Fort Royal and later seized by the British, who renamed it for their monarch. Built on a promontory with walls more than 4 feet thick, the fort was a master feat of engineering in its day. It has two levels with barracks, ammunition storage rooms, dungeons, and a maze of underground passages. The fort served as police headquarters for many years, and in 1983 it wit-

nessed the coup in which Prime Minister Bishop and many of his supporters were killed.

To visit the other forts, a drive is recommended, as the hillsides are very steep and the sun hot. Alternatively, you could drive or take a bus from Market Square to the top of a hill and walk down.

FORT FREDERICK Built in 1779 soon after the French recaptured the island from the British, Fort Frederick is located on the summit of Richmond Hill, between Fort Matthew to the north and Fort Adolphus to the south, occupying the most strategic position of all the fortresses and commanding extensive views. Its thick stone walls, barracks, watch towers, and underground tunnels are similar to those of Fort George. In the 1983 coup attempt, the fort was the headquarters of the People's Revolutionary Army, the faction that tried to seize power from Bishop. The carcass of a Soviet armored truck, left to rust where it was abandoned, seems a fitting reminder of the grim events.

BAY GARDENS East of Fort Frederick in the hillside suburb of St. Paul's on the site of an old sugar mill is a private three-acre spread with an estimated three thousand different species of flora found in Grenada and the Caribbean. Footpaths covered with nutmeg shells wind through exotic vegetation. In addition to spice and fruit trees—all labeled—Bay Gardens has sections for flowers and various kinds of orchids. The entrance fee includes a walk through the gardens with a guide.

THE TOWER A private home east of Bay Gardens on the St. Paul's Road is the estate house of a working fruit-and-spice plantation, set in gardens of exotic plants. The Tower, built in 1916, is one of the island's few remaining old houses constructed of volcanic rock. It is open to the public by appointment. The owner's private collection of Carib artifacts and antiques is on display.

A DRIVE AROUND THE ISLAND

ALONG THE WEST COAST

North of St. George's the road hugs the coast passing through small fishing villages and skirti

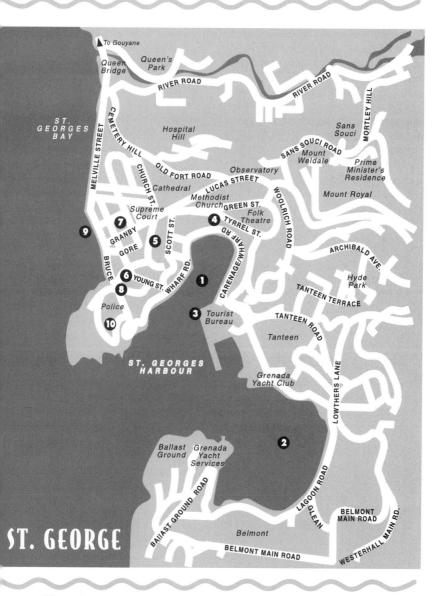

MAP LEGEND FOR WALKING TOUR OF ST. GEORGE

1. The Carenage
2. The Lagoon
3. Pier
4. Department of Tourism
5. St. George's Angelican Church
6. Grenada National Museum
7. Market Square
8. Sendall Tunnel
9. Esplanade
10. Fort George

magnificent scenery of lush, thickly carpeted mountainsides that drop almost straight into the sea and coves, their black-sand beaches almost hidden from view.

CONCORD VALLEY Inland from Halifax Harbour a road along the Black Bay River leads to the head of the Concord Valley, where a triple stage waterfall in a setting of dense tropical foliage cascades down the central mountains. Above Concord village the road stops directly in front of the falls' lower stage where concrete steps lead down to a swimming area.

The second stage has a much more beautiful setting, which is accessible thanks to a footpath laid by U.S. Peace Corps volunteers. Large rocks and a few small bridges were placed at strategic points, making it less difficult to cross the river against rushing water. Even so, the hike is not easy unless you are nimble and dressed appropriately in shorts, or bathing suit, and sneakers (the rocks are slippery). Your effort will be richly rewarded: The cascade spills through jungle-thick vegetation into a pool where you can have a delightful swim surrounded by magnificent scenery. The hike takes about 45 minutes to go and 25 minutes to return.

GOUYAVE Grenada is the world's second largest producer of nutmeg; the main production center is the area around Gouyave on the west coast north of St. George's. Inland about a half-mile immediately before Gouyave is Douglaston Estates, one of the island's oldest and largest nutmeg plantations. Its staff members explain the cultivation of nutmeg and other spices to visitors. In Gouyave you can have a free walk-through tour of a growers' cooperative that is the country's major nutmeg-processing station. You will see workers clean, grade, and prepare nutmeg for shipping.

Gouyave, the main fishing town on the west coast, was the site of the first British attempt to establish a colony in 1609, when they were forced to leave after encountering fierce Carib resistance. Today the town has a reputation for rowdiness.

THE NORTH COAST

CARIBS LEAP North of Gouyave the road passes through Victoria, a quiet town at the foot of 2,757-foot Mount St. Catherine, Grenada's highest peak, and continues to the town of Sauteurs (which in French means "leapers"). There a promontory

alongside St. Patrick's Roman Catholic Churc and Cemetery is a historic landmark. The steep faced north side of the promontory, known a Caribs Leap or Leapers Hill, drops more than 10 feet into the sea. The last of the Carib, the inhab tants of the island at the time of Columbus, leape to their death here rather than surrender to th French, who were intent on exterminating them

MORNE FENDUE On the south side of Sauteur the estate house of a former plantation, Morn Fendue, was built at the turn of the century in th traditional method: with hand-cut local stones an mortar made with lime and molasses. The owne Betty Mascoll—the island's best-known hostess kings, queens, and presidents—opens her hous for a Grenadian lunch—provided you call i advance (442–9330). This is not a restaurant; yo dine in Mrs. Mascoll's drawing rooms on loc dishes, usually fresh vegetables from her garde Similarly *Mount Rodney* (442–9420), a plantatic house also near Sauteurs, offers West Indian sp cialties that owners Lynn and Norris Nelson prepa and serve with style; lunch only. Fixed price, EC $4

LEVERA NATIONAL PARK East of Sauteurs is long white-sand beach popular with Grenadians weekends, but usually deserted during the wee The scenic coast is part of the Levera National Pa and nesting grounds for sea turtles, protected fro May to September. South of the park the coastli changes to gray sand and weathered rock cliffs.

LAKE ANTOINE AND RIVER ANTOINE DIS TILLERY South of Levera Park, the 18th-centu River Antoine Rum Distillery is a historic lan mark on a sugar plantation where cane for ru making is processed in the same way it was tw hundred years ago when the plant was built. Th distillery has an electrical pump and new boili machinery, but water from the river is still used turn the old waterwheel to power the plant. It the last operational waterwheel in Grenada. La Antoine, a crater lake, can be reached on a foo path from the distillery or nearby road.

THE CENTRAL HIGHLANDS

ANNANDALE FALLS On the highway from George's to the Grand Etang Forest Reserve, the mountain spine down the center of the islan short detour can be made to Annandale Falls, the most accessible waterfall in Grenada. Located only a few yards from the road in an area of lush tropical vegetation, the small hillside with steps leading to the falls is planted with an herb and spice garden. A welcome center at the entrance to the falls sells local spices and crafts.

Nearby at La Mode you can visit the St. George's estate where a local winery, Grenada Wine Cooler, which makes great fruit wines by traditional methods used in Grenada for two hundred years.

GRAND ETANG FOREST RESERVE The ridge of mountains that bisect the interior of Grenada are covered by the Grand Etang Forest Reserve, part of a new national parks system established by the government of Grenada with the help of U. S. development agencies, including the Peace Corps and the Organization of American States. The highway that zigzags up the forested mountains crosses the reserve almost at its center at a 1,910-foot altitude and within a few hundred yards of Grand Etang, an extinct volcano that gave the reserve its name; its crater is filled with a lake. (Grand Etang means "large pond" in French.) North of the crater is Mt. Qua Qua Peak, one of Grenada's three highest peaks. The flattop cone of Mt. St. Catherine can be seen on the north, with Mt. Sinai on the south.

Grand Etang Lake is only about 500 yards from the visitor's center, where there are displays and information on the self-guided nature trails. The trails range from 15 minutes to 3 hours and lead to the lake and surrounding rain forests, which have some of the island's most exotic vegetation and wildlife.

SEVEN SISTERS TRAIL Southwest of Grand Etang Lake a trail leads to an area with waterfalls that drop in several stages into a large pool delightful for swimming. The trail takes 3 hours round-trip for experienced hikers and crosses a cultivated area to reach the virgin forest. Parts of the trail, along steep ridges, are difficult, particularly during the rainy season when the ground is very muddy. An experienced nature guide is essential.

THE SOUTH COAST

From St. George's, along the Lagoon Road, the highway leads to Grand Anse Beach, one of the most beautiful beaches in the Caribbean, and the southern part of the island. At the southernmost point, Fort

Jeudy, the Atlantic crashes against high cliffs, and the scenery is magnificent. The entire south coast from Point Salines on the west, where the international airport is located, to Great Bacolet Bay on the east, is made up of hilly peninsulas, bluffs, and deep bays. Some fingers have hotels and marinas and others are elegant residential areas with pretty views.

LA SAGESSE NATURE CENTER In the southeast corner, La Sagesse is the site of the first European settlement on Grenada. A nature center here, developed as part of the national parks system, includes palm-fringed beaches and coral reefs, mangrove, a salt pond, woodlands, and an estuary with a large variety of birds. A small guesthouse with a delightful bar and outdoor restaurant has equipment for water sports.

You can return to St. George's via Marquis, Grenada's capital under the French. The road passes cacao and banana plantations and fields of wild pine whose fiber is widely used in making baskets and other straw handicrafts. In this area of the east coast, the island's French heritage is particularly evident in the names of people and places.

SHOPPING

The shopping area of St. George's is compact and easy to cover on foot in an hour or so. Some of the shops are on the waterfront by the Carenage, and others are in the "upper" town, where Young Street becomes Halifax and leads to Market Square. Most stores are open weekdays from 8:00 or 9:00 A.M.—noon and 1:00–4:00 or 4:30 P.M.; and Saturday 8:00 A.M.–noon. Not all close for lunch.

ART AND ARTISTS: *Yellow Poui Art Gallery I and II* (Young/Halifax Street and Cross Street; 3001). Gallery I features local artists including Grenada's best-known primitive artist, internationally known Canute Caliste, and such well-known Caribbean artists as Boscoe Holder from Trinidad. Both galleries have prints, rare antique maps and engravings, watercolors, and photographs. Also look for brightly decorated masks on calabash by local artist Ottley Dennis.

BOOKS AND MAPS: *Sea Change Book & Gift Shop* (Carenage) stocks American and British paperbacks and best-sellers; books on Grenada and the Caribbean.

CHINA AND CRYSTAL: *The Gift Shop* (Grand Anse Shopping Complex) has famous-name crystal and china, such as Wedgwood and Royal Copenhagen. *Bon Voyage* (Carenage) carries a large selection of china and crystal, fine jewelry, and other duty-free items.

CLOTHING AND ACCESSORIES: *Art Fabrik* (Halifax/Young Street) is a batik boutique and workshop. *Imagine* (Grand Anse Shopping Center) carries Caribbean handcrafts as well as island batiks and casual wear. *Vanity Ltd.* (Tryne Alley), which specializes in hand-painted garments, has men's and women's clothing, costume jewelry, handbags, and hair products.

CRAFTS AND SOUVENIRS: *Arawak Islands, Ltd.* (Belmont Road) has attractively packaged island products that make great gifts to take home. Sold in outlets around the island, the best of the collection are hand-made, hand-painted ladies' sachets and kits of island specialties packaged in a fabric pouch.

Blind Workshop (Carenage), is an outlet for handwork by local blind artisans. Gifts include straw bags, hats, and mats. Closed weekends. *Tikal* (Young Street), the leading store for handcrafts made in Grenada and other Caribbean islands, has batiks, hand-painted T-shirts, and jewelry.

JEWELRY: *Spice Island Jewellery* (Grenville Street) specializes in handmade gold and silver jewelry in West Indian designs. Closed weekends.

LIQUOR AND WINES: *Renwick-Thompson & Co.* (Carenage) claims to be "the best little liquor store in town." *Tourist Gift Shop* (St. George's Pier) stocks duty-free liquor and gifts.

PERFUMES AND COSMETICS: *Spice Island Perfumes* (Carenage) is a store and workshop that produces perfumes, lotions, potpourri and teas made from native flowers, spices, and herbs. The staff will explain the manufacturing process and let you sample scents such as frangipani, jasmine, or other unusual fragrances. Shampoo, body lotion, and suntan lotion also are available, and the shop sells colorful island sportswear and *pareos.*

PHOTO SUPPLIES: *Today's Wonder* (Market Hill) has cameras, tape recorders, film, and photographic equipment. Its second sto▯ (Grenville Street) carries clothing.

SPORTS EQUIPMENT: *Marine World* (Grenvi▯ Street) stocks a wide selection of fishing equipmer▯ including nets, sails, hooks, and diving masks.

DINING AND RESTAURANTS

Fresh fish, fresh vegetables and fruit, soups, ar▯ desserts made from exotic herbs and spices, ar▯ tangy cool drinks punched with island rum a▯ some of the taste treats of Grenadian cuisine, o▯ of the most original in the Caribbean. In additi▯ to traditional West Indian dishes, the Frenc▯ Chinese, Indian, and Middle Eastern influenc▯ have added a distinctive variety and nurtured ▯ interest in food not usually found in form▯ British colonies.

Restaurants are small and operated by th▯ owners, who take personal pride in every dis▯ Many close on Sunday. Major credit cards a▯ accepted unless noted otherwise. For lunch ine▯ pensive means under US $10; moderate, ▯ $10–$20; expensive, over US $20. A 10 perce▯ service charge and an 8 percent value added t▯ are added to the bill.

Boatyard (Spice Island Marina; 444–4662). ▯ part of the marina, the palm-shaded bar a▯ restaurant is something of a hangout for yach▯ men, where they can catch up on world events ▯ satellite television and enjoy local and intern▯ tional programs. On Friday nights it becomes▯ disco of sorts. Closed on Mondays. Moderate.

Canboulay (Moine Rouge; 444–4401). Un▯ recently, when the owner/chef went off to a job▯ Barbados, this was the best restaurant▯ Grenada. Recent reports indicate it has slipp▯ and may no longer be worth the expense. At a▯ rate, the view is still great.

Cicely's (Calabash Hotel, Lance Aux Epin▯ 444–4334). This is Grenada's best restaura▯ Award-winning chef Cicely Roberts and Graha▯ Newbould, former chef to the British Roy▯ Family, have combined their skills to cre▯ exquisite Continental cuisine with a Caribbe▯ touch in a heavenly *al fresco* setting. Excelle▯ service. Dinner only. Moderate to expensive.

Coconut's Beach (Grand Anse Beach; 444–4644). Delightful sand-in-your-feet setting for creole specialties or refreshing tropical drinks. No credit cards. Moderate.

Delicious Landing (Carenage; 440–9747). As popular for its view overlooking the harbor (you'll see your cruise ship) as for its food. Specialties are seafood and great tropical drinks, including one called the "U.S. Bomber." Friday Happy Hour starts at 4:30 P.M. Moderate.

La Belle Creole (Blue Horizons Hotel; 444–4316). Set in pretty tropical gardens, the hotel belongs to a family known throughout the Eastern Caribbean for its inventive, creole cuisine.

Mamma's (Lagoon Road; 440–1459). The late Insley Wardally, known to her fans as "Mamma," was the most widely written about chef in the Caribbean. Her fantastic meals of sixteen or more dishes of her own recipes are being continued by her children. Among the specialties are callaloo soup, breadfruit balls, tanya cakes, pig souse, baked bananas, and a variety of conch, turtle, lobster, fish, and opossum—and armadillo, when it is available. You must reserve in advance. Go with friends, and plan to spend several hours feasting. Do understand it's *very* local cuisine. Don't bother to go if you are a fussy eater or have any dietary requirements. No credit cards. Moderate.

Mount Rodney (See North Coast tour earlier in this chapter.)

Tropicana (Lagoon Road; 440–1586). West Indian and Chinese cuisine and the best Indian *rotis* (meat or chicken roll flavored with curry) in town. A local specialty is featured daily. Moderate.

NIGHTLIFE

In low-key Grenada nightlife means watching a magnificent sunset while sipping on an exotic sundowner, a leisurely dinner, and maybe a stop at a disco. Larger hotels have a West Indian buffet and live music on different nights of the week. The *Marryshow Folk Theatre* (Tyrrel Street) has concerts, plays, and special events from time to time.

The Rhum Runner (440–2198), a large catamaran, sails on Friday and Saturday evenings departing the Carenage at 7:30 P.M. There's music for dancing and free-flowing rum punch. Price is US $11; a dinner cruise on Wednesday evening, 6:00 to 9:00 P.M. for US $40 is also offered. Some cruise ships offer *The Rhum Runner* as a 3-hour excursion along the coast to a beach for a swim and rum drinks, US $27.

SPORTS

BEACHES/SWIMMING: Grand Anse Beach is a 2-mile band of beautiful white sand framed by palm trees bowing to a calm Caribbean Sea. It is not only the prettiest beach in Grenada, but one of the loveliest in the Caribbean and the island's resort and water-sports center. The south shore has quiet coves with white-sand beaches hidden between the fingers of its deeply indented coast. The west-coast beaches north of St. George's have steel gray, volcanic sand. Carriacou and its off-shore islands are rung by fabulous white-sand beaches that seldom see a footprint.

BOATING: Grenada is the southern gateway to the Grenadines and has long been known in yachting circles for its sheltered bays, which provide some of the best anchorages in the Caribbean. The south coast offers short excursions for snorkeling and beach picnics and complete charter facilities: *Grenada Yacht Service* (Lagoon Road; 440–2508) and *Spice Island Marine Services* (L'Anse aux Epines; 444–4342). *The Moorings* (Secret Harbour; 444–4439), one of the region's largest charterers, is based at *Secret Harbour,* its resort on Grenada's south coast, for cruising the Lower Caribbean, particularly the popular stretch between Grenada, the Grenadines, and St. Lucia.

DEEP-SEA FISHING: Fish are plentiful in Grenadian waters but sportfishing is not well developed here. The catch includes barracuda, kingfish, red snapper, and grouper offshore; ocean species are sailfish, black-fin tuna, and blue marlin, among others. *Sanvics* (Grenada Renaissance; 444–4371) arranges half-day charters for about US $350 and US $500 for 6 hours.

GOLF: *Grenada Golf and Country Club* (Woodlands; 444–4128) has a 9-hole course, which is one of the best natural courses in the Caribbean. Visitors may use the facilities for a small fee. Green fees are US $20 for 18 holes; club rental, US $8, caddie, US $10. Club hours: Monday to Saturday 8:00 A.M. to sunset; Sunday to 1:30 P.M.

HIKING: With its magnificent scenery and accessible self-guided nature trails in the Grand Etang National Park, hiking is one of Grenada's top attractions for nature lovers. To arrange more difficult hikes requiring a guide, contact *Telfour Bedeau* (440–8163) or Denis Henry of *Henry's Tours* (443–5313). The latter's rates range from US $70 for one person to US $30 per person for four or more persons for a hike to Concord or Seven Sisters falls.

SNORKELING/SCUBA DIVING: The best reefs are off Carriacou and her surrounding islands, but in the immediate vicinity of Grenada, you can find reefs along the west coast, some within swimming distance of shore. The south end of Grand Anse Beach is well suited for snorkeling. It has some of the largest sea fans in the Caribbean and a great variety of small fish. The north side of Grand Anse Beach at Martin's Bay is a popular dive site and has patch reefs in 30 to 50 feet of water. Molinière Reef, about 3 miles north of St. George's, is the most frequented area for diving. The reef begins at a 30-foot depth and slopes to 60 feet before dropping to 120 feet.

About 3 miles from Grand Anse Beach lies Costa Cruise Lines' former ship, *Bianca C,* which caught fire and sank in 1961. The wreck, one of the largest in the Caribbean, is in water more than 100 feet deep and attracts huge turtles, rays, and a variety of other fish. It is a very popular wreck for experienced divers.

Grand Anse Aquatics (Coyaba; 444–4129) and *Dive Grenada* (Grand Anse Beach; 444–1092) have daily excursions and certified diving courses at all levels. Sample prices are: US $60 for 2.5 hours for beginners; one-tank dive including equipment US $35, for certified divers; two tanks or *Bianca C,* US $45. Snorkeling is US $15 to US $20 per hour.

TENNIS: Public courts are located at the Tanteen Public Court and Grand Anse Public Court. The Richmond Hill Tennis Club allows visitors to use their facilities for a small fee, and most hotels have at least one court. An open-lawn tennis tournament is held annually in March.

WINDSURFING: Beachside hotels have windsurfing equipment. Board rentals cost about US $15.

FESTIVALS AND CELEBRATIONS

August is Grenada's month of celebration, with the year's three biggest events—Carriacou Regatta, Rainbow Festival, and Carnival—falling in the first two weeks.

Usually held the first weekend in August, the *Carriacou Regatta,* begun in 1965, has become one of the Grenadines' main sailing events. All types of boats participate—work boats, sloops, five-masted schooners, canoes, and even miniature sailboats propelled by hand. Banana boats exchange their cargo for people, and sailors from throughout the Grenadines converge on the island and camp on its nearby islets to be part of the three days of festivities. The biggest celebration is the Big Drum Dance, a ritual of the islanders' African heritage that has been reborn into the national culture of the Eastern Caribbean.

Either preceding or coinciding with the Carriacou Regatta is the *Rainbow Festival* in Grenville. The entire parish of St. Andrew, in which the town is located, turns out to paint the town with brilliant colors; music, food, and crafts fill the streets. In mid-August the festivities move into high gear on the "big island" with Carnival. The celebrations culminate in the final "jump-up," with the picturesque harbor of St. George's filled with color, music, and dance, and visitors joining the Grenadians in celebration.

CARRIACOU

Twenty-three miles northeast of Grenada is one of its two Grenadine Islands. Carriacou, a port of call for several small cruise ships, is a 13-square-mile island with an interesting history and a diverse cultural and natural heritage. It is scalloped with white-sand beaches and surrounded by tiny islets and cays with even more beautiful, pristine beaches—all set in turquoise waters with fabulous reefs. A national parks system is being developed to bring the main areas under protection.

About two-thirds of Carriacou is of volcanic origin, while the remainder is limestone and contains fossils that have made Carriacou particularly interesting to scientists. In its early colonial days, Carriacou was covered with deep fertile soil that led to intensive cultivation for sugar and, later, cotton. But erosion has changed the character of the land and vegetation, and today the island has a rather dry environment. Although Carriacou is mountainous, the mountains are not high enough to catch the moisture of the trade winds as in Grenada.

HILLSBOROUGH The port and main town is a village where time seems to have stood still. About 4 blocks long and 3 deep, it is worth a quick walkabout, particularly to visit the museum, where there is a collection of Amerindian and other artifacts. It is situated in the island's oldest house, which was recently restored. Sandy Island, facing the harbor, is a popular snorkeling location with a shallow-water reef only a few feet from shore. You can rent a boat at the pier for the five-minute ride to the island, but you'll need to bring your own snorkeling gear or rent it from the dive operator based at *Silver Beach Resort,* north of town.

Most parts of the island have adequate roads; you can make a tour in a leisurely hour's drive. From a hilltop on the north end of the island, known as the Hospital Scenic Overlook, you can get a grandstand view and a quick orientation of the island. High North Peak, the highest point in Carriacou, at 955 feet, is being made into a national park; it is the least altered area of the island. The forested northwest slope of the peak drops down to L'Anse La Roche, a beautiful reef-protected cove and beach. Here too are the stone ruins of an 18th-century plantation that once covered about 266 acres of forest and grazing lands.

The northeast coast at Petit Carenage Bay has extensive mangroves that attract a large variety of birds. South of the swamp at Watering Bay is the village of Windward, founded by Scottish seamen and known throughout the Eastern Caribbean for its skilled boat builders. You can often see them by the waterfront making their fishing and sailing boats, which they construct by hand without a blueprint in a traditional manner handed down from generation to generation.

Off the south coast are tiny Saline Island and White Island, surrounded on three sides by sandy white beaches and protected by the best coral reefs in Grenada's waters. Saline is interesting to scientists for its geological formations and to bird-watchers for its shore birds. Red-billed tropic birds, which grow tails up to 20 inches long, breed here from April to May.

Tyrrel Bay, in the southwest corner of Carriacou, a good anchorage for yachts, has a pretty secluded beach for swimming. North of the bay the village of Harvey Vale is the home of Grenada's leading primitive artist, Canute Caliste, who is in his 80s. He and some of his twenty-three children (yes, twenty-three!) welcome visitors. Caliste's inexpensive paintings are collector's items.

Silver Beach Diving (Silver Beach Resort), the first dive school on Carriacou, opened in 1989. It offers PADI and CMAS-certified international diving instruction and certification and a variety of dive packages. The thirty sites in the vicinity of Carriacou offer diverse diving grounds, from flat coral reefs to steep, sloped reefs.

Carriacou has small, attractive hotels with dining: *Caribee Inn*, at Prospect, on the northwest coast; *Cassada Bay,* on the southeast coast; and *Silver Beach Resort,* near Hillsborough. You can hire a taxi or rent a car to tour the island, and boats can be rented for day trips to nearby islands. Seafood is the specialty—with dining on the water's edge—at *Scraper's* (Tyrrel Bay; 443–1403). Carriacou, 18 minutes from Grenada on Airlines of Carriacou or Region Air Services, is an easy day-trip. The taxi fare from Carriacou Airport to Hillsborough is US $4; Windward, US $8. The *Osprey Express* hovercraft operates between Grenada and Carriacou daily.

PETIT MARTINIQUE Located 2.5 miles off the east coast of Carriacou is its sister island of Petit Martinique. The largest and only one of Carriacou's offshore islands that is inhabited, it covers 486 acres and is dominated by a 745-foot volcanic cone. The 600 residents are mainly fishermen and boat builders. The island is also served by the new high-speed hovercraft *Osprey Express.*

Barbados

BRIDGETOWN

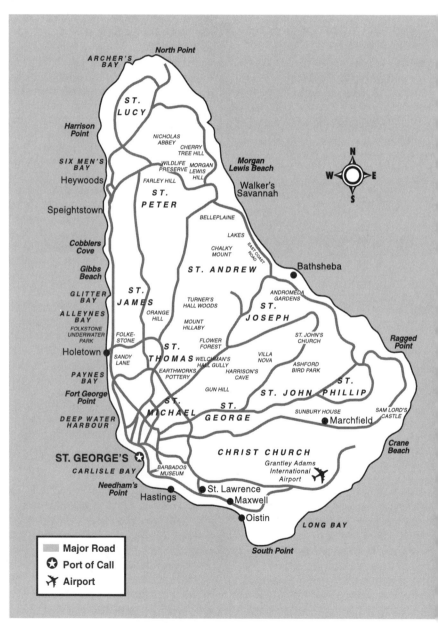

North Point

ARCHER'S BAY

ST. LUCY

Harrison Point

NICHOLAS ABBEY

CHERRY TREE HILL

SIX MEN'S BAY

WILDLIFE PRESERVE   MORGAN LEWIS HILL

Morgan Lewis Beach

Heywoods

FARLEY HILL

Walker's Savannah

ST. PETER

Speightstown

BELLEPLAINE

LAKES

Cobblers Cove

CHALKY MOUNT

EAST COAST ROAD

Gibbs Beach

ST. ANDREW

Bathsheba

GLITTER BAY

ST. JAMES

TURNER'S HALL WOODS

ANDROMEDA GARDENS

ALLEYNES BAY

ORANGE HILL

ST. JOSEPH

FOLKSTONE UNDERWATER PARK

FOLKE-STONE

MOUNT HILLABY

ST. JOHN'S CHURCH

Ragged Point

Holetown

FLOWER FOREST

SANDY LANE

ST. THOMAS

WELCHMAN'S HALL GULLY

VILLA NOVA

PAYNES BAY

EARTHWORKS POTTERY

HARRISON'S CAVE

ASHFORD BIRD PARK

Fort George Point

GUN HILL

ST. JOHN

ST. PHILLIP

DEEP WATER HARBOUR

ST. MICHAEL

ST. GEORGE

SUNBURY HOUSE

SAM LORD'S CASTLE

Marchfield

ST. GEORGE'S

CHRIST CHURCH

Crane Beach

CARLISLE BAY

BARBADOS MUSEUM

Grantley Adams International Airport

Needham's Point

Hastings

St. Lawrence

Maxwell

Oistin

LONG BAY

South Point

- Major Road
- Port of Call
- Airport

AT A GLANCE

CHAPTER CONTENTS

MASTERPIECE THEATER IN THE TROPICS

Barbados is an elegant sort of place in a quiet way. Whether it comes from the three hundred uninterrupted years of British rule, the pride and natural gentility of the Bajans—as its people are called—or from the blue-stocking vacationers who return annually like homing birds to their roost, this Caribbean island is tony. Something like *"Masterpiece Theatre"* in the tropics.

A limestone and coral island of soft, rolling green hills, Barbados is the easternmost land in the Caribbean, located 100 miles east of the Lesser Antilles. Surrounded by coral reefs that are often within swimming distance from shore, Barbados is fringed with white-sand beaches and calm Caribbean waters on the west and pounded by white-topped Atlantic rollers on the east.

The island's first inhabitants, the Barrancoids, were an Indian tribe from South America who came in the first century A.D. and remained six hundred years. There appears to have been a two hundred-year gap before the arrival of the peaceful Arawaks, another South American tribe that remained until they were forced north or conquered in about A.D. 1200 by the more warlike Caribs. Early in the 16th century, the Caribs met their fate at the hands of the Spaniards who took them as slaves to work in Hispaniola.

Thus when the Portuguese arrived in 1536, they found the island deserted but decided not to settle. A century later, due to a navigational miscalculation by the skipper, Henry Powell, the first English ship arrived in Barbados in 1625, on the west coast at the site Powell called Jamestown for the English monarch. Two years later he returned with eighty settlers to establish the first British colony at the site, known today as Holetown. The settlers raised crops such as yams, cassava, and tobacco, which they had learned from the Indians. But it was sugar, introduced in 1637, that brought Barbados the riches and gave birth to a plantation society that ran the island for almost three hundred years. Unlike most other Caribbean islands, which seesawed between rivaling European powers, Barbados remained British. This continuity helped to make her one of the most stable countries in the Caribbean.

Barbados lays claim to being the third-oldest democracy in the Commonwealth, having established its first parliament in 1639. But, of course, it was hardly a democracy for everyone. As the island developed the planters imported white indentured servants to fill the need for increased labor. But their treatment of these workers was so inhumane it led to riots in 1634 and 1649, and new arrivals fell to a trickle. To relieve the labor shortage, African slaves were introduced, but from the first slave uprising in 1675 until the abolition of slavery in 1833, rebellion was continuous. In the following century the majority black population matured politically and economically, and a middle class developed.

Although Barbados has been independent of British rule since 1966, in some ways it seems more British than the queen. Bridgetown, the capital, has a Trafalgar Square; bewigged judges preside over the country's law courts; and hotels stop for afternoon tea. Even the rolling countryside bears a striking resemblance to England.

FAST FACTS

POPULATION: 260,000

SIZE: 166 sq. miles

MAIN TOWN: Bridgetown

GOVERNMENT: Barbados, a member of the British Commonwealth, has two houses of parliament: the House of Assembly, the lower house, with twenty-seven members elected from each of Barbados's eleven parishes and the City of Bridgetown for five-year terms; the Senate, or upper house, with twenty-one appointed members. The governor-general is appointed by the queen.

 CURRENCY: Barbados dollar. US $1 equals B $1.98. U.S. dollars, traveler's checks, and major credit cards are widely accepted.

 DEPARTURE TAX: B $25 (US $12.50)

LANGUAGE: English

PUBLIC HOLIDAYS: January 1, New Year's Day; January 21 (or nearest Monday), Errol Barrow Day; Good Friday; Easter Monday; May 1, Labour Day; May 15, Whit Monday; October 2, United Nations Day; first Monday in August, Kadooment Day; November 30, Independence Day; December 25, Christmas Day; and December 26, Boxing Day.

 TELEPHONE AREA CODE: 246

AIRLINES: Barbados is one of the major transportation hubs of the Eastern Caribbean.

From the United States, direct service is provided by: Air Jamaica, American Airlines, and BWIA.

From Canada: Air Canada flies directly to Barbados.

Interisland: Air Martinique, American/American Eagle, BWIA, and LIAT.

INFORMATION:

In the United States, Barbados Board of Tourism:
New York: 800 Second Avenue, New York, NY 10017; (800) 221–9831; (212) 986–6516.

fax: (212) 573–9850.
Coral Gables: 150 Alhambra Circle, No. 1270, Coral Gables, FL 33134;
(305) 442–7471; fax: (305) 567–2844.
Los Angeles: 3440 Wilshire Boulevard, No. 1215, Los Angeles, CA 90010;
(800) 221–9831; (213) 380–2198; fax: (213) 384–2763.

In Canada, Barbados Board of Tourism:
5160 Yonge Street, No. 1800,
North York, ONT M2N 6L9;
(800) 268–9122; (416) 512–6569;
fax: (416) 512–6581.

In Port: Barbados Board of Tourism, Harbour Road, P.O. Box 242, Bridgetown; 427–2623; (800) 744–6244; fax: 426–4080.
The Inns and Outs of Barbados, an annual publication, contains a wealth of information.

BUDGET PLANNING

Barbados has a reputation for being an expensive island, but this may be unfair without some qualification. Certainly, if you travel by private taxi and dine at top restaurants and posh resorts, you will find prices on par with those in New York. But to enjoy Barbados you do not have to go the expensive route. It has good public transportation; taxis for touring, when shared with others, are not unreasonable; and Barbados has many areas where it is easy and pleasant to walk or hike. There are moderate-priced restaurants, particularly for Bajan food.

PORT PROFILE:

LOCATION/EMBARKATION: Bridgetown, the capital, is situated on the southwest corner of Carlisle Bay. Known as Deep Water Harbour, the port is about one mile west of the city center. Cruise ships dock next to the commercial port, which is part of an industrial park; however, it has a separate section of piers with a new terminal for cruise passengers. The terminal has a Tourist Information Desk and duty-free shops. Outside the terminal taxis authorized to be in the port area await passengers, most hoping to take you on a tour rather than merely transport you into town.

LOCAL TRANSPORTATION: Barbados has good public transportation serving all corners of the island. Buses operated by the state-owned Transport Board are blue with yellow trim; smaller, privately operated minibuses are yellow with blue trim. To ride the bus you need the exact fare, B $1.50, in Bajan currency; you can buy tokens at the bus depot in town. You need have no hesitation about using buses here, but be forewarned: Some bus drivers appear to be in training for the Indy 500. If they are not already deaf from the blast of their bus radios, they—or you—soon will be. Buses operate frequently, from 5:00 A.M. to midnight, but they are crowded from 3:00–7:00 P.M.

You can easily identify taxis by the TAXI sign on the roof and the letter "Z" on their license plates. They are not metered, but rates are regulated by law. As always, agree on the price with the driver in advance. Expect to pay about US $100 for a 4- to 5-hour tour; up to five persons may share the car. Drivers are supposed to be trained to act as guides, but you have to settle for potluck. (The taxi union here is very strong, and some of their members would do well to retire).

The taxi fare from the port to Bridgetown is B $6. Some one-way fares from Bridgetown: south to the Hilton, B $12; St. Lawrence Gap, B $18; airport, B $30 ; Harrison's Cave, B $30, west to Sandy Lane, B $22; Speightstown, B $30; and east to Bathsheba B $38.

ROADS AND RENTALS: Barbados has more than 800 miles of paved roads. The main arteries are fairly easy to follow, but the maze of small roads and country lanes bordered by tall khuskhus grass and sugarcane tend to look alike to newcomers and can sometimes make even the most accessible place hard to find. The road network starts from Bridgetown, in the southwest, and fans out across the island like sun rays. The main arteries are numbered 1 to 7 and branch

often to connect with other highways, creating a web across the island. A modern 12-mile highway between the airport and west coast skirts the congested Bridgetown/south coast area.

It is easy to take one road on the outbound and return by another route. For example, if you leave the port by Route 1, bordering the west coast where many top resorts are located, and return by Route 2, which is slightly inland from the west coast, you will pass near many of the main attractions.

Good maps are available, but adequate road signs are not. Fortunately Bajans are friendly and helpful. Their directions, however, are not always clear, because they use the name of the parish—rather than a town or specific locations—as a frame of reference. Bridgetown traffic is heavy; give yourself plenty of time to return to your ship so you won't be inadvertently stranded.

Cars, Mini-Mokes, and vans are available for rent. You can use your valid U.S. or Canadian driver's license, but you must register with the police and pay a fee of B $10. Your car-rental firm will handle all the formalities for you. Daily rates for cars start at about US $50 for standard shift and US $75 for automatic.

Mini-Mokes cost about US $40, motorscooters or mopeds about US $16, and bicycles about US $9–$11. Helmets are compulsory by law. Bikes and scooters are inexpensive, but they are also dangerous because most roads in Barbados are narrow, winding, and congested with drivers who love to speed. And remember, driving in this former British colony is on the LEFT.

Some companies will not rent cars for less than two days; it is wise to check in advance. Among those that offer one-day rentals are: *Courtesy Car Rentals* (431–4160) which has free pickup and delivery; *National* (426–0603); *P & S Car Rentals* (424– 2052) has mini-mokes and jeeps, also with free pickup and delivery; and *Sunny Isle Motors* (435–7979).

INTERISLAND AIR SERVICE: See Fast Facts.

EMERGENCY NUMBERS
Medical: Queen Elizabeth Hospital, 436–6450.
Ambulance, 426–1113;
Police: 112

AUTHOR'S FAVORITE ATTRACTIONS

BARBADOS MUSEUM
WELCHMAN HALL GULLY/HARRISON'S
    CAVE/FLOWER FOREST
ST. NICHOLAS ABBEY
MOUNT GAY RUM TOUR

SHORE EXCURSIONS

Because of its large number of sight-seeing attractions and the extensive road network, there are many routes to be taken for an island tour, and each local tour company has its version. Those described here are typical, but the excursions offered on your ship are likely to differ slightly. The first tour is the one most frequently used. The sites mentioned are described elsewhere in the chapter.

Harrison's Cave/St. Nicholas Abbey/Farley Hill National Park, 4.5 hours, US $37–$40. Drive through sugarcane fields of the central highlands to Harrison's Cave, St. Nicholas Abbey, and Farley Hill National Park. Return via Speightstown and the west coast to Bridgetown. Shorter versions available for about $30–$35.

Gun Hill/Flower Forest/Sunbury Plantation, 3.5 hours, US $35. Drive through Bridgetown via Trafalgar Square and Government House; to Gun Hill, the Flower Forest, and east to St. John's Church and return via Sunbury Plantation House, a private home open to the public.

Atlantis Submarine, 2 hours, US $72 adult; US $36 children. See *Sports* section for description.

Golf/Hiking/Biking Tours See *Sports* section.

Custom Tours (425–0099; fax: 425–0100). Margaret Leacock gives a personalized tour of Barbados highlighting its history and culture for a maximum of four people. Admission: US $30 per hour for a minimum of four hours.

BARBADOS ON YOUR OWN

Bridgetown, where approximately one-third of the population lives, has retained enough of its historic character to make a walk interesting.

A BRIDGETOWN WALKABOUT

When you come into Bridgetown at *Deep Water Harbour* (1), you drive (or walk) along Princess Alice Highway, a road built on reclaimed land and paralleling Broad Street, a thoroughfare to the north. You pass *Pelican Village* (2), a center for local arts and crafts; and, to the north, the 18th-century Church of St. Mary. The main road ends by *the Careenage* (3), the picturesque old harbor where the town began in 1628.

Still the heart of town, the Careenage lies at the mouth of Constitution River and is spanned by the two small bridges from which Bridgetown takes its name. On the north bank *Trafalgar Square* (4) has a statue of Admiral Nelson by Sir Richard Westmacott, dating from 1815 and predating by twenty-seven years the more famous Nelson Monument in London.

North of Trafalgar Square is a group of neo-Gothic buildings, which house the *Barbados Parliament* (5), originally constructed in 1635. The structures were rebuilt to replace buildings destroyed by fire in 1860. The west wing, dating from 1872, houses the Senate; and the east wing, built in 1874, is the House of Assembly. Note the stained-glass windows with portraits of British monarchs and the speaker's chair, which was a gift from the Indian government when Barbados got its independence.

From the square Broad Street runs west toward the port, crossing Prince William Henry Street, named for the young naval captain around whom one of the island's favorite tales was spun. It involves a character named Rachel Pringle, an

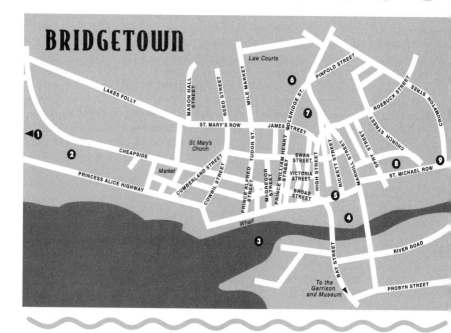

MAP LEGEND FOR WALKING TOUR OF BRIDGETOWN

1. Deep Water Harbour
2. Pelican Village
3. Careenage
4. Trafalgar Square
5. Barbados Parliament
6. Old Town Hall
7. Synagogue
8. St. Michael's Cathedral
9. Queen's Park

innkeeper and "madam" who ran the best little brothel in Barbados, where the prince and his rowdy sailor friends spent a raucous evening. Miss Rachel, history tells us, had no hesitation about sending the prince—who later ascended to the English throne as William IV—a bill for damages. He paid it.

North of Broad Street is Victoria Street, a narrow street with small shops, and Swan Street, a picturesque lane with old balconied buildings, stores selling clothing and jewelry, and pushcarts piled with tropical fruits. Farther north the 18th-century *Old Town Hall* (6), at James and Coleridge streets, houses the police headquarters. It neighbors the Supreme Court and the public library, built in 1905 with a grant from the Andrew Carnegie Foundation.

In a triangle east of the library on Magazine Lane (the name comes from a powder storehouse, or magazine, once here) you will see the Montefiore Fountain, donated by a member of the Jewish community in 1864. Across from it stands the recently restored *Synagogue* (7), the second oldest in North America. Originally built in 1656 by Jews from Brazil, the synagogue was rebuilt in the 19th century, but the building had long ceased serving as a temple and was in ruins when it was rescued from demolition in the early 1980s. It was restored through the efforts of the local Jewish community, National Trust and Jewish groups in the United States, Canada, and the United Kingdom.

Today the building's exterior appears much as it did in the 1830s and has a balustraded roofline, lancet-shaped windows, and thick walls rounded at the corners. Inside, all the additions made in this century—when it was used alternately as a racing club, warehouse, law library, and business office—were removed and walls stripped to the original coral stone and roof timbers.

To recreate the 1833 temple appearance, the original benches were copied in native mahogany, and eight chandeliers were copied from the originals (now in the Winterthur Museum in Delaware). The main gates, which had been at a private home, were returned to their place in the stone wall surrounding the property. The cemetery, with four hundred old graves, was cleaned and tombstones repaired. For information contact Synagogue Restoration, Box 256, Bridgetown; 432–0840.

East of Trafalgar Square, St. Michael's Row leads to *St. Michael's Cathedral* (**8**), built originally in 1665 and rebuilt in 1789 after being destroyed by a hurricane. It was elevated to a cathedral on the arrival of the first Bishop of Barbados in 1825. The Lady Chapel at the eastern end was added in the 1930s. On the south is Queen's College, a prominent girls' school, opened in 1880. At the end of the street is a public park, *Queen's Park* (**9**), that was once the residence of the commander of the British troops of the West Indies.

From the Careenage, Bay Street (which becomes Route 7) runs south past the Harbour Police Station and St. Patrick's Cathedral, the island's first Roman Catholic Church, built in 1849. The road passes the Carlisle Bay Centre, a recreational and water-sports center.

At the corner of Bay Street and Chelsea Road stands Washington House, once identified as the place where George Washington stayed with his brother in 1751 as a lad of nineteen. Recently, however, this historic error was corrected; and *Bush Hill House* in The Garrison was identified as the home where Washington stayed. A private house used for offices, Bush Hill House is not open to the public. In any event, Barbados was the only foreign land the first president of the United States ever visited.

At the south end of Carlisle Bay, Needham's Point is a popular resort area with hotels, pretty beaches, and sports and recreational facilities. On the tip are the ruins of Fort Charles and St. Anne's

Fort, which were part of a defense system begun in 1694. Behind the forts is *The Garrison Savannah,* a paradeground that is now the racetrack. It is surrounded by more than seventy historic buildings, one of which—a former colonial prison—houses the Barbados Museum.

BARBADOS MUSEUM For history buffs, a visit to the museum is a Barbados highlight where they can enjoy a magnificently displayed, comprehensive collection on the history, culture, and natural history of Barbados and the Caribbean. Among the outstanding exhibits are those tracing the routes of the pre-Columbian people into the Caribbean, along with displays of their artifacts. The museum has a fine library of old maps and documents on the West Indies and a good bookshop. Hours: Monday to Saturday 9:00 A.M.–5:00 P.M. Sunday 2:00 to 6:00 P.M. Admission, B $10 adult; B $5 children (427–0201).

Bordering the residential district of Belleville (too far to walk) on the east is *Government House,* set in lovely gardens. It has been the residence of the governor since 1702. Nearby *Ronald Tree House* (No. 2, Tenth Avenue, Belleville, Bridgetown; 426–2421) is the headquarters of the Barbados National Trust, a private organization concerned with the preservation of the country's cultural, historic, and natural heritage. It is housed in a restored Victorian townhouse named for the trust's founder, Ronald Tree, who also built the luxury hotel Sandy Lane. Many of the historic homes and sites maintained by the trust rank among the island's main attractions. On Wednesdays from mid-January to early April, the Trust sponsors Open Houses, which are a house and garden tour. The houses, often furnished with antiques and rare collections, have beautiful interiors. There is a charge.

TYROL COT HERITAGE VILLAGE (St. Michael; 424–2074) The latest addition to Barbados' heritage attractions is the house that belonged to both Sir Grantley Adams, the first premier of Barbados, honored as the "father of democracy," and his son Tom Adams, who followed in his father's footsteps and was the country's second prime minister. Built in 1854, and restored recently by the national trust, the manor is a good example of mid 19th century architecture. In the gardens is the *Heritage Village,* an outdoor "living" museum housed in chattel houses, the folk architecture of old Barbados. Each cottage displays the work of a traditional craftsman or artist, who usually can be seen at work. Traditional Bajan food and snacks are served in a "rum shop." Hours: weekdays 9:00 A.M. to 5:00 P.M. Admission: B $10 adults; B $5 children.

A DRIVE AROUND THE ISLAND

Barbados has so many historic homes, gardens, old churches, parks, nature reserves, and scenic sites that you could strike out in almost any direction and find plenty to fill a day. We have divided the excursions into segments to be taken separately as leisurely drives of 2 to 3 hours; they can also be combined, depending on your time.

NORTH TO SPEIGHTSTOWN

(Parishes: St. Michael/St. James/St. Peter)

From Bridgetown Route 1, skirting the palm-fringed beaches of the Caribbean known as the Platinum Coast, has many of Barbados's most fashionable resorts and fabulous villas.

SANDY LANE The dowager queen of the group is Sandy Lane Hotel and Golf Club, set in 380 acres of a former sugar plantation just south of Holetown. Designed by the well-known Caribbean architect Robertson "Happy" Ward, Sandy Lane was built in 1961 by Sir Ronald Tree, M.P., whose famous aristocratic friends helped him establish the resort's reputation as the most exclusive in the Caribbean. Built of coral stone, the imposing white-pillared entrance conveys the impression of an exclusive country club and is reminiscent of a grand hotel on the French Riviera in the Roaring Twenties. The lobby opens onto a crescent-shaped terrace—you almost expect to see Zelda and F. Scott Fitzgerald sitting here—overlooking one of the island's prettiest beaches. The golf-course clubhouse was once the plantation's sugar mill.

HOLETOWN The site of the island's first settlement, Jamestown, is marked by a memorial and the St. James Parish Church, first built about 1660 and thought to be the oldest on the island. The south porch has an old bell on a pillar, bearing an inscription to King William, 1696—making it older than the Liberty Bell in Philadelphia, which was cast in London in 1750. At the entrance to Holetown is *Chattel House Shopping Village,* which has craft and other shops in colorful cottages patterned after typical local houses.

FOLKSTONE PARK/BARBADOS MARINE RESERVE North of Holetown, the Folkstone Park is a picnic and swimming spot popular with Bajans and part of the complex that includes the Barbados Marine Reserve, a small marine museum, and the Belair Research Laboratory. Offshore, the marine park is divided into zones according to use for water sports or scientific research.

If you are short on time, you can turn east at Holetown on to Route 1A, for Harrison's Cave, Welchman Gully, and the Flower Forest.

GLITTER BAY Immediately upon entering the front gate, which opens onto twelve beachfront acres of landscaped gardens, you get the impression that someone important lived here. Glitter Bay, formerly the seaside retreat of Sir Edward Cunard of British steamship fame, was the gathering place of a glittering array of lords and ladies when Cunard's passengers came to winter in the tropics. English real-estate tycoon, Michael Pemberton, bought the property in the early 1980s. Cunard's mansion, or Great House, is the centerpiece of the baronial resort. Stately royal palms lead the way to flower-trimmed walkways, a mile-long beach, and a split-level swimming pool with a waterfall and footbridge. Pemberton added the equally stylish Royal Pavilion next door. Both resorts are now managed and partly owned by Princess Hotels.

COBBLERS COVE Farther north, Cobblers Cove is a small, romantic resort set snugly in three acres of tropical gardens overlooking a quiet crescent of pearly sand and just enough history to lend it charm. Cobblers Cove made its American television debut in 1982 when its former neighbor, actress Claudette Colbert, whose house shared the same beach, had ole chum Ron Reagan as a guest. The resort's centerpiece is a pale pink villa built as a summer home by a Bajan sugar baron early in this century.

SPEIGHTSTOWN Once an important sugar port, Barbados' second largest town was founded between 1630 and 1635 by a firm called Speight of Bristol (England). So close were the links in trade that the town was known as Little Bristol until the turn of the century. The Manse, the oldest building in the town, dates from the 17th century.

EAST TO FARLEY HILL

(Parishes: St. Peter, St. Andrew)

At Speightstown, Route 1 leaves the coast and turns east to Farley Hill.

FARLEY HILL NATIONAL PARK Approached by an avenue of royal palms and casuarina trees, the park is named after a mansion built in 1861 for the visit of Prince Alfred, Duke of Edinburgh. Later it housed George V and other members of the British royal family. After a fire in 1965, the house was taken over by the government, but not rebuilt. The grounds were made into a park of thirty wooded acres and gardens with picnic tables and children's playground. The views south and east of the Scotland District and the Atlantic coast are spectacular. Hours: daily from 7:00 A.M.–6:00 P.M.

BARBADOS WILDLIFE RESERVE Opposite the park entrance a track leads through a canefield to the Barbados Wildlife Reserve, primarily a sanctuary for the green, or vervet, monkey, created in 1985 by primatologist Jean Baulou of the Barbados Primate Research Centre. Monkeys, brought to Barbados from West Africa, were considered agricultural pests as early as 1680. In recent years they had become so numerous and destructive that the government turned to the Primate Research Centre to organize a humane trapping and wildlife management program.

The monkeys, although called green, are brownish gray with yellow and olive green flecks. Naturally shy and difficult to observe in the wild, the monkeys are uncaged here and can be seen in a mahogany grove along with agoutis, caimans, deer, opossums, raccoons, tortoises, and wallabies. The three-acre reserve has tree-shaded paths, a stream with otters, swans, and ducks and

a walk-in aviary of tropical birds. Hours: daily 10:00 A.M.–5:00 P.M. Admission, B $20 (US $10); children, half price.

ST. NICHOLAS ABBEY East of the park en route to Cherry Tree Hill is St. Nicholas Abbey, a plantation house built in 1650 and owned a decade later by Sir John Yeamans, the third governor of South Carolina. Still the estate house of a working sugar plantation, the well-preserved structure with curved gables and four chimneys is a fine example of Jacobean architecture. The mansion is open to the public year-round; tours include viewing an excellent 20-minute film with rare footage on plantation life and sugar processing early in this century. Open weekdays from about 10:00 A.M. to 3:30 P.M.; admission is B $5.

To the east, the 850-foot Cherry Tree Hill commands a fabulous view of the Atlantic coast and Scotland District, a large bowl-shaped area that differs geologically from the rest of the island. It is in St. Andrew parish, named for the patron saint of Scotland.

MORGAN LEWIS MILL About a mile south of Cherry Tree Hill stands the 17th-century Morgan Lewis Mill, the only windmill of the three hundred that once operated in Barbados that still has its wheelhouse and arms intact. It was built in Dutch style by Dutch Jews from Brazil who settled in Barbados and pioneered sugar cultivation. The mill was restored by the National Trust. Admission is B $4.

South of Morgan Lewis you can continue along the east coast to Bathsheba or join Route 2 to return to Bridgetown through the heart of the island. Mount Hillaby, Barbados's highest point, is in view, and inland, Turners Hall Woods is a 46-acre reserve of natural forest popular with hikers and naturalists.

THE CENTRAL HIGHLANDS

(Parishes: St. Michael, St. Thomas)

Three of Barbados's most popular attractions—Harrison's Cave, Flower Forest, Welchman Hall Gully—are located within a mile of one another about a 30-minute drive from the port on Route 2. A stop at Earthworks Pottery could be made enroute.

HARRISON'S CAVE Among Barbados's many limestone caverns, the most accessible and impressive is Harrison's Cave. First explored in 1781, the cave was developed in the 1970s as an attraction by the government with the aid of Danish speleologists. A battery-powered tram with a driver and guide takes visitors down into the lighted chambers. The spectacular Great Hall, which rises more than 150 feet, has a twin waterfall set among beautiful stalagmites and stalactites glittering under artificial lights. Near the bottom the tram rounds a curve where you see the falls again, plunging into a blue-green pool below. Tours operate daily every hour from 9:00 A.M. to 4:00 P.M.; admission is B $10; children, half price.

WELCHMAN HALL GULLY Across the road from the cave is the south entrance to Welchman Hall Gully, a split in the coral limestone where a nature reserve has been created. The gully, humid and protected from high winds, was converted into a tropical-fruit-and-spice garden in the mid-19th century but was later abandoned and by the turn of the century, it had gone back to nature. In 1962 the site was acquired and developed as an attraction by the National Trust. A half-mile-long path starts at the south entrance and meanders through the reserve, thick with vegetation that appears to be growing out of the rocks. It ends at the parking lot on the north side, having passed six different sections with trees and plants common to the Caribbean, including huge samples of the bearded fig. Open daily; admission is B $10. Harrison's Cave and Welchman Hall Gully can be reached by public bus.

THE FLOWER FOREST North of Harrison's Cave is a tropical garden developed on fifty acres by a private group of Bajans and foreigners as a "legacy of beauty, peace and quiet . . . to leave our children." Situated on Richmond Plantation, an old sugar estate at 850-feet in altitude, the gardens have a great variety of tropical fruit trees and herbs. Footpaths along the contours of the steep hillside lead past bougainvillea and other tropical flowers. The walk is a bit strenuous, but there are benches and lookouts where you can stop to enjoy views. There is a bar at the entrance serving exotic fruit drinks and also a gift shop.

Hours: daily 9:00 A.M.– 5:00 P.M. Admission: B $12 (US $6).

THE CENTRAL HIGHLANDS II

(Parishes: St. George, St. John)

Another excursion from Bridgetown through the central part of the island winds east, past tiny chattel houses and fields of swaying sugarcane, to the windswept Atlantic coast at Bathsheba on Routes 4 and 3B.

The parish Church of St. George, dating from the 17th century, was rebuilt after being devastated by a hurricane in 1780. It has an altarpiece painting by the 18th-century American painter Benjamin West.

GUN HILL About midway a secondary road leads uphill to Gun Hill at about a 700-foot elevation. Once an important British military camp, it was part of a chain of signal stations. On a hillside stands a huge British lion, 10 feet high and 16 feet long, hewn from a limestone outcrop in 1868. This emblem of Imperial Britain looks a bit incongruous now. Gun Hill, a National Trust property, is open daily. Admission is B $8.

VILLA NOVA Situated at a 900-foot elevation and hidden under huge tropical trees and flowering gardens, this restored plantation house was built in 1834 and once belonged to former British prime minister, Sir Anthony Eden. He wintered in Barbados and entertained Queen Elizabeth II here during her visit in 1966. The house was recently purchased by a Swiss company and is to be made into a hotel.

On the southwest, *Drax Hall,* built in 1650, is one of the oldest, finest plantation houses in Barbados and still owned by the Drax family. It is one of the private homes open to the public on the National Trust's homes and garden tours. *Francia Plantation House* is an elegant manor set on a wooded hillside with lovely terraced gardens. *Francia* was built in 1913 by a successful Brazilian farmer of French descent who married a Bajan woman. The beautifully maintained mansion is furnished with interesting antiques. Hours: weekdays 10:00 A.M. to 4:00 P.M. Admission: US $4.

THE EAST COAST

(Parishes: St. Philip, St. John, St. Joseph)

The lighthouse at Ragged Point marks the easternmost reach of Barbados; beyond, the next stop is the coast of Africa. North of the point the coast stretches for 16 miles along the Atlantic to Bathsheba and Pico Tenerife. The scenic area is popular for hiking and beach-combing.

CODRINGTON COLLEGE Founded in the 17th century by Christopher Codrington, a wealthy planter who became governor of the Leeward Islands, Codrington College is the oldest British school in the West Indies and one of the earliest institutions of higher education in the Western Hemisphere. Now a theological school, the entrance is marked by a fabulous avenue of stately royal palms—one of Barbados's most frequently pictured settings.

ST. JOHN'S CHURCH On a hillside above Codrington College is St. John's Church, built in 1836 to replace an earlier one destroyed by a hurricane. The churchyard contains tombstones from 1678; one is the grave of Ferdinando Palaeologus, said to be a descendant of Byzantine emperor Constantine. The hillside offers wonderful views of the Atlantic coast.

BATHSHEBA Overlooking beautiful Tent Bay and framed by the 1,000-foot-high limestone walls of Hackleton's Cliff, Bathsheba is a fishing village and holiday resort. Often described as Cornwall-in-miniature, it has room-size boulders resting at the water's edge, where large white-topped Atlantic waves break against the shore. Flying fish can be seen here. The Atlantis Hotel, famous for its Sunday brunch of Bajan cuisine, overlooks the dramatic landscape.

ANDROMEDA GARDENS A cliffside above Bathsheba is the site of the Andromeda Gardens, a mature tropical spread acquired by the National Trust in 1989. The gardens have a particular interest to botanists and horticulturists, because the late owner's hobby was to transplant species here from different climatic conditions around the world to test their ability to grow in the Caribbean's tropical environment. Laid out along the hillside by a meandering stream, the gardens

are known for their orchids. Hours: daily 9:00 A.M. to dusk. Admission: B $10.

TO THE SOUTH AND SOUTHEAST

(Parishes: Christ Church, St. Philip)

South of Bridgetown, Route 7 leads 16 miles to Ragged Point. A detour through St. Lawrence Gap or at Maxwell Road takes you through lanes that Bajans call "the Strip." But it's much tonier than the name might suggest, with small resorts and something of a Cape Cod ambience.

OISTINS From the fishing village of Oistins, one of the most historic towns on the island, a road leads to South Point, the southernmost tip of Barbados, where there is a lighthouse. The southeastern end of the island has rocky fingers and pretty bays protected by reefs lying just off the coast.

SAM LORD'S CASTLE The elegant Georgian mansion was built on the foundation of an old plantation house in the early 1800s by Samuel Hall Lord, who reputedly made his fortune as a wrecker—a pirate who lured ships onto the rocks to plunder them. Now a National Trust property, the mansion is the restored centerpiece of a hotel and boasts a fine collection of art and antiques. Tours are available; admission is B $10 adults; B $5, children.

SUNBURY PLANTATION HOUSE An early 18th-century plantation house that was extensively renovated after a fire in 1995, Sunbury House is furnished with antiques and artifacts meant to reflect life on a sugar estate in the colonial era. Hours: daily 10:00 A.M.–5:00 P.M. Admission is B $6.

SHOPPING

Broad Street in Bridgetown is the main shopping center of the island, complete with department stores, shopping malls, and a host of boutiques. The two largest department stores—*Cave Shepherd & Co.* and *Harrison's,* with branches at the port—stock duty-free imports such as perfumes and English bone china. Stores open weekdays from 8:00 A.M. to 4:00 P.M. and Saturdays to 1:00 P.M.

Colorful Swan Street is a place for bargains. Chic boutiques are found on Bay Street. Shopping villages have mushroomed around the island, making it easy to combine a sightseeing and shopping excursion.

ANTIQUES: *Greenwich House Antiques* (Greenwich, St. James), in an old plantation house, is crammed full of wonderful old china, furniture, books, and prints.

ART AND ARTISTS: The *Barbados Arts Council,* formed in the mid-fifties to encourage and promote local arts, and the *National Cultural Foundation* have created a national art collection through public donations and an annual competition made up of contemporary and older works. The collection is on view in its new home, which opened in 1996. The beautiful building is located at the top of Bush Hill in the historic Garrison area. For information: Art Collection Foundation, Box 312, Bridgetown.

The *Barbados Arts Council Gallery* (Pelican Village; 426–4385) has group and one-person shows year-round in its open-air gallery. It features everything from batik and photography to sculpture and ceramics. *Queen's Park Gallery* (Queens Park; 427–2345), operated by the National Cultural Foundation, stages month-long exhibitions throughout the year. The spacious gallery is open daily with changing hours: Sunday and Monday noon to 8:00 P.M.; Tuesday to Thursday 10:00 A.M. to 8:00 P.M.; and Friday and Saturday 10:00 A.M. to 6:00 P.M. *Verandah Art Gallery* (Broad Street; 426–2605) has a wide selection of art.

BOOKS AND MAPS: The best is the *Cloister Bookstore* (McGregor Street). Others are *Brydens* (Swan and Broad streets), *Cave Shepherd & Co.* (Broad Street), and *Barbados Museum Bookshop.*

CHINA AND CRYSTAL: *Cave Shepherd & Co.* (Broad Street and branches at deluxe hotels) stocks china and crystal such as Wedgwood, Royal Doulton, and Waterford, to name a few. *Louis Bagley* carries Lalique and other well-known crystal and china, as well as fine jewelry.

CLOTHING AND ACCESSORIES: In addition to department stores, you can find boutiques for beach and leisure wear throughout the island. The most interesting are those of Bajan designers. *Cotton Days Design Studio* (Rose Cottage, Lower Bay Street; 427–7191) is the studio and

boutique of designer Carol Cadogan, an extraordinary talent whose specialty is one-of-a-kind wearable art. She excels at casual evening wear of unusual designs full of fantasy and whimsy. *Gatsby,* with nine boutiques at Bridgetown Harbour and in west coast hotels, has international designer-label fashions. *Upbeat* (Broad Street and other locations) carries beachwear, including swimwear by local designers, such as Ripples. *Sandbox* (436–7388) sells handpainted swimwear and beachwear made in Barbados. *Sherigo* (Sandpaper Inn, St. James; 422–2251) specializes in fashions by local and Caribbean designers, as well as gifts and accessories for the home.

CRAFTS AND SOUVENIRS: The recent explosion of crafts has resulted in a bewildering variety of decorative and functional products by sophisticated artists, who set the standards and style, and by local craftspeople, who use their intuitive skills and ingenuity to transform clay, beads, seeds, rope, coral, wood, and grass into pottery, sculpture, jewelry, fabrics, and household items. The Industrial Development Corporation (IDC), a government agency that provides training, is credited with helping to improve the quality and sophistication of local crafts. IDC markets the products as *Pridecraft.* Craft fairs are held throughout the year. The main fairs are Holetown Festival, February; Oistins Festival, Easter; Crop Over, August; Barbados Museum Annual Craft Fair, December.

Pelican Village (Princess Alice Highway) is a cluster of small shops with curios and crafts. Nearby *Temple Yard* is the craft center of the Rastafarians, who specialize in leather and paintings with strong African identification.

Earthworks Pottery (Edghill, St. Thomas; 425–0223) is the workshop of Goldie Spieler whose imaginative collection ranges from decorative chattel houses to functional microwave and kitchenware. Hours: weekdays 8:00 A.M.–4:00 P.M.

Articrafts (Bridgetown) showcases the work of Roslyn Watson, an artist, designer, and handweaving specialist noted for pretty yet durable, basketry and tapestry. Quality work by other artists is also on display. *Best of Barbados* (outlets at hotels and tourist attractions) is both a group of shops and a marketing label for the distinctive work of Jill Walker, which is widely distributed throughout the Caribbean. She is best known for her watercolors of island folk scenes, which are reproduced in a wide range of gifts and small household items.

Wild Feathers (near Sam Lords Castle; phone/fax: 423–7758) is the small home studio, where Geoffrey and Joanie Skeete carve and recreate indigenous and migratory birds of Barbados. You usually can watch them at work. On display is their collection of more than thirty birds, including some made by their son and daughter-in-law. Larger carvings are made to order, but miniatures are available for sale. Joanie also paints watercolors of Caribbean birdlife. Call for an appointment. Hours: Monday to Saturday 9:30 A.M. to 4:30 P.M.

JEWELRY: You'll find fine jewelry at *Cave Shepherd*, *Harrison's*, and *Louis Bagley*. Craft stores and trendy boutiques carry handcrafted jewelry of local materials and semiprecious stones.

LIQUOR AND WINES: Bajan rum, some of the best in the Caribbean, has been made here since the early 17th century. Barbados claims to be the first island in the West Indies from which rum was exported. The best known is *Mount Gay*, whose factory (435–6900) offers one of the best and most comprehensive tours of a rum factory in the Caribbean. A popular brand of aged rum is *Cockspur Old Gold.*

PERFUMES AND COSMETICS: *Harrison's* (Broad Street; hotel outlets, and at the port) stocks most of the well-known French perfumes and at prices competitive with St. Thomas and other Caribbean islands.

DINING AND RESTAURANTS

Neither the gourmet capital of the Caribbean nor its creole center, Barbados nevertheless can hold its own for the range and variety of restaurants, and it's getting better with each passing year. More restaurants are offering West Indian dishes. Local seafood, especially Barbados's famous flying fish, a small fish that can be seen often skipping over the waves on the Atlantic coast, is the star, as are fresh fruits and vegetables.

Other Bajan specialties are pumpkin fritters; curried chicken; pepperpot (a savory stew derived from the Arawak Indians); *cou cou* (a cornmeal and okra dish); and pickled breadfruit, to name a few. *Mauby,* a traditional Bajan drink made from tree bark, has a pungent, bittersweet taste meant to stimulate the appetite.

Prices at the best restaurants are high. Inexpensive means under B $30; moderate, B $30–$40, and expensive, B $40 and up. Reservations are advised. Major credit cards are usually accepted, but inquire in advance. Dress is casual but conservative. Some hotel require a jacket for men at dinner. Some of the best restaurants serve only dinner. Those listed here serve lunch, but check locally for times as these vary.

BRIDGETOWN/CHRIST CHURCH AREA

Brown Sugar (Aquatic Gap near the Garrison; 426–7684). Casual setting in an airy West Indian house with a wraparound dining terrace, hanging plants, wicker furniture, and the Bajan buffet at lunch weekdays. Moderate.

Fisherman's Wharf (Bridge House, Cavan's Lane; 436–7778). You can enjoy seafood specialties here along with the picturesque setting of the Careenage. Moderate.

Josef's (St. Lawrence; 428–3379). Set in a renovated house with an airy touch, the cozy ambience conveys the feeling of dining at a friend's home. A garden has tables at the water's edge. Opened in 1987 with instant acclaim, the restaurant acquired new owners in 1990. Lunch weekdays; closed Sundays. Expensive.

WEST COAST

Carambola (Derricks, St. James; 432–0832). An excellent restaurant in a glorious seaside-terrace setting. Dinner only. Expensive.

Kokos (Prospect, St. James; 424–4557). An award-winning favorite for creative Nu-Bajan cuisine to be enjoyed on a covered patio overlooking the sea. Moderate to expensive.

The Cliff (Derricks, St. James; 432–1922). In a lovely seaside location and cleverly terraced to guarantee an ocean view for every table, this is the best restaurant in Barbados for sophisticated fare by the creative chef and manager team of Paul "Scally" Owens and "Mannie" Ward. Expensive.

NIGHTLIFE

The show "1627 and All That," an evening of feasting and festivity featuring Barbados's best dance troupe is performed at the Sherbourne Center on Thursday; cost is B $75 including transportation, dinner, and show (428–1627). Other dinner shows have Caribbean dances and music, but the atmosphere is that of nightclubs. Check local newspapers for days and times.

A *Caribbean Extravaganza* is staged every Wednesday, Thursday, and Friday from 6:30 P.M. at the *Plantation Garden Theatre* (St. Lawrence Road; 428–5048); Cost is US $52.50 and includes transportation, dinner, and drinks. Spice, the leading pop-music group, performs here regularly.

If you want to sample the island's late-night action, head for Baxters Road, a sort of ongoing food fair for Bajan snacks with more rum shops per block than any place on the island or maybe the Caribbean. It's busiest after midnight.

On the cultural scene, *Frank Collymore Hall* (436–6870), a modern concert and conference hall in Bridgetown, has a wide range of programs from poetry reading and jazz to ballet and symphony concerts. The year-round agenda is published in visitor newsletters. Theater has a long history in Barbados, and long-established groups stage plays by West Indian and international playwrights at island theaters regularly. Consult local newspaper or the tourism authority.

SPORTS

BEACHES/SWIMMING: All beaches are public, but access is often restricted by the presence of hotels that crowd the beaches on the west and south coasts. Hotels do not have the facilities for day visitors, but you can still use the beach. Much of the north and east coasts is rockbound, with stretches of beaches washed by strong Atlantic waves and too rough for swimming, except in certain places such as Bath, which is protected by a barrier reef. A government-operated picnic site here has showers and toilet facilities. Crane Beach, on the southeast, is one of the prettiest beaches, but it's often rough with Atlantic waves.

BIKING: *Mystic Mountain Bike Tours* (Prospect, St. James; 424–4730; iriemt@caribnet.net) The operator offers half- and full-day mountain bike excursions for riders of all abilities. Services include transfers, bikes and accessories, refreshments, lunch, a support vehicle and knowledgeable guides and a tour designed to your specifications. Prices start at B $95 per person. Open daily.

BOATING: At water-sports centers on the beach, Hobie-cats can be rented for B $30 per half-hour with skipper. Day sails along the west coast with food, drinks, snorkeling, and swimming are available from several companies. *Bajan Queen* (436–2149) a Mississippi-style riverboat, departs on Tuesday and Friday; and *Jolly Roger* (436–6424), a replica of a pirate ship, departs Monday to Saturday at 10:00 A.M. and returns about 2:00 P.M. Cost is B $80 and includes lunch, drinks, music, and snorkeling lessons, as well as transportation as needed. Both have offices at the port where their boats depart. *Tiami Catamaran Sailing Cruise* (Bridge House; 427–7245) and *Irish Mist II* (436–9201) depart daily from the Careenage. Boats often change their schedule seasonally; check locally. The *Barbados Yacht Club* (427–1125) is located east of Bridgetown on the south coast.

DEEP-SEA FISHING: Sportfishing is good here with bottom fishing over reefs, trolling along the coast, and deep-sea fishing for big game. Blue marlin is caught year-round, but more plentiful during the winter months. Other fish include wahoo, tuna, kingfish, bonito, mackerel, yellowtail, and amberjack. Anglers who cast from rocks or shallow water can catch small barracuda, jacks, snook, and tarpon. Half- and full-day char

rs are available from *Jolly Roger Watersports*
432–7090), *Dive Shop Ltd.* (426–9947), *Blue
ay Charters* (422–2098), and *Loisan II*
427–5485). Most half-day trips run from 8:00
M. to noon and 1:00 to 5:00 P.M., full-day trips
om 8:00 A.M. to 5:00 P.M.

OLF: Barbados's golf course most convenient to
e port is the 18-hole spread at *Sandy Lane
otel* (St. James; 432–1311); fees for nonguests
 winter are US $103, and less in summer.
arther north the *Royal Westmoreland* golf
ourse is a private club reserved for the owners of
e million-dollar homes in this pricey real estate
evelopment, their friends, and guests at hotels
ith whom the club has agreements. Perhaps if
ou know the "right people," you can get in to
ay the lovely course designed by Robert Trent
nes Jr. The Barbados Golf Association holds
ub tournaments and invitationals throughout
e year.

IKING: Barbados has many places to hike that
ombine beautiful scenery and interesting history.
n Sundays you can join an early-morning walk
rganized by the Barbados National Trust. Led by
ung Bajans, the hikes are designed to highlight
e island's history and natural beauty. They are
rganized into three groups—fast, medium, and
ow—start at 6:00 A.M. and last about 3 hours.
ear comfortable walking shoes or sneakers and
 wide brim hat for protection against the sun.
chedules are available from the national trust
809–426–2421) and published in local news-
apers.
Highland Outdoor Tours (Canefield Plantation,
. Thomas; 438–8069). Located near Mount
illaby, the island's highest point, *Highland* has
urs by a tractor-drawn jitney, horseback, or on
ot. The jitney ride is a leisurely 2-hour-tour
rough neighboring plantations and farms. You
n't need to be an accomplished rider to ride on
orseback: longer rides trek down to the beach
 the east coast. On foot, the Safari Hike is a
isurely walk via Mt. Hillaby and Turners Hall
oods down to the coast.

ORSEBACK RIDING: Several stables offer
ach, trail, and cross-country riding: *Brighton
ables* (425–9381), *Tony's Riding School* (St.
eter; 422–1549); and *Ye Old Congo Road*

Stables (St. Philip; 423–6180), for serious
equestrians.

KAYAK: *The Kayak and Surf Club* (South Coast
near Silver Sands Hotel at Kayaker's Point;
428–6750) welcomes visitors; equipment and
changing rooms are available.

POLO: Introduced in Barbados at the turn of
the century by the British Army, polo is
played at the *Polo Club* (St. James; 432–1802)
on Wednesday, Saturday, and Sunday from
September to March. Admission is B $5. Polo
ponies are bred on Barbados.

SNORKELING/SCUBA DIVING: Barbados is
surrounded by coral reefs—an inner one suitable for snorkeling and learning to scuba dive
and a barrier reef less than a mile from shore,
which has the main dive sites. The best area for
snorkeling is the quiet, clear waters of the
Caribbean on the west, where reefs in 20 to 30
feet of water are within swimming distance of
shore. Equipment is available for rent from the
dive shops and water-sport operators.

The main dive locations on the west coast are
reached by boat. The formation of the reefs is one
of peaks and valleys with the first dropoff ranging
from about 50 to 100 feet. North of Holetown, the
Barbados Marine Reserve has an artificial reef
and marine park with a marked underwater trail
for snorkelers and a segment of the 7-mile outer
reef for divers. An artificial reef lies about a half-
mile offshore at Prospect and was created by
sinking the Greek freighter *Stavronikita*, which
had been destroyed by fire in 1976. Most of the
ship rests from a 40- to 90-foot depth but the top
of the main mast, marked by a buoy, is only 15
feet below the surface.

Barbados has other shipwrecks nearby. Two in
Carlisle Bay, south of Bridgetown, are the closest.
The bay, too, is interesting for divers, because the
bottom is littered with bottles of different shapes
and sizes dating from colonial times, when the
Customs House was located here and ships
anchored in the bay.

The leading dive operators include *Dive Boat
Safari* (Hilton; 427–4350), *Coral Isle Divers*
(Careenage, Bridgetown; 481–9068), *Jolly Roger
Watersports* (432–7090), and *Dive Shop Ltd.*
(426–9947). Most have trips daily, departing at

9:30 or 10:30 A.M., 12:30, and 2:30 P.M. Cost is US $45 for one tank; US $65 for two tanks. Barbados is one of the few places in the Eastern Caribbean with a recompression chamber.

Atlantis II, a recreational submarine, takes passengers to depths of 100 feet on the barrier reef. Excursions leave about every 2 hours from 9:00 A.M. to 9:00 P.M. from the Careenage, where *Atlantis Submarine* (436–8929) is based, and take about 1.5 hours, with 45 minutes spent on the reef. Cost is US $72. *Seatrec,* a semi-sub, departs at 9:00 A.M., 11:00 A.M., and 1:00 P.M. from Monday to Thursday. Cost is B $59 per person.

SURFING: The Atlantic coast in the vicinity of Bathsheba has been the venue for several surfing championships. *Flying Fish* (Lawrence Gap) is a factory that makes custom-made surf and windsurfing boards. Inquire at the *Barbados Windsurfing Club* (Maxwell, Christ Church; 428–9095).

TENNIS & SQUASH: Tennis is available at two dozen hotels and at other sites operated by the government. For information, call 427–5238. The hotels nearest the port with the largest tennis complexes are *Hilton International* (426–0200) and *Sandy Lane Hotel* (432–1311). Call in advance for availability. Of the six squash facilities, those with air-conditioned courts nearest the port are *Barbados Squash Club* (The Marine, Christ Church; 427–7913); and *Rockley Resort* (Christ Church; 427–5890).

WINDSURFING: A combination of assets has made Barbados one of the prime windsurfing locations in the world with conditions particularly well suited for competition. The World Windsurfing Championships have been held here. The main location is the south coast where there is a reef almost 5 miles long. It protects the inner waters near the shore and provides a calm sea for beginners. Outside the reef, strong Atlantic waves break against and over the reef, providing a real challenge for competitors. Particularly exciting for advanced windsurfers is the sport of wave jumping. In addition, on the south coast the trade winds blow from the east for nine months of the year and enable windsurfers to reach for long distances. Barbados is a popular training base for competitors and has an active club, *Barbados Windsurfing Club* (Maxwell, Christ Church; 428–9095) with a small hotel.

FESTIVALS AND CELEBRATIONS

Crop Over, mid-July to early August, is an annual arts festival which is similar to Carnival in fanfare, but different in origin. Based on a 17th-century plantation tradition of celebrating the annual sugarcane harvest, the event was revived in the late 1970s as a local festival. It was so popular i evolved into the island's major annual event. In th old tradition the festival began on the last day o harvesting the cane, when the workers decorate themselves and drove to the mill singing that th "crop was over." The next day plantation owner. feted the workers with Crop Over parties. Today' version recreates some of these events with fu and frolic, beginning with the Ceremonial Deliver of Sugarcane and a Decorated Cart Parade. Ther are concerts, plays, regattas, fancy dress ball contests and parades, but the most importan event is the Calypso Contest.

PART V

THE SOUTHERN CARIBBEAN

Trinidad and Tobago

PORT OF SPAIN, TRINIDAD; SCARBOROUGH, TOBAGO; PIGEON POINT, TOBAGO

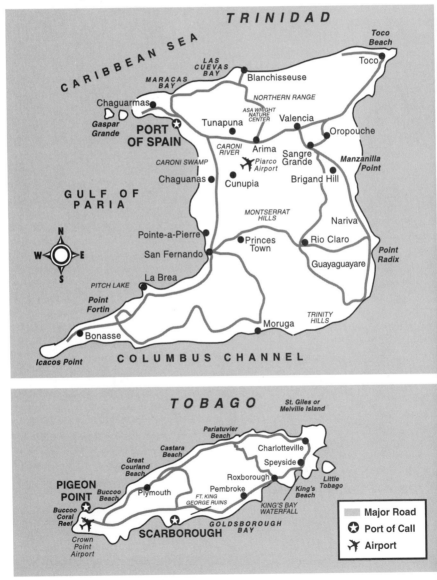

AT A GLANCE

CHAPTER CONTENTS

THE ODD COUPLE

A dual-island nation with some of the most spectacular scenery, wildlife, and unusual attractions in the Caribbean, Trinidad and Tobago are as different in life-style and tempo as any two islands in the region.

Trinidad, the birthplace of calypso and steel drums, is the ultimate Caribbean kaleidoscope with more than four dozen nationalities and ethnic groups making up this richly textured society. Hindu temples stand beside mosques, cathedrals, and Anglican steeples, and *roti* and *rijsttafel* count as local cuisine as much as pepperpot, fish cakes, and shishkebab. A veteran of oil boom and bust, Trinidad is the center of the country's commerce and trade, where visitors are usually more interested in business than beaches. But once a year all business stops and Trinidad explodes in C-A-R-N-I-V-A-L.

Twenty-two miles to the northeast lies tiny Tobago, a quiet and tranquil island so extravagantly beautiful it makes even the worst Caribbean cynic smile. Tobago is the ultimate tropical paradise, scalloped with palm-fringed alabaster beaches bathed by aquamarine waters and framed by lush green mountains that host hundreds of exotic birds.

Even the origin of the two islands differs. Trinidad, only 7 miles off the coast of Venezuela near the delta of the Orinoco River, was originally part of the South American mainland, although scientists are not sure exactly how or when the separation occurred. Tobago, however, was not part of South America; it was volcanic in origin and more closely associated with the islands of the Eastern Caribbean.

Trinidad is only 10 degrees north of the equator. It has three parallel mountain ranges, separated by wide plains, that run east-west across the island. The mountainous Northern Range, covering the northern third of the island, is considered to be an extension of the Andes of Venezuela. It

has the country's highest peaks, reaching more than 3,000 feet, which separate the Caribbean coast on the north from the rest of the country. The south side of the Northern Range gives way to the wide Caroni Plain, where nine rivers flow from the mountains into the Oropouche River, which runs east to the Atlantic; and the Caroni River, which meanders west through marshland to the Gulf of Paria.

Due to its proximity to and association with South America, Trinidad has flora and fauna found nowhere else in the Caribbean. In contrast to its bustling capital of Port of Spain, Trinidad's forest-clad countryside is home to 700 orchids, 600 varieties of butterfly, and more than 425 species of birds. It also has such strange natural phenomena as mud volcanoes and the world's largest asphalt lake.

Trinidad was first settled by the Arawaks from Venezuela and Guyana more than two thousand years ago. They called the island *iere,* meaning "land of the hummingbirds," and remained for many centuries before moving north to the Eastern Caribbean. The Arawaks were followed by the Caribs, also from South America, but apparently the Caribs did not stay long and moved north, too.

Columbus came upon Trinidad on his third voyage and went ashore at Moruga, on the south coast (some authorities say it was farther east at Erin). He named the island La Trinidad for the three peaks of the southeast mountains, which symbolized to him the Holy Trinity and are known today as the Trinity Hills. Trinidad seemed to have been a low priority for the rivaling European powers, thus enabling the Spaniards to hold it until 1797, when they were dislodged by the British.

In contrast, Tobago was so highly prized for its rich agricultural potential and its strategic location that it changed hands more than a dozen times between Spain, England, France and other European powers battling for control of the New World. Finally, in 1889, Tobago asked to become a part of Trinidad. The two islands received their independence from Britain in 1962 and became a republic in 1976.

FAST FACTS

POPULATION: 1.3 million

SIZE: Trinidad, 50 miles long, 37 miles wide; 1,900 sq. miles. Tobago, 27 miles long, 7.5 miles wide; approximately 200 sq. miles.

MAIN TOWNS: Port of Spain and San Fernando, Trinidad; Scarborough and Plymouth, Tobago.

GOVERNMENT: Trinidad and Tobago is a parliamentary democracy based on the British Westminster system. The president, elected by parliament, is chief of state and appoints the prime minister.

CURRENCY: Trinidad and Tobago dollar. US $1 equal about TT $5.70. Since both currencies are rendered as dollars, be sure you understand which currency is being quoted. U.S. and Canadian money can be exchanged at banks, where you receive an official receipt. It entitles you to reconvert your unused TT dollars back to your original currency on departure. Without this receipt you will not be able to reconvert TT dollars legally. Major U.S. credit cards and traveler's checks are accepted in most hotels, stores catering to tourists, restaurants, and car-rental firms; but at small operations and out-of-the-way places, be prepared to pay in the local currency.

DEPARTURE TAX: TT $85

ENTRY REQUIREMENTS: Currently, passports are required for U.S. and Canadian citizens.

LANGUAGE: English is the national language, but in this polylgot nation Chinese, Arabic, Urdu, Hindi, and other exotic languages are spoken, too.

PUBLIC HOLIDAYS: January 1, New Year's Day; Good Friday; Easter Monday; May or June, Whit Monday; June, Corpus Christi; June 19, Labor Day; first Monday in August, Emancipation/Discovery Day; August 31, Independence Day; September 24, Republic Day; December 25, Christmas Day; December 26, Boxing Day. *Eid-il-Fitr,* a Muslim feast, changes from year to year; as does *Divali,* a Hindu festival. Carnival is not a national holiday, but Carnival Week, and particularly the final two days, might as well be, since little business is transacted.

TELEPHONE AREA CODE: 868

AIRLINES:

From the United States, BWIA, the national carrier, flies daily from New York and Miami to Piarco International Airport, 20 miles southeast of Port of Spain. One flight from Miami goes directly to Tobago. Trinidad is served from New York by American Airlines and BWIA; American Eagle flies to Tobago directly from San Juan.

From Canada: From Toronto, BWIA and Air Canada; from Montreal, Air Canada.

Interisland: Air Caribbean (868) 623–2500 shuttles between Trinidad and Tobago every half hour, beginning at 6:30 A.M. LIAT also flies between the two islands.

INFORMATION:

In the United States:
 New Jersey: Tourism Services (SMARTS), 7000 Boulevard East, Guttenberg, NJ 07093; (201) 662–3403; fax: (201) 869–7628.

In Canada: RMR Group Inc., Taurus House, 512 Duplex Avenue, Toronto, Ont. M4R 2E3; (416) 485–8724; fax: (416) 485–8256.

In Port: Trinidad and Tobago Tourism and Industrial Development Company (TIDCO), 10–14 Philipps Street, Port of Spain, Trinidad, W.I.; (888) 595–4TNT; (868) 623–1932; fax: (868) 623–3848.

Tobago Tourist Bureau, Crown Port Airport, Unit 12, IDC Mall, Sangster's Hill, Scarborough; (868) 639–4333; fax: (868) 639–4514.

BUDGET PLANNING

For many years, the government of Trinidad and Tobago has had a love-hate relationship with tourists and an on-again–off-again desire to attract them. Until the oil bust in the mid-1980s, Trinidad had little need for tourism and indeed, its first prime minister, who ruled the country for thirty years, was openly hostile to it. This attitude manifests itself, I think, in the costs for visitors. You can get the impression that for Trinidadians, costs are reasonable, but if you are a tourist, costs are high. This assessment may be unfair, and rather, may simply reflect the absence of a well-developed tourist industry with competitive services. Another factor of cost is the 15 percent VAT, which is added to the price of most services.

Generally, food and public transportation are cheap. Taxis are expensive and tours are overpriced. If you know how to bargain or if a local person negotiates the price for you, the price of a taxi for the day can be reduced by as much as 30 to 50 percent.

PORT PROFILE: PORT OF SPAIN

LOCATION/EMBARKATION: Port of Spain, the capital and main port, is situated on the west coast of Trinidad, overlooking the Gulf of Paria. Its cruise-ship terminal is part of a complex covering four acres located at the foot of Port of Spain. The complex has a reception area, exchange bureau, post office, and communications center from which AT&T calls can be made collect; a shopping mall with duty-free shops. The Trinidad and Tobago Tourist Development Authority offices are on the second floor. Outside the terminal building is a craft market, a rustic outdoor pub, and *The Breakfast Shed,* one of the town's best inexpensive restaurants for local food.

LOCAL TRANSPORTATION: Taxis are available at the port to take you sight-seeing or to other parts of the city. Fares are posted on a board by the terminal door and in Port Authority literature.

In the heart of Port of Spain (walking distance from the port), walking is the most practical way to get around, as traffic moves at a snail's pace. Private taxis are expensive, but there are inexpensive collective taxis and minibuses (Port of Spain, yellow stripe; Tobago, blue stripe) called *maxi-taxis.* They follow specific routes, stopping to pick up and discharge passengers along the way. Fares are standard; occasionally drivers will take a passenger a short distance off the regular course for an extra fare. Maxi-taxis can be hailed by a hand signal. Port of Spain also has inexpensive bus service on main routes and between major towns.

Taxi rates increase by 50 percent after 9:00 P.M. All taxis have an 'H' as the first letter on their license plates. Sample rates from the port in Trinidad: to the Trinidad Hilton, TT $40; airport, TT $100; Asa Wright Nature Center, TT $300. Taxi for the day, about TT $500. In Tobago: from Pigeon Point to Plymouth, TT $50; to Scarborough TT $40; to Buccoo Point, TT $40; to Arnos Vale Hotel TT $60; Speyside, TT $200.

ROADS AND RENTALS: Trinidad has a fairly wide network of roads, including some super highways, reaching most areas of the country within 1 to 2 hours from the capital. Roads in and around towns are generally well signposted, but they have very heavy traffic. Small towns have secondary roads, but remote mountain and rural regions are reached by track or walking.

Two north-south roads connect Port of Spain with the northwest Caribbean coast. Directly north, Saddle Road winds up the mountains to the North Coast Road and continues to Las Cuevas and Blanchisseuse. East of the capital the only road across the Northern Range is a steep corkscrew route between Arima on the south and Blanchisseuse on the north coast.

East from Port of Spain, two parallel highways run along the south side of the Northern Range. Eastern Main Road, the older of the two, passes through densely populated suburbs to towns at the base of mountains, from which secondary roads climb the southern face of the mountains. Just before Valencia Eastern Main Road branches north to Toco, on the northeast tip, where it rounds the corner to the Caribbean coast. The other branch of the Eastern Main Road turns southeast via Sangre Grande, the largest town of the eastern region, to Manzanilla, on the Atlantic coast. The Beetham Churchill-Roosevelt Highway, the alternate expressway east from Port of Spain, terminates at Fort Reed (Wallerfield), a former U.S. Army base. It crosses several north-south roads, the main one being Uriah Butler (Princess Margaret) Highway, an expressway between Port of Spain and San Fernando, Trinidad's second largest city and the heart of the oil industry.

Car rentals are available. Rates start at about US $50 for a well-used car, plus 15 percent VAT (value added tax). Some firms require deposits. Check out your car carefully and make notes of all the dents and other signs of wear to avoid being charged for them when you return. U.S. and Canadian visitors with a valid driver's license may drive here for up to three months. At all times, drivers must have with them their driver's license and any travel document that certifies their date of arrival in Trinidad and Tobago. Driving in this former British colony is on the LEFT.

The Tourist Board has a list of car-rental companies and rates. In Port of Spain these include *Bacchus Taxi and Car Rentals* (622–5588); *Thrifty* (800–367–2277); *Econo-Car Rentals* (622–8072; fax: 622–8074); and *Singh's Auto Rentals* (625–4247).

In Tobago, *Baird's Car Rentals* (639–2528) and *Sweet Jeeps* (639–8533). In the Crown Point area: *Auto Rentals* (phone/fax: 669–2277).

INTERISLAND AIR SERVICE: See Fast Facts.

EMERGENCY NUMBERS:
Medical: Port of Spain General Hospital, 625–7869
Ambulance, dial 990
Tobago County Hospital, 639–2551
Police: dial 999

AUTHOR'S FAVORITE ATTRACTIONS

CARONI BIRD SANCTUARY
ASA WRIGHT NATURE CENTRE
DIVING IN TOBAGO
TOBAGO NATURE TRAIL

SHORE EXCURSIONS

FOR TRINIDAD

Local tour companies offer excursions as varied as a visit to a wildlife sanctuary or a working plantation to a day at the beach, golf, or fishing. Tours are expensive unless you are part of a group, and even some group tours are expensive. Prices vary considerably from one vendor to another; those below are average. Prices are subject to a 15 percent value added tax.

The first two tours described are likely to be offered as shore excursions by your ship. If you have a keen interest in natural attractions, an excursion led by an experienced nature guide will be more rewarding than traveling on your own. Trinidad has good nature guides who cater to birdwatchers and naturalists. One of the most outstanding is Jogie Ramial (Milepost 3¾ Blanchisseuse Road, Arima, Trinidad); write to him in advance to make arrangements. Sites mentioned here are described elsewhere in this chapter.

Caroni Bird Sanctuary, 4 hours, US $50 per person for two; US $34 for three persons or more. The 450-acre sanctuary for the scarlet ibis is visited at sunset to watch thousands of birds swoop in to roost for the night.

Port of Spain/Maracas/Saddle Drive, 3.5 hours, US $40 per person for two people; US $30 for three or more. City tour is followed by a drive over the Northern Range to the Maracas Valley and north coast. Or it may include less city sightseeing and more time at the beach.

Asa Wright Nature Centre, 5 hours, US $65 per person for two; US $50 for three or more. In the rain forest, about 1.5 hours' drive from Port of Spain, is an inn and study center for tropical wildlife with nature trails for self-guided hikes. Excursions are organized by the centre (P.O. Bag 10, Port of Spain; 914–273–6333; 800–426–7810) and by travel companies in the capital.

A list of tour companies is available from the Tourist Office. In Port of Spain these include *Travel Centre, Ltd.* (623–5096; fax: 868–623–5101); and *Trinidad & Tobago Sightseeing*

Tours (628–1051; fax: 868–628–1051). *Wild-ways Caribbean Adventure Travel* (phone/fax: 868–623–7332), specializes in biking, hiking, and kayaking nature tours for small groups in Trinidad and Tobago. Tour costs range from US $60 to $100 per person for a minimum of four people.

FOR TOBAGO

Buccoo Reef, 1.5 hours, US $14 plus transfers. Glass-bottom boat trip over the reef or a longer trip with snorkeling.

Island Tour, 2.5 hours, US $50 per person for two; or 5 hours, US $75 per person for two; $30 for three or more. Visit Scarborough, Plymouth, and Caribbean coast. A longer version continues along the windward coast to Speyside and Charlotteville and returns via part of the leeward coast.

Island Tour with Hiking, 4–5 hours, US $100 for up to three persons. Nature guide specialists combine an island tour with stops at places for birding, and Main Ridge Nature Trail for hiking. For Tobago nature tours, contact David Rooks (660–4360).

TRINIDAD ON YOUR OWN

If Trinidad and Tobago are the odd couple, Trinidad is a study in contradiction, beginning with the name of its capital. Facing south on the Gulf of Paria with the foothills of the Northern Range rising behind it, Port of Spain is turned inward to its city squares, savannah, and interior streets where the city pulsates. Hot, crowded, and congested, Port of Spain is a defiant city that almost dares you to like it. It is a vibrant, lived-in city with strong, competing images reflecting the multiracial, multifaceted society that makes up the twin-island nation. And, almost in spite of itself, it even has a plan. The quickest way to get a sense of Port of Spain is to walk through its heart where the architecture, music, museums, and restaurants mirror Trinidad's cultural mosaic.

A PORT OF SPAIN WALKABOUT

For 250 years under the Spanish, Port of Spain was little more than a tiny village amid swamps and mangroves. The actual Spanish capital, San José de Oruna, was 12 miles inland at St. Joseph, today a suburb. The early 1780s were a turning point, when French and other settlers who had been given land grants in Trinidad arrived and an agricultural and social transformation of the country began. To market their products and supply their needs, the port was improved and expanded. Then, in 1784, José Maria Chacon, the last of the Spanish governors, made Port of Spain the official capital. Merchants built townhouses, sugar barons added mansions, and the new prosperity attracted a great variety of people that further contributed to the town's growth. The British arrived in 1797 and added the streets that they named for their kings, queens, and admirals, and which are the heart of the city today.

A fire in 1808 destroyed much of the earlier town, but in 1813 a young and able British governor, Ralph Woodford, set about rebuilding it—a task he apparently relished. He was responsible for many of today's landmarks—two cathedrals, Woodford Square, Queen's Park Savannah, the Botanic Gardens—and his layout remains basically the same.

Now teeming with people, Port of Spain has grown far beyond its 19th-century heart into a complex of communities, each with a distinct identity. On the west are the old middle-class suburbs such as Newtown and Woodbrook. St. James, with streets named Bombay and Bengal, has a large Indian community whose ancestors came as indentured laborers to work the plantations after slavery was abolished. On the north you will see the newer affluent suburbs of St. Clair, Maraval, St Ann's, and Cascade climbing the hills; and on the east in the foothills are Belmont and Laventille, Afro-Trinidadian communities where the steel band was born and the air is filled with the pulsating rhythms of calypso.

As your ship sails into *port* (**1**), the twin towers of the Financial Complex, pictured on Trinidad

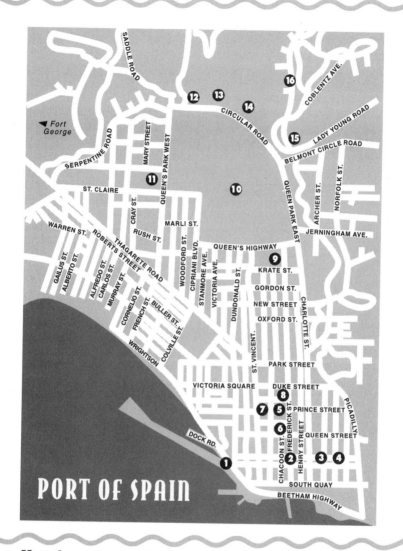

MAP LEGEND FOR WALKING TOUR OF PORT OF SPAIN

1. Cruise Ship Dock
2. Independence Square
3. Cathedral
4. Columbus Square
5. Woodford Square
6. Holy Trinity Cathedral
7. Red House (Parliament)
8. Town Hall
9. National Museum and Art Gallery
10. Queen's Park Savannah
11. Queen's Royal College
12. Emperor Valley Zoo
13. Botanic Gardens
14. President's House
15. Trinidad Hilton Hotel
16. Hotel Normandie

and Tobago currency and housing the Central Bank and Ministry of Finance, and the Holiday Inn, stand out in the foreground against the city, which is still mostly low rise. Some of the old buildings, which have been well restored, lend the city grace; those that have fallen into disrepair give it a tawdry touch; and here and there, a new high-rise lifts your eyes up from the shacks and rum shops that often greet your view at eye level.

The center of Port of Spain, from the harbor on the south to the Queen's Park Savannah on the north, is laid out in a modified grid of 10 blocks. From the port you cross Wrightson Road, the highway that separates the city from the port at the foot of Independence Square. Once lined with bars and brothels and dubbed the Gaza Strip, during World War II when Trinidad was home to an American army and navy base, Wrightson Road was built on part of the four hundred acres of landfill when the bay was dredged in 1935 to create a deep-water harbor.

Independence Square (2), a tree-lined plaza by the sea when it was laid out in 1816, is not a square but two parallel east-west streets. Normally it has the atmosphere and noise of a Middle Eastern bazaar and the confusion of an African market, with honking taxis and cars jostling people and pushcarts while calypso blares from sidewalk stands and storefronts.

(Although I have walked along these streets alone without fear or incident, many Trinis, as Trinidadians call themselves, do not consider the area safe, particularly for petty theft, and warn visitors to be careful with their purses and wallets.)

In the center of Independence Square at the base of Frederick Street is a statue of Arthur Andrew Cipriani, a pioneer of the independence movement and a former mayor of the city. The east end of Independence Square is anchored by the *Roman Catholic Cathedral* (3), one of the two cathedrals added by Woodford, but completed in 1832 after his death. Built of blue stone from the Laventille hills in the shape of a cross, the structure was renovated in 1984. When the cathedral was constructed, its eastern wall was on the seafront.

Behind the cathedral is *Columbus Square* (4), with a statue of a young Christopher Columbus—an area that is badly in need of renovation.

Frederick Street is the most direct connection between Independence Square and *Queen's Park Savannah*. Traditionally, it has been the main shopping street, but in recent years, as modern shopping centers have been built in the suburbs and the downtown streets have become congested with traffic, better-quality stores have moved away.

WOODFORD SQUARE (5) The main square, laid out by Woodford, is one of the town's prettiest areas, with enormous flowering trees shading its lawn and walkways. Down through history the square has been a favorite location for political rallies. On the south side is the *Cathedral of the Holy Trinity* (6), the Anglican cathedral built by Woodford to replace one destroyed by the fire of 1808. The church has a memorial statue of Woodford.

On the west is the *Red House* (7), the home of Parliament and other government departments. The sprawling neo-Renaissance structure got its name in 1897 when it was painted red for the diamond jubilee of Queen Victoria. Originally built in 1844, the enormous building was burned down in 1903 during demonstrations that started over hikes in water rates and ended in protest against the colonial government. Defiantly, the British rebuilt it. Again in the summer of 1990 the Red House was at the center of conflict when militants took the prime minister and parliament members hostage, and the building was badly damaged.

The north side of the square, once lined with townhouses, has *Town or City Hall* (8), built 1961 to replace an earlier structure destroyed by fire; the public library; and the modern Hall of Justice.

NATIONAL MUSEUM AND ART GALLERY (9) Founded in 1872 and housed in the Royal Victoria Institute (Keate and Frederick streets), the National Museum and Art Gallery has an art collection ranging from primitive to abstract to folklore; prints by Cazabon, a Trinidadian landscape artist whose paintings have provided a valuable historical record of Trinidad from about 1850 to his death in 1888. Periodic exhibitions of modern Trinidadian art are held here. The museum has a natural history section; exhibitions on the coun

y's oil industry, transportation, and the history
om the Arawaks to the colonial period. Hours:
esday to Saturday, 10:00 A.M.–6:00 P.M.

UEEN'S PARK SAVANNAH (10) Once an area
two hundred acres, the Savannah now covers
ghty acres of open land with enormous shade
d flowering trees. Stretching between the city
d the hills, it is both the city's lungs and play-
ound. In the northwest corner a depression
own as the Hollows, with enormous shade
es along walkways with flower beds, lily ponds,
d rock gardens, is a popular picnic spot. In
cent years the park has become a huge traffic
rcle, with cars circling it in a clockwise direc-
n—not entirely a new role, as the route was a
ll road in colonial times. Annually it is the cen-
r of Carnival activity.

A group of historic houses of imposing architec-
re frame the western perimeter of the park. Built
the turn of the century and known as the
agnificent Seven, each of the ornate structures
s distinguishing characteristics. From Frederick
reet, walking west along Queen's Park West, you
ss *Knowsley,* which houses the Foreign Ministry.
er the road bends north, you pass the American
nbassy, and then the stately *Queen's Royal
ollege* **(11)**, a boys' school; *Hayes Court,* the
sidence of the Anglican Bishop of Trinidad; and
omor, built in French baroque style, with soar-
g towers, pinnacles, dormers, and cupolas.
lle Fleurs is a typical townhouse, with lacy iron
twork; it is followed by the *Archbishop's House,*
e home of the Roman Catholic Archbishop of
inidad and Tobago.

Whitehall, which is in Moorish style, was built
1904 as a private residence and served until
cently as the office of the prime minister. The
t in line is *Stollmeyer's Castle,* also known as
llarney, also built in 1904. It is a copy of a
rman Rhine castle. Although not one of the
ven, *Boissiere House* (26 Queen's Park West),
eccentric structure known as the Gingerbread
use, is the photographer's favorite.

In the north side of the park is the home of the
esident of the republic.

PEROR VALLEY ZOO (12) Begun in 1952,
e zoo has animals from around the world, but
phasizes tropical fauna. Among the natives are

tree porcupine, ocelot, and two species of monkeys, weeping capuchin and red howler. There
are agouti, *lappe* (or paca), an enormous rodent
hunted in South America for its meat, and deer.
The large number of reptiles includes iguana;
spectacled caiman, a small crocodile called an
alligator locally; and some samples of Trinidad's
forty-seven types of snake. The most colorful
birds are the toucan and macaw, but, in fact, the
grounds of the zoo, gardens, and park are like an
aviary. The zoo gets its name from the once abundant Emperor Butterfly, one of Trinidad's six hundred varieties.

BOTANIC GARDENS (13) Laid out in 1820, the
seventy-acre Botanic Gardens have manicured
lawns with pretty walkways along an avenue of
palms and hedges of hibiscus and bougainvillea
shaded by large tamarind and saman. Among the
flowering trees is the wild poinsettia known as
Chaconia, named for the Spanish governor who
made Port of Spain the capital. The tree's brilliant
red blossom is the national flower.

THE PRESIDENT'S HOUSE (14) Built in 1857
in Italian Renaissance style, the home of the president of the republic has Victorian cast-iron
columns and railings. Its flowering gardens
adjoin the Botanic Gardens and Zoo.

Overlooking the park from the east is the
Trinidad Hilton **(15)**, known as the upside-
down hotel because of the manner in which it was
built into the hillside. You enter the lobby at the
upper level, where there is a magnificent view,
and from there descend to the restaurants and
guest rooms.

To the west of the capital, Fort George, built in
1804, has been restored as a historic monument.
It crowns a promontory at 1,100 feet with a fabulous view; the grounds are a popular spot for picnics. Next to the harbor Fort San Andres, built in
1785, is said to be the place Don Cosmo Damien
de Churruca, a Spanish naval officer and
astronomer to the king, fixed the first meridian of
longitude in the New World in 1792.

On the east edge of town is the most obvious
architectural reflection of Trinidad's multifaceted
society. The *Jinnah Memorial Mosque,* built in
1947 in South Asian-Islamic style, is named for
the founder of Pakistan.

A DRIVE AROUND TRINIDAD

Port of Spain makes a good base from which to see the countryside—as different from Port of Spain as Trinidad is from Tobago. Three of Trinidad's national parks—Chaguaramas on the west, Maracas on the north, and Caroni on the south—are less than 10 miles from the capital. Each park is completely different in nature from the other.

CHAGUARAMAS The Chaguaramas Peninsula, the northwestern reach of Trinidad, and its off-shore islands, are part of the Chaguaramas National Park, whose highest peak is 1,768-foot Mt. Catherine. About a mile off the south shore is Gasparee Grand, a local beach resort connected by daily boat service. The island has caves with stalactites and stalagmites that can be viewed along lighted walkways. There are picnic facilities near the cave entrance. Other islands are popular for sailing and water sports.

MARACAS On the north side of Port of Spain, Saddle Road winds up the mountains through the suburbs and descends along forested mountains to Maracas Bay on the Caribbean coast. Long strands of golden sands framed by the lush mountains of the Northern Range stretch from Maracas Bay to Las Cuevas Bay—all part of the Maracas National Park and the most popular beaches in the Port of Spain vicinity.

CARONI BIRD SANCTUARY NATIONAL PARK After meandering through the Caroni plains and mangroves, the Caroni River empties into the Gulf of Paria 7 miles south of Port of Spain. Within the mangroves, which cover 40 square miles, is the 450-acre Caroni Bird Sanctuary, the home of the scarlet ibis, Trinidad's national bird. Daily at sunset the brilliant scarlet birds stage one of nature's most spectacular shows. As the sun begins to drop a few of the bright red adults and their smokey pink juveniles appear in the sky. Then they arrive by the dozens, and finally by the hundreds, loudly flapping their 3-foot span of wings as they swoop down to perch on mangrove trees to roost for the night. They are joined by large numbers of snowy egrets and herons, and, by dusk the birds cover the green trees in such numbers that the sanctuary looks like a lake of Christmas trees.

Naturalist Frank Graham, Jr., writing i Audubon, the Magazine of the Natione Audubon Society (May 1987) says, "The arrival the scarlet ibises at their roosting place in the mar groves is the most spectacular exhibition in th avian world . . . ." The ibis gets its fire engine–re plummage from the carotene in the crabs, shrimp and snails on which it feeds. The birds need abou three years to achieve their intense sheen.

Boat trips are available from near the signposte entrance to the park, west of the Uriah Butle Highway. The boats wind through lagoons an mangrove swamps to the sanctuary. Along the wa a guide describes the vegetation and wildlife the swamp, which includes more than 15 species of birds, 80 kinds of fish, and a variety reptiles and other animals. Tours also leave dai from Port of Spain. Birders and those with a kee interest in nature should arrange to visit with naturalist guide, however, otherwise you will get standard tour—little more than a boat ride to th sanctuary at sunset.

POINTE-A-PIERRE WILD FOWL TRUST Le than an hour's drive south from Port-of-Spain an unlikely combination of conservation ar industry, which has resulted in one of the mo beautiful spots in Trinidad. Within the compour of the TRINTOC (Trinidad and Tobago Petroleu Company) refineries and petrochemical comple are two lakes surrounded by fifteen acres coastal wilderness turned into a bird refuge f endangered species and migrants. Established 1966 with the help of Texaco (former owner TRINTOC), the trust is a private, nonprofit effo to protect Trinidad's endangered species and he to rejuvenate their numbers to return them to th wild. It also serves as an environmental educ tional center, particularly for children.

On nature walks in a beautiful park setting, y can watch a great variety of water foul and fore species at close range. If you wish to make a d of it, bring a picnic lunch. The sanctuary is ope ated by volunteers, and visits must be arranged advance by contacting the trust (42 Sandov Road, Goodwood Park, Pt. Cumana, Trinida 868–637–5145).

DEVIL'S WOODYARD At Princes Town, east San Fernando, is a mud volcano known as t

Devil's Woodyard that is regarded as a holy site by some Hindus. Mud volcanoes are formations in the earth's surface created by methol gases sweeping through the subsurface mud. As the mud dries it builds up platforms that form cones sometimes as high as 20 feet. In 1852, when the mud volcano at Princes Town was formed, it was thought to be the only such phenomenon in the country. Twenty mud volcanoes have now been registered in southern Trinidad and are thought to be associated with oil production.

PITCH LAKE Trinidad's largest oil fields lie south of San Fernando. To the west, near the coast at La Brea, is *Pitch Lake*, the largest deposit of asphalt in the world, discovered in 1595 by Sir Walter Raleigh, who used the pitch to caulk his ships. Often described as resembling a gigantic parking lot, the lake covers approximately eighty-nine acres.

THE NORTHERN RANGE

MOUNT ST. BENEDICT The ridges and river valleys on the southern side of the Northern Range resemble the folds of an accordion. Almost any part of the mountains has great hiking and birding, but the areas most frequented are those near picnic, camping, or lodging sites. A popular one near the capital is Mt. Tabor where the Mount St. Benedict Guest House caters to bird-watchers and naturalists. A road there leads past the Abbey of St. Benedict to the peak of Mt. Tabor at 1,800 feet. Lookouts along the way provide fabulous views of Port of Spain and the Caroni Plains. The trees around the guesthouse and the abbey, particularly in the early morning and late afternoon, are alive with so many birds you can see three dozen or more species on a 2-hour walk.

Over the next ridge in the Caura Valley, the Forestry Division has a recreation center with picnic facilities, and over the next ridge, a road along the Arouca River leads to Lopinot, the valley's first coffee and cocoa plantation restored as a tourist attraction.

At Arima a 10-mile road crosses from the south side of the Northern Range to Blanchisseuse on the Caribbean coast. The spectacularly scenic route climbs from sea level to about 2,000 feet in 87 turns, passing through forests laced with gigantic bamboos and carpeted with ferns.

Logging tracks and old plantation roads branch from the main road and make good trails on which to explore the rain forest. Arima has about three hundred descendants of the Arawaks, the Amerindians who inhabited Trinidad when the Spaniards arrived. They have a social organization that is trying to keep their heritage alive. The most easily recognized tradition is their distinctive straw craft, similar in design and fabric to that of the Caribs in Dominica and Guyana.

ASA WRIGHT NATURE CENTRE Deep in a rain forest on the slopes of the Northern Range overlooking the Arima Valley is the Asa Wright Nature Centre (667–4655; fax: (868) 667–0493), a private institution unique in the Caribbean. Established in 1967 on the Spring Hill Estate, it is a former coffee, citrus, and cocoa plantation at 1,200 feet, located 7.5 miles north of Arima. The center includes a bird sanctuary and wildlife reserve with an inn (in the former estate house) and hiking trails that day visitors may use upon payment of a small fee. The William Beebe Tropical Research Station, begun by Dr. William Beebe of the New York Zoological Society in 1950, is part of the Nature Centre.

The inn's veranda, surrounded by dense tropical vegetation, is like an aviary, except that the birds come and go freely from the surrounding rain forest. The most celebrated species here is a nesting colony of oilbirds, which make their home in a cave located on the property. The oilbirds are found only here and in the northern parts of South America.

The center's five trails, ranging from half-hour strolls to 3-hour hikes, are designed to maximize viewing of particular species. The main trail runs downhill from the inn through orchards to the rain forest and is a good route to see tanagers, thrushes, and trogons. From it the bellbird trail branches west to where one can hear, if not see, the bearded bellbird, one of the most curious birds of the forest. He has two completely different calls: One is a loud clank like the pounding of metal; the other, from which its name derives, is soft like ringing bells. There is a US $6 fee for day visitors.

After crossing the ridge, the Arima-Blanchisseuse Road descends through a pass into the valley with magnificent views of the Northern Range and the

Caribbean. In Blanchisseuse, *Surf's Country Inn* (669–2475) is a daytime facility designed as a replica of a 17th-century ranch cottage. It has a bar, restaurant, and tea terrace overlooking the Caribbean Sea. You will find nature trails and boats available for a cruise along the north coast. About 3 miles west of Blanchisseuse are white-sand beaches for swimming. Las Cuevas is about 5 miles to the west. The northeast region is wild; even local naturalists do not go hiking without guides.

MATURA BEACH Matura, on the Atlantic coast, is the nesting beach of the leatherback turtle. The species is protected, and local environmentalists maintain a turtle watch during the nesting season, from March to September, when hunting is prohibited. Black with pink and white spots on its neck and flippers, the leatherback is the largest of the sea turtles and grows up to 7 feet in length and more than 1,000 pounds in weight.

BRIGAND HILL The best location in eastern Trinidad to enjoy magnificent views and see lots of birds is Brigand Hill, a little-known hilltop near the town of Plum. Once a cocoa plantation overtaken by rain forest, it is now a reserve with a Forestry station and lighthouse. The diverse concentration of colorful fruit and flowering trees and forest vegetation attracts an enormous variety of birds. From the summit you have a sweeping view of the east coast from Manzanilla Point on the north to Point Radix on the south, one of the longest stretches of golden sands in the Caribbean.

On the coast the Tourist Board maintains bathing and picnicking facilities. A undertow makes parts of the coast dangerous; ask locally before going into the water to swim, and always stay close to shore. This narrow strip of land, shaded for 17 miles by an estimated one million coconut palm trees, separates the waves of the Atlantic from the great expanse of the Nariva plains and swamp. There is no organized boat trip here such as those at Caroni Swamp, but there is a great variety of birds, easily spotted by the road and along the rice paddies that are characteristic of the area. A controversy is raging locally over proposed development of the region, pitting farmers and environmentalists against commercial and industrial interests.

SHOPPING IN TRINIDAD

Local crafts, good art, and an array of fashions by local designers are the attractions of shopping in Trinidad. Among the best crafts are wood carvings, hand-beaten copper, dolls, straw products, steel drums, paintings, fabrics, and jewelry. Don' overlook the locally made rum and world-famous Angostura bitters, which can be purchased at the Angostura shop in the port.

Port of Spain's main downtown shopping area is Frederick Street and nearby streets. The store more likely to be of interest to visitors, however are in the port terminal and at the *Trinidad Hilton* (Lady Young Road) and, particularly, the *Hotel Normandie* (10 Nook Avenue, St. Ann's) which has quality shops with jewelry and fashions by some of Trinidad's best designers. Shopping malls, popular with Trinis, are found on Frederick and Edward streets in town and Long Circular Road and Western Main Road in the suburbs.

The port terminal shopping plaza and the Trinidad Hilton are the most convenient place for cruise passengers to shop for china, crystal perfume, and similar duty-free items.

ART AND ARTISTS: *Art Creators* (Aldegond Park, St. Ann's Road; 624–4369) is one of the town's most serious galleries, with year-round exhibits of aspiring artists and established Trinidadian ones such as Boscoe Holders *Artspace* (66A Woodford Street; phone/fax 622–8682) has known and promising Trinidadian artists. *West Mall* has art exhibits and craft markets throughout the year.

BOOKS AND MAPS: *RIK Services* (16 Frederick Street) and *Ishmael M. Khan & Son* (20 Henry Street) are leading bookshops. Popular travel guides on Trinidad and Tobago are available in shops at the Trinidad Hilton and *Paria Publishing Co.,* which has a branch at the port terminal.

CLOTHING AND ACCESSORIES: The most attractive fashions by local designers are found in the boutiques that make up the Village Market the shopping gallery of the Hotel Normandie

These include *Greer's Textile Designs,* the boutique of Greer Jones-Woodham and Verena Mostyn-Numez, who make batiks of exotic designs on cotton, sold as fabrics and attractive fashions. *Meiling* (Satchel's House, 6 Carlos Street; 627–6975). Cool, breezy linen casuals are the trademark of one of Trinidad's best-known designers. Meiling's fashions are sold at the Coco Reef boutique on Tobago, too.

CRAFTS AND SOUVENIRS: *Athea Bastien* (The Batique; 43 Sydenham Avenue, St. Ann's; 624–3274). Athea Bastien is Trinidad's best-known batik artist. The *Trinidad and Tobago Blind Welfare Association* (118 Duke Street) has gifts, accessories, and household products of rattan, grass, and banana leaves made by the blind. *Trinidad and Tobago Handicraft Cooperative* (King's Wharf) sells hammocks, salad bowls, and small steel drums. *Kacal* (Trinidad Hilton) has wood carvings and art crafts. *Art Potters Ltd.* (port terminal) specializes in pottery. *Craft Mart* (Long Circular Mall and port) stocks crafts and souvenirs.

JEWELRY: *Baksh Bros* (66 Prince Street) has fine silver work. *Kanhai Ragubir* (13 Eastern Main Road, Curepe) is a jeweler in the port terminal.

MUSIC: Calypso and steel-band records and tapes can be found at *Rhyner's Record Shop,* which has branches at the Trinidad Hilton and at the port, and *Crosby Records,* suburb of St. James.

DINING IN TRINIDAD

Perhaps nothing reflects the multinational heritage of this dual-island nation better than its cuisine, which includes ingredients and dishes from its Spanish, French, Dutch, African, Indian, Chinese, Syrian, Portuguese, and English ancestry. Add to this melting pot an abundance of exotic fruits, herbs, and vegetables—and an imaginative people whose urge to create is as lively in the kitchen as it is in the costumes of Carnival. Moderate means under US $20. Check locally for days restaurants are open.

Rafters (6A Warner Street, off the Savannah; 628–9258). A popular old rum house with authentic brick walls and hand-hewn ceilings offers sandwiches, chili, and chicken wings in the pub bar; elegant dining in the room where Pat Bishop's colorful paintings brighten the walls. There's an à la carte menu of house specialties. Moderate.

Tiki Village (Kapok Hotel, 16 Cotton Hill; 622–6441). An excellent Chinese restaurant, it sits on the top floor of a hotel that has been in the Chan family since 1928.

Veni Mange (67A Ariapita Avenue, Woodstock; phone/fax: 624–4597). Cordon Bleu–trained Allyson Hennessy and her exuberant sister, Rosemary Hezekiah, prepare some of the best food in town from this small Victorian house. Not to be missed are specialties such as callaloo soup; stewed beef with eggplant fritters; Trinidad hot-pot; or oildown, a classic West Indian dish of breadfruit, pigs' tails, salted beef, and coconut. Lunch only, weekdays 11:30 A.M. to 2:30 P.M. On Fridays, people linger in an informal late-afternoon party atmosphere. No credit cards. Moderate.

NIGHTLIFE

Evenings in Port of Spain start when people elsewhere are ready for bed. Clubs pulsate with calypso and soca, and major hotels have everything from piano bars to limbo and steel bands. Check local publications to learn what's happening.

The *Roxy Entertainment Centre* (Roxy Roundabout, Tragarete Road; 622–1445) stages popular shows, concerts, and other cultural events. *Queen's Hall* (St. Ann's Road, off the northeast corner of Queen's Park Savannah) is a similar venue.

Cricket Wicket (149 Tragarete Road; no phone), a popular pub for after-work drinks, has varied music groups on weekends until 2:00 A.M. *Mas Camp Pub* (Ariapita Avenue and French Street; 627–8449) has calypso, pan, and dancing on weekends and live calypso talent night on Wednesdays. When the Mighty Sparrow—one of the world's best-known calypsonians—is in town, his *Hideaway* in Petit Valley is a great place to get into calypso.

SPORTS IN TRINIDAD

BEACHES/SWIMMING: The most popular beaches near the capital are on the Caribbean coast from Maracas Bay to Las Cuevas, where there are snack bars and changing facilities. Gasparee, Monos, and other islands off the northwest peninsula are popular for day trips. On the east coast, Salibia is the main resort and south of Manzanilla a palm-fringed beach stretches for 17 miles, but bathers must be careful about undertow. Don't overlook rivers and pools by waterfalls in the mountains where there are picnic facilities.

BOATING: Powerboat racing is a popular sport, with the major race, a 90-mile run between Trinidad and Tobago, in August. Sailing is big but only as a private sport. The Yachting Association holds races almost weekly and welcomes members of other yacht clubs with prior arrangements. Several tour companies offer cruises from Port of Spain to islands off the northwest peninsula, usually stopping at Gaspar Grande or one of the islands for a buffet lunch and swim. Contact *Travel Trinidad and Tobago* (625–2201).

DEEP-SEA FISHING: The Bocas Islands off Trinidad are the prime location for deep-sea fishing. Among the companies that arrange sports-fishing trips are *Classic Tours* (628–7053).

GOLF: The 18-hole Moka Golf Course (6,705 yards; 72 par), also known as *St. Andrews Golf Club* (in the suburb of Maraval; 629–2314), is the oldest on the island, having been established in the late 19th century.

HIKING: Trinidad's Northern Range is honeycombed with trails. Monthly field trips are arranged by the *Trinidad and Tobago Field Naturalists' Club* (624–3321). Visitors can be accommodated with prior arrangements. Its members are also the best source of information on trails.

SURFING: The north and northeast coasts are the main areas for surfing, a popular sport here. At Maracas Bay wave heights up to 10 feet are best for bodysurfing. The northwestern end of Las Cuevas, known as "the bowl," has strong wave action for experienced surfers. Damiens Bay, at Blanchisseuse, has the most consistent surf, with waves from 4 to 13 feet.

TENNIS: The courts closest to the port are at the *Trinidad Hilton,* where there are two. Public courts are poor quality.

WINDSURFING: The main areas for windsurfing are Chaguaramas Bay, on the west side of the capital, and the north coast.

TOBAGO ON YOUR OWN

Cloaked almost from end to end in deep green foliage brightened by flowering trees and colorful tropical flowers, tiny Tobago is an enchanted island scalloped with some of the Caribbean's most idyllic beaches and encircled by incredibly beautiful aqua waters. This quiet, tranquil Eden of tropical splendor rises almost directly from the sea to about 2,000 feet in the Main Ridge, a mountain spine down the center of the island. From the steep slopes covered with magnificent rain forests, hundreds of tiny streams carve their way through the mountains and cascade over rocky cliffs to the sea. The foothills are covered with cocoa and banana plantations and orchards.

Tobago has long been ambiguous toward tourists—most of whom come from Trinidad. An array of stop-and-go development projects of the government in Trinidad has left this out-of-the-way Nirvana with an assortment of rustic inns, funky guesthouses, and overpriced tourist-class hotels. In 1990 the island welcomed its first deluxe hotel, Grafton Beach Resort, in two decades. Yet, in this day of overdevelopment in Paradise, Trinidad's benign neglect may have been a blessing in disguise.

A new cruise-ship dock in Scarborough, the island's main town, opened in 1990; some ships also dock off the western tip and tender passengers to Pigeon Point, a spit of land with a picture-perfect, palm-fringed, white-sand beach overlooking the

Caribbean, within walking distance of many hotels. It has bathing facilities for day visitors (for a fee).

Tobago has a limited network of roads, which wind along the coast and twist through the mountains. The newest roads are excellent, the old ones are terrible, and others have simply been abandoned for lack of maintenance. One crosses the Main Ridge between the leeward and windward coasts, but no road completely circles the island.

You can rent a car or hire a taxi for the day. In planning an excursion, be aware that distances are deceiving, due to the nature of the terrain and the roads. For example, the 25-mile drive from Pigeon Point along the windward coast to Speyside takes more than 1.5 hours.

A DRIVING TOUR
OF TOBAGO

Scarborough, about 8 miles northeast of Pigeon Point, is a quiet West Indian village with a small Botanic Gardens and a *Handicraft Center* (Bacolet Street). Fort King George, a well-restored fortification built by the British in 1777, overlooks the town and provides a fabulous view of the Atlantic, or windward, coast. Its other historic buildings are St. Andrew's Church, constructed in 1819, and the Courthouse, which dates from 1825.

Directly north of Pigeon Point on the Caribbean, or leeward, coast and across the island from Scarborough is Plymouth, the island's second town. It, too, has a historic fort, Fort James, built in 1768. One of the island's prettiest strands is just south of the town: Great Courtland Bay, better known as Turtle Beach for the turtles who come to nest here in April and May.

BUCCOO REEF NATIONAL PARK In the quiet waters between Pigeon Point and Buccoo Bay is the Buccoo Reef National Park, a sea-and-land reserve with shallow-water reefs in the form of a wide horseshoe that shelters the inner reef and a lagoon at the center, where the water is less than 30 feet deep. An area of exceptionally clear water on the east is known as Nylon Pool. The gardens have a great variety of coral—staghorn, starlet, brain, sea fans, and others—that attracts an enormous array of fish.

At low tide the water in parts of the reef is only about 3 feet deep, a feature that has made it popular with snorkelers and nonswimmers who, unfortunately, walk around the reef in sneakers. Although there have been laws on the books for two decades to protect the reef, the government has never seriously enforced them, and the reef is in great danger of being destroyed by misuse. The Crusoe Reef Society, a marine research and conservation group in Trinidad, tries hard to pressure the government for greater conservation measures, but it has only limited results.

Bon Accord, another lagoon on the south side of the park, is edged by mangroves, which host a great number of birds, including the rufous-vented chachalaca, Tobago's national bird. A trail east of Pigeon Point borders the mangroves. Glass-bottom boat and snorkeling trips to Buccoo Reef leave daily from Pigeon Point.

THE LEEWARD COAST

Tobago's entire Caribbean coast is made up of one beautiful beach after another—some with resorts, others untouched. North of Plymouth, Arnos Vale, a tiny cove with a hillside hotel, is one of the most romantic spots in the Caribbean. Once part of a sugar plantation, the hotel's oldest building is completely encased in tropical foliage like a tree house, with a choir of birds to serenade it. Sunsets here are incredible. The idyllic cove has a fine coral reef suitable for snorkelers and novice divers. North of Arnos Vale an abandoned road of about 2 miles is now a hiking trail to Golden Lane and Culloden Bay.

West of Arnos Vale on the road between Scarborough and Golden Lane, the ruins of the Arnos Vale plantation (with a waterwheel and other machinery bearing 1857 markings), are the centerpiece of a lovely culture park and museum created by the owners of the Arnos Vale hotel. There is a guided nature trail through the surrounding woods to a waterfall. The open-air restaurant has an eclectic menu of local specialties and light fare.

North of Golden Lane along the Caribbean coast, the road snakes through forested mountains along steep cliffs that fall almost directly to the sea. From Mt. Dillon, a windswept promontory rising 800 feet above the sea, you can have a spectacular view of the leeward coast with Pigeon Point in the southwest and Trinidad on the horizon. Behind the white-sand beaches rise the green slopes of the Main Ridge.

Castara, a tiny village with a popular swimming beach, has bathing facilities. Farther north, Englishman's Bay, Parlatuvier Bay, and Bloody Bay—lovely enclaves of white-sand beaches shaded by giant ferns, bamboo, and palms—can be reached by short trails from the main road. Other trails inland lead to pretty waterfalls.

MAIN RIDGE RAIN FOREST TRAIL North of the island's midgirth a good road crosses the Main Ridge between Parlatuvier Bay, on the leeward coast, and Roxborough, on the windward side. At the crest of the ridge is the entrance to the Main Ridge Rain Forest Trail, the most accessible and best-maintained trail in the Tobago Forest Reserve, the oldest forest preserve in the Western Hemisphere (established in 1765). The entrance is marked by Bloody Bay Lookout Site, where the Forestry Department has a small cabin with a map of the trail. The Lookout sits high above Bloody Bay and offers magnificent views.

From here a looped footpath of 3 hours winds down the steep slopes through the rain forest along a stream that empties into Bloody Bay. After the trail crosses the stream, it levels out and returns on an easy walking path to the eastern entrance on the main highway, about 2 miles west of the Lookout.

THE WINDWARD COAST

Between Scarborough and Speyside, a fishing village near the north end of the island, the Windward Road hugs the serpentine coast, overhung with trees laden with mango, lime, and papaya as it weaves through fishing villages and bayside hamlets. Almost any road into the mountains leads to waterfalls, wooded slopes, and beautiful vistas. At the 110-foot Kings Bay Waterfall, the highest in Tobago, the Tourist Board has trails and facilities.

SPEYSIDE Set against the thick forests of the Main Ridge, the little fishing town of Speyside overlooks Goat Island, one of the most unusual dive sites in the Caribbean. A mile offshore is *Little Tobago*, a 280-acre bird sanctuary, also known as

Bird of Paradise Island. There in 1909 an Englishman introduced four dozen birds of paradise, hoping to establish a safe haven for th species, which was being decimated by poacher supplying feathers to the European fashion mar ket. The birds lived until 1963 when a hurricane devastated the island. Seven birds survived, bu none have been sighted since 1983. The island ha many other birds and wildlife and has been sanctuary since 1934. Nature trails lead to th eastern side of the island where the beautiful trop ic bird nests in the cliffs. Often birds on their nes can be observed and photographed at very clos range.

A boat from Speyside to Little Tobago take about 20 minutes and is often a rough crossin over white-capped seas. Be prepared for we landings, as there are no docks, and take wate because there is no supply on Little Tobago Arrangements are best made through a loca guide or the Blue Waters Inn in Speyside.

CHARLOTTEVILLE At the north end of Tobago on the leeward coast is Charlotteville, a fishing villag on Man o' War Bay. Directly behind the wide horse shoe bay rises heavily forested 1,890-foot Pigeon Peak, the tallest mountains. Due to its isolation Charlotteville has kept the island's folkways mor than any location on Tobago. The Man-O-War Ba Cottages on the north side of the bay is a small nat uralists' retreat on a one-thousand-acre cocoa plantation, open to visitors to wander at will.

DINING IN TOBAGO

The following restaurants are moderately priced ranging from about US $10 to $20.

Blue Crab (Main and Robinson streets Scarborough; 639–2737). In a hillside hous near the harbor, you will find home cookin offered for lunch. Flying fish, curried or rolle around sweet peppers and eggplant, is a specialt along with homemade ice cream and locall made fruit wines.

Gemma's Seafood Kitchen (south of Speyside 660–4066). The day's catch is cooked to order a this rustic beach tavern, where it's enjoyed on ttle "tree-house" veranda by the sea. Only a one-room shack a few years ago, *Gemma's* has grown into the best known restaurant on the island.

Grafton Beach Resort (Black Rock; 639–0191). One of Tobago's main hotels has a delightful terrace restaurant open to the breezes. Its buffet and à la carte menu have local specialties and international dishes, and they are all good.

Old Donkey Cart House (Bacolet Street, north of Scarborough; 639–3551). Wine bistro in a restored French colonial house that was Tobago's first guesthouse. Salads and light snacks. On special holidays they prepare armadillo and opossum (*manicou*).

Miss Esmee's stand at Store Bay Beach has great tamarind and sesame balls, coconut muffins, and *rotis* (Indian turnovers stuffed with meat or chicken and flavored with curry). If you are heading in a different direction, ask your driver to stop at his favorite *roti* maker. It's sure to be fresh, hot, and mighty good.

Sports in Tobago

BEACHES/SWIMMING: Almost any place on the island has powder-fine beaches, many that seldom see a footprint. Pigeon Point and Store Bay are the most convenient for ships anchoring off Pigeon Point. Parlatuvier and Bloody Bay, on the Caribbean coast, where bathers arrive by boat or hike in from the main road, are tranquil and secluded.

DEEP-SEA FISHING: The north shore of Tobago and the waters around nearby St. Giles Island are the main locations for game fishing. Arrangements must be made in advance through a local travel company.

GOLF: The 18-hole championship *Mount Irvine Golf Course* (6,800 yards; 72 par) at the Mount Irvine Hotel (639–8737) is about 5 miles from Pigeon Point. One of the Caribbean's most scenic golf courses, it is situated on 125 landscaped acres of gentle rolling hills overlooking the sea. The clubhouse, which is the headquarters of the Tobago Golf Club, is on a promontory with superb views. It has changing rooms, pro shop, and restaurant. Green fees are US $29 for 9 holes; US

$46 for 18 holes; cart US $21 and $35; caddy, US $7 and $10. All prices include taxes.

HIKING: Tobago offers endless opportunities for hiking. The most accessible is the Main Ridge Nature Trail, a loop off the main highway between Bloody Bay and Roxborough. You can take it as a short walk of an hour from its eastern entrance or try a 3-hour hike from the western one.

KAYAKING: Contact *Wildways Caribbean Adventure Travel* (phone/fax: 623–7332).

SNORKELING AND SCUBA DIVING: Tobago is almost completely surrounded by shallow-water reefs, most within swimming distance from shore and easily accessible to snorkelers and novice divers. Marine life is rich in color and the water exceptionally clear. Tobago was one of the earliest locations to be discovered by pioneer divers four decades ago, but the advanced skill needed for diving the best sites has left it as something of a last frontier. It offers great diversity, but the most interesting feature for advanced divers is drift diving.

The main area for snorkelers and novice divers is Buccoo Reef and the reefs along the Caribbean coast. Grouper Ground, on the western tip of the island opposite Pigeon Point, has gentle drift diving for experienced divers. Here basket sponges are the size of bathtubs. The clarity of the waters makes it a delight for underwater photographers.

The northeast coast around Goat Island offers some of the finest diving in the West Indies. Due to the strong surf and surge, the reefs have been dubbed "Flying Reefs" and are only for advanced divers with experience in drift diving. The most celebrated, *Japanese Garden,* begins in about 20 feet of water and drops to 110 feet. The shallow area has huge sea whips, sea fans, and sponges with a great variety of colors. Tobago has dive operators at Pigeon Point, Crown Reef, Turtle Beach, and Speyside.

Festivals and Celebrations

Carnival in Trinidad

Trinidadians say they have two seasons: Carnival and the rest of the year. Carnival in Trinidad is the biggest, most colorful and creative of all Caribbean Carnivals and the one after which the others are patterned.

Carnival is not simply another event, but a celebration of life—a folk festival, sports competition, art exhibit, and dance and music concert rolled into one, involving every age at every level of society. It's street theater where, after months of work, all the island's talent and energy are released in a few delirious days of mirth and madness. It's CAAR-NA-VAAL!

Although Carnival culminates in the last two days before Ash Wednesday and the start of Lent in the Catholic tradition, Carnival in Trinidad actually begins the day after the new year is born.

Trinidad's Carnival tradition began in 1783, when French settlers and others who were given land grants in Trinidad arrived in large numbers, and a festive season from Christmas to Ash Wednesday was initiated. Masked bands of people, often accompanied by musicians, paraded through the streets, stopping to visit friends at homes where elaborate balls were given. But this was sport for the privileged. "Free persons of color," as free Negroes and mixed races were known, were not forbidden to mask, but they did not participate in the affairs of high society. Negro slaves were prohibited by law from joining the festivities.

The most radical change came with the emancipation of the slaves in 1833, when the celebrations became the people's festival and the scene shifted from fancy dress balls for a few to the masses in the street. With it also came a confluence of national traditions that, over the century, became as mixed as a pot of callaloo, often totally reversing their original meanings. The music of the old bamboo bands was replaced by rudimentary pan bands whose metallic tones were beat out on dustpans, paint cans, and any other metal objects on which innately talented musicians could improvise rhythm and tone.

During World War II Carnival was suspended, but in the backyards of Trinidad the pan technique continued to develop (leading to the term "panyard"), and the number of instruments and their complexity grew. Not everyone embraced them; many people branded the players as hooligans and tried to prohibit them from playing in the streets.

In 1948 the commercial 55-gallon oil drum appeared in Trinidad for the first time. Soon the discarded drums were being used by pan players who found that tempered steel enabled them to extend their musical range. Rapidly the drum replaced all other pans in use, and a steel band association was formed. The first pan recital, with selections ranging from calypso to the classics, received such acclaim that the respectability of steel band music was assured. The steel band, which has been an essential element of Carnival, has recently become an endangered species during Carnival parade. Gigantic boom boxes mounted on flatbed trunks now accompany the paraders. The canned music is so loud that steel pans wouldn't stand a chance to be heard, even if they tried. Unfortunately, it's having a serious impact on Carnival, too; many revelers often seem as mechanical and uninspired as the canned music.

Today Mas Bands, as the masqueraders are known, are divided into three sizes—small, medium, and large—with the largest having four thousand people. Large groups are broken down into three dozen or more sections, each costumed differently to portray an element in an overall theme created by the band leader, who must excel as an artist, showman, director, and producer with the genius to choreograph theater on a grand scale. The winner of the Mas Band competition is crowned King of Carnival. What greater honor is there? The best are household names throughout the Caribbean.

Calypso is the very essence of Carnival. Always witty, rich in innuendo and satire, calypso contains a variety of verses followed by a set refrain. The lyrics often satirize island politics, society, and other local matters, so you are likely to miss the biting humor of the calypsonian, but this will not lessen your enjoyment. The music is infectious.

From December through the end of Carnival, top calypsonians and two or three dozen hopefuls perform their newest songs nightly at calypso tents. (Years ago the artists performed in outdoor tents and makeshift structures; today's calypsonians hold their shows in theaters with stages, but the term "tent" remains.) Each calypsonian has his or her own style and fans. The top ones are as well known in the Caribbean as Michael Jackson

Although the Road March, or Carnival Parade, is the greatest spectacle, the competitions for calypsonians, steel bands, and costumed bands are the heart of Carnival activity for Trinis. About three weeks before Carnival, the Steelband Panorama preliminaries are held over two days and bring together as many as one hundred steel orchestras from around the country, each with as many as fifty or one hundred players. The finals are held on the Saturday before Carnival, when a dozen or so orchestras compete for the championship.

Kiddies' Carnival is also held on the Saturday morning when children dressed in full regalia "play mas."

Dimanche Gras: On the Sunday before the two last days of Carnival, the finals of three major competitions take place: Calypso Monarch, the best calypsonian of the year; and the King and Queen of Carnival, chosen for the most beautiful, creative, and magnificently costumed male and female masqueraders. The Dimanche Gras show is staged at the Queen's Park Savannah.

Carnival Monday: Dawn, or *J'ouvert* (French for "the day begins"), is the official start of Carnival Monday and symbolizes the opening of the doors to let King Carnival in. At the end of the Dimanche Gras show, people join the crowds at *fêtes*—public parties that anyone can attend by buying a ticket. (Dozens of *fêtes* are advertised in daily newspapers, many being held at hotels.) On Carnival Monday the *fêtes* end at 4:00 A.M. when the dawn breaks and people spill into the streets to jump to the music of the steel bands. Everyone—young and old, visitors and Trinis—joins "Joovay" and lets the music move them along.

Carnival Tuesday: Early in the morning bands of brilliantly costumed masqueraders line up for the spectacular parade through the streets of Port of Spain to the Savannah, dancing to the music. Carnival ends at midnight with the "Las Lap," an expression for the wind down of the festivities—the last chance to jump in the streets before King Carnival disappears for another year.

OTHER FESTIVALS IN TRINIDAD

Steelband Music Festival in September/October is almost as important as Carnival. Trinidadians are justly proud of inventing the steel drum, the only new instrument to be added in the 20th century.

Festival of Hosay, a Muslim observance, is held in Muharram (first month of the Islamic calendar) and commemorates the martyrdom of Hassan and Hussein, the sons of Ali, at the battle of Kerbala in early Islam. The form it takes here is unique to Trinidad and stems from East Indian traditions. The most elaborate events are in the St. James section of Port of Spain, where East Indians are concentrated.

The Muslims prepare goat-skinned tassa drums and secretly build *tadjahs,* which are colorful, elaborate floats of intricate detail, made of paper, tinsel, reeds, and bamboo in the shape of mosques in Asian style. Three minicelebrations precede Hosay: *Flagnight* on the seventh day of Muharram, when pilgrims parade in the streets bearing flags honoring the battle of Kerbala; *Small Hosay,* the following night when miniature *tadjahs* (representing the tomb of the younger brother, Hussein) are carried through the streets; and *Big Hosay* (the following night), when the large *tadjahs* (symbolizing the tomb of the older brother, Hassan) are paraded. Hosay Day follows with a final parade of the *tadjahs* which, three days later, are ceremoniously cast into the sea.

Phagwa or Holi, the Hindu Festival of Color, has been celebrated in Trinidad and Tobago since 1845. The festival takes place on the full moon of Phagun (February to March), the most beautiful time of the year in North India at the dawn of spring.

Bonaire

KRALENDIJK

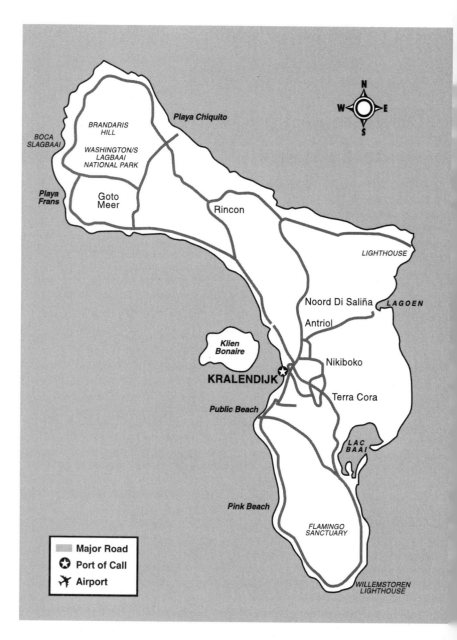

BOCA SLAGBAAI

BRANDARIS HILL

Playa Chiquito

WASHINGTON/S LAGBAAI NATIONAL PARK

Playa Frans

Goto Meer

Rincon

LIGHTHOUSE

Noord Di Saliña

LAGOEN

Antriol

Klien Bonaire

KRALENDIJK

Nikiboko

Terra Cora

Public Beach

LAC BAAI

Pink Beach

FLAMINGO SANCTUARY

WILLEMSTOREN LIGHTHOUSE

N W E S

Major Road
Port of Call
Airport

AT A GLANCE

Antiquities	★
Architecture	★★
Art and Artists	★
Beaches	★★★★
Colonial Buildings	★★★
Crafts	★
Cuisine	★★
Culture	★
Dining/Restaurants	★★★
Entertainment	★
Forts	★
History	★
Monuments	★
Museums	★
Nightlife	★
Scenery	★★★★
Shopping	★★
Sight-seeing	★★★
Sports	★★★★★
Transportation	★

CHAPTER CONTENTS

NATURE'S CHILD

Bonaire is an unspoiled island with small-town charm. Although it has seen considerable development in the past decade, the island is devoid of slick commercialism. It has only low-rise hotels along white-sand beaches fronting crystal-clear Caribbean waters within a 5- to 10-minute ride from town, the port, and the airport.

Shaped like a boomerang, the island is blessed with a bounty of natural beauty preserved in three nature parks—one for flora and wildlife, another for flamingos, and a third for its coastal waters and marine life. Bonaire has been a mecca for scuba divers from around the world since they discovered its fabulous underwater life three decades ago. But even for those who do not dive or have no higher aspirations than snorkeling, there is more than enough to see here to make a visit worthwhile.

The second-largest island of the Netherlands Antilles, Bonaire is located 86 miles east of Aruba and 30 miles east of Curaçao, its sister Dutch island; Venezuela is 50 miles to the south. The island's landscape is almost as diverse as its seascape and has three distinct areas: The north end, mostly covered by the national park, is hilly and greener than the rest of the island and has freshwater and saltwater lakes.

The central region is semi-arid, somewhat flatter, and has a landscape similar to the American southwest. The south end is the flattest part and is covered with salt pans, sand dunes, and mangroves. Less than a mile off Bonaire's south coast is *Klein* (meaning little) *Bonaire*, a flat, uninhabited island of about 3 square miles, which acts like a barrier reef protecting the main island's leeward waters.

In contrast to the calm south coast, Bonaire's north side is battered by strong waves that break against black volcanic and coral rocks, as well as unusual coastal formations with grottos and caves with Indian petroglyphs. Throughout the island the landscape is dominated by enormous candle and other cacti and the ever-present divi-divi tree, whose asymmetrical shape is sculpted by the strong winds that help keep Bonaire cool.

Bonaire, one of the Caribbean's youngest tourist destinations, was discovered nearly five centuries ago in 1499 by Amerigo Vespucci, the Italian navigator for whom the Americas were named. The tranquil island was inhabited by Arawak Indians at the time, and Vespucci named it *bo-nah* from the Arawak word meaning "low land." For the next century the Spaniards attempted to colonize it but failed. Instead they took the Arawak population to Hispaniola as slaves. In the years that followed, the island was colonized by the Dutch, fought over by the French and British, and leased to a New York merchant.

From 1639, and for the next 160 years, the island was managed by the Dutch West India Company, which developed salt production, and the Dutch imported African slaves to work the salt pans. In 1816 the Dutch government took over Bonaire, after an interlude of British control, and it has remained Dutch to the present.

FAST FACTS

 POPULATION: 13,400

SIZE: 24 miles long, 3 to 7 miles wide; 112 sq. miles.

MAIN TOWN: Kralendijk

 GOVERNMENT: Bonaire is part of the Netherlands Antilles, an autonomous region of the Kingdom of the Netherlands. The governor is appointed by the queen of the Netherlands. The locally elected legislative council has three elected Central Government senators and three elected island commissioners.

 CURRENCY: Netherland Antilles florin or guilder. US $1 equals NAf 1.77. U.S. dollars are readily accepted.

 DEPARTURE TAX: US $10 (NAf 17.70) on international flights; US $5.75 (NAf 10) to Curaçao.

LANGUAGE: Dutch is the official language, but papiamento is the island language. English and Spanish are widely spoken.

PUBLIC HOLIDAYS: January 1, New Year's Day; February, Carnival, Carnival Monday; Good Friday; Easter Monday; April 30, Coronation Day; May 1, Labor Day; Ascension Day; June 24, St. John's Day; June 29, St. Peter's Day; October, Sailing Regatta; September 6, Bonaire Day; December 25, Christmas Day; December 26, Boxing Day.

TELEPHONE AREA CODE: For international direct dialing from the United States, 011–599–7 plus four-digit local number.

AIRLINES:

From the United States: Flamingo International Airport is served by ALM Antillean Airlines daily from Miami via Curaçao, a Saturday non-stop from Atlanta, and Thursday and Sunday from Fort Lauderdale. Air Aruba has direct service from Baltimore, Miami, Newark, and Tampa to Bonaire via Aruba.

Interisland: The local services of ALM and Air Aruba connect Bonaire with Aruba and Curaçao several times daily.

INFORMATION:

In the United States: Tourism Corporation Bonaire, 10 Rockefeller Plaza, Suite 900, New York, NY 10020; 800–UBONAIR; (212) 956–5911; fax: (212) 956–5913.
In Port: Bonaire Government Tourist Bureau, 12 Kaya Simon Bolivar, Kralendijk, Bonaire, N.A.; (8322 or 8649/8322; fax: 8408.

BUDGET PLANNING

Bonaire is relatively inexpensive as Caribbean destinations go. Diving, deep-sea fishing, windsurfing, and most water sports are about the least expensive in the region. Tours are reasonably priced. Certain elements, such as good restaurants, however, can be expensive.

PORT PROFILE:

LOCATION/EMBARKATION: The pier is located on the south side of town, only a short walk from the town center and a few steps from the *Divi Flamingo Beach Hotel.*

LOCAL TRANSPORTATION: There is no public bus system, but there are taxis and rental cars. To see the most interesting sights, you need a car or a tour, which can be arranged through a local tour company or the Tourist Office.

ROADS AND RENTALS: Bonaire has a limited number of surfaced roads; the rest are dirt roads and tracks. A car or, in some places, a Jeep or four-wheel-drive vehicle, is necessary for exploring the island and can be arranged upon arrival. A valid driver's license is required. The minimum age is generally twenty-one, but it can be twenty-three for certain car models. Driving is on the right. The tourist office and local tour companies distribute a free booklet, "Bonaire Holiday," which has a road map.

From Kralendijk a surfaced road of 9 miles runs along the west coast, where most of the island's resorts are located, to the National Park boundary. Here it forks with the left road, which continues along the west shore to Nukove, a snorkeling area; the right fork runs east along Goto Meer, a lake, to Rincon, where a road leads northeast to the National Park entrance.

South of Kralendijk a surfaced road makes a loop around the southern tip of the island along the Pekelmeer Lagoon and returns north along the east coast.

Daily rates for cars, jeeps, and minivans range from US $40 to US $65 with air-conditioning. Rental companies in Kralendijk include: *Dollar* (phone/fax: 8888) and *Sunray Car Rental* (8600), among others; *Cycle Bonaire* (8761) has bikes for US $17 per day. *Caribbean Touring Scooters* (6877) rents a one seater for US $25; two seater, US $35.

INTERISLAND AIR SERVICE: See Fast Facts.

EMERGENCY NUMBERS:
> *Medical: Hospital,* 8900/8445;
> *Police:* 114

AUTHOR'S FAVORITE ATTRACTIONS

SNORKELING AND DIVING IN THE MARINE PARK

HIKING IN WASHINGTON/SLAGBAAI NATURE PARK

FLAMINGO SANCTUARY

SHORE EXCURSIONS

The Town and Country Tour is the most likely shore excursion to be offered on your ship. It was created by *Bonaire Tours* (Box 115, Kralendijk; 8778), the island's main tour company, especially for cruise-ship passengers. *Ayubi Tours* (5338) has similar programs for slightly lower prices. Transportation is by minivan or Jeep, depending on the number of people. Prices are per person. All locations are described further in this chapter.

Northern Island Tour, 2 hours, US $12 to $16. Drive along the north coast and through the hills inland to Rincon. Highlights are the Thousand Steps, Goto Lake to observe flamingos; the north coast to see Indian petroglyphs, and to Seroe Largo for a fabulous view.

Southern Island Tour, 2 hours, US $12 to $16. The low-lying south is a marked contrast to the hilly north. Highlights are 150-year-old salt pans with sparkling white hills; flamingo sanctuary; stone slave huts; and Lac Bay, a lagoon and wildlife area.

BONAIRE ON YOUR OWN

Hard by the sea on the west coast at about midisland is the capital Kralendijk, which means "coral dyke" in Dutch. It is a pretty little town of pastel buildings of Dutch colonial architecture, reflecting the island's commitment to preserve its cultural heritage as much as the parks preserve its natural one.

A KRALENDIJK WALKABOUT

Kralendijk (pronounced *KRAH*-len-dike) can be covered on foot in less than an hour. It comprises two parallel north-south streets, Kaya Hellmund/Kaya Craane (along the waterfront) and Kaya Grandi (the shopping street); and two east-west streets, Kaya Gerharts and Kaya Brion. A principal artery, Simon Bolivarstraat, begins at Kaya Grandi and cuts diagonally across Gerharts and Brion streets.

Kralendijk's historic and shopping areas are the same, making it easy to combine a walking and shopping excursion. Many of the shops, bars, and restaurants are housed in colorful old structures that give the town its special character. Some of the most historic buildings are located around Willheminaplein (Queen Wilhelmina Park), by the sea on the east side of town. The park has pretty shade trees and benches and three historical monuments: One commemorating Dutchman Van Welbeek's landing on Bonaire in 1634 is in the center of the park; another honoring Bonairean soldiers killed during World War II is by the sea; and the third remembers Eleanor Roosevelt's visit to Bonaire in 1944 when American troops were stationed here.

Directly behind the park on its east side is an 18th-century church; in front by the pier is the customs office; and on the south, Government House. South of Government House is the old fort, which is to be renovated for the *Instituto Folklore Bonaire* (Folklore Museum), a collection of musical instruments, old utensils, pre-Columbian and other artifacts.

A DRIVE AROUND THE ISLAND

TO THE NORTH

As you drive from town toward the island's north coast, the terrain changes from flat, desertlike errain with short, pale-colored bushes and hundreds of cactus plants to green rolling hills. The road winds along the west coast hugging the coastline of jagged, black coral rock. About 4 miles north of the capital at Barcadera (across from the Radio Antilles tower), there are seaside steps, known as *The Thousand Steps,* a popular dive site.

Another mile north are rock formations whose appearance is so grotesque they have been dubbed the *Devil's Mouth.* After another mile the road becomes one-way in a northbound direction. At Karpata the first of two roads goes inland to Bonaire's oldest village, Rincon. Karpata is the home of STINAPA, the Bonaire National Parks Foundation, which is responsible for the management of the land and marine parks, and of Karpata Ecological Center, a marine research facility. After another mile the road reaches the gate of Bonaire Petroleum's oil terminal, where the road forks. A left turn continues north to Nukove and Playa Frans, where you will find beaches for swimming, hidden caves, and some of the island's most popular picnicking and snorkeling locations; the right fork takes you along a lake on the southern border of the park to Dos Pos and south again to Rincon. There is no access to the park from the southwest.

GOTO MEER Lying outside the southwest border of the park is a beautiful lake, Goto Meer, once open to the sea and still fed by underground springs. The drive along the lake shore is the prettiest in Bonaire and should be a priority. The vegetation is typical of the park with candle cactus, acacia, mesquite, and other trees usually found in dry lowland tropical forests; it becomes leafy green during the rainy season. The southern end of the lagoon attracts large numbers of flamingo, particularly in November and December. Early in the morning you are also likely to see parrots and parakeets in the trees around the lake. The island's highest point, 784-foot Brandaris Hill, is in view on the northeast.

WASHINGTON/SLAGBAAI NATIONAL PARK

The northern end of Bonaire is covered by the 13,500-acre Washington/Slagbaai National Park, a wildlife sanctuary and the first of its kind in the Netherlands Antilles when it was established in 1974. Situated on the hilliest, greenest part of the island on a former plantation producing divi-divi trees, aloe, charcoal, and goats, the park showcases the island's flora and fauna and includes Brandaris Hill, which can be seen from most locations in the park.

In 1967 the heir of the Washington estate sold the land to the government on the condition that it would never be developed commercially. The land was designated for a national park, and the Netherlands Antilles National Parks Foundation was made the custodian. Three years later, in 1972, the family of the Slagbaai plantation sold the land to the Parks Foundation, and the two areas were reunited into the Washington/Slagbaai National Park.

The park has a wide variety of birds and landscape that ranges from dry lowland forest and salt licks to freshwater lakes, secluded white-sand beaches, unusual rock formations, and dramatic seascapes along rocky coasts. Candle cactus, which grows as tall as trees; prickly pear cactus; mesquite, a favorite perch of the Bonaire parrot; acacia; and divi-divi trees are abundant.

Bonaire, a flyover for migratory birds between North and South America, has as many as 150 species—some unique to the island. Among the most interesting are the beautiful black, yellow, and white trupial and the colorful parakeets and parrots. The endemic, yellow-winged Bonaire parrot, also called the Lora, is protected. The park can be seen by car or on foot.

There are two signposted routes over mostly dirt roads: a short one of 15 miles marked by green arrows and a longer one of 22 miles marked by yellow arrows. The routes can also be used for hiking, and there are additional footpaths to places not accessible by motor vehicles.

At the entrance, located on the southeastern side of the park, you can get a free pamphlet with map or purchase more complete guidebooks that detail the routes and the flora and fauna to be seen along the way. There is also a book on the birds of Bonaire. Hours: daily from 8:00 A.M. to 5:00 P.M. Entrance: US $5.

Both park roads begin at the entrance gate. The yellow one goes first to *Salina Mathijs,* a salt pond populated by flamingos during the rainy season (October to January). After another mile a side road to the right leads to *Playa Chiquito*, a rockbound cove with a beautiful beach, where the surf is too strong and the water too rough for safe swimming. A short walk north along the rocky coral coast at *Boca Chiquito*, huge waves crash against the shore with such force they send clouds of spray shooting 30 feet and more into the air.

The yellow route continues to the north end of the park at *Boca Cocolishi*, a small secluded cove divided into two parts—a deep, rough seaward side and a calm, shallow basin with a black-sand beach—separated by a coral ridge. The basin and beach were formed by small pieces of coral, mollusks and their shells (cocolishi means shell in papiamento). Hermit crabs can be seen on the beach and in the shallow water.

Inland along *Salina Bartol*, another salt pond, lies *Poos di Mangel*, a watering hole for a great variety of birds and a good bird-watching location. *Boca Bartol*, on the coast, is made up of coral rubble and flat, eroded rock. This bay has abundant elkhorn coral and sea fans and many colorful reef fish.

On the green route about three-quarters of the way from the east to the west coast, the road passes the trailhead for the 1.5-mile hike to the top of Mt. Brandaris. Farther on a side road leads to *Put Bronswinkel*, a watering hole for parakeets and other birds that is one of the park's best birding locations.

Playa Funchi, on the west coast, is the former harbor of the Washington Plantation. Here you can see dozens of multicolored geckos and iguana, particularly bright green baby ones. If you are quiet on the approach, the iguana often remain statue-still and can be photographed.

At Playa Funchi the green route turns south to *Boca Slagbaai*, a large bay with a white-sand beach popular for swimming, snorkeling, and diving. Used as a harbor for exporting salt and meat in the 1800s, the former storage buildings and customs office have been restored. Local scouts and other groups often rent the main house for overnight camping. The buildings sit on a strip of land that once dammed and separated the sea from *Salina Slagbaai*, the saline lake behind the bay. The lake has flamingos, particularly from about January to July.

ACROSS THE CENTRAL REGION AND NORTH COAST

The low-lying terrain and scattered hills of the central region stretch from Kralendijk to the north coast through green farm fields with old Dutch colonial farmhouses. The coast is as desolate as the moon, with large fields of coral terraces and deeply eroded rocks, some with petroglyphs. A good road from Kralendijk to Rincon and the entrance to the National Park runs through the *cunucu* (or *kunuku*), as the countryside is known in papiamento.

Immediately north of Kralendijk at Noord di Salina, a side road of about 1 mile leads up *Seroe Largo*, a hill of about 500 feet in altitude. There you will be rewarded with a fabulous view of Bonaire stretching from the national park on the north along the resorts of the west coast and Kralendijk to the salt mounds on the south.

Another 4 miles north on the main road brings you to a small sign marking the turnoff onto a dirt road for *Onima*, where there are Arawak petroglyphs on rock faces near the road. Here, too, strong waves break against the rocky shore.

On the main road, about 2 miles north of the Onima turnoff, you will reach Rincon, the first settlement on the island, dating from the 16th century. Set in a pretty green valley, the town is anchored by a brightly colored village church and surrounded by old red-tile–roofed houses of typical Dutch architecture. From Rincon to the national park entrance is less than 3 miles.

TO THE SOUTH

In contrast to the hilly north, the southern part of the island is flat, dry, and covered with white mountains of salt that shimmer in the bright sun. The salt pans, which are more than 150 years old, have been reactivated by Azko Salt Antilles Company, a Dutch enterprise, after many years of disuse. It takes seven months for the evaporation process to be completed to make salt. The modern plant can load salt by conveyor belt onto ships at the rate of 2,000 tons an hour. It is shipped to the eastern United States, throughout the Caribbean, and as far away as New Zealand for chemical, industrial, water softening, and iceontrol applications. On the coast south of the oading pier is *Witte Pan,* or Pink Beach, one of he longest stretches of beach on Bonaire. It parllels the south side of the *Pekelmeer Lagoon,* the arge canal that channels sea water to the salt ans.

LAMINGO SANCTUARY Between the salt pans nd the Pekelmeer Lagoon is a 135-acre flamingo anctuary, a nesting ground for about five thouand birds. You can tour the perimeter of the ans, but access to the sanctuary is prohibited ecause of the flamingo's extreme sensitivity. iewers usually leave their vehicles by the road nd walk quietly along the edge of the lagoon, vhere they can get close enough to see the birds vith binoculars and photograph them with tele-hoto lens.

On the south side of the salt works, you can see iny stone huts by the side of the road. Built round 1850—about a decade before slavery vas abolished here—the huts were used to house laves when they worked the salt pans.

On the southern tip of the island stands the *Villemstoren Lighthouse,* the oldest lighthouse n Bonaire, built in 1831. Here the road turns iorth for about 4 miles to *Lac Baai* (Lake Bay), vhich has extensive mangroves. On the south ide of the bay at Sorobon, there is a pretty beach vith a small naturalist hotel; its clothes-optional each may be used by nonguests upon payment f a fee.

BONAIRE MARINE PARK The growth of Bonaire as a diver's mecca and the development f tourism in the 1970s led to the need for a ong-term program to protect the island's extra-rdinary coral reefs and marine life. With the ielp of the International Union for the Conservation of Nature and Natural Resources, as vell as the World Wildlife Fund, the Netherlands antilles National Parks Foundation (STINAPA) eceived a grant in 1979 to create the Bonaire Marine Park.

It monitors the impact of coastal development, esource exploitation, visitor use and other vari-bles; and manages services and facilities for vis-tors, including park brochures, lectures, slide resentations, films, and permanent dive-site noorings.

The park incorporates the entire coastline of Bonaire and neighboring Klein Bonaire and is defined as the "seabottom and the overlying waters from the highwater tidemark down to 200 feet." It has more than eighty dive sites, often within wading distance from shore. All marine life is completely protected; fishing, spearfishing, and collecting of fish, shells, or corals—dead or alive—is prohibited. Boats of less than 12 feet may use a stone anchor, but all others must use permanent moorings and cannot anchor except in emergencies.

Bonaire's reefs contain some of the most beautiful coral formations in the Caribbean. They are famous for their variety—the park's guidebook describes eighty-four species—and include an abundance of sponges, particularly purple tube sponges, elkhorn and sheet coral, and four kinds of brain coral. More than 200 species of fish have been identified. *Guide to the Bonaire Marine Park,* available in local dive shops and gift stores, was written by the marine biologists who developed the Bonaire Marine Park, Tom van't Hof and Dee Scarr.

While divers and snorkelers derive the greatest pleasure from the park, non-divers can see a great deal on glass-bottom boat excursions, because visibility in Bonaire's waters is excellent and major coral formations are close to shore.

KLEIN BONAIRE Less than a mile west of Kralendijk is the small, dry, and rocky islet of Klein Bonaire. Covered with desert vegetation, it has several white-sand beaches, which are popular destinations for day-trippers. Its spectacular reefs are part of the Marine Park and range from shallow-water gardens thick with elkhorn coral to coral slopes with great varieties of sponges, gorgonians, large star and brain corals.

SHOPPING

Kralendijk has an assortment of small shops selling jewelry, crystal, leather, perfume, and sportswear at prices competitive with Curaçao and Aruba, but Bonaire is a place for casual, not serious, shoppers. Most shops on Kaya Grandi are housed in brightly painted colonial buildings. Harborside is a small mall in a renovated building with a Dutch colonial facade. Located between the Kaya Grandi and seaside, it has nine shops, an ice-cream parlor, bar, and restaurant. Hotels also have small gift shops, and these are likely to be your best place to find books on Bonaire, particularly its marine life.

Store hours generally are Monday through Saturday from 8:00 A.M. to noon and 2:00 to 6:00 P.M., although some stores remain open through the lunch hours. When cruise ships are in port on Sundays or holidays, tourist shops usually open for a few hours. U.S. dollars, credit cards, and travelers checks are accepted; stores often quote prices in dollars.

CHINA/CRYSTAL/JEWELRY: *Littman's Jewelers* (Harborside) is the agent for several well-known brands of European crystal and also carries delft china; it is best known for fine jewelry and quality dive watches.

CLOTHING AND ACCESSORIES: *Benetton* (19 Kaya Grandi; 5107) claims its prices are 30 percent less than those in the U.S. *Bye-Bye* (Harborside) has pretty coordinated sportswear at prices comparable to stateside ones. *Centro* (Kaya Grandi) is like a general store and has a local clientele for clothing, as well as perfume, toiletries, and pharmaceuticals.

CRAFTS AND SOUVENIRS: *Littman's Jeweler* boutique stocks hand-painted T-shirts, Dutch china and island souvenirs, and casual jewelry. A small deli section has Dutch chocolates, cheeses, and other specialties. *Bonaire Art Gallery* (10 Kaya Gerbats; 7120) carries works by local artists. *Donzie* (on the waterfront; 7642) and *Things Bonaire* (38c Kaya Grandi; 8423) stock art, accessories, custom jewelry and clothing. *Fundashon Arte Boneriano* (by the post office) has local handicrafts, souvenirs, and art.

DIVE AND SPORTING GOODS: Some stores in town have masks and fins, but you will find the best stocks of quality dive equipment in the dive shops at hotels. *S.G. Soliana/A. Kaluf & Co.* (Kaya Grandi) specializes in bicycles and sporting goods.

PERFUMES AND COSMETICS: *d'Orsy's* (Harborside), a member of a chain found in

Aruba and throughout the Netherlands Antilles has a good selection of French perfumes.

DINING AND RESTAURANTS

Bonaire has a surprising selection of restaurant offering fresh seafood and continental specialties but some of the best, such as *Beefeater,* are ope for dinner only. Those listed here are generall open daily, but some may close Sunday o Monday. Check locally. Entries range from inex pensive (less than $9) and moderate ($10–$20 to expensive (over $20).

Green Parrot (on the water by the Sand Dolla Beach Club; 5454). Large menu of fresh seafood broiled steaks, hamburgers, salads, and more for lunch and dinner. Moderate.

Harbor Village Beach, (by the yacht harbor 7500). Bonaire's prettiest and most charmin hotel has an attractive dining terrace overlookin the swimming pool and beautiful gardens Expensive.

Mi Poron Bar and Restaurant (1 Kay. Caracas; 5199). In the courtyard of a histori Bonairean home, you dine on home-cooke meals of local fare. At the entrance is a quaint lit tle museum, reflecting a typical Bonairean inte rior of bygone days. Open Tuesday to Saturda for lunch and dinner; Sunday, dinner onl Inexpensive.

La Sonrisa (Kaya Grandi; 5017). A bar/restau rant in town serves local cuisine in a local atmos phere. Some of the specialties are *calabas* (a ste of calabash, pig's feet, goat meat, and vegetable that's better than it sounds); *goat stew,* Caribbean favorite on many islands; and fres fish. Inexpensive.

't Ankertje (which means "little anchor" i Dutch) is a little outdoor cafe with about si tables run by Dutch couple, Elke and Gerbe Hartskeerl. Located near the pier overlookin the water, this unassuming place offers heap ing portions for a reasonable price. Inexpensive

Zeezicht Bar and Restaurant (10 Curaçao straat, near the pier). Established in 1929, it specialties are fresh fish and *nasi goring,* a

ndonesian dish. "Happy Hour" at 4:15 P.M.
eatures live musical entertainment. Moderate.

NIGHTLIFE

he nightlife on Bonaire is low-key, in keeping
ith the ambience of the island. *E Wowo* (Kaya
randi), a long-established disco and nightclub,
 on the second floor of one of its oldest and
ost picturesque Dutch colonial buildings in
ralendijk.

Bonaire has casinos at *Dive Flamingo Beach
lotel*, and *Plaza Resort Bonaire.* Minimum age
 eighteen.

SPORTS

3EACHES/SWIMMING: On Bonaire you have
he choice of powdery white sand, pretty pink, or
lack-sand beaches. Most are small reef-protected
oves with exceptionally clear water. The best
wimming is on the leeward, or western, side
/here the waters are calm. Swimming on the
/indward side is generally not recommended due
o the strong waves and currents.

Soroban Beach Resort is a clothes-optional
esort with a private beach on Lac Bay. Nonguests
re welcome to use the resort's facilities for a
mall fee.

Pink Beach on the southwest coast takes its
ame from the pinkish tint of the sand, enhanced
y the light of the late-afternoon sun. Popular with
Bonaireans on the weekends, it is delightfully
mpty during the week.

IKING: Bonaire has more than 100 miles of
rails ranging from goat paths to unpaved roads.
ocal bike shops offer bike rentals and guided
ours.

OATING: Sailing yachts offer half-day and full-
ay excursions; most serve beverages and snacks.
he *Oscarina* (8988) has trips to Klein Bonaire
or swimming and snorkeling, at $35 per person,
alf-day; $70 full day.

DEEP-SEA FISHING: Half- and full-day charters
with all provisions are available through water-
sports operators. Bonaire's offshore fishing
grounds beyond the Marine Park are abundant
with mackerel, tuna, wahoo, barracuda, and
swordfish, to name a few. *Piscatur Charters*
(Capt. Chris Morkos, 8774; fax: 599–7–8380)
has deep-sea fishing trips with gear, bait, beer,
soda, and sandwiches: half-day, 4 persons, $275;
and full-day, $425. The tackle shop also arranges
reef-fishing, as well as bonefishing and tarpon
fishing in the shallows.

HIKING: The best hiking is on the trails and footpaths of the national park. (See section on the
Washington/Slaagbaii National Park.) You can
arrange for a naturalist guide at the park entrance
for US $6.

HORSEBACK RIDING: *Warahama Ranch*
(599–7–5558), something of an American dude
ranch in the Caribbean, is in the southern wilderness of the island. It offers riding, horse shows,
and carriage rides, and two playgrounds and a
petting zoo for children.

KAYAKING: Kayaks can be rented from most dive
shops. Bonaire's calm waters are ideal for kayaking. Kayaks are available to explore Lac Bay, a
lagoon with mangroves, which are a nursery for
fish life; to view the coast; or to visit Klein Bonaire.

SNORKELING/SCUBA DIVING: Bonaire is one
of the world's leading scuba-diving locations
with more than eighty beautiful dive spots along
its magnificent reefs. Rave reviews come from
experienced divers because of the great variety
and quality of marine life; beginners like it
because of the ease and accessibility of the reefs.
Indeed there is no better place in the Caribbean
to learn to scuba or snorkel. In many places, you
can wade from the shore to the reefs, to enjoy
unlimited viewing and diving from the beach any
time of the day or night. Bonaire is also the first
Caribbean island to have a full-fledged snorkeling program. It teaches participants about the
reefs and provides trained guides to take them
on reef tours. Tours are available at twelve locations and each provides a different experience.
They are offered one to three times a day,
depending on demand; cost is about $20 plus
equipment rental (if you do not bring your own

gear). Tours can be booked through any dive shop in Bonaire.

The best reefs are within the protected lee of the island, where most of the diving and other recreational activity takes place. Here the reefs have a narrow, sloping terrace extending seaward to a dropoff at 33 feet. This is followed by a slope varying from 30 feet to a vertical wall, extending to a depth of 100 to 200 feet. Among the places for walk-in snorkeling and scuba are the Thousand Steps, on the north coast at Barcadera, and farther north at Nukove, where you can picnic and watch birds.

Bonaire is one of the Caribbean's best-equipped dive centers; all hotels cater to divers and have excellent dive shops on their premises. They offer lessons at every level of training, as well as in underwater photography. And divers can hire an underwater camera person to videotape their diving experiences. Deluxe live-aboard boats that carry their own dive equipment are based here. Among the dive operators closest to the port are *Bonaire Scuba Center* (Box 200; 8975; 800–526–2370; fax: 8846); *Dive Bonaire* (Divi Flamingo Beach Resort; 8285; 800–367–3484; fax: 8238) and *Habitat Dive Center* (Box 88; 8290; 800–327–6709; fax: 8240). A list of the island's dozen or so dive operators and their services is available from the Bonaire Tourist Office

WINDSURFING: The constant trade winds tha keep the island cool make Bonaire an idea location for windsurfing. All beachfront resort have windsurf equipment. *Windsurfing Bonaire* (Box 301; 5363) offers rentals: 1 hour, $20, t full day, $50, lessons, $25. A shuttle bus from west-coast resorts to Windsurfing Bonaire's bas at Lac Bay departs at 9:00 A.M. and 1:00 P.M.; an it returns at 1:00 P.M. and 5:00 P.M. There, *Jib City* (7363) rents boards for $20 an hour o $50 per day.

FESTIVALS AND CELEBRATIONS

Carnival is celebrated in the traditional pre Lenten period, and there is a big Fishin Tournament in March, but the biggest event of th year is the *Bonaire Sailing Regatta* in mi October. Started as a wager among friends tw decades ago, it has evolved into an official even Fishermen and yachtsmen from all over th Caribbean compete in different categories.

Curaçao

WILLEMSTAD

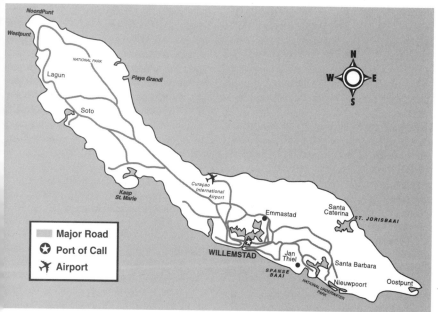

AT A GLANCE

CHAPTER CONTENTS

Curaçao

A DUTCH MASTERPIECE IN THE TROPICS

Known throughout its history as a center for international commerce with one of the world's busiest ports, Curaçao, the cosmopolitan capital of the Netherlands Antilles, has stepped into the role of a sun-drenched Caribbean resort rather recently. But over the past several years, in concert with private interests, the government has made up for lost time by renovating, upgrading, and expanding its many attractions. It has added sporting facilities, shopping plazas, a new cruise terminal and harborside park, as well as restored and beautified an extensive area around the port.

Lying 39 miles off the coast of Venezuela between Aruba and Bonaire, Curaçao is a surprising combination of worldliness and sophistication, resulting from its long trading tradition and polyglot culture, juxtaposed with a rugged landscape reminiscent of the American Southwest, with dry, cactus-covered reddish soil, undulating rocky hills, chalky mountains, and windswept shores. The land is greener toward the north and along the coast, where narrow waterways lead to large lagoons with fingers and islands used for commerce and sport. These waterways are Curaçao's most distinctive features and one of several elements that make it seem like a mini-Holland with palm trees.

Surrounded by beautiful reefs that divers are only now beginning to discover, Curaçao's rocky north coast is pounded by waves, while on the south a placid turquoise sea laps at small sandy coves. Uninhabited Klein Curaçao, lies to the southeast.

Cruise-ship passengers have the best vantage point for an introduction to this unusual island when they sail into Willemstad, the capital. There they are greeted by a colorful harborside of brightly painted and gabled Dutch colonial buildings dating from the 18th century. So distinctive is the setting that it has become Curaçao's signature and led others to call it a "Dutch masterpiece in the tropics."

The island's early inhabitants were the Caiquetios, an Arawak tribe that migrated north to the Caribbean from South America. Discovered in 1499 by the Spanish navigator Alonso de Ojeda, a lieutenant of Christopher Columbus, the Spanish made their first settlement here in 1527. But a century later the Dutch captured the island and founded their own settlement in 1634. It was made a colony of the Dutch West India Company, starting Curaçao's long trading tradition.

Over the next two centuries, the French and British, eager to have Curaçao for its natural harbors and strategic location, battled the Dutch for possession and dislodged them several times for a year or two. In 1642 a young Peter Stuyvesant was made governor, three years before being named director-general of the Dutch colony of New Amsterdam, which today we call New York.

Under the Dutch Curaçao was divided into plantations, some of which prospered on salt mining rather than agriculture. Slave trading was another important source of revenue. But after slavery was abolished here in 1863, Curaçao became a sleepy little island until 1914 when oil was discovered in nearby Venezuela.

Royal Dutch Shell Company, taking advantage of Curaçao's fine harbors, built one of the world's largest oil refineries here. It attracted trade, banks, and other commercial enterprises and created a prosperity that continued throughout the century. Curaçao's trading history had already made it an ethnic melting pot and the oil prosperity that brought workers from many nations enhanced the blend. Today Curaçao claims to be made up of more than forty nationalities.

FAST FACTS

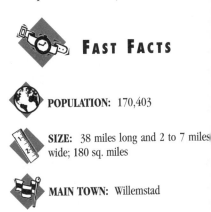

POPULATION: 170,403

SIZE: 38 miles long and 2 to 7 miles wide; 180 sq. miles

MAIN TOWN: Willemstad

GOVERNMENT: Curaçao is the largest, most populous of the Netherlands Antilles, which (with Aruba's departure 1 1986) consists of Curaçao, Bonaire, St. Maarten, Saba, and St. Eustatius. They form an autonomous region of the Kingdom of the Netherlands, with the seat of government in Willemstad. Their government is a parliamentary democracy with a governor appointed by the Dutch queen. There are three councils: legislative, executive, and advisory; and each island territory as its own legislative and executive body, called n Island Council whose members are elected for our years.

 CURRENCY: Netherlands Antilles guilder (NAf) divided into 100 florin or cents. US $1 equals NAf 1.77. U.S. dollars are widely accepted, and prices are often quoted in dollars.

 DEPARTURE TAX: US $12.50 (NAf 22.50) on international flights; US $9.00 (NAf 15) for interisland ones.

LANGUAGE: Dutch is the official language; English and Spanish are widely spoken. Papiamento is the local language and blends Dutch, Portuguese, English, French, Indian, and African words.

 PUBLIC HOLIDAYS: January 1, New Year's Day; Carnival Monday; Good Friday; Easter Monday; April 30, Queen's Birthday; May 1, Labor Day; Ascension Day; July 2, Flag Day; December 25–26, Christmas.

 TELEPHONE AREA CODE: From the United States, dial the prefix 011–599–9 followed by the local number.

 ## AIRLINES:

From New York and San Juan, ALM and American Airlines; and from Miami.

Interisland: ALM provides service to Trinidad and other destinations in the Caribbean and South America. ALM and Air Aruba serve the interisland routes between Curaçao, Aruba, Bonaire, and St. Maarten.

 INFORMATION:

In the United States: Curaçao Tourist Board: *New York:* 475 Park Avenue South, New York, NY 10016; (212) 683–7660; (800) 3–CURAÇAO; fax: (212) 683–9337. *Miami:* 330 Biscayne Boulevard, No. 808, Miami, FL 33132; (305) 374–5811; fax: (305) 374–6741.

In Port: Curaçao Government Tourist Bureau, Main office, Pietermaai 19, Curaçao, N.A.; (599) 461–6000; fax: 461–2305. STINAPA, Netherlands Antilles National Parks Foundation, P.O. Box 2090, Curaçao, N.A. 462–4242; fax: 462–7780.

 ## BUDGET PLANNING

Prices in Curaçao for restaurants and tourist services compare favorably with the rest of the Caribbean. Tourist attractions and facilities are rather spread out; hence touring by taxi tends to be expensive unless you can share costs. Car rentals are moderately priced and public buses inexpensive. You need have no hesitation about using buses since most people speak English and are helpful and friendly. If you like to walk and discover on your own you'll find Curaçao one of the most delightful ports in the Caribbean.

 ## PORT PROFILE:

LOCATION/EMBARKATION: Your ship's arrival in Curaçao will be one of the most interesting experiences of your cruise—don't miss it! Willemstad is built around Santa Anna Bay, a large deep-water lagoon, which is entered from the sea through a long, narrow finger whose waterfront is lined on both sides with colorful Dutch colonial buildings. The channel, which is 4,200 feet long and only 270 feet wide, opens onto the Schottegat, the inner harbor spanning 150 acres—the seventh-largest harbor in the world.

On the east side of the picturesque channel is the Punda, with Fort Amsterdam, the oldest part of town. The west side, where your ship docks, is known as Otrobanda (meaning, "the other side"). The two sides are connected by the Queen Emma Bridge, a century-old pontoon bridge that is a pedestrian walkway, near the dock.

Another bridge, the Queen Juliana—whose slender arched profile is in full view from the time your ship enters the harbor—is used for motor traffic. It spans Santa Anna Bay and connects the two sides of town to the roads that circumnavigate the bay. The bridge, 1,600 feet across, stands at a height of 185 feet; your ship is likely to pass directly under the bridge en route to its dock, and if the ship has a tall stack, watching the tricky maneuver can be a heart-stopping moment.

The port's passenger terminal has local and international telephones and a tourist information desk, and is walking distance to downtown shopping areas and attractions.

LOCAL TRANSPORTATION: Taxis are available at the port and taxi stands at hotels. Fares are set by the government, but should be agreed upon with the driver in advance. They are for up to four passengers; for a fifth passenger 25 percent is added; and there is an additional 25 percent surcharge after 11:00 P.M. Curaçao taxis can be identified by the sign on their roof and the letters TX after the license number. Sample fares from the port: to airport, $13 from Punda to Princess Beach, $10. Sight-seeing by taxi costs $20 an hour for one to four passengers, for a 1-hour minimum. Each additional quarter-hour or less is $5. To phone for a taxi, call 461–6711; to lodge a complaint, call 461–6577.

When you leave your ship (in Otrobanda) to go no farther than the downtown shopping area (Punda), it is better to walk across the pontoon bridge or take the free ferry; otherwise, a taxi must circle the long distance around the bay.

Public buses operate on regular schedules in Willemstad and to populated areas of the island. The central departure points are Waaigat (next to the post office) in Punda and Riffort in Otrobanda.

ROADS AND RENTALS: In its urban areas Curaçao has a good road network that fans out from Willemstad and the port on the south for radius of about 6 miles; and there are major east-west arteries crossing the island. But beyond these principal routes, rural roads are often dirt ones, which can become muddy after a heavy rain; inquire locally before leaving main highways. East and south of Willemstad, good roads run as far as Spaanse water (or Spanish Water), a large lagoon on the south coast beyond there are only a few dirt roads and tracks. On the west a major artery from Willemstad crosses the center of the island to the Christoffel Nature Park and Westpunt (West Point). En route it branches to the west coast in three places: Santa Marta Bay, San Juan, and Santa Cruz, where it continues via the coast to Westpunt. Road maps are available.

Car rentals are essential for touring on your own. You need a valid driver's license. Traffic moves on the right; road signs are in kilometers. Expect to pay about $40 and up for small car. Among the rental firms are Avis (461–1255); Budget (868–3198); Hertz (461–3622), which has Jeeps and Mini-Mokes and offers free pickup and delivery. Budget has Jeeps, too.

FERRY SERVICE: A free ferry crosses the harbor between Otrobanda and Punda regularly throughout the day; when the pontoon bridge is closed for traffic, pedestrians use the ferry.

INTERISLAND AIR SERVICE: See Fast Facts.

EMERGENCY NUMBERS:
Medical: St. Elisabeth Hospital,
Emergency, 462–4900.
Ambulance, 462–5822
Police: Dial 114

AUTHOR'S FAVORITE ATTRACTIONS

WILLEMSTAD WALKING TOUR WITH OLD CITY TOURS
DRIVE OR HIKE IN CHRISTOFFEL NATURE PARK
Animal Encounters AT THE SEAQUARIUM

SHORE EXCURSIONS

Cruise ships have tours to the island's best-known attractions, such as the Curaçao Seaquarium and Curaçao Liqueur Distillery, but Curaçao is not a cookie-cutter, beach-lined Caribbean island. It is different, and its differences are what make it interesting, particularly to those with curiosity, a fondness for history, and a sense of adventure. Several local companies offer tours for small groups that will give you a much better picture of this unusual island than standard tours can do. They also tailor tours to off-the-beaten-track places.

Walking Tours. The best walking tours of Willemstad are offered by *Old City Tours* (De Ruyterkade 53; 461–3554), whose architect/owner, Anko van der Woude, is the island's leading expert on historic architecture and usually leads the tour himself. The company has several programs of 2 to 3 hours, but with advance arrangements a program can be fitted to your interest.

Banda Ariba (East Side) or Banda Abao (West), 3.5 hrs., $15. The half-day tour to the east usually visits Landhuis Chobolobo, which houses the Curaçao Liqueur Distillery, and *Landhuis Rooi Catootje* (Curaçao Museum), with a collection of books, documents, and photos of Curaçao's history and its Jewish community; or Hato Caves.

A full-day tour to the west gives you a picture of country life in the 18th and 19th century and visits Landhuis Ascension, restored and furnished in its original style.

Trolley Train, 1.5 hours, $15. Guided city tour starting from Fort Amsterdam in a caboose-pulled open-sided trolley. Excellent guides. Operated by Miami-based ShorEx International (800–SHOREX–1).

Combination Tours, half-day, $28 per person. Some island sight-seeing, such as visiting the seaquarium, is combined with swimming or the Botanical Garden and Zoo, a drive west through the countryside, or a visit to a "cunucu" house or landhuis Jan Kok. *Taber Tours* (737–6637; fax: 737–9539).

CURAÇAO ON YOUR OWN

Willemstad is an architectural gem, best explored on foot. The heart of Willemstad, with its colorful historic buildings, straddles Santa Anna Bay. Punda, the east side, has a 5-block-square historic zone including Fort Amsterdam and the main shopping streets—all easily covered on foot. Otrobanda, the west side, is more residential and has clusters of old buildings, newly renovated as shopping and restaurant complexes.

A WILLEMSTAD WALKABOUT

Since 1987 Curaçao has put an extraordinary effort into the renovation of the city center, adding many new facilities. YOU ARE HERE signs with maps of the downtown shopping area are posted at the cruise terminal and other key locations.

QUEEN EMMA PONTOON BRIDGE (2) It is only a short walk from the dock (1) to the Queen Emma Pontoon Bridge that connects the Otrobanda and Punda. The bridge swings open regularly to allow ships to pass. The first pontoon bridge was built in 1888 by L. B. Smith, an American entrepreneur from Maine whose ships brought the first ice (packed in sawdust) to Curaçao; he was also involved in building Curaçao's first power and water plant. A series of postage stamps commemorates his achievements.

HANDELSKADE When you cross the ponton to the east bank, you arrive on Handelskade, the harborfront street lined with brightly painted 18th-century buildings complete with gables and red-tiled roofs. They were once offices of trading companies and warehouses, and were it not for their vivid colors under the bright Caribbean sun, you might imagine yourself in Amsterdam. The red tiles of the roofs came from Europe as ballast in ships. For their return voyages the ships were filled with salt, a major commodity in world trade in colonial days that was used in curing fish and preserving foodstuffs.

Directly in front is the *Penha building* (3), the town's oldest (corner of Handelskade and Breedestraat). Molded on the top is the date 1708, the year of its construction. As you walk along the narrow streets, you will see many old buildings similarly marked. The Penha building was once a social club with a gallery from which members could watch the passing harbor traffic; today it houses one of the town's leading department stores.

Breedestraat, historically, has been a major thoroughfare of Punda and Otrobanda and can be used as a focal point for your walk. (Incidentally, *straat* is Dutch for street; we have rendered street names as they appear locally in the conviction that they are easier to follow, if not always to pronounce.) On the south is Fort Amsterdam; on the north the shopping streets and several important historic buildings. Look down Breedestraat and you will see typical Dutch colonial–style galleries with their unusual short, round columns.

FORT AMSTERDAM (4) Originally constructed in 1634 to protect the harbor entrance, Fort Amsterdam was the largest and most important of the eight forts protecting Curaçao from 1648 to 1861, when the capital was a walled city. Now restored, the fort serves as the seat of government. Within its mustard-colored walls are the

governor's residence, several government offices and the 18th-century Dutch Reformed Church.

The governor's mansion is a classic colonial structure whose entrance opens onto a courtyard with buildings that house the offices of the Central Government. Some buildings have retained their old elements, such as heavy oak beams, wide-pegged floorboards, and hand-blown glass windows.

FORT CHURCH (5) Across the courtyard, the church dating from 1766 occupies the site where a church has stood since the Protestants first came to Curaçao in 1635. Owned by the United Protestant Community of Curaçao since 1824, the first church was probably a wooden shed that served the military garrison at the fort. According to old town maps, by 1707 it had been replaced by a stone building. The church was rebuilt and expanded many times.

By the southwest corner of the fort is a small *plaza* (6) with a statue of Manuel Piar, a gift from Venezuela to Curaçao in memory of one of Curaçao's native sons. Piar, a freedom fighter under the South American liberator Simón Bolívar, was the first foreigner to become a Venezuelan general.

WATERFORT ARCHES (7) On the south side of the fort, by the sea, the turreted and vaulted ramparts were added in 1826 and 1830 to strengthen the fortifications and house provisions. In 1988 the

MAP LEGEND FOR WALKING TOUR OF WILLEMSTAD

1. Dock
2. Queen Emma Pontoon Bridge
3. Penha building
4. Fort Amsterdam
5. Fort Church
6. Plaza Piar
7. Waterfront Arches
8. Wilhelmina Park
9. Police Office
10. Courthouse, Council, Bank of Boston
11. Temple Theatre
12. Mikve Israel-Emanuel Synagogue and Museum
13. Floating Market
14. Central Market
15. Post Office
16. Wilhelmina Bridge
17. Plaza Jojo Correa
18. Gomezplein
19. Riffort
20. Koral Agnosti

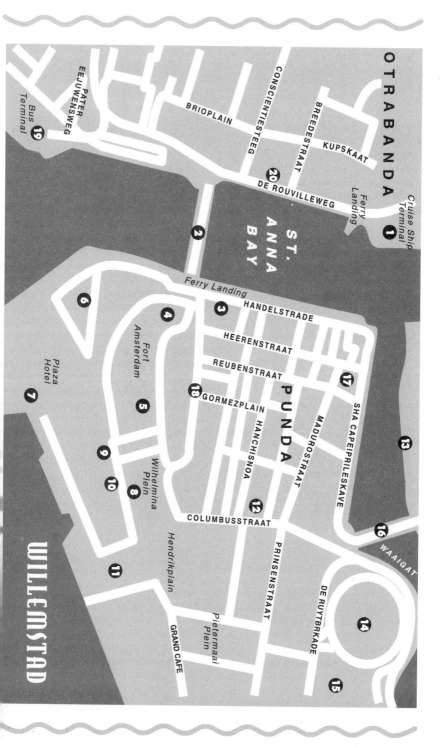

vaults adjacent to the Van der Valk Plaza Hotel were restored and converted into the Waterfort Arches, a plaza with shops, restaurants, and a seaside promenade where you can stroll along the ramparts. If you were on hand to watch your ship sail into port, you can see why the hotel, built directly on the foundations of fortress walls, is one of the few in the world with marine collision insurance.

Attached to the sea wall below the hotel are links of a heavy iron chain used in olden days for protection against invaders. The chain was placed across the mouth of the harbor, attaching it at the *Riffort* (19), the counterpart fortification on the west side. Built in 1828, the now restored Riffort houses a police station and *Bistro Le Clochard,* a restaurant with great harbor views.

WILHELMINA PARK (8) East of Fort Amsterdam beyond the *police office* (9) is the Wilhelmina-plein, a small park with a statue of Queen Wilhelmina. On its south are several imposing *buildings* (10). The first, with an impressive balustrade, houses the Council, or parliament, and Courthouse; another, in Georgian style, was built as a Masonic Temple in 1869.

If you were to continue east for a mile or so, beyond the Avila Beach Hotel—too far to walk—you would come to the Octagon House, a museum dedicated to Simón Bolívar. On two occasions Curaçao gave asylum to Bolívar during his struggle to free South America of Spanish rule. The house was visited by Bolívar when his sisters lived there. Hours: weekdays 8:00 a.m.–noon and 2:00–6:00 p.m. Admission is free.

Crossing to the north side of Wilhelmina Park, you read Columbusstraat, which marked the outer city walls until 1861.

MIKVE ISRAEL-EMANUEL SYNAGOGUE AND MUSEUM (12) At the corner of Hanchi Snoa is the oldest synagogue in continuous use in the Western Hemisphere. Built in 1732, some of its artistic treasures are even older than the synagogue itself, dating back to the founding of the congregation in 1651 by twelve families from Amsterdam. At services a prayer for the Dutch Royal Family is chanted in old Portuguese, which was once the common language of the Curaçao Jewish community.

The courtyard museum has artifacts, memorabilia, and replicas of the oldest, most elaborate gravestones in Beth Haim Cemetery, dating from 1659 and said to be the oldest Jewish cemetery in the Western Hemisphere. It is located on the north side of the bay. The architecture of the synagogue, with its curved gables and short columns, is interesting inside and out. As an example, the half columns on the facade do not support the building—they are hollow and function as drains for rainwater. The interior is rich with brasswork and woodwork. The symbolism of the white sand on the floor has several interpretations: the wandering of the Jews in the desert; the muffling of the sounds of secret services during the Spanish Inquisition; or God's promise to Abraham that his descendants would be "countless as the sand." Hours: weekdays 9:00–11:45 A.M. and 2:30–5:00 P.M. There is an entrance fee. Visitors are welcome to attend Sabbath services; tie and jacket are required.

FLOATING MARKET (13) Continuing on Columbusstraat to Madurostraat (another demarcation of the old city walls), you can turn left (west) to see some outstanding examples of rococo gables. The first lane on your right (north) leads to a canal with a picturesque floating market. Each week schooners from Venezuela come here to sell their fruits and vegetables in the open-air market shaded by the sails of the boats. There are also fishermen selling snapper, grouper, conch, and other fish from local waters. Up the street to the east, the large, round building is the *Central Market* (14), a modern town market—but with as much bustle as any Caribbean marketplace. It has a bar and native market-style buffet restaurant serving local food.

Behind the Central Market is the *post office* (15) which has a philatelic window. In front of the market, the *Wilhelmina Bridge* (16) connects Punda with Scharloo, formerly a wealthy residential quarter of early Jewish merchants. The architecture of this area ranges from 18th-century Dutch colonial to Victorian gingerbread. Over the past decade most of these mansions have been restored as private homes or offices; the drive along here is one of the main attractions of a city tour.

Walk west to *Plaza Jojo Correa* (**17**). You will probably see your ship docked across the bay. Stop and look back (northeast) across the channel to the Wilhelmina Bridge and Waaigat for a nice view. At the plaza turn south onto Heerenstraat, one of the main shopping streets, which has several buildings with elaborate gables. At the end of the street is the Penha building, where you began. If you want to take a break, Gomezplein (**18**) is a pretty pedestrian mall with park benches.

OTROBANDA

A walk around Otrobanda, except for the immediate vicinity of the port and Breedestraat, is difficult without a guide. The most picturesque parts are a labyrinth of narrow winding lanes lined with colorful old buildings and private houses, often unmarked and surrounded by garden walls. You need a guide to point out the historic and architectural features that have made them landmarks. A pamphlet, "Discover the Spirit of Historic Curaçao," has a walking tour with a useful map, prepared by the Chamber of Commerce and Curaçao Tourist Bureau. It is a little outdated, but if you have a good sense of direction and an adventurous spirit, you could use it for a self-guided walk. If you are truly interested in history, arrange to visit with Old City Tours, whose architect-owner has been a driving force behind the area's preservation.

Next to the port are the *Arawak Craft Products*, in a former warehouse, and *Kas di Alma Blou*, a new art gallery and gift shop in a 19th-century colonial house, which is gaily painted bright blue with white trim. South of the port terminal on the waterfront is a group of restored buildings known as *Koral Agostini* (**20**), which date from 1737. It has small shops, the *Carleton Cantina*, a sidewalk cafe, and *Rumrunners*, a popular balcony restaurant and tapa bar with live Latin and Caribbean music on weekends.

At Breedestraat, Otrobanda's main shopping street, turn west for 2 blocks to St. Anna Church (**21**). One block south is Conscientiesteeg, the oldest lane of the quarter; and directly south of it on Sebastopolstraat, the Sebastopol House is a good example of an 18th-century style that combined elements of a colonial townhouse with those of a plantation house.

West on Conscientiesteeg past *La Moda de Paris*, once the leading clothing shop in town, to the end of the street, a turn south for one block takes you to one of the most attractive areas, with a block of renovated townhouses called "The Four Alley." Farther south at Zaantjessteeg and Gravenstraat, there is a group of fine houses with their original entrances and pretty gardens facing Pater Eeuwensweg. The houses once overlooked a lagoon that had bridges leading to the Rif area, a sort of lovers' lane in olden days.

You can return to the port via the Riffort area or via Breedestraat for a stop at the *Netto Bar*, a famous neighborhood rendezvous where you can buy Cuban cigars (but smoke them before you go back through U.S. Customs, because agents are likely to confiscate them). On your return you will pass any number of wonderful houses that have been renovated.

CURAÇAO MUSEUM (Van Leeuwenhoeskstraat; 462–3777) A mile or more from Riffort is the Curaçao Museum, housed in a building dating from 1853. Originally it was used as a military hospital—and not a former plantation house, or *landhuis*, as is sometimes said, although the style is similar. The museum covers the island's history from pre-Columbian times to the Dutch colonial period and has some artifacts of this century.

Permanent exhibits include a replica of a typical kitchen of the colonial era, antique furniture, old industrial tools, and household utensils. You will find old maps of Curaçao and the Caribbean, a natural-history section, and a garden with island plants and trees. In addition to a permanent collection of contemporary art, the museum organizes exhibitions of works by local artists. In 1987 the *Children's Science Museum*, financed by the Rotary Club, was added. It has hands-on models of local industries. Hours: Tuesday to Saturday 9:00 A.M.–noon and 2:00–5:00 P.M.; Sunday 10:00 A.M.–4:00 P.M. Entrance is NAf 4 for adults; NAf 1 for children. On the first Sunday of each month, a concert is given in the gardens from 4:30 to 6:30 P.M.

On the south side of Otrobanda by the sea is

the Rif Recreation Center, and on the western edge, Piscadera Bay, a popular resort area with several hotels and the modern Convention and Trade Center. *Koredor,* a seafront recreational area on Piscadera Bay has a jogging track, playground, and picnic area, and the *Sundance Health & Fitness Center.*

The *Curaçao Sonesta Hotel,* which opened in 1992, was the island's first international chain hotel in two decades. The deluxe resort, set in tropical gardens, has three restaurants, a casino, pool with swim-up bar, a health club with four tennis courts, and water sports. A welcome addition, the outstanding hotel, designed in Curaçao's classic architecture, is credited with rejuvenating Curaçao's tourism (and hence its economy), and setting new standards for all the island's hotels and restaurants.

WILLEMSTAD ENVIRONS

You can circle Santa Anna Bay from Piscadera Bay on the west by taking the highway around the bay to the east, or cross over on Queen Juliana Bridge. East of the bridge on the right (south) on a hill is *Roosevelt House,* the U.S. Consul General's residence, a gift from Curaçao to the United States for its assistance in World War II.

After another mile along the highway, a large modern monument depicting six birds leaving the mother's nest commemorates the Netherlands Antilles becoming autonomous in 1954. North of the monument is the *Amstel Brewery,* said to be the only factory in the world that brews beer from distilled seawater. Tours are offered by appointment.

LANDHUIS CHOBOLOBO On the eastern edge of Willemstad in an 17th-century *landhuis* is the Curaçao Liqueur Distillery, where the orange-flavored liqueur Curaçao is made. (The distillery celebrated its 100th anniversary in 1996.) The early Spaniards planted the Valencia orange in Curaçao, and after adapting to the aridity and red-clay soil, it bore a fruit too bitter to eat—but an oil extracted from its skin proved to be suitable for making liqueur. The colorful bottles make distinctive gifts to take home. Tours are available weekdays 8:00 A.M.–noon and 1:00–5:00 P.M. (737–8459).

LANDHUIS ROOI CATOOTJE Since 185? another plantation house, on a hillside beyon the Curaçao Liqueur Distillery, has been in th Maduro family, one of Curaçao's oldest and best known families. After the owner died in 1974, hi heirs converted the home into a library to hous his unusual collection of books, documents, an photos relating to Curaçao's history, particularl its Jewish community. Visits are by appointmen (737–5119).

If you detour in a northerly direction alon Schottegatweg, you pass Peter Stuyvesant Hig School, which has a statue of Peter Styvesant in schoolyard—a reminder of Curaçao's early Nev York connection.

LANDHUIS BRIEVENGAT About 9 miles on th northeast, you will see an early 18th-centur plantation house that was a twelve-thousand acre cattle ranch until the mid-19th century. I was saved from demolition by the Preservation c Monuments Foundation, which restored it i 1954 as a cultural center. It has exhibits fron colonial times, a bar, and a restaurant with ea shattering music (737–8344).

A DRIVE AROUND THE ISLAND

WEST OF WILLEMSTAD

Too often cruise passengers confine their visit t Willemstad and miss some of Curaçao's be attractions: rugged windswept terrain, prett inland lagoons, adobe houses, and patchwor fields with fences of neatly crisscrossed candl cactus where sheep and goats graze, plus two the best nature parks in the Caribbean. These a all the more fascinating for their obvious contra to Curaçao's cosmopolitan capital.

The road crosses the tranquil countryside, c *cunucu (kunuku),* an Arawak word original used to mean a piece of land given by a landown to a slave to grow crops for his personal nee The dry landscape is covered with cactus th grows as tall as trees and the ever-present divi-d tree whose wind-sculpted branches grow in on direction at a right angle from the trunk.

Dotting the countryside are former plantation houses, or *landhuizen* some dating back to 1650. Most were surrounded by walls and fortified against marauding pirates and rebelling slaves. About sixty houses remain, and several are maintained as museums.

LANDHUIS DANIEL Just beyond the Santa Maria turn off at Daniel is one of the island's oldest plantation houses, dating from 1634. Landhuis Daniel was never a farmhouse, but a rest stop for travelers and their horses traversing the island. The house has been restored and once again is a rest stop with ten rooms, a pool, and facilities for diving nearby (864–8222).

LANDHUIS JAN KOCK At Daniel the road forks west to Sint Willibrordus, a village, and the 17th-century Landhuis Jan Kock, where once salt from nearby ponds was produced for the herring industry in Holland. The manor house has a bar, some furniture made from the mahogany that once grew on the plantation, and fanciful, crudely painted murals.

HATO CAVES Set on a bluff on the north coast near the airport, the ancient caves were recently renovated, lighted, and made more accessible. The caverns have stalagmites, stalactites, and bats. Beautiful orange and black orioles, known here as troupial, flit about in nearby trees, and iguanas scamper in the undergrowth near the snack bar and souvenir shop at the caves' entrance (868–0379). Hours: daily except Monday, 10:00 A.M. to 5:00 P.M.; guided tours on the hour until 4:00 P.M. Admission: US $4.25 adults; US $2.75 children.

CHRISTOFFEL NATURE PARK On the hilly north end of the island is a 3,500-acre nature park whose most prominent feature is Curaçao's highest peak: 1,238-foot Mt. Christoffel. The park begins north of Mt. Hyronimus, a tabletop mountain, and comprises three contingent plantations—Savonet, Zorgvlied, and Zevenbergen—acquired by the government and managed by STINAPA. The *Savonet Museum of Natural and Cultural History* near the park entrance is housed in Landhuis Savonet, the former estate house.

The park, opened to the public in 1978, has more than five hundred varieties of plants and trees, an estimated 150 resident and migrant bird species, iguana, feral donkeys, and the Curaçao deer. You can see unusual rock formations, caves with bats, and Indian petroglyphs. The vegetation is dry with abundant mesquite, century plants, divi-divi, and gigantic cactus.

Twenty miles of road, divided into four color-coded signposted routes, wind through the park. Three are driving routes of about an hour, each highlighting different points of interest. The fourth route is a footpath to the top of Mt. Christoffel. A nature guide for hiking, birding, and deer watching can be arranged through the tourist office. Hours: daily from 8:00 A.M. to 3:00 P.M.

Savonet Route is a good introduction to the park's vegetation and to the most common trees and plants of Curaçao. It starts at the visitor's center and winds through the eastern part to the north coast. You might see one of the two hummingbird species—ruby topaz and blue-tailed emerald—which breed here. Near the center of the area is a watch tower from which hikers can spot Curaçao deer come to a nearby watering trough.

Zorgvlied Route is a 90-minute circuit through the central and north areas; it returns along the eastern flank of Mt. Christoffel, crossing the footpath to the summit. Two abundant trees and plants are the *calabash,* whose large fruit has a hard shell used throughout the Caribbean since the time of the Arawaks as a bowl and cooking utensil; and the enormous *kadushi,* a type of candle cactus, used to make cactus soup.

Zevenbergen Route winds over the undulating hills of the southwest. The trail to the top of Mt. Christoffel offers grand vistas extending the length of the island, and, on a clear day, as far east as Bonaire and south to Venezuela. The hike from the visitor's center is a 3-hour round-trip, but by driving to the base of the mountain, you can cut off an hour.

WESTPUNT An old fishing town, Westpunt, or West Point, on the rocky cliffs at the north end of the island sits above a quiet, turquoise sea. Below is a small beach of coarse sand, surrounded by walls of rock. From Westpunt you can return south through the undulating hills of the west coast where there are rocky coves with pretty little beaches, some reached by dirt roads.

LANDHUIS KNIP This recently restored plantation house is a good example of the island's 17th-century–style *landhuis.* By the sea, the dive resort, *Habitat,* a sister to Bonaire's famous *Capt. Don's Habitat,* opened in late 1996, underscoring Curaçao's newly found appeal as a dive destination.

On the south side of Santa Cruz, Santa Marta Bay is a large serpentine lagoon with beaches and rocky shores surrounded by green hillsides. The cultivation of the orange tree, from which the liqueur Curaçao is made, is a specialty of the area.

EAST OF WILLEMSTAD

CURAÇAO UNDERWATER PARK The biggest boost to the development of Curaçao as a dive center has been the creation of the fifteen-hundred-acre Curaçao Underwater Park, stretching for more than 12 miles from the Princess Beach Hotel, just west of Jan Thiel Lagoon, to the eastern tip of the island. Developed by STINAPA, the Netherlands Antilles National Parks Foundation, with a grant from the World Wildlife Fund of the Netherlands, it protects some of Curaçao's finest reefs, which can be enjoyed by snorkelers as well as divers. Jan Thiel Beach and Santa Barbara Beach provide access to the park where visibility is up to 150 feet. An excellent guidebook by the marine biologist Jeff Symbesma has an explanatory profile of the reef.

There are sixteen permanent mooring buoys for boats. The first mooring in front of the Princess Beach Hotel has diverse and colorful formations typical of Curaçao's reef structure. It starts in shallow water, suitable for snorkelers, where elkhorn and staghorn corals and gorgorians are abundant, dropping to 30 to 40 feet, from which the reef slopes at a 45-degree angle. The upper slope has mountain star coral, leaf coral, flower coral, and yellow pencil coral, as well as a variety of sponges. On the lower slope are brain corals, sheet coral, and star corals. The fish seen here are typical of Curaçao reefs, too, and include chromis, wrasses, four-eyed butterfly fish, and sergeant majors, among others.

SEAQUARIUM On the west end of the Marine Park is the Curaçao Seaquarium, a private facility with more than four hundred species of marine life native to Curaçao waters. The Seaquarium uses no chemicals, pumps, or filters in the tanks, helping to promote the natural reproduction of sea life. Hours: daily 10:00 A.M.–10:00 P.M. Admission is $12.50. Cruise-ship shore excursions usually visit the Seaquarium.

ANIMAL ENCOUNTERS Here's your chance to face down a shark or pet a stingray. Next to the Seaquarium divers can enter a 15-foot-deep open-water enclosure, which is a natural tidal pool, to play with the ray, angelfish, grouper, and other fish. At one end of the enclosure, divers are separated by a mesh fence from large sea turtles; on the other side, they can watch reef, lemon, and nurse sharks through a thick Plexiglas wall while they pass food to the sharks through small openings.

Admission is $50, which includes a full dive tank, wetsuit, weights, a bucket of fish, and a hour of basic instruction on the use of dive gear from a professional diver who will accompany you. Photographs or a video of you can be taken for an additional charge. It's probably as close to a shark as most people ever want to be, but it still thrilling. About half of those who participate are donning dive gear for the first time. (I recommend, however, that you have at least taken resort course.) Non-swimmers can watch from semi-submersible submarine at the site. Hours 8:30 A.M. to 5:30 P.M.

SPANISH WATER Near the eastern end of the island, Spaanse Water, or Spanish Water, one of the island's largest and most beautiful lagoons, is a sheltered natural harbor with many hilly green fingers and coves, islands and beaches, and long, very narrow opening to the sea. It is the island's boating and fishing center, with marinas and other water-sports facilities. The Curaçao Yacht Club is based here, and many Willemstad residents have weekend houses here.

East of Spanish Waters you can see a chalktable mountain, 637-foot Tafelberg, from almost any height on the island. At one time as much as 100,000 tons of phosphate were mined here yearly; mining continues on a small scale. Beyond to the east is an arid, desolate area of rocky, rugged terrain.

CURAÇAO OSTRICH FARM Across the island from the Seaquarium on the north coast at St. Jonis Bay is a farm, unique to Curaçao and the Caribbean; it's one of the biggest ostrich ranching operations outside Africa. Here you can see the majestic creatures, which are the world's fastest animals on two legs, and learn about all aspects of ostrich ranching in an Africa-like environment. Reservations: 560–1276.

SHOPPING

Willemstad's cosmopolitan ambience is reflected in its shops filled with goods from around the world, including an abundance of European items: from fine jewelry to designer fashions, perfumes, and Japanese electronics. Cruise passengers are usually most interested, however, in Dutch goods, such as chocolate, rounds of Edam and Gouda cheese, delftware, and even wooden clogs. Breedestraat and Heerenstraat are the main streets of Punda, where quality stores are housed in colorful 18th-century colonial buildings.

Curaçao is not a duty-free port, but in 1988 the government removed tariffs on most luxury items, so prices represent a savings of 20 to 30 percent off those in the United States. A knowledge of stateside prices is the best way to recognize a good bargain. "Curaçao Holiday," a free tourist pamphlet, has a keyed map of store locations that is a convenient reference guide.

Punda stores are open Monday to Saturday from 8:00 A.M. to noon and 2:30 to 6:00 P.M. Some remain open during lunch, particularly when cruise ships are in port. They also open for cruise passengers on Sundays and holidays, except Christmas and Good Friday.

ARTS AND ARTISTS: *Gallery 86* (Trompstraat, 3rd floor; on the waterfront; 461–3417) specializes in works by local and contemporary artists and has changing exhibitions. *Kas di Alma Blou* (67 De Rowieleweg, by the cruise terminal; 462–8896) sells art and gifts by local artists.

BOOKS AND MAPS: *Van Dorp* (Breedestraat) is one of the main bookstores.

CAMERAS AND ELECTRONICS: *Boolchand's* (Heerenstraat) and *Palais Hindu* (Heerenstraat) have large selections of photographic equipment and electronic gadgetry. Come with prices from home.

CLOTHING AND ACCESSORIES: The most easily recognized store in Curaçao is the yellow-and-white rococo front of *Penha & Sons,* a department store in the town's oldest building. It has a wide variety of goods from perfumes and designer clothes to delft china and cashmere sweaters. *Bamali Boutique* (Waterfort Arches) carries stylish fashions in Indonesian batik, plus art and wood carvings. *Benetton* (Madurostraat), the Italian coordinates king, claims discounts of 30 percent off European and stateside prices, but generally we have not found this to be the case. *Gifi* (Trompstraat 20) specializes in Italian designers such as Valentino, Krizia, and Armani. *Emilia* (Gomezplein), another trendy boutique, specializes in chic French and Belgian apparel for men, women, and children, including Naf Naf and European footwear.

CRAFTS AND SOUVENIRS: *Obra di Man* (Bargestraat in Scharloo) is both a shop and workshop for handmade folkloric dolls, wall hangings, ceramics, and other local crafts, with an outlet on Gomezplein. *Kas di Arte* (Breedestraat 126) stocks local crafts. *Arawak Craft Products* (at the port; 462–7249) makes replicas of *landhuizen,* plates, tiles, and other souvenirs; their products are also sold at souvenir shops.

GOURMET FOOD PRODUCTS: Rounds of Gouda or Edam can be purchased at supermarkets at about a 30 percent savings over U.S. prices. And don't forget Curaçao liqueur. *Zuikertuintje* (meaning "the sugar garden") is a supermarket in a 17th-century *landhuis* on the east side of town, just beyond the Curaçao Liqueur factory. It has selections of Dutch cheese and chocolates and a large assortment of European gourmet products—plus a cafe where you can sample some of the products.

JEWELRY: Among the best-known names is *Gandelman Jewelers* (Breedestraat 35), which creates its own designs, also sells Piaget and Movado watches and Gucci accessories.

LINENS: *New Amsterdam* (Breedestraat) is a variety store, with goods ranging from sports gear and Gottex swimsuits to Chinese cloisonné and Lladro figurines, but it is best known for fine linens. *Little Holland* (Breedestraat) has lovely linens, too.

PERFUMES AND COSMETICS: *Yellow House* (Breedestraat), the leading perfume shop, is as pretty as it is complete in its stock of French and other perfumes and cosmetics. It also carries Hummel figurines and other gifts.

DINING AND RESTAURANTS

Curaçao's long trading history and diverse population made up of Dutch, Portuguese Jews, Africans, Chinese, Indians, Indonesians, and a host of Europeans is reflected in its food and wide selection of restaurants. They range from pizza parlors and Dutch taverns to French bistros and elegant continental restaurants. Some offer harbor views, while others are set in historic forts and charming old plantation houses. Entries range from moderate (under $10) and moderately expensive ($10 to $25) to expensive (over $26).

For "criollo," or local fare, try *empana,* a pastry inherited from the Spaniards; *sopito,* a fish-and-coconut soup served with *funchi,* a cornbread taken from the Africans; *keshi yena,* a cheese shell filled with meat, learned from the Dutch; and *rijsttafel,* a multidish treat the Dutch learned in Indonesia.

Belle Terrace (Penstraat, Avila Beach Hotel; 461–4377). A small hotel that was once a governor's mansion has one of the leading restaurants near the harbor, specializing in old Curaçao recipes and seafood. Moderate.

Bistro Le Clochard (Riffort, Otrobanda; 462–5666). In this restaurant set in an old fortification and former prison by the harbor, you can sit almost close enough to touch the passing ships. The menu is French and continental with fresh seafood, veal, cheese fondue, and sinful desserts. Expensive.

De Taveerne (Landhuis Groot Develaar; 737–0669). Northeast of town in a charming old *landhuis* and furnished with 18th-century antiques, it offers international cuisine, grilled lobster, and some irresistible desserts. Moderately expensive.

Fort Nassau (461–3086). Known for its view, it offers a pretty hilltop setting overlooking Willemstad, as well as an ideal perch for an aperitif on its terrace bar. Moderately expensive.

Portofino Restaurant (Sonesta Beach Hotel; 736–8800). Situated in an air-conditioned dining room and an outdoor garden terrace, the delightful restaurant features a variety of Northern Italian dishes. The atmosphere is casual, but elegant. Moderately expensive.

Rijsttafel Indonesia (Mercuriusstraat 13; 461–2606). In Salinja, just east of Princess Beach, it has as good a *rijstaffel* as you will find east of Indonesia. Moderate.

Golden Star (Socratesstraat 2; 465–4795). The informal Curaçaoan bar/restaurant is not much to look at, but it's everyone's favorite for criollo cuisine. You can try a zesty *carco stoba* (conch stew), *bestia chiki* (goat-meat stew), *bakijou* (salted cod), *locrio* (a chicken-mixed rice), *concomber stoba* (stewed meat and cucumber), fish, and *funchi.* Moderate.

NIGHTLIFE

Most of Curaçao's nightlife centers around hotels, restaurants that have music for listening or dancing, and discos. Five hotels have casinos; the closest to the port is *Van der Valk Plaza Hotel,* and the newest is the *Curaçao Sonesta Beach.* There are popular bars for happy hour, piano bars for a quiet rendezvous, and seaside cafes where you can watch the parade of people and ships.

Facade (Salinja; 461–4640), a nightclub, has live music several nights a week. *Blues Cafe* (Avila Beach Hotel; 461–4377) offers jazz by leading local musicians at the center of the night action on the east side of town. The Latin in the Curaçaoans comes out most in their popular music and dance. Tumba music is Curaçao's answer to salsa.

SPORTS

Most of the island's hotels and water-sports centers are located along the south coast immediately east and west of Willemstad. They welcome day visitors.

BEACHES/SWIMMING: Several beaches on the leeward coast within a mile or so of Willemstad have been developed. They have changing facilities and water sports; there is an admission fee. There are pretty bays and coves with beaches, which swimmers are likely to have to themselves, except perhaps on weekends. You will find free public beaches at Westpunt, Knip, Klein Knip, and Daaibooi. Private beaches, charging a fee per car, are Blauw Bay and Jan Thiel, which have changing facilities. On the southeast Santa Barbara, at the entrance to Spanish Water, is a popular beach with Curaçaoans. The windward coast generally is too turbulent for safe swimming.

BOATING: A cruise along the coast to Klein Curaçao off Curaçao's eastern end, to enjoy its sandy beaches and snorkeling is a favorite sailing excursion offered by water-sports operators. A full-day sail on the *Insulinde*, a 120-foot traditionally rigged sailing vessel, is $55 (560–1340); *Vira Cocha* (767–6003), a Norwegian sailing ship, departs daily from the Seaquarium Marina on picnic and snorkeling cruises for $25–$29 per person.

DEEP-SEA FISHING: Half-day charters for about $300 and full-day ones for about $600 leave from major hotels and the marinas at Spanish Water almost daily, offering great deep-sea fishing for four to six persons, with tackle and bait provided. Arrangement can be made through water-sports operators. Anglers go for marlin, tuna, wahoo, sailfish, and other large fish. Only hook and line fishing is permitted in the Curaçao Underwater Park.

GOLF AND SQUASH: The *Curaçao Golf and Squash Club* (Wilhelminalaan, Emmastad; 37–3590) welcomes visitors. The strong winds and sand greens of the 10-hole course are the challenge. Clubs and pullcarts are available for rent. Green fee $15. There is a clubhouse with bar, open daily in the morning. The club also has two squash courts open daily from 8:00 A.M. to 6:00 P.M. There are special hours for visitors.

HIKING: The best hiking is in the Christoffel Nature Park where marked routes highlight special features and show the variety of Curaçao's natural features and attractions. Many parts of the north coast have only dirt tracks, where hikers can enjoy the wild desolate scenery of strong waves breaking against rock shores.

HORSEBACK RIDING: *Rancho Alegre* (Landhuis Groot St. Michiel; 868–1181) and *Ashari Ranch* (Kaya Groot Piscadera A-23; 869–0315) offer riding in the countryside. Arrangements should be made in advance.

SNORKELING/SCUBA DIVING: Long overshadowed by its sister island of Bonaire for diving, Curaçao is only now beginning to get the attention it deserves. The island is surrounded by fringing reef, much of which is virgin territory. The structure comprises gently sloping terraces, shallow walls, and sheer dropoffs. The marine park protects some of Curaçao's finest reefs and can be enjoyed by snorkelers as well as divers. (See the Curaçao Underwater Park section earlier in this chapter.)

In addition, Curaçao has more than three dozen coves and beaches with reefs within swimming distance from shore at places that can be reached by car. One of the most convenient is Blauw Bay, 5 miles from Willemstad, just west of Piscadera Bay.

Curaçao Watersports Operator Association (868–8044; fax: 868–8114) is made up of the island's main water-sports operators, dive shops, and tourism interests. Most operators are located at hotels and can make arrangements for fishing, water skiing, day sailing, and glass-bottom boat excursions, as well as diving and snorkeling.

TENNIS: Courts are available at the Curaçao Caribbean, Sonesta Beach, Holiday Beach, and Princess Beach hotels.

WINDSURFING: The strong trade winds that cool the island and shape the divi-divi trees have also made windsurfing one of Curaçao's most popular sports, with international recognition and an

Olympic champion. Annually in June, the *Curaçao Open International Pro-Am Windsurf Championship* attracts the masters from around the world. The meet is an official stop on the Caribbean World Tour and is sanctioned by the Professional Windsurfer's Association as a part of the World Cup title. The most popular windsurfing area is on the southeast coast between Princess and Jan Thiel beaches, which is also the venue for the annual championships. The protected waters of Spanish Water are best for novices. *Top Watersports Curaçao* (by the Seaquarium; Box 3102; 461–6666; fax: 461–3671) specializes in windsurfing. It rents boards and offers lessons. It also rents other water-sports equipment.

FESTIVALS AND CELEBRATIONS

Curaçao gets the year off to a good start with *Carnival* and closes it with a big *Christmas*— after all, jolly ole St. Nick was Dutch. In between there is a full calendar of sports and cultural events. In addition to the international windsurfing competitions, Curaçao hosts a big fishing tournament in spring, the *Troubadours Song Festival* usually in July, and the *Curaçao Jazz Foundation Festival* in November.

Aruba

Oranjestad

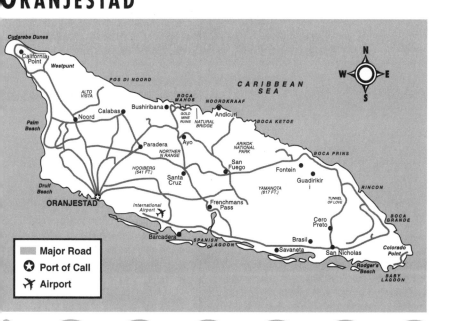

AT A GLANCE

Antiquities	★
Architecture	★
Art and Artists	★
Beaches	★★★★★
Colonial Buildings	★★
Crafts	★
Cuisine	★★★
Culture	★
Dining/Restaurants	★★★★
Entertainment	★★★
Forts	★
History	★
Monuments	★
Museums	★
Nightlife	★★★★
Scenery	★★★
Shopping	★★
Sight-seeing	★★★
Sports	★★★★
Transportation	★★★

CHAPTER CONTENTS

Aruba

ISLAND OF SURPRISES

By any measure Aruba is an unusual island. It combines city polish, frontier ruggedness, and a people who are as warm and gracious as they are ingenious. Dutch orderly and clean, this modern miracle was little more than sand and brush four decades ago. Now the island is one of the most popular, sophisticated destinations in the Caribbean, with tourist facilities catering to visitors from three continents. And it never stops. New hotels, restaurants, shops, and other attractions continue to pop up, adding to Aruba's already impressive range and variety.

In contrast to the glitter and glamour of its resorts, Aruba's arid, rocky terrain is similar to the American Southwest. The land is flat, except for the 541-foot-Hooiberg—a conical-shaped hill rising in the center of the island—and small, undulating hills on the north side. Yet for a small, low-lying island, Aruba has surprisingly diverse landscape and natural attractions.

Located only 15 miles off the coast of Venezuela, Aruba is rung by coral reefs. Its leeward coast, where tourist development has been concentrated, has miles of calm, palm-fringed white-sand beaches, which are among the most beautiful in the Caribbean. In contrast, strong winds and big waves crash against the northeast coast, where the landscape is as desolate as the surface of the moon. Along the rockbound shores are coves with white-sand or black-pebble beaches, caves with prehistoric drawings, and sand dunes. The countryside is dotted with tiny, colorful Dutch colonial villages and farms against a landscape of gigantic rock formations sculpted by the strong winds, and shrub and cactus fields that overnight can turn from a lifeless brown to flowering green after a good rain.

Inhabited by Amerindians from South America as early as 2,500 B.C., little is known about their civilization, although excavations as recently as 1989 have yielded important artifacts that are shedding new light for archaeologists. The island was claimed for Spain in 1499 by Alonso de Ojeda and became a Dutch possession in 1636. Except for a short period of British control in the 19th century, it has remained Dutch.

No Europeans settled on Aruba until 1754, but it was another forty years before colonization began. Aruba was largely ignored until 1824 when gold was discovered. Its production lasted almost a century and was followed by an oil prosperity that began in 1924 when the Lago Oil and Transport Co. built an oil refinery here. Eight years later the company became a subsidiary of Exxon and prospered until 1985, when Exxon closed its refinery due to the drop in world demand. It was a move that might have devastated most islands, but not Aruba. Almost without skipping a beat, the Arubans quickly got their affairs in order—including leaving the Netherlands Antilles in 1986 to become a separate entity under the Dutch crown—and redirected their energies into developing other sectors of their economy.

Arubans say their population is made up of forty-three nationalities. One look at the astonishing range of physical and facial characteristics of the people will convince you the claim is not far fetched. But the most pronounced feature the Arubans have retained is the legendary Arawak traits of a gentle, smiling nature. For most visitors this is Aruba's biggest attraction.

 **FAST FACTS**

 POPULATION: 80,000

SIZE: 20 miles in length and 6 miles in width; 70 sq. miles.

MAIN TOWN: Oranjestad

 GOVERNMENT: Aruba was a member of the Netherlands Antilles until 1986 when it became a separate entity within the Kingdom of the Netherlands with political autonomy, which allows Aruba to conduct its affairs without ratification by the Central Government at required of the other five Dutch Islands. The Netherlands government is responsible for defense and foreign affairs. Aruba has a governor appointed by the queen for a six-year term of office. The parliament is made up of twenty-one members elected for four-year terms. The Council of Ministers forms the executive power, headed by a prime minister.

 CURRENCY: Aruba's currency is the florin, divided into 100 cents. US $1 equals Afl 1.77. Dollars and traveler's checks are widely accepted.

 DEPARTURE TAX: Afl 35 (US $20). U.S. passengers returning home from Aruba pass through U.S. immigration in Aruba before their departure.

 LANGUAGE: Dutch is the official language, but papiamento is the local language, used increasingly in the schools. It evolved from Spanish, Dutch, and Portuguese and is sprinkled with African, English, and French words. Most Arubans have an amazing aptitude for languages and often speak Dutch, English, and Spanish.

 PUBLIC HOLIDAYS: January 1, New Year's Day; Carnival Monday; March 18, Flag Day; Good Friday; Easter Monday; April 30, Coronation Day; May 1, Labor Day; Ascension Day; December 25 and 26, Christmas.

 TELEPHONE AREA CODE: To call Aruba from the United States, dial 011–297–8 plus the five-digit local number.

 AIRLINES:

From the United States:
From New York and Newark, daily flights on Air Aruba, American Airlines, and Continental Airlines; from Miami, Air Aruba and ALM Antillean Airlines; from Houston, ALM; and from Tampa, Air Aruba.

Interisland:
From Puerto Rico, daily service on American Airlines; from Curaçao, daily on Air Aruba or ALM. Oduber Aviation (26975) is a local air-taxi service.

 INFORMATION:

In the United States, Aruba Tourism Authority:
New Jersey: 1000 Harbor Boulevard, Main Floor, Weehawken, NJ 07087; 800–TO–ARUBA; (201) 330–0800.
Atlanta: 199 Fourteenth Street, Northeast No. 2008; Atlanta, GA 30309; (404) 892–7822; fax: (404) 873–2193.
Houston: 12707 North Freeway, No. 138; Houston, TX 77060; (713) 87–ARUBA; fax: (713) 872–7872.
Miami: 2344 Salzedo Street, Miami, FL 33134, (305) 567–2720; fax: (305) 567–2721.

In Canada:
Toronto: 86 Bloor Street West, No. 204, Toronto, Ont. M5S 1M5; (416) 975–1950; (800) 268–3042; fax: (416) 975–1947.

In Port: Aruba Tourism Authority, 172 Lloyd G. Smith Boulevard, Aruba (P.O. Box 1019); 21019; 34702.

 # BUDGET PLANNING

Aruba can be expensive if you travel by taxi and dine at the top restaurants. Bus transportation is reliable and cheap, however; car rentals are reasonable and the best mode of travel; sight-seeing tours are moderately priced and well executed; and there is a wide range of restaurants. If you want to tour off-the-beaten-track, you will probably need a guide on rural roads, because there are very few signs and no gasoline stations. On the other hand, if you are adventurous and have a good sense of direction, you can probably manage on your own. Arubans are so friendly and helpful, you are not likely to be lost for long.

 # PORT PROFILE:

LOCATION/EMBARKATION: Ships pull dockside at the port, which is located on the west side of Oranjestad, the capital, less than a quarter mile from the town center and within walking distance of the main shopping area.

LOCAL TRANSPORTATION: Taxis are on hand at the port to meet arriving ships, and they can be requested by phone from a taxi dispatch office (22116). Taxis are expensive, unless you share the cost with others. They do not have meters, but rates are fixed and should be agreed upon in advance. The one-way fare from the port to a Palm Beach hotel is $6; from Palm Beach hotels to the airport, $12; and from the port or town to the airport, $7. All taxi drivers participate in the government's Tourism Awareness Program and receive a Guide Certificate.

Local buses are inexpensive and can be recommended. Drivers speak English and are very helpful. The buses run at 30-minute intervals along Smith Boulevard, the main seaside thoroughfare paralleling the port. Buses heading east from the port take you to the downtown area and the bus station on Zoutmanstraat. Buses going west take you to the resorts along Eagle and Palm beaches. Bus stops are marked BUSHALTE. One-way fare is $1 and can be paid in U.S. currency. There is also a free "shopping bus," which operates from hotels to town. *Arubus* (27089) and the Tourist Bureau have information on buses and schedules.

ROADS AND RENTALS: Aruba has a network of paved and rural roads that make it possible to drive to any part of the island. "Aruba Holiday," a free tourist guide with a road map, is available from the Aruba Tourism Authority. Most roads radiate from Oranjestad, from which the main arteries run west to the resort center of Palm Beach, east to the airport, and southeast to San Nicolas. No road completely encircles the island, but by using a series of connecting roads you can make a loop from Palm Beach around the northwest end and return via Noord to the Natural Bridge.

Toward the south beyond the airport, the highway continues to Spanish Lagoon, Savaneta, and San Nicolas. You can loop through San Nicolas to the southeast coast and return via Santa Cruz, a crossroad town almost in the center of the island, with roads branching north to the Natural Bridge; west along the Hooiberg, Casibari, and to Palm Beach; and south through Frenchman's Pass (Franse Pas) to Barcadera.

Car rentals are abundant and the best mode of transportation around the island. Cars range from $35 and up per day. An open-air Jeep, the most popular choice, costs about $60 to $70 per day. A valid foreign driver's license is needed to rent and drive a car. The minimum driving age for rental cars is twenty-one. Major U.S. car-rental companies have licensees in Aruba, and there are reliable local companies. Driving is on the right side of the road.

George's Cycle and Jeeps (25975) rents Jeeps, scooters, and motorcycles and has pickup service. Bikes cost about $10, scooters $15 to $18.

EMERGENCY NUMBERS:
> *Medical:* Dr. Horacio Oduber Hospital, Smith Boulevard; 24300
> *Police:* 24555/24000/24100;
> *Alarm Center,* dial 115

AUTHOR'S FAVORITE ATTRACTIONS

A *cunucu* (OR COUNTRYSIDE) TOUR
LEARNING TO WINDSURF
DEEP-SEA FISHING EXCURSION

SHORE EXCURSIONS

An island tour can be taken several ways: a standard motorcoach or jeep excursion, on horseback or by hiking with a nature guide or other specialist visiting the less accessible parts of the island and focusing on its more unusual aspects. Prices are per person.

Island Tour, 3 hours, $15. A drive around the island from the port passes the Hooiberg en route to the Natural Bridge. The return probably will be via Ayo and the resorts along Palm Beach.

Cunucu Safari, 6 hours, $38 with lunch. An excursion with more emphasis on the natural environment accompanied by a naturalist guide takes you to the interior of Aruba. You travel by jeep or hike.

earn to Windsurf, 2 hours; lesson package '40–$44. Aruba is one of the Caribbean's major windsurfing locations. Lessons are available at beachside hotels and Windsurf Village.

ARUBA ON YOUR OWN

The capital of Oranjestad is a neat, clean town of Dutch colonial and modern architecture. It s easy to cover in an hour's stroll or to combine with a shopping excursion. From the port you can walk along Smith Boulevard to the Seaport Village complex, a mall with moderate-priced boutiques and outdoor cafes overlooking the harbor. Farther along is Wilhelmina Park, a small tropical garden named for the Dutch queen.

AN ORANJESTAD WALKABOUT

From Schuttestraat, turn right on Oranjestraat for block to reach Fort Zoutman, the oldest-standing structure on Aruba. It was built in 1796 to protect Aruba's harbor; the Willem III Tower was added in 1868 to serve as a lighthouse. The fort houses the *Aruba Historical Museum* (26099), which focuses on the last one hundred years of Aruba's history. Hours: 9:00 A.M. to noon; 1:30 to 4:30 P.M.

The *Bon Bini Festival,* a folkloric fair, takes place in the courtyard of the fort every Tuesday evening from 6:30 to 8:30 P.M. year-round. Admission is Afl 1. It features a folkloric show, native food, and crafts by local artisans. The fair proceeds go to local charities whose members man the stalls. (*Bon Bini* in papiamento means "welcome.")

As an alternative route from Smith Boulevard, just before the small bridge over the Sonesta Hotel lagoon, you can detour through the Seaport Village, a shopping complex of the Sonesta Hotel the town center. Guests board a boat, directly from the lobby, to go to Sonesta's private beach. An escalator in the atrium takes you from the

street level by the lagoon to the main floor, where the casino and disco are located. The north side of the hotel has a sidewalk cafe overlooking the town square.

ARUBA ARCHAEOLOGICAL MUSEUM (at corner of Wilhelminastraat and Zoutmanstraat; 28979). The museum, inaugurated by Princess Margriet of the Netherlands in 1986, was created to preserve the artifacts of Aruba from precolonial times to the present. Aruba is placing increased emphasis on its cultural and historic heritage for the benefit of its citizens as well as visitors. Hours: weekdays 8:00 A.M.–1:00 P.M. and 2:00–4:30 P.M. A booklet, "The Indians of Aruba," published by the museum, is helpful in understanding the island's ancient history.

Across from the museum is the Protestant Church, dating from 1846 and rebuilt in the 1950s in Dutch-Aruban architecture. It faces a small square, which was redesigned in the late 1980s as the town plaza and pedestrian mall, surrounded on all sides by shopping complexes behind colorful facades of Dutch colonial architecture. The north side of the square is Nassaustraat, the traditional commercial street. West of the square is Havenstraat, with several of Aruba's best restaurants.

The *Numismatic Museum* (Zuidstraat No. 27, behind the police station; 28831) displays more than thirty thousand different coins and paper money, some dating from ancient Greek and Roman times. Hours: weekdays 7:30 A.M.–noon and 1:00 P.M.–4:30 P.M. There is no entrance fee, but donations are accepted.

The *De Man Shell Collection* (18 Morgenster Street; 24246) is one of the world's most complete private collections, with many rare and unusual pieces. It is housed in the owner's home and is open to the public. Phone in advance.

WEST OF ORANJESTAD

At Druif Bay, where the coastline bends north, a talcum powder-fine white sand stretches for almost 7 miles. It is the most developed part of Aruba, containing the majority of its luxury hotels, casinos, restaurants, and water-sports facilities. The first mile or so, known as *Eagle Beach,* has a jogging track at the western end and on its north side are wetlands known as *Bubali Pond,* a bird sanctuary, and *De Olde Molen,* a 19th-century Dutch windmill, now a restaurant and next to The Mill resort.

PALM BEACH The next stretch of 5 miles is gorgeous Palm Beach. Each of its seaside hotels is surrounded by flowering gardens that provide privacy and relieve an otherwise-barren landscape with color. Each hotel has its own swimming pool, beach bar, and water sports. The prettiest of the group is the deluxe *Hyatt Aruba,* designed in Spanish architecture with tropical gardens and terraced pools and lagoons interconnected by waterfalls overlooking a beautiful palm-graced beach. It is the headquarters of *Red Sail Sports* (31603 or in the United States 800–255–6425), which also handles sports arrangements for day visitors.

CALIFORNIA POINT The scenic northern end of Aruba is marked by the California Lighthouse, a historic landmark. It takes its name from the ship *Californian,* wrecked in 1891 and lying in 15 to 30 feet of water off the northwest tip.

En route to the Point after Palm Beach is a stretch of beach known as Fisherman's Huts; it is the island's prime windsurfing area and home of *Windsurf Village.* At the foot of the lighthouse is *Tierre del Sol,* Aruba's new golf course (See Sports).

The main road from California Point returns southeast along a stretch of dry, desolate terrain characterized by towering rocks and scattered hills. The highest is Alto Vista, 236 feet, from which there are lovely views. Here too is the chapel of Alto Vista, consecrated in 1750. In the village of Noord, St. Anna Church, with a 17th-century Dutch hand-carved altar, is one of the island's oldest churches and a fine example of Dutch colonial architecture.

A DRIVE AROUND THE ISLAND

Aruba's surprising diversity can be revealed only on a tour of the island—a total change from the beaches and glittering casinos of the south coast. After leaving the placid turquoise waters and

white sands on the leeward shores, the road north passes an area of gigantic rock formations and the ever-present Aruban landmark, the divi-divi tree, whose curious shape is sculpted by strong prevailing winds.

HOOIBERG East from Oranjestad toward the airport is the conical-shaped 541-feet Hooiberg known as "the Haystack," in view on the eastern horizon. Located almost in the center of the island, the curious volcanic formation is visible from most any location. It is covered with dry woodlands of *kibrahacha,* or yellow *poui,* common tree of the Caribbean that usually blossoms after a rain. A flight of several hundred steps leads to the summit, where you can see the coast of Venezuela in the distance on a clear day. Among the birds populating the hill is the spectacular orange and black trupial (or troupial).

On the south side of the Hooiberg, the Canashito area has caves with Arawak petroglyphs—one of several places where they are found. The area between the Hooiberg and Casibari, on the north, is littered with huge boulders that have been carved and weathered into bizarre shapes by the strong winds that blow across the island.

AYO Directly east of Hooiberg, an area strewn with enormous rocks has been dubbed "the Stonehenge of Aruba." Footpaths make it easy to walk through the area and exam the formations at close range. If you are very quiet, you will probably see a variety of birds, particularly colorful parakeets that populate these parts.

THE NATURAL BRIDGE Across the island from Oranjestad on the northeast coast between Boca Mahos and Andicuri Bay, the land drops sharply into a turbulent sea where waves crash endlessly against the rocky shores. At a natural bridge—prime tourist attraction (and, unfortunately, with a tourist souvenir shop)—the force of the water is so great it has given rise to the popular notion that the bridge was carved out of the coral by the sea. Scientists say, however, that the bridge and other similar formations along the coast were formed when weak spots in the coral terrace, which make up the north coast, were dissolved and washed away by abrasive action of fresh rain water. They explain that the sea could have po

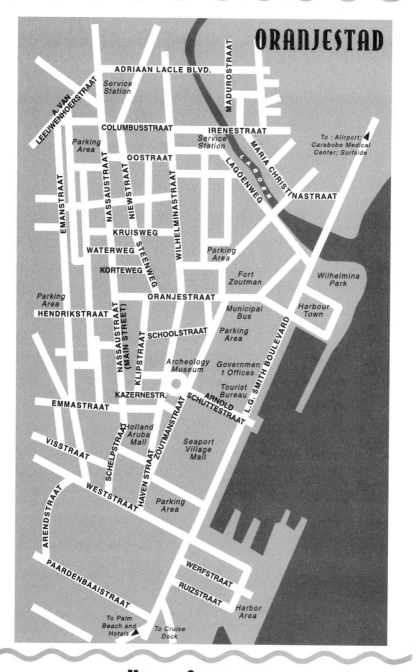

MAP OF ORANJESTAD

ished, enlarged, and even smashed the bridge by its force, but only freshwater could have dissolved the rock on the land side. Another bridge, known as Boca Druif, or Dragon Mouth, can be seen at Boca Prins on the windward coast.

The road between Santa Cruz and Boca Prins runs through the Miralamar Pass between Aruba's highest hills and the countryside of rolling hills, farms, and colorful *cunucu* houses. Originally, *cunucu* in the Arawak language meant a plot of land for agriculture; now it is widely used to mean rural areas. Arubans also use the Spanish word *campo* for countryside.

ARIKOK NATIONAL PARK Mt. Arikok, 577 feet, is the island's second-highest peak and the center of the Arikok National Park, which lies between Boca Prins, San Fuego, and Boca Ketoe. It was created by FANAPA, Aruba Foundation for Nature and Parks, the principal group working to preserve Aruba's natural heritage. At the foot of the hill is a restored country house with a small garden that has samples of trees and bushes found on Aruba.

Aloe vera grows wild throughout Aruba. Widely cultivated for medical purposes in the past, its production declined due to competition from lower-priced synthetics, and most plantations were abandoned. Small-scale cultivation continues, and a few of the outdoor ovens where the juice of the leaves is boiled and hardened are still in use on the island. The juice is used in making sunscreen lotions and cosmetics at a local plant. You can treat a cut or sunburns simply by breaking off a leaf and rubbing the sap on your skin.

MOUNT YAMANOTA The south side of the San Fuego/Boca Prins Road is known as Yamanota (or Jamanota), an area that has been earmarked as a national park and includes the island's highest hill, 617-foot Mt. Yamanota. You can take a paved road to the summit, where you will find grand views of the island. The Yamanota area is the home of the Aruban parakeet, a bright green-and-yellow bird that is almost as large as a parrot.

GUADIRIKIRI AND FONTEIN CAVES The most accessible of Aruba's many caves are two on the east coast: the Fontein Cave, with fine Arawak petroglyphs; and the large Guadirikiri Cave, with two high ceiling chambers, one with an opening at the top that allows in some light. A third chamber, entered by a small low opening, is home to a large number of bats. Be forewarned: The room is hot and humid.

SOUTH OF ORANJESTAD

SPANISH LAGOON The road south from the airport returns to the coast at Barcadera, where there is a long island waterway, Spanish Lagoon, with mangroves and a bird refuge at its northeastern end.

About 600 yards from shore in front of Barcadera Harbor is a reef that starts at the surface and drops to about an 80-foot depth. It is part of a 2-mile reef along the south coast and is popular for snorkeling and diving. The *Atlantis* submarine is based here, and there are also two beach developments: The north one belongs to the Sonesta Hotel; the south one is De Palm Island, a privately developed recreation and sports center. The area is also a favorite for sport fishing.

Savaneta, on the south side of Spanish Lagoon, was the first European settlement and the former capital of Aruba.

FRENCHMAN'S PASS A road inland around the north end of Spanish Lagoon goes through Frenchman's Pass (Franse Pas), a tree-lined drive and site of a historic battle between French and Spanish buccaneers in 1700. Tracks from the main road go to the ruins of the Balashi gold mine, a relic of Aruba's gold rush, built in 1898.

SAN NICOLAS (or Sint Nicolaas), Aruba's second-largest settlement, grew up around the refinery, owned by Standard Oil of New Jersey until it closed in 1985. Now, the town will have a new lease on life when an ambitious urban renewal project—to make it a cultural and tourism center—is completed. *Charlie's Bar*, the heart of the town, is an island mainstay not to be missed. Charlie came to Aruba several decades ago to work in the oil refinery, but after a time decided a bar was more fun. So too is the bar's decor—everyone who visits is supposed to leave something, and they have! South of the oil installation, there are two secluded beaches, popularly known as Rodger's Beach and Baby Lagoon, where you can snorkel from shore. Both beaches lie at the foot of Seroe Colorado, a residential community originally built for Exxon Oil executives.

The southeastern end of the island, marked by the Colorado Lighthouse, overlooks some of Aruba's main dive locations. Along the east coast Boca Grandi, a wide bay, is a popular picnic spot. The area is popular for windsurfing and sports fishing.

North of San Nicolas is an arid, windswept region with little vegetation, even during the rainy season, where the divi-divi tree is abundant. Its asymmetrical shape is caused by the *passaat*, the papiamento name for the strong winds that blow mainly from the east. Although all wind-sheared trees with this shape are commonly called divi-divi, several species grow in this manner. Divi-divi means "ear" in the Arawak language and is derived from the *watapana* tree, which has thick, curled pods resembling a human ear.

SHOPPING

Aruba is not officially a free port, but in 1989 duties on luxury items were lowered from 40 to 3.5 percent, turning it into a shopping mecca. Of greatest interest to most visitors are the Dutch products, such as delft blue pottery, Dutch pewter; Gouda, Edam, and a variety of other Dutch cheeses and chocolates; and Indonesian crafts.

Traditionally, Nassaustraat (Calle Croes) has been the shoppers' street, but a downtown renewal project, begun with the opening of the Sonesta Hotel in 1988, changed the face of the town center. Several complexes set behind pastel-colored facades of traditional Dutch Caribbean architecture, complete with gables, added many stores. The town square is anchored on the east by the Strada, a long-established department store, which has been rebuilt as a complex with eleven boutiques. On the west is the Holland Aruba Mall, another shop-and-restaurant complex. On the south is Seaport Village, the shopping and restaurant complex of the Sonesta Hotel. By the waterfront is HarbourTown on the east. Together these malls have more than one hundred stores with

sports and casual wear, leather, shoes, swimwear, designer fashions, jewelry, and crafts—all within walking distance of the docks.

Stores are open Monday to Saturday, from 8:00 A.M. to noon and from 2:00 to 6:00 P.M.; however, many stores remain open during the lunch hour. When cruise ships are in port on Sundays and holidays, some shops are open from 9:00 A.M. to noon.

ART AND ARTISTS: *Artesania Arubiano* (142 Smith Boulevard, next to Aruban Tourism Authority; 37494) has charming Aruban handmade pottery, silk-screen T-shirts and wall hangings, and folklore objects. *Creative Hands* (5 Scotorolaan) carries ceramic cunucu houses and divi-divi trees. *Gaspirito,* on a country road near Palm Beach, and *Que Pasa?* (20 Schelpstraat) are both restaurants and art galleries with local and Caribbean art. *Mopa Mopa* (5 Havenstraat) sells unusual gifts that appear to be hand-painted but are not. The specialized craft is made from the buds of the mopa mopa tree, which are boiled to form a resin. Vegetable colors are added to the resin, which the artist then stretches by hand. The material is cut into small pieces and layered to form intricate designs on wood.

CHINA AND CRYSTAL: *Aruba Trading Company* (Nassaustraat 12) is a large department store, established in 1930, with a section for china and crystal. *Little Switzerland* (Nassaustraat) is one of the Caribbean's mainstays for fine china and crystal. *Ecco* (Main Street) has hand-painted delft pottery and Dutch souvenirs.

CLOTHING AND ACCESSORIES: There are many boutiques of women's fashions in the various shopping malls, but if you are looking for high fashion, *Studio Italia* (Seaport Village) has Dior and other designer labels. *Bennetton* (Holland Plaza) is here too, but a check of prices did not reflect a savings over New York stores; the same can be said of *Fendi,* whose store is located on the town square. For funky upscale fashions, *Tropical Wave* (Seaport Village) has Indonesian batiks and French-designer outfits.

FOOD SPECIALTIES: *Le Gourmet,* in the Aruba Trading Company (Strada), stocks pâté, caviar, fine Dutch chocolates and cheeses, liqueurs, wines, spices, and more. Supermarkets, such as *Pueblo* and *Ling & Sons,* are good places to buy Dutch cheese, chocolates, and other edibles, as well as liquor.

JEWELRY: The best-known jewelers are *Gandelman* (Nassaustraat 5A and Alhambra, Americana Hotel, Hyatt Regency), a long-established quality store, has a large selection of fine gold jewelry and watches, and a customer-service office in the U.S., and *Lucor Jewelers* (Nassaustraat 20).

LEATHER: *Gucci* (Seaport Mall) has its own store facing the town square, where the savings are about 20 percent over U.S. ones. There are many stores in Oranjestad selling Louis Vitton–type handbags and luggage at prices considerably lower than in the United States. You would need to be familiar with the manufacturer's goods to know if those here are the genuine item or merely good replicas. But if you don't care, they are very good buys.

PERFUME AND COSMETICS: Every shopping complex in town and at resort hotels has perfume shops. *Aruba Trading Company* (Nassaustraat 12) has a well-stocked perfume-and-cosmetics section. *D'Orsy's* specializes in perfumes, and *Sardini's* (Holland Plaza) has a large selection and exceptionally pleasant staff.

DINING AND RESTAURANTS

Oranjestad has a surprising range and variety of restaurants—Chinese, American, Italian, French, Indonesian, and more—reflecting the multifaceted nature of the country. In recent years, too, Aruban specialties have come out of home kitchens onto restaurant menus at places specializing in local cuisine. Some of the best restaurants—*Chez Matilda, Gasparito, Mama & Papa's, Papiamento, Que Pasa?*—are open for dinner only; some may open for lunch during the winter season. Most restaurants close Sunday or Monday. Inquire in advance.

Le Petit Cafe (Schelpstraat; 26577). Fresh and lively cafe on the town square where your chicken or meat is cooked on a hot-stone platter in front

of you. They also serve salads, sandwiches, hamburgers, and light meals. Moderate to expensive.

Warung Djawa (Wilhelminastraat 2; 33928) Surinam and Indonesian dishes are served at lunch and dinner in the setting of an old house—the name means "Javanese cottage." Moderate.

Mi Cushina (La Quinta Hotel, L.G. Smith Boulevard; 48335). Typical Aruban dishes, such as fried fish with *funchi* (cornmeal) and stewed lamb with *pan bati* (local pancake), are specialties. International dishes are also on the menu. The decor includes light fixtures of old wagon wheels, family photographs, and a small museum of old tools and musical instruments used by past generations. Moderate to expensive.

Brisas del Mar (by the sea near San Nicolas 47718). This open-air restaurant with fishnets hanging from the ceiling and a direct view of the Caribbean is a 30-minute drive from Oranjested—but well worth it for seafood and local cuisine. Phone in advance to know if lunch is being served. Expensive.

For some budget-easy alternatives, try *Cheers Cafe Bistro* (Ports of Call Marketplace; 30838) which becomes a disco in the evening; *Coco Plum* (100 Caya Croes; 31176), which serves Dutch specialties in an open-air cafe; *The Grill House* (31 Zoutmanstraat; 31611), which has Aruban-style fish and Dutch steak in cozy setting, and *New York Delicatessen* (Alhambra Center 35000), which offers soups and oversized deli sandwiches.

NIGHTLIFE

Aruba has a sophisticated nightlife. Each hotel has a nightclub with international entertainment of disco with a distinct ambience. *The Visage* (Smith Boulevard) is the hottest disco, but if you are over twenty-five, you might feel out of place.

The island's ten casinos are found mostly in hotels. *The Alhambra,* a large independent gaming house, is part of an entertainment-and shopping complex near Eagle Beach. The complex also has a theater, shops, restaurants including a New York deli—and an entertainment center with a Roseland Ballroom featuring the big

nd sound, as well as a cabaret with jazz and
ribbean music.

SPORTS

hotels here have a swimming pool and water
orts, and they can arrange scuba, fishing, and
ndsurfing. De Palm Island, south of Oranjestad,
a water-sports center of *De Palm Tours*
4400; in United States, 800–533–7265).

ACHES/SWIMMING: The most beautiful
ters for swimming are along the soft sands of
lm Beach, but you can find other white-sand
aches with calm waters along the leeward
ast. At Baby Beach on the southern coast, the
ter is only 4 to 5 feet deep. Its calm waters are
pecially suited for children.

ATING: Water-sports operators offer sail and
orkel cruises on catamarans and other sail-
ats and glass-bottom ones for viewing the
ral.

EP-SEA FISHING: Sports fishing is a big sport
Aruba. Less than a mile or so from shore, the
is rich with kingfish, tuna, bonito, wahoo,
e and white marlin, and more. About a dozen
at operators offer half- and full-day, fully
lipped charters, some for a maximum of four
sons; others for up to six persons. The price
ges from $200 to $300 per person for half-
. You can obtain a list is available from the
rist Office. *De Palm Tours* has daily depar-
es at 8:00 A.M. and 1:00 P.M.

LF: *Tierre del Sol,* Aruba's first 18-hole cham-
nship golf course (6,811 yards; par 71) was
igned by the Robert Trent Jones II Group and
managed by Hyatt Resorts Caribbean. It can
ommodate golfers of all ages and abilities.
re is a driving range, putting green, and prac-
chipping area complete with a bunker.
ated near the California Lighthouse, it is part
planned community with apartments and vil-
health club, a handsome clubhouse with a
ular restaurant, swimming pools, and tennis
nplex. The development has its own irrigation
em and water supply (a major consideration
this arid island). During construction of the

course, which is landscaped with Aruba's indigenous plants, environmentalists were consulted to
protect local wildlife, particularly the birds at a
nearby sanctuary.

HIKING: Aruba does not have marked hiking
trails, but there are many tracks branching from
main arteries to almost any place of interest.
Nature hikes, birding, archaeological excursions,
and jeep safaris lasting three to six hours are lead
by naturalists from *De Palm Tours* (24400;
800–766–6016) and through *Martin Booster
Tracking* (Diamontbergweg 40, San Nicolas;
2–978–41513). The latter organizes all-day tours
with an archaeologist and hiking excursions to
the less accessible parts of the island. They can
also be arranged through *De Palm Tours.*

HORSEBACK RIDING: *Ponderosa Ranch* (30
Papaya; 25027), *Rancho Daimari* (60239),
Rancho del Campo (22 East Sombre; 20290),
and *Rancho El Paso* (44 Washington; 63310)
offers trail rides daily except Sunday. The mounts,
imported from South America, are the famous
paso fino horses noted for their smooth gait. Trips
can be arranged for all levels of skill.

SNORKELING/SCUBA DIVING: Aruba is surrounded by coral reefs, and there are interesting
shipwrecks. The reefs in the calm leeward waters
range from shallow-water corals within swimming distance of shore—suitable for snorkelers
and novice divers—to deep-water reefs and walls
that drop 100 feet and more. Snorkeling and diving can be arranged directly with dive operators,
most of whom are located at the hotels on Eagle
and Palm beaches. A beginner's dive lesson costs
about $50.

Arashi Beach, north of Palm Beach, is ideal for
snorkeling and shallow-water dives directly from
the beach. The reef of elkhorn coral lies on a
sandy bottom in 20 to 40 feet of water. There are
two shipwrecks that can be viewed by snorkelers
as well as divers. The *Pedernales,* an oil tanker
from World War II, lies in 20 to 40 feet of water
near the Holiday Inn; the *Antilla,* a German cargo
ship scuttled by the Germans at the start of the
Second World War, lies at 60 feet in two parts.

At Barcadera, a 2-mile reef runs along the south
coast and has abundant gorgonians and elkhorn
and staghorn corals, which attract a great variety

of fish common to the Caribbean. Farther south Baby Lagoon offers the greatest visibility for snorkeling.

TENNIS: Most hotels have tennis courts, but Aruba's strong winds are not conducive to play, except at well-protected courts.

WINDSURFING: The same strong winds that shape the divi-divi tree and keep the island cool have made Aruba one of the leading windsurfing locations in the Caribbean. Most of the year the winds blow at 15 knots and, at times, up to 25 knots. Windsurfers from around the world meet here annually in June for the *Aruba Hi-Winds Pro-Am World Cup,* where the winds get up to 25 knots or more. The most popular windsurfing areas are north of Palm Beach at Fisherman's Huts, the beach fronting *Windsurf Village.* All beachside hotels have windsurfing equipment. If you want to learn or polish your skills, the *Sailboard Vacations Flight School* at the Windsurf Village is best. Lessons from a skille full-time instructor costs $40 per hour or $15 for five hours and are given in the warm shallo waters of Fisherman's Huts where winds are co sistent.

FESTIVALS AND CELEBRATIONS

Carnival, celebrated during the pre-Lenten per od, has long been the main celebration in Arub and it has all the costumes, color, and calyps parades, and floats of any Caribbean Carniva More recently the annual *Aruba Jazz and Lat Music Festival* in June has captured the island heart. Begun in 1988, it was an instant succe and attracted such well-known artists as Rub Blades and José Feliciano. (For information, ca 23777).

PART VI

South America's Caribbean and the Panama Canal

VENEZUELA

Venezuela is a country of dazzling variety. On its West are the snowcapped Andes Mountains soaring to more than 16,000 feet; on the north lie more than 1,000 miles of Caribbean coast; and to the south and east, the Amazon jungle. Deep in the southland of strange table-top mesas is Angel Falls, the tallest waterfalls in the world; through the central plains flows the Orinoco River, the second longest in South America.

The people come from backgrounds as varied as the Venezuelan landscape. In addition to the Amerindians, whose Arawak ancestors populated the Caribbean at the time of Columbus, and the Spaniards who conquered South America, Venezuela has had large influxes of Europeans, Mediterraneans, and Asians, and after the discovery of oil, a steady stream of Texas oilmen and New York bankers. The hodgepodge is what Venezuelans call their own brand of *crillos.*

Clearly, one day—or even one month—is not enough time to see this diverse country. And even with the little time you have during a day in port, what you see of the country depends on which of Venezuela's ports your ship visits.

La Guaira

Located about midpoint on Venezuela's Caribbean coast, La Guaira is the port for Caracas, the capital, situated on the south side of the Avila Mountains, which rise almost directly from the coast. All cruise ships offer a day's motorcoach excursion to Caracas; most also have one to Angel Falls, which departs from the international airport, about a 10-minute drive from the port.

La Guaira is a scruffy port town with very little to recommend it, except for some good seafood restaurants and the old section of pastel colonial buildings and cobblestone streets centered around Plaza Vargas. *Guipuzcoana House,* on the shore road, is the former trading and customs house built in the early 18th century and restored as the town hall. It houses the local tourist office. Behind it is the *Boulton Museum,* which displays antiques and memorabilia of John Boulton, a wealthy 19th-century English trader whose descendants lived in the house until the 1960s.

East of La Guaira are the main beach resorts of the north coast. Be careful about where you swim, as some places have strong undertow; *balnearios,* or public beaches, with changing facilities and lifeguards, and hotel beaches are best. Macuto has the deluxe Macuto Sheraton and Melia Caribe, which has good sports facilities.

Caracas

Stretching 12 miles east-west along the Cuaire River Valley, Caracas sits at 3,000 feet above sea level, enjoying spring weather year-round, even though it is only 10 degrees north of the equator. Free-spending and fun-loving, the oil-rich capital has grown from a small town of 400,000 to a sophisticated metropolis of almost 4 million in less than four decades.

One of South America's most modern and dynamic cities, with a skyscraper skyline to rival New York or São Paolo, it is also one of the oldest, founded by the Spaniards in 1567. Its historic heart is *Plaza Bolívar,* a tree-shaded square with an equestrian statue of Simon Bolívar, the native son who led the revolution that liberated Venezuela—and, ultimately, most of South America—from Spanish rule. His birthplace *Casa Natal,* a lovely restored colonial home, the *Bolívar Museum,* and the *National Pantheon* where the Great Liberator's ashes are enshrined are nearby. Also on the plaza is the *Cathedral of Caracas,* first built in 1595, containing works by Rubens and Murillo and other art treasures; to the southwest is the *Capitol* building.

Modern Caracas is best reflected in the monolithic Parque Central, a complex of ultramodern towers housing offices and apartments with the striking *Museum of Modern Art* at the center. Two other museums, the *Museum of Fine Arts,* where Venezuela's many fine artists are displayed, and the *Museum of Natural Science (Ciencia*

Naturales), with pre-Columbian artifacts and a fauna collection, are at the entrance to *Los Caobos Park.* Other attractions include the *Botanical Gardens, University City* (started in 1725), and *La Rinconada Racetrack,* one of the most beautiful in the world.

Caracas has super restaurants and shopping, particularly for stylish but inexpensive fashions, in high-rise malls. It is famous for its nightlife, which, unfortunately, cruise passengers will need another visit to enjoy—most ships stay in port only long enough for a day tour. This short time points to a potential problem in visiting Caracas on anything but your ship's organized tour. Traffic is horrendous, despite a network of superhighways stretching forever. Some have suggested that instead of being called the city of eternal spring, Caracas might more appropriately be named the city of eternal traffic jams. A new subway, which is fairly easy to use and costs about 10 cents, has made getting around the city easier for people who want to be on their own.

That's the good news. The bad news is that the 12 miles between Caracas and your ship in La Guaira—normally a 30-minute drive—has been known to take 2 hours. If your tour bus gets stuck in traffic, the ship will not leave without you. So if you do decide to go off on your own—and many do—be sure to allow ample time for the return to port.

EXCURSION TO ANGEL FALLS Angel Falls and nearby Canaima, a remote base camp and airstrip, are hidden deep in the Gran Sabana, a 14,000-square-mile region of towering, tabletop mesas with truncated peaks known as *tepuis,* likened to the Grand Canyon in the jungle. The only way to get there is by air on Avensa, the domestic airline, which has regular service. En route the plane flies into the canyon of Auyantepuy, or Devil Mountain, whose top covers an area of 180 square miles at 5,000 feet in height. It is said to be the setting of Authur Conan Doyle's classic, *Lost Worlds.*

At the head of the canyon, through the clouds and mist, passengers see slender Angel Falls sprouting from the top of the mountain and dropping for 3,212 feet—twice the height of the Empire State Building and fifteen times that of

Niagara Falls. The falls were named for American pilot Jimmie Angel, who discovered them in 1933. As the plane flies through the narrow canyon, the walls seems so close you wonder how the pilot can avoid scraping the plane's wingtips. This is not a trip for the fainthearted!

Canaima has a lodge, also operated by Avensa, set on a beach by an amber-hued lagoon whose color comes from the water's high tannic acid content. In the distance *La Hacha Falls,* made up of seven cascades on the Carrao River, roars into the lake. You can take a canoe trip on the lake for a closer look at the cascades, swim, and have lunch before flying back to your ship.

LOS ROQUES ARCHIPELAGO: Directly north of La Guaira is an atoll of coral islands and reef surrounding a transparent lagoon protected as a national park. It is an occasional stop for small cruise ships where passengers can enjoy snorkeling and scuba diving to see the rich marine life. Los Roques are only some of the seventy-two islands that dot Venezuela's Caribbean coast.

PUERTO LA CRUZ

Set on a wide bay in an amphitheater of green hills, Puerto La Cruz is one of Venezuela's fastest growing resort towns and an occasional cruise port. The port in town is near hotels, which offer water sports, tennis, racquetball, a health spa, and a golf course. The beachfront *Melia,* which has swimming pools, tennis courts, and water sports, is at the head of Paseo Colon, a seaside boulevard with restaurants and shops.

The principal sight-seeing attraction is *Barcelona,* the capital of the state of Anzoátegui, 8 miles from Puerto La Cruz. Founded by the Spaniards in 1693, Barcelona is a typical Spanish colonial town with neat, narrow cobblestone streets lined with whitewashed houses and a plaza with the Church of San Cristobal, the municipal building, and a museum. Next to the plaza are the ruins of *Casa Fuertes,* called the Venezuelan Alamo. It was formerly a monastery where Simon Bolívar established his headquarters during the War of Independence.

CUMANÁ: Forty-five miles east of Puerto La Cruz, Cumaná is the oldest city in South America, an occasional port of call, and a ferry departure point for Margarita Island. It is rich in history, churches, and other colonial buildings and boasts the *Museum of the Sea*. It can be visited on a day trip from Puerto La Cruz. From either Puerto La Cruz or Cumaná, a day's excursion can be made to the *Guacharo World Sanctuary*, a one-thousand-acre national park with wildlife and caves with rare oilbirds, known in Spanish as *guacharo*.

MARGARITA ISLAND

Famous for pearls, pirates, and earthly pleasures, Margarita Island is one of Venezuela's leading resorts, popular for its pretty beaches and duty-free shopping. Located 23 miles off the coast, northeast of Puerto La Cruz, Margarita and its satellites of Cubagua and Coche make up Venezuela's three-island state of Nueva Esparta.

On Cubagua in A.D. 1500, the Spaniards founded *Nueva Cadiz*, their first settlement in South America, which thrived on pearling until the Spaniards depleted the oyster beds and mother nature finished the Spaniards with a tidal wave. The Spaniards then took up residence on Margarita, fending off pirates who preyed on ships carrying treasures from the Spanish Main.

Mountainous and green, Margarita—about 40 miles long and 20 miles wide—comprises two islands joined by the narrow, 10-mile-long Isthmus of La Arestinga bordered by a large mangrove, which is protected as a national park. *Porlamar*, the port and tourist center, is booming with new shops, restaurants, cafes, and resorts. Elegant shops with duty-free European fashions are found along Cuatro de Mayo and Santiago Marino avenues; the *Museum of Contemporary Art* and more shops are located between Calles Iguaidad and Zamora.

In town and elsewhere are a great variety of restaurants—seafood, creole, Spanish, Italian, Chinese—but the highlight of any menu is the prices. Margarita is one of the Caribbean's least expensive islands. The main beaches are east of the town, from Bella Vista to El Morro; others edge the north shores.

Porlamar has more than a dozen car-rental agencies, including Avis, Budget, Hertz, and National. Most are located at the airport, but some have offices in town and at leading hotels. Porlamar is connected to other parts of the island by good roads, which lead to another world of colonial towns, mountain vistas, quiet fishing villages, and deserted beaches.

La Asunción, 6 miles north of Porlamar, is the state capital, founded in 1565. Nestled in the Santa Lucia Valley, surrounded by green hills, its location was selected for its relative inaccessibility to pirates in olden days. Among its historic sites are the *Cathedral of Nuestra Señora de La Asunción*, built in 1568 and considered the model for churches built in Venezuela up to the 19th century; *Museum of Nueva Cadiz*, housed in the former government headquarters; and the 17th-century *Fort of Santa Rosa*, which guarded the eastern approach to the capital. It is one of three forts, underscoring the island's strategic location to the Spanish fighting off the English and others in colonial times.

Pampatar, a pretty whitewashed colonial town on the east coast, has the *Fort of San Carlos Borromeo*, dating from 1662 and restored as a museum in 1968. *Casa Amarilla*, the seat of the short-lived Republic Government during the War of Independence against Spain, has been restored as the customs house.

About 2 miles northwest of Porlamar, *El Valle del Espiritu Santo*, dating from 1529, was the first capital of Margarita. Here the *Sanctuary of the Virgin of the Valley*, long venerated by fishermen and boatmen, was consecrated by Pope John Paul II as the patron saint of the Venezuelan Navy. The virgin's feast day, September 8, is cause for a week-long celebration.

The 26,000-acre *La Restinga National Park*, 22 miles west of Porlamar, is one of the island's main attractions. Boats take you through the beautiful bayous, rich in plant and wildlife. You are likely to see cormorants, heron, white ibis, and an occasional scarlet ibis. The oysters attached to the roots of the mangrove trees are so abundant that you can hear them clicking their shells. Further west, the *Macanao Peninsula*—the other island of Margarita beyond the isthmus—is mostly wilderness with beaches that seldom see a footprint.

ORINOCO RIVER

Some nature-oriented cruises combine visits to the Roques Archipelago with a voyage on the Orinoco, the eighth-largest river in the world. Its serpentine course flows over 12,500 miles from its Andean sources to the huge delta where thirty-seven "mouths" empty into the Atlantic. When your ship enters the delta, you see the color of the water change immediately from deep blue to muddy brown.

The most interesting cruises take passengers by zodiacs or other small inflatable boats into the tributaries to see birds and other wildlife and to visit remote villages. About 60 miles up the river, *Uraipo,* a village of about 1,000 Warao Indians, has houses on stilts to protect them when the river rises 60 feet during the rainy season of July and September. The step back in time here is quite a contrast to the industrial area around *Ciudad Guayana* from which passengers can take an excursion to Angel Falls.

INFORMATION: Venezuela Tourist Office, c/o Embassy of Venezuela, 2445 Massachusetts Avenue, NW; (202) 797–3800. The language of Venezuela is Spanish and the currency, the bolivar. US $1 equals about 700 bolivars. You need a valid driver's license to rent a car; driving is on the right side of the road. *A note of caution:* When you go ashore, do not take valuables with you, and at the beach, even on the most secluded beaches of Margarita, never leave your personal belongings unattended.

COLOMBIA

CARTAGENA

Cartegena, about midpoint on Colombia's Caribbean coast, is both a historic monument and a modern beach resort. Founded in 1533, the city became the main port of Spain's New World empire, serving as the staging ground for conquest and plunder of the continent. It was the departure port for treasure ships laden with the gold, emeralds, and other riches that sailed with their loot to the mother country.

The Old City was protected by 7 miles of walls, 40 feet high and wide enough for cars to drive along the ramparts. Inside the walls you will discover narrow lanes with whitewashed houses and flower-filled balconies. In one place the dungeons and storerooms have been converted into an arcade of craft shops, where you can find excellent regional crafts. Among the architectural gems to visit are the *Palace of the Inquisition,* housing the *Colonial Museum,* facing Plaza Bolívar and its statue of Simon Bolívar; several churches; and the restored mansion of the Marques de Valdehoyos, where the *National Tourist Office* is located.

The 16th-century *Fort San Felipe,* standing guard above the Old City, is considered the best-preserved example of Spanish military architecture in the Western Hemisphere. Outside the city atop a hill called *La Popa* is the Monastery of Santa Cruz, from which you will find a grand view of Cartagena and the Caribbean.

Today Cartegena is Colombia's main Caribbean resort, with deluxe hotels in the modern beachfront stretch of Bocagrande, offering a wide range of sports and fashionable shops with resort wear, leather goods, and emeralds for which Colombia is famous. Shore excursions usually end here. Be prepared for your tour guides to hustle you into certain shops—the ones where they get the highest commissions—and where you will stay much too long, if you are not a shopper.

Cartegena has a golf course, tennis courts, and charter boats for deep-sea fishing. Boat excursions are available to nearby *Bocachica* offering beautiful beaches, snorkeling; and diving, and to *Pirate's Island,* one of fifty Rosairo Islands, which are protected as a nature preserve.

A Note of Caution: When you go ashore do not take valuables with you, and when at the beach, never leave your personal belongings unattended.

 **INFORMATION:**

Colombian Consulate,
10 E. 46th Street, New York, NY 10022;
(212) 949–9898.

PANAMA

THE VITAL LINK

History is replete with great endeavors but few were as bold, difficult, dangerous, and controversial—yet successful and beneficial—as the Panama Canal. An engineering triumph by any measure, the Big Ditch, as it is often called, is a 50-mile-long channel traversing Panama at the narrowest point between the Atlantic and Pacific oceans. A vital link in international trade for almost 100 years, it has had a profound effect on world economic and commercial development. Annually, as many as 13,721 ships pass through it, carrying almost 200 million tons of cargo bound for destinations in the four corners of the globe.

From the time the Spanish explorer Vasco Nuñez de Balboa crossed from the Atlantic to glimpse the Pacific in 1513, the dream of a waterway through the Isthmus of Panama was born. Under Charles I of Spain, the first survey for a proposed canal was made in 1534. During the California gold rush of 1849, when the lack of a safe way across the U.S. by land hampered those

in the eastern U.S. from participating in t[ ] bonanza, the search for a short-cut acro[ ] Panama found new motivation. With the permi[ ] sion of Colombia, which controled the isthm[ ] area, a group of New York businessmen financ[ ] the building of a railroad, completed in 1855. [ ] provided travel from the eastern U.S. to Panam[ ] by sea, crossing the Isthmus of Panama by r[ ] and sailing up the Pacific coast to California.

Yet the idea of a waterway persisted. In 187[ ] Colombia gave a French financial syndica[ ] headed by Lt. Lucien Napoleon Bonaparte Wys[ ] a French army officer, permission to construct[ ] canal. The syndicate engaged Ferdinand [ ] Lesseps, who built the Suez Canal, for the proje[ ] De Lesseps, with little evidence to support it, sa[ ] that a canal at sea level was feasible.

Despite tremendous support, enthusiasm, ar[ ] feverish activity, the project was doomed from t[ ] start. For reasons of geography and topograph[ ] engineers say, digging a canal at sea level wou[ ] not have worked regardless of how much mone[ ] men, and machines De Lesseps had used. And[ ] technical miscalculations had not been enoug[ ] to defeat the French, tropical diseases wer[ ] Approximately 20,000 men died from yello[ ] fever, malaria, and other illnesses in the tw[ ] decades the French toiled. To these trials we[ ] added mismanagement and financial chicane[ ] by no less than De Lesseps's son Charles ar[ ]

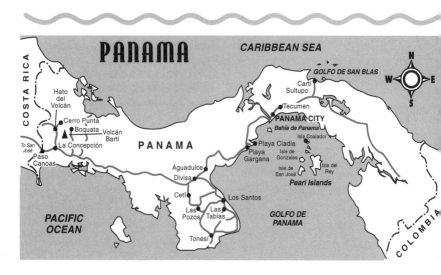

Gustave Eiffel, builder of the Paris tower. After 300 million in payout, the syndicate went bankrupt in 1889.

Meanwhile, Theodore Roosevelt, a visionary who personified the American spirit of the times, wanted the U.S. to build a canal, which he saw as strategic for an expanding America and the link between the eastern U.S. and its new Pacific possessions—Hawaii and the Philippines—gained from the Spanish-American War in 1898.

After engineers studied sites in Nicaragua and Panama and a long, public debate was held, Congress approved Panama in 1902. But the battle was not over. Colombia said no and demanded more money for granting the U.S. permission. The Panamanians, wanting the canal and eager for independence from Colombia, had their own ideas. With French aid and U.S. encouragement, they revolted; U.S. troops prevented Colombia from moving forces to stop them.

In 1903, the U.S. and Panama signed a treaty allowing the U.S. to build the canal. The following year, the U.S. bought the rights, property, and equipment of the French Canal Company for $40 million. Ironically, the equipment had deteriorated so much by then that most of it was worthless.

Faced with the difficulties of removing the rock necessary to create a sea-level canal, U.S. engineers, headed by Col. George W. Goethals, an Army Corps of Engineers career officer, concluded that a lock system would be less costly and provide better control. But the first order of business was to improve health conditions and particularly to control the mosquitoes that carried yellow fever and malaria. The job was given to Col. William C. Gorgas, who set about draining swamps and installing sewer systems. By 1906, yellow fever had been brought under control and malaria reduced dramatically.

Building the canal entailed three major projects on a grand scale: cutting a channel through the Continental Divide; digging an earthen dam—the largest ever built up to that time—across the Chagres River to create Gatum Lake, which became the largest artificial lake of its time; and designing and building three sets of enormous parallel locks and gates.

Cutting the 9-mile channel through Panama's mountain spine at the Culebra Cut—later named Gaillard Cut for Col. David DuBose Gaillard, the engineer in charge—was the most difficult part and took ten years. Enormous amounts of rock and shale were removed and hauled by rail to the Pacific to fill in marshes and build a causeway. Like the French, the U.S. team was plagued by rock and mudslides caused by the area's heavy rains.

The canal opened to traffic on August 15, 1914, six months ahead of schedule and at a cost of $387 million—$23 million below estimates. In the intervening years, the U.S. has invested more than $3 billion in the canal, 70 percent of which has been recovered, but basically, the original structure is intact. Even though ships have gotten larger, the canal can still handle 90 percent of the world's ocean-going liners. By the time the canal had marked its 75th anniversary in 1989, more than 5 billion tons of goods and 700,000 ships had transited it.

In his *The Path Between the Seas,* the leading book on the history and construction of the Panama Canal, author David McCullough says that of its many achievements, perhaps the most remarkable is that "so vast and costly an undertaking . . . [was] done without graft, kickbacks, payroll padding [or] any of the hundred and one forms of corruption endemic to such works . . . . nor has there been even a hint of scandal . . . [or] charge of corruption in all the years that it has been in operation."

The canal's value is impossible to calcuate. Just one example provides a dramatic illustration: From San Francisco, the voyage around South America is 13,000 miles and takes three weeks; via the canal, it's 4,600 miles and can be made in a week.

TRANSITING THE PANAMA CANAL

As many as two dozen cruise ships offer transcanal cruises regularly in the winter season, and another three dozen offer them seasonally in spring and fall when they make their way between the Caribbean and Alaska, or the West Coast and the East Coast, or en route to and from South America in winter and Europe for the summer. See the chart at the end of the book for specific ships.

The Isthmus of Panama, the neck of land connecting North and South America and traversed by the canal, lies northeast/southwest across mountainous, tropical jungle terrain. Due to the lay of the land, ships sail mostly on a north/south course, rather than east/west as might be assumed.

Ships approaching from the Caribbean enter the waterway at the Port of Cristobál in Limón Bay; Colón, Panama's second largest town, is to the east. Port Cristobál is also the northern terminus of the railroad that runs alongside the canal. There may be as many as 50 ships waiting to transit but cruise ships are given priority over cargo vessels. Normally, cruise ships complete the crossing in about eight hours, but it can take longer, depending on the number and speed of the ships ahead. Pilots from the Panama Canal Commission board all ships to guide them through the canal. The commission also provides every cruise ship with a commentator who gives a running account over the ship's public address system of the vessel's passage through the canal and of the history and operation of the canal.

From Cristobál, your ship follows a 6.5-mile course at sea level along a 500-foot-wide channel south to the Gatun Locks, the first of three locks where your ship is lifted 85 feet in three stages to the level of Gatun Lake. As your ship inches forward on its own steam into the first and lowest of the three chambers, a tow line is tossed to the Panamian seaman, who connects it to a messenger line from an electric 55-ton towing locomotive known as a mule, which runs on rails at the top of the lock on each side, pulling the ship into place in the chamber. Each mule can pull 70,000 pounds; the number attached to a ship is determined by the ship's size.

Above the first chamber is the control tower where the operator controls the flow of water through huge 18-foot culverts, or tunnels, located in the center and side walls of the locks. When the pilot gives the signal, the mules begin to roll forward to position your ship into the first chamber; slowly the great doors at the stern close.

With your ship inside the huge chamber, the tower operator opens the valves and water spills out through the culverts at the rate of three million gallons a minute. It is like being on the bottom of a gigantic swimming pool, watching you ship rise as water fills the enclosure. No pump are used to fill or empty the chambers; the syste works by gravity, with water flowing from on level to another through the large culverts smaller culverts that open to the floor of th chambers.

The huge chambers—1,000 feet long by 11 feet wide—have concrete walls from 8 to 50 fe thick and floors from 13 to 20 feet deep. Each s of locks has parallel chambers of the same size allow passage in both directions at the same time Each lock holds 65.8 million gallons of wate every time a ship makes a complete transit, 5 million gallons of water flow into the sea. Th colossal steel doors or gates—still the orig nals—at the end of each chamber are 65 fe wide and 7 feet thick, and vary from 47 to 82 fe in height; the largest weighs more than 700 ton Yet they can be opened and closed with only a 4C horsepower motor.

When the water in the first chamber reaches th level of the water in the next lock, the gate between the two open, the mules pull your shi forward, and the doors behind your ship clos Again, water fills the chamber, and your ship rise to the water level of the third and final stag When that step is completed, your ship sails ont Gatun Lake.

Covering an area of 163.38 square miles, Gatu Lake was created by carving out an enormou earthen dam across the Chagres Valley at th north end of the canal. The Chagres River flow into Gatun and Madden lakes on the north side c Continental Divide, and together with Miraflore Lake on the south side, supplies the water t operate the locks. The lakes' water levels are con troled by dams, ensuring a constant supply.

Your ship sails under its own power for 2 miles across Gatun Lake to the Gaillard Cu through a pretty landscape of forested hills an islets (the tops of submerged hills), where yo can observe some of the region's wildlife. Th most frequent visitors around your ship ar brown pelican; the treetops are often heavy wit vultures; and high in the sky, magnificent frigat birds glide overhead. If you are good at spottin birds, off in the forest you might see toucan an macaw; and as the ship moves closer to th acific, you might begin to see bobbies.

You will also be able to watch ships transiting he canal from the other direction; most will be argo vessels, but occasionally, a small private acht or another cruise ship will pass, too. Expect shower or two; depending on the time of year, he air can be balmy and pleasant or steamy. This s, after all, the middle of the jungle, even if it appears mechanized and manicured.

A few cruise ships on one-week Caribbean ruises go only as far as Gatun Lake, where hey turn around and depart through the Gatun Locks back to the Atlantic side.

At about the midpoint of the canal, your ship eaves Gatun Lake and sails into the Gaillard Cut. This V-shaped channel, cut from granite and volanic rock, is the narrowest stretch of the canal and was the most difficult to build. More than 230 million cubic yards of earth and rock were excavated from the 9-mile stretch to make it navigable. Orginially, the channel was 300 feet wide; later, it was widened to 500 feet, and there is discussion about widening it farther. It has a depth of 42 feet. While the sides have been stabilized, they are monitored constantly and dredging never stops. About halfway along the cut on the west side, a bronze plaque honors the builders of the canal and the workers who died.

The cut ends at the entrance to the first of two sets of locks: Pedro Miguel Locks with only one step of 31 feet, followed by the Miraflores Lake and the Miraflores Locks, which drop 54 feet in two steps. Here, the process is reversed. Your ship will enter a chamber full of water, and as the water is drained out, your ship is lowered to the next level, and finally to the level of the Pacific. At the exit of the final lock is the Port of Balboa and, off in the distance to the south, Panama City. Directly in front is the lofty *Bridge of the Americas,* the bridge connecting the two sides of the waterway and part of the Interamerican Highway between North and South America.

Trivia buffs may like to know that the largest cruise ship to pass through the canal is Cunard's *QE2,* which is 963 feet long with a beam of 105—just 5 feet short of the locks' 110 feet. Princess Cruises' *Crown Princess* holds the record for paying the highest fees, based on tonnage, which was $156,100 in 1996; the least is still the 36 cents paid by Richard Halliburton to swim the canal in 1928.

THE PANAMA CANAL OPERATION

Under treaties signed by the U.S. and Panama in September of 1977, full control of the canal will be turned over to Panama on January 1, 2000. Meanwhile, the canal administrator, who was a U.S. citizen with a Panamanian deputy prior to 1990, is a Panamanian nominated by Panama, appointed by the U.S. president, and approved by U.S. Congress; his deputy is a U.S. national.

The treaty also created the Panama Canal Commission with a policy-making board comprised of five U.S. citizens and four Panamanians to operate the canal. As an agency of the United States Government, the Panama Canal Commission has a legal obligation to operate on a break-even basis, recovering through tolls all costs of operating, maintaining, and improving the canal. Toll rates have been increased only six times since the opening of the canal in 1914.

The Panama Canal operation is the model of efficiency. It operates 24 hours a day and 365 days a year, with as many as 40 ships passing through daily. For most ships, the average Canal Waters Time—the total time spent at the Panama Canal, including waiting time and in-transit time—is just under 24 hours. A reservation system is available to provide a guaranteed priority transit upon request.

Its ability to work at peak efficiency is attributed to its skilled technicians and year-round maintenance, which accounts for about one-quarter of the canal's annual operating budget, or about $221 million. These include annual major overhauls of the lock gates, culverts, and valves; towing locomotives, which are reconditioned at a repair facility designed especially for them, and tow track; and continuous dredging of the 50-mile channel and anchorages. Millions are also invested in new plant and equipment, and more than $5 million goes to training annually.

Some of the new equipment includes more powerful tugboats designed to canal requirements; new towing locomotives that provide faster transit through the locks; and high mast lighting with clusters of 1,000-watt metal halide lamps on 100-foot poles that light the inner walls of lock chambers, providing pilots with better visibility for nighttime transiting.

THE SAN BLAS ISLANDS

Of all the exotic destinations cruise ships visit in the Western Caribbean, none is more ususual that the San Blas Islands off the northeast Caribbean coast of Panama. An archipelago of low-lying islands, upon approach their thatched-roof dwellings shaded by crowds of palm trees look more like the islands of the South Seas than the Caribbean.

These islands are the home of the Cuna Indians, the only tribe of island dwellers in the Caribbean who have both survived and been able to maintain their ancient folkways, more or less, intact despite 500 years of contact with Europeans and other alien cultures.

The San Blas Islands are comprised of about 400 islets plus a strip of land on the Panamanian coast, over which the Cuna claim sovereignty and maintain self-rule. There are 48 Cuna villages with a total population of about 40,000, represented in a tribal council. The people move between the islands in dugout canoes, little changed from those of their ancestors. Their main crop is coconut, which they use as currency. Despite their isolation on these islands, they are unusually worldly and have accepted certain innovations, such as communications and education, while retaining their traditional way of life.

Normally, your first glimpse of the Cuna will be from your cruise ship, where as many as ten boats, full of Cuna women, will be doing a brisk business selling their colorful, unique molas for which they are famous. Do not think these are the last of their stock. When you go ashore to visit a Cuna village, you will see the molas displayed on clotheslines strung the entire length of the village. Some are squares that can be made into pillow covers or framed; others appear on shirts and dresses. All are remarkably inexpensive, ranging from $10 to $40 depending on the intricacy of the design. There is no need to try bargaining; these

women may not be able to speak your language but they understand money.

Molas represent a Cuna woman's wealth, like a dowry. They are elaborate reverse-applique in bold, bright colors, incorporating stylized flowers, animals, birds, and super-natural motifs, and are made originally for the front and back panels of the blouse which the petite Cuna women wear. Occasionally you will see a mola that incorporates current events, such as the U.S. landing of troops in Panama, which crept into designs in 1990. To a newcomer, molas may all seem alike but upon closer examination, the fineness of the stitches and sophistication of the motifs are the telling signs of a master craftswoman.

Cuna women also wear beaded bracelets drawn tightly on their arms and legs, gold nose rings, and layers of gold around their necks. They are a colorful bunch, irresistible to photographers. Most are happy for you to take their picture, often posing with a bright green parakeet, monkey, or iguana, but you must pay them—25 cents per click.

The villagers are friendly, although rather stone-faced unless you take the time to admire some-one's beautiful child—a gesture that usually draws a broad smile from the young mother. Their straight hair is jet black and their facial features are similar to those of other Indian tribes of South America's Caribbean coast whose common ancestors were the Arawaks once populating all the islands of the Caribbean.

More and more, the San Blas Islands are being included on transcanal itineraries, particularly the westbound ones sailing from the Caribbean to the Panama Canal. See the chart at the end of the book for specific ships.

 **INFORMATION:**

Office of Public Affairs,
Panama Canal Commission,
APO Miami 34011;
(800) 622-2625 (Panama),
202-634-6441.

Appendix

CHART OF CRUISE SHIPS SAILING THE EASTERN/SOUTHERN CARIBBEAN

*E*very effort has been made to ensure the accuracy of the information regarding the ships' ports of call and prices, but keep in mind that cruise lines often change itineraries for a variety of reasons. Before you make plans, you should obtain the most current information from the cruise line or your travel agent.

Prices are for "cruise only" unless indicated otherwise and are based on per person, double occupancy rates, ranging from the least expensive cabin in low season to the best cabin in high season. Rates for holiday and special cruises and owners, president's and other top suites are not included (unless all the ship's accommodations are suites).

Itinerary codes are given in parentheses: (A) alternating itineraries (not all ports are included in every cruise, nor are they necessarily visited in the order listed); (B) same itinerary except for holidays; (C) same itinerary year-round or during season or months indicated.

Ship (Cruise Line)	Ports of Call*	Price Range	Duration/ Season
Amazing Grace (Windjammer Barefoot Cruises)	Bahamas or Trinidad to Freeport, Grenada, Antigua, St. Lucia, St. Vincent, Dominica. (A)	$1,075 to $2,900	13 days June–Oct/ Nov.–May
Carnival Destiny (Carnival Cruise Line)	Miami to San Juan, St. Croix, and St. Thomas; or Playa del Carmen, Cozumel, Grand Cayman, Ocho Rios. (C)	$1,309 to $2,059*	7 days Year-round
Century (Celebrity Cruises)	Ft. Lauderdale to San Juan, St. Thomas, St. Maarten, Nassau; or, Playa del Carmen/Calica, Grand Cayman, Cozumel, Key West. (C)	$975 to $1,125*	7 days Year-round
Club Med 1 & 2 (Club Med)	Martinique to St. Lucia, Tobago Cays, Bequia, Mayreau, Barbados, Carriacou; or Los Roques, Blanquilla, Carriacou, Barbados, Mayreau; or Les Saintes, St. Barts, Virgin Gorda, Jost Van Dyke, St. Thomas, St. Kitts; or St. Lucia, Union, Grenada, Blanquilla, Trinidad, Mayreau; or Les Saintes, St. Martin, Tintamarre, San Juan, Virgin Gorda, St. Kitts. (C)	$2,128 to $3,384 w/air	7 days Nov. '97- March '98
CostaRomantica (Costa Cruises)	Ft. Lauderdale to San Juan, St. Thomas/St. John, Serena Cay/Casa de Campo, Nassau; or Key West, Playadel Carmen/Cozumel, Ocho Rios, Grand Cayman.	$849 to $2,449	7 days Dec.–Apr.

Ship (Cruise Line)	Ports of Call*	Price Range	Duration/ Season
CostaVictoria (Costa)	Ft. Lauderdale to San Juan, St. Thomas/St. John, Serena Cay/Casa de Campo, Nassau; or to Key West, Playa del Carmen, Cozumel, Ocho Rios, Grand Cayman.	$849 to $2,449	7 days Nov.–April
Crown Princess (Princess Cruises)	Ft.Lauderdale to Cartegena, Panama Canal partial transit, San Blas, Cozumel.(C)	$2,370 to $4,370	10 days Jan.–April
Crystal Harmony (Crystal Cruises)	Los Angeles/Acapulco via the Panama Canal, Aruba, Grenada, St. Lucia to Barbados; or reverse; or, Grand Cayman, Playa del Carmen, Cozumel to New Orleans; or reverse; or, Aruba, Tortola, St. John, St. Thomas to San Juan; or reverse.(A)	$3,790 to $8,310*	8-15 days Jan.–May
Crystal Symphony (Crystal)	Barbados to Acapulco via St. Lucia, Grenada, Aruba and Panama Canal; or reverse; or, Acapulco via Panama Canal, Aruba, St. Maarten, St. Thomas to San Juan; or reverse; or Acapulco via the Panama Canal, Grand Cayman, Playa del Carman/Cozumel to Ft. Lauderdale; or reverse with San Andres Island. (A)	$4,425 to $7,590*	10-14 days Nov./Dec.
Dawn Princess (Princess)	San Juan to Aruba, Caracas, Grenada, Dominica and St.Thomas; or Barbados, St. Lucia, Martinique, St. Maarten, St. Thomas. (C)	$1,149 to	7 days Oct.-Apr
Enchantment of the Seas (Royal Caribbean International)	Miami to St. Maarten, St. Thomas/St. John, CocoCay; or Key West, Playa del Carmen/Cozumel, Ocho Rios, Grand Cayman. (B)	$1,199 to $2,299*	7 days Year-round
Fantome (Windjammer)	Belize City to Goff's Cay, Lighthouse Reef/Half Moon Cay, Roatan, Cayos Cochinos, and Glovers Reef/Northern Cay; or, Placencia, Puerto Cortes, Roatan, and Utila/Half Moon Cay. (A)	$875 to $1025	6 days Apr.-Oct.
Fascination (Carnival)	San Juan to St. Thomas, St. Maarten, Dominica, Barbados, and Martinique. (C)	$1,109 to $2,009*	7 days Year-round
Flying Cloud (Windjammer)	Tortola to Salt Island, Virgin Gorda, Beef Island, GreenCay, Sandy Cay, Norman Island, Deadman's Bay, Cooper Island, Jost Van Dyke, Peter Island. (A)	$650 to $975	6 days June-Oct./ Nov.-May
Galaxy (Celebrity)	San Juan to Catalina Island (Dominican Republic), Barbados, Martinique, Antigua, St. Thomas. (C)	$1,075 to $1,175*	7 days Winter

Ship (Cruise Line)	Ports of Call*	Price Range	Duration/Season
Grandeur of the Seas (Royal Caribbean)	Miami to Labadee, San Juan, St. Thomas, CocoCay. (B)	$1,199 to $2,299*	7 days Year-round
Horizon (Celebrity)	Ft. Lauderdale to St. Maarten, St. Lucia, Barbados, Antigua, St. Thomas; or, to Curacao, La Guaira, Grenada, Barbados, Martinique, St. Thomas. (C)	$1,294 to $1,504*	10, 11 days Winter
Inspiration (Carnival)	San Juan to St. Thomas, Guadeloupe, Grenada, St. Lucia and Santo Domingo. (C)	$1,109 to $2,009*	7 days Year-round
IslandBreeze (Dolphin)	Santo Domingo to Barbados, St. Lucia, Guadeloupe, St. Maarten, St. Thomas; or to Curacao, Caracas, Grenada, Martinique and St. Croix. (C)	$895 to $2,095*	7 days Dec.-Apr.
Mandalay (Windjammer)	Antigua or Grenada to Palm Island, Mayreau, Tobago, Bequia, St. Vincent, St. Lucia, Martinique, Dominica, Isle des Saintes, Nevis, Montserrat, and Carriacou. (A)	$775 to $875	6 days June-Oct./ Nov.-May
Monarch of the Seas	San Juan to St. Thomas, Martinique, Barbados, Antigua, St. Maarten. (B) to $2,599* (Royal Caribbean)	$1,099	7 days Year-round
Nantucket Clipper (Clipper)	St. Thomas to St. John, Jost Van Dyke, Tortola, Virgin Gorda, Salt and Norman islands in U.S. and British Virgin Islands. (A)	$1,950 to $3,050	7 nights Winter
Niagara Prince (American Canadian Caribbean Line)	Virgin Islands; or St. Maarten to Antigua; or Antigua to Grenada; or Trinidad/Orinoco/ Tobago; or Venezuela Islands, Bonaire, Curaçao; or Turks & Caicos to Nassau. (A)	$1,405 to $2,499	12 days Winter
Nordic Empress (Royal Caribbean)	San Juan to St. Thomas and St. Maarten, St. Croix. (C)	$499 to $1,399*	3, 4 days Sept–March
Norway (Norwegian Cruise Line)	Miami to St. Maarten, St. John/St. Thomas, Great Stirrup Cay; or, occasional cruises to Ochos Rios, Grand Cayman, Playa del Carmen/ Cozumel, Great Stirrup Cay. (C)	$499 to $3,549**	7 days Winter
Norwegian Sea (NCL)	San Juan to Santo Domingo, Barbados, Dominica, Antigua, St. Thomas; or Santo Domingo, St. Lucia, St. Kitts, St. Maarten, St. Thomas. (B)	$549 to $2,499	7 days

Ship (Cruise Line)	Ports of Call*	Price Range	Duration/ Season
Norwegian Wind (NCL)	San Juan to Barbados, St. Lucia, St. Barts, or Tortola optional ferry to Virgin Gorda), St. Thomas. (A)	$699 to $2,799*	7 days to Dec. 1997
Polynesia (Windjammer)	St. Maarten to St. Barts, St. Kitts, Saba, Nevis, PricklyPear, Anguilla, and Montserrat. (A)	$650 to $975	6 days June–Oct./ Nov.–May
Radisson Diamond (Radisson Seven Seas)	San Juan to Curacao, Cartagena, San Blas Islands, transit Panama Canal, Puerto Caldera, San Jose (Costa Rica). (A)	$4,795 to $5,695	9 days January
	San Jose to Puerto Caldera, transit canal, San Blas Islands, Cartagena, Curacao, Aruba; or, reverse. (A)	$4,395 to $5,295	8 days Jan.-Feb./Apr.
Regal Princess (Princess)	San Juan to St. Thomas, Martinique, Grenada, Caracas, Curacao, transit Panama Canal, Acapulco; or Acapulcoto Puerto Caldera, transit canal, Cartagena, Aruba, St. Thomas, San Juan.	$2,370 to $4,524*	10, 11 days Oct.-Apr.
Rhapsody of the Seas (Royal Caribbean)	San Juan to Aruba, Curacao, St. Maarten, St. Thomas. (C)	$1,199 to $2,199*	7 days Winter
Ryndam (Holland America Line)	Ft. Lauderdale to St. Kitts, Martinique, Trinidad, Roseau/Cabrits (Dominica), St. Thomas, Half MoonCay (Bahamas); or, St. Maarten, Castries/ Soufriere (St. Lucia), Barbados, Basse-Terre/ Pointe-a-Pitre (Guadeloupe), St. John/St. Thomas, Nassau; or, Nassau, St. Thomas, St. Maarten, Castries/Soufriere,Barbados, Half Moon Cay. (C)	$2,048 to $3,808	10 days Oct.-April
Seabreeze (Dolphin)	Miami to Nassau, San Juan, St. Thomas/St. John; or Playa del Carmen/Cozumel, Montego Bay, Grand Cayman. (C)	$795 to $1,745*	7 days Year-round
Seabourn Pride (Seabourn Cruise Line)	Ft. Lauderdale to St. John, St. Barts, St. Thomas, St. Martin, Virgin Gorda. (B)	$1,995 to $7,600+	5, 10 days Nov.–Dec. '97
	Ft. Lauderdale to St. John, St. Barts, St. Thomas, Virgin Gorda, St. Martin. (B)	$2,990 to $9,780	5, 10 days Nov.–Dec. '98
Sea Goddess I (Cunard)	St. Thomas to St. Barts and Jost Van Dyke; or, St. Barts, St. Martin and Virgin Gorda. (C)	$1,900 to $3,500	3, 4 days November
	St. Thomas to St. John, St. Martin, St. Barts, Antigua, Virgin Gorda, Jost Van Dyke	$4,700 to $7,100	7 days Nov.–March

Ship (Cruise Line)	Ports of Call*	Price Range	Duration/ Season
Sea Goddess II (Cunard)	St. Thomas to St. John, St. Martin, St. Barts, Antigua, Virgin Gorda, Jost Van Dyke; or Virgin Gorda, St. Barts, St. Kitts, Martinique, St. Lucia, Mayreau, Barbados; or, reverse; or, Barbados to Tobago, Oronoco/Ciudad, Guayana (Venezuela), Grenada. (C)	$4,700 to $8,100 w/air	7 days Jan./March
	St. Thomas to St. Barts, Jost Van Dyke; or, St. Barts, St. Martin and Virgin Gorda. (C)	$1,900 to $3,500	3, 4 days April
Seawind Crown (Seawind Cruise Line)	Aruba to Curaçao, La Guaira/Caracas, Barbados, St. Lucia. (C)	$970 to $1,700 *	7 days Year round
Sensation (Carnival)	San Juan to St. Thomas, St. Maarten. (C)	$1,109 to $2,009 *	7 days Year-round
Splendour of the Seas (Royal Caribbean)	Miami to Playa del Carmen/Cozumel, Grand Cayman, Ocho Rios, St. Thomas, San Juan, Labadee. Or, Key West, Curacao, Aruba, Ocho Rios, Grand Cayman, Playa del Carmen/Cozumel. (B)	$1,899 to $3,399*	10,.11 days Nov.–Apr.
Star Clipper (Star Clippers)	Barbados Carriacou, Grenada, Union Island, St. Vincent, St. Lucia; or Martinique, Dominica, St. Lucia, Tobago Cays, Bequia. (C)	$1,095 to $2,595	7 days Nov.–Jan.
Statendam (HAL)	Ft. Lauderdale to Curacao, Bonaire, Grenada, Roseau/Cabrits (Dominica), St. John/St. Thomas, Nassau; or, St. Kitts, Martinique, Trinidad, Roseau/Cabrits, St. Thomas, Half Moon Cay, Bahamas. (C)	$2,048 to $3,808	10 days Nov.–March
Tropicale (Carnival)	San Juan to St. Thomas, Martinique, Barbados, Grenada, St. Lucia, St. Barts, Antigua, St. Maarten; or, St. Thomas, St. Barts, St. Lucia, Aruba, partial transit of Panama Canal, Ocho Rios. (A)	$1,499 to $1,809*	10, 11 days Winter '98
Veendam (HAL)	Ft. Lauderdale to St. Kitts, St. John/St. Thomas, Nassau (1997)/ Half Moon Cay (1998), Bahamas; or, Key West, Playa del Carmen/Cozumel, Ocho Rios, Grand Cayman. (C)	$1,248 to $2,568	7 days Year-round
Westerdam (HAL)	1997-Ft. Lauderdale to St. Maarten, St. John/ St. Thomas, Nassau 1998-Nassau, San Juan, St. John/St. Thomas, Half Moon Cay, Bahamas. (C)	$1,248 to $2,178	7 days Year-round

Ship (Cruise Line)	Ports of Call*	Price Range	Duration/ Season
Wind Song (Windstar)	Puerto Caldera via Panama Canal to San Blas Island, Cartagena, Aruba, Curacao, Bonaire, Los Roques (Venezuela)Grenada, Bequia, Barbados; and reverse. (A)	$3,395 to $6,695	7, 8, 14 days Apr. & Oct. '98
Wind Spirit (Windstar)	St. Thomas, Saba, St. Martin, Iles des Saintes, St. Barts, Virgin Gorda, Jost Van Dyke. Or, to Iles des Saintes, Vieux Fort (St. Lucia), Bonaire, Aruba, Curacao, Santo Domingo, St. Croix, St. Barts. (C)	$2,495 to $3,395	5, 7, 14 days Nov.– Dec. '97
	St. Thomas, St. John, St. Martin, St. Barts, Tortola, Virgin Gorda, Jost Van Dyke. (C)	$3,495 to $3,895	7 days Jan.–Mar./ Nov.–Dec. '98
Wind Star (Windstar)	Barbados to Tobago Cays, Tobago, Bequia (Grenada in 1998), Martinique, Iles des Saintes, Pigeon Island (St. Lucia); or, Nevis, St. Martin, St. Barts, Iles des Saintes, Bequia. (A)	$3,395 to $3,595	7 days Nov. '97– Mar. '98
Wind Surf (Windstar)	Barbados to Nevis, St. Martin, St. Barts, Iles des Saintes, Bequia; or, to Tobago Cays, Tobago, Grenada, Martinique, St. Lucia. (A)	Prices to be determined	7 days Nov '98.– Mar. '99
Yankee Clipper (Windjammer)	Grenada to Petit St. Vincent, Bequia, Mayreau, Palm Island, Union Island, Young Island, or Carriacou. (A)	$775 to $975	6 days June–Oct./ Nov.–May
Yorktown Clipper (Clipper)	St. Lucia or Grenada to the Grenadines; or Curacao to Trinidad via Bonaire, Orinoco River and Tobago. (A)	$1,950 to $4,665	6, 7, 10 days Winter
Zenith (Celebrity)	San Juan to St. Thomas, Guadeloupe, Grenada, La Guaira, Aruba.	(C)$899 to $1,175 *	7 days Winter

* Prices include port charges
+10th Anniversary Cruise Only Tariffs (1997 only)

Index

ABOUT THE AUTHOR

Kay Showker is a veteran writer, photographer, and lecturer on travel. Her assignments have taken her to more than one hundred countries in the Caribbean and around the world. She has appeared as a travel expert on CNN, ABC, CBS, and NBC, and radio stations across the country; and as guest host on *America On Line* and *The Travel Channel*.

Showker has written 13 travel guides; five on the Caribbean. Her newest book, *Caribbean Ports of Call: Western Region* (Globe Pequot) is third of a three-book series. Her other books include *The Unofficial Guide to Cruises* (Macmillan) named "The Best Guidebook of the Year" by the Lowell Thomas Travel Awards in 1996; *The 100 Best Resorts of the Caribbean* (Globe Pequot); *The Outdoor Traveler's Guide to the Caribbean* (Stewart, Tabori, & Chang), and two Fodor guides—*Egypt* and *Jordan and the Holy Land*. She writes regularly for *Travel and Leisure, Caribbean Travel and Life, Cruise & Vacation Views,* and other publications. She served as senior editor of *Travel Weekly,* the industry's major trade publication, with which she was associated for eleven years.

A native of Kingsport, Tennessee, Ms. Showker received a Master's degree in international affairs from the School of Advanced International Studies of Johns Hopkins University in Washington, D.C. In 1996, she became the first journalist to receive Martinique's *Sucrier d'Or,* a professional achievement award. She was the 1989 recipient of the Marcia Vickery Wallace Award given annually by the Caribbean Tourism Organization and the Government of Jamaica to the leading travel journalist on the Caribbean and the 1990 Travel Writer of the Year award of the Bahamas Hotel Association. She was the first recipient of the Caribbean Tourism Association Award for excellence in journalism and has served as a consultant to government and private organizations on travel and tourism.